FIFTH EDITION

Law in the Schools

WILLIAM D. VALENTE
Villanova University School of Law

with

CHRISTINA M. VALENTE
Villanova University

Merrill
Prentice Hall

Upper Saddle River, New Jersey
Columbus, Ohio

Library of Congress Cataloging-in-Publication Data

Valente, William D.
    Law in the schools / William D. Valente and Christina M. Valente.—5th ed.
        p. cm.
    Includes bibliographical references and index.
    ISBN 0-13-030546-4
    1. Educational law and legislation—United States. I. Valente, Christina M. II. Title.

KF4119 .V28 2001
344.73'07—dc21   00-055907

Vice President and Publisher: Jeffery W. Johnston
Acquisitions Editor: Debra A. Stollenwerk
Editorial Assistant: Penny S. Burleson
Production Editor: Kimberly J. Lundy
Design Coordinator: Diane C. Lorenzo
Cover Designer: Rod Harris
Production Manager: Pamela D. Bennett
Director of Marketing: Kevin Flanagan
Marketing Manager: Amy June
Marketing Services Manager: Krista Groshong

This book was set in Palatino by Carlisle Communications, Ltd. It was printed and bound by
R. R. Donnelley & Sons Company. The cover was printed by The Lehigh Press, Inc.

Merrill
Prentice Hall

10 9 8 7 6 5 4 3 2 1
ISBN: 0-13-030546-4

❖ PREFACE

The need for this revised edition is best explained by the unusual number of law changes that have occurred since the last edition. Under the press of demands that schools achieve better educational results and better control of school-centered violence, drug use, and sexual misconduct, the courts and legislatures modified the rights and duties of all segments of the school community. Decisions breaking new ground, particularly from the United States Supreme Court, necessitate a fresh look at the law on teacher and student rights and on the counterbalancing rights and obligations of school officials and administrators. As the Supreme Court observed some years ago:

> Maintaining order . . . has never been easy, but in recent years, school disorder has often taken particularly ugly forms: drug use and violent crime in the schools have become major social problems. . . . [*New Jersey v. T.L.O.*, 469 U.S. 325 (1985) (White, J.)]

The emphasis on personal liberties of teachers and students, which followed the "rights" revolution of the 1960s and 1970s, has given way to "zero tolerance" policies and severe sanctions for their violation. The scope of changes that must be noted or anticipated by all concerned parties is indicated by the following sampling of new law.

The growing use of computer and Internet technology, particularly in distance learning projects, opens new vistas of legal problems as well as educational opportunities. The *Dawson* case in Chapter 1 probes new issues on the legality of commercially produced materials that are electronically transmitted into schoolrooms. The drive to wire all schools for computerized education may also have influenced the seismic shift, noted in Chapter 9, in Supreme Court reasoning on the constitutionality of state loans of computers for use by students in religiously affiliated schools.

Chapter 3 traces the latest constitutional rulings on student and community group uses of prayer and religious expression at public school sites and events. New materials on teacher employment discrimination in Chapters 5 and 9 include decisions that significantly alter and clarify the prior law on gender, disability, and age discrimination. New cases that revise the constitutional bounds of teacher freedom of speech and of random, suspicionless searches of teachers, including urinalysis testing, are reported in Chapter 6.

Kindred issues of student speech and of suspicionless student searches are revisited in Chapter 7 in light of recent court decisions. One first of its kind case there explores largely open issues on "Do not resuscitate" orders which pit normal school obligations, to give first aid to an afflicted student against the rights of parents to control medical decisions and treatment of their children. The changes in the rights of students with handicaps under the 1997 IDEA amendments and under the Supreme Court's 1999 decision on the scope of "related services" that school districts must provide under that act are also reported in Chapter 7.

Chapter 8 reviews the layers and interoperation of uncoordinated discrimination statutes. Of particular note are the new lead cases on school district or supervisor liability for student-on-student sexual harassment under Title IX (*Davis*); teacher sexual abuse of students (*Doe*); and student suicides (*Hasenfus*). The *Walker* case provides a good essay on the untidy state of discrimination laws regarding the allowance or disallowance of alternative or cumulative remedies under different civil rights statutes.

Chapter 9 on alternatives to public education updates the unique legal status of home education, private schools, and charter schools. New additions include the unresolved divisions among the states on the validity of tuition vouchers and the latest Supreme Court pronouncements on the use of government-employed teachers and government-supplied computers in parochial school classrooms.

The incorporation of the above and other updates reinforces the theme of prior editions—that law and educational practice develop and interact in response to changing societal needs or demands. Because educational judgments necessarily involve shared elements of educational policy and law, the text aims to provide readers with sufficient information and insights to identify and address potential legal problems without foregoing the use of sound educational judgment, and to recognize those instances where the state of the law is such as to suggest the need for expert legal advice.

CHAPTER ORGANIZATION

This edition slightly reorganizes the chapter arrangement of the prior edition. The major changes involve the relocation of the torts chapter (previously Chapter 7) to Chapter 4; the addition to the renumbered Chapter 5 on teacher employment of topics on employment discrimination; and the consolidation of former Chapters 9 and 10 into one Chapter 9 on alternative education. But for these changes, the chapters cover the same general topics as prior editions. The chapter title and topical sections are listed in a detailed outline at the beginning of each chapter. Some section headings were revised to provide more concrete specification of covered subjects.

To simplify reading the principal case opinions at the end of each chapter, we have omitted the court footnotes and dissenting opinions unless otherwise indicated. Omitted sections of case opinions are indicated within the text using the symbol (✧ ✧ ✧). We also chose to employ a simplified, nontechnical form of case citation that indicates the case name and year of decision, and the particular state or federal court that rendered the cited decision.

ACKNOWLEDGMENTS

In completing this edition, we remain indebted and grateful to many persons, too numerous to list here, for indispensable support and encouragement. We wish to note the special contributions by the following individuals.

Here at Villanova University Law School, we are particularly indebted to Dean Mark Sargent for his generous offer of law school resources; to Associate Dean William James and to his research and computer staff whose efficient assistance preserved us from unmeasurable delays and manuscript errors; to Joan De-Long, ever reliable faculty secretary, for managing the many manuscript drafts; and to our student research assistants, particularly Colleen O'Day and Rebecca Craggs.

At Prentice Hall, our special thanks go to Debbie Stollenwerk, senior editor; Kimberly Lundy, production editor; Penny Burleson, editorial assistant; and Lorretta Palagi, copy editor, for their indispensable encouragement, direction, and assistance in shepherding this edition into print.

Finally, we are grateful to the following reviewers for their helpful comments and suggestions: Brian E. Boettcher, Minnesota State University, Mankato; Martha Bruckner, University of Nebraska at Omaha; Margaret Grogan, University of Virginia; David Gullatt, Louisiana Tech University; Karen B. Lieuallen, Marian College; and Ralph D. Mawdsley, Cleveland State University.

William D. Valente
Christina M. Valente
Villanova University
Villanova, Pennsylvania

RELATED TITLES

Karen L. Hanson
Preparing for Educational Administration Using Case Analysis
ISBN: 0-13-0230243

Taher A. Razik and Austin D. Swanson
Fundamental Concepts of Educational Leadership, Second Edition
ISBN: 0-13-0144916

Ronald W. Rebore
The Ethics of Educational Leadership
ISBN: 0-13-7879202

❖ BRIEF CONTENTS

❖ CONTENTS

Law in the Schools

❖ CHAPTER 1

Education under the American Legal System

❖ **CHAPTER OUTLINE**

3. Access to Courts—Technical Barriers
   a. Standing—Who Can Sue?
   b. Exhaustion—When May a Party Sue?
4. Court Review of Administrative Decisions
   a. Judicial Cure of Administrative Errors

❖ **CHAPTER DISCUSSION QUESTIONS**

❖ **CASES**

1.1 Dawson v. East Side Union High School District, 34 Cal. Rptr. 2d 108 (1994)[†]

1.2 Conover v. Board of Education of Nebo School District, 267 P.2d 768 (Utah 1954)[†]

❖ **ENDNOTES**

[†]Indicates cases with review questions.

3

THE RELATION OF LAW, POLITICS, AND EDUCATION

Contests for Control

Education is inherently subject to a struggle for control. ". . . In our history, the schools have been not only an institution in which to teach . . . but an arena where interest groups fight to preserve their values, or to revise the judgments of history, or to bring about fundamental social change. Given the diversity of American society, it has been impossible to insulate the schools from pressures that result from differences. . . ." [D. Ravitch, *Multiculturalism: E Pluribus Unum*, 56 The Key Rptr. 1 (Autumn 1990); see also J. Coleman, *The Struggle for Control of Education and Social Policy* 64 (1970).]

The root issue in schooling is one of control. Who does or should control child education? The government, parents, students, teachers, church and other private institutions, special-interest organizations, taxpayers? All have acknowledged interests but the extent to which each party has legal power to influence school decisions on study content or methods, noncurricular services, school budgets, or day-to-day school activity is settled ultimately by the law and its recognition of their respective interests.

Control issues are fueled by continued dissatisfaction with the performance of public schools and by continued demands to elevate educational goals, testing programs for teacher certification and for student promotion or graduation, as well as stricter sanctions for teacher or student misconduct.

School Violence and Crime

The unprecedented violence that has erupted in American schools since 1995 raises special problems of control that are beyond the range of ordinary school discipline. The safety of the school population and the security of school property have been shaken by bombings and vandalism and by assaults, ranging from individual and gang beatings to life-threatening shootings, stabbings, and surreal massacres. The presence at school of firearms, explosives, and all manner of weapons, and of illegal drugs is a major concern of current school management. In addition, the psychological violence of harassment, ridicule, intimidation, and extortion have become disturbingly commonplace. The federal Departments of Education and Justice recently took a lead in developing school policies to identify, treat, and regulate students with symptoms of abnormal violent tendencies. Documented studies on school violence and legislative responses to control it through state safe school statutes are noted in the endnote.[1]

The West Virginia statute that authorized student expulsion from public schools for weapons possession for up to one year is illustrative. The law and a student's expulsion for one year was upheld as constitutional under the state's constitution.[2]

Administrative control of school violence requires far stricter restraints on individuals than was customary under prior administrations that gave broad sway to personal freedoms of movement, expression, and privacy. In tightening those restraints, school supervisors have to reckon with the legal limits of their authority to prohibit, prevent, and punish threats of violence, even as legislatures and courts are upholding zero tolerance prohibitions against possession of weapons or illegal drugs at school. Preemptive school searches of teachers and students and tighter bans on use of intimidating language or "gang" symbols are testing the legal bounds of school discipline and the correlative bounds of teacher and student rights. Security measures that impact personal freedoms such as free speech, association, and freedom from unreasonable searches must still be carefully crafted to avoid potential liabilities under civil rights laws which apply to many of the topics in later chapters.

THE LEGAL INTERESTS OF PARTICIPANT PARTIES

The sorting out of the respective rights and responsibilities of educational agencies and administrators, school staff, special-purpose organizations, individual teachers, parents, and students is influenced by manifold law sources of federal and state constitutions, statutes, regulations, and court decisions. The sorting of rights process is largely undertaken in terms of the recognized legal interests of each of the foregoing participants.

Government Interests

States

Public education is *primarily* but not exclusively the province of the states. State constitutions mandate the creation of a state system of public education. State requirements of compulsory school attendance are exercises of inherent state police powers, to act for the general welfare.

The National Government

The national Constitution in specifying the powers of the federal government makes no mention of education. Nevertheless, a number of federal interests justify federal regulation of many public school operations. In advancing federal interests, Congress, federal courts, and federal agencies pervasively influence public schools. With respect to federal rights, the topics of Chapters 3 through 9 are shot through with issues concerning religion, employment discrimination, teacher and student rights, school segregation, and state regulation of private schools.

With respect to curriculum development, federal subsidies provide powerful inducements for schools to adapt their courses to serve federal goals, such as foreign language studies that facilitate the conduct of international relations, and science studies that improve military proficiency and national defense.

School operations that affect interstate businesses are subject to the broad power of Congress to regulate interstate commerce, including the power to compel public schools to comply with federal statutes governing employment practices.

Supremacy of Federal Law

Where federal jurisdiction attaches, it supercedes and displaces any inconsistent state laws by reason of the Supremacy Clause of the national Constitution which reads:

> This Constitution, and the laws of the United States which shall be made in pursuance thereof; and all treaties made . . . under the authority of the United States, shall be the *supreme law of the land; and the judges in every state shall be bound thereby, anything in the Constitution or laws of any state to the contrary notwithstanding.* (Article VI, § 2, U.S. Constitution) (Emphasis added)

Individual Interests

Students and Parents

Students and parents possess recognized interests in a wide range of school events, both as beneficiaries of public education and as citizens. The protection of their interests is exemplified by the constitutional right of parents to control the upbringing of their children and to resist laws or decisions that infringe that right. Thus, while states may compel parents to satisfy state education requirements for children, they cannot force parents to send their children to public schools. When so enrolled, schools may have to exempt students from public school activities that violate their religion. The resolution of competing claims of parents and public school authorities is a common feature of school law.

School Authorities, Teachers, and Staff

The obligations of school administrators, supervisors, teachers, and other employees in the conduct of school affairs involve their respective legal rights, the limits of which are also a perennial issue in school law.

Citizen and Organizational Interests

The interests of citizens, taxpayers, and organizations also enjoy legal protection insofar as those interests are affected by particular school policies or actions. A party's interest in a school dispute determines whether that party may obtain or be denied a court hearing and relief in a given school dispute.

THE AMERICAN LEGAL SYSTEM—STRUCTURE AND SOURCES

The United States republic is comprised of two systems of laws and governments: one for the nation as a whole, and one for each of the 50 constituent states. The coordinated powers of different government entities are expressed by the term "jurisdiction," which denotes law-based *authority*, as opposed to an assertion of power that has no valid legal foundation. Where federal jurisdiction exists, it governs the states. Where state jurisdiction exists, it governs only the home state. Where federal and state laws conflict, the above quoted Supremacy Clause makes federal law paramount. In most cases, however, federal and state laws operate in harmony and concurrently.

Within each jurisdiction, one finds another hierarchy of law sources, namely, constitutional law, legislated law (statutes), administrative law, and court or case law. The distinguishing features of each form dictate its rank vis-à-vis other forms of law. A constitution ranks highest and supersedes any inconsistent statute, administrative ruling, or case decision, while statutes and court decisions rank higher than administrative law. To sustain a challenged decision, therefore, a school administrator must be satisfied that, though authorized by one level of law, the decision does not offend a higher level of law. One cannot rely on a statute or regulation that offends the higher constitution or on a regulation that was previously voided by court decision. This interplay of law sources will become increasingly familiar in later chapters.

Constitutional Law—The Basic Charter

Constitutions are basic written charters of government that are adopted by the people. They are worded broadly to serve conditions over long periods of time and are seldom formally amended, if only because amendment is politically difficult to achieve. Courts must interpret, i.e., referee, the contested meaning and application of open-ended constitutional language (such as "due process") in order to decide the validity of challenged school actions. In that function, courts may be said to supply the law.

Statutory Law—The Role of Legislatures

Elected legislatures enact laws called statutes, which are subject to ongoing revision by current and successor legislatures. This continuous legislative authority cannot be exhausted by any prior statute. "The legislature, having tried one plan, is not precluded from trying another. It . . . may change its plans as often as it deems necessary or expedient." [*State v. Haworth*, 23 N.E. 946, 948 (Ind. 1890).]

Many education-related statutes are officially compiled in school codes, and helpful summaries of school laws are published by government agencies and educational organizations. As with constitutions, courts are called on to supply the authoritative interpretation of statutes whose meaning is contested.

Control of public schools is vested in the state legislature, not in local school districts. School districts cannot, therefore, ignore or disobey state legislative directives, no matter how fervently the community espouses the idea of local control. For example, state legislatures can (1) create, alter, and abolish school districts and school boards; (2) remove incumbent school board members and abolish their offices; (3) prescribe school calendars and curricula; (4) determine the sources and procedures for providing school revenues and expenditures; (5) fix the appointment, term, and qualifications of teachers; (6) fix admission policies for local schools; and (7) impose penalties for noncompliance with state regulations.

Administrative Law—The Role of Administrators

Legislative Delegation of Authority

Educational agencies and administrators have only those powers that are granted to them, expressly or impliedly, by statutes or by the state constitution. The legal doctrine on delegation of authority to school administrators has a crucial effect on school governance. State legislatures sometime exercise direct, central authority by enacting mandatory rules, such as statutes that fix school calendars, school election dates, and attendance requirements. In most instances, however, specific legislative direction is not possible, and legislatures delegate authority to administrators to determine at their own discretion whether, when, and how to achieve broad legislative goals.[3]

The law on delegated power is deceptively simple: A state legislature may not transfer *lawmaking* authority since that power is vested by state constitutions exclusively in elected legislatures. But the legislature may delegate *administrative* authority to implement legislative policy. Courts differentiate "administrative" from "lawmaking" powers by the norm that a power will be considered "administrative" if it is accompanied by legislative (statutory) guidelines that are *reasonably adequate* to indicate the legislative will to be followed.[4] Courts generally find broad guidelines "adequate" for administrative direction, though they may require more precise guidelines for decisions that implicate important civil rights or that carry substantial penalties.

The principle that limits delegation of authority also limits redelegation or subdelegation of power by administrators to other parties. Unless the delegating statute contemplated such redelegation, a board cannot transfer its discretion to others. Redelegation issues are commonplace in challenges to hiring decisions. Thus a school board attempt to transfer its hiring or firing discretion to a supervisor would be an unauthorized redelegation that would nullify the supervisor's hiring decision.[5] The limits on redelegation apply only to transfer of *discretionary* authority, and not to instructions to perform nondiscretionary (called ministerial) acts. Executing a direct administrative order would not fall under the redelegation ban.[6]

In exercising lawfully delegated authority, school administrators make law in the sense that their regulations and decisions have a legally enforceable effect. This species of law is called *administrative law*. However, when administrators act beyond the scope of their delegated authority, their acts are *ultra vires* (meaning beyond the conferred power), and are void or voidable in law.[7] For example, a school board acted *ultra vires* in attempting to empower the teachers' union to determine how negotiated employment benefits should be allocated among its members.[8] Similarly, a commission's authority to supervise creation of independent school districts was held not to include authority to order one district to annex territory of another district.[9] Recent battles between community and central school boards over hiring authority essentially involved the issue of their respective scope of authority.[10]

Expressed and Implied Powers. Administrative authority may be implied as being reasonably necessary or incidental to carrying out expressly delegated powers. Many assertions of implied power go unchallenged, and courts tend to uphold liberal implication of administrative powers. They will not, however, imply a power that contradicts or is inconsistent with an express duty or the manifest intent of the law. Thus a school board could not claim implied power to determine tenure policy or to delimit areas of tenure when those subjects are fixed by tenure statutes.[11] Nor could a board claim implied authority to lease a building for school purposes from its express authority to construct school buildings.[12] A legislature can always settle implied power questions by enacting statutes that expressly grant or deny a disputed power.[13]

Administrative Structure of Public Education

State legislatures establish the structure and organization of public education, with most states employing a three-tier system of state-level, regional (intermediate), and local administrative agencies. A minority of states employ a two-echelon (state and local) structure, while Hawaii has a single statewide administration.[14] Agency organization varies from state to state.[15] The following summary indicates the more prominent parallels found in most states.

State–Level Agencies. Central state agencies typically include a state Department of Education; a state Board of Education; a Chief State School Officer, variously designated as Commissioner, Superintendent, or Secretary of Education; and special service divisions or departments. State Boards of Education develop policies and regulations on specified topics, e.g., school district organization, school closings, reductions of professional staff, and state-level review of appeals from local boards.

The Chief State School Officer often acts as the executive head of state education departments,[16] which may contain divisions for specialized services such as research, administration, finance, teacher certification, and instructional services. The mentioned agencies also perform regulatory functions relating to their assigned tasks.[17]

Regional Agencies. Mid-tier regional entities deliver state-mandated special services (such as special education and transportation) to school districts in their territory. They may be authorized to conduct or coordinate nonmandated programs, which their constituent local districts voluntarily undertake. A number of states have replaced older county boards of education with *intermediate unit* entities having assigned territories that may span more than one county.

Local School Districts. School districts, acting through their school boards, manage the public schools. They have, in addition to delegated government powers, certain corporate powers, e.g., to sue and be sued, make contracts, hold property, and receive grants from private sources as well as from governments. State legislatures may create different classes of school districts with different powers. Where school districts are by law subjected to legal controls of an overlying municipality, they are called "dependent"; those that are free of such controls are called "independent." School administrators must observe the laws that define the authority of their particular school district.

Local attempts to defeat state legislation that requires school districts to be reorganized can only succeed if the state law is unconstitutional. Such attacks commonly allege that the state has taken local property without compensation or has unconstitutionally impaired the affected district's contracts. But altering school district bounds, assets, and obligations is not "taking" anything from the district because public school property is, in law, state, not district, property.[18] On the contract impairment claim, courts have held that local districts do not have any legal right or power to sue their parent state. Only district creditors could assert a contract impairment if district assets had been pledged to secure payment of their debt claims and are transferred to another entity. But if, as is more common, the creditor never had a property pledge but only an unsecured promise of payment from the school district, there is no impairment as long as the promising district continued to exist.[19] State legislatures may elect to avoid reorganization burdens or windfalls between reorganized districts by enacting prescribed adjustments of district assets and obligations.[20]

Local School Boards. School boards derive their powers and duties from school statutes. Where the legislature enacts a specific method of operation, local boards may not adopt alternative methods, as by making a teacher contract run longer than the term fixed by statute.[21]

State law also governs the composition, selection, term, and qualifications for board office, e.g., age, residency, noncriminal history, the absence of prohibited kinships to district personnel, and avoidance of conflicts of interest.[22] Legislatures may not, however, disqualify persons for unconstitutional reasons, such as political party affiliation.[23]

As a general rule, a school board can only make official decisions as a single corporate entity, i.e., as a whole at a duly covened official board meeting.[24]

Board members may not redelegate their discretion to other individuals. Board attempts to authorize a school superintendent to determine whom to hire were, therefore, *ultra vires* and void.[25] State laws require that official board actions be taken only at a meeting that is convened pursuant to proper public notice, is attended by a required quorum of board members, and is open to the public. A court of equity may refuse to apply these formal requisites where a board unjustly sought to void a teacher's contract for lack of formal board approval after misleading the teacher into believing that the board had duly approved his appointment.[26]

Notice of scheduled meetings must be given to each board member as well as the public, and must afford a reasonable opportunity for notified parties to prepare for and attend the meeting.[27] School boards may set their meetings at any reasonable time or place, but meetings set at unreasonable distances from the district may be voided.[28]

A majority of board members must be present to constitute a necessary quorum for an official meeting, but the legislature may vary the quorum requirement for specified circumstances or topics, as noted in the endnote.[29] The legal effect of a member's withdrawal from a meeting or of abstention from voting will also depend on particular case circumstances and the interpretation of statutory wording in different states. Some case illustrations are listed in the endnote.[30]

An assortment of statutes, known as open meeting, sunshine, freedom of information, and public records laws, aims to guarantee public access to board records as well as board meetings.[31] Open meeting laws generally provide exceptions for certain confidential material, the disclosure of which could prejudice public or individual interests, such as deliberations on labor negotiations, plans to acquire property, or discussion of accusations, which if false could irreparably harm an individual's reputation.[32] A common point of contention is whether those laws exempt particular board gatherings or data from public access and disclosure.[33]

Board members may meet unofficially and informally as long as they defer official decision on discussed matters to a later open meeting. Courts are not agreed, however, on the question whether a board may, after discussing a matter at a closed (executive) session, lawfully act on it without further discussion or deliberation at a later open meeting. The state variations on that question and on the penalties for open meeting violations appear in the endnote.[34]

Whether particular records qualify as public records subject to public inspection and copying (at reasonable times and places on payment of reasonable copying costs) will depend on the definition of a public record under the governing statute. Some statutes even apply to unofficial board records, such as school files (if not privileged as confidential), payroll records, and even the names of job applicants.[35]

As reported in the *Conover* opinion at the end of this chapter, courts of different states have drawn diverse conclusions as to when notes of a board meeting become official minutes subject to public inspection. Board minutes remain subject to timely board correction and clarification whether or not they are deemed "public records."[36] Minutes of an executive board session were held subject to public inspection in one state, even though the law did not require that the board make or keep such minutes.[37] With regard to student records, however, many state provisions have been effectively superseded by the federal student records statute, which is discussed in Chapter 7.

Case Law—The Role of Courts

Courts have the last say on the meaning and effect of questioned laws and on the processes by which a party may seek or obtain relief. In addition, they have created rights and duties that are not based on the written law of constitutions, statutes, and administrative regulations. To state a few obvious examples, courts:

- Create law known as common law and equity law.
- Create the rules for allowing or disallowing court consideration of a complaint.
- Determine when presented evidence is sufficient or insufficient to justify a case result, including resolution of conflicting testimony or evidence.
- Determine whether or not a school administrator lawfully exercised his or her authority or unlawfully abused administrative discretion.
- Determine what process is due or required for different types of school hearings or decisions.

The power of individual judges to shape case facts, issues, and outcomes is illustrated by the *Dawson* case, which appears at the end of this chapter; by the *Lee* opinions at the end of Chapter 3; and by the contrasting treatment of sex-oriented classroom presentations given by the judges of the First and Eighth Circuit Courts of Appeal in the *Brown* and *Lacks* cases, which appear, respectively, at the end of Chapter 3 and Chapter 6.

Structure and Jurisdiction of American Courts

America's federal and state courts have distinct structures, subject matter jurisdiction, and territorial jurisdiction. These differences largely explain their influence on the schools. The federal courts have primary jurisdiction on federal law questions, while state courts have primary jurisdiction on the laws of their home state, so that state courts are bound to follow federal court decisions on federal law, and federal courts follow state law and state court decisions on state law.[38] Each court's jurisdiction with regard to other courts is further defined by its assigned territory of operation and by its assigned function as a trial court or a court of appeal.

Federal Courts.   Federal courts operate at three basic tiers, as indicated in Figure 1.1.

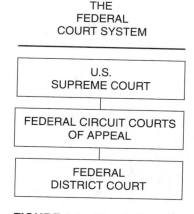

FIGURE 1.1   The Federal
Court System

At the base trial level, the District Courts (about 92 in number) hear and decide lawsuits arising within their territories. At the intermediate level, the Circuit Courts of Appeal (13 in number) hear appeals taken from District Courts within their respective circuit territories. The Circuit Courts and their boundaries are indicated in Figure 1.2.

District and Circuit Court decisions bind only their respective territories, which explains why cases from different federal venues often do not agree. Later chapters provide many examples where federal Circuit Court conflicts produce different law in different federal circuits unless and until the Supreme Court resolves such a conflict. Federal Circuit Courts have significant impact in that their decisions remain binding for long periods because the Supreme Court can only accept and review a tiny percentage of appeals from lower courts. Schools authorities must, therefore, be particularly attentive to the decisions of their federal circuit that remain unreviewed by the United States Supreme Court.

The Supreme Court of the United States is the only court of nationwide territorial jurisdiction that binds all other courts, federal and state, on federal law questions.

State Courts.   As with federal courts, most state systems consist of three tiers: trial courts, intermediate appeal courts, and courts of final appeal. The assigned territory of state trial courts normally coincides with county boundaries, while the intermediate and high courts of appeal take cases from all parts of the state. Appeals on federal questions may be taken from the highest state court to the United States Supreme Court.

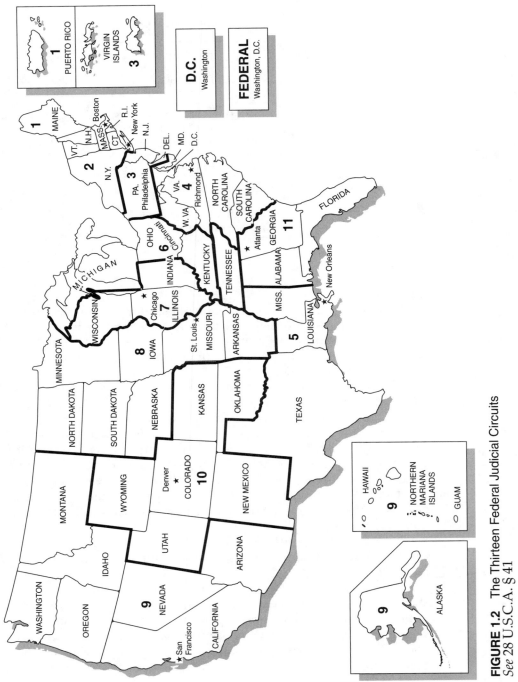

FIGURE 1.2 The Thirteen Federal Judicial Circuits
See 28 U.S.C.A. § 41

Judge-Made Law—Common Law and Equity Law

Over time courts have built up two categories of law known as common law and equity law. The common law was built from court decisions and legal principles thought to reflect the customs and values of the court territory. Under the practice of *stare decisis* (meaning "let the past decision stand") courts tend to follow prior case law. The law on contracts, property, and torts originated in and still rests substantially on common law principles.

When the common law, through rigid adherence to case precedents, proved inadequate or resulted in harsh outcomes, a separate court system known as chancery or equity was created to provide relief not available in common law courts. By looking less to precedents than to supervening principles of justice and conscience, judges in equity fashioned a body of doctrines and remedies unknown to the common law, such as court decrees to enjoin, i.e., coerce, wrongdoers under penalties of fines or imprisonment for contempt of court, to desist from ongoing harmful actions, or to take affirmative action to undo past harms. The court injunction, a product of equity law, continues to have a crucial impact in labor disputes and discrimination cases. As the Supreme Court noted in a recent desegregation case:

> The essence of a court's equity power lies in its inherent capacity to adjust remedies in a feasible and practical way to eliminate the conditions or redress the injuries caused by unlawful action. Equitable remedies must be flexible if these underlying principles are to be enforced with fairness and precision. [See *Freeman v. Pitts*, 112 S. Ct. 1430, 1444 (1992).]

While the originally separate courts of common law and equity have been merged and unified in most states, the doctrines created by common law and equity endure as distinct branches of law in the unified courts.

Access to Courts—Technical Barriers

Unless conferred by statute, a party must meet judge-made standards for "judicial review" in order to be heard by a court. The rich law on the limits of judicial review cannot be canvassed here, but two doctrines have special import for school cases, namely, standing to sue, which limits party access to courts, and the exhaustion doctrine, which determines when a suit may be brought.

Standing—Who Can Sue?   To gain court hearing, a party must establish a personal right to be heard, which in technical terms is called "standing to sue." Unless a right to sue is conferred by legislation, that party must have suffered a concrete injury-in-fact (as distinguished from an abstract, ethical, aesthetic, or philosophical grievance); that is, the person must have a personal stake in the challenged decision and must be seeking a form of relief that the court is empowered to provide. Standing requirements are concerned only with the legal interest of the particular suitor in the presented case, and not with the validity of the challenged decision. Thus citizens who have no real or threatened legal interest at stake will not be heard. For example, taxpayers have standing to sue on matters regarding the levy or expenditure of their taxes, but do not have standing to seek relief from an unjust suspension of unrelated students.[39]

Exhaustion—When May a Party Sue?   Courts generally require that a party first "exhaust" all available channels of administrative hearing and relief before they will hear a case.[40]

> The exhaustion doctrine serves to prevent premature interruption of administrative review, to permit school agencies to function efficiently with reasonable opportunity to correct its own errors, and to provide a reviewing court with the benefit of a full record of administrative hearings. [*Weinberger v. Salfi,* 422 U.S. 749, 756–66 (1975)]

Courts recognize several exceptions to the exhaustion rule, namely, where the legislature grants a right of appeal to courts without administrative exhaustion; and where courts find that the use of the exhaustion rule would not serve its essential purposes, e.g., where the appeal is taken on a pure question of law; or where delays incident to further administrative proceedings would irreparably jeopardize the complainant's rights; or where the administrative body could not, in any event, provide appropriate legal relief.[41] Exhaustion would not be required for a situation in which an administrative hearing on a student's exclusion from a school program could not be completed before that program would expire, or where a school district, by repeated failure to provide a due process hearing required by law for children with handicaps, frustrated any adequate relief by further administrative hearings.[42] The strongest exceptions to the exhaustion rule are made where the delays of administrative hearings would jeopardize alleged violations of important civil rights, such as freedom of speech.[43]

Court Review of Administrative Decisions

Once courts decide to hear an appeal, they normally do not reconsider the entire case, but only those questions for which review is allowed, and then only on the basis of the written record of the administrative proceedings.[44] A court will not consider questions that were not properly raised or tried before the administrative tribunal. This narrowing process explains why courts often bypass important questions, and why a series of cases is sometimes needed to settle all important aspects of a school problem.

The three principal grounds for judicial reversal of an administrative decision are that the decision:

1. Was based on an error of law, or
2. Was not supported by substantial evidence on important case facts, or
3. Manifested an abuse of discretion by the administrative decisionmaker.

For questions of pure law, i.e., where facts are not disputed, courts need only identify and apply the governing law. Thus a board's failure to follow required procedures or actions based on a misreading of pertinent law are grounds for reversal.[45] When faced with conflicting evidence on important facts, courts generally limit their review to the question whether the administrative record contained substantial evidence to support the administrative findings. In so doing, they do not decide afresh whether they would have viewed the evidence differently than the administrator, but only whether the record presented "such relevant evidence as a reasonable mind might accept as adequate to support a conclusion."[46]

In like fashion, on the question whether administrators abused their discretion, courts only consider the reasonableness of the administrator's judgment, not whether they would arrive at the same judgment.[47] Educational judgments for which educators are presumptively the primary experts, e.g., decisions regarding curricular development,[48] command greater judicial deference than decisions on legal standards (such as due process procedures) on which judges are the primary experts.[49] Still, administrative decisions enjoy a rebuttable presumption of correctness, with challengers having the burden of proving administrative error.

Judicial Cure of Administrative Errors.   To minimize disruptions that are occasioned by overturning administrative actions, courts have devised several doctrines to cure or mitigate such errors. The *harmless error* doctrine allows a court to hold that some errors are insufficient to invalidate the questioned action. Secondly, a court may excuse defective performance of an administrative duty if it finds that the violated law was only *directory* (i.e., merely presenting a helpful direction) and not *mandatory* (i.e., a strict precondition for lawful action). While the mandatory/directory distinction theoretically rests on the intent of the applicable statute, courts candidly acknowledge that they are influenced by practical considerations in finding a statute to be directory or mandatory. Thus in suits challenging defectively conducted elections, courts tend to find that the alleged errors involved "directory" duties only, and to uphold the election, unless the errors seriously affected the election outcome.[50] In sum, the gravity of the error, the magnitude of public cost involved in overturning the action, and the presence or absence of official fault or bad faith are factors that influence case applications of the mandatory/directory classification.

Administrators may also rectify past errors by timely substitution of corrective proceedings. Where that is not feasible, there still remains a doctrine to avoid nullification by retroactive validation of the ineffective action, i.e., "ratification." The ratification doctrine allows an authorized official or agency to adopt and approve a past action that could have been, but was not, properly adopted. The technical requisites for ratification must be left to specialized texts, but the essential preconditions for ratification are as follows:

1. A board can only ratify actions that it was legally authorized to take, both at the time it initially took faulty action and at the time it seeks to ratify that action.
2. Ratification must follow the same formalities as would have been required for the initial action.

3. The board cannot ratify unknowingly or accidentally. It must specifically intend to affirm the past action with full knowledge of all material facts.
4. The board must ratify the entire past action or none of it.
5. Ratification cannot be made if it results in fraud or unfair consequences to third parties.
6. A board cannot ratify action of a party who did not purport to act on its behalf or under its authority.[51]

Ratification normally requires affirmative administrative action, but in limited circumstances a court may find a ratification from board inaction, e.g., where a school board accepted in silence the benefits of a defectively executed contract.[52] Inasmuch as the operation of the ratification doctrine may require technical legal analysis, interested parties should consult legal counsel on ratification questions.

Chapter 1 Discussion Questions

Where the answer to a question may be qualified by special circumstances, explain the potential qualification.

1. What is the legal difference and ranking between a constitution, a statute, and a school board regulation?

2. What do the following terms signify in law?
   a. Jurisdiction
   b. *Ultra vires*

3. Name the principal federal law grounds for the exercise of federal government jurisdiction over public education.

4. Where federal and state laws conflict, why does the federal law supercede state law to control the covered subject?

5. Where a school board decision is not unconstitutional or *ultra vires*, on what other grounds may a court overturn that decision?

6. Does the state or local school district have ultimate legal control over the disposition and use of public school property? On what basis?

7. Name some important areas of day-to-day school operations that are controlled by state education agencies rather than by local school districts.

8. What legal body has authority to:

a. Alter or abolish your school district without its consent?
b. Alter the legal powers of your school board?
c. Determine public school course requirements and textbook selection?

9. Are the persons serving in the following positions classified as public officers or public employees?
   a. School board members
   b. Teachers
   c. School principals
   d. School superintendents

10. How does the superintendent's position differ from that of:
    a. School board members?
    b. School supervisors?
    c. Teachers?

11. Name the principal requirements for an official school board meeting.

12. May an official school board meeting be held outside the school district? Explain.

13. What does "standing to sue" mean, and what must a party show in order to have "standing to sue"?

14. What is the difference between common law and equity law? Give an example of each.

15. Where cases are appealed to the courts, why do courts, rather than legislatures or school administrators, have the final word in school disputes?

❖ CASES

Case 1.1

DAWSON v. EAST SIDE UNION HIGH SCHOOL DISTRICT
34 Cal. Rptr. 2d 108 (1994)

> [***Focus Note.*** *Whittle Communications, L.P., a for-profit publisher, developed an educational network and audio-video channel to transmit into schools a daily program consisting of 10 minutes of current events and 2 minutes of commercial ads by vendors of teen products. The commercial ads were distinguished from the current events portion of the video. Whittle offered its program and the necessary receiving equipment to schools free of charge, and profited from the sale of the advertising time to the commercial vendors. The state Superintendent of Public Instruction opposed use of "Channel One" in public schools. The California State Board of Education took the position that such use was lawful and within the decisional authority of the local school districts. The school board of the East Side Union High School District decided to use Channel One for its high school (Overfelt). The superintendent and others brought suit to enjoin that use. The trial court denied the injunction, and the appeals court affirmed that ruling. The following opinion illustrates the importance of administrative law doctrines.]*

BAMATTRE-MANOUKIAN, ASSOCIATE JUSTICE.

❖ ❖ ❖

The essence of the plaintiffs' position . . . is that it is unlawful in any circumstances for a public school district to contract for use in its classrooms of video programming which contains commercial advertising.

❖ ❖ ❖

Our consideration . . . will take account of two broad and interrelated principles: That in California local school districts are granted substantial discretionary control of public education, and that in the exercise of this discretion the school districts have some latitude to adopt or permit uses or procedures which in and of themselves are not strictly educational so long as the uses or procedures are no more than incidental to valid educational purposes.

❖ ❖ ❖

1. Local Control

❖ ❖ ❖

By the terms of the [state constitution] . . . primary authority over public education is vested in the Legislature. . . .

The Legislature has explicitly recognized that "because of economic, geographic, physical, political, educational, and social diversity, specific choices about instructional materials need to be made at the local level" (Ed. Code, § 60002), that it has given school district governing boards "broad powers to establish courses of study. . . . " (id. § 60003).

❖ ❖ ❖

It follows that courts should give substantial deference to the decisions of local school districts and boards within the scope of their broad discretion, and should intervene only in clear cases of abuse of discretion.

2. Incidental Noneducational Matters

. . . [E]very activity of a California public school must be focused upon valid educational purposes. . . . Nevertheless it has long been recognized that activities or procedures other than those which can be characterized as purely and universally educational may be deemed suitable to further the purposes of education. . . .

❖ ❖ ❖

Under the principles of local control . . . the essentially factual question whether particular noncurricular matters are or are not incidental must be addressed in the first instance to the broad discretion of local school districts and boards, and a court would be justified in disturbing the local decision only upon a clear showing of abuse of the local district's or board's sound discretion.

❖ ❖ ❖

The Issues

. . . [W]e shall conclude that the trial court correctly rejected the plaintiffs' contentions that classroom video advertising can never be deemed incidental to valid education purpose. . . . We shall also conclude that the trial court correctly determined that the "Channel One" advertising . . . could lawfully be used in classrooms only so long as students were not coerced to view it.

1. Could "Channel One's" Advertising Ever Be Incidental?

. . . The school district's implicit determination that "Channel One's" current-events programming served a valid educational purpose is supported by the record and was well within the sound discretion of the school district.

. . . Neither Whittle nor anyone else suggests that the school district could properly have given Whittle carte blanche to display classroom video advertising without limitation as to content or duration. . . .

As thus framed by the parties, the primary issue before us is whether the concededly noncurricular "Channel One" advertising could be deemed incidental to the valid educational purpose of the current-events programming.

✧ ✧ ✧

. . . [T]he determination whether the advertising was incidental was to be entrusted in the first instance to the broad discretion of the local school district, and the trial court's only concern . . . would have been whether the district's determination constituted a clear abuse of the district's discretion. . . .

. . . We should point out, however, that our concurrence does not and cannot extend beyond the precise circumstances of record in this case: In another case, a showing of more intrusive commercial content, or of less effective editorial content, might warrant a conclusion that it would be an abuse of discretion for a school district to enter into such a contract. Nor should we be understood to suggest that it would have been a clear abuse of discretion for this (or another) school district to have declined to enter into the Whittle contract. . . . We must emphasize once again that a local school district's discretion to make such determinations is broad and must be judicially respected as such.

. . . [T]he plaintiffs attack neither the abstract concept that public school students may be exposed to noncurricular matter incidental to a valid educational purpose, nor the sufficiency of the factual record. . . . Instead, the plaintiffs argue, that as a matter of law, a school district may never lawfully contract for, or display, classroom video advertising such as "Channel One's." . . . The plaintiffs assert that "[i]t is the advertising scheme itself that is the problem, not the educational resources purchased with the revenue from the advertising." . . .

✧ ✧ ✧

We shall agree with the trial court that contracts for classroom video advertising are not illegal as a matter of law.

✧ ✧ ✧

Next the plaintiffs propose that "[t]elevision advertising should be treated the same as partisan political campaigning."

✧ ✧ ✧

. . . Their argument appears to be that there is a broader principle—that publicly provided resources or opportunities may not be used to advocate a course of action . . . which not all members of the underwriting public might otherwise choose. . . .

The plaintiffs' broader principle is too broad to be persuasive, or even useful. . . . The principle could as readily be applied to any element of orthodox school curriculum as to which a difference of opinion could be anticipated. . . .

✧ ✧ ✧

The plaintiffs argue that statutes require . . . that "all instructional materials shall be 'accurate, objective, and . . . suited to the needs of pupils' and must 'encourage thrift,' " but that . . . "Channel One's" advertisements "exag[g]erate and glorify consumption by pandering to adolescent desires for popularity, status, glitter, and sexual attractiveness." . . . To support this argument the plaintiffs cite three statutes:

✧ ✧ ✧

The plaintiffs argue, broadly, that "[t]he advertising scheme embodied by 'Channel One' is inconsistent with each of these statutory purposes and State Board policies."

✧ ✧ ✧

We are satisfied that the various statutes and State Board policy statements the plaintiffs cite by no means establish as a matter of law that classroom video advertising will be illegal in all circumstances.

c. "Core Values"

Finally, the plaintiffs assert that "[w]hile this case presents novel and difficult issues, it must ultimately be resolved by reliance upon our core values regarding 'public education.' "

(1) Commercial Advertising

The crux of the plaintiffs' core-values argument appears to be their perception that the motives and methods of commercial advertising are simply and irreconcilably antithetical to the ideals of public education.

✧ ✧ ✧

. . . In the plaintiffs' view, "we are dealing with a commercial advertising scheme that uses student attendance and attention as saleable property." . . .

✧ ✧ ✧

The plaintiffs generalize, broadly . . . but they identify no specific harm to students . . . .

That Whittle stands to make a great deal of money from "Channel One" has nothing whatsoever to do with whether, from the educational standpoint . . . the "Channel One" advertisements were incidental to a valid educational purpose. . . .

✧ ✧ ✧

. . . [T]he plaintiffs do not deny, that student exposure to many forms of advertising has long been tolerated. . . . Vending machines . . . commercial logos on computer equipment and . . . scoreboards . . . assigned reading materials from magazines or newspapers . . . yearbooks, . . . class photographers, brand-name . . . food service products. . . .

The plaintiffs undertake to distinguish these forms of commercialism . . . from "the invasive nature of the televised program known as 'Channel One' " which, in the plaintiffs' view, "clearly crosses the line of appropriateness. . . ."

❖ ❖ ❖

2. Must Student Viewing be Voluntary? . . .

We agree . . . that public school students cannot be compelled to watch class-room video advertising. [The court then decided that the school's exemption of students who desired not to watch the program removed the legal difficulty.]

Review Questions 1.1

1. Could the court have reasonably viewed the authority of the state board more liberally to arrive at a contrary result? Could courts in other states do so?
2. What guidance does the opinion provide for administrators when considering potential educational uses of commercially driven Internet technology?

Case 1.2

CONOVER v. BOARD OF EDUCATION OF NEBO SCHOOL DISTRICT
267 P.2d 768 (Utah 1954)

> [***Focus Note.*** *In deciding what is a "public record" open to public inspection under Utah law, the following opinion noted the variations in both the legislative and judicial treatment of public record statutes from state to state.*]

HENRIOD, JUSTICE.

On Feb. 16, 1953, . . . the State Superintendent of Public Instruction . . . advised the [school board] Clerk that minutes of local board meetings were not official until approved by the board . . . . On Feb. 18, the board held a meeting. . . . The Clerk took notes of what transpired, and transcribed them into minutes for board approval and placement in his Journal. On Feb. 19 the plaintiffs asked permission to examine and copy the minutes so transcribed, but the Clerk . . . advised that they would not be available for inspection until the board approved them at its next meeting. . . .

Plaintiffs urge that the notes of the Clerk, or at least the transcribed minutes, prepared for Journal entry, subject only to board approval, were a public writing . . . and should have been open to inspection immediately after preparation, and that preparation immediately should have followed the meeting. Defendants say this might lead to public misinformation and embarrassment . . . because of possible inaccuracies in what they claim were tentative minutes, unofficial until approved and placed in the Journal.

The statutes and cases relating to public writings are divergent as the shading of the spectrum. There appears to be no formula for determining what is or is not a public writing, except by defining the terms, looking at the facts, and relying on court decisions. . . . To hold that a public writing includes the unexpurgated scribbled notes of a Clerk, legible, perhaps, to him alone, would be unreasonable. . . . It would be unreasonable also to hold that any record made by the Clerk short of approval by a board and placement in a Journal, is not a public writing. . . . We hold, therefore, that the Clerk's untranscribed notes reasonably are not classifiable as a public writing under the statute, whereas the transcribed minutes, in final form, but awaiting only approval and placement in the Journal, are a public writing in contemplation of the statute. In so holding, we are aware of those authorities stating that not every memorandum of a public officer is a public record. We believe, however, that the more pertinent cases are found in a long line holding that whenever a written record of a transaction of a public officer in his office is a *convenient and appropriate* mode of discharging the duties of his office, and is kept by him as such, whether required by express provision of law or not, such a record is a public record. To hold that the minutes in this case were not, but the Journal was, a public writing, would attach a magic significance to the word "journal," and might repose in boards a power to act on matters of great public moment without opportunity for public scrutiny.

Here the Clerk did everything he intended to do by way of recording the meeting. Under the statute he could have placed the minutes in the Journal as soon as prepared. The board's policy of having him refrain from doing so until approval was had cannot justify circumvention of a statute requiring him to prepare the minutes, nor the withholding of information from the public for an unreasonable length of time. . . .

The parties here have requested that we address ourselves also to the matter of when the minutes should be available for public inspection. . . . We believe that what is a reasonable time to prepare a record of a public board meeting depends entirely on the facts of each case. If the board action called for the purchase of textbooks advocating communism, the record reasonably should be prepared for public release at once after the meeting, while a resolution to dismiss school on Washington's Birthday perhaps need never be documented. . . . It seems to us that the reasonable time when the record of such meetings should be made available to the public, may vary with the exigencies of the particular case, and the time for preparation and dissemination would be directly proportional to the importance of the action taken.

Both sides concede that the public is entitled to know what happened at school board meetings within a reasonable time. . . . We believe further, that a reasonable time after the meeting for making available the record of actions taken there would be some time *before* any important action was to take place. If available only *after* action taken, such information would have little or no news value. . . .

✧ ✧ ✧

There is the further problem as to when *information* of what transpired at the meeting should be made available to the public, quite apart from documentation in a public writing. It would seem that, unless matters were of such a delicate nature or of the type where public policy dictates nondissemination, the meeting itself should be open to the public and press, and information concerning what transpired there should be made available at least in a general way . . . at any time thereafter by him whose duties require its recordation. . . . We . . . hold that although the Clerk's action in refusing permission to inspect his minutes was reasonable for the purpose of obtaining an adjudication of correlative rights and duties, it would be unreasonable in preventing the public and press from obtaining information as to what happened at the meeting.

Review Questions 1.2

1. If legislative intent was not expressly stated, on what basis did this court answer the following questions?
    a. That untranscribed notes are not public records, but transcribed notes may be.
    b. That transcribed, but unapproved, notes must be made available for inspection within a "reasonable time."
    c. That "reasonable time" depends on the court's mentioned factors.
    d. That information of a meeting not noted in writings must be made available.
2. In filling in the gaps of written law, did the court make law in deciding how it operated?

❖ ENDNOTES

1. The National Center for Education Statistics reported, *inter alia,* that more than half of U.S. public schools reported experiencing at least one crime incident in school year 1996–97, and 1 in 10 schools reported at least one serious violent crime during that school year. See *Violence and Discipline Problems in U.S. Public Schools: 1996–97 (1998)* (www.nces.ed.gov/pubs98/violence).

   Safe school acts have been enacted in California, Connecticut, Iowa, Louisiana, Massachusetts, Michigan, New York, Pennsylvania, Tennessee, Texas, West Virginia, and Wisconsin. [Missouri and Georgia also recently enacted school safety laws] and such laws commonly require schools to adopt and enforce student codes of conduct. See Robert C. Cloud, Federal, State, and Local Responses to Public School Violence, 120 *Ed. Law Rep.* 877 (1997). Department of Justice statistics from 1996 reported the numbers and types of school assaults, the numbers of students staying home or dropping out of school out of fear, and the numbers of students reported for bringing weapons to school.

2. Cathe v. Doddridge County Board of Education, 490 S.E.2d 340 (W. Va. 1997).

3. Floyd v. Waiters, 133 F.3d 786 (11th Cir. 1998); Lockhart v. Cedar Rapids Community School Dist., 577 N.W.2d 845 (Iowa 1998); Packer v. Board of Educ. of Town of Thomaston, 717 A.2d 117 (Conn. 1998).

4. Where state constitutions directly delegate specified powers to a named agency or source, the state legislature cannot alter that arrangement. City of Eastlake v. Forest City Enterprises, Inc., 426 U.S. 668 (1976).

5. Jacob v. Fremont R-1 School Dist., 697 P.2d 414 (Colo. Ct. App. 1984); Boyce v. Alexis I. duPont School Dist., 341 F. Supp. 678 (D. Del. 1972).

6. Boyd v. Mary E. Dill School Dist., 631 P.2d 577 (Ariz. 1981).

7. Brandon Valley Indep. School Dist. v. Minnehaha County Board of Educ., 181 N.W.2d 96 (S.D. 1970).

8. Chatham Assn of Educators v. Board of Pub. Educ., 204 S.E.2d 138 (Ga. 1974).

9. State *ex rel.* Dix v. Board of Educ., 578 P.2d 692 (Kan. 1978); Elk Point Indep. School Dist. v. State Comm. of Elementary and Secondary Educ., 187 N.W.2d 666 (S.D. 1971).

10. *The N. Y. Times,* Section B, p. 1 (12-24-96); Section A, p. 1 (12-23-96).

11. Haschke v. School Dist., 167 N.W.2d 79 (Neb. 1969). *See also* Elroy Kendall Witton Schools v. Coop Educ. Service Agency Dist. 12, 302 N.W.2d 89 (Wis. 1981).

12. Bower v. Arizona State School for the Deaf and the Blind, 704 P.2d 809 (Ariz. App. 1984); Baer v. Nyquist, 357 N.Y.S. 442 (1974).

13. *See, e.g.,* Carter v. Allen, 250 N.E.2d 30 (N.Y. 1969), where a subsequent statute negated a previously implied power.

14. Survey of the State Administrative Structures in Pa. Dept. of Educ., PREP Rep. No. 23 (1971), at 3, 4.

15. *See, e.g.,* U.S. Dept. of Health, Education, and Welfare, State Departments of Education, State Boards of Education, and Chief State School Officers, DHEW Pub. No. (OE) 73-07400 (1973).

16. *E.g.,* Pordum v. State, 492 N.Y.S.2d 204 (A.D. 1985).

17. National Institute of Education, U.S. Department of Health, Education, and Welfare, A Study of State Legal Standards for the Provision of Public Education (1979).

18. Moses Lake School Dist. No. 161 v. Big Bend Community College, 503 P.2d 86 (1972), *appeal dismissed,* 412 U.S. 934 (1973); New Castle County School Dist. v. State, 424 A.2d 15 (Del. 1980).

19. The fuzzy scope of the Contracts Clause is discussed in U.S. Trust Co. of New York v. New Jersey, 431 U.S. 1 (1977); Camardo v. Board of Educ. of City School Dist., 434 N.Y.S.2d 514 (1980).

   A court might find no contract impairment if the surviving reorganized district succeeds to prior contract obligations. Shirley v. School Bd., 332 P.2d 267 (Kan. 1958). *See also* Michigan Educ. Assn v. North Dearborn Heights School Dist., 425 N.W.2d 503 (Mich. 1988).

20. School Dist. No. 47 of Hall County v. School Dist. of City of Grand Island, 186 N.W.2d 485 (Neb. 1971).

21. Wecherly v. Board of Educ., 202 N.W.2d 777 (Mich. 1972); Nethercutt v. Pulaski County Special School Dist., 475 S.W.2d 517 (Ark. 1972). Savino v. Bradford Central School Dist. Board of Educ., 429 N.Y.S.2d 108 (1980).

22. *Age requirements:* Human Rights Party v. Secretary of State, 370 F. Supp. 921 (E.D. Mich. 1973). *Residency requirements:* Brown v. Patterson, 609 S.W.2d 287 (Tex. 1980); State v. Thomas, 293 So.2d 40 (Fla. 1974). *Family relationships:* Rosenstock v. Scaringe, 357 N.E.2d 347 (N.Y. 1976).

    The laws on board conflicts of interest, plural job holding, and nepotism vary greatly from state to state. Annot., *Teacher as a Member of School Board*, 70 A.L.R. 3d 1188 (1976). *Re* ouster of board member for nepotism, *see* Cross v. Comm. *ex rel.* Cowan, 795 S.W.2d 65 (Ky. 1990). *Re incompatible dual positions, see* Cranston Teachers Alliance Local No. 1704 v. Miele, 495 A.2d 233 (R.I. 1985).

23. Socialist Workers Party v. Hardy, 607 F.2d 704 (5th Cir. 1977); Communist Party of Indiana v. Whitcomb, 414 U.S. 441 (1974).

24. State v. Cons. School Dist., 281 S.W.2d 511 (Mo. 1955); School Board v. Goodson, 335 So.2d 308 (Fla. 1976); Konovalchik v. School Comm. of Salem, 226 N.E.2d 222 (Mass. 1967) (voiding teacher hire for lack of school board approval in official meeting).

    Ministerial delegation upheld. Whalen v. Minn. Special School Dist., 245 N.W.2d 440 (Minn. 1976); Dugan v. Bollman, 502 P.2d 113 (Colo. 1972).

25. Big Sandy School Dist. v. Carroll, 433 P.2d 325 (Colo. 1967) (discretionary delegation—held void). *See* Nuxabee County School Bd. v. Cannon, 485 So.2d 302 (Miss. 1986); Board of Educ. of Baltimore County v. County of Ballard, 507 A.2d 192 (Md. 1986).

26. Mullen v. Board of School Directors of DuBois Area School District, 259 A.2d 877 (Pa. 1969).

27. *Appropriate notice:* Mead School Dist. v. Mead Educ. Assn, 530 P.2d 302 (Wash. 1975). *Reasonable opportunity to attend:* Rhea v. School Board, 636 So.2d 1383 (Fla. App. 1994); News & Observer Pub. v. Interim Board of Educ., 223 S.E.2d 580 (N.C. 1976).

    The consequences of notice defaults vary from state to state—from nullifying action taken at the meeting, to imposing only personal penalties against offending board members. Rhea v. School Board, 636 So.2d 1383 (Fla. App. 1994).

    An agreement that some board members act for the board is not a lawful waiver of notice. School Dist. No. 22 v. Castell, 150 S.W. 407 (Ark. 1912).

    Courts may excuse notice defaults in special circumstances, e.g., in an emergency that requires immediate board action before notice could be given, or would serve no purpose because the non-notified board member party was so ill or distant that he could not have attended in any event. Cons. School Dist. of Glidden v. Griffin, 206 N.W. 86 (Iowa 1925).

28. Quast v. Knudson, 150 N.W.2d 199 (Minn. 1967).

29. Endeavor-Oxford Union Free H.S. Dist. v. Walters, 72 N.W.2d 535 (Wis. 1955). Some states require a higher than majority quorum, and a supermajority affirmative vote of the entire board for action on some subjects, such as dismissal of tenured teachers or adoption of school district budgets. Jacob v. Board of Regents, 365 A.2d 430 (R.I. 1976); Wesley v. Board of Educ., 403 S.W.2d 28 (Ky. 1966).

30. True withdrawal may destroy the necessary quorum, but mere removal from the board table was not considered a withdrawal. State v. Vanosdal, 31 N.E. 79 (Ind. 1892).

    Where a majority vote is required, some courts treat failure to vote as agreement with the voting majority. If, however, the law requires a specified procedure on a given topic, an abstention may be treated as either concurrence or dissent depending on the interpretation of the governing statute. For subjects requiring a specified number of affirmative votes, abstention has the same effect as a negative vote. Edwards v. Mettler, 129 N.W.2d 805 (Minn. 1964); Mullins v. Eveland, 234 S.W.2d 639 (Mo. 1950); Bunsen v. County Board of School Trustees, 198 N.E.2d 735 (Ill. 1964). *See also* Wesley v. Board of

Educ., 403 S.W.2d 28 (Ky. 1966); Oldham v. Drummond Board of Educ., 542 P.2d 1309 (Okla. 1975).

31. Rathman v. Board of Directors of Davenport Community School Dist., 580 N.W.2d 773 (Iowa 1998).

32. *See, e.g., re student discipline:* Hanten v. School Dist. of Riverview Gardens, 13 F. Supp. 2d 971 (E.D. Mo. 1998); Davis v. Churchill County School Bd., 616 F. Supp. 1310 (D. Nev. 1985); Racine Union School Dist. v. Thompson, 321 N.W.2d 334 (Wis. 1982). *Re labor negotiations:* Bassett v. Braddock, 262 So.2d 425 (Fla. 1972). *Re potential land purchase:* Collinsville Comm. Unit School Dist. No. 10 v. White, 283 N.E.2d 718 (Ill. 1972). *Re employment matters:* McCown v. Patagonia Union School Dist., 629 P.2d 94 (Ariz. 1981). *Re teacher discharge:* School Dist. for City of Royal Oak v. Schulman, 243 N.W.2d 673 (Mich. 1976).

33. *Disapproved closed meetings:* Marxsen v. Board of Directors, 591 A.2d 867 (Me. 1991); Ridenour v. Board of Educ., City of Dearborn, 314 N.W.2d 760 (Mich. 1981); Orford Teachers Assn v. Watson, 427 A. 2d 21 (N.H. 1981).

34. *Compare* Bagby v. School Dist. No. 1, 528 P.2d 1299 (Colo. 1974); Reeves v. Orleans Parish School Bd., 281 S.2d 719 (La. 1973); *with* Board of Educ. v. State Board of Educ., 443 P.2d 502 (N.M. 1968).

    Some courts nullified board actions, while others decline to do so on the view that nullification of board action would entail unreasonable public costs or harm to innocent third parties. White v. Battaglia, 434 N.Y.S.2d 537 (1980); Matter of Order Declaring Annexation, 637 P.2d 1270 (Okla. 1981); Toyah Indep. School Dist. v. Pecos-Barstow Indep. School Dist., 466 S.W.2d 377 (Tex. 1971); Dobrovolny v. Reinhardt, 173 N.W.2d 837 (Iowa 1970).

    In several states, courts limit the remedy for open meeting violations to individual penalties on individual board members, such as personal fines, suspension, loss of school board office, or monetary liability to parties injured by the statutory violation. Griswold v. Mt. Diablo Unified School Dist., 134 Cal. Rptr. 3 (1976); Channel 10 Inc. v. Independent School District, 215 N.W.2d 817 (Minn. 1974).

35. Atty. Gen. v. School Comm. of Northampton, 375 N.E.2d 1188 (Mass. 1978) (names of appointive candidates); Mans v. Lebanon School Bd., 290 A.2d 866 (N.H. 1972) (payroll records).

36. Haight v. Board of Educ., 329 N.E.2d 442 (Ill. App. 1975).

37. Orford Teachers Assn v. Watson, 427 A.2d 21 (N.H. 1981).

38. Erie R. Co. v. Tompkins, 204 U.S. 64 (1938).

39. Brandon v. Ashworth, 955 P.2d 233 (Okl. 1998); Fort Wayne Educ. Assn. v. Indiana Dept. of Educ., 692 N.E.2d 902 (Ind. App. 1998); Coughlin v. Seattle School Dist., 621 P.2d 183 (Wash. 1980). For standing to sue on federal questions, *see* Flast v. Cohen, 392 U.S. 83 (1968).

40. *See* Kincel v. Supt. of Marion County Schools, 499 S.E.2d 862 (W.Va. 1997); Assn for Community Living v. Romer, 992 F.2d 1040 (10th Cir. 1993); Honig v. Doe, 484 U.S. 305(1988).

41. *Question of law:* Matthews v. Barrios-Paoli, 676 N.Y.S.2d 757 (1998). *Futility of administrative hearing:* Meehan v. Pachogue-Medoford School, 29 F. Supp. 2d 129 (E.D. N.Y. 1998); Grove City College v. Bell, 465 U.S. 555 (1984). *Harmful delays:* Middough v. Board of Trustees, 119 Cal. Rptr. 826 (1975); State Board of Educ. v. Anthony, 389 So.2d 279, 284 (La. 1974); Hickey v. Board of School Directors, 328 A.2d 549 (Pa. 1975).

42. Indiana H.S. Athletic Assn v. Blanche, 329 N.E.2d 66 (Ind. 1975); Meehan, *supra* note 41.

43. LaCroix v. Board of Educ., 505 A.2d 1233 (Conn. 1984); Hayes v. Cape Henlopen School Dist., 341 F. Supp. 823 (D. Del. 1972).

44. Antwerp v. Board of Educ. for Liverpool Central School Dist., 668 N.Y.S.2d 737 (1998).

45. McKelvey v. Colonial School Dist., 348 A.2d 445 (Pa. Cmwlth. 1975); Hill v. Dayton School Dist., 517 P.2d 223 (Wash. 1974).

46. Tarbox v. Greensburgh Central School Dist., 375 N.Y.S.2d 610 (1975); Sherefield v. Sheridan County School Dist., 544 P.2d 870 (Wyo. 1976). *See also* Wilson v. Board of Educ., 411 S.W.2d 551 (Tex. 1974).

47. Wolf v. Cuyahoga Falls City School Board of Educ., 556 N.E.2d 511 (Ohio 1990); MidValley

Taxpayers v. MidValley School, 416 A.2d 590 (Pa. 1980)

48. State of Mo. v. Schoenlaub, 507 S.W.2d 354 (Mo. 1974); Older v. Board of Educ., 266 N.E.2d 812 (N.Y. 1971).

49. Smith v. Siders, 183 S.E.2d 433 (W. Va. 1971). See discussion of procedural due process in Chapter 6.

50. Butsche v. Coon Rapids Comm. School Dist., 255 N.W.2d 337 (Iowa 1977); Little v. Alto Indep. School Dist., 513 S.W.2d 626 (Tex. 1974) (school bond election).

51. American Law Institute, Restatement of the Law, Agency 2d, §§ 82–104. (1) Comeaux v. School Employees Retirement Sys., 241 So.2d 298 (La. 1970) (board could not ratify an *ultra vires* contract). *Accord:* Zevin v. School Dist. No. 11, 12 N.W.2d 634 (Neb. 1944). (2) Grippo v. Dunmore School Board, 365 A.2d 678 (Pa. 1976).

52. Sabin v. La. State Board of Educ., 289 So.2d 554 (La. 1974) (holding board to have ratified lease by conduct other than express words).

CHAPTER 2
Public Schools: Programs and Services

❖ **CHAPTER OUTLINE**
  I. Attendance and Admission
     A. Compulsory Attendance Laws
     B. Admission Standards
        1. Residence
        2. Immunization and Health Requirements
        3. Age Requirements
     C. School Assignments
  II. Studies Program
     A. Curriculum
        1. Prescribed Courses and Activities
        2. Textbooks and Reading Materials
     B. Extracurricular Activities
        1. Student Clubs
        2. Interscholastic Athletic Associations
     C. Placement, Grading, Promotion, and Graduation
  III. Student Services
     A. Transportation
        1. Distance Limits
        2. Bus Routing
     B. Fees and Charges

❖ **CHAPTER DISCUSSION QUESTIONS**

❖ **CASES**
  2.1 Cardiff v. Bismark Public School District, 263 N.W.2d 105 (N.D. 1978)
  2.2 Board of Education v. Pico, 457 U.S. 853 (1982)

❖ **ENDNOTES**

This chapter deals with the traditional public schools that are the principal vehicles for state-sponsored education. Alternative education, at nonpublic schools or in home education programs, and more recently at state-created charter schools, is discussed in Chapter 9.

ATTENDANCE AND ADMISSION

Attendance laws require parents to enroll their children in a state-qualified school or education program, while admission laws require local school authorities to assure the proper admission of students to public schools.

Compulsory Attendance Laws

Children of specified ages must attend public schools if they do not receive alternative qualified education. State laws typically exempt certain classes of children from compelled attendance such as emancipated youngsters (married or self-supporting beyond a certain age); youngsters who must work to provide essential family support, and children whose disabilities render them incapable of benefitting from normal schooling.

Religious exemptions may be constitutionally required if continued school attendance would place a "substantial" (not merely inconvenient or distasteful) burden on religious beliefs and practice, and if the state cannot demonstrate a compelling interest in requiring continued schooling. The Supreme Court so held in *Wisconsin v. Yoder* in ruling that Amish children could not be compelled to attend school beyond eighth grade contrary to their religious precepts, because the state failed to show that Amish children required further schooling in order to become self-sufficient, responsible citizens. *Yoder* made clear, however, that philosophical and culturally based objections do not suffice for constitutional exemption. Religious exemption claims have been denied in most cases because the petitioners did not convince a court that compulsory schooling would coerce them to act against basic religious tenets or obligations.[1] Native American complaints that public schools do not adequately teach about Indian culture and heritage or that the school's hair length regulation conflicted with Native American religious tradition were found insufficient to require constitutional exemption.[2]

Constitutional exemption from specific school activities, such as flag salute and pledge of allegiance exercises, has been allowed for students and teachers whose religion forbids such practice. However, parents who object to a particular exercise may not totally withdraw the child from the school, but must request that the child be excused from the practice that would violate their religion.

Child safety has been recognized as a reason to excuse nonattendance at an assigned school,[3] but a parent has the burden of proving that a serious danger exists and that the school authorities will not or cannot eliminate it. Judicial assessments of alleged dangers can vary widely. In one case, evidence of extortion, threats, and physical assault sufficed to require reassignment of the child to another school, while another case in the same state found evidence of violent student assaults with sharp instruments insufficient to show school inability to protect the student.[4] Similar variations appeared in New York where one court found child mistreatment insufficient ground for excusal, while another court upheld a parent's removal of a child to a different school by using a false address in order to avoid the allegedly dangerous school.[5] If a school's location renders a child's attempt to reach it dangerous, a court may exempt the child from attending that school.[6]

Compulsory education laws may be enforced by criminal prosecution of parents for child neglect, by court removal of a child from their custody,[7] or by actions against truants, including placement of truants in custodial schools.[8] Academic penalties for truancy, such as expulsion or lengthy suspensions, are generally disfavored as counterproductive. Where severe criminal penalties are sought against noncooperative parents, state prosecutors must prove charges of neglect by "clear and convincing evidence."[9]

Admission Standards

To be entitled to tuition-free admission to a public school, children must meet state-specified conditions in terms of age, residence, immunization, and other conditions that school authorities may reasonably impose.[10]

Residence

Residency requirements for school admission have withstood constitutional challenge.[11] In most states, districts may admit nonresidents only under legally specified arrangements, including that parents or government agencies pay the admitting district its cost of educating the nonresident child.

Local residency means a bona fide place of abode with intention to remain there indefinitely. Legally emancipated minors have their own residence, but an unemancipated minor is presumed to reside with his or her parents or with a legal custodian, for instance, when parents are divorced, separated, or away.[12] Exceptions to this presumption are allowed where it is not justified, e.g., in cases of parental abandonment or death.[13] In such cases, courts consider the best interests of the child and the good faith of caretakers.[14] Thus, where a child remained with a natural parent and not the legally appointed guardian, the child was deemed to reside with the parent.[15]

Homeless children are subject to special rules. The federal Homeless Assistance Act of 1987 defines a homeless person as one who lacks a regular nighttime residence or whose residence is a temporary living accommodation. This law directs each state to adopt a plan for the education of homeless children within its borders, including adequate rules and records to ensure that they are afforded transportation and other school services.[16]

Immunization and Health Requirements

The protection of school populations from disease is a sufficiently strong state interest to override religion-based constitutional objections to compelled immunization of students.[17] Even so, a number of states have chosen, as a matter of policy, to exempt religious objectors from such immunizations.

The HIV virus was initially thought to present a sufficient danger of transmission to justify exclusion of HIV-infected students and staff, but courts have found insufficient medical evidence to establish such a danger or to exclude infected individuals.[18]

Age Requirements

Minimum admission ages, when set directly by statute, must be observed unless state laws grant local school boards the discretion to exempt children from such age limits. Local school decisions to deny early admission may, however, be overturned if permitted by law and found to be an abuse of administrative discretion.[19]

School Assignments

Where state law restricts transfers between schools, local boards cannot make prohibited transfers for other reasons, however beneficial they may be.[20] However, where school statutes vest local school authorities with discretion to allow or deny school assignments, courts will not overturn their decisions unless they committed a serious error of law or abused their discretion.[21]

In making school assignments, administrators may subordinate the interests of an individual student to the needs of the total school population, particularly where limited resources confine school choices.[22] Even so, courts may overturn assignments that are arbitrary and capricious, e.g., where a musically talented student was reassigned from a school that offered music studies to one that provided none.[23]

School reassignments necessitated by school closings must also comply with assignment provisions of school closing statutes.[24] The question of whether the consolidation of classes from different schools constitutes a school closing will depend on the interpretation of the governing statute. Partial grade elimination was not deemed to be a closing under North Dakota's statute.[25] The special impacts of antidiscrimination laws on student assignments are reviewed in Chapter 7.

STUDIES PROGRAM

School programs may be classified in many ways. For example, curriculum may be viewed narrowly to refer only to courses given regularly for credit, or viewed broadly to embrace most life experiences, including extracurricular activities. The following discussion considers school programs in terms of curriculum and of extracurricular activities.

Curriculum

Curricular arrangements may have different objectives, i.e., "return to basics," "multicultural" studies, or some combination of traditional and progressive themes of education. Educators may, therefore, differ in structuring their school curriculum and course offerings beyond those mandated by state law. The general parameters of control over curriculum are summarized in the following, though somewhat dated, report.

> In all states the local district must offer a curriculum that the state prescribes. . . . In about half the states the local district must offer the curriculum prescribed by the state. . . . Even in those states where districts retain some discretion, course offerings must still be chosen within state guidelines. . . . For example, all schools must offer courses in American history and government. . . . In addition, the choice of the district is often limited by state board guidelines regulating the number, content or quality of the courses. Some states provide that a district must offer a specified number of courses. . . . Sanctions for noncompliance would include . . . loss of state aid. . . . The local district selects its curriculum offerings on the basis of the . . . authority delegated by the State. (National Institute for Education, A Study of State Legal Standards for the Provision of Public Education, 1974, p. 28)

Subject to the foregoing constraints, school administrators have broad authority to expand or modify their curriculum. Physical education, health inspection, medical treatment, career training, and counseling are now accepted parts of a school's mission.

Prescribed Courses and Activities

In the landmark flag-salute case, Justice Jackson wrote prophetically that "As government pressure towards unity becomes greater, so strife becomes more bitter as to whose unity it shall be." [*W. Va. Board of Educ. v. Barnette*, 319 U.S. 624, 641 (1943)]

The issue of control comes to the fore as parents, the school management, teachers, churches, and the local community strive to promote or suppress particular programs, instructional content or methods. District residents cannot force local school boards to add or delete particular courses unless a state legislature invests that power in them, or unless a challenged course violates civil rights. Absent such grounds, school officials may eliminate or reduce courses and services not mandated by state law, especially when faced with declining enrollment. Conflicts are particularly acute over subjects previously consigned to private or family initiative, such as courses and services dealing with sexual topics such as pregnancy, contraception, abortion, homosexuality, and AIDS. These topics are discussed further in later chapters.

Parental demands to choose a child's course of study have been largely limited by courts to the question whether school authorities abused their discretion. Nor may students demand that they be offered courses or services available at other schools.[26] Relief can be had, however, where school authorities unreasonably disregard the welfare of a student.[27]

Provision of kindergarten programs is mandated in some states and left to local district option in others. Where the standards for first-grade admission are set by state law, school districts may not alter them by adding other requirements.[28]

Graduation requirements must also comply with higher law. The requirement that students perform community service in order to graduate raised unconstitutional challenges that it abridged student liberty and subjected students to involuntary servitude, but it was upheld.[29]

Textbooks and Reading Materials

The law on textbook selection varies from state to state. In some states local districts must select class texts from a state-approved list. In others, local districts may adopt supplementary texts that are not on the state list. A few states provide recommended book lists, without restricting local district discretion in selecting course books.

Complaints are perennially raised against the use of particular books, on the grounds that they ignore or disparage particular racial, ethnic, gender, religious, or political groups or that they undermine social morality, patriotism, or religious beliefs. To prevail on such complaints, challengers face—and often cannot meet—a high burden of proving that the book contents irremediably injure the challengers.

> "[D]eference to local control . . . is a recognition of the varying wants and needs of the Nation's diverse and varied communities, each with its unique character, standards and sense of social importance of a variety of values."[30]

Religious objections to book content are considered in greater detail in Chapter 3.

Student and teacher attempts to overturn book selections or removals have been notably unsuccessful.[31] In *Board of Education v. Pico*, reported at the end of this chapter, the Supreme Court provided some guidance. *Pico* presented the question of whether a school board could constitutionally remove books from a high school library over teacher, parent, and student objections. In returning that case for trial, seven of the nine Justices wrote individual opinions that expressed at least three different constitutional viewpoints. Even so, the majority of Justices agreed on the following points:

- That school boards could constitutionally select course books based on their educational judgment without being limited by the desires or opinions of parents, teachers, or students;
- That school board decisions on classroom texts are less open to challenge than decisions regarding library books for optional student use; and
- That school boards could constitutionally undertake to "inculcate" community values by removal of materials that they in good faith consider to be "educationally" unsuitable.

The *Pico* opinions left a central question unanswered—how to determine whether the motivation for a book removal is "educational" or "political." Later courts interpreted *Pico* to support school board authority to ban, as educationally unsuitable for high school students, Chaucer's *Miller's Tale* and Aristophanes' *Lysistrata*,[32] and to uphold board authority to overrule teacher selections of supplemental classroom readings.[33]

Board control over teacher reading assignments and the distribution of noninstructional literature on school property raise related First Amendment issues, which are discussed in Chapters 6 and 7.

Special education laws provide a wide range of programs to accommodate physical, intellectual, and emotional disabilities. Those laws must comply with federal subsidy conditions and with federal laws governing persons with disabilities. Those laws are reviewed in later chapters.

Extracurricular Activities

In many states, public schools are expressly required to conduct specified nonacademic activities. In addition, local districts have implied power to sponsor extracurricular activities that reasonably relate to the school's educational goals. The scope of that power remains an issue in extracurricular disputes.

Student Clubs

Schools may prohibit "secret" or "oath bound" clubs, or clubs that exclude students based on preferences of existing members. The school's educational interests in discouraging undemocratic practices outweigh student First Amendment rights of association.[34]

Interscholastic Athletic Associations

School board joinder in interscholastic associations that regulate institutional and student conduct in interscholastic contests, both academic and noncurricular, have survived the challenge in most states that such joinder involved an unlawful redelegation of board authority.[35]

Association rules and decisions are subject to reversal for abuse of discretion,[36] but they have been generally upheld as reasonable. Rules to suspend or disqualify students or schools from interscholastic competition for talent raiding, school jumping, residency violations, redshirting, extramural training with outside teams, and student exclusion from interscholastic competition for academic deficiency or misconduct have survived legal challenge.[37] A suspension of a school from association competition was upheld even though the suspension prevented the school from honoring its game contracts with other schools.[38]

As agents of member schools, athletic associations are engaged in "state action." They may not discriminate on the basis of race, gender, or marriage, or among schools, and they must afford due process in disciplinary proceedings that affect student rights.[39] However, in the view of most courts, a student's interest in participating in school athletics does not rise to the level of a constitutional "right" and does not require the highest level of constitutional due process.[40] Association rules that bar coed competitions raise issues of gender discrimination, which are reviewed more fully in Chapter 7. Association rules that exclude or impose different burdens on nonpublic schools or their students have, however, been upheld as having a reasonable basis.[41]

Placement, Grading, Promotion, and Graduation

Class placement, grading, and promotion are generally left to local control. Students have no inherent right to promotion, and courts are disinclined to interfere with school placement policies or decisions.[42] They have accordingly upheld board demand that a child register for kindergarten before taking a test for advanced placement.[43] Courts will, however, strike down decisions that discriminate between new students admitted to higher grades on the basis of age, while requiring existing students of like age to pass tests for like advancement.[44] The question of advancing a bright child to a higher grade involves discretionary judgment that courts are inclined to uphold.

> Certainly, the court may not hold as arbitrary or capricious the respondent's determination that chronologically determined physical, social, and emotional maturity are vital and proper factors to be considered. . . .[45]

The use of academic penalties, adverse placements, grade reductions, or denials of promotion to punish student nonacademic misconduct risks court disapproval as unreasonable, though these types of penalties have been sustained in some circumstances.[46]

Promotion requirements are set locally when not fixed by state law. A growing number of states have imposed minimum achievement or competency requirements for the award of a standard high school diploma. Unless found to be unfair or discriminatory, these requirements have withstood legal challenge.[47] In some states students must pass a prescribed exit examination, while in others local boards have the option to set achievement conditions or prescribe their own tests for graduation.[48]

A student who satisfies the academic requirements for graduation cannot be denied a diploma for nonacademic misconduct or defaults, such as failure to pay school fees.[49] Courts have even overturned denials of diploma for academic infractions where that sanction was deemed unreasonable and excessive.[50] A graduating student's right to participate in graduation ceremonies presents a different question, but there also courts have disagreed on the question whether exclusion from the graduation exercise for disciplinary reasons was reasonable or an abuse of discretion.[51]

STUDENT SERVICES

Transportation

Courts have refused to imply school board authority to provide school transportation services,[52] but nearly all states have statutes that expressly authorize school transportation.[53] States may constitutionally prescribe different transportation for different classes of schools or students, as long as the classifications are deemed reasonable.[54] Unless mandated by state law, however, local boards may refuse to provide school transportation service, provided they do so in a nondiscriminatory manner.[55] Parents may not demand transportation to a district school other than the student's assigned school, or to a school outside the district,[56] unless such a right is expressly granted by transportation laws, such as laws enacted for the benefit of students who are exceptional or who have disabilities.[57]

Distance Limits

Minimum home-to-school distances for school busing are generally set by school boards where statutes authorize "reasonable" transportation without fixing specific distances. A board's refusal to provide transportation for a small number of poor students from an inaccessible part of the district was overruled as an abuse of discretion,[58] but safety factors may justify board denial of busing services over unsafe roads.[59] Excessive meticulousness in applying distance standards in order to deny transportation may also be overturned as capricious, for instance, where the minimum distance was measured to a student's driveway (disqualified) rather than to his home (qualified).[60]

Bus Routing

In setting bus routes and pickup or discharge points, a board may not require pupils to walk unreasonable distances, unless the transportation statute fixed the distance. Many states provide exceptions from distance or route restrictions for students who lack safe walking paths or encounter hazardous crossings.

The legality of school payments for privately provided school transportation, in lieu of school bus service, has not been widely litigated, but was upheld where roads were unsafe for school bus operation.[61]

Fees and Charges

The growing practice of charging student fees for select school materials or services has raised objections that the fees violate a student's "right" to a free public education under state law. The scope of that right may be interpreted broadly to entitle students to receive at no charge all materials and services provided by public schools, or more narrowly to entitle students only to receive such materials and services as are deemed essential or reasonably related to "public education." The variations among the states on public school fees

arise partly from different wording of their laws and partly from judicial disagreements as to which school activities should be considered part of a free
public education.[62] As school fees proliferate on a wide range of benefits, the
law on their legality may be expected to grow.

A school district may not charge residents for full-time admission to regular school year classes, whether that charge be labeled tuition, matriculation, or
registration fee, but it may charge parents or legal custodians of nonresident students for such admittance. With regard to summer school classes, nonrequired
courses, or other programs outside the normal school year, the law varies from
state to state, depending on each state's classification of contested charges as
falling within or beyond the scope of that state's "free" public education.

A number of courts have upheld fees for textbooks and school supplies,
as illustrated by the case samplings in the endnote.[63] The *Cardiff* case, which
appears at the end of this chapter, surveys the varied state law.

Similar variations exist on activity fees. The Supreme Court of California
ruled that its state constitution prohibited assessment of any extracurricular activity fee (though the same court later held that school transportation fees were
permissible under California law).[64] That view of the scope of free public education does not appear to prevail in a majority of states.

Chapter 2 Discussion Questions

Where the answer to a question may be qualified by special circumstances, explain the potential qualification.

1. Do state agencies, local school boards, or both regulate the following
   functions?
   a. School zones and school assignments
   b. Extracurricular programs
   c. Grading, promotion, and graduation
   d. School transportation
   Explain your answers.

2. Name the principal grounds on which a school district may deny a child
   admission to public schools.

3. What are the general requirements to establish a legal residence at a
   particular location?

4. Does an expelled pupil still have a right to public education? Explain.

5. On what grounds may parents challenge or overturn school assignment
   of their children to "special classes"? Explain.

6. When, if ever, may a parent overturn school requirements of immunization of pupils from contagious diseases?

7. In the absence of a busing statute, may a school district refuse to provide school transportation to its students? Explain.

8. What law sources determine whether or not a school district may charge student fees for:
   a. Course textbooks?
   b. Admission to participate in extracurricular activities?
   c. Swim suits?

❖ CASES

Case 2.1

CARDIFF v. BISMARK PUBLIC SCHOOL DISTRICT
263 N.W.2d 105 (N.D. 1978)

> [***Focus Note.*** *School fees. Parents of elementary school children brought suit to overturn school rental fees for required textbooks. In deciding whether the fees violated the state constitutional guarantee of a free public education, the court surveyed the range of positions in sister states under their respective laws.]*

SAND, JUSTICE.

❖ ❖ ❖

The basic issue . . . is whether or not . . . the North Dakota Constitution . . . prohibits the Legislature from authorizing school districts to charge for textbooks. . . .

To resolve the first issue we must examine and construe the provisions of § 148 of the North Dakota Constitution. . . .

In 1968 this section was amended, as follows:

The legislative assembly shall provide for a uniform system of free public schools throughout the state. . . .

❖ ❖ ❖

In 1895 the North Dakota Legislature enacted chapter 109, the title of which provides as follows: "AN ACT to Provide for Free Text Books and School Supplies for the Use of the Pupils in the Public Schools of North Dakota." The body of the Act, however, conditions the free textbooks upon a favorable election by a majority of qualified electors of the district. . . . The title of the Act is misleading when compared to the body of the Act. . . .

From this examination we are left with a firm conviction that the legislative acts referred to do not lend any significant comfort or aid to the resolution of the basic question under consideration. . . . The Journal entries of the constitutional convention are not very helpful in determining the meaning of the language, "free public schools."

❖ ❖ ❖

From this brief review it is clear that the framers consistently had in mind a free public school.

A short survey of the constitutional provisions of other states and their case law will shed some light on our question.

Arizona: . . . In *Carpio v. Tucson High School District No. 1 of Pima County,* 111 Ariz. 127, 524 P.2d 948 (1974) . . . the court had under consideration Article XI, § 6 of the Arizona Constitution. The court held that textbooks were not required to be furnished to high school students. However, the court referred to an earlier decision . . . where the court held that these constitutional provisions had been satisfied when the legislature provided for the means of establishing required courses, qualifications of teachers, textbooks to be used in common schools, etc. Considering this statement and the statement in *Carpio* that "textbooks have not been provided free in high schools as they have been in the common schools" leaves the impression that under the constitutional provisions of Arizona textbooks in common schools were provided free of charge.

Colorado: . . . In *Marshall v. School District RE # 3 Morgan County,* 553 P.2d 784 (Colo. 1976), the court held that the school district was not required to furnish books free of charge to all students.

Indiana: . . . In *Chandler v. South Bend Community School Corporation,* 160 Ind. App. 592, 312 N.E.2d 915 (1974), the court held that this constitutional provision did not require textbooks to be provided free, but merely to provide a system of common schools where tuition would be without charge.

Illinois: . . . In *Beck v. Board of Education of Harlem Consolidated School District No. 122,* 63 Ill. 2d 10, 344 N.E.2d 440 (1976), the court held that workbooks, and other educational material, were not textbooks so as to come within the statutory provision of free textbooks, and as such it did not preclude the school board from charging the parents a fee for supplying the students with such material.

Earlier, in *Hamer v. Board of Education of School District No. 109,* 47 Ill. 2d 480, 265 N.E.2d 616 (1970), the court was specifically concerned with the constitutional provision and held that under its provisions the school board was not prohibited from purchasing textbooks and renting them to pupils. . . .

Wisconsin: . . . The court in *Board of Education v. Sinclair,* 65 Wis. 2d 179, 222 N.W.2d 143 (1974), held that the schools may charge a fee for the use of textbooks and items of similar nature authorized by statute and that such did not violate the constitutional provision commanding that schools shall be free without charge for tuition for all children. . . .

Idaho: . . . In *Paulson v. Minidoka County School District No. 331,* 93 Idaho 469, 463 P.2d 935 (1970), the court held that school districts could not charge students for textbooks under the state constitutional provision. . . .

Michigan: . . . The Michigan court in *Bond v. Public Schools of Ann Arbor School District,* 383 Mich. 693, 178 N.W.2d 484 (1970), held that the 1963 constitutional provision meant that books and school supplies were an essential part of the system of free public elementary and secondary schools and that the schools should not charge for such items. . . .

Montana: . . . In *Granger v. Cascade County School District No. 1,* 159 Mont. 516, 499 P.2d 780 (1972), the school district, as the school district here, contended that the pertinent language simply meant "tuition-free" as far as required courses were concerned and did not prohibit fees and charges for optional extra-curricular or elective courses and activities. . . . The Montana Supreme Court answered the question in the following manner:

> We believe that the controlling principle or test should be stated in this manner: Is a given course or activity reasonably related to a recognized academic and educational goal of a particular school system? If it is, it constitutes part of the free, public school system commanded by Art. XI, Sec. 1 of the Montana Constitution and additional fees or charges cannot be levied, directly or indirectly, against the student or his parents. If it is not, reasonable fees or charges may be imposed.

The court, however, pointed out that its decision does not apply to supplementary instruction offered by the school district . . . during the summer recess or at special times. . . .

New Mexico: . . . The court, in *Norton v. Board of Education of School District No. 16,* 89 N.M. 470, 553 P.2d 1277 (1976), held that . . . courses required of every student shall be without charge to the student. However, reasonable fees may be charged for elective courses. The court also recognized that the board of education shall define what are required or elective courses in the educational system of New Mexico.

South Dakota: . . . We have found no South Dakota case law on the question of tuition or textbooks.

West Virginia: . . . The court in *Vandevender v. Cassell,* 208 S.E.2d 436 (W. Va. 1974), held that furnishing textbooks free to needy students satisfied the constitutional requirement. But two of the five judges . . . stated that they did not interpret "free" as pertaining only to indigent pupils. . . .

Missouri: . . . The court held in *Concerned Parents v. Caruthersville School District No. 18,* 548 S.W.2d 554 (Mo. 1977), that under this [Missouri] constitutional provision school districts were prohibited from charging registration fees or course fees in connection with courses for which academic credit was given.

Washington: . . . The Supreme Court of the State of Washington, in *Litchman v. Shannon,* 90 Wash. 186, 155 P. 783 (1916), said: "Public schools are usually defined as schools . . . open without charge to the children of all the residents of the town or other district."

. . . From this study we have concluded that the courts have consistently construed the language "without payment of tuition" or . . . such similar language to mean that a school is prohibited from charging a fee for a pupil attending school. This language has also been construed as not prohibiting the charging of fees for textbooks.

However, as to constitutions containing language such as "free public schools" or "free common schools" or similar language, the courts have generally held, with a few exceptions, that this language contemplates furnishing textbooks free of charge, at least to the elementary schools. The exceptions have generally relied upon extrinsic material such as contemporary construction, history, or practices, as well as the language itself. Although the cases involving language similar to that contained in the North Dakota Constitution are not in themselves conclusive, they nevertheless are helpful, if not persuasive.

A comparison of the key constitutional provisions and existing case law of states which entered the Union at the same time and under similar conditions as North Dakota will be very helpful and valuable in determining the intent of the people of North Dakota in adopting § 148 of the North Dakota Constitution. . . .

The key language in the constitutional provisions of the four States are as follows:

Montana: ". . . thorough system of public, free common schools."

South Dakota: ". . . uniform system of public schools wherein tuition shall be without charge."

North Dakota: ". . . uniform system of free public schools throughout the state. . . ."

Washington: ". . . uniform system of public schools. . . ."

We are impressed with the different language employed in the constitutions of the four states . . . Montana, South Dakota, North Dakota, and Washington, which came into the Union at the same time and under the same Enabling Act. . . .

It is significant to note that Montana and North Dakota adopted the "free common schools" and the "free public schools" concept, whereas South Dakota adopted the "public schools wherein tuition shall be without charge" concept, and Washington merely provided for a "uniform system of public schools."

. . . If the framers of the North Dakota Constitution and the people of North Dakota had in mind only to provide public schools without charging tuition they could have, and probably would have, used the language "without payment of tuition" or "wherein tuition shall be without charge," rather than the language "free public schools." The term "free public schools" without any other modification must necessarily mean and include those items which are essential to education.

It is difficult to envision a meaningful educational system without textbooks. . . .

. . . We cannot overlook the fact that attendance at school . . . was compulsory from the very beginning. . . . This lends support to the contention that textbooks were to be included in the phrase "free public schools."

✧ ✧ ✧

. . . After a review of the case law and constitutional provisions of other states . . . we have come to the conclusion that the term "free public schools" means and includes textbooks, and not merely "free from tuition." . . .

Sections 15-43-07, 15-43-08, 15-43-09, 15-43-10, and 15-43-12, North Dakota Century Code, to the extent that they apply to elementary textbooks, are in conflict with § 148 of the North Dakota Constitution and are therefore invalid and unconstitutional as to elementary school textbooks. . . .

Case 2.2

BOARD OF EDUCATION v. PICO
457 U.S. 853 (1982)

> [*Focus Note*. School book selection. Suit to challenge school board removal of nine books from school libraries. The Second Circuit Court of Appeals ordered a trial to determine whether the board was acting from unconstitutional motives in removing the books. The Supreme Court by a 5–4 vote affirmed that order, but a majority of justices could not agree on the constitutional basis for the outcome. The following excerpts of their separate opinions indicate the range of possible views leading to a common result.]

JUSTICE BRENNAN *announced the judgment of the Court [in an opinion not signed or joined by a majority of the Nine Supreme Court Justices].*

We emphasize at the outset the limited nature of the . . . question presented. . . . . . . For as this case is presented to us, it does not involve textbooks, or indeed any books that Island Trees students would be required to read. Respondents do not seek . . . to impose limitations upon their school board's discretion to prescribe the curricula of the Island Trees schools. . . . [T]he only books at issue in this case are *library* books, books that . . . are optional rather than required reading. Our adjudication of the present case thus does not intrude into the classroom, or into the compulsory courses taught there. . . . Rather, the only action challenged in this case is the *removal* from school libraries of books originally placed there by the school authorities. . . . . . .

❖ ❖ ❖

We are therefore in full agreement . . . that local school boards must be permitted "to establish and apply their curriculum in such a way as to transmit community values," and that "there is a legitimate and substantial community interest in promoting respect for authority and traditional values be they social, moral, or political."

❖ ❖ ❖

Of course, courts should not "intervene in the resolution of conflicts which arise in the daily operation of school systems" unless "basic constitutional values" are "directly and sharply implicate[d] in those conflicts." *Epperson v. Arkansas*, 393 U.S., at 104. But we think that the First Amendment rights of students may be directly and sharply implicated by the removal of books from the shelves of a school library. . . . And we have recognized that "the State may not, consistently with the spirit of the First Amendment, contract the spectrum of available knowledge." . . . In keeping with this principle, we have held that in a variety of contexts "the Constitution protects the right to receive information and ideas. . . ."

This right is an inherent corollary of the rights of free speech and press. . . . . . .

More importantly, the right to receive ideas is a necessary predicate to the *recipient's* meaningful exercise of his own rights of speech, press, and political freedom. . . .

❖ ❖ ❖

. . . It appears . . . that use of the Island Trees school libraries is completely voluntary. . . . Their selection of books . . . is entirely a matter of free choice. . . . . . .

❖ ❖ ❖

. . . Petitioners rightly possess significant discretion to determine the content of their school libraries. But that discretion may not be exercised in a narrowly partisan or political manner. . . . Thus whether petitioners' removal of books . . . denied respondents their First Amendment rights depends upon the motivation behind petitioners' actions. If petitioners *intended* . . . to deny respondents access to ideas with which petitioners disagreed, and if this intent was the decisive factor in petitioners' decision, then petitioners have exercised their discretion in violation of the Constitution. . . . On the other hand, respondents implicitly concede that an unconstitutional motivation would not be demonstrated if it were shown that petitioners had decided to remove the books at issue because those books were pervasively vulgar. . . . And again, respondents concede that if it were demonstrated that the removal decision was based solely upon the "educational suitability" of the books in question, then their removal would be "perfectly permissible. . . ."

❖ ❖ ❖

. . . In brief, we hold that local school boards may not remove books from school library shelves simply because they dislike the ideas contained in those books and seek by their removal to "prescribe what shall be orthodox in politics, nationalism, religion, or other matters of opinion." *West Virginia Board of Education v. Barnette*, 319 U.S., at 642. . . .

JUSTICE BLACKMUN, concurring in part and concurring in the judgment.

To my mind, this case presents a particularly complex problem. . . . On the one hand, as the dissenting opinions demonstrate . . . the Court has acknowledged the importance of the public schools "in the preparation of individuals for participation as citizens, and in the preservation of the values on which our society rests." *Ambach v. Norwick,* 441 U.S. 68, 76 (1979). . . . Because of the essential socializing function of schools, local education officials may attempt "to promote civic virtues," *Ambach v. Norwick,* 441 U.S., at 80. . . .

❖ ❖ ❖

In my view, then, the principle involved here is both narrower and more basic than the "right to receive information" . . . I do not suggest that the State has any affirmative obligation to provide students with information or ideas. . . . And I do not believe, as the plurality suggests, that the right at issue here is somehow associated with the peculiar nature of the school library . . .; . . . Certainly, the unique environment of the school places substantial limits on the extent to which official decisions may be restrained by First Amendment values. But that environment also makes it particularly important that some limits be imposed. . . . In starker terms, we must reconcile the schools' "inculcative" function with the First Amendment's bar on "prescriptions of orthodoxy."

In my view, we strike a proper balance here by holding that school officials may not remove books for the *purpose* of restricting access to the political ideas or social perspectives . . . when that action is motivated simply by the officials' disapproval of the ideas involved. . . .

. . . School officials must be able to choose one book over another, without outside interference, when the first book is deemed more relevant to the curriculum, or better written, or when one of a host of other politically neutral reasons is present. . . . First Amendment principles would allow a school board to refuse to make a book available to students because it contains offensive language . . . or because it is psychologically or intellectually inappropriate for the age group, or even, perhaps, because the ideas it advances are "manifestly inimical to the public welfare." *Pierce v. Society of Sisters*, 268 U.S. 510, 534 (1925). . . .

[Concurring opinion of JUSTICE WHITE omitted.]

CHIEF JUSTICE BURGER, with whom JUSTICE POWELL, JUSTICE REHNQUIST, and JUSTICE O'CONNOR join, dissenting.

❖ ❖ ❖

I agree with the fundamental proposition that "students do not 'shed their constitutional rights to freedom of speech or expression at the schoolhouse gate.' " . . . Here, however, no restraints of any kind are placed on the students. They are free to read the books in question, which are available at public libraries and bookstores. . . . Despite this absence of any direct external control on the students' ability to express themselves, the plurality suggests that there is a new First Amendment "entitlement" to have access to particular books in a school library. . . .

❖ ❖ ❖

In short . . . there is not a hint in the First Amendment, or in any holding of this Court, of a "right" to have the government provide continuing access to certain books.

❖ ❖ ❖

[Dissenting opinion of JUSTICE POWELL omitted.]

JUSTICE O'CONNOR, *dissenting.*

If the school board can set the curriculum, select teachers, and determine initially what books to purchase for the school library, it surely can decide which books to discontinue or remove from the school library so long as it does not also interfere with the right of students to read the material and to discuss it. As Justice Rehnquist persuasively argues, the plurality's analysis overlooks the fact that in this case the government is acting in its special role as educator.

I do not personally agree with the Board's action with respect to some of the books in question here, but it is not the function of the courts to make the decisions that have been properly relegated to the elected members of school boards. . . . I therefore join the Chief Justice's dissent.

[Dissenting opinion of JUSTICE REHNQUIST omitted.]

[The nine books in the high school library were: Slaughterhouse Five, *by Kurt Vonnegut, Jr.;* The Naked Ape, *by Desmond Morris;* Down These Mean Streets, *by Piri Thomas;* Best Short Stories of Negro Writers, *edited by Langston Hughes;* Go Ask Alice, *of anonymous authorship;* Laughing Boy, *by Oliver LaFarge;* Black Boy, *by Richard Wright;* A Hero Ain't Nothin' But a Sandwich, *by Alice Childress; and* Soul on Ice, *by Eldridge Cleaver. The book in the junior high school library was* A Reader for Writers, *edited by Jerome Archer. Still another listed book,* The Fixer, *by Bernard Malamud, was found to be included in the curriculum of a twelfth grade literature course. . . .]*

❖ ENDNOTES

1. State v. Kasubowski, 275 N.W.2d 101 (Wis. 1978) (religious exemption claim denied as based on philosophical, not truly religious grounds).

2. Matter of McMillan, 226 S.E.2d 693 (N.C. 1976); Hatch v. Goerke, 502 F.2d 1189 (10th Cir. 1974).

3. As to unsafe school conditions, *see* Annot., *Conditions at Schools as Excusing or Justifying Nonattendance,* 9 A.L.R. 4th 122 (1981); and cases in next note. As to dangerous travel conditions, *see, e.g., Re* Richards, 7 N.Y.S.2d 722 (1938).

4. *Compare* School Dist. of Pittsburgh v. Zebra, 325 A.2d 330 (Pa. 1974), *with* Comm. *ex rel.* School Dist. v. Ross, 330 A.2d 290 (Pa. 1975).

5. Matter of Baum, 382 N.Y.S. 2d 672 (1976); *in re* Foster, 330 N.Y.S.2d 8, 10 (1972).

6. Williams v. Board of Educ., 99 P. 216 (Kan. 1908).

7. Scoma v. Ill., 391 F. Supp. 452 (N.D. Ill. 1974); Matter of McMillan, 226 S.E.2d 693 (N.C. 1976).

8. *Re* T.V.P., 414 N.E.2d 209 (Ill. 1980).

9. Santosky v. Kramer, 450 U.S. 993, (1982).

10. Hammond v. Marx, 406 F. Supp. 853 (D. Me. 1975) (minimum age requirements for admission to public school upheld); O'Leary v. Wisecup, 364 A.2d 770 (Pa. 1976).

11. Martinez v. Bynum, 461 U.S. 321, 75 L. Ed. 2d 879 (1983).

12. Mathias v. Richland School Dist., 592 A.2d 811 (Pa. 1991); Matter of Montcrieffe, 467 N.Y.S.2d 812 (1983).

13. Sleesman v. State Board of Educ., 753 P.2d 186 (Ariz. 1988) (custody recognized in grandparents of child with unknown father and of mother with unknown address). *See also* Simms v. Roosevelt Union Free School Dist., 420 N.Y.S.2d. 96 (1976); Luoma v. Union School Dist. of Keene, 214 A.2d 120 (N.H. 1965).

14. Sleesman *supra* note 13; University Center, Inc. v. Ann Arbor Pub. Schools, 191 N.W.2d 302 (Mich. 1971).

15. Matter of Proios, 443 N.Y.S.2d 828 (1981); School Dist. No. 3 of Maricopa County v. Dailey, 471 P.2d 736 (Ariz. 1970).

16. 42 U.S.C.A. § 11302. P. First and G. Cooper, *Access to Education by Homeless Children,* 53 Ed. Law Rep. 757 (1989); Harrison v. Sobol, 705 F. Supp. 870 (S.D. N.Y. 1988).

17. Jacobson v. Cmwlth. of Mass., 197 U.S. 11 (1905); Calandra v. State College Area School Dist., 512 A.2d 809 (Pa. Cmwlth. 1986).

18. *See generally* Annot., *AIDS Infections as Affecting Right to Attend Public Schools,* 60 A.L.R. 4th 15 (1988); Hammett, *Protecting Children with AIDS against Arbitrary Exclusion from School,* 74 Cal. L. Rev. 1373 (1986); L. Rothstein, *Children with AIDS,* 12 Nova L. Rev. 1259 (1988). Martinez v. School Board of Hillsborough County, 861 F.2d 1502 (11th Cir. 1988); Doe v. Dolton Elementary School Dist., 694 F. Supp. 440 (N.D. Ill. 1988).

19. *Compare, e.g.,* Zweifel v. Joint Dist. No. 1, Belleville, 251 N.W.2d 822 (Wis. 1977); (sustaining board decision), *with* Blessing v. Mason County Board of Educ., 341 S.E.2d 407 (W. Va. 1985) (overturning decision as abuse of discretion).

20. Board of Educ. v. Oklahoma School Board of Educ., 521 P.2d 390 (Okla. 1974); Board of School Directors v. Dock, 318 A.2d 370 (Pa. 1974).

21. Ramsdell v. N. River School Dist. NO 200, 704 P.2d 606 (1985); Fitzpatrick v. Board of Educ., 578 F.2d 858 (10th Cir. 1978).

22. Bronestine v. Geinsendorfer, 613 S.W.2d 465 (Mo. 1981) (transfer of certain classes to non-neighborhood school); Zoll v. Anker, 414 F. Supp. 1024 (S.D. N.Y. 1976) (shortened school hours).

23. *In re* Reassignment of Hayes, 135 S.E.2d 645 (N.C. 1964).

24. Bartlett v. Board of Trustees, 550 P.2d 416 (Nev. 1976).

25. Choal v. Lyman Indep. School Dist., 214 N.W.2d 3 (N.D. 1974).

26. *Re* course reductions, *see* Board of Educ. of Okay Indep. School Dist. v. Carrol, 513 P.2d 872 (Okla. 1973). *Re* service reductions, *see* Borough v. Governing Bd. of El Segundo Unified School

Dist., 173 Cal. Rptr. 729 (1981). *Re* elective elimination, see Messina v. Sobol, 553 N.Y.S.2d 529 (A.D. 1990).

27. *In re* Reassignment of Hayes, *supra* note 23.

28. *See, e.g.,* Morgan v. Board of Educ., 317 N.E.2d 393 (Ill. 1974).

29. Herndon v. Chapel Hill-Carrbora City Board of Educ., 89 F.3d 174 (4th Cir. 1996); Immediato v. Rye Neck School Dist., 73 F.3d 454 (2d Cir. 1996); Stirer v. Bethlehem Area School Distr., 987 F.2d 989 (3rd Cir. 1993).

30. Mercer v. Michigan State Board of Educ., 379 F. Supp. 580, 585 (E.D. Mich.), *aff'd,* 419 U.S. 1081 (1974).

31. *See, e.g.,* Pratt v. Indep. School Dist. No. 831, 670 F.2d 771 (8th Cir. 1982); Zykan v. Warsaw Comm. School Corp., 631 F.2d 1300 (7th Cir. 1980); Sheck v. Baileyville School Comm., 530 F. Supp. 679 (D. Me. 1982); Mozert v. Hawkins County Board of Educ., 827 F.2d 1058 (6th Cir. 1987) (as offensive to christianity); Williams v. Board of Educ., 388 F. Supp. 93 (S.D. W. Va. 1975) (as offensive to parents' beliefs); Rosenberg v. Board of Educ., 92 N.Y.S.2d 344 (1949) (as offensive to Jews).

32. Virgil v. School Board, 677 F. Supp. 1547 (M.D. Fla. 1988).

33. On board authority to overrule teacher selection, *see* Fisher v. Fairbanks N. Star Borough School, 704 P.2d 213 (Ala. 1985).
   On unconstitutional motive for book removal, *see also* Campbell v. St. Tammany Parish School Board, 64 F.3d 184 (5th Cir. 1995); Case v. Un. School Dist. No. 233, 908 F. Supp. 864 (D. Kan. 1995).

34. Passel v. Ft. Worth Indep. School Dist., 453 S.W.2d 888 (Tex. 1970); Robinson v. Sacramento City Unified School Dist., 53 Cal. Rptr. 781 (1966).

35. *Upheld:* Dennis J. O'Connell H.S. v. Virginia H.S. League, 581 F.2d 81 (4th Cir. 1978) (regulation of literary and debating competition as well as athletics); ABC League v. Missouri State H.S. Activities Assn., 530 F. Supp. 1033 (E.D. Mo. 1982) (statewide regulation of speech, debate, and music competition as well as athletics). *Overturned:* Bunger v. Iowa H.S. Athletic Assn., 197 N.W.2d 555 (Iowa 1972).

36. Crane v. Indiana High School Athletic Assn., 975 F.2d 1315 (7th Cir. 1991) (overturning as abuse of discretion use of school transfer rule to disqualify student moving to reside with a parent).

37. Kirby v. Mich. H.S. Assn., 585 N.W.2d 290 (Mich. 1998); Alerding v. Ohio H.S. Athletic Assn., 779 F.2d 315 (6th Cir. 1985); OSAA v. Stout, 692 P.2d 633 (Or. 1984); E. New York Youth Soccer Assn. v. New York State Pub. H.S. Athletic Assn., 488 N.Y.S.2d 293 (1985), *aff'd,* 490 N.E.2d 538 (1986). *Suspension for academic failure and for misconduct:* Brands v. Sheldon Comm. School Board, 671 F. Supp. 627 (N.D. Iowa 1987) (citing supporting cases from 5th, 6th, 8th, and 10th Circuit Courts of Appeal).

38. State v. Judges of the Court of Common Pleas, 181 N.E.2d 261 (Ohio 1962).

39. *State action found:* Arkansas Activities Assn. v. Meyer, 805 S.W.2d 58 (Ark. 1991). *Discrimination prohibited:* Clark v. Arizona Interscholastic Assn., 695 F.2d 1126 (9th Cir. 1982); Dobson v. Arkansas Activities Assn., 469 F. Supp. 394 (E.D. Ark. 1979); Haas v. S. Bend Comm. Corp., 289 N.E.2d 495 (1972) (sex). *See also* Mahan v. Agee, 652 P.2d 765 (Okla. 1982) (age). *Due process:* Duffley v. New Hampshire Interscholastic Athletic Assn., 446 A.2d 462 (N.H. 1982).

40. Bailey v. Truby, 321 S.W.2d 302 (W. Va. 1984); Tennessee Secondary School Athletic Assn. v. Cox, 425 S.W.2d 597 (Tenn. 1968) (finding that no student "right" but only a privilege to participate in athletics, and therefore no right to a due process hearing).

41. Griffin H.S. v. Ill. H.S. Assn., 822 F.2d 671 (7th Cir. 1987); Windsor Park Baptist Church, Inc. v. Arkansas Activities Assn., 658 F.2d 618 (8th Cir. 1981); Walsh v. Louisiana H.S. Athletic Assn., 616 F.2d 152 (5th Cir. 1980); Dennis J. O'Connell H.S. v. Virginia H.S. League, 581 F.2d 81 (4th Cir. 1978); Christian Brothers Institute v. N. New Jersey Int. League, 432 A.2d 26 (N.J. 1981).

42. Arundar v. DeKalb County School Dist., 620 F.2d 493 (5th Cir. 1980); Erik V. v. Causby, 977 F. Supp. 384 (E.D. N.C. 1997); Sandlin v. Johnson, 643 F.2d 1027 (4th Cir. 1981).

43. Frost v. Yerozunis, 385 N.Y.S.2d 181 (1976); Rosenstein v. N. Penn School Dist., 392 A.2d 788 (Pa. 1975).

44. Catlin by Catlin v. Sobol, 569 N.Y.S.2d 353 (1991).

45. Ackerman v. Rubin, 231 N.Y.S.2d 112, 114 (1962).

46. *Compare* Jones v. Latexo Indep. School Dist., 499 F. Supp. 223 (E.D. Tex. 1980), *with* Donaldson v. Board of Educ., 424 N.E.2d 737 (Ill. 1981).

47. Brookhart v. Ill. State Board of Educ., 697 F.2d 179 (7th Cir. 1983); Williams v. Austin Ind. School Dist., 796 F. Supp. 251 (W.D. Tex. 1992); Board of Educ. v. Ambach, 436 N.Y.S.2d 564 (1981), *aff'd,* 458 N.Y.S.2d 680 (1982).

48. Brookhart, *supra* note 47.

49. *See* Annot., *Student's Right to Compel School Officials to Issue Diploma,* 11 A.L.R. 4th 1182 (1982). Shuman v. Cumberland Valley School Dist. Board of Directors, 536 A.2d 490 (Pa. Cmwlth. 1988).

50. Ryan v. Board of Educ., 257 P. 945 (Kan. 1927) (overturned denial of diploma for student possession of unauthorized materials during a test); State *ex rel.* Miller v. McLeod, 605 S.W.2d 160 (Mo. App. 1980) (overturned denial for shortfall by one-half credit).

51. *Compare, e.g.,* Ladsen v. Board of Educ., 323 N.Y.S.2d 545 (1971) (overturning exclusion of student who struck principal), *with* Fowler v. Williamson, 251 S.E.2d 889 (N.C. App. 1979) (upholding exclusion of student not attired for graduation per the school's regulation).

52. Conecuh County Board of Educ. v. Campbell, 162 So.2d 233 (Ala. 1964).

53. The following report, though outdated, indicates the range of variations in state laws.

In almost all states the responsibility for providing pupil transportation rests with the local school districts. However, the districts are almost equally divided between [those] having mandatory and discretionary provisions. . . . Transportation distances vary considerably from state to state. . . . A few states . . . set different distance standards for elementary and secondary schools. . . . A few states require . . . transportation under legislated standards which allow the district a certain amount of discretion. . . .

In all states the fixing of school bus routes is left to the local districts, but many state education agencies issue regulations concerning bus routes. . . . In most instances, state education agencies have detailed regulations concerning bus equipment. . . . (National Institute of Education, *A Study of State Legal Standards for the Provision of Public Education,* 1974, p. 57)

54. Kadrmas v. Dickinson Pub. Schools, 487 U.S. 450 (1988).

55. Plesnicer v. Kovach, 430 N.E.2d 648 (Ill. 1981); Abraham v. Wallenpaupak Area School Dist., 422 A.2d 1201 (Pa. 1980). Shrewsbury v. Board of Educ., 265 S.E.2d 767 (W. Va. 1980).

56. Davis v. Fentress County Board of Educ., 402 S.W.2d 873 (Tenn. 1966); Hatch v. Board of Educ., Ithaca City School Dist., 439 N.Y.S.2d 466 (1981) (transportation denied student attending non-neighborhood schools under open enrollment program).

57. Morrisette v. DeZonia, 217 N.W.2d 377 (Wis. 1974); Sparrow v. Gill, 304 F. Supp. 86 (M.D. N.C. 1969).

58. Manjares v. Newton, 411 P.2d 901 (Cal. 1966).

59. State v. Grand Coulee Dam School Dist., 536 P.2d 614 (Wash. 1975); Randolph v. School Unit 201, 270 N.E.2d 50 (Ill. 1971).

60. Nelson v. Board of Educ., 587 A.2d 1327 (N.J. 1991); Madison County Board of Educ. v. Grantham, 168 So.2d 515 (Miss. 1964).

61. State v. Grand Coulee Dam School Dist., *supra* note 59.

62. *See generally* Annot., *Validity of Public School Fees,* 41 A.L.R.3d 752 (1972, Supp. 1998).

Re summer schools fees: compare Washington v. Salisbury, 306 S.E.2d 600 (1983) (permitted) *with* Cal. Teachers Assn. v. Board of Educ., 167 Cal. Rptr. 429 (1980) (prohibited).

Re charges for elective courses: compare, Norton v. Board of Educ., 553 P.2d 1277 (N.M. 1976) (permitted) *with* Concerned Parents v. Caruthersville School Dist., 548 S.W.2d 554 (Mo. 1977) (prohibited).

Re use of "related to education" test for such charges: see Grange v. Cascade School Dist., 499 P.2d 780 (Mont. 1972); Vandevender v. Cassell, 208 S.E.2d 436 (W. Va. 1974).

63. On fees for books and supplies, *compare* Marshall v. School Dist., 553 P.2d 784 (Colo. 1976) (upheld); Carpio v. Tucson High School

Dist., 524 P.2d 948 (Ariz. 1976) (for elementary school only) *with* Union Free School Dist. v. Jackson, 403 N.Y.S.2d 621 (1978) (disallowed).

On fees for swim suits and musical instruments, *compare* Board of Educ. v. Sinclair, 222 N.W.2d 143 (Wis. 1974) (upheld) *with* Grange v. Cascade County School Dist., 499 P.2d 780 (Mont. 1972) (disallowed). For examples of fee exemptions for needy students, *see* Marshall v. School Dist., *supra;* Chandler v. South Bend Comm. School Corp., 312 N.E.2d 915 (Ind. 1974); Hamer v. Board of Educ., 292 N.E.2d 569 (Ill. 1973).

64. Arcadia Unified School Dist. v. State Dept. of Educ., 825 P.2d 438 (Cal. 1992) (school transportation fee—upheld).

CHAPTER 3

Public Schools: Religion-Related Problems

❖ **CHAPTER DISCUSSION QUESTIONS**

❖ **CASES**

3.1 Lee v. Weisman, 505 U.S. 577 (1992)[†]
3.2 Capitol Square Review and Advisory Board v. Pinette, 515 U.S. 753 (1995)
3.3 Rosenberger v. Rector and Visitors of the University of Virginia, 515 U.S. 819 (1995)
3.4 Santa Fe Independent School District v. Jane Doe—U.S.—(2000)
3.5 Brown v. Hot, Sexy and Safer Productions, Inc., 68 F.3d 525 (1st Cir. 1995)[†]

❖ **ENDNOTES**

[†]Indicates cases with review questions.

CONSTITUTIONAL CONSTRAINTS

> Congress shall make no law respecting *an establishment of religion,* or prohibiting *the free exercise thereof;* . . . (Amendment I, U.S. Constitution) (Emphasis added)

This First Amendment provision, though addressed only to Congress, also applies to state agencies, including public schools, by way of the Fourteenth Amendment. *Cantwell v. Connecticut, 310 U.S. 296 (1940).* The immediate impetus for the religious clauses of the First Amendment was to avoid creation of a national religion and church–state conflicts that had occurred in the colonies. Beyond that clear objective, the clauses leave much room for interpretation. There is no constitutional definition of "religion" and the Supreme Court has expressly refused to define religion for First Amendment purposes.[1] In considering the two religious clauses, the Establishment Clause and the Free Exercise Clause, courts have, wherever feasible, interpreted and applied each clause as a separate, isolated command, but as seen in this chapter, they are often forced to consider the combined effect of both clauses. Talismanic phrases like "church–state separation" do not provide ready answers for many government–religion issues because students, parents, and citizens have strong individual interests in government–religion interaction that may not coincide with the institutional interests of churches and states.

The Establishment and Free Exercise Clauses

Once general agreement is reached that the Establishment and Free Exercise Clauses prohibit control of religion by government or the control of government by religion, there is no prevailing consensus on how the clauses should be applied. As the Supreme Court has noted, each clause could, if pressed as absolutes, clash with the other. *Lemon v. Kurtzman, 397 U.S. 664, 668–69 (1970).*

Establishment Clause

The Supreme Court has uttered various interpretations of the Establishment Clause, declaring that it:

a. Requires *strict and absolute separation* of state functions and religion [*Everson v. Board of Education,* 330 U.S.1 (1947)];
b. Permits government *accommodation of religion* [*Zorach v. Clauson,* 343 U.S. 306 (1953)];
c. Requires that school activity serve a *secular (vs. religious) purpose and have a "primary" secular (vs. religious) effect* [*Lemon v. Kurtzman,* 403 U.S. 602 (1971)];
d. Forbids *"excessive entanglement"* of government with religion [*Walz v. Tax Comm'n,* 397 U.S. 664 (1970)];

    e. Only requires that government *does not in fact or appearance endorse religion*, regardless of its incidental benefit or burden on religion [*Capitol Square Review and Advisory Board v. Pinette*, 115 S.Ct. 1995)]; and

    f. Aims for government *"neutrality"* to religion.

State creation of a special education district with boundaries that embrace a specific religious community (Orthodox Jews) was held an unconstitutional support, and not an accommodation, of religion under the Establishment Clause.[2] With regard to other school settings, the Justices have divided on the application of the mentioned tests to specific facts, e.g., what constitutes "accommodation"? "Excessive entanglement"? "Endorsement"? "Neutrality"? For example, the *Everson* case announced the strict church-state-separation/ no-aid-to-religion test but decided by a 5–4 vote that publicly supported school transportation for parochial school children was constitutional as a neutral child-benefit program. Neither the "wall of separation" nor the child-benefit rationale minimized later conflicts on nonpublic school aid, as noted in Chapter 9. The purpose/effect, "excessive" government–religion entanglement, and "endorsement" tests only widened the range of argument. Indeed, Justice Sandra O'Connor disavowed any fixed constitutional test:

> In the end, I would recognize that the Establishment Clause inquiry cannot be distilled into a fixed, per se rule. Thus, "[e]very government practice must be judged in its unique circumstances to determine whether it constitutes an endorsement or disapproval of religion." (From *Capitol Square Review and Advisory Board v. Pinette*, reported at the end of this chapter.)

> [What] is crucial is that a government practice not have the effect of communicating a message of government endorsement or disapproval of religion. [*Lynch v. Donnelly*, 465 U.S. 668 (1984)]

The continuing evolution of Establishment Clause jurisprudence is evident from the sharply divided Supreme Court opinions at the end of this chapter and at the end of Chapter 9.

Free Exercise Clause

The Free Exercise Clause does not require government accommodation of religious belief and practice in all cases. The Amish attendance decision, discussed in Chapter 2, did hold that government may not impose a "substantial" burden on religious conduct unless it shows a "compelling" need to impose such burdens, but the Supreme Court later limited that rule to cases where the law is directed at a particular religion or specific practice. Laws that apply generally to all citizens, notwithstanding incidental religious burdens on some persons, have been held constitutional.[3] What remains, therefore, is that the Free

Exercise Clause, absent a compelling government purpose, prohibits government coercion of religious belief or of a practice that violates one's religion.

Religion-Related Speech

The constitutional guarantees of free speech, free press, and equal protection of the laws provide different constraints that tend to counter Establishment Clause limitations. Government may not bar or discriminate against expression because of its religious content or purpose, unless it has an overriding need to do so. The Supreme Court sought to differentiate between speech that the government can sponsor and speech that it must allow:

> There is a crucial difference between government speech endorsing religion, which the Establishment Clause forbids, and private speech endorsing religion, which the Free Speech and Free Exercise Clauses protect. [*Board of Educ. of Westside Community Schools v. Mergens*, 496 U.S. 226, 250 . . . (1990)]

When public school authorities open school property for optional uses by students or by the public during noninstructional time, the question arises whether government must allow equal access to religious groups to avoid violation of free speech, free exercise, or equal protection rights, or whether it must deny such access to avoid government aid to religion. In *Lamb's Chapel* (summarized in the *Capitol Square* opinion at the end of this chapter), the Supreme Court held that once public school facilities are opened to the public for nonschool uses, school authorities may not constitutionally exclude persons based on the religious content or purposes of their expression; and that the Establishment Clause did not require such exclusion. The Supreme Court in the later *Rosenberger* case, also reported at the end of this chapter, extended the *Lamb's Chapel* reasoning to require equal access to school student activity funds for students who desire to use the funds for their religious club purposes. The lower courts after *Lamb's Chapel* also ruled that school districts could not constitutionally deny use of school facilities to student religious clubs and church groups even for religious promotions if those facilities were open to the public or other nonreligious student groups.[4]

The federal Equal Access Act of 1985 mirrored the constitutional rulings in that it required school recipients of federal aid to grant equal access to all "noncurriculum-related student groups" during noninstructional time. The Supreme Court upheld the Act and rejected the challenge that it violated the Establishment Clause.[5] These developments negate prior laws and case decisions that prohibited such uses of school property. The allocation of mandatory student activity fees to student organizations that use the funds to engage in ideological causes to which other students object raises related issues that are controlled not by the religion clauses, but by the First Amendment doctrines on freedom of speech and association.

It is important to note, however, that several situations are not covered by equal access obligations. The Second Circuit recently concluded that the Establishment Clause would still bar public school use for formal church services.[6] Equally important is the conclusion that the Constitution and the equal access act do not require public school authorities to open school facilities for nonacademic uses.[7] They may lawfully deny school use for non-school activities to *all* comers, including students. Third, two courts recently held that school authorities may limit outside uses to a particular class of activity, e.g., for discussion of religious materials, but not for religious instruction, or as a community theater, but not for a Bible lecture on the origins of the human race.[8] The limited use rationale raises the additional question whether a requested use falls within the announced class of limited uses, e.g., whether allowance of school auditorium use only for education, athletic activities, and live plays would include or exclude a Bible seminar sponsored by a religious organization. The Second Circuit found that the Bible seminar was not included in the allowed educational use.[9] In addition, school authorities may not falsely classify a favored nonacademic use as part of the school curriculum in order to allow it. The Supreme Court expressly anticipated the problem:

> . . . [W]e think that the term "noncurriculum related student group" is best interpreted broadly to mean any student group that does not *directly* relate to the body of courses offered by the school. . . . A student group directly relates to a school's curriculum if the subject matter of the group is actually taught . . . in a regularly offered course; if the subject matter . . . concerns the body of courses as a whole; if participation in the group is required for a . . . course; or if participation in the group results in academic credit. . . . [*Board of Educ. v. Mergens,* 496 U.S. 226 219 (1990)] (Emphasis added)

The question whether participation by teachers and other school employees in noncurricular school-site uses by religious groups would create an unconstitutional endorsement of religion, or whether such participation would be protected as freedom of speech, has not been fully considered by the courts. The impact of the foregoing principles to prayer at school sites or events is discussed below.

State Constitutional Constraints

Most state constitutions contain stricter limitations than federal limits on public school–religion relationships. As noted in Chapter 9, some forms of government aid to religious schools that are permitted by federal law may still be barred by state law.[10] However, state law may not forbid what federal law requires, and state officials may not avoid federal law by reading it differently than federal authorities. Federal authorities may cut off federal educational subsidies to states whose laws prohibit their compliance with federal aid conditions.[11]

SCHOOL–RELIGION CONFLICTS

Prayer, Bible Reading, and Meditation

The law on public access to school property for noninstructional uses does not apply to school-sponsored activity. The legality of public school prayer, Bible reading, or meditation depends on the circumstances of their use, principally the time, place, and specific nature of the event in question, and the presence or absence of official involvement in those activities.

Classroom Prayer

School organized *classroom* prayer and recitation of verses from the Bible violate the Establishment Clause, whether conducted by teachers or by students, and whether or not they are voluntary or nondenominational.[12] The barriers to classroom religious exercises cannot be overcome by formalistic devices, such as omitting the word "God" from a classroom prayer or by furnishing classroom Bibles at private rather than state expense.[13] Arguments persist as to what other school activities amount to a prohibited religious exercise. For example, courts have upheld flag salute and pledge of allegiance exercises notwithstanding the pledge's reference to a nation "under God."[14]

Classroom periods of silence for student meditation, though affording an opportunity for silent prayer, appear to be constitutional, if neutrally administered. The Supreme Court struck down an Alabama meditation statute that was found to be enacted for the unconstitutional purpose of promoting classroom prayer,[15] but suggested that moment-of-silence statutes would be constitutional if not religiously motivated, and if school authorities remained neutral as to student use of the meditation period. Later courts accordingly upheld neutral classroom meditation periods as constitutional.[16]

Nonclassroom Prayer

The conduct of a school commencement inside a church and the lease of a school building to permit its use for a church baccalaureate service have been held unconstitutional.[17] The lower courts have been seriously divided on the constitutionality of less direct forms of nonclassroom student prayer, such as graduation ceremonies, or extracurricular athletic or social events. Their divisions were substantially narrowed by two recent Supreme Court decisions, namely, *Lee v. Weisman*, decided in 1992 with regard to graduation prayer, and *Santa Fe Independent School District v. Jane Doe*, decided in June 2000, with regard to prayer at athletic events. Excerpts of those landmark decisions are reproduced at the end of this chapter and deserve close reading.

The *Lee* case held that delivery of a nondenominational invocation at a high school commencement by a rabbi at the invitation of school authorities violated the Establishment Clause, though the students were not required to attend the commencement. Following the *Lee* decision and prior to the *Santa Fe*

decision, the lower courts continued to disagree on the scope of the constitutional prohibition.

A series of Fifth Circuit cases held that (a) *Lee* did not prohibit public
schools from giving students the option, on their own initiative and free of direct school control, to have a member of the graduating class deliver a commencement message, with or without a prayer, as long as the school policy
ensured that any optional student prayer was nonsectarian and nonproselytizing; but that (b) school allowance of student-led prayers at sporting events
games was unconstitutional, because the justification for solemnizing graduations by prayer did not extend to athletic events, and further that (c) the use of
volunteer clergy in a course on "civic virtues and morality," though unattended by religious symbols or by religious identification of the instructor, unconstitutionally aided and entangled religion with government, notwithstanding exemption options for objecting students.[18] The Eleventh Circuit Court
adopted the Fifth Circuit approach to uphold student-initiated graduation
prayer, while the Third Circuit Court rejected that view and held that such
graduation prayers violated the Establishment Clause.[19] The Sixth Circuit
Court held (a) nonsectarian invocations at college commencements to be constitutional; but (b) that an opening prayer at a school board meeting attended
by students was not constitutional, which decision was rejected by a federal
district court in California, which held school board opening prayer to be constitutional, even though some students were present and addressed the
board.[20] The Ninth Circuit originally upheld a high school policy of allowing
merit students to deliver an address at graduation commencement on any
topic they chose, including prayers, but the court later withdrew that opinion
for rehearing on a "standing to sue" question.[21]

In *Santa Fe* the Supreme Court revisited the issue whether student-initiated prayer at nonclassroom sites is to be viewed as government-sponsored
prayer in violation of the Establishment Clause or as private student speech,
regardless of its religious content. The Court there decided that the school's
policy of allowing a student "statement or invocation" to be broadcast to the
entire stadium audience over the public address system at all varsity football
home games violated the Establishment Clause. The court held that the
school policy was an unconstitutional government endorsement of religion
and that, in light of past *Santa Fe* district efforts to encourage student prayer,
the policy served the unconstitutional government purpose of advancing religion. The Court, therefore, rejected the district's argument that it sought
only to allow student freedom of speech under the Free Speech Clause of the
First Amendment and that the policy was not governed by the Establishment
Clause.

The following statements from the *Santa Fe* opinions indicate the crucial
role played by circumstances in the determination of whether nonclassroom
student prayer or religious speech involves an unconstitutional government
purpose or effect of advancing or endorsing religion, or a constitutional purpose and effect of allowing freedom of private speech.

From the majority opinion:

It [the school district] reminds us that "there is a crucial difference between government speech endorsing religion, which the Establishment Clause forbids, and private speech endorsing religion, which the Free Speech and Free Exercise Clauses protect." *Board of Ed. of Westside Community Schools (Dist. 66) v. Mergens,* 496 U.S. 226, 250. . . (1990) (opinion of O'CONNOR, J.). We certainly agree with that distinction, but we are not persuaded that the pregame invocations should be regarded as "private speech." . . . Our inquiry into this question not only can, but must, include an examination of the circumstances surrounding its enactment. Whether a government activity violates the Establishment Clause is "in large part a legal question to be answered on the basis of judicial interpretation of social facts. . . . Every government practice must be judged in its unique circumstances. . . . " . . .

From the dissenting opinion:

The Court so holds despite that any speech that may occur as a result of the election process here would be private, not government, speech. The elected student, not the government, would choose what to say. Support for the Court's holding cannot be found in any of our cases. . . . See *Lee, supra,* at 630, n. 8 (SOUTER, J., concurring). ("If the State had chosen its graduation day speakers according to wholly secular criteria, and if one of those speakers (not a state actor) had individually chosen to deliver a religious message, it would be harder to attribute an endorsement of religion to the State".)

The following questions, which consider other occasions when student religious speech might be challenged, highlight the kinds of circumstances that were not directly analyzed or covered by the Supreme Court in *Santa Fe,* and the potential impact of different circumstances on the constitutional distinction between government endorsement and private speech:

1. Where class presidents, valedictorians, homecoming, or prom queens could possibly decide whether or not to include a prayer or religious message in their public speeches, must the school authorities take steps to ensure that their speech is free of prayer or religious messages, either by imposing an advance prohibition against religious content in the student's address, or by requiring the student to prepare and submit the speech in advance to school authorities for their review, and if necessary censoring any religious content? Or would such requirements be treated as unconstitutional censorship of personal speech?

2. What if team members form a huddle for silent prayer before beginning a school competition, athletic or otherwise? What if cheer leaders do the same? What if team coaches join such huddles? What if coaches or other faculty members form their own huddle without students?

3. What if a student spectator stands up and shouts an invitation to all within hearing to join him or her in a prayer for the school team's success?

What if he or she uses a powerful private bullhorn to reach more people? What if an adult nonstudent takes like actions?

4. Finally, does it matter whether these actions take place inside a school building or outdoors?

Other questions not ruled on by the Supreme Court involve school use of classical music with religious themes or school choir use of Christian music. One lower court upheld these practices as constitutional, whereas another held that the formation of a school gospel choir was unconstitutional.[22]

The legality of nonclassroom silent prayer or reading of religious literature by school employees while off duty during the regular school day also requires case clarification under the Constitution and under Title VII of the Civil Rights Act, which, as discussed in Chapter 5, requires reasonable employer accommodation of religion.

Holiday Commemorations

Traditional acceptance of religious symbols and art on government property, including in the Supreme Court courtroom,[23] does not extend to religious displays or themes in the public schools. Religious symbols arguably serve secular, cultural purposes or convey religious messages, or both. Case outcomes have, therefore, varied with specific case facts. A classroom plaque containing the Ten Commandments was held to serve an impermissible religious purpose because several commandments made explicit reference to human obligations to God.[24] Similarly, displays of school art identified with the person and life of Jesus Christ were held unconstitutional as conveying a Christian religious message.[25]

Disputes over holiday displays with religious origins (such as Christmas, Easter, and Hanukkah) have also produced mixed case rulings on the details of each display. In the lead case of *Allegheny County v. Greater Pittsburgh American Civil Liberties Union*,[26] the Supreme Court held that placement at private expense of a crèche, unaccompanied by other secular holiday symbols, in the lobby of a county courthouse conveyed government sponsorship of a religious message in violation of the Establishment Clause, but that placement of a privately owned 18-foot menorah next to a Christmas tree at the entrance to a city-county building did not communicate government sponsorship of a religious message, and thus did not offend the Establishment Clause. The Seventh and Eleventh Circuit Courts of Appeal thereafter ruled that a menorah display *inside* government buildings would not violate the Establishment Clause, but the Third Circuit Court of Appeals took a contrasting view.[27] Some lower courts have read *Allegheny* as permitting school holiday displays, plays, or songs with some religious elements, as long as the display served a secular purpose and effect, and the religious elements of those exercises did not so dominate over the secular holiday symbols to convey government endorsement of a religious message.[28] The Supreme Court has not reconciled these case variations.

School Excusals for Religious Purposes

School excusal of students from scheduled classes to pursue religious ends also received varied court responses, depending on the circumstances of such excusal. The Supreme Court struck down, as unconstitutional aid to religion, a school program whereby students were *released* from regular classes on parental request to attend private religious instruction in another part of the public school building.[29] But the Court later upheld, as an accommodation of religion, *dismissal* of students from school to attend religious studies away from the school.[30] Lower courts have followed the distinction between internal and external religious study to uphold dismissals from school.[31]

The Supreme Court recently declined to review a decision that found that a public school holiday that coincided with a major Christian holiday (Good Friday) was constitutional, either as serving a secular purpose or as an accommodation of religion.[32] Courts also upheld school rules that prohibited extracurricular school activities during the sabbath periods of various sects, i.e., Friday evenings, Saturdays, and Sunday mornings.[33] One court sustained a school rule that prohibited public school dances, in response to vocal community opposition.[34] To say that schools *may* accommodate religion, however, is not to say that they *must* do so. The Constitution does not require schools to reschedule graduations or sporting or other school events because a religious observer could not attend those events due to conflicting religious obligations. A school was held not bound to schedule graduation ceremonies on a day that did not conflict with the Jewish Sabbath.[35]

The right of teachers or students to be excused from normal school attendance to observe religious obligations will depend on whether the urgency of school need outweighs the individual's interest in religious observation. In balancing school and individual needs, courts have overturned school denials of excused absences for religiously compelled observance where such excusal would not create a material operational hardship.[36] Conversely, excusals for compulsory religious observations may be denied where the frequency of absences for weekly religious holidays would defeat the educational program.[37] Accommodation of religion claims are buttressed by the federal employment discrimination statute known as Title VII which mandates "reasonable accommodation" of employee religion by employers in the absence of employer hardship. But neither the Constitution nor Title VII requires a school district to *subsidize* religious observance by *paid* (rather than unpaid) leave where paid leave is not afforded other employees for their personal needs.[38] However, the lower courts have divided on the question of whether teacher contracts may constitutionally provide for *paid* holidays on religious holidays.[39] Academic penalties for religiously grounded student conduct may penalize and violate freedom of religion. The denial of a diploma to a student who could not in religious conscience fulfill a school graduation requirement was stricken where there was no compelling state interest to insist on that requirement.[40]

Religion-Related Courses and Programs

Religiously controversial courses and services continue to incite lawsuits. Under Supreme Court precedents, it is easier to ban courses on Establishment Clause grounds than on Free Exercise grounds. To prevail on an Establishment Clause objection, a party need only show that a course gives favorable treatment to religion, whereas to prevail under the Free Exercise Clause, objectors must prove that religiously offensive courses or programs "coerce" them personally in the practice of their religion.

> The Establishment Clause, unlike the Free Exercise Clause, does not depend upon any showing of direct governmental compulsions and is violated . . . whether those laws operate directly to coerce nonobserving individuals or not. [*Engel v. Vitale*, 370 U.S. 421 (1962)]

Courts have upheld public school distribution of condoms, though religiously offensive to some, because offended parents or students could opt out of those programs and thus were not "coerced" for Free Exercise purposes.[41] The shifting uses of the coercion argument for establishment and free exercise purposes appear in the contrasting findings of "peer pressure" to invalidate graduation prayers under the Establishment Clause (*Lee v. Weisman*, above) on one hand, and the judicial denial that "peer pressure" deters students from opting out of religiously offensive sex education courses. Courts insist that "the [First] Amendment does not guarantee that nothing about religion will be taught in the schools, nor that nothing offensive to any religion will be taught in the schools,"[42] but the paradoxical difference in measuring neutrality under the Establishment and Free Exercise clauses remains:

> First, the mere fact that certain students are permitted to leave makes the court question whether students are being indoctrinated to religion rather than being taught within the permissible boundaries. If the course is taught within constitutional limits, every student should be required to attend. . . . While permitting non-attendance does not ordinarily raise constitutional questions, it does indicate that a constitutionally questionable course is being taught. . . . If the course is being properly taught within the constitutional limits, there is no reason for nonattendance by any student. [*Vaughn v. Reed*, 313 F. Supp. 431, 433–34 (W.D. W. Va. 1970)]

Evolution

Laws prohibiting public instruction of Darwinian evolution theory have been overturned as unconstitutional attempts to favor a fundamentalist religious view of human creation.[43] Conversely, laws that required equal instruction on "creation science" were held unconstitutional as intended to advance the fundamentalist religious view on evolution.[44] Although a Supreme Court footnote once declared that secular humanism is a form of "religion," the argument that instruction on a materialist version of evolution advances the religion of secular humanism has not prevailed.[45] A school board requirement that high school science teachers read a disclaimer that evolution lessons "are not intended to influence or dissuade the Biblical version of creation or any other concept" was also held to lack a secular purpose in violation of the Establishment Clause.[46]

The Bible as History and Literature

In ruling against school-sponsored Bible recitation, the Supreme Court stressed that public schools could constitutionally teach *about* religion, and could employ the Bible for secular educational purposes, e.g., as a source reference for historical, literary, political, and comparative cultural courses. The issue whether Bibles are being used for secular or religious purposes must be decided case by case. Class discussion of the parables of Jesus as illustrating a method of teaching, and discussion of the biblical account of the rise of the kingdom of Israel were upheld, while study of the prophecies of Daniel, of biblical accounts of worship of the golden calf, and of the fall of Sodom and Gomorrah were held unconstitutional as conveying religious messages.[47]

Sexuality and Reproduction

The expansion of "sex education" courses and services regarding student sexual activity, pregnancies, and sex-related diseases has spurred suits to challenge their validity. Courts upheld such programs as authorized by law and as falling reasonably within the educational mission of the schools. The constitutional objection that they infringe parental or religious rights presents complex questions that have not yet reached the Supreme Court.[48] For Establishment Clause purposes, courts upheld such courses as not involving government preference of the moral beliefs of sects that favor the courses over those of sects that oppose them.[49] In suits claiming violation of the Free Exercise Clause and of parental and student liberty, the cases found no violation where the challenged course or service was optional, and thus did not subject students or parents to religious coercion.[50] Where, however, a court cannot find elective escape from a particular sex education program, the constitutional issue becomes more difficult.

　　Cases on school distribution of condoms on student request are somewhat in conflict. Courts in Massachusetts and Pennsylvania sustained the practice, whereas a New York court overturned it.[51] The opinion in the *Brown v. Hot, Sexy and Safer Productions Inc.*, which appears at the end of this chapter, and the questions presented there illustrate the tasks courts face in deciding how to characterize the content and mode of presenting particular sex-oriented material to elementary and high school students. It may be that the *Brown* court's flippant characterization, as justified harmless humor, of an admitted bawdy parade of explicit sexual skits over a period of one-and-a-half hours to unconsenting adolescents in a mandatory school assembly would not command respect in other courts or school districts. Although the issues in *Brown* are technically different than the *Lacks* case which appears at the end of Chapter 6, the stark contrast between the court's review of comparably lewd presentations in *Brown* and *Lacks* points up the power of a judge to shape crucial issues of evidence and of law.

Sex-oriented student publications raise free press as well as religious issues, and these are discussed in Chapter 7 on student civil rights.

Textbooks and Readings

Course textbooks, like course offerings, invite study concerning whether they favor or disfavor religion. Complaints largely fail because objectors cannot meet the high burden of proving a constitutional violation. The omission of reference to religious influence in history was held not to convey a government hostility to religion or preference of a materialist view of history.[52] Objection that a book (*Slaughterhouse Five*) was anti-Christian in content, including derogatory references to Christianity, was turned aside where the court did not agree that the novel's materials were antireligious and where it further assumed that teacher neutrality in discussing the book would cure its antireligious potential.[53] The Sixth Circuit Court of Appeal sustained a school board's refusal to excuse students from required readings of material they deemed antithetical to their religion, on its view that compelled exposure to religiously objectionable material did not force students to affirm or deny the reading and thus did not burden their freedom of religion.[54] Another court avoided the issue by exempting students from required use of religiously offensive reading material.[55]

Distribution of outside religious literature to public school classrooms is a clearer case of aid to religion in violation of the Establishment Clause.[56]

School Conduct Requirements

The state's substantial interest in fostering patriotism is not sufficiently compelling to override free exercise objections that a flag salute or pledge of allegiance would violate objector's religious tenets.[57] Nor was the state's interest in class regularity and discipline sufficiently compelling to burden religious practice by requiring students to wear gym costumes or engage in dancing exercises that were condemned as sinful by their religion.[58] Courts have not developed sure guides for deciding when a religiously offensive dress requirement (gym or swimming outfits) rises to the level of an unconstitutional burden on religion.

State interests in protecting health and safety are, however, sufficiently compelling to override religious mandates. Statutes requiring student inoculation against communicable diseases are uniformly upheld, notwithstanding prohibitions of the student's religion,[59] even to the point of upholding state authority to appoint a guardian to enforce immunizations against the wishes of natural parents: "A person's right to exhibit religious freedom ceases where it . . . transgresses the rights of others."[60] The immunization laws of some states exempt religiously conscientious objectors, in which case courts must decide whether a claim of exemption rests on a sincerely held "religious" tenet rather than a broader philosophical objection.[61]

Public School Services to Church-School Students

As a general proposition, public schools may not promote the religious mission of any sect,[62] but as explained in Chapter 9, the legality of public school distribution of government aid benefits to nonpublic schools or their students will depend on the source, nature, and form of such assistance and the place and mode of their delivery.

Federally Funded Programs

Public school districts receiving federal funds for distributing benefits to church-related schools or students must comply with the federal subsidy conditions or forego the aid, even where state laws prohibit such public school distributions. The Supreme Court agreed that Congress could not force school authorities to violate state law, but held that Congress could require noncompliant states to return federal funds where the federal conditions could not be met.[63] Many states avoid this problem by construing their state law restrictions on aid to religious schools as limited to state funds and as not applicable to federal funds.

State-Funded Programs

The law on funding of full-time public education differs from the law on funding of school programs for the benefit of the general public, including nonpublic school students, such as summer and evening courses, work training courses, and community recreational programs. The latter generally present no serious legal problems regarding religion, but the admission of nonpublic school students to regular public school classes, a practice known as "dual enrollment," presents a hybrid situation. Local boards have no obligation to open regular public school classes to part-time dual enrollment[64] unless state law mandates part-time admission.[65] In several states "dual enrollment" or "shared time" programs are authorized when conducted by public school personnel in public schools and in classes jointly attended by students from public and nonpublic schools. These laws were held not to aid religion or violate the Establishment Clause.[66] Where, however, public school courses were taught by public school personnel in church school facilities, with religious artifacts removed from the classroom, that practice was held to violate the Establishment Clause of the federal Constitution and the state constitutions of Oregon and Montana.[67] *Kindred* and later aid cases are reviewed in Chapter 9.

Direct School–Church Dealings

School Uses of Church Property

School districts may lease private property, including church-owned buildings, for public school uses, provided the public school controls and operates the leasehold without religious furnishings or instruction.[68] But leases of parochial school buildings where religious furnishings and religious garb of teachers were maintained were voided for excessive entanglement with religion under the Establishment Clause.[69] Courts are reluctant to uphold leases of only part of a church-owned building because of the proximity of religious and secular functions in different parts of the facility. The use of a Catholic school for part of the time as a public school and as a Catholic school at another time was, however, upheld where the court found that the school–church contacts were sufficiently minimal to avoid unconstitutional entanglements.[70]

Church Uses of School Property

Public school property may be leased for a fixed term to a religious organization if the lease terms are commercially fair and neutral. Leases of public school and state college properties at reasonable, fair market rentals, when not used for public school operations, have been upheld as lawful commercial transactions with no implication of religion aid, though the lease was taken for a religious purpose.[71] Leases whose terms favor or discriminate against religious groups will, however, be disapproved.[72]

Chapter 3 Discussion Questions

Where the answer to a question may be qualified by special circumstances, explain the potential qualification.

1. What is the significance of "precedent" in court cases involving the interpretation of the religion clauses of the Constitution?

2. On what reasoning or tests do courts decide when a religion-related conflict is governed by the constitutional prohibition of establishment of religion, on one hand, and by the constitutional guarantee of free exercise of religion and freedom of speech, on the other?

3. Explain what, if any, constitutional differences may be drawn between:
   a. Recitation of classroom prayer and classroom meditation.
   b. In-class student prayer and out-of-class student prayer.
   c. "Released time" and "dismissed time" to permit student attendance at privately sponsored religious instruction.
   d. Religious references to the Bible and historical references to the Bible.
   e. The prohibition against teacher religious garb and student religious garb. (Have the courts resolved this question?)
   f. Public and nonpublic schools.
   g. Federally funded and state-funded school benefits.
   h. Evolution and creation science courses.

❖ CASES

Case 3.1
LEE v. WEISMAN
505 U.S. 577 (1992)

> [**Focus Note.** *Lee, a high school principal, invited a rabbi to offer a nondenominational invocation at the school's graduation commencement where student attendance was optional. A graduating student and her father unsuccessfully sued to block the invocation. After the commencement, which she attended, they pressed their suit to the Supreme Court, which ruled, 5–4, that the invocation violated the Establishment Clause.*]

JUSTICE KENNEDY delivered the opinion of the Court.

❖ ❖ ❖

This case does not require us to revisit the difficult questions dividing us in recent cases. . . . . . . We can decide the case without reconsidering the general constitutional framework by which public schools' efforts to accommodate religion are measured. . . . The government involvement with religious activity in this case is pervasive, to the point of creating a state-sponsored and state-directed religious exercise in a public school. . . .

❖ ❖ ❖

. . . The degree of school involvement here made it clear that the graduation prayers bore the imprint of the State and thus put school-age children who objected in an untenable position. . . . . . . It is argued . . . that prayer at a high school graduation does nothing more than offer a choice. By the time they are seniors, high school students no doubt have been required to attend classes and assemblies and to complete assignments exposing them to ideas they find distasteful or immoral or absurd or all of these. Against this background, students may consider it an odd measure of justice . . . to be denied a brief, formal prayer ceremony that the school offers in return. This argument cannot prevail, however.

❖ ❖ ❖

It is of little comfort to a dissenter, then, to be told that for her the act of standing or remaining in silence signifies mere respect, rather than participation. . . . We do not address whether that choice is acceptable if the affected citizens are mature adults. . . . Research in psychology supports the common assumption that adolescents are often susceptible to pressure from their peers towards conformity. . . . . . .

❖ ❖ ❖

Inherent differences between the public school system and a session of a State Legislature distinguish this case from *Marsh v. Chambers,* 463 U.S. 783 (1983) [which upheld invocations at the opening of a state legislature]. . . .

. . . We do not hold that every state action implicating religion is invalid if one or a few citizens find it offensive. People may take offense at all manner of religious messages, but offense alone does not in every case show a violation. . . . But, by any reading of our cases, the conformity required of the student in this case was too high an exaction to withstand the test of the Establishment Clause. . . .

❖ ❖ ❖

JUSTICE SCALIA, with whom the CHIEF JUSTICE, JUSTICE WHITE, and JUSTICE THOMAS join, dissenting.

Three Terms ago, I joined an opinion recognizing that the Establishment Clause must be construed in light of the "[g]overnment policies of accommodation, acknowledgement, and support for religion [that] are an accepted part of our political and cultural heritage." . . . It said that "[a] test for implementing the protections of the Establishment Clause that, if applied with consistency, would invalidate longstanding traditions cannot be a proper reading of the Clause." [quoting Kennedy J. concurring opinion in *Allegheny County v. Greater Pittsburgh ACLU,* 492 U.S. 573, 657, 670 (1989)]

In holding that the Establishment Clause prohibits invocations and benedictions at public-school graduation ceremonies, the Court . . . lays waste a tradition that is as old as public-school graduation ceremonies themselves. . . .

❖ ❖ ❖

From our Nation's origin, prayer has been a prominent part of governmental ceremonies and proclamations. The Declaration of Independence . . . "appeal[ed] to the Supreme Judge of the world. . . ." . . . In his first inaugural address, after swearing his oath of office on a Bible, George Washington deliberately made a prayer a part of his first official act as President:

❖ ❖ ❖

. . . Thomas Jefferson . . . prayed in his first inaugural address. . . . In his second inaugural address, Jefferson acknowledged his need for divine guidance and invited his audience to join his prayer. . . .

❖ ❖ ❖

Most recently, President Bush . . . asked those attending his inauguration to bow their heads, and made a prayer his first official act as President. . . .

Our national celebration of Thanksgiving likewise dates back to President Washington. . . .

❖ ❖ ❖

. . . And this Court's own sessions have opened with the invocation "God save the United States and this Honorable Court". . . .

❖ ❖ ❖

. . . According to the Court, students at graduation who want "to avoid the fact or appearance of participation," . . . are *psychologically* obligated by "public pressure, as well as peer pressure . . . to stand as a group or, at least, maintain respectful silence" during those prayers. . . . This assertion—*the very linchpin of the Court's opinion*—is almost as intriguing for what it does not say as for what it says. It does not say, for example, that students are psychologically coerced to bow their heads . . . pay attention to the prayers, utter "Amen," or in fact pray. . . . It claims only that students are psychologically coerced "to stand . . . *or,* at least, maintain respectful silence." . . .

❖ ❖ ❖

. . . Since the Court does not dispute that students . . . at graduation ceremonies retain . . . the free will to sit . . . there is absolutely no basis for the Court's decision. . . .

❖ ❖ ❖

. . . Many graduating seniors, of course, are old enough to vote. Why, then, does the Court treat them as though they were first-graders? . . .

❖ ❖ ❖

Our religion-clause jurisprudence has become bedeviled (so to speak) by reliance on formulaic abstractions that are not derived from, but positively conflict with, our long-accepted constitutional traditions. Foremost among these has been the so-called *Lemon* test. . . . The Court today demonstrates the irrelevance of *Lemon* by essentially ignoring it. . . . Unfortunately, however, the Court has replaced *Lemon* with its psycho-coercion test. . . .

. . . Given the odd basis for the Court's decision, invocations and benedictions will be able to be given at public-school graduations next June. . . . All that is seemingly needed is an announcement, or perhaps a written insertion to the effect that, while all are asked to rise for the invocation and benediction, none is compelled to join in them, nor will be assumed, by rising, to have done so. . . . . . .

Review Questions 3.1

In reading the foregoing opinions, consider the following questions:

1. Does the majority opinion rest primarily on the finding of coercive peer pressure to conform or on a finding of school sponsorship and endorsement of religion?

2. If an invocation creates material peer pressure to participate, can future graduation prayers be validated, as the dissent suggests, by school announcement that students are free to leave, sit, or ignore the invocation?

3. In future graduations, can a school disclaimer that it is not endorsing, but only accommodating, religion and student wishes avoid the endorsement objection?

4. Does the court's acceptance of the peer pressure argument in this case square with the rejection of peer pressure objection to sex education courses?

5. Does the court's opinion of high-school-age students as more susceptible to pressure than adults for prayer purposes square with its treatment of such students as sufficiently mature to obtain abortions without parental notification or consent where the legislature does not mandate such notification?

Case 3.2

CAPITOL SQUARE REVIEW AND ADVISORY BOARD v. PINETTE
515 U.S. 753 (1995)

[**Focus Note.** *The city of Columbus, Ohio, refused to grant the Ku Klux Klan a permit to erect a private, unattended cross in a public square on the grounds that the display of a religious symbol on government property was prohibited by the Establishment Clause. The Supreme Court held that the Establishment Clause did not bar granting of the permit, and that the Free Speech clause required equal treatment of religious expression in public areas that have been opened to use by the public.*]

JUSTICE SCALIA announced the judgment of the Court.

✧ ✧ ✧

Respondents' religious display . . . was private expression. Our precedent establishes that private religious speech . . . is as fully protected under the Free Speech Clause as secular private expression. . . .

❖ ❖ ❖

. . . Petitioners advance a single justification for closing Capitol Square to respondents' cross: the State's interest in avoiding official endorsement of Christianity, as required by the Establishment Clause. . . .

❖ ❖ ❖

. . . We have twice previously addressed the combination of private religious expression, a forum available for public use, content-based regulation, and a State's interest in complying with the Establishment Clause. Both times, we have struck down the restriction on religious content.

❖ ❖ ❖

In *Lamb's Chapel*, a school district allowed private groups to use school facilities during off-hours for a variety of civic, social and recreational purposes, excluding, however, religious purposes. We held that . . . the school district violated an applicant's free-speech rights by denying it use of the facilities solely because of the religious viewpoint of the program. . . . We rejected the district's . . . Establishment Clause defense (the same made here) because . . . the district was not directly sponsoring the religious group's activity, and "any benefit to religion or to the Church would have been no more than incidental." . . . The *Lamb's Chapel* reasoning applies a fortiori here. . . .

❖ ❖ ❖

. . . We find it peculiar to say that government "promotes" or "favors" a religious display by giving it the same access to a public forum that all other displays enjoy. . . . . . .

❖ ❖ ❖

. . . "[T]here is a crucial difference between government speech endorsing religion, which the Establishment Clause forbids, and private speech endorsing religion, which the Free Speech and Free Exercise Clauses protect." . . .

❖ ❖ ❖

Religious expression cannot violate the Establishment Clause where it (1) is purely private and (2) occurs in a traditional or designated public forum, publicly announced and open to all on equal terms. . . .

Justice O'Connor, with whom Justice Souter and Justice Breyer join,. . . .

I . . . concur in the judgment. . . .

❖ ❖ ❖

In the end, I would recognize that the Establishment Clause inquiry cannot be distilled into a fixed, per se rule. Thus, "[e]very government practice must be judged in its unique circumstances to determine whether it constitutes an endorsement or disapproval of religion." . . .

❖ ❖ ❖

JUSTICE STEVENS, dissenting.

The Establishment Clause should be construed to create a strong presumption against the installation of unattended religious symbols on public property. . . .

Case 3.3

ROSENBERGER v. RECTOR AND VISITORS OF THE UNIVERSITY OF VIRGINIA
515 U.S. 819 (1995)

[**Focus Note.** *A student group, called Wide Awake Productions (WAP), that published a newspaper titled* Wide Awake *with a Christian editorial viewpoint. WAP requested a grant from the university fund that was created from student activity fees to support student publications. The university denied the grant on the grounds that it would violate the Establishment Clause. The Supreme Court, by a 5–4 vote, held that the University's denial violated the student First Amendment freedom of the press; and that such denial was not required by the Establishment Clause.]*

JUSTICE KENNEDY *delivered the opinion of the Court.*

❖ ❖ ❖

. . . In the realm of private speech or expression, government regulation may not favor one speaker over another. . . . Discrimination against speech because of its message is presumed to be unconstitutional. . . . . . .
. . . [W]e hold that the regulation invoked to deny SAF [Student Activity Fund] support . . . is a denial of their right of free speech guaranteed by the First Amendment. It remains to be considered whether the violation . . . is excused by the necessity of complying with the Constitution's prohibition against state establishment of religion. . . .

❖ ❖ ❖

The governmental program here is neutral toward religion. There is no suggestion that the University created it to advance religion or adopted some ingenious device with the purpose of aiding a religious cause. . . .

❖ ❖ ❖

It does not violate the Establishment Clause for a public university to grant access to its facilities on a religion-neutral basis to a wide spectrum of student groups, including groups which use meeting rooms for sectarian activities, accompanied by some devotional exercises. See *Widmar,* 454 U.S., at 269, . . . *Mergens,* 496 U.S., at 252. . . .

❖ ❖ ❖

There is no Establishment Clause violation in the University's honoring its duties under the Free Speech Clause. . . .

JUSTICE SOUTER, with whom JUSTICE STEVENS, JUSTICE GINSBURG, and JUSTICE BREYER join, dissenting.

The Court today, for the first time, approves direct funding of core religious activities by an arm of the State. . . .

The Court . . . has never before upheld direct state funding of the sort of proselytizing published in Wide Awake. . . .

❖ ❖ ❖

. . . At the heart of the Establishment Clause stands the prohibition against direct public funding. . . .

❖ ❖ ❖

Given . . . the Establishment Clause's bar to funding the magazine, there should be no need to decide whether . . . the University would violate the Free Speech Clause. . . . . . .

Case 3.4

SANTA FE INDEPENDENT SCHOOL DISTRICT v. JANE DOE
—U.S. — (2000)

[***Focus Note.*** *The treatment of voluntary student prayer at graduation and athletic events. The following opinion extended the constitutional ban to student prayer at school varsity football games. Note the court's emphasis on the particular history and practices of student prayer in the defendant school district. Further, note that the decision rests on two separate court findings, namely, of an unconstitutional purpose to advance religion and of an unconstitutional effect of endorsing religion, either of which would independently suffice for the case.]*

Justice Stevens DELIVERED THE OPINION OF THE COURT.

Prior to 1995, the Santa Fe High School student who occupied the school's elective office of student council chaplain delivered a prayer over the public address system before each varsity football game for the entire season. This practice . . . was challenged . . . as a violation of the Establishment Clause. . . . While these proceedings were pending . . . the school district adopted a different policy that permits, but does not require, prayer initiated and led by a student at all home games. The District Court entered an order modifying that policy to permit only nonsectarian, nonproselytizing prayer. The Court of Appeals held that . . . the football prayer policy was invalid. . . .

❖ ❖ ❖

The August policy, which was titled "Prayer at Football Games," was similar to the July policy for graduations. . . . On August 31, 1995, according to the parties' stipulation, "the district's high school students voted to determine whether a student would deliver prayer at varsity football games. . . . The students chose to allow a student to say a prayer at football games." *Id.* at 65. A week later, in a separate election, they selected a student "to deliver the prayer at varsity football games." *Id.* at 66.

The final policy (October policy) is essentially the same as the August policy, though it omits the word "prayer" from its title, and refers to "messages" and "statements" as well as "invocations." It is the validity of that policy that is before us.

❖ ❖ ❖

The decision of the Court of Appeals [in a prior proceeding] followed Fifth Circuit precedent that had announced two rules. In *Jones v. Clear Creek Independent School Dist.*, 977 F.2d 963 (1992), that court held that student-led prayer that was approved by a vote of the students and was nonsectarian and nonproselytizing was permissible at high school graduation ceremonies. On the other hand, in later cases the Fifth Circuit made it clear that the *Clear Creek* rule applied only to high school graduations and that school-encouraged prayer was constitutionally impermissible at school-related sporting events. Thus, in *Doe v. Duncanville Independent School Dist.*, 70 F.3d 402 (1995), it had described a high school graduation as "a significant, once in-a-lifetime event " to be contrasted with athletic events in "a setting that is far less solemn and extraordinary." *Id.* at 406–407.

In its opinion in this case, the Court of Appeals explained:

The controlling feature here is the same as in *Duncanville*: The prayers are to be delivered at *football games*—hardly the sober type of annual event that can be appropriately solemnized with prayer. The distinction . . . is simply one without difference. Regardless of whether the prayers are selected by vote or spontaneously initiated at these frequently-recurring, informal, school-sponsored events, school officials are present and have the authority to stop the prayers. Thus, as we indicated in *Duncanville,* our decision in *Clear Creek II* hinged on the singular context and singularly serious nature of a graduation ceremony. Outside that nurturing context, a Clear Creek Prayer Policy cannot survive. We therefore reverse the district court's holding that [the District's] alternative Clear Creek Prayer Policy can be extended to football games, irrespective of the presence of the nonsectarian, nonproselytizing restrictions. 168 F.3d at 823.

❖ ❖ ❖

We granted the District's petition for certiorari, limited to the following question: "Whether petitioner's policy permitting student-led, student-initiated prayer at football games violates the Establishment Clause." 528 U.S. 1002 (1999). We conclude, as did the Court of Appeals, that it does.

❖ ❖ ❖

. . . In *Lee v. Weisman,* 505 U.S. 577 . . . (1992), we held that a prayer delivered by a rabbi at a middle school graduation ceremony violated that Clause. Although this case involves student prayer at a different type of school function, our analysis is properly guided by the principles that we endorsed in *Lee.*

❖ ❖ ❖

In this case the District first argues that this principle is inapplicable to its October policy because the messages are private student speech, not public speech. It reminds us that "there is a crucial difference between *government speech* endorsing religion, which the Establishment Clause forbids, and *private speech* endorsing religion, which the Free Speech and Free Exercise Clauses protect." *Board of Ed. of Westside Community Schools (Dist. 66) v. Mergens,* 496 U.S. 226, 250. . . (1990). . . . We certainly agree with that distinction, but we are not persuaded that the pregame invocations should be regarded as "private speech."

These invocations are authorized by a government policy and take place on government property at government-sponsored school-related events. Of course, not every message delivered under such circumstances is the government's own. We have held, for example, that an individual's contribution to a government-created forum was not government speech. See *Rosenberger v. Rector and Visitors of Univ. of Va.,* 515 U.S. 819. . . (1995). Although the District relies heavily on *Rosenberger* and similar cases involving such forums, it is clear that the pregame ceremony is not the type of forum discussed in those cases. The Santa Fe school officials simply do not "evince either 'by policy or by practice,' any intent to open the [pregame ceremony] to 'indiscriminate use,' . . . by the student body generally." *Hazelwood School Dist. v. Kuhlmeier,* 484 U.S. 260, 270 (1988). . . . . . .

Granting only one student access to the stage at a time does not, of course, necessarily preclude a finding that a school has created a limited public forum. Here, however, Santa Fe's student election system ensures that only those messages deemed "appropriate" under the District's policy may be delivered. That is, the majoritarian process implemented by the District guarantees, by definition, that minority candidates will never prevail and that their views will be effectively silenced.

Recently, in *Board of Regents of Univ. of Wis. System v. Southworth*, 529 U.S. — (2000), we explained why student elections that determine, by majority vote, which expressive activities shall receive or not receive school benefits are constitutionally problematic:

> To the extent the referendum substitutes majority determinations for viewpoint neutrality it would undermine the constitutional protection the program requires. The whole theory of viewpoint neutrality is that minority views are treated with the same respect as are majority views. Access to a public forum, for instance, does not depend upon majoritarian consent. That principle is controlling here. *Id.* at — (slip op., at 16–17).

Like the student referendum for funding in *Southworth*, this student election does nothing to protect minority views. . . . . . the District's elections are insufficient safeguards of diverse student speech.

In *Lee,* the school district made the related argument that its policy of endorsing only "civic or nonsectarian" prayer was acceptable because it minimized the intrusion on the audience as a whole. We rejected that claim by explaining that such a majoritarian policy "does not lessen the offense or isolation to the objectors. . . ." 505 U.S. at 594. Similarly, while Santa Fe's majoritarian election might ensure that *most* of the students are represented, it does nothing to protect the minority; indeed, it likely serves to intensify their offense.

Moreover, the District has failed to divorce itself from the religious content in the invocations. It has not succeeded in doing so, either by claiming that its policy is " 'one of neutrality rather than endorsement' " or by characterizing the individual student as the "circuit-breaker" in the process. Contrary to the District's repeated assertions that it has adopted a "hands-off" approach to the pregame invocation, the realities of the situation plainly reveal that its policy involves both perceived and actual endorsement of religion. In this case, as we found in *Lee,* the "degree of school involvement" makes it clear that the pregame prayers bear "the imprint of the State and thus put school-age children who objected in an untenable position." 505 U.S. at 590.

The District has attempted to disentangle itself from the religious messages by developing the two-step student election process. . . . The elections take place at all only because the school "board *has chosen to permit* students to deliver a brief invocation and/or message." . . . The elections thus "shall" be conducted "by the high school student council" and "upon advice and direction of the high school principal." *Id.* at 104–105. The decision whether to deliver a message is first made by majority vote of the entire student body, followed by a choice of the speaker in a separate, similar majority election. Even though the particular words used by the speaker are not determined by those votes, the policy mandates that the "statement or invocation" be "consistent with the goals and purposes of this policy," which are "to solemnize the event, to promote good sportsmanship and student safety, and to establish the appropriate environment for the competition." *Ibid*.

In addition to involving the school in the selection of the speaker, the policy, by its terms, invites and encourages religious messages. The policy itself states that the purpose of the message is "to solemnize the event." A religious message is the most obvious method of solemnizing an event. . . . Indeed, the only type of message that is expressly endorsed in the text is an "invocation." . . . Thus, the expressed purposes of the policy encourage the selection of a religious message, and that is precisely how the students understand the policy. . . .

The actual or perceived endorsement of the message, moreover, is established by factors beyond just the text of the policy. Once the student speaker is selected and the message composed, the invocation is then delivered to a large audience assembled as part of a regularly scheduled, school-sponsored function conducted on school property. The message is broadcast over the school's public address system. . . . . . .

In this context the members of the listening audience must perceive the pregame message as a public expression of the views of the majority of the student body delivered with the approval of the school administration. In cases involving state participation in a religious activity, one of the relevant questions is "whether an objective observer . . . would perceive it as a state endorsement of prayer in public schools." *Wallace*, 472 U.S. at 73, 76 (O'CONNOR, J., concurring in judgment). . . . . . . [A]n objective Santa Fe High School student will unquestionably perceive the inevitable pregame prayer as stamped with her school's seal of approval.

❖ ❖ ❖

Most striking to us is the evolution of the current policy from the long-sanctioned office of "Student Chaplain" to the candidly titled "Prayer at Football Games" regulation. This history indicates that the District intended to preserve the practice of prayer before football games. The conclusion that the District viewed the October policy simply as a continuation of the previous policies is dramatically illustrated by the fact that the school did not conduct a new election, pursuant to the current policy, to replace the results of the previous election, which occurred under the former policy. Given these observations, and in light of the school's history of regular delivery of a student-led prayer at athletic events, it is reasonable to infer that the specific purpose of the policy was to preserve a popular "state-sponsored religious practice." *Lee*, 505 U.S. at 596.

. . . The delivery of such a message—over the school's public address system, by a speaker representing the student body, under the supervision of school faculty, and pursuant to a school policy that explicitly and implicitly encourages public prayer—is not properly characterized as "private" speech.

The District next argues that its football policy is distinguishable from the graduation prayer in *Lee* because it does not coerce students to participate in religious observances. Its argument has two parts: first . . . because the pregame messages are the product of student choices; and second, that there is really no coercion at all because attendance at an extracurricular event, unlike a graduation ceremony, is voluntary.

The reasons just discussed explaining why the alleged "circuit-breaker" mechanism of the dual elections and student speaker do not turn public speech into private speech also demonstrate why these mechanisms do not insulate the school from the coercive element of the final message. . . .

. . . Although it is true that the ultimate choice of student speaker is "attributable to the students," Brief for Petitioner 40, the District's decision to hold the constitutionally problematic election is clearly "a choice attributable to the State." *Lee*, 505 U.S. at 587.

The District further argues that attendance at the commencement ceremonies at issue in *Lee* "differs dramatically" from attendance at high school football games, which it contends "are of no more than passing interest to many students" and are "decidedly extracurricular," thus dissipating any coercion. . . .

There are some students, however, such as cheerleaders, members of the band, and, of course, the team members themselves, for whom seasonal commitments mandate their attendance, sometimes for class credit. The District also minimizes the importance to many students of attending and participating in extracurricular activities as part of a complete educational experience. . . . Undoubtedly, the games are not important to some students. . . . For many others, however, the choice between whether to attend these games or to risk facing a personally offensive religious ritual is in no practical sense an easy one. The Constitution, moreover, demands that the school may not force this difficult choice upon these students. . . .

Even if we regard every high school student's decision to attend a home football game as purely voluntary, we are nevertheless persuaded that the delivery of a pregame prayer has the improper effect of coercing those present to participate in an act of religious worship. . . . The constitutional command will not permit the District "to exact religious conformity from a student as the price" of joining her classmates at a varsity football game.

The Religion Clauses of the First Amendment prevent the government from making any law respecting the establishment of religion or prohibiting the free exercise thereof. By no means do these commands impose a prohibition on all religious activity in our public schools. See, e.g., *Lamb's Chapel v. Center Moriches Union Free School Dist.*, 508 U.S. 384, 395 (1993); *Board of Ed. of Westside Community Schools (Dist. 66) v. Mergens*, 496 U.S. 226 (1990); *Wallace v. Jaffree*, 472 U.S. 38, 59 (1985). . . . Thus, nothing in the Constitution . . . prohibits any public school student from voluntarily praying at any time before, during, or after the school day. But the religious liberty protected by the Constitution is abridged when the State affirmatively sponsors the particular religious practice of prayer.

Finally, the District argues repeatedly that the Does have made a premature facial challenge to the October policy. . . . The District emphasizes, quite correctly, that until a student actually delivers a solemnizing message under the latest version of the policy, there can be no certainty that any of the statements or invocations will be religious. Thus, it concludes, the October policy necessarily survives a facial challenge.

This argument, however, assumes that we are concerned only with the serious constitutional injury that occurs when a student is forced to participate in an act of religious worship. . . . But the Constitution also requires that. . . we guard against other different, yet equally important, constitutional injuries. One is the mere passage by the District of a policy that has the purpose and perception of government establishment of religion. . . .

. . . Our Establishment Clause cases involving facial challenges, however, have not focused solely on the possible applications of the statute, but rather have considered whether the statute has an unconstitutional purpose. . . . Under the *Lemon* standard, a court must invalidate a statute if it lacks "a secular legislative purpose." *Lemon v. Kurtzman*, 403 U.S. 602, 612 (1971). . . .

As discussed, *supra*. . . the text of the October policy alone reveals that it has an unconstitutional purpose. . . .

This case comes to us as the latest step in developing litigation brought as a challenge to institutional practices that unquestionably violated the Establishment Clause. . . . The narrow question before us is whether implementation of the October policy insulates the continuation of such prayers from constitutional scrutiny. It does not. Our inquiry into this question not only can, but must, include an examination of the circumstances surrounding its enactment. Whether a government activity violates the Establishment Clause is "in large part a legal question to be answered on the basis of judicial interpretation of social facts. . . . Every government practice must be judged in its unique circumstances. . . ." *Lynch,* 465 U.S. at 693–694 (O'CONNOR, J., concurring). . . .

The District, nevertheless, asks us to pretend that we do not recognize what every Santa Fe High School student understands clearly—that this policy is about prayer. . . . We refuse to turn a blind eye to the context in which this policy arose, and that context quells any doubt that this policy was implemented with the purpose of endorsing school prayer.

Therefore, the simple enactment of this policy, with the purpose and perception of school endorsement of student prayer, was a constitutional violation. We need not wait for the inevitable to confirm and magnify the constitutional injury. . . .

Therefore, even if no Santa Fe High School student were ever to offer a religious message, the October policy fails a facial challenge because the attempt by the District to encourage prayer is also at issue. Government efforts to endorse religion cannot evade constitutional reproach based solely on the remote possibility that those attempts may fail.

❖ ❖ ❖

The judgment of the Court of Appeals is, accordingly, affirmed.
It is so ordered.

Dissent:

CHIEF JUSTICE REHNQUIST, with whom JUSTICE SCALIA and JUSTICE THOMAS join, dissenting.

The Court distorts existing precedent to conclude that the school district's student-message program is invalid on its face. . . . But even more disturbing than its holding is the tone of the Court's opinion; it bristles with hostility to all things religious in public life. Neither the holding nor the tone of the opinion is faithful to the meaning of the Establishment Clause, when it is recalled that George Washington himself, at the request of the very Congress which passed the Bill of Rights, proclaimed a day of "public thanksgiving and prayer, to be observed by acknowledging with grateful hearts the many and signal favors of Almighty God." Presidential Proclamation, 1 Messages and Papers of the Presidents, 1789–1897, p. 64 (J. Richardson ed. 1897).

We do not learn until late in the Court's opinion that respondents in this case challenged the district's student-message program at football games before it had been put into practice. As the Court explained in *United States v. Salerno*, 481 U.S. 739, 745, 95 L. Ed. 2d 697, 107 S. Ct. 2095 (1987), the fact that a policy might "operate unconstitutionally under some conceivable set of circumstances is insufficient to render it wholly invalid." . . . Therefore, the question is not whether the district's policy *may* be applied in violation of the Establishment Clause, but whether it inevitably will be.

The Court. . . decides that it "need not wait for the inevitable" and invalidates the district's policy on its face. . . . To do so, it applies the most rigid version of the oft-criticized test of *Lemon v. Kurtzman*, 403 U.S. 602. . . (1971).

❖ ❖ ❖

Even if it were appropriate to apply the *Lemon* test here, the district's student-message policy should not be invalidated on its face. . . .

❖ ❖ ❖

But the Court ignores these possibilities by holding that merely granting the student body the power to elect a speaker that may choose to pray, "regardless of the students' ultimate use of it, is not acceptable." *Ante*, at 25. The Court so holds despite that any speech that may occur as a result of the election process here would be *private*, not *government*, speech. The elected student, not the government, would choose what to say. . . .

❖ ❖ ❖

The Court also relies on our decision in *Lee v. Weisman*, 505 U.S. 577 (1992). . . . In *Lee*, we concluded that the content of the speech at issue, a graduation prayer given by a rabbi, was "directed and controlled" by a school official. . . . In other words, at issue in *Lee* was *government* speech. Here, by contrast, the potential speech at issue would be a message or invocation selected or created by a student. That is. . . it would be *private* speech. . . .

❖ ❖ ❖

. . . The students may have chosen a speaker according to wholly secular criteria—like good public speaking skills or social popularity—and the student speaker may have chosen, on her own accord, to deliver a religious message. Such an application of the policy would likely pass constitutional muster. See *Lee, supra,* at 630, n. 8 (SOUTER, J., concurring) ("If the State had chosen its graduation day speakers according to wholly secular criteria, and if one of those speakers (not a state actor) had individually chosen to deliver a religious message, it would be harder to attribute an endorsement of religion to the State").

❖ ❖ ❖

The policy at issue here may be applied in an unconstitutional manner, but it will be time enough to invalidate it if that is found to be the case. I would reverse the judgment of the Court of Appeals.

Case 3.5

BROWN v. HOT, SEXY AND SAFER PRODUCTIONS, INC.
68 F.3d 525 (1st Cir. 1995)

[***Focus Note.*** *Suit by parents and public high school students against the school district, school officials, and Hot, Sexy and Safer Productions, Inc., a contractor retained by the school district to make a presentation to a high school assembly as a vehicle to promote AIDS awareness. The program consisted of a continuous one-and-a-half hour series of explicit sexual skits. Students were required to attend the assembly, and the school defendants also attended and observed the presentation. The defendant school officials did not notify student parents of the program or allow them to have their children decline to attend the Hot, Sexy presentation, as required by official written school policy. The following opinion affirmed the trial court's dismissal of the suit.]*

TORRUELLA, CHIEF JUDGE.

❖ ❖ ❖

. . . The plaintiffs' complaint alleges the following facts, which we take as true for purposes of this appeal. On April 8, 1992, Mesiti and Silva attended a mandatory, school-wide "assembly" at Chelmsford High School. Both students were fifteen years old at the time. The assembly consisted of a ninety-minute presentation characterized by the defendants as an AIDS awareness program (the "Program"). The Program was staged by defendant Suzi Landolphi ("Landolphi"), contracting through defendant Hot, Sexy, and Safer, Inc., a corporation wholly owned by Landolphi.

Plaintiffs allege that Landolphi gave sexually explicit monologues and participated in sexually suggestive skits with several minors chosen from the audience. Specifically, the complaint alleges that Landolphi: 1) told the students that they were going to have a "group sexual experience, with audience participation"; 2) used profane, lewd, and lascivious language to describe body parts and excretory functions; 3) advocated and approved oral sex, masturbation, homosexual sexual activity, and condom use during promiscuous premarital sex; 4) simulated masturbation; 5) characterized the loose pants worn by one minor as "erection wear"; 6) referred to being in "deep sh—" after anal sex; 7) had a male minor lick an oversized condom with her, after which she had a female minor pull it over the male minor's entire head and blow it up; 8) encouraged a male minor to display his "orgasm face" with her for the camera; 9) informed a male minor that he was not having enough orgasms; 10) closely inspected a minor and told him he had a "nice butt"; and 11) made eighteen references to orgasms, six references to male genitals, and eight references to female genitals.

Plaintiffs maintain that the sexually explicit nature of Landolphi's speech and behavior humiliated and intimidated Mesiti and Silva. Moreover, many students copied Landolphi's routines and generally displayed overtly sexual behavior in the weeks following the Program, allegedly exacerbating the minors' harassment. The complaint does not allege that either of the minor plaintiffs actually participated in any of the skits, or were the direct objects of any of Landolphi's comments.

❖ ❖ ❖

The complaint names eight co-defendants along with Hot, Sexy, and Safer, and Landolphi, alleging that each played some role in planning, sponsoring, producing, and compelling the minor plaintiffs' attendance at the Program. . . .

❖ ❖ ❖

. . . All the defendants were physically present during the Program.

A school policy adopted by the School Committee required "[p]ositive subscription, with written parental permission" as a prerequisite to "instruction in human sexuality." The plaintiffs allege, however, that the parents were not given advance notice of the content of the Program or an opportunity to excuse their children from attendance at the assembly.

❖ ❖ ❖

The plaintiffs seek . . . relief, alleging that the school sponsored program deprived the minor plaintiffs of: (1) their privacy rights under the First and

Fourteenth Amendments; (2) their substantive due process rights under the First and Fourteenth Amendments; (3) their procedural due process rights under the Fourteenth Amendment; and (4) their First Amendment rights under the Free Exercise Clause (in conjunction with a deprivation of the parent plaintiffs' right to direct and control the upbringing of their children). Plaintiffs also allege that the Program created a sexually hostile educational environment in violation of Title IX of the Education Amendments of 1972. . . .

❖ ❖ ❖

I. Privacy Rights and Substantive Due Process

. . . There are two theories under which a plaintiff may bring a substantive due process claim. . . . Under the second, a plaintiff is not required to prove the deprivation of a specific liberty or property interest, but, rather, he must prove that the state's conduct "shocks the conscience." . . .

A. Conscience Shocking Behavior

Plaintiffs' claim that the defendants engaged in conscience shocking behavior when they compelled the minor plaintiffs to attend the Program. The Supreme Court set the standard for analyzing claims of conscience shocking behavior in *Rochin*. In that case, the Court held that the government could not use evidence obtained by pumping a defendant's stomach against his will because the state actor's conduct was so egregious that it "shock[ed] the conscience". . . . . . . Although we have not foreclosed the possibility that words or verbal harassment may constitute "conscious shocking" behavior in violation of substantive due process rights . . . our review of the case law indicates that the threshold for alleging such claims is high and that the facts alleged here do not rise to that level.

❖ ❖ ❖

The facts alleged at bar are less severe than those found insufficient in *Souza* and *Pittsley* [police and prosecutor misconduct cases]. The minor teenagers . . . were compelled to attend a sexually explicit AIDS awareness assembly without prior parent approval. While the defendants' failure to provide opt-out procedures may have displayed a certain callousness towards the sensibilities of the minors, their acts do not approach the mean-spirited brutality evinced by the defendants in *Souza* and *Pittsley*. We accordingly hold that the acts alleged here, taken as true, do not constitute conscience shocking and thus fail to state a claim under *Rochin*.

B. Protected Liberty Interests

The Supreme Court has held that the Fourteenth Amendment encompasses a privacy right that protects against significant government intrusions into certain personal decisions. . . .

1. Right to Rear Children

❖ ❖ ❖

. . . We need not decide here whether the right to rear one's children is fundamental because we find that, even if it were, the plaintiffs have failed to demonstrate an intrusion of constitutional magnitude on this right.

The *Meyer* and *Pierce* cases, we think, evince the principle that the state
cannot prevent parents from choosing a specific educational program. . . . That
is, the state does not have the power to "standardize its children". . . . We do
not think, however, that this freedom encompasses a fundamental constitutional right to dictate the curriculum at the public school to which they have
chosen to send their children. . . . . We cannot see that the Constitution imposes such a burden on state educational systems, and accordingly find that
the rights of parents as described by *Meyer* and *Pierce* do not encompass a
broad-based right to restrict the flow of information in the public schools.

2. Right to be Free from Offensive Speech

The minor plaintiffs maintain that the defendants' conduct violated their privacy right to be free from "exposure to vulgar and offensive language and ob-
noxiously debasing portrayals of human sexuality." Plaintiffs cite no cases—
and we have found none—indicating that such a fundamental privacy right
exists. Rather, they attempt to extract the claimed privacy right from the
Supreme Court's First Amendment cases which uphold the state's limited
power to regulate or discipline speech to protect minors from offensive or vulgar speech. See *Bethel Sch. Dist. No. 403 v. Fraser*, 478 U.S. 675, 685, . . . (1986)
(cited for the proposition that "[a] high school assembly or classroom is no
place for a sexually explicit monologue directed towards an unsuspecting audience of teenage students"). . . . We agree with the district court that these
cases "do not create a private cause of action against state officials for exposure" to patently offensive language.

II. Procedural Due Process

The plaintiffs' third claim alleges that their procedural due process rights under the Fourteenth Amendment were violated when the defendants compelled
the minor plaintiffs to attend the Program without giving the parents advance
notice and an opportunity to opt out of attending.

❖ ❖ ❖

The plaintiffs contend that state law and the School Committee's policy
on "Sex Education" confers a protected liberty interest, and that the defendants' actions deprived them of it without due process. Specifically, the complaint alleges that the defendants failed to follow the school's Sex Education
Policy. . . .

Defendants concede . . . that the Sex Education Policy confers a liberty interest in freedom from exposure to the content of the Program and in being afforded an opportunity to opt out. They argue, however, that the plaintiffs still fail to state a claim because the violation of the Sex Education Policy was a "random and unauthorized" act within the confines of the Parratt-Hudson doctrine. . . .

❖ ❖ ❖

Parratt and Hudson preclude § 1983 claims for the "random and unauthorized" conduct of state officials because the state cannot "anticipate and control [such conduct] in advance." . . .

❖ ❖ ❖

The plaintiffs contend that the deprivation cannot be characterized as "random and unauthorized" because the performance was planned well in advance. . . . The deprivation alleged here is not the staging of the Program itself, but rather the defendants' failure to follow the procedures mandated by the Sex Education Policy. . . . Rather, the Sex Education Policy states that "[p]ositive subscription, with parental permission, will be a prerequisite to enrolling," and, accordingly, vested no discretion in school officials. We therefore conclude that the failure to follow the Sex Education Policy was a "random and unauthorized" act within the confines of the Parratt-Hudson doctrine.

III. Free Exercise Clause

Plaintiffs' fourth claim seeks . . . relief, alleging that the defendants' endorsement and encouragement of sexual promiscuity at a mandatory assembly "imping[ed] on their sincerely held religious values regarding chastity and morality," and thereby violated the Free Exercise Clause of the First Amendment.

In *Employment Div., Oregon Dep't of Human Resources v. Smith,* 494 U.S. 872, . . . (1990), the Supreme Court addressed a free exercise challenge to a facially neutral and generally applicable criminal statute. . . . The Court explained that the First Amendment was not offended by neutral, generally applicable laws, unless burdening religion was the object of the law. . . .

❖ ❖ ❖

. . . The plaintiffs do not allege . . . that the compulsory attendance at the Program was anything but a neutral requirement that applied generally to all students. . . .

❖ ❖ ❖

IV. Sexual Harassment

The plaintiffs' fifth claim alleges that the defendants engaged in sexual harassment by creating a sexually hostile environment, in violation of Title IX of the Education Amendments of 1972. Title IX provides in relevant part:

No person in the United States shall, on the basis of sex, be excluded from participation in, be denied the benefits of, or be subjected to discrimination under
any education program or activity receiving Federal financial assistance. . . .

Because the relevant case law under Title IX is relatively sparse, we apply Title
VII caselaw by analogy. . . .
    Title VII, and thus Title IX, "strike at the entire spectrum of disparate treat-
ment of men and women," including conduct having the purpose or effect of
. . . creating an intimidating, hostile or offensive environment. *Meritor Sav.
Bank, FSB v. Vinson*, 477 U.S. 57, 64–65. . . .

❖ ❖ ❖

    Title IX is violated "[w]hen the [educational environment] is permeated
with 'discriminatory intimidation, ridicule, and insult' that is 'sufficiently severe or pervasive to alter the conditions of the victim's employment and create an abusive . . . environment.' " *Harris*, 510 U.S. at—, 114 S.Ct. at 370 . . .
While a court must consider all of the circumstances in determining whether
a plaintiff has established that an environment is hostile or abusive, it must
be particularly concerned with (1) the frequency of the discriminatory conduct; (2) its severity; (3) whether it is physically threatening or humiliating
rather than a mere offensive utterance; and (4) whether it unreasonably interferes with an employee's work performance. See *Harris*, 510 U.S. at—. . . .

❖ ❖ ❖

    . . . If the conduct is not so severe or pervasive that a reasonable person would
find it hostile or abusive, it is beyond Title IX's purview. . . . Thus, the court must
consider not only the actual effect of the harassment on the plaintiff, but also the
effect such conduct would have on a reasonable person in the plaintiff's position.
    Turning to the case at bar, we find that the facts alleged here are insuffi-
cient to state a claim for sexual harassment under a hostile environment theory. . . . First, plaintiffs cannot claim that the offensive speech occurred frequently, as they allege only a one-time exposure to the comments.
    We also think that the plaintiffs' allegations do not establish that Landolphi's
comments were so severe as to create an objectively hostile environment. . . . . . .
    Moreover, during his introductory remarks, defendant Gilchrist advised
students that the purpose of the Program was to educate them about the dangers of sexual activity. . . . stating:

> We see young people in their twenties who are infected with the AIDS virus. . . .
> It means they caught the virus when they were in high school, and will be dead
> before they are thirty years old. . . . And today, we have a very special messenger,
> who uses probably one of the most effective forms of communication—humor. I
> want you to listen carefully. Enjoy it, but also remember the message.

Similarly, Landolphi stated in her opening remarks that "[w]e're going to talk
about AIDS, but not in the usual way." These prefaces framed the Program in

such a way that an objective person would understand that Landolphi's allegedly vulgar sexual commentary was intended to educate the students about the AIDS virus rather than to create a sexually hostile environment.

. . . In this context, while average high school students might have been offended by the graphic sexual discussions alleged here, Landolphi's remarks could not reasonably be considered physically threatening or humiliating so as to create a hostile environment.

Similarly, the plaintiffs' allegations establish that the Program did not significantly alter their educational environment from an objective standpoint. The Program consisted of two ninety-minute sex-education presentations, and although the plaintiffs allege that "coarse jesting, sexual innuendo, and overtly sexual behavior took place for the weeks following the Program," they fail to explain how the coarse jesting and overtly sexual behavior "create[d] an atmosphere so infused with hostility toward members of one sex that [it] alter[ed] the [educational environment] for them." . . . If anything, then, they allege discrimination based upon the basis of viewpoint, rather than on the basis of gender, as required by Title IX. We therefore find that their claim under Title IX fails.

✧ ✧ ✧

Review Questions 3.5

Consider the following questions on the court's treatment of the case facts and legal issues.

1. Did the court fairly characterize the admitted facts as harmless humor, and characterize the violation of the official school policy as an excusable isolated event? Compare the treatment of sexual vulgarity in the *Lacks* case, by the Eighth Circuit Court of Appeal, which appears at the end of Chapter 6.

2. How do you think that federal courts beyond the liberal First Circuit would answer the following questions addressed in *Brown?*
   a. Was the authorization and compliant observation of the Sexy program by school authorities sufficient to "shock the conscience" for a constitutional "substantive due process" violation? Whose conscience or value judgments? The Court's? The community's? The education profession?
   b. Were the police brutality cases that the *Brown* court cited germane to the question whether the Sexy presentation to a school mandated captive audience of adolescent students conscience shocking?

3. In Part B of the *Brown* opinion the court stated that "The Supreme Court has held that the Fourteenth Amendment encompasses a privacy right that protects against significant government intrusions into certain

personal decisions." In that light, did the *Brown* court fairly describe the parental claim as an attempt *to dictate* the school curriculum, rather than as a claim of right, conferred by state law and school policy, *to be exempt from* the curricular program?

4. In the absence of any precedent case on these facts (a common problem in all cases of first impression), should the court have distinguished away the Supreme Court decision (*Bethel*) which upheld a school's authority to protect students from unwelcome lewd speech to a school assembly, by punishing the lewd student speaker? Are students more accountable for lewd speech than school authorities?

5. In characterizing the defendants' conduct as "random and unauthorized" in dismissing the Due Process claim, could the court fairly ignore the period of administrative preplanning and contract making that led to the actual assembly presentation? Was the authorization of the program truly a random act? Was the failure to notify the parents throughout the preplanning period random and unauthorized? Did the presence of nonobjecting school authorities during a ninety-minute period of lewd skits render the program random and unauthorized?

6. On the free exercise claim, the court noted that the school written exemption *policy* was "neutral" and therefore constitutional, but did it confront the question of whether the defendant's *conduct* throughout the planning, non-notification and presentation was neutral, rather than a form of "deliberate indifference", e.g., (a) in failing to inquire of the program content? (b) In failing to intervene during the presentation once the content became obvious? Return to this question after completing study of the "deliberate indifference" basis for § 1983 federal tort liability in Chapter 8.

7. On the Title IX claim, could the court have reasonably viewed the Hot, Sexy program as creating a sexually harassing environment? Under Title IX, which is discussed in Chapter 8, the test of violation is the *effect* of school actions on student educational benefits, not subjective intent.

8. On the court's conclusion, "We also think that the plaintiffs' allegations do not establish that Landolphi's comments were so severe as to create an objectively hostile environment," what more do you think that court would have required for an objective sexual harassment in a mandatory school assembly, short of physical sexual assault? The court appeared to credit the defense that Landolphi indicated that she was only kidding. Do you think violators of sexual harassment laws escape liability whenever they announce that they were only kidding? We return to this problem in Chapter 8.

❖ ENDNOTES

1. "There is no right in a state or an instrumentality thereof to determine that a cause is not a religious one." Cantwell v. Conn., 310 U.S. 296 (1940). For purposes of interpreting the federal military draft statute, the Supreme Court construed the term *religion* very broadly. United States v. Seeger, 380 U.S. 163, 165–66 (1965).

2. Board of Educ. of Kiryas Joel Village School Dist. v. Grumet, 512 U.S. 687 (1994); Grumet v. Pataki, 675 N.Y.S.2d 662 (N.Y. 1998).

3. Employment Division v. Smith, 110 S. Ct. 1595 (1990). The Supreme Court overturned the Religious Freedom Restoration Act of 1993, which attempted to reverse the Smith decision. City of Boerne v. Flores, 117 S. Ct. 2157 (1997). A move by Congress to develop a new law to change the Smith result had not resulted in actual legislation as of this writing.

4. *Religious group use:* Peck v. Upshur County Board of Educ., 155 F.3d 274 (4th Cir. 1998); Garnett v. Renton School Dist., 987 F.2d 641 (9th Cir. 1993); Hoppock v. Twin Falls School Dist., 772 F. Supp. 1160 (D. Idaho 1991); Youth Opportunities Unlimited v. Board of Public Educ. of the School Dist. of Pittsburgh, 769 F. Supp. 1346 (W.D. Pa. 1991) (nonprofit corporation summer religious program).

   Re rental of school facility to religious groups, *see:* Seas v. School Dist., 811 F. Supp. 183 (E.D. Pa. 1993); Randall v. Pegan, 765 F. Supp. 793 (W.D. N.Y. 1991) (lease of school auditorium); Grace Bible Fellowship, Inc., v. Maine School Administrative Dist., 941 F.2d 45 (1st Cir. 1990) (refusal to rent facility otherwise leased to outside groups).

   *Religious fund raiser:*Travis v. Owego-Appalachian School Dist., 927 F.2d 688 (2d Cir. 1992) (counseling organization fund raiser with religious purpose).

   Testimonial to Christ: Gregoire v. Centennial School Dist., 907 F.2d 1366 (3d Cir. 1990).

5. Westside Community Schools v. Mergens, 496 U.S. 226 (1990). To like effect, *see* Cisneros v. Board of Trustees of San Diego School Dist., 106 F.3d 878 (9th Cir. 1997); HSU v. Roslyn Union Free School Dist., 85 F.3d 839 (2d Cir. 1996). *See*

   also Good News/Good Sports Club, 28 F.3d 1501 (8th Cir. 1994) (outside religious club); Pope v. E. Brunswick Board of Educ., 12 F.3d 1244 (3d Cir. 1993); Hedges v. Wauconda Comm. School Dist., 9 F.3d 1296 (7th Cir. 1993) (student distribution of religious literature); Annot., *Use of Public School Premises for Religious Purposes during Nonschool Time,* 79 A.L.R. 2d 1148 (1961).

6. Bronx Household of Faith v. Community School Dist. No. 10, 127 F.3d 207 (2d Cir. 1997). *Cf.* Verbena United Methodist Church v. Chilton County Board of Educ., 765 F. Supp. 704 (M.D. Ala. 1991) (refusal to rent school auditorium to religious organization for baccalaureate service).

7. The Good News Club v. Milford Central School, 21 F. Supp. 2d 147(N.D. N.Y. 1998).

8. Campbell v. St. Tammany's School Board, 64 F.3d 184 (5th Cir. 2000); Saratoga Bible Training Inst. v. Schuylerville, 18 F. Supp. 2d 178 (N.D. N.Y. 1998).

9. Travis v. Oswego-Appalachin School Dist., 972 F.2d 688 (2d Cir. 1991).

10. *See* Lanner v. Wimmer, 662 F.2d 1349 (10th Cir. 1981); Smith v. Smith, 523 F.2d 121 (4th Cir. 1975); State v. Thompson, 225 N.W.2d 678 (Wis. 1975).

11. Wheeler v. Barrera, 417 U.S. 402 (1974).

12. Engle v. Vitale, 370 U.S. 421 (1962) (school-sponsored prayer); School Dist. of Abington Twp. v. Schempp, 374 U.S. 203 (1963) (classroom recitation of the Lord's prayer and Bible verses). *See also* Roberts v. Madigan, 921 F.2d 1047 (10th Cir. 1991); Walker v. San Francisco Unified School Dist., 761 F. Supp. 1463 (N.D. Cal. 1991); Doe v. Shenandoah County School Bd., 737 F. Supp. 913 (W.D. Va. 1990).

13. *E.g.,* "We thank You for the flowers so sweet; we thank You for the food we eat; we thank You for the birds that sing, we thank You for everything." DeSpain v. DeKalb County Comm. School Dist., 384 F.2d 836 (7th Cir. 1967); *see also* Berger v. Rensalaer Central School Corp., 982 F.2d 1160 (7th Cir. 1993).

14. *Cf.* Board of Educ. v. Barnette, 319 U.S. 624 (1943); Sherman v. Comm. Consol. School Dist.

21 of Wheeling Twp., 758 F. Supp. 1244 (N.D. Ill. 1991) (pledge of allegiance statute held not to violate Free Exercise Clause).

15. Wallace v. Jaffree, 473 U.S. 38 (1985).

16. *E.g.,* DeBord v. Board of Educ., 126 F.3d 1102 (8th Cir. 1997); Bown v. Gwinnett County School District, 112 F.3d 1464 (11th Cir. 1997).

17. Lemke v. Black, 376 F. Supp. 87 (E.D. Wis. 1974); *cf.* Bronx Household of Faith, *supra* note 6.

18. (a) Jones v. Clear Creek Indep. School Dist., 977 F.2d 963 (5th Cir. 1992).

    (b) Doe v. Duncanville Ind. School Dist., 70 F.3d 402 (5th Cir. 1995). *See also* Ingebretson v. Jackson Public School Dist., 88 F.3d 274 (5th Cir. 1996)

    (c) Doe v. Beaumont School Dist., 173 F.3d 274 (5th Cir. 1999).

19. Adler v. Duvall County School Board, 206 F.3d 1070 (11th Cir. 2000) petition for certiorari to U.S. Supreme Court filed 5-22-00 (S. Ct. Docket 99-1877). *Contra:* ACLU of New Jersey v. Black Horse Pike Regional Board of Educ., 84 F.3d 1471 (3rd Cir. 1996)

20. (a) Chaudhuri v. State of Tenn., 130 F.3d 232 (6th Cir. 1997)

    (b) Coles v. Cleveland Board of Educ., 171 F.3d 369 (6th Cir. 1999). *Contra:* Bacus v. Palo Verde Un. School Dist., 11 F.Supp. 2d 1192 (C.D. Cal. 1998).

21. Doe v. Madison School Dist., 147 F.3d 832 (9th Cir. 1998), withdrawn 165 F.3d 1265 (1999). The 1998 opinion distinguished Collins v. Chandler Unified School Dist., 644 F.2d 759 (9th Cir. 1981) because the students in Collins were selected for the express purpose of delivering a prayer.

22. *Compare* Baumann v. West High School, 132 F.3d 542 (10th Cir. 1997) (rejecting challenge of Jewish choir member to teacher's choice of Christian music, and choir performance of Christian songs at Christian sites) *with* Sease v. School Dist. of Philadelphia, 811 F. Supp. 183 (E.D. Pa. 1993) (disapproving student-organized gospel choir under school secretary supervision).

23. Lynch v. Donnelly, 465 U.S. 668, 677 (1984)

24. Stone v. Graham, 449 U.S. 39 (1980).

25. Washagesic v. Bloomingdale Public Schools, 33 F.3d 679 (6th Cir. 1994) (portrait of Jesus Christ);

Joki v. Board of Educ., 745 F. Supp. 823 (N.D. N.Y. 1990) (student art of a crucifixion).

26. 492 U.S. 473 (1989). *See also* Lynch v. Donnelly, 465 U.S. 668 (1984)

27. Grossbaum v. Indianapolis-Marion County Bldg. Authority, 63 F.3d 581 (7th Cir. 1995); Chabad-Lubavitch of Georgia v. Miller, 5 F.3d 1383 (11th Cir. 1993); Americans United for Separation of Church and State v. Grand Rapids, Mich., 980 F.2d 1538 (6th Cir. 1992) (privately funded 20-foot menorah in public square with city's permission does not violate the Establishment Clause). *But see contra:* American Civil Liberties Union v. Schundler, 104 F.3d 1435 (3d Cir. 1997), which held display of crèche and menorah unconstitutional.

28. Clever v. Cherry Hill Twp. Board of Educ., 838 F. Supp. 929 (D. N.J. 1993) (classroom calendars depicting religious and other holidays, and classroom displays containing religious symbols). Florey v. Sioux Falls School Dist., 619 F.2d 1311 (8th Cir. 1980) (singing of Christmas carols—allowed).

29. McCollum v. Board of Educ., 333 U.S. 203 (1948).

30. Zorach v. Clauson, 343 U.S. 306 (1952).

31. *E.g.,* Springfield School Dist. v. Dept. of Educ., 397 A.2d 1154 (Pa. 1979).

32. Koenick v. Felton, 190 F.3d 259 (4th Cir. 1999), *cert denied,* 120 S.Ct.938 (1999) (statute providing school holidays on Good Friday— held constitutional; *but see* Metzl v. Leininger, 57 F.3d 618 (7th Cir. 1995) (voiding state setting of school holiday on Good Friday). *See generally* Annot., *Validity of Laws Making Day of Religious Observance a Legal Holiday,* 90 A.L.R. 3d 752 (1979).

33. Student Members of the Playcrafters v. Board of Educ. of the Twp. of Teaneck, 424 A.2d 1192 (N.J. 1981) (school ban on extracurricular activity on religious sabbaths). *See also* Cammack v. Waihee, 932 F.2d 765 (9th Cir. 1991).

34. Clayton v. Place, 884 F.2d 376 (8th Cir. 1989).

35. Smith v. Board of Educ., 708 F.2d 258 (7th Cir. 1983).

36. *Student request:* Church of God Worldwide Tex. Region v. Amarillo, 670 F.2d 46 (5th Cir. 1982).

Teacher request: Niederhuber v. Camden County Vocational Technical School Dist. Board of Educ., 495 F. Supp. 273 (D. N.J. 1980); *aff'd,* 671 F.2d 496 (3d Cir. 1981).

37. Cmwlth. v. Bey, 70 A.2d 693 (Pa. 1953) (Mohammedan Friday Sabbath); *in re* Currence, 248 N.Y.S.2d 251 (1963) (Wednesday and Thursday Sabbath).

38. DiPasquale v. Board of Educ. 457 (W.D. N.Y. 1985).

39. *Compare* California School Employees Assn. v. Sequoia Union H.S. Dist., 136 Cal. Rptr. 594 (1977) (upheld paid holiday), *with* Hunterdon Central High School Board of Educ. v. Hunterden Central High School Teachers Assn., 416 A.2d 980 (N.J. 1980) (paid holiday—voided).

40. Spence v. Bailey, 465 F.2d 797, 798–800 (6th Cir. 1972).

41. Parents United for Better Schools v. School Dist. of Philadelphia, 148 F.3d 260 (3d Cir. 1998); Curtis v. School Committee, 652 N.E.2d 580 (Mass. 1995).

42. Williams v. Board of Educ., 388 F. Supp. 93; *aff'd,* 530 F.2d 972 (4th Cir. 1975). *See also* Davis v. Page, 385 F. Supp. 395 (D. N.H. 1974).

43. Epperson v. Arkansas, 393 U.S. 97 (1968).

44. Edwards v. Aguillard, 482 U.S. 578 (1987) (statute requiring teaching of creation science violated Establishment Clause). *See also* McClean v. Ark. Board of Educ., 529 F. Supp. 1255 (E.D. Ark. 1982); Daniel v. Waters, 515 F.2d 485 (6th Cir. 1975).

45. "Among religions in this country which do not teach . . . a belief in the existence of God . . . [are] Ethical Culture, Secular Humanism, and others." *See* Torcaso v. Watkins, 376 U.S. 488, 495, at n. 11 of the court's opinion (1961). Ploza v. Capistrano Unified School Dist., 782 F.Supp. 1412 (C.D. Cal. 1992); Wright v. Houston Indep. School Dist., 486 F.2d 137 (5th Cir. 1973).

46. Freiler v. Tangipahoa Parish Bd. of Educ., 185 F.3rd 337 (5th Cir. 1999), cert. den.—U.S.—(6-19-2000).

47. Wiley v. Franklin, 497 F. Supp. 390 (E.D. Tenn. 1980); Annot., *Bible Distribution or Use in Public Schools,* 111 A.L.R. Fed 121 (1993; Supp. 1998).

48. See Annot., *Validity of Sex Education Programs in Public Schools,* 82 A.L.R. 3d 570 (1978, Supp. 1998).

49. *See, e.g.,* Citizens for Parental Rights v. San Mateo County Board of Educ., 124 Cal. Rptr. 68 (1975); Smith v. Ricci, 446 A.2d 501 (N.J. 1982).

50. Hopkins v. Board of Educ., 289 A.2d 914 (Conn. 1971); *aff'd,* 305 A.2d 536 (Conn. 1973) (upholding sex education). *But see* Mercer v. Mich. State Board of Educ., 379 F. Supp. 580 (E.D. Mich. 1974) (state law barring birth control instruction, upheld), Ware v. Valley Stream High School Dist.; Hobolth v. Greenway, 218 N.W.2d 98 (Mich. 1974); Medeiros v. Kyosaki, 478 P.2d 314 (Hawaii 1970).

51. *Compare* Curtis v. School Committee, 652 N.E.2d 580 (Mass. 1995) (program of condom availability and instruction upheld as not violating parental rights or student free exercise of religion); *accord:* Parents United for Better Schools, Inc. v. School Dist. of Philadelphia 148 F.3d 260 (3d Cir. 1998), *with* Alfonso v. Fernandez, 606 N.Y.S.2d 259 (1993) (a similar program struck down on both constitutional and state law grounds). *See generally* Annot., *Propriety of Prophylactic Availability Programs,* 52 A.L.R.5th 477 (1997); E. Bjorklun, *Condom Distribution in the Public Schools: Is Parental Consent Required?* 91 Educ. Law Rep. 11 (1994).

52. Smith v. Board of School Commissioners, 827 F.2d 684 (11th Cir. 1987).

53. Todd v. Rochester Comm. Schools, 200 N.W.2d 90 (Mich. 1972).

54. Mozert v. Hawkins County Board of Educ., 827 F.2d 1058 (6th Cir. 1987). *See also* Ware, *supra* note 50; *cf.* Frost v. Hawkins County School Board, 851 F.2d 822 (6th Cir. 1988).

55. Grove v. Mead School Dist., 753 F.2d 1528 (9th Cir. 1985).

56. Berger v. Renselaer Cent. School Corp., 982 F.2d 1160 (7th Cir. 1993); Meltzer v. Board of Public Instruction, 548 F.2d 559 (5th Cir. 1977).

57. W. Va. Board of Educ. v. Barnette, 319 U.S. 624 (1943) (student); Russo v. Central School Dist., 469 F.2d 623 (2d Cir. 1972) (teacher). *But see* discussion in Palmer v. Board of Educ., 603 F.2d 1271 (7th Cir. 1979) on circumstances where teacher cannot reject curriculum directive for

classroom patriotic exercises, based on her religious grounds.

58. Mitchell v. McCall, 143 So. 2d 629 (Ala. 1962); Hardwick v. Board of School Trustees, 205 P. 49 (Cal. 1921).

59. Jacobson v. Cmwlth. of Massachusetts, 197 U.S. 11 (1905); Calandra v. State College Area School Dist., 512 A.2d 809 (Pa. Cmwlth. 1986) (condition of participation in school athletics); *In re* Clark, 185 N.E.2d 128 (Ohio 1962).

60. Cude v. State, 377 S.W.2d 816, 819 (Ark. 1964).

61. *E.g.,* Mason v. General Brown Cent. School Dist., 851 F.2d 47 (2d Cir. 1988) (Universal Life Church held a system of ethics, not a religion). *Compare* State v. Miday, 140 S.E.2d 325 (N.C. 1965), *with* McCartney v. Austin, 293 N.Y.S.2d 188 (1968).

62. Americans United for Separation of Church & State v. Paire, 348 F. Supp. 506 (D. N.H. 1972); Moore v. Board of Educ., 212 N.E.2d 833 (Ohio 1965); Zellers v. Huff, 236 P.2d 949 (N.M. 1951); State v. Taylor, 240 N.W. 573 (Neb. 1932).

63. Wheeler v. Barrera, 417 U.S. 402 (1974).

64. Citizens to Advance Public Educ. v. Porter, 237 N.W.2d 232 (Mich. 1976); Morton v. Board of Educ., 216 N.E.2d 305 (Ill. 1966); *in re* Proposal C, 185 N.W.2d 9 (Mich. 1971).

65. *E.g.,* 24 Pa. Stat. Ann. § 5–502.

66. Snyder v. Charlotte Public School Dist., 333 N.W.2d 542 (Mich. 1983).

67. Fisher v. Clackamas Cty. School Dist., 507 P.2d 839 (Or. 1973); State v. School Dist. No. 10, 472 P.2d 1013 (Mont. 1970).

68. Brown v. Heller, 273 N.Y.S.2d 713 (1966).

69. Fisher *supra* note 67; State v. Taylor, 240 N.W. 573 (Neb. 1932); Zellers v. Huff, 236 P.2d 949 (N.M. 1951).

70. Thomas v. Schmidt, 397 F. Supp. 203 (D. R.I. 1975). A good analysis of the entanglement issue is contained in Buford v. S.E. DuBois County School Corp., 472 F.2d 890 (7th Cir. 1973).

71. Pratt v. Arizona Board of Regents, 520 P.2d 514 (Ariz. 1974) (lease of state college arena); Cooper v. County School Board, Fla. Sup. Ct. No. 81–3625 (11-2-82) (lease to a Catholic mission).

72. Fairfax Covenant Church v. Fairfax County School Board, 17 F.3d 703 (4th Cir. 1994) (school charging higher rent for religious than for nonreligious users); Resnick v. E. Brunswick Twp. Board of Educ., 343 A.2d 127 (N.J. 1975). Cases are collected in Annot., *Schools—Use for Religious Purposes,* 79 A.L.R. 2d 1148 (1961).

❖ CHAPTER 4

Tort Liability under State Law

III. Limitations on Tort Recovery
   A. Governmental Immunity
       1. Nuisance Exceptions
       2. Governmental vs. Proprietary Functions
       3. Discretionary vs. Ministerial Functions
   B. Individual Immunity
   C. Notice and Time Limits and Dollar Caps
       1. Statutes of Limitations
       2. Dollar Recovery Limits

❖ **CHAPTER DISCUSSION QUESTIONS**

❖ **CASES**
4.1 Grant v. Lake Oswego School District No. 7, 515 P.2d 947 (Or. App. 1973)
4.2 Simonetti v. School District of Phila., 454 A.2d 1038 (Pa. Super. 1982)
4.3 Ayala v. Philadelphia Board of Public Education, 305 A.2d 877 (Pa. 1973)

❖ **ENDNOTES**

GENERAL PRINCIPLES OF STATE TORT LAW

This chapter deals with traditional tort liability under the laws of individual states. Liability for violations of federal laws are considered in Chapters 5 and 8.

Under state tort law, a person who causes injury to another through violation of some legal duty has committed a tort and is liable to pay compensation to the injured party. A *tort* is a civil wrong arising out of a breach of duty that is imposed by law. Torts are not crimes. Only the government can prosecute someone for committing a crime and guilt must be proven beyond a reasonable doubt.[1] The victim of a tort, on the other hand, may file his own civil lawsuit and need only prove fault by a preponderance of evidence, which is an easier standard to satisfy. While some torts are also crimes (for instance, intentional assaults), many torts are not crimes. Tort law obligations are different from contract obligations because torts arise from duties imposed by law, not from obligations imposed by a contractual arrangement.

Tort law governs school districts, their officers, and their employees. Group insurance is often purchased by school districts to help absorb the risk of loss through tort claims. In some states, indemnity statutes reimburse and hold school officers and employees harmless from tort liability incurred in the course of their duties. Nonetheless, even with insurance and indemnity statutes, tort litigation can be burdensome and provides ample incentive for school districts and their employees to minimize tortious conduct.

Tort law is primarily judge-made law (also known as "common law"), and is usually grounded in the concept of *fault*. Generally speaking, public schools have no duty to ensure the safety of students and other members of the school community at all times.[2] A school district is not liable for every accidental injury but only for injuries caused intentionally or by negligence of employees and officials:

> . . . [A] school district is not the insurer of complete safety of school children, nor is it strictly liable for any injuries which may occur to them. [*Benton v. School Board of Broward County*, 386 So.2d 831, 834 (Fla. App. 1980)]

In limited instances, the law may impose "strict liability" for injuries without regard to intent or fault. Those relatively rare situations are not covered in this text. Cases of intentional injury by school personnel are also uncommon and will receive only occasional mention.

The principal questions to be resolved in tort claims are these:

1. Did the sued party have a duty of care under the law to avoid the injury suffered by the claimant?
2. If so, was that duty actually breached?
3. If a breach of duty occurred, was it the proximate (or direct) cause of the injury?
4. If so, is the sued party shielded from liability by a *privilege* or *immunity* conferred by law?

5.   If there is liability, does the law place a dollar limit on the money damages that the claimant may recover?

In resolving these questions, courts and juries must initially determine if the evidence is sufficient to find negligence. The diverse results of seemingly similar tort cases arise from different fact findings in similar cases. However, courts have the power to dismiss an insufficient case without submitting it to the jury or to reverse a jury verdict that is clearly against the law or the evidence.

Duty of Care Requirement

Whether a duty of care exists in a given situation is a question of law to be decided by courts.[3] If such a duty exists, courts permit a jury, under court instructions, to determine whether the duty has in fact been breached. The answer often depends on the jury's view of conflicting testimony and evidence.[4]

In the overwhelming majority of states, the duty of care is that duty which a reasonable person of ordinary prudence would exercise for the safety of others in like circumstances.[5] To determine whether an act was negligent, the courts look at what the sued party should reasonably have foreseen and done under the circumstances. "The risk reasonably to be perceived defines the duty to be obeyed."[6] The precise risk that caused the injury need not be foreseeable; it is enough if risks of the same general character as that which caused injury were foreseeable.[7]

The law does not oblige a party to assume impractical and unreasonable burdens to prevent harm to others. Failure to take *every* precaution against *all* foreseeable injury to another does not *necessarily* constitute negligence. That would amount to making one an insurer. The existence of compulsory attendance laws does not so restrict a student's freedom of action that schools have an affirmative "due process" duty to protect students under all circumstances.[8] In sum, the risk must be both foreseeable and reasonably preventable.

Because there is no fixed measure of due care for the limitless variety of risk relationships in schools, the "reasonable person" standard reflects community norms of reasonable conduct as they evolve from time to time and place to place. Generally speaking, the age, relationship, and physical characteristics of the parties involved, the gravity and probability of danger presented in specific circumstances, and the necessity and utility of the risk-creating conduct must all be weighed to determine the required level of care and reasonable response.

The required "duty of care" standard can be modified by state laws, such as those limiting school liability to cases of willful or wanton misconduct, and those that impose higher "special duties" for certain situations.

The Causation Requirement

A tort claimant must prove that the defendant's act or omission was the *proximate* cause of the claimant's injury; i.e., that the defendant's conduct was a *material* and *substantial* factor in producing the harm, "but for" which the harm would not have occurred.[9] The defendant's conduct need not be the immediate, or even the primary, cause of injury, but it must be a necessary link in the chain of events that resulted in injury.

Proximate cause often becomes an issue in tort suits when some intervening act of an unsupervised student or other person was the immediate cause of injury. The court or jury must decide whether proper supervision could have prevented or deterred the intervening student conduct that directly caused the injury.[10] When a student was killed in a fight during recess, one court ruled that the jury should decide the question of proximate cause.[11] However, in another case of student misconduct during recess, the court found that teacher negligence was not the proximate cause of the victim's injury.[12] A teacher and a principal who negligently failed to report the unauthorized absence of a 13-year-old girl, who was later found murdered, were found not to have proximately caused her death.[13] The lack of evidence as to how and when the crime occurred prevented any inference that a prompt report would have prevented her death. It would be unwise, however, to conclude that failure to note an absence would be similarly treated in other circumstances. These examples show how particular facts critically affect the application of the proximate cause standard.

General Defenses

If a claimant proves that negligence caused the injury, his recovery of money damages may still be barred. Several doctrines prevent a tort victim from recovering money damages. Some of these were recognized by the common law, and others were later created by legislation. Defenses that can bar recovery of tort damages include

- Privileged conduct,
- Victim fault,
- Waiver of claims,
- Scope of wrongdoer's authority,
- Dollar recovery limitations,
- Notice requirements and time bars, and
- Party immunity from liability.

The special defenses of dollar recovery limits, notice and time bars, and party immunity are discussed later in the section titled "Limitations on Tort Recovery."

Privileged Conduct

Teachers and administrators are legally empowered to engage in certain conduct, technically called a legal privilege. Privileged conduct is not tortious. For example, the use of reasonable force in self-defense or to quell a fight would be privileged conduct, even if it causes injury to a student. Examples of this *privilege* defense and the special circumstances that create or limit it are discussed later.

Victim Fault

In some states, students who knowingly assume a risk of injury, or whose own negligence contributes to it, may be denied recovery against another person whose negligence also caused that injury, or may be limited in the amounts they may recover for such injury.[14] These doctrines of "assumption of risk" and "contributory negligence" vary from state to state. Originally, they were applied to bar any recovery, regardless of the degree to which another person contributed to the injury. In recent times, however, an increasing number of states have modified these defenses to take into account the comparative fault of the tort actor and the victim. Many states modified the defense of contributory negligence by a doctrine of *comparative negligence*, which does not completely extinguish a wrongdoer's liability for negligence, but reduces the victim's recovery to the extent that he contributed to his own injuries.[15] For instance, if the victim and another person both acted negligently and were equally responsible for the victim's injuries, the victim's recovery of money damages would be reduced by half. Comparative negligence can only be attributed to persons who are sufficiently mature to recognize the risks that can cause injury. Similarly, assumption of risk applies only where the injured individual could reasonably recognize the assumed danger:

> A child is not held to the same degree of care as an adult. Rather, the test is whether the particular child, considering his age, background, and inherent intelligence, indulged in gross disregard of his own safety in the face of known, understood, and perceived danger. . . .

> A defense of assumption of risk is, however, narrowly . . . restricted by requirements that a party must have full knowledge and appreciation of the danger, yet voluntarily expose himself to the risks and embrace the known danger. [*Simmons v. Beauregard Parish School Bd.*, 315 So. 2d 883, 888 (La. 1975)]

Teachers should not, therefore, rely too heavily on these defenses in dealing with students, especially the very young. Consider the following examples: (a) a kindergarten child who wandered off school grounds into a busy street was found not to be contributorily negligent; (b) a student injured by an explosion in preparing a science project was found not to have assumed the risk of explosion; (c) a 13-year-old was found not contributorily negligent in placing his hand inside a door jamb; but (d) a 17-year-old who ran around a darkened school stage and fell into a hatchway was held contributorily negligent, as was (e) a visitor who chose to walk across an unlit portion of open school grounds; and (f) a strong high school student athlete who challenged a coach to a wrestling match was held to have assumed the risk of injury.[16] A student's knowing violation of school safety rules may constitute comparative negligence.

Juries are often left to determine the extent of a victim's fault. The *Grant* opinion at the end of this chapter illustrates the foregoing principles.

Written Waivers of Tort Claims

Schools often request written parental consent for student participation in special activities, such as field trips and athletic competitions. The consent forms often require parents to release the school and its employees from all legal responsibility for any injury the child may sustain in the activity. These releases may have the psychological effect of deterring parents from bringing tort actions, but they have limited *legal* effect. First, many courts hold such releases to be void as contrary to public policy.[17] Second, even in states where a parent can surrender her own tort claim, that parent cannot legally surrender the independent claim of a minor child for pain and suffering and for any loss of future earning power.[18] In most cases, minors lack the legal capacity to make binding agreements so their signature on a release form would be equally unenforceable.

By definition, a release is an "intentional" abandonment of a "known" right. A release can always be challenged as having been obtained or signed without full disclosure or knowledge of the relevant risks of the school activity. Also, the release would not be valid if the signor was not knowledgeable about the rights he was relinquishing in the release. The relatively few reported court cases in this area indicate that school authorities frequently do not prevail on the basis of such releases.[19]

School District Vicarious Liability

A school district is a fictional legal "person" and, hence, can only be *vicariously* liable for the torts of its human servants, i.e., its acts of teachers, staff, and officials that may be *legally imputed* to the district. This doctrine is based on the maxim, *respondeat superior*, meaning "Let the master answer for the conduct of his servant." Generally, the law holds school districts liable only for those acts of its employees that are within the scope of their authority or employment.[20] A school district is accountable for conduct that it has the power to control, but it is not responsible for tortious conduct that is beyond the authority given the actor by the district. Courts and juries must decide when a particular act departs so far from an employee's scope of employment or authority that it should be treated as a purely personal act, and not that of the school district.[21]

Determining the scope of authority or employment involves difficult factual issues. When an employee intentionally injures another, courts disagree on whether that misconduct should be imputed to the employer school district.[22] Previous court reliance on an artificial distinction between active wrongdoing (misfeasance) and passive wrongdoing (nonfeasance) has not effectively resolved this issue.

COMMON TORT SITUATIONS

Corporal Punishment

Constitutionality

In the case of *Ingraham v. Wright*,[23] the U.S. Supreme Court upheld the constitutionality of corporal punishment where permitted by state law. If there are no statutory limitations, school authorities can administer corporal punishment without prior notice, hearing, or consent of students or their parents. In its extensive survey of state law variations on corporal punishment, the Court noted that Massachusetts and New Jersey generally prohibit disciplinary corporal punishment, while California requires parental consent for its use.[24]

When Corporal Punishment Is Not Tortious

Corporal punishment that is administered in a *privileged* manner is not a tort. In most states, corporal punishment is privileged only when it is administered by authorized individuals and is reasonable as to its purpose, method, and degree of force.[25] Many school employees are not privileged to use corporal punishment except where force is necessary to preserve the safety of students.[26] The so-called *in loco parentis* privilege of teachers "to act in the place of parents" is not equivalent to the broader privileges of natural parents.[27]

In states that permit corporal punishment, school boards may regulate its use. Many boards have limited the grounds for corporal punishment and the way it can be administered. Many districts require the school principal, rather than individual teachers, to determine whether and how corporal punishment should be carried out. Often, boards require the presence of another adult under conditions calculated to avoid unnecessary abuse or embarrassment of students.[28] Only rarely have schools and courts allowed corporal punishment for purely instructional purposes.[29]

Purpose of Punishment.   Courts have denied any "privilege" to administer corporal punishment that served no reasonable educational purpose. The child or parent has the burden of proving that corporal punishment is unreasonable (and therefore not privileged), and in close cases juries decide whether corporal punishment was reasonable. The standard of "reasonableness" reflects local community attitudes and can vary from region to region. Typical considerations include the nature of the student infraction; the student's past record, age, sex, and mental and physical condition; and the suitability of the instrument and force employed. A student's intent (willful misbehavior vs. mistake) and a teacher's motivation (benign vs. vindictive) are also relevant.[30] A parent's objection to punishment does not prevent a school disciplinarian from claiming a defense of privilege, unless state law or school board regulation expressly requires parental consent to use corporal punishment.[31]

Reasonableness of Force.   The fact that punishment produces pain or minor bruises does not automatically demonstrate that excessive force was used.[32] Indeed, the use of increased force may be considered reasonable in dealing with chronically recalcitrant students.[33] But corporal punishment that produces physical dislocations (bleeding, deep bruises, sprains, or fractures) is likely to be considered excessive and tortious.[34] Courts have also disapproved the use of certain instruments, such as cattle prods or broken paddles, regardless of the degree of force employed.[35]

A teacher is not liable for injuries when she cannot reasonably anticipate that normal corporal punishment would produce serious injury because of a child's undisclosed or unknown medical condition.

Deciding how much corporal force may be used calls for caution. Courts are more likely to uphold spanking and paddling of healthy students as privileged,[36] but excessive force was found when (a) a teacher beat a boy with a broken paddle, resulting in bruises to the boy's head and body; (b) a 190-pound principal sat on a disobedient 10-year-old student; and (c) a teacher struck an 8-year-old, puncturing the child's eardrum.[37] Disciplinary restraints on student movement (e.g., in-school detention during and after school hours) are not considered corporal punishment, but are also privileged if used reasonably.[38]

Defensive Use of Force.   It is clear that teachers and employees have the same legal privilege to use reasonable force to defend persons or property as would any other person. In stressful circumstances, a person of ordinary prudence may reasonably act with less detachment and control than he or she would under normal circumstances. The greater the threat of danger, the greater the justification for quick and forceful defensive action. Even the use of a "sneeze gun" to ward off student attack was held reasonable where the accosted teacher thought it necessary to protect herself.[39] The privilege of defense is lost when retaliation against a student assailant becomes vindictive and excessive.[40] In subduing an emotionally upset, mentally retarded student, a teacher was found to have used excessive force and was held liable for the consequent injuries.[41]

Premises Liability

Tort law imposes a duty of care in maintaining safe premises, but it does not require owners and possessors of land and buildings to keep premises absolutely safe at all times and for all persons. The law considers not only the condition of the premises, but also the purpose for which the injured person was there.

Standard of Care for Premises Safety

Persons invited to school premises, such as students and attendees of school functions, are considered *invitees*. They have a right to expect that the premises they visit are reasonably safe. Invitees may recover money damages for injuries caused by negligent failure of school authorities to make the premises reasonably safe.[42] If school authorities take reasonable measures, such as periodic inspections and repairs, victims of unforeseeable accidents cannot recover.[43] Juries are often left to decide whether there is enough evidence to prove negligence. Under the principle of *res ipsa loquitur* ("the thing speaks for itself"), a court or jury may infer negligence from clear circumstantial evidence.[44] Courts have found negligence where school personnel actively created the hazard or permitted it to continue after it became known or should have been discovered.[45] School authorities are not generally required to discover and remedy every premises defect that they did not create.[46] However, in states that enacted tort statutes that render districts liable for injuries caused by a "dangerous condition" of school property, a district may be liable for injuries caused by that condition, even in the absence of proven negligence.[47]

Tort law imposes a lower duty of care for "trespassers" and "licensees" than for "invitees." *Licensees* are persons who are allowed entry to the school but who have not been invited there for a school purpose. *Trespassers* are those who unlawfully enter the property. Schools generally have no duty to make the premises safe for trespassers or licensees. However, if school authorities learn that licensees or trespassers are on school grounds, they have a limited duty to warn these entrants of known but concealed hazards and to avoid affirmative acts that place them in jeopardy.[48] The usual rule that an owner of property has no duty of care to trespassers does not always apply to children. Potentially dangerous sites or facilities (such as construction sites) that may reasonably be expected to attract child trespassers are known as *attractive nuisances*. Some states encourage owners and possessors of land to keep children out of unsafe areas through the attractive nuisance doctrine, which treats child trespassers as if they were invitees. The attractive nuisance doctrine has been applied sparingly to normal school building conditions.

School authorities are not obliged to expend great resources to ensure the safety of every child trespasser. For example, a district was held not liable when a 12-year-old used a ladder hanging from the side of a school to climb to the building's roof.[49] But new construction activity and excavations at school sites may fall within the attractive nuisance doctrine.

Examples of Premises Liability

Students have been awarded tort damages for injuries resulting from sticky or slippery floors; defective bleachers, handrails, gates, and doors; poorly lighted or darkened passageways; unstable and unsecured lockers, furniture, equipment, or stacked materials; and building protrusions against which children were likely to fall.[50] While school districts and school boards are the dominant targets of tort suits for premises liability, school principals and teachers with supervisory duties may also be held personally liable for their negligent supervision.[51]

Supervision Liability

Most school-related torts are brought under a theory of negligent supervision. Negligent acts or omission include the failure to warn students of dangers; failure to report, avoid, and correct unsafe situations; failure to arrange student activities in a safe manner; and failure to aid ill or injured students. Supervision cases raise three basic questions: (1) Was there any duty to supervise students in the circumstances? If so, (2) what kind and degree of supervision would be reasonable under those circumstances and (3) was the lack of proper supervision a proximate cause of the claimed injury?

When the Duty of Supervision Arises

A duty to supervise arises only when a reasonable person would anticipate the need for supervision. But a volunteer who has no duty of supervision and nevertheless seeks to protect a student is held to the same duty as one who has a legal obligation to supervise.[52]

To determine the extent of supervision required, courts consider a number of factors: the nature and location of the activity, the number and ages of the students, and the practicability and expense of providing varying degrees of supervision. The law demands only what is reasonable in light of these factors, unless a "safe school" statute imposes a higher district responsibility for "dangerous conditions" of school property.[53] While educators share a general obligation for student safety, the level of supervisory duties of each individual is largely defined by his or her position in the schools. Generally speaking, prudent supervision has two major aspects: (1) care not to create danger by one's own negligent conduct (such as ordering activities that endanger students) and (2) care to avoid perils created by others.[54]

General vs. Special or Direct Supervision

Teachers cannot observe every movement of every child and are generally duty bound only to exercise reasonable general supervision rather than special, direct supervision of students. The *Simonetti* case at the end of this chapter, and the cases it cites from other states, summarizes well the law in this respect. Only general supervision is required where students are engaged in many activities that are not usually dangerous. However, teacher knowledge of an assaultive student triggers a higher duty of care to protect other students from that assailant.[55] Special supervision is required whenever a school activity poses special danger, such as instruction on hazardous activity with which students are not familiar or adept.[56] The failure to provide direct supervision on occasions where students were known to engage in rough horseplay may form the basis of tort liability.[57]

Under earlier common law, the criminal conduct of third parties was generally thought to be unforeseeable and therefore there was no duty to protect against it. However, the more recent case trend has been to hold schools liable for the failure to protect students from criminal conduct if past experience shows that the criminal conduct was reasonably foreseeable.[58] Failure to supervise students with known violent tendencies and to warn a substitute teacher about such students are both grounds for holding principals and teachers liable.[59] The student suicide cases present special issues and are discussed below.

Properly published safety rules and procedures may relieve school districts and supervisors of liability for injuries caused by violations of those rules, unless student ignorance or disobedience of the rules was reasonably to be anticipated.[60] Whether proper supervision could have prevented one student from injuring another raises the thorny fact issues on proximate causation, about which courts and juries often disagree.[61]

Circumstances Affecting Degree of Supervision

Supervisory duties are determined by the nature, time, and place of student activity.

School Grounds. Supervision of school grounds may be required where students are known to congregate immediately before or after school.[62] Liability has been imposed for playground injuries sustained before the opening of school, whether caused by regular play, student misconduct, unsafe conditions, or scuffling at school bus delivery points.[63] A stronger case arises where school rules explicitly require such supervision.[64] Absent these circumstances, school authorities are not obliged to supervise dismissed children who remained on school grounds indefinitely to await private transportation.[65]

When school is in session, failure to provide special supervision over normal playground activity is generally held not to be negligent.[66] The school's failure to provide off-hour supervision to prevent snowball fights was also held not to be negligent especially where school rules prohibited them.[67] But where school authorities knew or should have known that students were throwing iceballs and attacking isolated children in the schoolyard, the district was held liable for failing to undertake necessary supervision to protect the injured student.[68]

Once undertaken, supervision must be adequate under the circumstances.[69] One court upheld a jury finding of insufficient supervision where some 23 teachers were assigned to supervise a heavily attended school carnival.[70]

Classrooms and Corridors. A teacher who is temporarily distracted or absent from the classroom when an accident occurs is not automatically considered negligent. The fact-finder must consider whether the temporary absence was reasonable in light of the purpose and duration of the absence, the distance the teacher was removed from his or her charges, the class makeup and its conduct history, and the assignment given to students during the teacher's absence. A kindergarten music teacher who momentarily looked away before a child fell from the piano was not negligent,[71] nor was a teacher who failed to anticipate and prevent a classroom assault while she stood outside the door shepherding children into the room.[72] However, teachers who left a class unsupervised for an extended period, during which time students were injured, were found negligent.[73]

Two Louisiana cases indicate the difficulty of predicting how a jury will assess case facts. In one, a teacher was held liable for a brief absence from a normal class; in the other, the teacher of a special education class was absolved when she left the class unattended for a five-minute coffee break.[74] If the absence from class is brief and for school purposes, and if the class has a good behavior record, most courts will not consider brief absences to be negligent.[75]

Cases that exonerated teachers for injuries caused by students jostling each other confirm the general principle that only prudent general supervision is required in normal circumstances.[76]

When the school is used by outside groups for nonschool activities, the duty of supervision shifts to the outside party, and school personnel are not liable unless they affirmatively assumed a duty of care or created a dangerous condition.[77]

Athletics and Physical Education.   Inadequate supervision of physical education and athletic exercises commonly results in tort claims. The following are typical grounds for liability: dangerous placement of gym equipment; mismatching of contestants; imprudent inducement to perform exercises for which pupils are not physically or psychologically prepared; and placement of different activities in dangerously congested areas.[78] Liability does not result from any one factor. A football player did not prove negligence simply because he was tackled by a much larger lineman.[79] Nor was the act of permitting adjoining games in the same gym per se unreasonable,[80] but an instructor's violations of school safety rules, and provision of faulty safety equipment, such as ill-fitting football helmets, will expose the instructor and the school district to liability.[81] Instructors are not obliged to head off unknown risks to a student with an unreported medical condition that renders the student abnormally vulnerable, such as an unexplained drowning in a supervised swimming pool that could have resulted from an unforeseen or unpreventable medical condition.[82] However, schools have a duty not to aggravate a student's vulnerable condition. For example, it was held negligent to refuse to excuse heat stroke victims from team exercises or to permit careless movement of an injured player by fellow students.[83] Negligence is less likely to be found where mature and properly trained athletes sustain injuries from risks that are inherent in their athletic activities.[84] For such cases, general supervision satisfies the duty of care.[85] But courts found a need for special supervision when an instructor ordered a seven-year-old child to climb a cargo net or failed to monitor wrestling matches.[86] Spectators at school athletic events do not require special supervision.

Laboratory and Shop Facilities.   Due care is commensurate with the hazards presented. For this reason, laboratory and shop instructors are typically held to a higher degree of care in the uses of dangerous chemicals or equipment and in providing proper safety instructions.[87] The defenses of contributory or comparative negligence and assumption of risk do not apply to uninformed students who cannot appreciate the risks of their conduct in these situations.[88] However, students who removed chemicals from storage without permission to conduct unauthorized experiments were held to be contributorily negligent.[89]

Instructor violations of state safety laws may constitute negligence per se. Failure to secure shop equipment (such as power presses, grinders, saws, and cutting equipment) or to supply effective safety devices (pressure gauges or goggles) may be found to be negligence per se.[90] In the absence of a safety statute, an instructor's failure to establish safety rules in apparently dangerous situations still constitutes negligence, as was the case with an instructor who did not stop student horseplay in a school shop.[91]

Where shop injuries arise from sudden, unauthorized student actions, courts have found no liability, e.g., when a student, after the shop class closed, threw a power switch thereby activating a power tool that was being cleaned, and when a student threw nails toward the trash box rather than dropping them into the box as ordered by the instructor.[92]

Student Transportation.   Absent a transportation statute, public schools have no obligation to provide or supervise student transportation between school and home.[93] Where school transportation is provided, most courts apply the general standard of reasonable care, with a small minority applying a special rule of automatic (i.e., absolute) liability for accidents caused by defective equipment that does not meet the requirements of school bus safety statutes.[94] Liability does not arise for unavoidable accidents, such as when a severe bee sting caused a driver to lose control of the bus.[95]

Transportation-related torts most often arise from (1) unsafe equipment, (2) negligent bus operation, or (3) negligent supervision of students at bus stops.[96] Typical examples include blowouts of defective tires and lack of on-board supervision to head off foreseeable harms by unruly students.[97] But where student-to-student injury could not be reasonably anticipated, the driver was not held negligent.[98] Cases of negligent bus operation include (a) driving too fast on school grounds, (b) sudden stops and starts, (c) sudden turns at unsafe speed, (d) failing to flash warning lights at crossings, and (e) discharging passengers at unsafe places.[99]

Courts have stressed the need for special caution at bus stops, especially for very young children who can be expected to run alongside a moving bus or dart into traffic. Failure to guard against this conduct is tortious.[100] In disembarkation cases, bus drivers are obliged to caution children of approaching traffic. A driver who observed moving traffic but failed to warn crossing students was found liable.[101] The occurrence of a boarding accident does not alone automatically prove driver negligence.[102]

School authorities have a duty to select reasonably safe bus stop locations, but they are not obliged to select the safest points, and they are not responsible for injuries at unassigned stops.[103] Unless a statute requires it, school authorities have no general duty to provide safety patrols for student pedestrians. However, if a school employs crossing guards, it will be responsible for negligent failure to deploy them properly.[104] While school is in session, a court may find a duty to supervise student pedestrians, such as when students cross a public highway to reach a particular class.[105]

Off-Campus Activities.   The duty of supervision extends to school-sponsored activities, whether on or off school property, but no duty to supervise exists for nonsponsored off-campus activities.[106] School club moderators were held liable for failure to supervise school club initiations that caused student injury.[107] The degree of required supervision for field trips depends on the nature of the trip. A child injured on a seashore outing after the teacher abandoned supervision to pursue other interests was entitled to have a jury determine if the teacher was negligent,[108] but a teacher who allowed a student to wander out of her presence during a class visit to a museum was held not negligent.[109]

First Aid.   The duty to render first aid to students arises when the need is apparent, but not where there is no reasonable indication that first aid is needed.[110] However, teachers who volunteer medical assistance to students will be held liable for injuries caused by their negligence.[111]

Student Suicides and Homicides.   The sharp rise in student suicides and homicides, at and away from school, has opened a new area of state tort law by way of suits against school districts and their employees. Suits for failure to prevent suicides present two theories, namely, that the school district was negligent in failing to implement a suicide prevention program and in failing to warn the suicide's parents of known or recognizable suicidal tendencies. Suits on these grounds usually add federal law claims based on a more complex theory of student constitutional rights to bodily security. That law is explored in Chapter 8.

State tort claims of a duty-to-protect suicidal students builds indirectly on the developing law regarding the duty of licensed physicians and psychotherapists to warn appropriate parties of suicidal or homicidal threats by their patients, notwithstanding the fact that those threats were disclosed by the patient to the physician in a confidential physician–patient relationship.[112]

While there is no general duty to anticipate and prevent student suicides or threats of harm by others, absent special circumstances,[113] recent student suicide cases found that school authorities and their employees have, as part of their general duty of supervision for student safety, a duty to take reasonable steps to prevent suicide by students with detected suicidal tendencies, and to warn parents of such tendencies.[114] The threshold question whether school authorities knew or should have reasonably suspected suicidal tendencies will in doubtful cases rest with a jury.

On the issue whether such omissions are the proximate cause of the suicide, or are too remote from the suicidal act to be a proximate cause, or whether the act of suicide should be considered a supervening cause that broke the chain of causation from any original negligence, the courts are not in agreement. Most of the recent cases leave those questions to jury determination.[115] But a Wisconsin court held that a student's suicide is, as a matter of law, a superceding cause of death, which relieved the school superiors and teachers of any tort liability for the student's death, even though they knew that the student was severely upset and pressured by numerous failing grades and by his removal from the school basketball team and that they failed to report to his parents his unexcused absence from school on the day of his suicide, as required by official school policy.[116]

With regard to assaults on students, recent cases found no reason for school authorities to anticipate school site stabbings and shootings by outsiders who unlawfully entered the school.[117] Those cases can be readily distinguished from foreseeable threats of student violence. If plaintiffs establish that the school authorities knew or could by prudent diligence have identified violent-prone students and failed to take reasonable measures to control them, a court and jury may well find them negligent and liable for resulting injuries.[118] The widespread adoption of strict security measures and zero-tolerance policies regarding weapons in the aftermath of school site massacres in several states is itself a recognition of a duty to protect students from potential grave danger.

A school district claim of tort immunity for failure to adopt a suicide prevention policy or to warn parents of a student's suicidal tendencies was considered in a recent Idaho test case in which the teacher knew but failed to alert the suicide's parents that the suicide student recorded suicidal thoughts in a school class journal. The court held that, with regard to the district's alleged negligence in failing to implement a suicide prevention program, it was immune since that decision involved a "discretionary" function. However, with regard to the failure to warn the student's parents, it ruled that the district as well as the teacher could be held liable for failure to protect the student because the decision not to warn the parents was an "operational" decision and not part of an immune discretionary decision.[119] See the later section on tort immunity.

Defamation (Libel or Slander)

At common law, defamation (libel or slander) is a communication of a false or misleading statement that damages the victim's reputation. Defamation may be committed indirectly by innuendo; a person who repeats a defamatory statement by others may also be guilty of libel or slander. Not every unpleasant criticism is defamatory. A leading authority on tort law describes defamation as follows:

> Defamation is made up of the twin torts of libel and slander—the one being, in general, written, while the other in general is oral. . . . In either form, defamation is an invasion of the interests in reputation and good name. . . . Consequently,

> defamation requires that something be communicated to a third person that may affect that opinion. Derogatory words and insults directed at the plaintiff himself (but not communicated to another person) cannot form the basis for a defamation suit. . . . Defamation is rather that which tends to injure "reputation" in the popular sense, to diminish the esteem, respect, good will or competence in which the plaintiff is held, or to excite adverse, derogatory or unpleasant feelings or opinions against him. [W. Prosser, *Law of Torts* 737, 739 (4th ed.)]

In a suit for defamation, the plaintiff must prove these elements: (1) The statement asserts a fact rather than an opinion; (2) it is untrue; (3) the speaker knew or had reason to know the statement was false; (4) the statement was communicated to a third party; and (5) it injured the claimant's reputation. If a person did not intend and could not reasonably foresee that the statement would reach anyone other than the subject of the statement, there is no liability for defamation. Likewise, no liability attaches if the speaker has no reason to know that the statement is untrue. Perhaps the most contentious defense is that the statement was one of opinion, rather than of fact.

There are several special defenses to defamation claims. Truth is always an absolute defense because a true statement cannot be defamatory. If the party has a legal right or duty to make statements that would be defamatory in other contexts, e.g., for the good of the school community,[120] courts find that the potential harm to an individual's reputation is outweighed by the public's need for the information. Typical examples of this privilege involve school hearings or discussions of a teacher's fitness, in which administrators or even parents make adverse comments that relate to official consideration of the teacher's competence, as long as those statements are not actually known by the speaker to be false.[121] Similar conditional privileges apply to comments made by teachers about students for appropriate school purposes.

Defamatory statements about "public officials" or "public figures" receive extraordinary constitutional protection. For a statement about a public figure to be defamatory, the speaker must make it with *actual knowledge* that it was false *or* with *reckless disregard* of its truth or falsity. The law thus opens public debate on matters of public interest by shielding news agencies and others from liability for *negligent* falsehoods about public officials and public figures.[122] Though the case law on public figures in the school context is relatively sparse, it is worth noting that in addition to school board members, school superintendents and principals may be considered public officials, at least in certain circumstances, and so be exposed to defamatory statements that are not actionable unless they are knowingly false or reckless.

Educational Malpractice

The term "educational malpractice" blurs two related tort claims, namely, failure of school authorities to properly test, evaluate, and place a student, with consequent injury to that student's development, and failure to bring a student up to satisfactory levels of learning and achievement. Courts have declined to impose any tort liability for these purely academic shortfalls, since they lack objective standards to measure educational performance and to reckon the effect of numerous education-related factors that are beyond educators' control. The cases do not, however, eliminate the possibility of recovering for negligent or wanton misconduct in the testing and evaluation of special student needs.[123] Nor do they preclude damage claims for violations of federal statutes that require special programs for children with special needs, such as children with disabilities.

LIMITATIONS ON TORT RECOVERY

In addition to the defenses noted above, state laws accord other defenses to school districts and their employees such as immunity from tort liability; statutory limits on dollar recovery; statutory indemnity of teachers and supervisors for their litigation expenses and liability; and statutory bars to tort suits for failure to give timely notice of tort claims and for failure to institute suit within statutory time deadlines. These defenses vary with the law of each state.

Governmental Immunity

As frequently noted, the law has, for various reasons of policy, conferred on various classes of government and individual defendants an "immunity" from otherwise binding obligations. In the field of tort liability, state and federal governments have in varying degree conferred immunity from tort liability on school districts and individuals, regardless of the factual merits of a tort claim. Tort immunity, unlike defenses of "privilege" (such as inflicting corporal punishment where legal) or of "justification" (such as use of reasonable force in self-defense), does not rest on *case facts* that might validate otherwise tortious conduct, but on the *legal shield* for immune defendants. The defense goes to a party's protected legal position, and not to justifying circumstances.

The scope and limits of tort immunities vary with the public policy of each state. That policy may be expressed by the state's courts, or by its legislature, which may opt to modify the judge-made law on tort liability and immunity. In like vein, federal law determines who and to what extent government entities or individuals are given immunity from liability for violations of federal law. Federal law immunity doctrines are discussed in Chapters 5 and 8, with reference to defendants charged with disability and age discrimination in employment, and with reference to alleged violations of federal civil rights. The following discussion relates to tort immunity under state tort law.

Tort immunity developed historically in two distinct branches, namely, *sovereign immunity*, which attaches to sovereign state and federal governments, and *governmental immunity*, which attaches to state subdivisions and actors whose actions are not considered to be acts of the state itself. Sovereign immunity is absolute and bars suit against the state on the theory that the state cannot be sued without its consent. Governmental immunity is based not on sovereign status, but on a policy of protecting government functions and actors for conduct not considered to be acts of the sovereign state itself. Although the distinction between sovereign and governmental or official immunity has been blurred and rendered moot in a growing majority of states that have consented to be sued and whose courts or legislatures have abrogated or limited tort immunity, sovereign immunity defenses remain significant in the few states that still accord school districts the shield of sovereign immunity.[124] Even in those states, the sovereign immunity of school districts and officials does not extend to teachers and other school employees unless the state legislature extended tort immunity to them.[125] Recent legislative developments of tort immunity law are given in the endnote.[126]

Courts of most states have abrogated or delimited the earlier tort immunity doctrines, and many state legislatures continue to refine the grounds of tort liability and immunity, often on a selective basis. One can still note broad principles of tort immunity that are generally shared in most states.

Tort immunity has been delimited in many states by judicial and legislative exceptions, the most prominent of which cover injuries caused by a "nuisance"; by school activities that are deemed to be "proprietary" rather than "governmental" in nature; by actions that are deemed "ministerial" rather than "discretionary"; or by defective conditions of school property or equipment, particularly where the injury is attributable to a violation of a school safety statute. Some examples of these exceptions are discussed shortly.

School districts may waive their governmental immunity, and in some states, districts that have liability insurance to cover the tort claim are deemed to have waived immunity to the extent of the insurance coverage.[127] A number of states also deny district tort immunity for certain classes of injury, such as injuries from defective equipment or property conditions.[128] The uneven development of tort immunity doctrines[129] is evident in an Illinois case which held that a child injured on a defective playground slide could fully recover tort damages if the city owned the playground, but could recover only in certain circumstances if the school district owned the playground, and could not recover at all if a park district owned the site.[130] Where an injury is caused by equipment that violates safety statutes, courts must decide whether the policy of promoting safety (by imposing tort liability) or the policy of immunizing government entities should prevail. In such cases, many courts elected to impose liability on school districts.[131]

Nuisance Exceptions

Some states favor school district liability for nuisances[132]:

> A municipal corporation has no more right to create and maintain a nuisance than does a private person. To constitute a nuisance . . . the condition must in some way constitute an unlawful invasion of the property rights of others. And it has been said that the invasion . . . must be inherent in the thing or condition itself,

beyond that merely from its negligent or improper use. [*Stein v. Highland Park Indep. School Dist.*, 540 S.W.2d 551, 553 (Tex. 1976)]

Under this concept of nuisance, school districts retain immunity for injuries resulting from negligent *uses* of property rather than from its defective *condition*.[133] Many tort statutes have broadened the common law nuisance exception to permit tort recovery for personal injuries resulting from specified property conditions whether or not they fit the common law definition of a nuisance.[134]

Conditions that have been classified as nuisances include (a) a sewage lagoon that pollutes an adjoining dairy farm, (b) a wall that diverts natural surface drainage away from the school onto neighboring land, and (c) a school building's unlawful encroachment of another property, causing students continually to trespass and throw litter on the adjoining property.[135]

Governmental vs. Proprietary Functions

Courts are hopelessly divided about treating particular functions as "proprietary" or "governmental" for purposes of granting or denying tort immunity to school districts.

> . . . Moreover, the distinction between governmental and proprietary functions is probably one of the most unsatisfactory known to the law, for it has caused confusion not only among the various jurisdictions but almost always within each jurisdiction. (See *Ayala* opinion at the end of this chapter.)

Broadly speaking, activities that resemble a commercial enterprise more than a governmental service are deemed proprietary.[136] As school operations become more education related, they are more likely to be considered governmental.[137] In a minority of cases, the charge of a fee to school events was cited to hold fee-funded operations to be proprietary functions subject to tort liability.[138] However, in other cases nominal school charges for community uses of the school did not render the operation "proprietary."[139]

Discretionary vs. Ministerial Functions

Many states confer governmental and/or personal immunity for discretionary acts, but not for ministerial ones. The classification of immune "discretionary acts" and nonimmune "ministerial acts" has been a source of continuing confusion in case law.[140]

> The expression "discretionary function" is clearly a standard, requiring measured judgment in its application, and its meaning cannot be reduced to a set of specific rules. (*Restatement of Law 2d*, Torts, Section 895D, Comment b)

In theory, discretionary acts are those that involve the exercise of judgment regarding school policy or planning, while ministerial acts purportedly involve activities that do not require significant exercises of judgment regarding school policy. While the distinction has an abstract logic, it is fuzzy and difficult to apply.

Individual Immunity

The personal tort immunity of board members (when sued as individuals), teachers, and other "employees" differs from governmental immunity accorded to school districts and to board members when sued for actions taken in their official capacity. Suits against board members in their official capacity are treated as suits against the school district itself.[141] A growing number of state legislatures have extended limited personal immunity to supervisors and teachers.[142] State law variations are referenced in the endnote.[143]

Personal tort immunity is intended to encourage public servants to perform their duties without fear of tort suits, but it is largely confined to actions that involve the use of educational discretion rather than routine workplace conduct. Thus even school officials who fail to maintain safe premises or who dismiss teachers in violation of tenure law are not deemed to be exercising educational judgment and accordingly are not granted personal tort immunity.[144] The courts are divided on the question of whether personal immunity extends to willful or intentional misconduct, even though that conduct arguably involves the exercise of discretion.[145]

A supervisor is normally not liable for the tortious conduct of a subordinate *unless* the supervisor personally fostered that conduct.[146]

A number of states further protect school officials and employees from personal losses by *indemnification* statutes that require school districts to pay for tort litigation costs and judgments that an employee or official suffers from actions taken within the scope of his or her duties.[147]

Notice and Time Limits and Dollar Caps

Many states impose notice requirements and time deadlines for pursuing tort claims and also set dollar ceilings on the amount of damages that can be recovered for particular classes of torts.

Notice statutes aim to ensure government agencies that they will have a fair opportunity to investigate and evaluate the legitimacy of tort claims, and to cure defective conditions following notice of their existence. Claimants against a school district must give timely written notice of their tort claim, usually within three to six months of the injury, in the form and to the officials specified by the notice statute. Failure to do so will bar the claimant from suing on that claim.[148] Notice statutes are construed liberally by most courts to allow exemptions for excusable failures to comply.[149] Notice requirements were satisfied or excused when the defendant entity was not prejudiced by the lack of statutory notice (having adequate notice from other sources); the claim notice substantially, though not fully, met statutory requirements; the required notice was prevented by excusable conditions (physical or mental incapacity; minority or incompetency); or the sued district waived the right to notice.[150]

Statutes of Limitations

Many states have short statutes of limitations for lawsuits against government agencies, usually one year from the date of injury. Here also, courts may allow late filing in special circumstances.

Dollar Recovery Limits

Many statutes set specific dollar caps for tort money damages against school districts. The caps often vary with the type of tort or nature of the injury. The state-to-state variations on such caps range from a modest ceiling of several thousand dollars in one state to a ceiling of several hundred thousand dollars in another.[151]

Chapter 4 Discussion Questions

Where the answer to a question may be qualified by special circumstances, explain the potential qualification.

1. What is a tort?

2. What are the limits of school district *respondeat superior* liability for the acts of its employees?

3. What constitutes "negligence" in tort law?

4. Are school district tort obligations and liability coextensive with school teacher tort obligation and liability? Explain.

5. What do the terms *respondeat superior* and *vicarious liability* mean?

6. Are the defenses of tort immunity the same for school districts as for teachers? Explain.

7. Are statutory dollar limits on tort recovery the same for school districts as for teachers? Explain.

8. Explain how juries play a more crucial role than courts in tort cases.

9. Under state tort law, to what extent are school districts obliged to protect students from physical or sexual abuse? From their own suicidal acts?

10. Under tort law, to what extent are teachers obliged to protect students from physical or sexual abuse? From their own suicidal acts?
    Note: Additional federal law obligations, as discussed in Chapter 8, do not relieve school districts and teachers from obligations under state tort law.

❖ CASES

Case 4.1

GRANT v. LAKE OSWEGO SCHOOL DISTRICT NO. 7
515 P.2d 947 (Or. App. 1973)

> [**Focus Note**. *Proximate cause; contributory negligence. Suit by a 12-year-old seventh-grade student against the school district and her physical education teacher for personal injuries sustained when she jumped off a springboard stored in an alcove and struck her head on the low doorway beam.*]

LANGTRY, JUDGE

Plaintiff alleged that defendants were negligent:

1. In placing a springboard under a low ceiling and doorway.
2. In failing to turn the springboard on its side or otherwise making it harmless.
3. In failing to warn the students of the danger of hitting the low ceiling and/or doorway.
4. In failing to supervise the students in the use of dangerous exercise equipment.

Defendants School District and Berke alleged that the plaintiff was contributorily negligent in jumping on the board without permission at a time and place when and where it was not supposed to be used . . . and in failing to maintain a proper [student] lookout. Evidence showed that . . . a class of 17 seventh grade girls was having its first instruction in gymnastics in a school "exercise room" with a high ceiling. . . . Near the end of the class plaintiff and three other girls, on instruction of defendant Toni Berke, dragged the springboard from the middle of the exercise room to an entrance alcove where the springboard was normally stored. The alcove had a low ceiling. . . .

After instructing the girls to move the springboard, defendant Toni Berke turned her attention elsewhere. . . . She was standing in position where she had no view into the entrance alcove. . . . Plaintiff then jumped off the springboard. She felt that she would propel herself into the exercise room. The lighting was good and she was aware of the low clearance of the doorway. She struck her head on the beam above the door and fell, injured. . . . The jury returned a verdict for plaintiff. . . . Upon motion by defendants the trial judge granted judgment notwithstanding the verdict. . . .

❖ ❖ ❖

(1) The child was not barred from recovery by contributory negligence as a matter of law. A child may be, under proper evidence, so barred. . . .

Whether the question of a child's contributory negligence is regarded as one of capacity, standard of care, or compliance with that standard, the courts are in substantial agreement that normally, if not always, a question of fact for the jury is presented, rather than one of law for the court. . . . Annotation, 77 A.L.R. 2d 917, 932 (1961).

This rule appears to apply in Oregon. . . .

✧ ✧ ✧

In the case at bar there is no testimony to the effect that plaintiff knowingly embarked on a course of dangerous conduct. Her contributory negligence, if any, was in her failure to appreciate the danger of her act, not in her failure to perceive the source of her danger. She knew the beam was there but jumped anyway, thinking she would miss it. If she should have known this was dangerous and did it anyway, then she would be guilty of negligence. . . . However, the question of what she should have known (absent testimony that she actually knew) is a question that depends upon what a hypothetical child of like age, intelligence, and experience should have known given similar circumstances. From the evidence presented in this case, that this was plaintiff's first experience with the use of a springboard and the apparent absence of in-depth instruction in its use and characteristics, a reasonable jury could have concluded that a similar child would not have appreciated the danger. . . .

. . . Defendant School Board's negligence is predicated on a finding that its servant Toni Berke was negligent. . . .

The evidence presented a conflict as to whether Toni Berke told the girls to "just drag [the springboard] over here" or to put the springboard away and "tip it on its side." . . .

✧ ✧ ✧

Here there was sufficient evidence to support a jury finding that the injury suffered was foreseeable. Toni Berke testified that inexperienced students should not use the springboard. The question of plaintiff's experience was as we have noted above a jury question.

Plaintiff's second two specifications of negligence—"(3) in failing to warn the students of the danger of hitting the low ceiling and/or doorway (4) in failing to supervise the students in the use of dangerous exercise equipment"—are also interrelated. Failure to warn can be viewed as a specific instance of failure to supervise.

✧ ✧ ✧

However, the facts of this case indicate that it can reasonably be found that proper supervision could have prevented this accident for the teacher would have noticed that the springboard was not being stored properly before plaintiff jumped off and struck her head on the beam. A quick admonition could have prevented her injury.

. . . We have concluded . . . that there was a jury question presented on all four specifications of negligence. This is contrary to the trial court's conclusion. . . . It follows that the ruling below must be reversed and remanded with instructions to reinstate the jury verdict. . . .

Case 4.2

SIMONETTI v. SCHOOL DISTRICT OF PHILA.
454 A.2d 1038 (Pa. Super. 1982)

WIEAND, JUDGE.

Richard Simonetti, a fifth grade student, returned to the classroom from recess and was struck in the left eye by a pencil which had been propelled from the hand of a classmate. . . . The teacher . . . was outside the classroom, standing at the door, when Simonetti was injured. There she was engaged in monitoring the return of her students from recess and talking with another teacher. The student who dropped or threw the pencil and two other students had been required to remain in the classroom during recess as punishment for misbehavior at breakfast. They . . . were instructed to take their seats when the teacher stepped outside the classroom to supervise the return of the students from recess.

. . . [I]t was contended by Simonetti that the teacher had been negligent in failing to provide adequate classroom supervision. The case was tried . . . and damages of $15,000 were awarded to the minor plaintiff and his mother. This appeal followed.

✧ ✧ ✧

There is no liability predicated on lack or insufficiency of supervision where the event in connection with which the injury occurred was not reasonably foreseeable. . . . The courts frequently state that a teacher is not required to anticipate the myriad of unexpected acts which occur daily in and about school . . . or to watch all movements of children. Where injury results from an unforeseen, sudden, impulsive, or spontaneous act of another pupil, such act has been held the intervening proximate cause of the injury. . . . Thus . . . failure of supervision is not that proximate cause of an accident where injury results from an unanticipated act of a fellow pupil, since the teacher cannot be expected to watch all movement of pupils in the absence of anything to place the teacher on notice to guard against the occurrence.

. . . [C]ases from other jurisdictions illustrate . . . these principles. In *Ohman v. Board of Education of City of New York* . . . the facts were remarkably similar to those of the instant case. There, a thirteen-year-old student sustained injury when struck in the eye by a pencil. The pencil had been thrown by one student to another, and when the boy for whom it was intended ducked, the pencil hit the minor plaintiff. The accident occurred while the teacher in charge of the classroom was temporarily absent for the purpose of sorting and storing supplies in a corridor closet. The court held that the teacher's absence from the room was insufficient to impose liability upon the Board of Education, saying: [A] teacher may be charged only with reasonable care such as a parent of ordinary prudence would exercise under comparable circumstances. . . .

In *Swaitkowski v. Board of Education of the City of Buffalo* . . . (1971), the Court held that the Board of Education was not liable for injuries sustained by a student who, upon returning to his seat, sat on the point of a pencil placed on the seat by another student while the teacher was absent from the classroom for a short period to assist another teacher locate books in a bookroom 10½ feet away with the doors open. The Court said: Nor can respondents prevail on their claim of inadequate supervision by the teacher in leaving the classroom unattended for the short space of time she was required to be absent. . . . [T]he injury resulted from "the act of an intervening third party which under the circumstances could hardly have been anticipated in the reasonable exercise of the teacher's legal duty toward the plaintiff. . . ."

❖ ❖ ❖

From these decisions it can safely be concluded that momentary absence from a classroom is not negligence. This is particularly true where . . . the absence was for the authorized and compelling reason of monitoring the return of about thirty students from recess. . . .

It is common knowledge that children may indulge in horseplay. . . . In the instant case, the teacher attempted to guard against any horseplay by instructing the three students who were in the classroom to return to their seats and remain there. While these students were . . . being punished for unrelated misconduct at breakfast, there is no evidence that they were hellions who required constant custody. . . .

The dissenting opinion contends that the teacher was negligent because she positioned herself so that she could neither see nor hear what was transpiring in the classroom. This is not in accord with the facts found by the trial judge. . . .

❖ ❖ ❖

To require the teacher to anticipate the events which occurred while she was outside the classroom door would be to hold that a teacher is required to anticipate the myriad of unexpected acts which occur daily in classrooms in every school in the land. This is not the law, and we perceive no good reason for imposing such an absolute standard on teachers and school districts.

❖ ❖ ❖

Case 4.3

AYALA v. PHILADELPHIA BOARD OF PUBLIC EDUCATION
305 A.2d 877 (Pa. 1973)

[**Focus Note**. *Suit by 15-year-old student for injuries suffered in upholstery class when his arm was caught in a shredding machine, necessitating its amputation.*]

ROBERTS, JUSTICE.

❖ ❖ ❖

Appellants alleged that appellee school district, through its employees, was negligent in failing to supervise the upholstery class, in supplying the machine for use without a proper safety device, in maintaining the machine in a dangerous and defective condition, and in failing to warn the children of the dangerous condition. Appellee, the Philadelphia Board of Public Education, interposed preliminary objections asserting the defense of governmental immunity. These objections were sustained and the Superior Court affirmed in a per curiam order.

❖ ❖ ❖

We now hold that the doctrine of governmental immunity . . . is abolished in this Commonwealth. In so doing, we join the ever-increasing number of jurisdictions which have judicially abandoned this antiquated doctrine. See, e.g., *Spencer v. General Hospital of District of Columbia* . . . 425 F.2d 479 (1969); *Campbell v. State*, 284 N.E.2d 733 (Ind. 1972) . . . ; . . . *Flournoy v. School District No. 1*, 174 Colo. 110 . . . (1971); *Smith v. State*, 93 Idaho 795 . . . (1970); *Willis v. Department of Conservation and Econ. Dev.*, 55 N.J. 534 . . . (1970); *Becker v. Beaudoin*, 106 R.I. 562 . . . (1970); *Johnson v. Municipal University of Omaha*, 184 Neb. 512 . . . (1969); . . . *Parish v. Pitts*, 244 Ark. 1239 . . . (1968); *Veach v. City of Phoenix*, 102 Ariz. 195 . . . (1967) . . . ; *Haney v. City of Lexington*, 386 S.W.2d 738 (Ky. 1964); *Sherbutte v. Marine City,* 374 Mich. 48 . . . (1964); *Rice v. Clark County*, 79 Nev. 253 . . . (1963); *Scheele v. City of Anchorage*, 385 P.2d 582 (Alaska 1963); . . . ; *Spanel v. Mounds View School District No. 621*, 264 Minn. 279 . . . (1962); *Holytz v. City of Milwaukee*, 17 Wis. 2d 26, 115 . . . (1962); *Muskopf v. Corning Hospital District*, 55 Cal.2d 11 . . . (1961); *Williams v. City of Detroit*, 364 Mich. 231 . . . (1961); *Molitor v. Kaneland Community United District No. 302*, 18 Ill. 2d 11 . . . (1959); *Hargrove v. Town of Cocoa Beach*, 96 So. 2d 130 (Fla. 1957). . . .

I

It is generally agreed that the historical roots of the governmental immunity doctrine are found in the English case of *Russell v. Men of Devon*, 2 T.R. 667, 100 Eng. Rep. 359 (1788). . . . There, the court . . . expressed the fear that if suits against such political subdivisions were permitted, there would be "an infinity of actions." . . . Finally, Justice Ashurst . . . observed that "it is better that an individual should sustain an injury than that the public should suffer an inconvenience." *Id.*

❖ ❖ ❖

Although the English courts abandoned the doctrine . . . this Commonwealth continued to deny recovery. . . . Thus, until the present action, we have retained the archaic and artificial distinction between tortious conduct arising out of the exercise of a proprietary function and tortious conduct arising out of exercise of a governmental function.

II

Today we conclude that no reasons whatsoever exist for continuing to adhere to the doctrine of governmental immunity. . . .   . . .

❖ ❖ ❖

. . . Moreover, the distinction between governmental and proprietary functions "is probably one of the most unsatisfactory known to the law, for it has caused confusion not only among the various jurisdictions but almost always within each jurisdiction."

❖ ❖ ❖

. . . [A]ppellee does not attempt to justify retention of immunity on policy grounds. Rather, it contends that abrogation, if it is to be achieved, should be accomplished by legislative direction rather than by judicial determination.

. . . [W]e stated in *Flagiello v. Pennsylvania Hospital, supra,* 417, Pa. at 503, 208 A.2d at 202: "[T]he controverted rule of charitable immunity is not the creation of the Legislature. *This Court fashioned it, and, what it put together, it can dismantle* (Emphasis added). . . .

Similarly, here, the doctrine of governmental immunity—judicially imposed—may be judicially terminated. . . .

❖ ❖ ❖

. . . [T]he order sustaining appellee's preliminary objections is reversed and the record remanded for proceedings consistent with this opinion.

❖ ENDNOTES

1. State v. Hoover, 450 N.E.2d 710 (Ohio 1982) (criminal assault charge against teacher).

2. Brown v. Calhoun County Board of Educ., 432 So. 2d 230 (Ala. 1983).

3. Barrett v. Phillips, 223 S.E.2d 918 (N.C. 1976).

4. District of Columbia v. Connelly, 465 A.2d 395 (D.C. Cir. 1983); Tiemann v. Indep. School Dist., 331 N.W.2d 250 (Minn. 1983); Benton v. School Board of Broward County, 386 So. 2d 831 (Fla. App. 1980).

5. *Re* heightened special duties, *see* Barth v. Board of Educ., 490 N.E.2d 77 (Ill. App. 1986) (special duty to protect); Rodriguez v. Inglewood Unified School Dist., 230 Cal. Rptr. 823 (1986) (duty to render school safe from criminal assaults); Phyllis P. v. Superior Court, 228 Cal. Rptr. 776 (Cal. 1986) (duty to notify parents of sexual assaults). *See generally* Annots., *Pub. Schools—Torts—Supervision*, 38 A.L.R. 3d 30 (1971); *Public Schools—Torts—Student Activity*, 36 A.L.R. 3d 330 (1970).

6. Cardozo, J., *in* Palsgraf v. Long Island R.R. Co., 162 N.E. 99, 100 (N.Y. 1928).

7. Smith v. Archbishop of St. Louis, 632 S.W.2d 516 (Mo. 1982).

8. Wyke v. Polk County School Board, 129 F.3d 560 (11th Cir. 1997).

9. This "but for" test is generally reliable, but not exact. Proximate cause may be found where the same harm would have occurred if either of two concurrent acts were solely involved.

10. State Farm Mutual Auto. Insurance Co. v. Pharr, 808 S.W.2d 769 (Ark. 1991); Hoyem v. Manhattan Beach City School Dist., 585 P.2d 851 (Cal. 1978) (question of whether motorist action was intervening cause of injury to unsupervised student—left to jury decision). *See generally* Ehlinger v. Board of Educ., 465 N.Y.S.2d 378 (1983); Dibartolo v. Metropolitan School Dist., 440 N.E.2d 506 (Ind. 1982); Ankers v. Dist. School Board, 406 So.2d 72 (Fla. 1981).

11. Daily v. L.A. Unified School Dist., 470 P.2d 360 (Cal. 1970).

12. Fagan v. Summers, 498 P.2d 1227 (Wyo. 1972) (dictum).

13. Levandoski v. Jackson City School Dist., 328 So.2d 339 (Miss. 1976).

14. Walcott v. Lindenhurst Union Free School Dist., 662 N.Y.S.2d 931 (1997) (assumption of risk in wrestling competition); Berman by Berman v. Philadelphia Board of Educ., 456 A.2d 545 (Pa. 1983); Hutchison v. Toews, 476 P.2D 811 (Or. 1970) (high school student injured by explosive made without permission from chemicals he knew to be dangerous, held barred from recovery by contributory negligence); Becker v. Beaverton School Dist., 551 P.2d 498 (Or. 1976) (student violation of school rule); Levin v. Board of Educ., 388 N.Y.S.2d 645 (1976).

15. Summerall v. Quachita Parish School, 665 So.2d 734 (La. App. 1995). *See* Annots., *Effect of Comparative Negligence in Assumption of Risk*, 16 A.L.R. 4th 700 (1982); *Modern Trends in Contributory Negligence*, 32 A.L.R. 4th 56 (1984).

16. (a) Ballard v. Polly, 387 F. Supp. 895 (D. D.C. 1975); (b) Simmons v. Beauregard Parish School Board, 315 So.2d 883, 888 (La. 1975). *But see* Kush v. City of Buffalo, 462 N.Y.S.2d 831 (1983) (injuries caused by unsecured stolen chemicals); (c) Robinson v. City of New York, 377 N.Y.S.2d 576 (1975); (d) Tannenbaum v. Board of Educ., 214 N.E.2d 378 (N.Y. 1966); (e) Shannon v. Addison Trail High School, 339 N.E.2d 372 (Ill. 1972); (f) Kluka v. Livingston Parish School Board, 433 So. 2d 302 (La. 1983).

17. Wagenblast v. Odessa School Dist., 758 P.2d 968 (Wash. 1988) (tort claim not waivable by student); *semble:* Whittington v. Sowela Technical Inst., 438 So. 2d 236 (La. 1983) (adult student).

18. A.L.I. Restatements, Torts § 575.

19. Apicella v. Valley Forge Military Academy, 630 F. Supp. 20 (E.D. Pa. 1985) (parent, but not child, bound by release and waiver); Haynes v. County of Missoula, 517 P.2d 370 (Mont. 1973) (voiding waiver).

20. Gaston v. Becker, 314 N.W.2d 728, 731–732 (Mich. 1982). No liability for the acts of independent contractors. *See* Hunter v. Board of Educ., 439 A.2d 582, 587 n. 8 (Md. 1982), and the authorities there cited.

21. Withers v. Charlotte-Mecklenburg Board of Educ., 231 S.E.2d 276 (N.C. 1976) (board not liable for collision of school bus driven by unauthorized student).

22. Kimberly M. v. Los Angeles Unified School Dist., 263 Cal. Rptr. 612 (Cal. App. 1989) (no *respondeat superior* liability for abuse of authority by teacher molester). *Compare* Galli v. Kirkeby, 248 N.W.2d 149 (Mich. 1977) *with* Adam v. Tatsch, 362 P.2d 984 (N.M. 1961). Annot., *Vicarious Liability for Intentional Assault*, 17 A.L.R. 4th 870 (1982).

23. 430 U.S. 651 (1977).

24. But even there, the use of bodily force in self-defense or to halt other assaults is permitted.

25. Roberts v. Way, 398 F. Supp. 856 (Vt. 1975); Illinois v. DeCaro, 38 N.E.2d 196 (Ill. App. 1974); Indiana St. Personnel Board v. Jackson, 192 N.E.2d 740 (Ind. 1963).

26. Allen v. LaSalle Parish School Board, 341 So. 2d 73 (La. 1977) (bus driver dismissed for administering corporal punishment).

27. Axtell v. LaPenna, 323 F. Supp. 1077 (W.D. Pa. 1971).

28. Glaser v. Marietta, 351 F. Supp. 555 (W.D. Pa. 1972).

29. *See* Hogenson v. Williams, 542 S.W.2d 456 (Tex. 1976) (helmet slapping by a football coach), which reviewed case authorities on corporal punishment for instructional purposes.

30. Tinkham v. Kole, 110 N.W.2d 258 (Iowa 1961); Suits v. Glover, 71 So. 2d 49 (Ala. 1954).

31. Baker v. Owen, 395 F. Supp. 294 (M.D. N.C. 1975)

32. Guillory v. Ortego, 449 So. 2d 182 (La. Ct. App. 1984)

33. Simms v. School Dist. No. 1, 508 P.2d 236 (Or. 1973); Andreozzi v. Rubano, 141 A.2d 639 (Conn. 1958).

34. Commonwealth v. Douglas, 588 A.2d 53 (Superior Ct. Pa. 1991) (excessive paddling of seven-year-old boy). People v. Smith, 335 N.E.2d 125 (Ill. 1975) (bleeding nose and swollen eye).

35. Rolando v. School Directors, 358 N.E.2d 945 (Ill. 1976) (use of cattle prod); Johnson v. Horace

Mann Mutual Insurance Co., 241 So. 2d 588 (La. 1970) (use of broken paddle); Berry v. Arnold School Dist., 137 S.W.2d 256 (Ark. 1940).

36. Suits v. Glover and Indiana St. Personnel Board v. Jackson, 71 So. 2d 49 (Ala. 1954).

37. (a) Johnson v. Horace Mann Mutual Insurance Co., 241 So. 2d 588 (La. 1970); (b), (c) Calway v. Williamson, 36 A.2d 377 (Conn. 1944); Tinkham v. Kole, 110 N.W.2d 258 (Iowa 1961).

38. *See* Small v. Board of Educ., 450 N.Y.S.2d 987 (1982). A teacher grabbing a student's face to get his attention is also not corporal punishment. Daniels v. Gordon, 503 S.E.2d 72 (Ga. 1998).

39. *See* Small, *supra* note 38; Owen v. Comm. of Kentucky, 473 S.W.2d 827 (Ky. 1971).

40. Frank v. Orleans Parish School Board, 195 So. 2d 451 (La. 1967).

41. Williams v. Cotton, 346 So. 2d 1039 (Fla. 1977).

42. Smith v. Broken Arrow Pub. School, 655 P.2d 858 (Okla. 1983) (patron at school supper). *See* Annots., *Public School Premises Liability*, 37 A.L.R. 3d 712, 738 (1971); *Tort Liability of Public Schools . . . for Accidents due to Condition of Buildings and Equipment*, 34 A.L.R. 3d 1166 (1970).

43. Hernandez v. Renville P. S. Dist. No. 654, 542 N.W.2d 671 (MN 1996) (student fall from nondefective playground slide); Narcisse v. Continental Insurance Co., 419 So. 2d 13 (La. 1983) (no duty to install door closures); Kass v. Board of Educ., 193 N.E.2d 643 (N.Y. 1963) (stage screen tipover).

44. Douglas v. Board of Educ., 468 N.E.2d 473 (Ill. 1984); Watts v. Town of Homer, 301 So. 2d 729 (La. 1974) (collapsing schoolyard slide).

45. *Cf.* Milliken v. City of Lewiston, 580 A.2d 151 (Me. 1990); Giosa v. School Dist. of Philadelphia, 562 A.2d 417 (Pa. Cmwlth. 1989) (icy walks); Gurule v. Salt Lake City Board of Educ., 661 P.2d 957 (Utah 1983): Lostumbo v. Board of Educ., 418 A.2d 949 (Conn. 1980); Kingsley v. Indep. Dist. No. 2, 251 N.W.2d 634 (Minn. 1977) (ragged-edged metal locker).

46. Jackson v. Cartwright School Dist., 607 P.2d 975 (Ariz. 1980) (insufficient time to learn of fresh hazard); Quigley v. School Dist., 446 P.2d 177 (Or. 1968) (no recovery for fall of recently delivered equipment); Duncan v. Board of

Educ., 159 N.Y.S.2d 745 (1957) (broken door-check); Dausend v. Board of Educ., 138 N.Y.S.2d 633 (1955) (floor clean-up at reasonable intervals).

47. Constantinescu v. Conejo Valley Unified School Dist., 20 Cal. Rptr. 2d 734 (Calif. App. 1993) (school pickup area could be held a statutory basis for liability).

48. Brewer v. Ind. School Dist., 848 P.2d 566 (Okla. 1993) (no liability for playground injury to licensee child); Slovin v. Gauger, 200 A.2d 565 (Del. 1964) (no liability to visitor falling from stage exit).

49. Heva v. Seattle School Dist., 188 P.776 (Wash. 1920); *see also* Jackson v. Board of Educ., 441 N.E.2d 120 (Ill. 1982) (attractive nuisance not excepted from governmental immunity). *But see* Yeske v. Avon Old Farm School, Inc., 470 A.2d 704, 710–11 (Conn. 1984).

50. *E.g.,* Ackler v. Odessa-Montour School Dist., 663 N.Y.S.2d 352 (1997) (sticky gym floor); Tieman v. Indep. School Dist., 331 N.W.2d 259 (Minn. 1983) (gym horse without handles); Hampton v. Orleans Parish School Board, 422 So. 2d 202 (La. 1982) (examples of building hazards); Bessette v. Enderlin School Dist., 310 N.W.2d 79 (N.D. 1981) (defective slide); Board of Educ. v. Fredericks, 147 S.E.2d 789 (Ga. 1966) (stadium seats); Wiener v. Board of Educ., 369 N.Y.S.2d 207 (1975) (loose handrail); Cappel v. Board of Educ., 337 N.Y.S.2d 836 (1972) (unanchored hockey cage).

51. Caltavuturo v. City of Passaic, 307 A.2d 115 (N.J. 1973) (school principal liable for injury from torn fence).

52. Barnes v. Bott, 615 So. 2d 1337 (La. App. 1993); Greene v. City of New York, 566 N.Y.S.2d 40 (1991); Padgett v. School Board, 295 So. 2d 504 (Fla. 1981); Guerreri v. Tyson, 24 A.2d 468 (Pa. 1842).

53. Texas Education Code, Title 2, subtitle G, *Safe Schools* (1996). California "Safe Schools Act of 1990." *See* Constantinescu, *supra* note 47 (crowded pickup area); Pa. Stat Ann., 24 P.S. § 13-1303-A (1995).

54. Reed v. Pawling Cent. School Dist., 664 N.Y.S.2d 483 (N.Y. A.D. 1997); Malik v. Greater Johnstown Enlarged School Dist., 669 N.Y.S.2d 729 (N.Y. A.D. 1998) (student can recover under theory of negligent supervision only where victim can show that acts of fellow students could have been reasonably anticipated by school employees).

55. *See also* Maynard v. Board of Educ., 244 A.2d 622 (N.Y. App. 1997).

56. *See* Note, *School Liability for Athletic Injuries*, 21 Washburn L.J. 315, 321, n. 52 (1982). Justus v. Jefferson County School Dist., 683 P.2d 805 (Colo. 1984) (school, by its rules and regulations, assumed duty to prevent first grader from leaving school grounds).

57. Titus v. Lindberg, 228 A.2d 65 (N.J. 1967) (schoolyard before start of classes).

58. Hill v. Safford Unified School Dist., 952 P.2d 754 (Ariz. App. 1997); Gross v. Family Services, Inc., 716 So. 2d 337 (Fla. App. 1998) ("special relationships" exception to the general rule that there is no duty to protect one from criminal conduct); Bell v. Board of Educ. of the City of New York, 687 N.E.2d 1325 (N.Y. 1997) (rape of sixth-grade student left behind in park after school trip; board of education held liable for child's injuries). *Compare* Dickerson v. City of New York, 684 N.Y.S.2d 584 (N.Y. 1999) (no school duty to protect student who was shot by intruder in school hallway).

59. Garufi v. School Board, 613 So. 2d 1341 (Fla. App. 1993) (assault by violent student); Ferraro v. Board of Educ., 221 N.Y.S.2d 279 (1961) (principal's failure to warn substitute teacher of problem student); Korenak v. Curative Work Shop Adult Rehabilitation Center, 237 N.W.2d 43 (Wis. 1976) (exposing student to person with criminal tendencies); Lauricella v. Board of Educ., 52 A.D.2d 710 (N.Y. 1976) (racially troubled school).

60. Schuyler v. Board of Educ., 205 N.E.2d 311 (N.Y. 1965); Morris v. Ortiz, 437 P.2d 652 (Ariz. 1968). *But see* Hoyem v. Manhattan Beach City School Dist., 150 Cal. Rptr. 1 (1978).

61. James v. Gloversville Enlarged School Dist., 548 N.Y.S.2d 87 (1989). *Compare* Raymond v. Paradise Unified School Dist., 31 Cal. Rptr. 847 (1963) (whether duty existed—held question of law for the court), *with* Fazzolari v. Portland School Dist., 717 P.2d 1210 (Or. 1986) (whether duty existed before school opening—held question for the jury); School Board v. Anderson, 411 So. 2d 940 (Fla. 1982). Supervision cases are

collected in Annots., *Public Schools—Torts—Supervision*, and *Public Schools—Torts—Student Activity, supra* note 5.

62. *Ibid.* Constantinescu, *supra* note 47 (crowded pickup area); Broward County School v. Ruiz, 493 So. 2d 560 (Fla. 1985) (after-school cafeteria assault).

63. *Regular play:* Tymkowicz v. San Jose Unified School Dist., 312 P.2d 388 (Cal. 1957) (10-year-old injured shortly before school hours). *Student misconduct:* Titus, *supra* note 57. *But see* Sly v. Board of Educ., 516 P.2d 895 (Kans. 1973) (no notice of prior misconduct). *Unsafe conditions:* Rice v. School Dist., 248 P. 388 (Wash. 1926) (student electric shock on radio aerial recently installed by janitor). *But see contra:* Fitzgerald v. Montgomery County Board of Educ., 336 A.2d 795 (Md. 1975) (exposed wire).

64. Tashjian v. N. Colonie Central School Dist., 353 N.Y.S.2d 467 (1975) (permitting third grader to play baseball contrary to school rules); Briscoe v. School Dist., 201 P.2d 697 (Wash. 1949) (permitting football in playground contrary to school rules).

65. Lee v. School Dist., 324 N.W.2d 632 (Mich. 1982). *Cf.* Sutton v. Duplessis, 584 So. 2d 363 (La. App. 1991).

66. *See* Gordon v. Deer Park School Dist., 426 P.2d 824 (Wash. 1967) (student spectator struck by bat).

67. Lawes v. Board of Educ., 16 N.Y.S.2d 302 (1965).

68. Cioffi v. Board of Educ., 278 N.Y.S.2d 249 (1967).

69. Decker v. Dundee Central School Dist., 151 N.E.2d 866 (N.Y. 1958) (child fell from bleachers, 1,000 feet from the sole supervisor); Charronat v. San Francisco Unified School Dist., 133 P.2d 643 (Cal. 1943) (failure to assign more than one supervisor to playground).

70. Beck v. San Francisco Unified School Dist., 37 Cal. Rptr. 471 (1964). *See also* Gibbons v. Orleans Parish School Board, 391 So. 2d 976 (La. 1980) (one supervisor for several hundred children—held inadequate). *Compare* Glanker v. Rapides Par. School Board, 610 So. 2d 1020 (La. App. 1992) (three teachers, plus 11 parents, held adequate to supervise 78 kindergarten children).

71. Barbato v. Board of Educ., 182 N.Y.S.2d 875 (1959).

72. Swaitkowski v. Board of Educ., 319 N.Y.S.2d 783 (1971) (teacher briefly absent to aid another teacher—held not liable for injurious student prank).

73. See Simonetti case in this chapter; Collins v. School Board, 471 So. 2d 560 (Fla. App. 1985) (absence during 10-minute sexual assault—supported finding of negligence); Gonzales v. Mackler, 241 N.Y.S.2d 254 (1963) (half-hour absence from class for children with mental retardation); *contra* Jackson v. Chicago Board of Educ., 549 N.E.2d 829 (Ill. App. 1989).

74. *Liable for absence:* Schnell v. Travelers Insurance Co., 260 So. 2d 346 (La. 1972). *Not liable:* Banks v. Terrebone Parish School Board, 339 So. 2d 1295 (La. 1976).

75. James for James v. Charlotte-Mecklenburg Board of Educ., 300 S.E.2d 21 (N.C. 1983).

76. *Cf.* Sutton v. Duplessis, 584 So. 2d 362 (4th Cir. 1991); Lewis v. St. Bernard Parish School Board, 350 So. 2d 1256 (La. 1977).

77. Brand v. Sertoma Club of Springfield, 349 N.E.2d 502 (Ill. 1976) (no liability for injurious activity); Sims v. Etowah City Board of Educ., 337 So. 2d 1310 (Ala. 1976) (liability for defective bleachers).

78. Grant v. Lake Oswego School Dist., in this chapter; Benitez v. New York City Board of Educ., 73 N.Y.S.2d 650 (1989); Summers v. Milwaukee Unified High School Dist., 481 P.2d 369 (Or. 1971) (girl with history of falls); Kefesee v. Board of Educ., 23 N.Y.S.2d 300 (1962) (placing inexperienced girls in soccer game); Bauer v. Board of Educ., 140 N.Y.S.2d 167 (1955) (16 three-man teams, on eight adjoining gym areas); Dobbins v. Board of Educ., 335 A.2d 23 (N.J. 1975) (racing over macadam surface).

79. *Adjoining games:* see prior note.

80. Gerrity v. Beatty, 373 N.E.2d 1323 (Ill. 1977) (ill-fitted helmet); Armlin v. Board of Educ., 320 N.Y.S.2d 402 (1971) (violation of gym safety rules); Brown v. Board of Educ., 326 N.Y.S.2d 9 (1971) (drowning case).

81. *Unknown medical condition:* Kerby v. Elk Grove Unified School Dist., 36 P.2d 431 (Cal. 1934) (student with undetected aneurism killed by head blow). *Cf.* Rodriguez v. San Jose Unified School Dist., 322 P.2d 70 (Cal. 1958) (fatal fall of

child with cerebral palsy and heart disease where parent advised school that child could take care of himself).

Unexplained drowning: Wong v. Waterloo Comm. School Dist., 232 N.W.2d 865 (Iowa 1975) (11-year-old); Stephens v. Shelbyville Central Schools, 318 N.E.2d 590 (Ind. 1974) (14-year-old).

82. *Heat stroke:* Lovitt v. Concord School Dist., 228 N.W.2d 479 (Mich. 1975); Peck v. Board of Educ., 30 N.Y.2d 700 (1972); Mogabgab v. Orleans Parish School Board, 239 So. 2d 456 (La. 1970). *Negligent movement of injured student:* Welch v. Dunsmuir Joint Union High School Dist., 326 P.2d 633 (Cal. 1958).

83. For cases involving organized sports, *see* Annots., *Schools—Liability—Athletic Events,* 35 A.L.R. 3d 725 (1971); *Schools—Liability—Physical Training,* 36 A.L.R. 3d 361 (1970). *Compare* Berman by Berman v. Philadelphia Board of Educ., 456 A.2d 545 (Pa. 1983) (negligence re 11-year-old student injury in hockey), *with* Smith v. Vernon Parish School Board, 442 So. 2d 1319 (La. 1983) (no negligence re 15-year-old injury on trampoline); Fosselman v. Waterloo School Dist. 229, N.W.2d 280 (Iowa 1975) (gym game of "bombardment"); Passantino v. Board of Educ., 395 N.Y.S.2d 628 (1977) (baseball contest).

84. Banks v. Terrebonne Parish School Board, 339 So. 2d 1295 (La. 1976) (no liability for absence during gym recess); Seda v. Board of Educ., 152 N.Y.S.2d 356 (1956) (student falling from horizontal bar).

85. Ragnone v. Portland School Dist., 633 P.2d 1287 (Or. 1981); Carabba v. Anacortes School Dist., 435 P.2d 936 (Wash. 1967).

86. Shop and laboratory cases are collected in Annot., *Schools—Tort Liability—Shop Training,* 35 A.L.R. 3rd 758 (1971).

87. Velmer v. Baraga Area Schools, 424 N.W.2d 770 (Mich. 1988) (milling machinery); Bush v. Oscoda Area Schools, 250 N.W.2d 759 (Mich. 1977) (explosion from science experiment); Simmons v. Beauregard Parish School Board, 315 So. 2d 883 (La. 1975) (work with explosives).

88. Lemelle v. State through Board of Secondary and Elementary Educ., 435 So. 2d 1162 (La. 1983) (welding shop); Isard v. Hickory City Board of Educ., 315 S.E.2d 765 (N.C. 1984) (power saw). Compare Lorte v. Board of Educ., 395 N.Y.S.2d 262 (1977) (no negligence where student upset bottle of acid); *cf.* Bottorf v. Waltz, 369 A.2d 332 (Pa. 1976) (negligence question left to jury where candle mold fell).

89. Hutchison v. Toews, 476 P.2d 811 (Or. 1970) (15-year-old); Frace v. Long Beach City High School Dist., 137 P.2d 60 (Cal. 1943) (17-year-old student). *But see* Kush v. City of Buffalo, 59 N.Y.S.2d 831 (1983).

90. Scott v. Indep. School Dist., 256 N.W.2d 485 (Minn. 1977) (failure to enforce safety goggle law); Lehmann v. Los Angeles Board of Educ., 316 P.2d 55 (Cal. 1957) (unguarded printing press); Matteucci v. High School Dist., 281 N.E.2d 383 (Ill. 1972); Ayala v. Philadelphia Pub. Board of Educ., 305 A.2d 877 (Pa. 1973).

91. *Absence of safety rules:* Steffani v. Baker, 387 N.Y.S.2d 355 (1976) (unsupervised car lift); Govel v. Board of Educ., 60 N.E.2d 133 (N.Y. 1944) (shop repair of loaded gun).

92. Meyer v. Board of Educ., 86 A.2d 761 (N.J. 1952); Ressle v. Board of Educ., 395 N.Y.S.2d 263 (1977); Hammond v. Scott, 232 S.E.2d 336 (S.C. 1977); Morris v. Ortiz, 437 P.2d 652 (Ariz. 1968).

93. Plesnicav v. Kovach, 430 N.E.2d 648 (Ill. 1981); Hoyem v. Manhattan Beach County School Dist., 139 Cal. Rptr. 769 (1977); Oglesby v. Seminole City Board of Instruction, 328 So. 2d 515 (Fla. 1976); Lunsford v. Board of Educ., 374 A.2d 1162 (Md. 1972).

94. *Reasonable care standard:* Cooper v. Millwood Ind. School Dist., 887 P.2d 1370 (Okla. 1994); Gardner v. Biggart, 417 S.E.2D 858 (S.C. 1992); Mitchell v. Guilford County Board of Educ., 161 S.E.2d 645 (N.C. 1968).

Safety statutes: Van Gaasbeck v. Webatuck Central School Dist., 243 N.E.2d 253 (N.Y. 1967) (failure to use bus light signals); State Use of Parr v. Board of County Commissioners, 113 A.2d 397 (Md. 1955) (defective emergency door).

95. Schultz v. Cheney School Dist., 371 P.2d 59 (Wash. 1962).

96. For a review of cases in this field, see Annots., *Schools—Transportation,* 23 A.L.R. 5th 1 (1994); *Schools—Transportation—Student Injury,* 34 A.L.R. 3d 1210 (1970).

97. *Reason to expect student misconduct:* Cooper v. Millwood, 887 P.2d 1370 (Okla. 1994); Brantly v. Dade County School Board, 493 So. 2d 471 (Fla. 1986); Blair v. Board of Educ., 448 N.Y.S.2d 556 (1982).

98. Garza v. McAllen Indep. School Dist., 613 S.W.2d 526 (Tex. 1981); Arnold v. Hayslett, 655 S.W.2d 941 (Tenn. 1983) (thrusting head out of bus window).

99. (a) Crawford v. Wayne County Board of Educ., 168 S.E.2d 33 (N.C. 1968); (b) Coral Gables v. Patty, 162 So. 2d 530 (Fla. 1964); (c) Croghan v. Hart City Board of Educ., 549 S.W.2d 306 (Ky. 1977); Slade v. New Hanover County Board of Educ., 179 S.E.2d 453 (N.C. 1971); *cf.* Sparrow v. Forsyth County Board of Educ., 198 S.E.2d 762 (N.C. 1973) (swerving reaction to avoid snowball, held not negligent); (d) County School Board v. Thomas, 112 S.E.2d 877 (Va. 1960); Van Gaasbeck, *supra* note 94; and (e) Scott v. Thompson, 363 N.E.2d 295 (Mass. 1977).

100. Mitchell v. Guilford County Board of Educ., 161 S.E.2d 645 (N.C. 1968).

101. Anderson v. Ohm, 258 N.W.2d 114 (Minn. 1977); Slade v. New Hanover Board of Educ., 178 S.E.2d 316 (N.C. 1971). *See also* Van Gaasbeck, *supra* note 94.

102. Bailey v. Gallatin County Board of Educ., 383 S.W.2d 63 (Ky. 1964) (student shoved out of stationary bus); Norris v. American Casualty Co., 176 So. 2d 677 (La. 1965) (student pushed or fell under bus).

103. *Re safe route selection:* Pratt v. Robinson, 360 N.Y.S.2d 349 (1974); Sanderlin v. Central School Dist., 487 P.2d 1399 (Or. 1971). *Re student use of other stops:* DeCerbo v. Raab, 516 N.Y.S.2d 995 (1987).

104. Barnes v. Bott, 615 So. 2d 1337 (La. App. 1993)

105. Gilbert v. Sacramento Unified School Dist., 65 Cal. Rptr. 913 (1968); Verbel v. Indep. School Dist., 359 N.W.2d 579 (Minn. 1984); Whorley v. Brewer, 315 So. 2d 511 (Fla. 1975).

106. Coates v. Tacoma School Dist., 347 P.2d 1093 (Wash. 1960).

107. Chappel v. Franklin Pierce School Dist., 426 P.2d 471 (Wash. 1967) (failure to provide substitute for absent instructor).

108. Morris v. Douglas County School, 403 P.2d 775 (Or. 1965); Williamson v. Board of Educ., 375 N.Y.S.2d 221 (1975).

109. Mancha v. Field Museum of Natural History, 283 N.E.2d 899 (Ill. 1972). *See also* Arnold v. Hafling, 474 P.2d 638 (Colo. 1970) (no duty to supervise high school students at mountain camp).

110. Applebaum v. Nemon, 678 S.W.2d 533 (Tex. 1984) (no duty to provide aid that required special training); Peck v. Board of Educ., 319 N.Y.S.2d 919 (1970) (gym student kicked in the head). *Compare* Declouet v. Orleans Parish School Board, 715 So. 2d 69 (La. App. 1998) (failure to call ambulance promptly for student suffering severe asthma attack).

111. O'Brien v. Twp. High School Dist., 392 N.E.2d 615 (Ill. 1980); Guerrieri v. Tyson, 24 A.2d 468 (Pa. 1942).

112. *Re actionable medical negligence, see, e.g.,* Snow v. State of New York, 469 N.Y.S.2d 959 (1983). *See generally* Annot., *Liability of One Treating Mentally Afflicted Patients for Failure to Warn or Protect Third Persons Threatened by Patient,* 83 A.L.R. 3rd 1201 (1978). Tarasoff v. Regents, Univ. of Cal., 551 P.2d 334 (Cal. 1976); McIntosh v. Milano, 403 A.2d 500 (N.J. 1979); *cf.* Lipari v. Sears Roebuck & Co., 497 F. Supp. 185 (D. Neb. 1980). For other views, *see* Cole v. Taylor, 301 N.W.2d 766 (Iowa 1981); Durflinger v. Artiles, 673 P.2d 86 (Kan. 1983); Doyle v. U.S., 530 F. Supp. 1278 (C.D. Cal. 1982); Leedy v. Hartnet, 510 F. Supp. 1125 (M.D. Pa. 1981); Thompson v. County of Alameda, 614 P.2d 728 (Cal. 1980).

113. Hammond v. Board of Educ. of Carroll County, 639 A.2d 223 (Md. App. 1994) (no liability under federal rights statute for lack of official notice of the suicide threat).

114. Brooks v. Logan, 903 P.2d 73 (Idaho 1995); Eisel v. Board of Educ., 97 A.2d 447 (Md. 1991). *See generally Restatement (Second) of Torts,* § 315(1965).

115. Brown v. Board of Educ., 681 A.2d 996 (Conn. 1996); Eisel v. Board of Educ., 597 A.2d 447 (Md. App. 1991). *See also Restatement (Second) of Torts* § 315 (1965); Eugene C. Bjorklun, *School Liability for Student Suicides,* 106 Ed. Law. Rep. 21 (March 1996).

116. McMahon v. St. Croix Falls School Dist., 596 N.W.2d 875 (Wis. 1999).

117. Dickerson v. City of New York, 684 N.Y.S.2d 584 (N.Y. 1999) (student stabbing by outsider); Rodrigues v. Englewood School Dist., 230 Cal. Rptr. 823 (1986) (student shooting by outsider). *See also* notes 58 and 59 and related text.

118. Maynard v. Board of Educ., 244 A.2d 622 (N.Y. App. 1997).

119. Brooks v. Logan, 903 P.2d 73 (Idaho 1995).

120. *Compare* Grostick v. Ellsworth, 404 N.W.2d 685 (Mich. 1987) (superintendent's negative comments, held qualifiedly privileged), *with* Santavicca v. City of Yonkers, 518 N.Y.S.2d 29 (1987) (superintendent's comments held absolutely privileged). *See also* Morrison v. Mobile County Board of Educ., 495 So. 2d 1086 (Ala. 1986); Berlin v. Supt. of Pub. Instruction, 448 N.W.2d 764 (Mich. App. 1989). Annot., *Libel—School Board Members Privilege*, 85 A.L.R. 3d 1137 (1978).

   Re privilege under child-abuse reporting statutes, *see* Annot., *State Statute Requiring Doctor or Other Person to Report Child Abuse*, 73 A.L.R. 4th 782 (1989).

121. *Ibid. Board members:* Malia v. Monchak, 543 A.2d 184 (Pa. Cmwlth. 1988); Freir v. Indep. School Dist., 356 N.W.2d 724 (Minn. App. 1984); Mancuso v. Oceanside Unified School Dist., 200 Cal. Rptr. 535 (1984). *See generally* Annot., *Libel and Slander—School Board Members Privilege*, 85 A.L.R. 3d 1137 (1978) and 1996 pkt. part.

   Parents: Martin v. Kearney, 124 Cal. Rptr. 281 (1975); Schulze v. Coykendall, 545 P.2d 392 (Kan. 1976); *but see* Everett v. Cal. Teachers Assn., 25 Cal. Rptr. 120 (1962) (liability for knowingly false statement).

122. New York Times Co. v. Sullivan, 376 U.S. 254 (1964). *Public figures:* Scott v. News-Herald, 496 N.E.2d 699 (Ohio 1986) (school superintendent); Garcia v. Board of Educ., 777 F.2d 1403 (10th Cir. 1985) (board members); Stevens v. Tillman, 855 F.2d 394 (7th Cir. 1988) (school principal). *Not public figures:* Franklin v. Elks Lodge, 97 C.A.3d 915 (1979) (teachers); Jones v. Maness, 648 S.W.2d 629 (Mo. 1983) (students).

123. (1) *Failure to achieve satisfactory educational levels—no cause of action:* Heilbig v. City of New York, 597 N.Y.S.2d 587 (1993); Rich v. Kentucky Country Day, 793 S.W.2d 832

(Ky. 1990); Smith v. Philadelphia School Dist., 679 F. Supp. 479 (E.D. Pa. 1988); Donohue v. Copiague Union Free School Dist., 391 N.E.2d 1352 (N.Y. 1979).

   (2) *Failure to properly test, evaluate, and place student—cause of action:* Daniel B. v. Wis. Dept. of Pub. Instruction, 581 F. Supp. 585 (E.D. Wis. 1984); Tubell v. Dade County Public Schools, 419 So. 2d 388 (Fla. 1982) (misclassification and misplacement in special educational program); Doe v. Board of Educ., 453 A.2d 814 (Md. 1982) (misclassification and misplacement, as brain injured); D.S.W. v. Fairbanks N. Star Borough School Dist., 628 P.2d 554 (Alaska 1981) (misclassification and misplacement of dyslexic students); Hoffman v. Board of Educ., 400 N.E.2d 317 (N.Y. 1979) (misclassification of student as retarded); *accord:* Smith v. Alameda County Social Services, 153 Cal. Rptr. 712 (1979). *But see contra:* B.M. v. State, 649 P.2d 425 (Mont. 1982) (misclassification and misplacement of student as having mental retardation).

   See generally Annot., *Tort Liability—Educational Malpractice*, 1 A.L.R. 4th 1139 (1980); Note, *Nonliability for Negligence in the Public Schools—Educational Malpractice*, 55 Notre Dame L. Rev. 814 (1980).

124. The differences between state sovereign immunity and school district immunity are noted in Mt. Healthy School Dist. v. Doyle, 429 U.S. 274 (1977). *Denial of state sovereign immunity:* Ohio Valley Contractors v. Board of Educ. of Wetzel County, 293 S.E.2d 437 (W. Va. 1982). *Granting state sovereign immunity:* Hutt v. Etowah County Board of Educ., 454 So.2d 973 (Ala. 1984).

125. Davis v. DeKalb County School Dist., 996 F.Supp. 1478 (N.D. Ga. 1998) (state Tort Claims Act did not waive immunity for school districts; therefore, school district could not be held liable for teacher sexual molestation of student).

126. For a good summary of state legislative changes in tort law, *see* J. Martinez, *Contemporary Trends in State Public Tort Law*, 18 McQuillin Municipal Law Report, No. 6, pp. 7–10 (June 2000).

   Re legislative extension of tort immunity to school district teachers and employees, *see, e.g.,*

Bankston v. Pulaski County School Board, 65 S.W.2d 859 (Ark. 1984); McManus v. Anahuac Indep. School Dist., 667 S.W.2d 275 (Tex. 1984); Bodano v. Wayne-Westland Comm. School, 318 N.W.2d 613 (Mich. 1982); Daniels v. Gordon, 503 S.E.2d 72 (Ga. App. 1998) (official immunity extends to employees of school districts); S.W. v. Spring Lake Park School Dist. No. 16, 580 N.W.2d 19 (Minn. 1998).

127. Alter v. City of Newton, 617 N.E.2d 656 (Mass. 1993). *Waiver found by taking out insurance:* Durham City Board of Educ. v. National Union Fire Ins. Co., 426 S.E.2d 451 (N.C. 1993); Crowell v. School Dist. No. 7 of Gallatin County, 805 P.2d 522 (Mont. 1991); School Board of Orange County v. Coffey, 524 So. 2d 1052 (Fla. App. 1988); James v. Charlotte-Mecklenburg Board of Educ., 300 S.E.2d 21 (N.C. 1983); Vendrell v. School Dist., 360 P.2d 282 (Or. 1971). *Contra:* Dugger v. Sprouse, 364 S.E.2d 275 (Ga. 1988); Nelson v. House, 402 N.W.2d 639 (Minn. App. 1987); Bartley v. Special School Dist., 649 S.W.2d 864 (Mo. 1983); Bernhard v. Kerrville Indep. School Dist., 547 S.W.2d 685 (Tex. 1977). *Cf.* Guillaume v. Staum, 328 N.W.2d 259 (S.D. 1982).

128. Wilson v. Ridgway Area School Dist., 596 A.2d 1161 (Pa. Cmwlth. 1991); Bonamico v. City of Middletown, 706 A.2d 1386, *on remand,* 713 A.2d 1291 (Conn. App. 1998).

129. Oklahoma confers school district immunity against attractive nuisance claims, while Missouri denies immunity for injuries caused by "dangerous conditions." Brewer v. Ind. School Dist., 848 P.2d 566 (Okla. 1993); Goben v. School Dist. of St. Joseph, 848 S.W.2d 20 (Mo. 1992). *See also* McGeregor v. Middletown School Dist., 190 A.3d 923 (N.Y. 1993) (New York statutory exceptions to immunity); Edmonson v. Brooks County Board of Educ., 423 S.E.2d (Ga. 1992) (state immunity for injury on property open to public recreation uses). Annot., *Schools—Torts—Sovereign Immunity,* 33 A.L.R. 3d 703 (1970) and 1996 pkt part.

130. Bankenship v. Peoria Park Dist., 647 N.E.2d 287 (Ill. App. 1994); Harvey v. Clyde Park Dist., 203 N.E.2d 573, 577 (Ill. 1964).

131. *Cf.* Scott v. Indep. School Dist., 256 N.W.2d 485 (Minn. 1977).

132. Grames v. King, 332 N.W.2d 615 (Mich. 1983); Stein v. Highland Park Indep. School Dist., 540 S.W.2d 551 (Tex. 1976); Kreiner v. Turkey Valley Comm. School Dist., 212 N.W.2d 526 (Iowa 1973). *Contra:* Kellam v. Board of Educ., 117 S.E.2d 96 (Va. 1960).

133. Sly v. Board of Educ., 516 P.2d 895 (Kan. 1973) (negligent supervision—held not a nuisance).

134. *E.g.,* Everhart v. Board of Educ., 310 N.W.2d 338 (Mich. App. 1981); Canon-McMillan School Dist. v. Bioni, 555 A.2d 901 (Pa. 1989).

135. (a) Kreiner, *supra* note 132. (b) Sturges v. School Dist., 33 Pa. D. & C. 525 (1938). (c) Stein, *supra* note 132.

136. *See, e.g.,* Ross v. Consumer Power Co., 363 N.W.2d 641 (Mich. 1984); Marilyn S. v. City of New York, 521 N.Y.S.2d 485 (1987); Matthews v. Elder; 400 So. 2d 251 (La. App. 1981).

137. Lovitt v. Concord School Dist., 228 N.W.2d 479 (Mich. 1975) (school games); Rennie v. Belleview School Dist., 521 S.W.2d 423 (Mo. 1975); Coleman v. Beaumont Indep. School Dist., 496 S.W.2d 245 (Tex. 1973) (playground maintenance).

138. Sawaya v. Tuscon High School Dist., 281 P.2d 105 (Ariz. 1955) (lease of school stadium to another school district); *contra:* Watson v. School Dist., 36 N.W.2d 195 (Mich. 1949).

139. Smith v. Board of Educ., 464 P.2d 571 (Kans. 1970).

140. *Compare e.g.,* Burns v. Board of Educ., 638 A.2d 1 (Conn. 1994) (discretionary immunity superseded), *with* Doe v. Park Center High School, 592 N.W.2d 131 (Minn. App. 1999) (execution of policy is discretionary not ministerial). *See also* Lipman v. Brisbane Elementary School Dist.

141. Scott, *supra* note 131.

142. Barr v. Bernhard, 562 S.W.2d 844 (Tex. 1978); Morrison v. Comm. Anita School Dist., 358 N.E.2d 389 (Ill. 1976); Baird v. Hosmer, 347 N.E.2d 533 (Ohio 1976) (citing numerous authorities from other states); Lovitt v. Concord School Dist., 228 N.W.2d 479 (Mich. 1975); Caldwell v. Griffin Spalding County Board of Educ., 503 S.E.2d 43 (Ga. App. 1998) (supervision of student safety is a discretionary function; school officials are

entitled to immunity even for negligent supervision.)

143. *See* Annot., *Student Injury—Teacher Liability*, 34 A.L.R. 4th 228, 234–46 (1984); Moore v. Port Arthur Indep. School Dist., 751 F. Supp. 671 (E.D. Tex. 1990); Vitale v. Lentine, 358 N.W.2d 2 (Mich. 1984).

144. *Failure to maintain safe premises:* Elgin v. Dist. of Columbia, 337 F.2d 152 (D.C. Cir. 1964); Whitt v. Reed, 239 S.W.2d 489 (Ky. 1951). *Violation of tenure law:* Babb v. Moore, 374 S.W.2d 516 (Ky. 1964); Bronaugh v. Murray, 172 S.W.2d 591 (Ky. 1951).

145. Reckless, unauthorized, or unlawful acts are often excluded from such immunity. Holman v. Wheeler, 677 P.2d 645 (Okla. 1983); Board of Trustees v. Holso, 584 P.2d 1009 (Wyo. 1978).

146. Wood v. Board of Educ., 412 S.W.2d 877 (Ky. 1967); Annots., *Personal Liability of Public School Teacher*, 34 A.L.R. 4th 228 (1984); *Personal Liability of Public School Executive or Administrative Officer*, 34 A.L.R. 4th 272 (1985); *Personal Liability in Negligence Action of Public School Employee Other than Teacher or . . . Administrative Officer*, 34 A.L.R. 4th 328 (1985).

147. Annot., *Indemnification of Public Officer or Employee*, 71 A.L.R. 3d 90 (1976).

148. *See, e.g.*, Baldi v. Mt. Sinai School Dist., 679 N.Y.S.2d 89 (1998); Doe v. Town of Blandford, 525 N.E.2d 403 (Mass. 1988); Professional Detail Service, Inc. v. Board of Educ., 479 N.Y.S.2d 40 (1984) (notice to wrong source); Faucher v. Auburn, 465 A.2d 1120 (Me. 1983).

149. *See generally* Annot., *Notice of Tort Claims against Municipality*, 59 A.L.R. 3d 93 (1974). SENA School Bus Co. v. Board of Educ., 677 P.2d 639 (N.M. 1984); Brown v. Portland School Dist., 617 P.2d 665 (Or. 1980).

Michigan, Nevada, and Washington courts found short-notice statutes to be unconstitutional. Hunter v. N. Mason High School, 539 P.2d 845 (Wash. 1974); Friedman v. Farmington Twp. School Dist., 198 N.W.2d 785

(Mich. 1972); Turner v. Staggs, 510 P.2d 879 (Nev. 1973).

150. *Re waiver of notice requirement:* Flandera v. Jamesville-Dewitt Cent. Schools, 369 N.Y.S.2d 920 (1975).

Re excuse for incapacity: Draper v. City of Los Angeles, 276 Cal. Rptr. 864 (1990); Welsh v. Berne-Knox-Westerlo Central School Dist., 479 N.Y.S.2d 567 (1984) (minor).

Re excuse for substantial compliance: Oliber v. Sioux City Comm. School Dist., 389 N.W.2d 665 (Iowa 1986); Urban v. Waterford-Halfmoon Unified Free School, 483 N.Y.S.2d 462 (1984); Lucas v. Indep. School Dist., 674 P.2d 1131 (Okla. 1983). *But see* Scarborough v. Granite School Dist., 531 P.2d 480 (Utah 1975).

Re excuse where no prejudice from delay: Murray v. LeRoy Cent. School Dist., 491 N.E. 2d 1100 (N.Y. 1985); Shope Enterprises Inc. v. Kent School Dist., 702 P.2d 499 (Wash. 1985).

Re excuse where notice received from other sources: Friedman v. Syosset Central School Dist., 545 N.Y.S.2d 814 (1989).

Other good cause: Valiquette v. City School Dist., 391 N.Y.S. 2d 23 (1977).

Variations in state law are noted in Annots.: *Tort Claims against Public Entity—Notice*, 44 A.L.R. 3d 1108 (1976); *Municipality—Notice of Injury—Waiver*, 65 A.L.R. 2d 1278 (1959) and 1996 pkt. part.; *Incapacity . . . as Affecting Notice of Claim Required as Condition of Holding Local Govt. Unit Liable for Personal Injury*, 44 A.L.R. 3d 1108 (1976) and 1996 pkt part; . . . *Minority as Affecting Notice of Claim Requirement*, 58 A.L.R. 4th 402 (1987).

151. *See, e.g.*, Turrentine v. Brokhaven Miss. School Dist., 794 F. Supp. 620 (S.D. Miss. 1992) (dollar cap for school bus accident—upheld); Doe v. Board of Educ., 453 A.2d 814, 822 (Md. 1982); *cf.* Thompson v. Sanford, 603 S.W.2d 932 (Ark. 1984); Packard v. Joint School Dist., 661 P.2d 770 (Idaho 1983).

❖ CHAPTER 5

Professional Employees: Rights and Obligations

❖ **CHAPTER DISCUSSION QUESTIONS**

❖ **CASES**

❖ **ENDNOTES**

[†]Indicates case with review questions.

There are many parallels of law among the states on school employment, but also some important variations. School nurses are classified and treated as professional employees in Pennsylvania, but not in Texas.[1] Teacher classifications (e.g., as substitute, temporary, probationary, or tenured) affect employment rights though all such employees perform substantially the same work. State variations also arise from diverse court interpretations of similar statutes. Thus where a teacher accepted temporary duty as a principal at a principal's salary scale, the court had a choice of deciding whether his claim for overtime pay was governed by the fixed compensation for principals or by his regular teacher contract. The law of the home state must, therefore, be considered with regard to teacher rights and duties.

STATUTORY AND NEGOTIATED PROVISIONS

Employment rights and obligations are basically defined by teacher contracts and by employment discrimination statutes. The first three major sections of this chapter address the various sources of contract obligations. The last section reviews the principal statutes governing discrimination in employment. Contract terms include those contained in individual teacher contracts, in union contracts, and in school statutes, which are by law made a part of all teacher contracts. School boards and teachers cannot surrender or alter terms imposed by school statutes and by lawful union agreements.

This chapter deals only with those laws specifically addressed to the employment relation. Other laws that also affect public school employees are considered in the following chapter.

EMPLOYMENT RIGHTS AND DUTIES

Employment Prerequisites

School districts may set job qualifications for teaching positions, provided they are reasonable and consistent with state law. However, a district's failure to follow its own employment standards and procedures is ground to overturn its employment decisions.[2]

State Certification

A person must have credentials specified by state law, often in the form of a state certificate, in order to be eligible for employment as a teacher.[3] The cases are divided on the question whether a school board may pay for work actually done by an uncertificated teacher.[4] Certification standards and records are administered by central state agencies in most states, but a state legislature may vest that authority in local school districts. Local school boards cannot waive certification requirements unless so authorized by statute.[5]

Two counter movements influence teacher certification. The movement to increase certification requirements for new teachers and for recertification of employed teachers arises from dissatisfaction with teaching results. The counter trend, to relax or change traditional certification standards, seeks to mitigate anticipated teacher shortages. The literature in the endnote indicates the varied certification standards of different states.[6]

Teaching eligibility is limited to the subjects or area covered by the issued certificate. A teacher certified for foreign language instruction may not be hired to teach English, nor can a teacher claim seniority rights to a position for which that teacher lacks certification. Conversely, a teacher may not, without cause, reject assignment to a position that is covered by his or her certificate.[7]

Many states require that certificates be registered with the employing school district *before* an employment contract is made or before commencement of work. The penalty for filing defaults varies with state law, from dismissal without pay, to surrender of employment rights for the period preceding proper filing, to excusal from any penalty if the filing default is considered harmless error.[8] Courts may also extend filing deadlines in special circumstances, e.g., for emergencies or bureaucratic delays.[9]

Suits to invalidate certification tests as biased because they result in disproportionate failures of one racial group have been largely rejected for reasons that are explained in Chapter 8.

Decertification. A teaching certificate is considered a species of "property" protected by constitutional law, so that its holder is entitled to due process hearings before it may be revoked. Grounds for decertification are specified by statutes (e.g., grave misconduct, disabling mental illness, or drug addiction). In some states such grounds must be shown to be job related. Courts decide what conduct or conditions are job related or adversely affect job performance based on the facts of each case.[10]

Decertification statutes operate independently of teacher dismissal statutes. For example, a school board may dismiss a teacher whose position is abolished, but it may not for that reason decertify the teacher, nor may nonrenewal of a teacher's contract affect the teacher's certification.[11]

Personal Conditions

Residency. School boards may require their employees to reside within the employing district, or may allow exemptions from in-district residency conditions unless denied that power by state law.[12] A minority of states prohibit local boards from imposing in-district residence for teacher employment.

Health. Physical and medical examinations, such as vision and hearing tests, and tests for communicable diseases and for addiction or mental disabilities may be lawfully required to ensure employee job fitness and the safety and health of others. Boards may suspend or dismiss employees whose condition poses a danger to the school population.[13] As explained in Chapter 6, employees may challenge medical examinations as being unreliable, or intrusive upon personal privacy, especially where the examination involves extraction and testing of body fluids or other body-invasive procedures.[14]

Citizenship.   School districts may constitutionally deny teaching posts to noncitizens, but may not require citizenship as a condition of employment in nonteaching, nonconfidential positions.[15] Teachers may be constitutionally required to take a loyalty oath, to uphold constitutional government against overthrow by force or violence, and may be denied employment for refusal to take a lawfully worded oath,[16] provided that the oath is limited to disavowal of subversive *action,* as opposed to avowal or disavowal of *ideas.*[17] The constitutional right to espouse ideas, however, does not include a right to refuse to cooperate in a school investigation of others.[18]

Conflicts of Interest.   Personal interests that conflict with official or work duties, be they financial, political, or familial, may disqualify an individual from holding school office or employment. State laws on conflicts of interest vary widely in defining the nature, magnitude, and duration of disqualifying conflicts, and in setting penalties for prohibited conflicts. A sampling of these variations is provided in the endnote.[19] The major disfavored conflicts involve (1) nepotism (i.e., favoritism of close relatives by blood or marriage), (2) holding outside employment or office, and (3) interests in outside organizations that do business with the school district.

Teacher Performance

School Assignments

Teachers have no general right to particular school or class assignments,[20] except in the uncommon instance where state law or contract agreement confers such a right.[21] The same is true of disciplinary assignments, so that school boards need not grant a due process hearing to an affected teacher.[22] To overturn a placement decision in court, a teacher must prove that the decision is based on an error of law or an abuse of administrative discretion, such as board violation of its own assignment rules, or transfers made to punish constitutionally protected speech, such as nonschool political activity or teacher criticism at a school-sponsored public forum.[23]

Implied Duties

Job duties, though not expressly specified in a contract, may be implied from the nature of the position. Courts decide what duties may be implied, but they will not imply a duty that is contrary to law or to an express contract provision. Implied duty disputes have diminished as union contracts increasingly specify that certain duties must be subject to additional negotiation or compensation.

Absent written negation, courts tend to uphold implication of noninstructional duties which they consider to be part of normal school operations and reasonable, e.g., supervision of study halls, cafeterias, and school-sponsored events (social or athletic) or attendance at open house, and teacher workshops.[24] Conversely, school authorities may not demand that teachers undertake work not reasonably related to their particular positions, such as supervision of after-school bowling that is not school sponsored, or the coaching of sports by a mathematics teacher.[25] Assignment of coaching duties to a physical education teacher was upheld as reasonable.[26] The availability of school volunteers or hired assistants to conduct nonacademic work does not of itself prevent assignment of teachers to such tasks.[27]

Teacher Evaluations and Ratings

Teacher evaluations have crucial career consequences, i.e., they affect job assignments, contract renewals, tenure eligibility, order of layoff, and disciplinary sanctions.[28] In most states, rating systems are developed by state education agencies for local district use, and may vary from the sparest categories of a "satisfactory" or "unsatisfactory" rating, to multiple scoring systems that rate different aspects of teacher performance.

Courts tend to insist on strict compliance with rating laws and procedures and to overturn ratings for lack of such compliance, unless rating defaults have no harmful consequences.[29] Where state law or union-bargained agreements give teachers a right to a hearing on contested ratings, school authorities have the burden of proof to support the adverse rating.[30]

Demotions

Administrative authority to change teacher assignments is limited where the transfer amounts to a demotion, but the law does not treat every disadvantageous transfer as a demotion,[31] and it does not forbid all demotions. Demotions are presumptively valid,[32] so that an aggrieved teacher must first prove that the transfer amounted to a demotion and then that the demotion was unlawful.

The definition of a "demotion" varies with state law. In some states a demotion occurs only if the transfer results in reduced compensation; in others a demotion occurs if a transfer results in a loss of professional rank, reputation, or prestige, as well as compensation; while in still other states, a demotion occurs only when the transfer produces a change in the teacher's certification or tenure area.[33] Where diminished professional prestige is considered a demotion, the teacher may show adverse community reactions or a loss of professional reputation or responsibility (namely, from principal to classroom teacher).[34]

Where state law requires a notice and hearing procedure on a proposed transfer, courts differ about whether those procedures are strictly required or loose directions, the absence of which may be excused as harmless error.[35] If a teacher fails to make timely demand for a demotion hearing, or to comply with statutory procedures, he or she may be barred from complaining of the alleged demotion.[36] Acceptance of a new assignment pending a hearing on an alleged demotion was not deemed to waive the objection, and even a resignation in protest of the challenged reassignment was held not to waive the right to contest it at a demanded hearing.[37] A well-publicized board resolution to eliminate a teaching position was held to satisfy the notice requirement for a demotional transfer, but other forms of indirect notice were held insufficient in law.[38]

Lawful and Unlawful Demotion. Demotions may be made for disciplinary reasons[39] or for nondisciplinary reasons, such as transfers necessitated by staff reductions where no comparable position survives the staff reductions. The rights of senior or tenured teachers to move into available positions provide independent grounds to resist a demotional transfer. Transfers made for unlawful reasons, such as a board's desire to avoid contract salary obligations, may always be challenged.[40] In special circumstances, state law barriers to demotional transfers may be superseded by superior federal law, e.g., where teacher reassignments are required to achieve racial desegregation of the teaching staff.[41]

Teacher Job Security

Job security provisions in school statutes and teacher contracts are not the same for tenured and nontenured teachers.

Nontenured Teachers—Nonrenewal

Teachers appointed for a limited time or purpose, such as temporary, substitute, or probationary teachers, are not on a tenure track. Probationers generally gain tenure upon completion of a prescribed period of satisfactory service, but until they gain tenure, school boards may decline to renew their contracts at the expiration of their current contract without giving a particular form of notice, hearing, or a statement of reasons for nonrenewal, unless their discretion is expressly constrained by statute or by union agreements.[42] A court may, of course, overturn a nonrenewal decision for board abuse of discretion.[43] It is not typical, however, for school boards to be given unbridled discretion for nonrenewal decisions. The law in most states requires school boards to notify probationers in writing before a specified calendar deadline of the district's intention not to renew the current contract.[44] Failure to provide the nonrenewal notice normally entitles the teacher to a renewal contract. The required details of nonrenewal notices vary with each state's law and each school district's union contract. The right to receive a statement of the board's reasons for nonrenewal, and some additional protections, such as the right to appeal nonrenewal decisions to a higher agency or court and a preservation of probationer rights of recall to newly opened positions, have been added in varying degree by school statutes in a number of states and by union-bargained agreements.[45]

Union-bargained procedures for nonrenewal must also be followed, even where they are stricter than those provided by statute. Minor notice defaults are treated strictly by courts in some states, but excused as harmless error by courts of other states.[46] Teachers may not willfully frustrate timely delivery of a notice and then seek to defeat it as legally defective.[47] A board may of course cure a notice default by a timely substitute notice. As with other challenges to administrative action, probationers seeking to overturn nonrenewals must prove that the board committed an error of law or abuse of discretion.

As explained in the next chapter, non-tenured teachers cannot claim a constitutional *property* interest in a teaching position. Most states do not create a *property* interest in probationary employment.[48] However, probationers may constitutionally challenge a nonrenewal decision that was made to punish the probationer for exercising a constitutional *liberty*, such as freedom of speech to promote unionization of teachers.[49] Here also the challenger has the burden of proving unconstitutional retaliation.[50]

Termination of employment before the expiration of an existing contract is governed by contract law and not by the law on renewals of expired contracts. Contracts may not be unilaterally terminated[51] except for a material contract breach. For such terminations, the burden would be on school authorities to prove that the teacher breached the employment contract.

Tenured Teachers

Job security is the central value of tenure status. One author described tenure well as "the right of employment for a continuing or indefinite period of time, subject to removal only for a cause prescribed by . . . law."[52] Tenure can only be created by state law, and does not exist under common law or constitutional law. Therefore, the rights incident to tenure may be altered by subsequent legislation.[53] In most states, tenure vests only on probationer completion of the designated period of continuous satisfactory service. Temporary or substitute teachers are not generally eligible for tenure, regardless of their length of service.[54]

The positions eligible for tenure depend on the law in each state.[55] Some states extend separate tenure to administrative positions while others limit tenure to teaching positions, even for principals or other administrators. In such states, a tenured teacher with greater service seniority may have a priority of retention right over a school principal.[56] Vested tenure is a constitutional property interest entitled to constitutional due process protection, but tenure statutes often provide even greater protective procedures.

Tenure rights are subject to cutoff or suspension only for statutorily specified grounds, such as position abolitions, staff reductions, or for "cause" that justifies teacher dismissal. Because tenure status creates a presumption of fitness for continued employment, school authorities must establish and prove the pertinent statutory grounds for a layoff, suspension, or discharge of a tenured teacher.

Required Service Period. The required period of satisfactory service to acquire tenure, usually three years, as set by statute, may not be waived, ignored, or modified.[57] The service period usually begins with commencement of service not date of hire.[58] Discontinuous part-time teaching does not generally qualify for tenure, unless state legislation allows credit for it. Part-time teachers are given service credit toward tenure under the laws of New York and Oklahoma, but not of Alaska and Louisiana.[59] In several states, service credit accrues only if the teacher devoted at least half of work time to the area or subject for which tenure is sought.[60] A teacher who breaks continuous service by resignation or voluntary (not maternity) leave may be held to forfeit service credit.[61] Maternity leave may no longer be treated as a break in employment service by reason of superceding federal laws on gender discrimination.

State laws vary on the portability of service credit earned in one school district toward tenure service in another district within the same state, with some states permitting such transfer of service and others prohibiting it.[62] Portability may also be affected by special statutes governing school reorganizations and school district consolidations. The portability of tenure also varies with the peculiarities of each state's law.[63]

Scope of Tenure.   Where tenure is confined to teaching, nonteaching service may be excluded in calculating tenure credit or seniority rank.[64] In Pennsylvania, a teacher's tenure extends to all positions for which the teacher is certified, regardless of teaching lack of service in positions covered by the certificate, while other states limit tenure to the area of actual teaching service.[65] New York's complex system of tenure by area rather than subjects actually taught must be left to fuller study elsewhere, but under that system, courts must determine which positions fall within a recognized tenure area.[66]

Tenure by Official Default.   Where official misconduct would cause denial of tenure, courts of equity may order that tenure be granted, but such extraordinary relief lies wholly within a court's discretion.[67] A school board that failed to complete removal proceedings prior to expiration of the teacher's probationary period, was enjoined from denying tenure,[68] but where a board revoked preliminary approval for tenure following the probationer's arrest and consequent inability to complete his current contract, the court upheld the denial of tenure.[69] Where a board failed to give legally required notices of intention not to reemploy a probationer for the final year of required service for tenure, some courts ordered that tenure be granted, while others upheld denials of tenure and limited the teacher remedy to recovery of money damages or to another year of employment.[70]

Union Contract Terms

The law on teacher unionization and collective bargaining is too massive for full treatment here, yet too important to ignore completely. The following overview sketches the major issues on teacher collective bargaining.

Bargaining Authority

Teachers have a constitutional right to form or join labor organizations,[71] but that right does not include a right to compel school districts to bargain with their association. The overwhelming majority of courts found no right to collective negotiation at common law; school districts may refuse to engage in collective bargaining unless required to do so by state legislation. The National Labor Relations Act excludes state and local agencies from its requirements. Since 1959, practically every state has enacted laws to permit some form of teacher collective activity, but the states have not developed a common model of teacher labor relations,[72] and state legislatures failed to dovetail their new teacher labor relations statutes with older school statutes, thereby raising additional problems for court solution.

The question whether school boards could claim implied authority to engage in collective negotiations voluntarily is now largely mooted by bargaining statutes that cover board authority to bargain collective contracts.

Union Representation

Bargaining Units. The size and composition of bargaining units affect both the employees placed in a given unit and the unions that compete to represent the unit. The dominant legal standards for determining the composition of a unit are not always harmonious, namely, that the fewer the number of units in an enterprise, the better for the sake of efficiency and economy; but that employees in each unit should have a "community of interest" rather than conflicting interests in the setting of bargaining goals or priorities.[73] The separation of professional and nonprofessional employee bargaining units may avoid bargaining tensions between their respective interests, but such separation may be impractical and therefore not required in very small school districts.[74] State labor boards generally determine the "appropriate bargaining unit," and also determine and certify which union organization is entitled to act as the "bargaining representative" of that unit. For specified employee groups, e.g., supervisors, security personnel, or confidential secretaries, a legislature may require they be placed in an exclusive bargaining unit.[75]

In most states, the officially certified union representative becomes the *exclusive* bargaining agent for all unit members, including those who do not wish to be so represented.[76] Exclusive representation was held constitutional on the grounds that the state's strong interest in effective labor relations through exclusive unit representation outweighs the burden on the constitutional right of dissidents not to associate with the selected union.[77]

Bargainable Matters. The scope of collective negotiations largely turns on the following questions: What subjects are required to be bargained, or may optionally be bargained, or can only be "discussed" with final decision reserved to the school discretion as part of its "management rights"? When labor disputes arise, what methods of settling them are mandated or permitted by law? "Bargaining" requires the parties to negotiate on bargainable issues until they arrive at a mutually satisfactory agreement or at an impasse for which the law would allow other means of resolution. Some states require the parties to bargain on specified labor topics; while others permit, but do not mandate bargaining, and still others allow only "meet and discuss" negotiations for some or all subjects of negotiation.[78] In some states, state labor boards determine whether disputed topics are subject to particular types of bargaining.

Mandatory Bargaining.   Most states permit mutual bargaining on all topics other than those expressly classified as "management rights" or "meet and discuss" issues. Statutory descriptions of nonbargainable subjects vary from nonspecific categories, e.g., "managerial rights," to specific subject itemization, e.g., tenure rights, pension rights, or budget items.[79] A wide path has been cut around "managerial rights" limits in a growing number of states by court decisions that distinguish inability to bargain the substance of managerial rights from a right to bargain on the impacts of managerial decisions on working terms and conditions, including the procedures for implementing management decisions.[80] For example, in Connecticut, a government employer was required to negotiate the impact of a managerial decision to institute a smoke-free workplace policy, and in New York a school district could not impose a non-negotiated smoking ban in empty buses because the labor law was held to require bargaining on secondary impacts, even though a state smoke-free environment statute authorized the ban.[81] In New York class size was not mandatorily bargainable but teacher workloads (affected by class size) were held bargainable.[82]

In the absence of legislative direction, some courts adopted other tests, with most favoring a balancing approach to determine whether exclusive school board control over a given subject outweighs or is outweighed by employee interests in that subject.[83] The case-by-case approach has produced varied results from state to state. The courts of different states have not agreed on the bargainability of class size,[84] and on the setting of working hours and length of the school day.[85] The school calendar was considered bargainable in Wisconsin with dictum hinting that curriculum matters were not bargainable.[86] Legislatures can, of course, override court interpretations, as did the Nevada legislature, which reacted by enacting laws to exclude from mandatory bargaining such items as class size, school calendar, workload, and teacher selection.[87] A sampling of other items subject to diverse treatments is given in the endnote.[88]

Permissive Bargaining.   Where bargaining is neither mandated nor prohibited, "permissive" bargaining offers an important alternative, and it has been upheld[89] when not found to be *ultra vires* or contrary to public policy. The case trend, particularly in industrial states, favors permissive bargaining on any subject not "explicitly and definitely prohibited by statute."[90]

School Statute–Labor Law Conflicts.   Most states lack a universal rule regarding the impact of labor and education statutes where they overlap or conflict. In Connecticut and Ohio, a bargained agreement "shall prevail" over any conflicting law or regulation, but in Massachusetts, prior school laws were held to prevail over later inconsistent labor laws.[91] Courts may read their labor laws narrowly to restrict the scope of bargaining, while others read education statutes broadly to make them control in doubtful situations.[92] Courts may subordinate a labor statute to a school statute where the latter affords greater teacher protections than bargained agreements or labor arbitration (e.g., on dismissal, maternity leave, superannuation benefits, layoff, and seniority credit).[93] Nor would courts permit a bargained procedure to allow "back door" grant of tenure or union control over distribution of negotiated wage benefits.[94] While labor agreements may lawfully affect layoffs in ways not contemplated by school statutes, courts will not allow such agreements to diminish rights accorded teachers under tenure statutes.[95]

Union Fees and Privileges.   In a majority of states, union representatives may bargain for certain union rights and privileges, such as employer collection of union dues or fees by payroll deductions, but state laws vary considerably in detail.[96] The Supreme Court upheld the constitutionality of such bargaining, but it limited union assessment of representation fees against nonunion employees to amounts that are reasonably related to union representation costs.[97] In a minority of states "right to work" laws restrict payroll collections of union dues and service fees.[98] Union bargaining for use of school facilities by the union representation, including agreement to exclude other unions from like privileges, was held constitutional as justified by the state interest in promoting effective labor relations.[99]

Dispute Resolution

Labor statutes generally prescribe and limit the means of resolving different kinds of labor disputes, namely, *representation disputes,* which involve contests for union appointment and certification as bargaining representatives; *interest disputes,* which involve disagreements on contract negotiation questions; and *grievance disputes,* which involve disputes on the interpretation and performance obligations under an existing union contract.

Mediation and Arbitration.   In mediation, a designated third party attempts to bring negotiating parties into agreement, but unlike arbitration, mediation relies only on persuasion. In some states, mediation efforts must be exhausted before either party can terminate bargaining and resort to other measures.

Arbitration involves submission of dispute questions to an arbitrator or panel of arbitrators. A number of states make *grievance arbitration* mandatory while making *interest arbitration* optional,[100] except for security personnel (guards and safety employees), for whom interest arbitration is also often made compulsory.

Arbitration issues parallel those of bargaining, i.e., what matters are arbitrable, whether arbitration is mandatory or optional, whether arbitration is binding or advisory, and the scope of arbitrator authority to order particular remedies. As with bargaining, the treatment of these questions varies from state to state. If a disputed matter is considered a managerial right, it cannot be a subject of arbitration.[101] In several states interest arbitration is banned on particular subjects, such as position elimination, board examination of teachers' files, teacher evaluation, leaves of absence, teacher nonrenewal, and teacher discharge for cause.[102] Other illustrations of state divisions on the arbitrability of particular topics appear in the endnotes.[103]

Where the law or contracts are unclear on the scope of arbitration, many courts favor the following rules: Any subject not excluded by law or agreement is arbitrable; and the scope of grievance arbitration is to be determined by the "essence" of the entire labor agreement, including the negotiating background as well as contract language.[104] However, where the labor agreement expressly subjects particular matters of disputes to an alternative settlement procedure, grievance arbitration may be foreclosed.[105]

Arbitration decisions are presumptively valid and upheld as long as they are rationally related to and derived from the parties' agreement,[106] but courts will overturn awards that are contrary to law or to the terms of arbitration.[107] The cases are mixed on the forms of relief that an arbitrator may give. One case overturned an arbitrator's orders to renew a teacher's contract while another upheld arbitrator authority to award monetary recovery for the same grievance.[108] Courts may, but are loathe to, sustain arbitration orders that require the grant of tenure, even to an improperly dismissed teacher.[109]

Grievance Arbitration.   While grievance issues often involve contract interpretation, they also involve disagreements on facts, i.e., conflicting versions of events that led up to the grievance. The filing of a grievance usually effects a "stay" or freeze of the status quo to prevent disciplinary measures against a teacher, unless one party can convince a court to lift that stay.[110] The freeze, time delays, and costs incurred in pursuing a grievance may deter pursuit of contesting grievances.

Strikes.   Public school strikes were not recognized at common law and must be authorized by legislation,[111] but a growing number of states have granted teachers a limited right to strike under specified conditions.[112]

A labor statute may define a strike in very broad terms: Strike means concerted action in failing to report for duty; the willful absence from one's position; the stoppage of work, a slowdown, or the absence in whole or in part from the full, faithful, and proper performance of the duties of employment for the purpose of inducing, influencing, or coercing a change in the conditions, compensation, or other rights, privileges, or obligations of employment. Some forms of concerted action, such as slowdowns, "going by the book" (refusing to perform duties not specified in written contracts), and massive sick call-ins, are used occasionally as a negotiation weapon, but they carry the risk of being adjudged unlawful stoppages.[113] The legality of labor picketing depends on its form and purpose. Purely *informational* picketing is constitutionally protected *speech*, but picketing that trespasses or blockades others, or incites an illegal stoppage, is not.[114]

Strike Limitations. Many labor statutes limit the purposes, timing, and duration of teacher strikes. For example, strikes may not be permitted to protest grievances under existing contracts, or unfair labor complaints, or to support organization drives or strikes by other groups. Most statutes prohibit strikes before the parties have arrived at a negotiation impasse and have exhausted statutory mediation and fact finding. They typically authorize court termination of legally commenced strikes where the strike poses a danger to public health, safety, or public welfare.[115] The degree of danger that justifies strike injunctions is left largely to court discretion, but inconvenience alone is not sufficient.[116] Courts may refuse to enjoin even an admittedly harmful strike if they conclude that the public interest in achieving labor settlement is of greater importance than the resumption of school service.[117]

Strike Sanctions. Participants in an illegal strike are subject to contempt of court penalties of monetary fines or imprisonment, and in some states to statutory fines and penalties.[118] The ultimate sanction of discharge may be imposed by law on various grounds, i.e., unauthorized absence, insubordination, or abandonment of the striker's position.[119]

SUSPENSION AND TERMINATION OF EMPLOYMENT

In nonstrike situations, professional employment may be terminated voluntarily by resignation or abandonment, or involuntarily by nonrenewals, layoffs, suspensions, or discharge for cause.

Resignation and Abandonment

A teacher can forfeit all employment rights, including tenure by resignation or abandonment.[120] It is imperative, therefore, to know what acts effect a binding resignation or abandonment.

Unless a statute requires specific resignation formalities,[121] any statement or act that manifests an intent to abandon a position may effect a resignation, such as not showing up for work, acceptance of another full-time job, or rejection of tendered work assignments.[122] Other examples of conduct manifesting an intent to resign appear in the endnotes.[123] Courts have ruled both ways on the question whether absences of striking teachers convey an intent to abandon their position.[124]

A resignation must be knowing, voluntary, and express a clear intent to abandon. School authorities may not seize on equivocal statements to claim a resignation such as objection to a new assignment or calling in sick.[125] A resignation must be accepted as tendered, and any material change of its terms by the recipient may invalidate the acceptance.[126] Resignations obtained by coercion or undue influence, or if made under excusable mistake of material facts, are legally void,[127] but resignations submitted to avoid adverse board charges or as part of a settlement agreement are not deemed coercive.[128]

A generally worded resignation may surrender all employment with the school district,[129] but a resignation that referred only to a subordinate position was held not to surrender rights to the other positions.[130] In some states, written resignations become final and irrevocable only when formally accepted by the school board, so that a teacher could withdraw a resignation before board acceptance, but in others, resignations become irrevocable on proper delivery, without need for board acceptance.[131]

Nonrenewal of Probationer Contracts

See the earlier section titled "Nontenured Teachers—Nonrenewal."

Reductions in Force (RIF)

RIF statutes authorize reductions in school staff in specified circumstances and in no way impugn the reputation of released teachers.

RIF dismissals are not subject to the rules that govern non-RIF dismissals, such as dismissals of tenured teachers or nonrenewal of probationers.[132]

The major RIF issues were crisply summarized as follows: "when to RIF, whom to RIF, and how to RIF,"[133] i.e., whether statutory grounds exist to conduct a RIF; whether the RIF was properly implemented; and whether the legally required order of teacher retention, reassignment, and dismissal was observed. Because RIF statutes vary in significant details they must be reviewed in each case. The following discussion outlines major considerations that are common to most RIFs.

Grounds for RIF.   RIFs may only be undertaken for purposes listed in the RIF statute,[134] the most common being fiscal shortfalls, declining enrollments, and substantial reorganizations of schools and school programs. Fiscal shortfall, though an important factor, may not always suffice.[135] Courts have overturned position abolitions in fiscally distressed districts where abolished positions were deemed necessary to carry out state-mandated duties or to maintain quality education.[136]

The determination whether necessary conditions exist to authorize a RIF lies initially with a school board so that challengers have the burden of proving that the board's findings were erroneous.[137] Board decisions may be overturned if nominally abolished positions were not truly eliminated, but only retitled.[138] On the other hand, redistribution of the duties of an eliminated position to a different surviving position is lawful.[139]

Order of Release and Recall.   The ranking of teacher priority of retention and recall is generally set by law. Priority of retention is normally given to qualified tenured teachers over nontenured teachers,[140] followed by seniority preferences among qualified teachers within the same rank.[141] Tenured teachers on leave retain their priority rank, and probationers may be released to make way for returning tenured teachers.[142]

The calculation of seniority service has significant impact. For example, service credit for military, maternity, or approved leaves may be required by federal or state law,[143] while other types of leave (e.g., leaves without pay) may not count toward seniority credit.[144] Seniority rank that is forfeited by resignation and retirement may not be revived by subsequent reemployment.[145]

The law does not require a school district to retain unneeded teachers.[146] In school district mergers, the seniority rankings of the merged staff will depend on the governing statute. Some courts read their law to credit teacher service in either system,[147] but a statute that created a new regional school vested staffing discretion in the board of the new school, without reference to previously earned seniority.[148]

The law in many states requires school boards to realign the positions not eliminated by a RIF in order to ensure fairness to teachers with seniority, but the case law on the proper criteria of a "reasonable" realignment is far from uniform.[149]

Discharge for Cause

As used in this section, *discharge* refers to termination of employment for a "just cause," usually one specified by school statutes. Unlike nonrenewals and RIF dismissals, just cause discharges may be made at any time with respect to any employee, and terminates all employment rights with the employer district. In most states, the statutory grounds for discharge are exclusive, and statutory hearings must be accorded to discharged teachers who request them. Discharge for reasons or under procedures other than those specified by law are subject to reversal.[150] Indeed, a wrongful discharge could constitute a breach of contract, rendering the district liable to reinstate the employee with compensation for back wages, lost fringe benefits, and possibly for monetary damages for injury to the teacher's reputation.[151]

Grounds for Discharge

The statutory grounds for discharge encompass a broad range of acts, many of which permit discharge under several listed grounds. The principal grounds—*incompetency, incapacity, insubordination, unprofessional conduct, neglect of duty, immorality, intemperance,* and *sufficient cause*[152]—have withstood constitutional challenge that they are unconstitutionally vague.[153]

Practically every ground for discharge embraces the core idea of "fitness" to be a teacher, but even that standard invites diverse readings. Some courts construe discharge statutes as applying only to ability to function as a teacher while others read them to prohibit conduct that undermines a teacher's broader duty to be a role model for students. Courts further differ on the impact of particular conduct, thus reflecting different expectations and mores.[154] They can widen or narrow the meaning and operation of a given ground as well as excuse otherwise condemned conduct in "extenuating circumstances." The burden of proving grounds for discharge lies with the school board, and its findings must be supported by substantial evidence.[155]

Discharge statutes raise other issues, namely, whether the governing law requires that a teacher be given a warning and an opportunity for "remediation" (i.e., rehabilitation) before discharge proceedings are undertaken, and whether the discharge proceedings afforded the teacher "due process." Courts may always overturn a discharge which they find to be unreasonable and excessive.[156] Discharge statutes *authorize,* but generally do not *command,* school boards to impose the strongest penalty of discharge for teacher misconduct, so that school boards have the discretion to impose lesser disciplinary penalties.

Where remediation efforts are required, the threshold issue is whether the alleged misconduct is in fact "remediable." Only if it is must remediation be attempted.[157] Board failure to follow statutory procedures or procedures required by union agreements will void a discharge, regardless of the teacher's alleged misconduct.

Incompetence.   "Incompetence" is a sufficiently expansive concept to encompass most other specified grounds for discharge. It may embrace performance deficiency, or personal incapacity or character defect,[158] and may cover the following conditions:

1.   Physical or mental incapacity,
2.   Lack of knowledge or inability to impart knowledge,
3.   Failure to adapt to new teaching methods,
4.   Physical mistreatment of students,
5.   Violation of school rules,
6.   Violation of duties to superiors or coworkers,
7.   Lack of cooperation,
8.   Persistent negligence,
9.   Failure to maintain discipline, or
10.   Personal misconduct, in or out of school[159]

Isolated incidents of incompetence may be sufficiently serious to sustain discharge, but incompetence charges usually involve a pattern of behavior.

Incapacity.   Serious physical, mental, or emotional illness or disability of an indefinite duration is generally grounds for discharge,[160] but discharge for accommodatable disability has been foreclosed by the Americans with Disabilities Act, which is discussed later in this chapter.

Insubordination.   Insubordination commonly involves a series of acts, but a single incident, if sufficiently serious, may support discharge. Courts look to the gravity and persistence of insubordination in deciding whether discharge is warranted.[161] Examples of insubordination include unauthorized absence from work, encouraging student disobedience or disrespect, violation of corporal punishment regulations, and untoward criticism of school superiors.[162] Teacher initiation of a federal narcotics investigation without the knowledge or approval of superiors, and teacher failure to report suspicious student conduct were held to support discharge for insubordination.[163]

Innocent mistakes are not insubordinate, as where a teacher who was late the first day of the school term due to her registration for graduate studies at a nearby university[164] but a school principal who left students unsupervised to register for summer programs was held insubordinate.[165]

Unprofessional Conduct.   Like "conduct unbecoming a teacher," this standard potentially includes the use of offensive language, abuse of corporal punishment, threats and insults to fellow teachers, taking time off without permission, and shoplifting.[166] Other examples are use of classroom time to promote partisan political causes, distributing poems that herald the joys of marijuana, encourage students to ignore family morals, improper sexual contacts, and fomenting teacher disloyalty.[167] As with other grounds, court appraisals of conduct range from strict to indulgent. One court held that a teacher who fought with a rowdy student and a teacher who had private consensual sexual relations with a former student could not be dismissed for unprofessional conduct.[168] But a teacher who dressed and undressed a publicly exposed mannequin in a lewd and suggestive manner was dischargeable for unprofessional conduct.[169]

Immorality.   The Supreme Court library book removal case noted in Chapter 2 recognized the educational interest in moral standards:

> We are, therefore, in full agreement . . . that there is a legitimate and substantial interest in promoting . . . traditional values, be they social, moral, or political. [*Board of Educ. v. Pico,* 457 U.S. 853 (1982)]

Immorality charges chiefly involve dishonesty, sexual misconduct, and criminal acts. Courts have divided on the question whether alleged immoral conduct must be shown to adversely affect teaching performance and school relationships, or need only undermine the teacher's role as exemplar for school children, regardless of teaching proficiency or community support.[170] They also differ widely on the relevance of surrounding circumstances, i.e., whether the misconduct occurs at or away from school, with students or school personnel; whether it is treated in law as a crime; whether it gained public notoriety; and how it affected relationships within the school and with the surrounding community. Some examples of these variations appear in the endnotes.[171]

Dishonesty may justify discharge,[172] but here also courts must decide if a particular offense is sufficiently grave to warrant discharge. Misappropriation of school funds sustained discharge, while negligent mishandling of funds did not.[173] Acquittal of a criminal charge does not preclude school discharge of a teacher on the same evidence.[174] Regional variations appear in drug abuse cases. Private possession of marijuana was grounds for discharge in Florida and Illinois, but not in West Virginia and California.[175]

Charges of sexual misconduct pose special problems for school administrators. On one hand, they risk criticism and potential liability for failure promptly to investigate and prosecute sexual misconduct. On the other hand, they face criticism for failure to deal fairly with accused teachers. Court appraisals of sexual immorality vary widely, but the eruption of teacher sexual abuse of school students will likely induce stricter standards than those previously indulged. Two courts recently upheld school board discharge of tenured teachers for sexual abuse of students that occurred 16 and 24 years prior to its disclosure and to board initiation of discharge proceedings.[176] They found no denial of due process since the boards acted promptly on receipt of admittedly late reports by the former students.

Immorality decisions rest heavily on particular case circumstances.[177] For instance, a recent Missouri case sustained teacher discharge although the school district could not prove actual sexual contact between a teacher and student. In that case, a private detective hired by the parents of a 14-year-old eighth-grade student observed her enter and remain at the home of a probationary teacher-coach until nearly midnight and reported his observations to the police. The police went to the probationer's residence to inquire of the child, but the teacher denied them entry, and when asked if he had contact with her, he admitted that he had spoken to her by phone. The police left, but kept the house under observation, and shortly thereafter caught the girl leaving the property by the back alley. Following his discharge for immorality, the teacher argued that the student's presence in his home was insufficient to prove immorality, but the court upheld the discharge.[178]

With regard to extramarital cohabitation and pregnancy, one case line disfavors teacher discharge unless there is clear factual proof that such circumstances adversely affect job performance.[179] Episodic adultery, though publicly known, was held insufficient cause for discharge where the general community supported the adulterous teacher.[180]

The case law on discharge for homosexual conduct (here used also to denote lesbian sexual acts) remains somewhat mixed. Distinctions may be drawn between the state's power to criminalize sodomy, which was upheld by the Supreme Court,[181] and the intent of teacher discharge statutes. Further distinctions must be noted between expression and conduct. Advocating acceptance of homosexual lifestyles is constitutionally protected expression, while oppressing persons because of their homosexual orientation is prohibited by antidiscrimination laws.[182] The question of whether homosexual *conduct* falls within the immorality ban of teacher discharge statutes presents a different issue. Circumstances will control the finding whether homosexual conduct, such as teacher publication of homosexual relations, suffices to sustain discharge, and whether a court must find that such disclosure destroys teacher effectiveness or fitness as a role model.[183]

Vulgar Language.   Grossly offensive language is grounds for discharge in some states, but is often an element of other charges.[184] Case treatment of vulgarity varies with the place and circumstances of its delivery. One court overturned the discharge of a teacher who wrote a grossly vulgar letter addressed to a former student that was read by the addressee's mother, on its reasoning that the letter might not have been so offensive to the son as it was to his mother.[185] Another court reinstated a teacher who failed to halt a school presentation that included profane, obscene, distasteful, and inappropriate language because it found extenuating circumstances in the failure of school authorities to interrupt the program, the improbability of a repetition, and the lack of proof of adverse impact on teaching ability.[186] The *Brown* case (reported at the end of Chapter 3), the *Lacks* case (reported at the end of Chapter 6), and the *Bethel* decision (reported at the end of Chapter 7) confirm the varied perception of vulgarity among judges.

Remedies for Wrongful Discharge

Wrongfully discharged teachers may recover lost back wages and fringe benefits, less any substitute earnings they made or reasonably could have made following the breach.[187] The general duty under contract law to mitigate damages does not require teachers to take inferior employment or incur unreasonable burdens, such as pursuing work in a distant region.[188] The school board has the burden of proving that the teacher failed to mitigate damages.[189] Where monetary damages alone cannot adequately compensate for a contract breach, i.e., where the breach resulted in loss of tenure or other important status, courts may order reinstatement to the prior position and status.

EMPLOYMENT DISCRIMINATION

Federal antidiscrimination laws fall into three distinct categories: laws that specifically address discrimination in employment; laws that prohibit discrimination only in federally aided programs; and laws that protect citizen rights generally, without regard to employment or federal aid status. This section discusses the laws that relate only to employment discrimination. The broader group is discussed in Chapter 8. State discrimination laws, which often mirror the more intensely used federal laws, are not reviewed here.

The major employment specific discrimination statutes are Title VII of the Civil Rights Act of 1964; the Equal Pay Act of 1964; the Americans with Disabilities Act of 1990 (ADA, Title I); and the Age Discrimination in Employment Act of 1967 (ADEA).

It is helpful to note preliminarily that these laws have some common features with respect to the parties they cover and the proofs and defenses those parties must present in order to prevail. Employers and unions are subject to these laws. Individual supervisors, teachers, or other employees are not subject to personal liability under them for their discriminatory acts.[190] Relief against such individuals must be sought under other law.

Prohibited discrimination under these statutes may be shown either by proof of *intentional adverse treatment* against a member of the protected class, or indirectly by proof that a challenge practice has *disparate adverse impacts* on the protected class. In disparate impact cases, courts impose a shifting burden of proof whereby evidence of disparate impacts raises a rebuttable inference of discrimination, notwithstanding lack of proof of actual discriminatory intent. This shifts the burden of defense to the employer who must produce a justifying nondiscriminatory reason for the challenged practice in order to avoid liability. Only if such rebuttal evidence is produced does the burden of proof shift back to the complainant to show that the asserted justification is only a pretext or that the employer could have achieved a justified need by less discriminatory means.[191]

Title VII of the Civil Rights Act of 1964

Title VII, the most widely litigated employee grievance statute, prohibits *employment discrimination* by employers and unions with regard to an individual's *race, color, religion, sex*, or *national origin*. The law specifically exempts from its prohibitions employment preferences or differentials that are based on bona fide seniority or merit systems, occupational qualifications, or business necessity. It also *exempts* decisions based on religion, sex, or national origin, where those traits are bona fide job qualifications for the conduct of a particular enterprise (religious or business necessity). Title VII covers all aspects of employment, from hiring to discharge, and all policies or actions regarding ". . . compensation, terms, conditions, or privileges of employment" including actions that "limit, segregate, or classify . . . employees . . . in any way which would deprive . . . any individual of employment opportunities. . ." § 703(a). The Pregnancy Discrimination Act amended Title VII expressly to require that pregnancy, childbirth, or related medical conditions be treated no less favorably than other work-limiting conditions.[192]

Title VII is not a minority protection statute. It protects caucasians as well as nonwhites from race-based discrimination; males as well as females from gender discrimination; and, as recently decided, same-sex harassment and gender orientation harassment. Title VII also prohibits affirmative action preferences that are not justified to remedy for past discrimination. These aspects of Title VII coverage are elaborated in the *Taxman, Oncale,* and *Burlington* cases, which appear at the end of this chapter.

Taxman overturned a public school affirmative action policy and appointment whereunder race was used to decide which of two equally qualified women with equal seniority should get the only available teaching position following a school RIF. In like manner, the same court held that an affirmative action hiring preference of a black applicant for a technician job over an equally qualified white applicant also violated Title VII.[193] The *Oncale* case explained the basis for holding an employer liable for same-sex workplace harassment. *Burlington* modified the prior law by promulgating different rules for different kinds of harassments. In that connection, it refined the law governing employer burdens of proof in cases of *supervisor* harassment. The *Burlington* ruling defies simplification but is fairly summarized in its following holding:

> An employer is subject to vicarious liability to a victimized employee for an actionable hostile environment created by a supervisor with immediate (or successively higher) authority over the employee. *When no tangible employment action is taken, a defending employer may raise an affirmative defense to liability or damages.* . . . The defense comprises two necessary elements: (a) that the employer exercised reasonable care to prevent and correct promptly any sexually harassing behavior, and (b) that the plaintiff employee unreasonably failed to take advantage of any preventive or corrective opportunities provided by the employer or to avoid harm otherwise. . . . . . . And while proof that an employee failed to fulfill the corresponding obligation of reasonable care to avoid harm is not limited . . . a demonstration of such failure will normally suffice to satisfy the employer's burden. . . . *No affirmative defense is available, however, when the supervisor's harassment culminates in a tangible employment action,* such as discharge, demotion, or undesirable reassignment. (Emphasis added)

The question whether workplace mistreatment creates a "hostile working environment" or whether the complainant invited or was unfazed by alleged harassing conduct is governed by the following Supreme Court guideline:

> Conduct that is not severe or pervasive enough to create an *objectively* hostile or abusive working environment— . . . that a *reasonable* person would [not] find hostile or abusive—is beyond Title VII's purview. Likewise, if the victim does not *subjectively* perceive the environment to be abusive . . . there is no Title VII violation. . . . This is not, and . . . cannot be a mathematically precise test. [*See Harris v. Forklift Systems Inc.,* 114 S. Ct. 367, 370–1 (1993)]. (Emphasis added)

Harris and later cases suggest consideration of the following factors: the frequency and severity of the conduct; whether it was physically threatening or humiliating; and whether it affected the psychological well-being, work performance, or economic condition of the claimant. Thus, particular offensive actions may be sufficiently severe or pervasive to create a hostile workplace environment in some work contexts, but not in others. A stark example appeared in a recent decision by the Eleventh Circuit Court of Appeals, which held that while a male supervisor's alleged staring, sniffing, and bumping of a female subordinate over an 11-month period was offensive, it was not, as a matter of law, sufficiently severe or pervasive to constitute an actionable Title VII sexual harassment.[194] The court there cited cases from six other federal circuits that considered even more offensive conduct to be insufficient to meet the Title VII severity/pervasive test of sexual harassment.

Acts of overt discrimination, such as passing over a female candidate to appoint a less qualified male candidate and using impermissible factors of race or gender in making employment-related decisions, present straightforward cases for VII relief.[195] Employers may rebut a discrimination charge by showing a valid nondiscriminatory reason for a hiring preference, e.g., hiring a male rather than a female applicant who had a higher degree because the male applicant could be hired at a lower salary and perform supplemental coaching duties.[196] Changes in employment status or compensation that may be considered adverse or discriminatory, absent employer justification (such as poor job performance or position eliminations), include reduced compensation or benefits, loss of supervisory rank, or significant responsibilities, or other disadvantages that are unique to a particular situation.[197]

Title VII also effected a major change in employment and benefits plans. The Supreme Court decided that Title VII prohibited the use of gender-based life expectancy tables for calculating employee retirement contributions or benefits.[198] However, benefit plans that incidentally have unequal impacts but are not tied to gender remain lawful, e.g., plans that provide extra benefits to heads of households (though more males fit that category).

Equal Pay Act of 1964

The Equal Pay Act of 1964 prohibits wage discrimination on account of sex; hence, an employer may not pay different wages to men and women for work in like positions that require equal skill, effort, and responsibility. Like Title VII, this Act exempts wage differentials based on a *seniority* or *merit system* and it prohibits affirmative action preferences of higher pay to women than to men for equal work.[199] The question of what positions involve "equal work" arises where positions within the same salary class involve different "workload" hours. Higher pay for a boys' coaching position that involves longer hours than a girls' coaching position would not violate the act as long as access to the higher pay position is restricted only by bona fide employment qualifications or by business needs. Even so, one court relied on salary classification rather than workload in holding that a female professor whose teaching hours doubled those of a male professor had no Equal Pay Act complaint, though she might assert a Title VII complaint for gender bias in work assignments.[200] The argument that the Equal Pay Act required like compensation for work of "comparable worth" though performed in different positions has not taken hold in the law.

Americans with Disabilities Act of 1990 (ADA)

The ADA complements the Rehabilitation Act of 1973, which is not confined to employment issues. Title II of the ADA prohibits discrimination, by any government entity, including school districts, in all aspects of employment from hire through discharge. The broader aspects of the ADA, along with the Rehabilitation Act (§ 504), will be discussed in Chapter 8.

The ADA does not cover all personal impairments or workplace limitations, hence the interpretation of its key provision is crucial to determining what employees can claim its protections. The act provides that no employer or union "shall discriminate against a *qualified individual with a disability because of* the disability. . . ." It defines *disability* as "(A) a physical or mental *impairment that substantially limits* one or more of the *major life activities of such individual*" and it defines *qualified individual* as "an individual . . . who, *with or without reasonable accommodation,* can perform *the essential functions* of the employment position that such individual holds or desires." 42 U.S.C. § 12111(8) (Emphasis added) The *Salmon* case at the end of this chapter illustrates the interpretive problems raised by the ADA. In sum, a grievant must show that he or she (1) has a "disability"; (2) is "a qualified individual" for the benefit in question; and (3) was discriminated against "because of" the disability.

What Is an ADA "Disability"?

The Supreme Court recently held that a correctable impairment is not a "disability" within the meaning of the ADA, so that persons suffering correctable impairments are not covered by or entitled to ADA relief. The Court there held that pilots with severe myopia did not have a "disability" that "substantially limits" a major life activity because their myopia was correctible with proper lenses, and because they could find work in a broad class of jobs for which they were trained, though not the work they preferred as commercial airline pilots. For like reasons, it held that a driver with medically correctable hypertension could not claim ADA disability or job discrimination.[201] These decisions significantly shrink the range of impairments covered by the ADA, but they also confirmed prior rulings that employers may not presume that particular illness or limitation renders a person unqualified to perform the essential functions of a particular job. School districts may not, therefore, deny employment opportunities on that basis, but must consider the relation of a specific impairment to specific job requirements, even if an illness is contagious, such as tuberculosis or HIV infection.[202] In considering whether a teacher's (HIV) condition endangered others at school enough so as to justify her transfer, the Eleventh Circuit noted:

> This inquiry must include: (a) the nature of the risk (how the disease is transmitted), (b) the duration of the risk (how long is the carrier infectious), (c) the severity of the risk (what is the potential harm to third parties), and (c) the probabilities the disease will be transmitted and will cause varying degrees of harm. [*Doe v. Dekalb County School Dist.,* 145 F.3d 1441, 1446 (11th Cir. 1998)]

Employers may require an applicant or a current employee to undergo mental or physical examinations if the tests are limited to ascertaining the employee's fitness for duty and ability to perform essential job functions. Thus a school district could require an examination by a long-term teacher whose disruptive behavior was not typical of her past work experience.[203] In such circumstances, the employee could not claim that the employer impermissibly presumed that she had a disability.

Employer "Accommodation" of a Covered Disability

As noted in the *Salmon* case, the ADA requires only "reasonable" employer accommodation to enable a person with a disability to perform the "essential functions" of a position. No duty to accommodate arises if (a) accommodation could not make the employee qualified to perform essential job functions or (b) the requested accommodation would impose undue hardship on the employer's enterprise. While the developing case law is not unanimous, the cases suggest that there is no duty to provide accommodations that require undue financial and administrative costs, fundamental alteration of the nature of a job, lowering of performance standards, reallocation of essential job functions, creation of new jobs, or reassignment of employees with disabilities to positions already occupied by others.[204] A physical impairment that might not seriously impede work as a classroom teacher might well impede work as a security officer or bus driver. Examples of reasonable accommodation include work schedule modifications that do not defeat the utility of the employee's work, and granting of a leave of absence where such leaves are allowed to nondisabled employees.[205] Examples of unreasonable accommodation include a request for a late starting schedule that is incompatible with job requirements, as in the *Salmon* case, and acceptance of unpredictable lateness and absences by an employee with a disability. As these examples demonstrate, the question whether a requested accommodation is reasonable turns on the specific circumstances of each request.

On the important allied question whether reasonable accommodation under the ADA requires an employer to reassign an existing employee from a current position which that employee cannot continue to perform with reasonable accommodation to a different position that the employee can perform with or without reasonable accommodation, the federal circuit courts are in disagreement, with the Seventh, Ninth, and Tenth Circuits indicating a duty to reassign, and the Third and Fourth Circuits finding no ADA duty to offer an alternative position.[206]

The question whether states are immune from liability for alleged violations of the ADA by reason of the Eleventh Amendment to the national Constitution has produced a conflict of opinion among the lower federal courts.[207] The Supreme Court has not directly resolved that conflict, but its recent decision, reported in endnote 217, recognizing state Eleventh Amendment immunity from suit under the ADEA suggests that like Eleventh Amendment immunity would extend to states that are sued under the ADA. That decision implicitly covers central state education agencies, but it does not directly consider or rule upon the question whether local school districts and local school officials are entitled to Eleventh Amendment immunity. As explained in the Chapter 4 discussion of sovereign immunity, as distinguished from local government immunity, most states have not extended state sovereign immunity (which the Eleventh Amendment adopts) to their local school districts, so that it is not likely that the courts would accord Eleventh Amendment immunity to school districts and their officials for federal law violations. However, in the few states with laws that treat school district actions as acts of their sovereign state, the possibility remains that the courts would accord them Eleventh Amendment immunity from ADA claims. Even there, however, the only prudent course for public school administrators would be to assume that they and their subordinates remain exposed to liability for federal law violations. Any other course runs some risk until the Supreme Court clearly settles the availability of Eleventh Amendment immunity under each specific federal statute because the interoperation of state and federal laws raises complex issues of constitutional law and statutory interpretation which the Supreme Court alone can finally settle.

Age Discrimination in Employment Act of 1967 (ADEA)

ADEA is modeled after, and operates in much the same manner as, Title VII, with regard to discrimination on account of age:

> It shall be unlawful for an employer to fail or refuse to hire or to discharge any individual or otherwise discriminate against any individual with respect to his compensation, terms, conditions, or privileges of employment, because of such individual's age. [29 U.S.C. § 623(a)(1)(1994)]

As with Title VII, the lower courts have held that teachers claiming age discrimination must produce evidence that they were qualified for and denied an employment opportunity because of their age, by intentional discriminatory treatment or by the disparate effects of an employer's decision, subject to the employer rebuttal evidence of a legitimate nondiscriminatory reason for the challenged action, which would shift the burden of proof back to the employee to show that the district's proffered reason is a pretext and untrue.[208] The latest Supreme Court decision on required proofs under the ADEA allows courts and juries to decide the sufficiency of proof of discrimination based on all circumstances.[209]

The ADEA does not prohibit good faith employment decisions based on nondiscriminatory criteria, such as physical incapacity, performance skills, competitive superiority or job performance, or on business necessity and bona fide seniority systems. An older person could not claim discrimination because younger workers with superior qualifications were given employment preference, or because a new school assignment increased the commuting distance to work, or because he received an otherwise justified unfavorable performance rating.[210] But, as with a disability, age may not be used as a proxy to decide performance capability.[211] Although costs and efficiency factors may negate a finding of discrimination, cost motives do not always justify discharge of older employees in a school staff reduction, or justify changing "continuing" contracts to "annual" contracts.[212] In each case, the courts consider all factors relevant to the presented situation to determine whether age was the basis of a contested action. The treatment of transfers of older employees as reasonable or discriminatory must, therefore, be decided on the basis of case facts.[213]

ADEA prohibits mandatory age retirements[214] and age-based differentials in compensation, including fringe benefits (health and retirement plans). Congress amended ADEA to require that employer cost expenditures for older workers under retirement plans be no less than those expended for younger workers.[215] The validity of early retirement plans that offer incentives for voluntary early retirement will depend on whether the retirement incentives and conditions are truly voluntary and nondiscriminatory or coercive and discriminatory. The *Auerbach* case, which appears at the end of this chapter, traces the ADEA history on this issue, and illustrates how courts determine the fairness and voluntariness of retirement plans. To head off age discrimination suits following layoffs, employers have resorted to offering severance packages in exchange for written releases by the laid-off employee that could bar future discrimination suits by the laid-off employee. Such agreements have been held lawful unless the employee could prove that they were not made knowingly and voluntarily.[216]

The recent Supreme Court decision that the ADEA could not be enforced against *state* employees by reason of state Eleventh Amendment immunity would shield direct arms of state government, such as central state agencies, from suit under the ADEA. However, as noted in the preceding section, the Supreme Court decision does not speak to the immunity of persons acting for school districts that are not treated (in the majority of states) as arms of the parent state.[217] Only in the few states that treat their school districts as partakers of state sovereign immunity (see Chapter 4 discussion on governmental immunity) could public school officials assert a colorable claim to Eleventh Amendment immunity. Also as noted in the preceding section, even in such circumstances, the law on federal Eleventh Amendment immunity is not fully clarified or settled.

Chapter 5 Discussion Questions

Where the answer to a question may be qualified by special circumstances, explain the potential qualification.

1. May a relative of a school board member be employed as a teacher in the same district? Explain.

2. How does a teacher's certification limit the positions in which he or she can be employed?

3. What are the main grounds to revoke a teacher's certificate?

4. How does certification affect teacher recall rights following a layoff?

5. When must a teacher submit to a school medical examination, and when can the teacher refuse to do so?

6. Do school counselors, nurses, psychologists, or home and school visitors have an absolute legal privilege to refuse to disclose information that was disclosed to them in confidence? Explain.

7. What rights, if any, do probationary teachers have with respect to the following?
   a. Contract continuation from year to year
   b. Notice and hearings on nonrenewal of annual employment
   c. Performance ratings

8. Do school principals attain tenure as teachers or as principals? Explain.

9. What is a demotion?

10. Can a teacher be lawfully "demoted" for nondisciplinary reasons? Explain.

11. On what grounds may
    a. Original tenure be denied?
    b. Existing tenure be terminated?

12. Can tenure rules be altered by mutual agreement between the school board and the teacher? Between the board and employee unions? Explain.

13. Are school districts required to enter into collective bargaining with their teachers in these circumstances?
    a. Under the constitution
    b. Under the federal National Labor Relations Act
    c. Under state labor laws

14. What elements of the following employment discrimination laws provide different definitions and different remedies for the same acts of discrimination?
    a. Title VII
    b. Rehabilitation Act
    c. Americans with Disabilities Act
    d. Age Discrimination in Employment Act

15. Can harassment between members of the same sex constitute gender discrimination under Title VII?

16. How did the Supreme Court change the Title VII measure of sexual harassment in the *Burlington Industries* case reported at the end of this chapter?

17. When, if ever, may a teacher demand excusal from a work assignment under Title VII for religious reasons? Explain.

CASES

Case 5.1

POOLE v. LITTLE VALLEY CENTRAL SCHOOL DISTRICT
472 N.Y.S.2d 226 (1984)

> [**Focus Note.** *Following a hearing under the state Education Law on school district misconduct charges that resulted in his termination from district employment, Poole and his union representative filed a grievance and requested arbitration on his discharge. The district refused to arbitrate on the grounds that his statutory hearing was final. The question on appeal was whether he was entitled to arbitration as well as the statutory hearing.*]

JOSEPH P. KUSZYNSKI, JUSTICE.

. . . Poole, and the respondent Teachers Association did not avail themselves of a review either by an appeal to the State Commissioner of Education or by a . . . proceeding as provided in Section 3020–a(5) Education Law, but filed a grievance . . . and demanding arbitration as described in the 1980 Collective Bargaining Agreement ("Agreement") entered into by the School District and the Teachers Association.

Petitioner School District submits that the filing of a grievance . . . is an impermissible attempt to circumvent the statutorily prescribed appeal process provided for in Section 3020–a(5) Education Law. . . .

. . . The School District points out that Poole's dismissal arises not from a contract violation, but from acts spelled out in Education Law Section 3020. . . .

Petitioner [School District] contends also that the respondents no longer have any recourse to the Agreement's grievance procedure, no matter how broad the contract definition may be of a grievance. . . .

❖ ❖ ❖

The 1977 amendment changed the effect of Section 3020. . . . Previously a [hearing] Panel's determination served only as a recommendation to the Board of Education. Now the amendment makes such determinations binding upon a school district.

❖ ❖ ❖

The rationale advanced by [prior cases] . . . favoring an arbitral review no longer has any application after 1977, when by legislative fiat only two (2) methods are available to a chastised teacher for a review of the adverse determination of charges. . . . Once the issues have been submitted to such a hearing, the binding aspects of the panel's determination upon the School District have stripped the School District of any discretion to agree to a submission of the controversy to any processing under the grievance procedures of the [Labor] Agreement. . . .

The amendment to . . . the Education Law changed the three way option previously available to a disciplined teacher. . . . Here, respondent Poole, having invoked the panoply of the statutorily provided hearing forum . . . under the Education Law, is bound to a review of its determination only by the two statutorily provided for avenues, an appeal to the State Commission of Education or the Courts. . . . *Abramovich v. Board of Education,* 46 N.Y.2d 450, 414 N.Y.S.2d 109, 386 N.E.2d 1076 (1979), cited by respondents, concerns itself with arbitration absent any 3020–a Education Law Panel determination. Clearly, once a 3020–a Education Law Panel has been convened and has decided charges . . . the recommended penalty is binding upon a school district barring any claim of irregularity. It follows then, that a school district cannot agree to a resubmission of the same issues or the penalty imposed, which would be tantamount to a retrial of the issues, to an arbitral processing as a grievance under the Agreement. . . .

The arbitration is permanently stayed and the motion to compel arbitration is denied in its entirety.

Case 5.2

TAXMAN v. BOARD OF EDUCATION
91 F.3d 1547 (3d Cir. 1996)

MANSMANN, CIRCUIT JUDGE.

In this Title VII matter, we must determine whether the Board of Education of the Township of Piscataway violated that statute when it made race a factor in selecting which of two equally qualified employees to lay off. Specifically, we must decide whether Title VII permits an employer with a racially balanced work force to grant a non-remedial racial preference in order to promote "racial diversity".

It is clear that the language of Title VII is violated when an employer makes an employment decision based upon an employee's race. The Supreme Court determined in *United Steelworkers v. Weber,* 443 U.S. 193, 99 S.Ct. 2721, 61 L.Ed.2d 480 (1979), however, that Title VII's prohibition against racial discrimination is not violated by affirmative action plans which first, "have purposes that mirror those of the statute" and second, do not "unnecessarily trammel the interests of the [non-minority] employees," . . .

We hold that Piscataway's affirmative action policy is unlawful because it fails to satisfy either prong of *Weber*. Given the clear antidiscrimination mandate of Title VII, a non-remedial affirmative action plan, even one with a laudable purpose, cannot pass muster. We will affirm the district court's grant of summary judgment to Sharon Taxman.

The Board's affirmative action policy did not have "any remedial purpose"; it was not adopted "with the intention of remedying . . . prior discrimination or identified underrepresentation of minorities within the . . . School System." At all relevant times, Black teachers were neither "underrepresented" nor "underutilized" in the Piscataway School District work force. . . .

In May, 1989, the Board accepted a recommendation from the Superintendent of Schools to reduce the teaching staff in the Business Department at Piscataway High School by one. At that time, two of the teachers . . . were of equal seniority. . . . One . . . was . . . plaintiff Sharon Taxman, who is White, and the other was Debra Williams, who is Black. . . .

Decisions regarding layoffs by New Jersey school boards are highly circumscribed by state law. . . . Thus, local boards lack discretion to choose between employees for layoff, except in the rare instance of a tie in seniority between the two or more employees eligible to fill the last remaining position.

. . . In prior decisions involving the layoff of employees with equal seniority, the Board had broken the tie through "a random process which included drawing numbers out of a container, drawing lots or having a lottery." . . . [N]one of those instances, however, had the employees involved been of different races.

. . . Superintendent of Schools Burton Edelchick recommended to the Board that the affirmative action plan be invoked in order to determine which teacher to retain. Superintendent Edelchick made this recommendation "because he believed Ms. Williams and Ms. Taxman were tied in seniority, were equally qualified, and because Ms. Williams was the only Black teacher in the Business Education Department."

While the Board recognized that it was not bound to apply the affirmative action policy, it made a discretionary decision to invoke the policy to break the tie between Williams and Taxman. As a result, the Board "voted to terminate the employment of Sharon Taxman, effective June 30, 1988. . . ."

✧ ✧ ✧

Following the Board's decision, Taxman filed a charge of employment discrimination with the Equal Employment Opportunity Commission. Attempts at conciliation were unsuccessful, and the United States filed suit under Title VII against the Board. . . . Taxman intervened, asserting claims under both Title VII and the New Jersey Law Against Discrimination (NJLAD).

. . . The district court . . . granted partial summary judgment to the United States and Taxman. . . .

A trial proceeded on the issue of damages. By this time, Taxman had been rehired by the Board and thus her reinstatement was not an issue. The court awarded Taxman damages in the amount of $134,014.62 for backpay, fringe benefits and prejudgment interest under Title VII. A jury awarded an additional $10,000 for emotional suffering under the NJLAD. . . .

The Board appealed, contending that the district court erred in granting Taxman summary judgment. . . . The Board also contends, in the alternative, that the court erred in awarding Taxman 100% backpay and in awarding prejudgment interest. . . . Taxman cross-appealed, contending that the district court erred in dismissing her claim for punitive damages. Subsequently, the United States sought leave to file a brief. . . . We treated the position of the United States . . . as a motion to withdraw as a party, which we granted. Thus, the only parties before us on this appeal are the Board and Taxman.

❖ ❖ ❖

. . . [T]he parties do not dispute that Taxman has established a prima facie case or that the Board's decision to terminate her was based on its affirmative action policy. The dispositive liability issue, therefore, is the validity of the Board's policy under Title VII.

❖ ❖ ❖

Title VII was enacted to further two primary goals: to end discrimination on the basis of race, color, religion, sex or national origin, thereby guaranteeing equal opportunity in the workplace, and to remedy the segregation and underrepresentation of minorities that discrimination has caused in our Nation's work force.

❖ ❖ ❖

. . . It is only because Title VII was written to eradicate not only discrimination per se but the consequences of prior discrimination as well, that racial preferences in the form of affirmative action can co-exist with the Act's antidiscrimination mandate.

Thus . . . we are convinced that unless an affirmative action plan has a remedial purpose, it cannot be said to mirror the purposes of the statute. . . .

We see this case as one involving straightforward statutory interpretation. . . . . . . The statute . . . provides that race cannot be a factor in employer decisions. . . . If exceptions to this bar are to be made, they must be made on the basis of what Congress has said. The affirmative action plans at issue in *Weber* and *Johnson* were sustained only because the Supreme Court . . . found a secondary congressional objective in Title VII that had to be accommodated—i.e., the elimination of the effects of past discrimination in the workplace. Here, there is no congressional recognition of diversity as a Title VII objective requiring accommodation.

❖ ❖ ❖

. . . Our analysis . . . convinces us that a non-remedial affirmative action plan cannot form the basis for deviating from the antidiscrimination mandate of Title VII.

The Board admits that it did not act to remedy the effects of past employment discrimination. . . . Nor does the Board contend that its action here was directed at remedying any de jure or de facto segregation. . . .

✧ ✧ ✧

Finally, we are convinced that the harm imposed upon a nonminority employee by the loss of his or her job is so substantial and the cost so severe that the Board's goal of racial diversity, even if legitimate under Title VII, may not be pursued in this particular fashion. This is especially true where, as here, the nonminority employee is tenured. . . .

✧ ✧ ✧

. . . The parties have agreed that the legal analysis required by the state statute is essentially the same as that undertaken in Title VII cases. . . .

. . . Analysis of this case under the NJLAD would, therefore, lead to the same result as that which we have reached under Title VII. Sharon Taxman is entitled to summary judgment on her claim made under the NJLAD.

Case 5.3

ONCALE v. SUNDOWNERS OFFSHORE SERVICES INC.
118 S. Ct. 998 (1998)

JUSTICE SCALIA delivered the opinion of the Court.

This case presents the question whether workplace harassment can violate Title VII's prohibition against "discriminat[ion] . . . because of . . . sex," 42 U.S.C. § 2000e-2(a) (1), when the harasser and the harassed employee are of the same sex.

. . . [W]e must assume the facts to be as alleged by petitioner Joseph Oncale. . . . In late October 1991, Oncale was working for respondent Sundowner Offshore Services on a Chevron U.S.A., Inc., oil platform in the Gulf of Mexico. He was employed as a roustabout on an eight-man crew which included respondents John Lyons, Danny Pippen, and Brandon Johnson. Lyons, the crane operator, and Pippen, the driller, had supervisory authority. . . . On several occasions, Oncale was forcibly subjected to sex-related, humiliating actions against him by Lyons, Pippen and Johnson in the presence of the rest of the crew. Pippen and Lyons also physically assaulted Oncale in a sexual manner, and Lyons threatened him with rape. Oncale's complaints to supervisory personnel produced no remedial action. . . . Oncale eventually quit—asking that his pink slip reflect that he "voluntarily left due to sexual harassment and verbal abuse." . . .

Oncale filed a complaint . . . alleging that he was discriminated against in his employment because of his sex. Relying on the Fifth Circuit's decision in *Garcia v. Elf Atochem North America,* 28 F.3d 446, 451-452 (C.A.5 1994), the district court held that "Mr. Oncale . . . a male, has no cause of action under Title VII. . . . On appeal, a panel of the Fifth Circuit . . . affirmed. . . .

Title VII of the Civil Rights Act of 1964 provides, in relevant part, that "[i]t shall be an unlawful employment practice for an employer . . . to discriminate against any individual with respect to his compensation, terms, conditions, or privileges of employment. . . ." . . . We have held that this not only covers "terms" and "conditions" in the narrow contractual sense, but "evinces a congressional intent to strike at the entire spectrum of disparate treatment of men and women in employment." *Meritor Savings Bank, FSB v. Vinson.* . . .

Title VII's prohibition of discrimination . . . protects men as well as women, *Newport News Shipbuilding & Dry Dock Co. v. EEOC* . . . and in the related context of racial discrimination in the workplace we have rejected any conclusive presumption that an employer will not discriminate against members of his own race. "Because of the many facets of human motivation, it would be unwise to presume as a matter of law that human beings of one definable group will not discriminate against other members of that group." *Castaneda v. Partida.* . . . In *Johnson v. Transportation Agency, Santa Clara Cty.* . . . a male employee claimed that his employer discriminated against him because of his sex when it preferred a female employee for promotion. Although we ultimately rejected the claim on other grounds, we did not consider it significant that the supervisor who made that decision was also a man. . . . If our precedents leave any doubt on the question, we hold today that nothing in Title VII necessarily bars a claim of discrimination "because of . . . sex" merely because the plaintiff and the defendant or the person charged with acting on behalf of the defendant are of the same sex. . . .

We see no justification in the statutory language or our precedents for a categorical rule excluding same-sex harassment claims from the coverage of Title VII. As some courts have observed, male-on-male sexual harassment in the workplace was assuredly not the principal evil Congress was concerned with when it enacted Title VII. But statutory prohibitions often go beyond the principal evil to cover reasonably comparable evils, and it is ultimately the provisions of our laws rather than the principal concerns of our legislators by which we are governed. Title VII prohibits "discriminat[ion] . . . because of . . . sex". . . . Our holding that this includes sexual harassment must extend to sexual harassment of any kind that meets the statutory requirements.

Respondents and their amici contend that recognizing liability for same-sex harassment will transform Title VII into a general civility code for the American workplace. But that risk is no greater for same-sex than for opposite-sex harassment. . . . Title VII does not prohibit all verbal or physical harassment in the workplace; it is directed only at "discriminat[ion] . . . because of . . . sex." We have never held that workplace harassment . . . is automatically discrimination because of sex merely because the words used have sexual content or connotations. "The critical issue . . . is whether members of one sex are exposed to disadvantageous terms or conditions of employment to which members of the other sex are not exposed." . . .

✧ ✧ ✧

. . . Because we conclude that sex discrimination consisting of same-sex sexual harassment is actionable under Title VII . . . the case is remanded for further proceedings consistent with this opinion.

❖ ❖ ❖

Case 5.4

BURLINGTON INDUSTRIES, INC. v. ELLERTH
118 S. Ct. 2257 (1988)

[**Focus Note.** *Ellerth worked in defendant's two-person Chicago office where she was supervised by her office colleague, who in turn answered to a supervisor, one Slowik, in New York who had authority to make hiring and promotion decisions, subject to the approval of his supervisor. She sued Burlington, alleging that she was forced to quit work there by Slowick's constant sexual harassment of her, including three incidents where Slowik's comments could be construed as threats to deny her tangible job benefits. Ellerth knew that the company had a policy against sexual harassment, but did not inform anyone in authority about Slowik's conduct because she thought that her immediate supervisor in Chicago had the duty to report incidents of sexual harassment. After quitting her job, she originally sent a letter giving reasons for leaving that were unrelated to the alleged sexual harassment, but several weeks later she faxed another letter explaining that Slowik's behavior caused her to quit. The District Court granted summary judgment to Burlington, but the Court of Appeals reversed that judgment. The Supreme Court in turn reversed the Court of Appeals and sent the case back for further proceedings in light of the following opinion in which the Court reviewed the complex history of Title VII and reformulated the grounds for establishing Title VII employer liability for the acts of its supervisors. The emphases in italics are the authors' and not the Court's.]*

JUSTICE KENNEDY *delivered the opinion of the Court.*

We decide whether, under Title VII . . . an employee who refuses the unwelcome and threatening sexual advances of a supervisor, yet suffers no adverse, tangible job consequences, can recover against the employer without showing the employer is negligent or otherwise at fault for the supervisor's actions.

❖ ❖ ❖

. . . The premise is: a trier of fact could find in Slowik's remarks numerous threats to retaliate against Ellerth if she denied some sexual liberties. The threats, however, were not carried out or fulfilled. Cases based on threats which are carried out are referred to often as quid pro quo cases, as distinct from bothersome attentions or sexual remarks that are sufficiently severe . . . to create a hostile work environment. The terms *quid pro quo* and *hostile work environment* are helpful, perhaps, in making a rough demarcation between cases in which threats are carried out and those where they are not . . . but beyond this they are of limited utility.

✧ ✧ ✧

. . . "Quid pro quo" and "hostile work environment" do not appear in the statutory text. The terms appeared first in the academic literature. . . . . . . Nevertheless . . . they acquired their own significance. . . . If the plaintiff established a quid pro quo claim, the Courts of Appeals held, the employer was subject to vicarious liability. . . . . . . [T]he issue of real concern to the parties is whether Burlington has vicarious liability for Slowik's alleged misconduct. . . .

We do not suggest the terms quid pro quo and hostile work environment are irrelevant to Title VII litigation. To the extent they illustrate the distinction between cases involving a threat which is carried out and offensive conduct in general, the terms are relevant. . . . When a plaintiff proves that a *tangible employment action* resulted *from* a refusal to submit to a supervisor's *sexual demands,* he or she establishes that the employment *decision itself constitutes a change in the terms and conditions of employment that is actionable under Title VII.* For any sexual *harassment preceding the employment decision* to be actionable, however, the conduct must *be severe or pervasive.* Because Ellerth's claim involves only unfulfilled threats, it should be *categorized as a hostile work environment claim* which requires a showing of severe or pervasive conduct. . . . For purposes of this case, we accept the District Court's finding that the alleged conduct was severe or pervasive. . . .

When we assume discrimination can be proved, however, the factors we discuss below, and not the categories quid pro quo and hostile work environment, will be controlling on the issue of vicarious liability. . . .

. . . We turn to principles of agency law, for the term "employer" is defined under Title VII to include "agents." 42 U.S.C. § 2000e(b). . . . In express terms, Congress has directed federal courts to interpret Title VII based on agency principles. Given such an explicit instruction, we conclude a uniform and predictable standard must be established as a matter of federal law. . . .

. . . The EEOC has issued Guidelines governing sexual harassment claims under Title VII, but they provide little guidance on the issue of employer liability for supervisor harassment. . . .

✧ ✧ ✧

An employer may be liable for both negligent and intentional torts committed by an employee within the scope of his or her employment. . . . The Restatement defines conduct, including an intentional tort, to be within the scope of employment when "actuated, at least in part, by a purpose to serve the [employer]" . . . even if it is forbidden by the employer. Restatement § § 228(1)(c), 230. . . . For example, when a salesperson lies to make a sale . . . the tortious conduct is within the scope of employment because it benefits the employer . . . even though it may violate the employer's policies. . . .

✧ ✧ ✧

When a supervisor makes a tangible employment decision, there is assurance the injury could not have been inflicted absent the agency relation. . . .
. . . Tangible employment actions are the means by which the supervisor brings the official power of the enterprise to bear on subordinates. . . .
For these reasons, a tangible employment action taken by the supervisor becomes for Title VII purposes the act of the employer. . . .

✧ ✧ ✧

. . . [W]e adopt the following holding in this case and in *Faragher v. Boca Raton* . . . also decided today. An employer is subject to vicarious liability to a victimized employee for an actionable hostile environment created by a supervisor with immediate (or successively higher) authority over the employee. When no tangible employment action is taken, a defending employer may raise an affirmative defense to liability or damages. . . . The defense comprises two necessary elements: (a) that the employer exercised reasonable care to prevent and correct promptly any sexually harassing behavior, and (b) that the plaintiff employee unreasonably failed to take advantage of any preventive or corrective opportunities provided by the employer or to avoid harm otherwise. While proof that an employer had promulgated an anti-harassment policy with complaint procedure is not necessary in every instance . . . the need for a stated policy . . . may appropriately be addressed in any case. . . . And while proof that an employee failed to fulfill the corresponding obligation of reasonable care to avoid harm is not limited to showing any unreasonable failure to use any complaint procedure provided by the employer, a demonstration of such failure will normally suffice to satisfy the employer's burden. . . . No affirmative defense is available, however, when the supervisor's harassment culminates in a tangible employment action, such as discharge, demotion, or undesirable reassignment.

✧ ✧ ✧

. . . In light of our decision, Burlington is still subject to vicarious liability for Slowik's activity, but Burlington should have an opportunity to assert and prove the affirmative defense to liability. . . .

Review Question 5.4

1. The Burlington opinion drew a crucial difference between employer defenses between claims based on threats that are carried out and those where threats are not carried out. How is this classification of

defenses different from the earlier legal classification of "quid pro quo" (seeking sexual favors) and non quid pro quo "harassment"? Why do you think the court thought its restatement of the law an improvement over prior law?

Case 5.5

SALMON v. DADE COUNTY SCHOOL BOARD
4 F.Supp.2d 1157 (S.D. Fla. 1998)

Order Granting Defendant's Motion for Summary Judgment

GOLD, DISTRICT JUDGE.

Zilpha Salmon . . . filed this action . . . alleging that the defendant failed to provide a reasonable accommodation for her disability and . . . denied her an equal chance for promotion. . . .

. . . She is the only guidance counselor at the Eneida Hartner Elementary School which has over one-thousand low-income, socially and emotionally deprived students, ranging in age from five to eleven years old. . . . Counselors and teachers are required to report to school by 8:15 A.M. and remain at school during scheduled working hours, which conclude at 3:20 P.M.

Salmon suffers from a back condition—a permanent partial disability. . . . Because of this back problem, she is unable to sit or stand for long periods of time and cannot climb stairs. . . . . . . Salmon was frequently tardy and her arrival times were unpredictable.

To accommodate Salmon's disability, the school principal provided her with a special chair and moved her counseling sessions from the second floor to the first. . . . Teachers were instructed to walk their students to Salmon's office so that Salmon would not have to walk long distances. . . . Salmon complained that driving . . . exacerbated her back problems and asked that she be permitted to arrive at work five to twenty-five minutes late on a regular basis in order to stretch and rest her back after the car ride. The principal denied this request, telling Salmon that as the only guidance counselor in a school of 1,200 students she needed to arrive at school on a regular and punctual basis in order to serve the needs of the children. No substitute counselors are available for an absent or late counselor. . . . The principal suggested that Salmon leave home a little earlier . . . to give herself time to stretch and rest her back.

✧ ✧ ✧

Salmon filed this lawsuit . . . alleging that it [school board] discriminated against her . . . by refusing to grant her a reasonable accommodation by allowing her to arrive late or transferring her to another school closer to her home. . . .

❖ ❖ ❖

. . . In demonstrating a viable claim under the ADA a plaintiff must demonstrate three elements: (1) that she has a disability; (2) that with or without reasonable accommodations she can perform the essential functions of her job; and (3) that she was discriminated against because of her disability. . . . Defendant contends, however, that the plaintiff is not a "qualified individual with a disability." . . . According to the defendant . . . arriving to work on time is an essential element of Salmon's job and that . . . the School Board had no duty to accommodate her request to come in late. . . .

An employee with a disability must be qualified for a job in order to be entitled to the non-discrimination protections guaranteed by the ADA. . . . . . . *Southeastern Community College v. Davis*, 442 U.S. 397, 406, . . . (1979) (the employee must be "able to meet all of a program's requirements in spite of his handicap"). . . . Therefore, the initial inquiry . . . is whether Salmon was capable of performing the essential functions of her job. If the Court finds that Salmon was unable to perform the essential functions of her job, the Court must then determine whether the plaintiff has demonstrated a genuine issue of material fact regarding her ability to perform those functions with any reasonable accommodation. . . .

. . . The term "essential functions" is defined as the fundamental job duties of a position. . . . For example, a job function may be considered essential because the reason the position exists is to perform that function. . . .

Unlike other jobs that can be performed off site or deferred until a later day, a guidance counselor must counsel students at the school during the hours in which the children are in attendance. . . . When a guidance counselor is absent or tardy, no substitute is available so counseling services are simply not provided. . . . The defendant's position . . . has not been disputed by the plaintiff. . . . [T]he Court must accept the defendant's unrebutted claim that arriving promptly for work is a necessary part of Salmon's position and that plaintiff was unable to meet this essential requirement.

. . . As the second step, the Court must determine whether any reasonable accommodation by the employer would enable Salmon to perform her job functions. . . . Reasonable accommodation includes modifications or adjustments to the work environment or the manner in which the position is customarily performed to enable an individual with a disability to perform the essential functions of that position. . . . Reasonable accommodation may include a change in work schedule.

Under the ADA, an employer is not required to provide an accommodation that would require significant difficulty or expense . . . or where it would impose undue financial and administrative burdens, or where it would require a fundamental alteration in the nature of the program. . . . Additionally, the duty to accommodate does not require an employer to lower its performance standards, reallocate essential job functions, create new jobs, or reassign disabled employees to positions that are already occupied. . . . . . .

Plaintiff bears the burden to identify an accommodation that would have allowed her to perform her job. She must also demonstrate that such an accommodation is reasonable. . . .

❖ ❖ ❖

. . . The undisputed facts show that Salmon was the only guidance counselor at the school and no substitute counselor was available to fill in for her when she was late. . . . Under these circumstances, permitting the employee to come in late to work is not a reasonable accommodation.

Plaintiff also claims that the School Board failed to accommodate her disability by transferring her to a school which afforded her a shorter commute. But plaintiff's commute to and from work is an activity that is unrelated to and outside of her job. . . . [A]n employer is not required to eliminate those barriers which exist outside the work environment. . . .

❖ ❖ ❖

She failed to rebut the School Board's claim that arriving to school on time is an essential element of a counselor's responsibilities at Eneida Hartner Elementary School. . . .

❖ ❖ ❖

. . . [T]he Court enters summary judgment in favor of the School Board. . . .

Case 5.6

AUERBACH v. BOARD OF EDUCATION OF THE HARBORFIELDS CENTRAL SCHOOL DISTRICT
136 F.3d 104 (2d Cir. 1997)

[**Focus Note.** *Public school teachers brought suit under the Age Discrimination in Employment Act to challenge the validity of a collectively bargained early retirement incentive plan. The following opinion traces the shifting case and legislative history of the ADEA provisions regarding early retirement incentive plans.*]

CARDAMONE, CIRCUIT JUDGE.

We are called upon . . . to determine the validity of an early retirement incentive plan for teachers employed at a Long Island, New York, school district. The critical question is whether the plan discriminates against older teachers in a manner that violates federal law prohibiting discrimination in employment on account of age. . . .

. . . All plaintiffs were or are members of defendant United Teachers of Harborfields (the Union). . . .   . . .

The defendant Union and the defendant School District entered into a collective bargaining agreement. . . . It contains a provision entitled "Retirement Incentive Plan/Payment for Unused Sick Leave". . . .

Under the plan's terms, a participating teacher must actually retire at the conclusion of the school year in which he or she first becomes eligible to retire (the optimum year) in order to secure the $12,500 fixed sum payment and the accumulated sick leave payment (together, the retirement incentive benefits). Teachers older than 55, but who have not yet fulfilled the service requirements, must retire in the year they complete the service requirements, regardless of their actual age, to receive the retirement incentive benefits. Conversely, a teacher who has already completed the service requirements by the time he or she reaches age 55 must retire at the conclusion of the school year during which he or she becomes 55 in order to obtain these benefits. Otherwise, the benefits are forever lost.

❖ ❖ ❖

We affirm the order dismissing the six unretired plaintiffs' claims as not ripe for adjudication. Although we also agree with the dismissal of the remaining eight teachers' causes of action, we take a somewhat different path to reach that result.

❖ ❖ ❖

Here the eight remaining plaintiffs fulfilled the retirement plan's job service requirements and reached the requisite age of 55 or older. But because they did not retire in the precise year when they first fulfilled the requirements of the plan, they are forever precluded from receiving the retirement incentive benefits. Thus, age is a trigger for the denial of their employee benefits. . . .

Consequently, we think it plain that age, not years of service, is the factor behind the disparate treatment of teachers. . . . Nonetheless, we agree . . . that the retirement plan is a valid early retirement incentive plan under the ADEA as a matter of law. To put our reasoning in proper perspective, a review of ADEA legislative history is helpful.

❖ ❖ ❖

Congress enacted the ADEA in 1967. . . . Section 4(f)(2) of the Act, 29 U.S.C. § 623(f)(2), addresses the issue of employee benefit plans, including retirement incentive plans. . . . Thus, § 4(f)(2), as originally enacted, allowed an employer to offer disparate employee benefit plans so long as the plan was not a "subterfuge to evade the purposes" of ADEA. . . .

In 1977 the Supreme Court first construed the meaning of this "subterfuge" provision. . . . The Court . . . held instead that the provision was intended to protect from invalidation almost all retirement plans. . . .

❖ ❖ ❖

The next year Congress amended the ADEA to overrule McMann. It added a final clause to § 4(f)(2) requiring that an employee benefit plan be voluntary in order to be valid under the ADEA. . . .

❖ ❖ ❖

In 1989, the Supreme Court reconsidered the meaning and scope of § 4(f)(2) in *Ohio Pub. Employees Retirement Sys. v. Betts*, 492 U.S. 158 . . . (1989). . . . According to the Court, § 4(f)(2) provided a broad exemption for employee benefit plans under the ADEA. . . . . . . This interpretation would effectively validate virtually all age-based restrictions in retirement incentive plans . . . absent the requisite showing by an employee that the employer subjectively intended to discriminate. . . .

❖ ❖ ❖

Congress . . . quickly responded by amending § 4(f)(2) in the course of passing the Older Workers' Benefit Protection Act of 1990. . . . That Act changed § 4(f)(2) to its modern form: . . .

. . . Section 4(f)(2)(B)(i) governs employee benefits and expressly adopts the "equal benefit or equal cost" principle. . . .

Section 4(f)(2)(B)(ii) controls early retirement incentive plans and, significantly, contains no such increased cost language. In other words, the "equal benefit or equal cost" rule has no application in the retirement incentive plan context. Thus, § 4(f)(2)(B)(ii) does not require that an employer provide identical early retirement incentives for employees of different ages or incur the same costs for all employees. Rather, the early retirement incentive plan need only be voluntary and consistent with the ADEA's relevant purpose(s). . . .

❖ ❖ ❖

Whether such a plan "furthers the purposes of the Act" is ultimately an inquiry to be made on a case-by-case basis, taking into account all of the relevant facts and circumstances. . . . A court examining the validity of these plans should consider whether the plan (1) is truly voluntary, (2) is made available for a reasonable period of time, and (3) does not arbitrarily discriminate on the basis of age. . . . For the following reasons, we conclude that the subject retirement plan . . . furthers the purposes of the ADEA.

1. Voluntariness. . . . The present early retirement plan provides older teachers with an uncoerced, free choice. No teacher is required to accept the plan. Moreover, the record shows that neither fraud, threats of imminent layoffs, intimidation nor subtle coercion are present. Instead, teachers receive complete and accurate information regarding the benefits available to them

under the plan. Those who elect not to retire in the optimum year continue to teach and receive all of the benefits of the collective bargaining agreement, including annual salary increases. Hence, the plan meets Congress' test of voluntariness.

2. Reasonable Period of Time. . . . Under the plan, qualifying teachers must submit to the School District a letter of resignation no later than January 1 of their final full year of service. This requirement gives teachers approximately four months . . . to reflect and weigh their options. Under these circumstances, the district court correctly held that the retirement plan provides a reasonable amount of time for teachers to consider their options.

3. No Arbitrary Discrimination. . . . The plan grants every teacher the opportunity to receive a $12,500 cash payment and an accumulated sick leave payment once he or she reaches the age of 55 and has served the requisite number of years. Teachers who decline to participate in the plan . . . continue to work as valued employees . . . without any corresponding loss of benefits or job status.

The Harborfields Plan is easily distinguished from the plan considered by the *Seventh Circuit in Karlen v. City Colleges of Chicago*, 837 F.2d 314 (7th Cir. 1988), on which plaintiffs rely. . . .

The *Karlen* plan arbitrarily discriminated on the basis of age. . . . . . . The incentives gradually increased between ages 55 and 64, but dropped off precipitously for those participants who retired after age 64. . . . The employer offered no reason other than age for this downward sliding scale of incentive benefits.

An early retirement incentive plan that withholds or reduces benefits to older retiree plan participants . . . so as to encourage premature departure from employment by older workers conflicts with the ADEA's stated purpose. . . . . . . In contrast, the present plan does not provide for an age-based phase out of a lump sum incentive payment. . . . By offering the same incentives . . . to all plan participants who reach the age of 55, it treats those participants equally, regardless of the actual age at which they retire. . . . Consequently, the subject retirement incentive plan does not arbitrarily discriminate on the basis of age. . . .

❖ ❖ ❖

❖ ENDNOTES

1. Dodd v. Meno, 857 S.W.2d 575 (Tex. App. 1993).

2. Heifner v. Board of Educ., 335 N.E.2d 600 (Ill. 1975).

3. Hunt v. Sanders, 554 N.E.2d 285 (Ill. App. 1990); Green Bay Ed. Assn. v. State Dept., 453 N.W.2d 915 (Wis. App. 1990).

4. *Compare* Luz v. School Comm. of Lowell, 313 N.E.2d 925 (Mass. 1974), *with* Sorenson v. School Dist. No. 28, 418 P.2d 1004 (Wyo. 1966).

5. *Requirement not waivable by local board:* Bradford Cent. School Dist. v. Ambach, 436 N.E. 2d 1256 (N.Y. 1982). *Statutory exception for emergencies:* Cranston Teachers Assn. v. Cranston School Comm., 424 A.2d 648 (R.I. 1982)

6. State v. Project Principle, Inc., 724 S.W.2d 387 (Tex. 1987); Texas State Teachers Assn. v. State, 711 S.W.2d 421 (Tex. 1987). *But see* Allen v. Alabama State Board of Educ., 816 F.2d 575 (11th Cir. 1987).

   The National Center for Education Statistics reported:

   . . . school districts rely on teacher credentials, such as state certification, or teacher tests to determine the qualifications of a candidate.

   From 1987–88 to 1993–94, increasing percentages of public school districts required passage of state tests of basic skills and subject knowledge in the teacher hiring process, although teacher credentials were the most widely used criteria at each survey point.

   . . .

   In 1993–94, state tests were relied upon more frequently than the NTE in the South and Midwest; in the Northeast, this pattern was reversed.

   . . . the NTE was the most frequently used teacher assessment in the Northeast, with half of all districts requiring passage of the national exam. Following the NTE, similar percentages of Northeastern districts relied on state tests of basic skills and subject knowledge. . . . In the West, districts most frequently required passage of state tests of basic skills. . . . Across all four regions, district-level tests were required less frequently than national and state tests. Issue Brief, *Credentials and Tests in Teacher Hiring: What Do Districts Require?* (February 1997)

   The National Center for Education Statistics in 1998 reported on a survey of teachers that found the following: More than 90% of the teachers were fully certified in their main teaching field, and the percentage of teachers teaching out of their field ranged from 4 to 10%. (See nces.ed.gov/pubsinfo. asp?pubid=199080)

   A recent report of a study by The Education Trust stated, *inter alia:*

   —Only 29 states require teacher candidates to pass tests in subjects they wish to teach; and that eligibility examinations are "insultingly easy" to pass.

   —States whose school districts face severe teacher shortages may hesitate to require more rigorous testing for fear of intensifying the shortage.

   —Some states, notably California, are being sued and accused of discrimination because their teacher tests result in disproportionate failure rates of minority group candidates.

   [News Article, *Study Says States Don't Require a Lot from Teacher,* The Philadelphia Inquirer, p. A13 (5-28-99); *see also* Lines, *Teacher Competency Testing,* 23 Ed. Law 811, 827 (1985).]

7. *Wrong subject placement and seniority:* Matter of Proposed Placement, 381 N.W.2d 476 (Minn. App. 1986); Giowacki v. Ambach, 385 N.Y.S.2d 819 (1976). *Uncertified position:* Audet v. Board of Regents, 606 F. Supp. 423 (D.R.I. 1985).

8. *Discharge:* Luz v. School Comm. of Lowell, 313 N.E.2d 925 (Mass. 1974). *Contra:* Bates v. Hinds, 324 F. Supp. 528 (D.C. Tex. 1971). *Nonforfeiture of pay for work prior to proper filing:* Mass v. Board of Educ., 394 P.2d 579 (Cal. 1964). *No forfeiture for harmless default:* Woodrum v. Rolling Hills Board of Educ., 421 N.E.2d 859 (Ohio 1981).

9. Board of Educ. of Taos v. Singleton, 712 P.2d 1384 (N.M. 1985); Altoona Area Vo-Tech. School v. Pollard, 520 A.2d 99 (Pa. Cmwlth. 1987).

10. A teacher convicted for marijuana possession was held fit in Comings v. State Board of Educ., 100 Cal. Rptr. 73 (1972), *but* not in Walton v. Turlington, 444 So. 2d 1082 (Fla. 1984).

11. Bloomburg-Dubin v. Board of Educ., 43 N.Y.S.2d 956 (1981). *Position abolition:* Steele v. Board of Educ. of City of N.Y., 354 N.E.2d 807 (N.Y. 1976). *Nonrenewal:* Ambrose v. Comm. School Board, 367 N.Y.S.2d 550 (1975).

12. *See* cases in Annot., *Validity, Construction, and Effect of Municipal Residency Requirements for Teachers, Principals, and Other School Employees,* A.L.R. 4th 272 (1990). *Residency upheld:* McClellan v. Paris Public Schools, 742 S.W.2d 907 (Ark. 1988); Wardwell v. Board of Educ., 529 F.2d 625 (6th Cir. 1976). *Grandfather exemption upheld:* Pittsburgh Fed'n of Teachers v. Aaron, 417 F. Supp. 94 (W.D. Pa. 1976).

13. Daury v. Smith, 842 F.2d 9 (1st Cir. 1988); Garrett v. Los Angeles County Unified School Dist., 172 Cal. Rptr. 170 (1981).

14. *See generally* J.D. Weeks, *Public Employee Drug Testing,* 20 The Urban Lawyer 445 (1988).

15. Ambach v. Norwick, 441 U.S. 68 (1979); Sugerman v. Dougall, 413 U.S. 634 (1973).

16. Cole v. Richardson, 405 U.S. 676 (1972); Connell v. Higginbotham, 403 U.S. 207 (1971) (oath upheld).

17. Idem.

18. Beilan v. Board of Public Educ., 357 U.S. 399 (1958).

19. *Nepotism:* Chapman v. Gorman, 839 S.W.2d 232 (Ky. 1992) *See also* cases collected in Annot., *Nepotism in Public Service,* 11 A.L.R. 4th 826 (1982) and pocket part. Some states permit employment of close relatives of a board member provided that member takes no part in the employment decision, while some states only ban such employment for "first hirings." Schere v. Roch Hill Local School Dist. Board of Educ., 597 N.E.2d 525 (Ohio 1990).

Some states permit relatives to serve on the same school board: Hinek v. Bowman Public School Dist. No.1, 232 N.W.2d 72 (N.D. 1975)

The cases are divided on the following questions:

—Whether teacher spouses may work in the same school. *Cf.* Waters v. Gaston County, 57 F.3d 422 (4th Cir. 1995); Solomon v. Quinones, 531 N.Y.S.2d 349 (1988).

—Whether a board member may concurrently hold another public office. Craighead County Board of Educ. v. Henry, 748 S.W.2d 132 (Ark. 1988) (school nurse and guidance counselor allowed to hold elective municipal office); Schulman v. O'Reilly-Lando, 545 A.2d 241 (N.J. 1988); Cmwlth. v. Tekavec, 319 A.2d 1 (Pa. 1975) (intermediate unit supervisor was not disqualified from election to school board); Gretick v. Jeffrey, 465 N.E.2d 412 (Ohio 1984) (school principal could act as county commissioner); Jenkins v. Bishop, 589 P.2d 770 (Utah 1978) (school administrator serving in state legislature). *But see contra:* LoBusco v. Dunn, 502 N.Y.S.2d 200 (1986) (employee barred from board office); Contesi v. Atty. Gen., 416 N.W.2d 410 (Mich. App. 1987); Cranston Teachers Alliance Local No. 1704 v. Miele, 495 A.2d 233 (R.I. 1985) (rehabilitation specialist barred from service on school committee); Town of Cheshire v. McKenney, 438 A.2d 88 (Conn. 1980) (teacher barred from office on town council).

Under "resign to run" statutes, a person seeking election to public office may not retain public school employment. Yonts v. Comm. *ex rel.* Armstrong, 700 S.W.2d 407 (Ky. 1985) and authorities there reviewed.

20. Malynn v. Morgan Hill Unified School Dist., 187 Cal. Rptr. 303 (1982); Glanville v. Hickory County Reorganized School, 637 S.W.2d 328 (Mo. App. 1982); Maupin v. Indep. School Dist., 632 P.2d 396 (Okla. 1981).

21. *See, e.g.,* Lavender v. McDowell County Board of Educ., 327 S.E.2d 691 (W. Va. 1984); Silavent v. Buckeye Cent. Local School Dist. Board of Educ., 500 N.E.2d 315 (Ohio App. 1985).

22. *Disciplinary transfers:* Brough v. Board of Educ., 463 P.2d 567 (Utah 1970) (disobeyed order to attend a workshop).

Hearing rights: Wheeler v. School Dist. No. 20, 535 P.2d 206 (Colo. 1975); State v. Berger, 314 So. 2d 700 (Ala. 1975).

23. Givhan v. Western Line Consol. School Dist., 439 U.S. 410 (1979); Calhoun v. Cassady, 534 S.W.2d 806 (Ky. 1976).

24. Blair v. Robstown Indep. School Dist., 556 F.2d 1331 (5th Cir. 1977) (high school football game); Fox v. Board of Educ., 236 S.E.2d 243 (W. Va. 1977) (parent conference).

25. Pease v. Millcreek Twp. School Dist., 195 A.2d 104 (Pa. 1963); Parrish v. Moss, 106 N.Y.S.2d 577 (1951).

26. Lockhart v. Board of Educ., 735 P.2d 913 (Colo. App. 1986).

27. Dist. 300 Educ. Assn. v. Board of Educ., 334 N.E.2d 165 (Ill. 1975).

28. Banks v. Comm. School Board No. 29, 364 N.Y.S.3d 379 (1975) (nonrenewal for unsatisfactory rating).

29. Tyler v. Jefferson City-DuBoise Area Voc. Tec., 359 A.2d 761 (Pa. 1976) (failure to rate); Morse v. Wozniak, 398 F. Supp. 597 (E.D. Mich. 1975) (failure to give proper notice); Longarzo v. Anker, 578 F.2d 469 (2d Cir. 1978) (noncompliance with district bylaws). *Compare* Smith v. Board of School Directors, 328 A.2d 883 (Pa. 1974) (harmless error).

30. Gunter v. Board of Trustees of Pocatello School Dist., 854 P.2d 253 (Id. 1993).

31. Ala. State Tenure Comm'n v. Shelby County Board of Educ., 474 So. 2d 723 (Ala. 1985).

32. Kaczmarcik v. Carbondale Area School Dist., 625 A.2d 126 (Pa. Comm. 1993).

33. *Re* loss of pay or prestige, *compare*, Ellis-Adams v. Whitfield County Board of Educ., 356 S.E.2d 219 (Ga. 1987); Kenaston v. School Admin. Dist. No. 40, 317 A.2d 7 (Me. 1974).

   Re loss of pay only, *see* Glanville v. Hickory County Reorganized School Dist., 637 S.W.2d 328 (Mo. App. 1982).

   Re loss of certification or tenure, King v. Board of Educ., 447 S.E.2d 667 (Ga. 1994); Preuss v. Board of Educ., 667 S.W.2d 391 (Ky. 1984).

34. *Ibid;* Glennon v. School Committee of Boston, 378 N.E.2d 1372 (Mass. 1978).

35. Hatcher v. Board of Public Educ., 809 F.2d 1546 (11th Cir. 1987); White v. Banks, 614 S.W.2d 331 (Tenn. 1981); Candelari v. Board of Educ., 428 A.2d 331 (Conn. 1980).

36. Williams v. Cody, 545 P.2d 905 (Or. 1976); Clark v. Mt. Greylock Regional High School Dist., 336 N.E.2d 750 (Mass. 1975).

37. Board of School Directors v. Pittinger, 305 A.2d 382 (Pa. 1973); Calhoun v. Cassady, 534 S.W.2d 806 (Ky. 1976).

38. *Compare* Clark, *supra* note 36 (publicized board resolutions satisfied notice obligation).

39. *Disciplinary demotions:* Harris v. School Dist., 624 A.2d 784 (Pa. Cmwlth. 1993).

40. Kotan v. School Dist. No. 110C, 509 P.2d 452 (Or. 1973).

41. Lee v. Macon County Board of Educ., 463 F.2d 1174 (5th Cir. 1972); Singleton v. Jackson Mun. Sep. School Dist., 425 F.2d 1211 (5th Cir. 1970).

42. *Compare* Durant v. Ind. School Dist., 990 F.2d 560 (10th Cir. 1993) (hearing not required), *with* English v. Central Educ. Agency, 866 S.W.2d 73 (Tex. App. 1993); Tucker v. Board of Educ., 624 N.E.2d 643 (N.Y. 1993) (hearings required by statute).

   On differences among states and federal circuits, *see* Marxsen v. Board of Directors, 591 A.2d 867 (Me. 1991); Irving v. School Dist., 813 P.2d 417 (Mont. 1991).

43. Cronacher v. Scribner, 369 N.Y.S.2d 780 (1975).

44. Giangreco v. Mulless, 939 P.2d 596 (N.M. 1997). But board delay of nonrenewal notice to afford teacher opportunity to convince board to renew did not void nonrenewal. Carl v. S. San Antonio Indep. School Dist., 561 S.W.2d 560 (Tex. 1978). For authorities on nonrenewal notices in 41 states, *see* Annot., *Sufficiency of Notice,* 52 A.L.R. 4th 283 (1987) and pocket part.

45. *Advance statement or hearing:* Gibson v. Board of Educ. of Jackson County, 805 S.W.2d 673 (Ky. App. 1991) (statutory entitlement to statement of reasons); Kruse v. Board of Directors, 231 N.W.2d 626 (Iowa 1975).

46. *Formal failures not excused:* Bently v. School District, 586 306 (Neb. 1998) (notice from superintendant, due from the board). *See also* Rhoads v. Board of Trustees, (WL432161); Sills v. Ala. State Tenure Comm'n., 718 So. 2d 1145 (Ala. 1998) (timely mailing, not received by statutory deadline). *Defect excused as harmless error:* Joanou v. Board of Educ., 345 A.2d 46 (Conn. 1974).

47. Conte v. School Committee, 356 N.E.2d 261 (Mass. 1976).

48. Roth v. Board of Regents, 408 U.S. 564 (1972); Perry v. Sindermann, 408 U.S. 593 (1972).

49. Givhan v. Western Line Cons. School Dist., 439 U.S. 410 (1979); Hanover Twp. Fed'n. of Teachers v. Hanover Comm., 318 F. Supp. 757 (D. Ind. 1970).

50. Mt. Healthy City Board of Educ. v. Doyle, 429 U.S. 274 (1977).

51. Wertz v. St. Cloud Unified School District, 542 P.2d 339 (Kan. 1975).

52. Bolmeier, *School in the Legal Structure* 192 (1973).

53. Alexander v. Delano Jt. Unified High School, 188 Cal. Rptr. 705, 708–9 (1983).

54. Buckner v. School Board, 718 So. 2d 862 (Fla. 1998); Welk v. Iowa City Comm. School Dist., 470 N.W.2d 57 (Iowa App. 1991).

55. *See, e.g.,* Wrightgorman v. Board of Educ., 491 A.2d 644 (N.J. 1985) (custodians covered); State *ex rel.* Haak v. Board of Educ., 367 N.W.2d 461 (Minn. 1985) (some supervisory positions covered); Roberts v. Comm. School Board, 486 N.E.2d 818 (N.Y. 1985) (some substitute service covered).

56. Jefferson v. Compton Unified School Dist., 17 Cal. Rptr. 2d 474 (Cal. App. 1993). *States with separate tenure for administrators:* Wooten v. Alabama Tenure Comm'n., 421 So. 2d 1288 (Ala. 1982); Paqua v. LaForche Paris School Board, 408 So. 2d 438 (La. 1981). *States where administrators hold tenure as teachers:* Snipes v. McAndrew, 313 S.E.2d 294 (S.C. 1984); Waltz v. Board of Educ., 329 N.W.2d 131 (S.D. 1983); Fuller v. N. Kansas City School Dist., 629 S.W.2d 404 (Mo. 1982).

57. Halsey v. Board of Educ. of Garrett County, 331 A.2d 306 Md. (1975); *cf.* City Univ. v. Board of Higher Educ., 330 N.Y.S.2d 688 (1972).

58. Kletzkin v. Board of Educ., 642 A.2d 993 (N.J. 1994).

59. Dist. v. Lollar, 547 P.2d 1324 (Okla. 1976); People v. Kapp, 389 N.Y.S.2d 645 (1976) (kindergarten teacher on half-day sessions). *But see* Fairbanks N. Star School v. NEA-Alaska, 817 P.2d 923 (Alaska 1991); Thompson v. E. Baton Rouge Parish School Board, 303 So. 2d 855 (La. 1974). Dial v. Lathrop R-11 School Dist., 871 S.W.2d 444 (Mo. 1994).

60. Copella v. Board of Educ., 367 A.2d 444 (N.J. 1976); Rhee v. Allegheny Intermediate Unit No.

3, 315 A.2d 644 (Pa. 1974); *cf.* Stang v. Indep. School Dist., 256 N.W.2d 82 (Minn. 1977).

61. *Voluntary leave:* Solomon v. School Committee of Boston, 478 N.E.2d 137 (Mass. 1985). *Compare* Matthews v. School Committee of Bedford, 494 N.E.2d 38 (Mass. 1986). *Resignation:* Williams v. Lafayette Parish School Board, 533 So. 2d 1359 (La. App. 1988).

62. *Prohibited:* Britt v. Red Mesa Unified School Dist., 748 P.2d 1202 (Ariz. 1987); Nagy v. Board of Educ., 500 P.2d 987 (Colo. 1972).

    Permitted: cf. Oak Harbor School Dist. v. Oak Harbor Educ. Assn., 545 P.2d 1197 (Wash. 1976) (seniority determined by total service in the state); Harbe v. Hazelwood School Dist., 532 S.W.2d 848 (Mo. 1975).

63. Lee-Warren v. School Board, 403 S.E.2d 691 (Va. 1991) (principalship tenure lost upon removal to another district). Teachers in some federally funded positions were held eligible for tenure credit in Alabama and Massachusetts but not in Louisiana or Delaware. Berry v. Pike County Board of Educ., 545 So. 2d 43 (Ala. 1987); Brophy v. School Comm., 383 N.E.2d 521 (Mass. 1978); Board of Educ. of Newcastle v. Savino, 494 A.2d 1258 (Del. 1985). *See also* Annot., *Teachers Service Period—Computation,* 2 A.L.R. 2d 1033 (1948).

64. Sadler v. Board of Educ., 851 S.W.2d 707 (Mo. App. 1993).

65. *See* Nagy v. Board of Educ., 500 P.2d 987 (Colo. 1972); Coates v. Ambach, 383 N.Y.S.2d 672 (1976); McNamara v. Board of Educ., 389 N.Y.S.2d 682 (1976) (prekindergarten teachers held to be within elementary tenure area).

66. Hicksville Congress of Teachers v. Hicksville Union Free School Dist. Board of Educ., 499 N.Y.S.2d 774 (1986).

67. Loftus v. Board of Educ. Town of Fairfield, 509 A.2d 500 (Conn. 1986); Roberts v. Comm. School Board, 486 N.E.2d 818 (N.Y. 1985).

68. Elisofon v. Board of Educ., 379 N.Y.S.2d 145 (1976); *but cf.* LaBarr v. Board of Educ., 425 F. Supp. 219 (D. N.Y. 1977).

69. Williams v. Board of Public Instruction, 311 So. 2d 812 (Fla. 1975).

70. *Tenure grant ordered:* Board of Educ. of Harrodsburg v. Powell, 792 S.W.2d 376 (Ky.

App. 1990); Dav v. Prowers County School District, 725 P.2d 14 (Colo. 1986); Hyde v. Willpinit School Dist., 648 P.2d 892 (Wash. 1982); *cf.* Wilt v. Flannigan, 294 S.E.2d 189 (W. Va. 1982) (board policy violated).

Tenure grant denied, but other relief awarded: School Dist. v. Norwood, 644 P.2d 13 (Colo. 1984); LaBorde v. Franklin Parish School Board, 510 F.2d 590 (5th Cir. 1975); Mugavin v. Nyquist, 367 N.Y.S.2d 604 (1975); Snell v. Brothers, 527 S.W.2d 114 (Tenn. 1975).

71. Tex. State Teachers Assn. v. Garland Indep. School Dist., 777 F.2d 1046 (5th Cir. 1985); Saye v. St. Vrain Valley School Dist., 785 F.2d 862 (10th Cir. 1986); Mo. Nat'l Educ. Assn. v. New Madrid County R-1 Enlarged School Dist., 810 F.2d 164 (8th Cir. 1987).

72. *See* U.S. Dept. of Labor, Labor Management Services Admin., Summary of Public Sector Labor Relations Policies (1981); Education Commission of the States, State Education Collective Bargaining Laws, Elementary/ Secondary Sector (July 1984).

73. United Teachers Org. v. WERC, 342 N.W.2d 709 (Wis. 1984); School Board of Polk County v. Fla. PERC, 399 So. 2d 520 (Fla. App. 1981); Detroit Board of Educ. v. Local No. 28, 308 N.W.2d 247 (Mich. App. 1981).

74. Anthony Oto Comm. School Dist. v. Public Employment Relations Board, 404 N.W.2d 140 (Iowa 1987).

75. *Teachers:* The law in some states required all teachers to be in a single unit. Connecticut, Delaware, and Hawaii required separation of professional employees according to certification classes or administrative duties. *See also* Board of Trustees of Speedway v. Ind. Educ. Employee Relations Board, 498 N.E.2d 1006 (Ind. App. 1986). Pennsylvania law gives teachers the option to include nonprofessionals in their bargaining unit.

Supervisors: Rhode Island and Wisconsin prohibited union representation of supervisors, but other states allow such representation in a separate unit. Appeal of Manchester Board of School Comm., 523 A.2d 114 (N.H. 1987); Annot., *Who Are Supervisors for Purposes of Bargaining Unit Determination,* 96 A.L.R. 3d 723 (1980) and pkt. part. Other states left the matter to labor boards. Anthony Oto Comm. School

Dist., *supra* note 74; Mo. N.E.A. v. Mo. State Board of Mediation, 695 S.W.2d 894 (Mo. 1985). "Wall-to-wall" bargaining units include all employees (professional and nonprofessional) of a single employer, notwithstanding potential adverse interests. Sandburg Faculty Assn. v. Ill. Educ. Labor Relations Board, 618 N.E.2d 989 (Ill. App. 1993).

76. Very few states provide for proportional (union members only) representation. Fayette Co. Educ. Assn. v. Hardy, 626 S.W.2d 217 (Ky. 1980); Minnesota State Board of Comm. Colleges v. Knight, 465 U.S. 271 (1984).

77. Lehnert v. Ferris Faculty Association, 111 S. Ct. 1950 (1991).

78. Rogers v. Board of Educ., 2 F.3d 163 (6th Cir. 1993). *See* Annot., *Negotiable Issues in Public Employment,* 84 A.L.R. 3d 242 (1978) and pkt. part.

79. For updates on state legislative actions, *see* Government Employee Relations Reporter (Bureau of National Affairs, Special Reports, Labor Relations in Secondary and Elementary Education).

A school's duty to bargain is suspended during an illegal teachers' strike. Melvindale-Northern Allen Park Fed. of Teachers v. Melvindale-Northern Allen Park Public Schools, 549 N.W.2d 6 (Mich. 1996).

80. *E.g.,* Board of Educ. v. Kansas Dept. of Human Res., 856 P.2d 1343 (Kan. App. 1993) (appraisal procedures); Ind. School Dist. v. School Service Employees' Union, 503 N.W.2d 104 (Minn. 1993) (effects of outsourcing). *See also* School Board of Seminole County v. Morgan, 582 So. 2d 787 (Fla. App. 1991); Board of Educ. v. Illinois Educ. Labor Relations Board, 556 N.E.2d 857 (Ill. 1990).

81. Local 1186 v. State Board of Labor Relations, 620 A.2d 766 (Conn. 1993); Newark Valley Central School Dist. v. Public Empt. Relations Board, 632 N.E.2d 443 (N.Y. 1994).

82. W. Irandequoit Teachers Assn. v. Helsby, 35 N.Y.2d 46 (1974); Yorktown Faculty Assn. v. Yorktown Cent. School Dist., 7 N.Y.P.E.R.B. 3030 (1974). *But see* Susq. Valley C. School Dist. v. Susq. Valley Teachers Assn., 358 N.Y.S.2d 235 (1974).

83. Aberdeen Educ. Assn. v. Aberdeen Board of Educ., 215 N.W.2d 837 (S.D. 1974); Sutherland Educ. Assn. v. Sutherland School Dist., 548 P.2d 647 (Or. 1976); Pa. Labor Relations Board v. State College Area School Dist., 337 A.2d 263 (Pa. 1975).

84. *Held bargainable:* W. Hartford Educ. Assn. v. deCourcey, 295 A.2d 536 (Conn. 1972); Hawaii Public Employee Relations Board decision [Govt. Emp. Relations Rptr. E-1 (1972)]. *Held not bargainable:* Aberdeen Educ. Assn., *supra* note 83; Nat'l Educ. Assn. of Shawnee Mission v. Board of Educ., 512 P.2d 426 (Kans. 1970).

    Where the labor statute is unclear, some courts leave the question of mandatory bargaining to state labor boards. Central City Ed. Assn. v. Illinois Educational Labor Relations Board, 599 N.E.2d 892 (Ill. 1992).

85. W. Hartford Educ. Assn., *supra* note 84.

86. Joint School Dist. No. 8 v. Wis. Employees' Relation Board, 155 N.W.2d 78 (Wis. 1967). *Compare* Hillsborough Classroom Teachers Assn. v. School Board, 423 So. 2d 969 (Fla. 1982), *with* Eastbrook Comm. School Corp. v. Ind. Educ. Employment Relations Board, 446 N.E.2d 1007 (Ind. 1983).

87. Nev. Rev. Stat. § 228.150.

88. The bargainability of promotional and supervisory appointments, teacher evaluations, transfers, tenure, and nonrenewal of contracts receives conflicting treatment under the laws of different states. *Held not bargainable:* Board of Educ. v. NEA-Goodland, 785 P.2d 993 (Kan. 1990); Marsh v. St. Vrain School Dist., 644 P.2d 41 (Colo. 1981); Minn. Fed'n of Teachers v. Minn. Spec. School Dist., 258 N.W.2d 802 (Minn. 1977); Newman v. Board of Educ., 325 A.2d 387 (Del. 1974); School Dist. of Seward Educ. Assn. v. School Dist., 199 N.W.2d 753 (Neb. 1972). On teacher evaluation, *compare* Aplington Comm. School Dist. v. Iowa PERB, 408 N.W.2d 495 (Iowa 1986) (bargainable), *with* Wethersfield Board of Educ. v. Conn. State Board of Labor Relations, 519 A.2d 41 (Conn. 1986); Miller v. Board of Educ., 744 P.2d 113 (Kan. 1988) (nonbargainable). *Held bargainable to some extent:* Alton Comm. School Dist. v. E.L.R.B., 567 N.E.2d 671 (Ill. App. 1991); Board of Educ. of Yonkers City School Dist. v. Yonkers Fed'n of Teachers, 514 N.Y.S.2d 465 (1987); Wright v. Board of Educ., 491 A.2d 644 (N.J.

1985) (tenure rights bargainable within statutory limits).

Re bargaining on budget reductions and job eliminations, *see* School Comm. of Hanover v. Curry, 325 N.E.2d 282 (Mass. 1975); City of New Rochelle v. New Rochelle Fed'n of Teachers, 4 PERB 3060 (N.Y. 1971); Pa. Labor Relations Board v. Mars Area School Dist., 344 A.2d 284 (Pa. 1975); Board of Educ. of W. Orange v. W. Orange Educ. Assn., 319 A.2d 776 (N.J. 1974). *Contra:* Cent. City Educ. v. Ill. Educ. Labor Relations Board, 557 N.E.2d 418 (Ill. App. 1990); Barrington School Comm. v. Rhode Island State Labor Relations Board, 388 A.2d 1369 (R.I. 1978).

Bargainability of "outsourcing" of work that might be performed by unit employees remains particularly contentious. A California statute authorizing school districts' use of private contractors for pupil driver training was upheld, but courts in Pennsylvania, Michigan, and Wisconsin held that outsourcing contracts for bus and food services was subject to mandatory bargaining. *Compare* Ind. School Dist. v. School Serv. Employees Union, 503 N.W 2d 104 (Minn. 1993) (contracting out held not bargainable), *with* Elizabeth Forward School Dist., 624 A.2d 215 (Pa. Cmwlth. 1992) (contracting out, held a mandatory subject of bargaining). *But see* Midland Borough School Dist. v. Pa. Labor Relations Board, 560 A.2d 303 (Pa. 1989); Bay City Educ. Assn. v. Bay City Public Schools, 397 N.W.2d 219 (Mich. App. 1986); Unified School Dist. v. Wisconsin Employment Relations Comm'n, 259 N.W.2d 724 (Wis. 1977); *cf.* Southwestern Vermont Educ. Assn., 396 A.2d 123 (Vt. 1978) (board contract for outside janitorial during a labor dispute held an unfair labor practice); Cent. City Educ. v. Ill. Educ. Labor Relations Board, 557 N.E.2d 857 (Ill. App. 1990); Board of Educ. v. Poughkeepsie P.S. Teachers Assn., 436 N.Y.S.2d 50 (1981).

89. Board of Educ. of Yonkers City School Dist. v. Yonkers Fed'n of Teachers, 383 N.E.2d 569 (N.Y. 1976) (no layoff provision, a subject of permissive bargaining). *Contra:* Westtown Educ. Assn. v. Westtown Public School Board of Educ., 337 N.W.2d 533 (Mich. 1983); Fortney v. School Dist. of W. Salem, 321 N.W.2d 225, 230–1 (Wis. 1981).

90. *See, e.g.,* Montgomery County Educ. Assn. Ind. v. Board of Educ., 534 A.2d 980 (Md. 1987); City of Beloit v. WERC and Beloit Educ. Assn., 242 N.W.2d 231 (Wis. 1976).

91. The distinction between subject matter and "effects" bargaining was adopted in Kansas and Minnesota. Board of Ed. v. Kansas Dept. of Human Resources, 856 P.2d 1343 (Kans. App. 1993) (appraisal criteria not bargainable, but appraisal procedures are); Independent Sch. Dist. v. School Service Employees Union, 503 N.W.2d 104 (Minn. 1993) (effects of contracting out food services, a managerial right, must be negotiated). *See also* Brown v. Milton-Union Ex. Vil. Board of Educ., 531 N.E.2d 1297 (Ohio 1988). *But see* Elizabeth Forward School Dist. v. Pa. Labor Relations Board, 624 A.2d 215 (Pa. Cmwlth. 1992) (proposal to outsource work of bargaining unit employees held subject to mandatory bargaining).

92. *Compare* Boston Teacher's Union v. School Comm., 434 N.E.2d 1258, 1266 (Mass. 1982), *with* Niagara Wheatfield Cent. School Dist., 375 N.E.2d 37 (N.Y. 1978).

93. Martel v. Teachers Retirement Board, 479 N.E.2d 191 (Mass. 1985); Johnson v. Nyquist, 361 N.Y.S.2d 531 (1974) (probationer dismissal, contrary to education statutes—held void); Union Free School Dist. No. 6 v. N.Y. Human Rights App. Board, 320 N.E.2d 859 (N.Y. 1974) (bargained maternity leave, contrary to later statute—held void); Dauphin County Tech. School Educ. Assn. v. School Board, 357 A.2d 721 (Pa. 1976) (dismissal for failure to pay union dues—held void). *Re* layoff and seniority credit, *see* Oak Harbor School Dist. v. Oak Harbor Educ. Assn., 545 P.2d 1197 (Wash. 1976).

94. Chatam Assn. of Educators v. Board of Public Educ., 204 S.E.2d 138 (Ga. 1974) (union distribution of negotiated benefits).

95. McKee v. Board of Educ., 627 A.2d 951 (Conn. App. 1993); Piquard v. Board of Educ., 610 N.E.2d 757 (Ill. App. 1993).

96. *E.g.,* Schaffer v. Board of Educ., 869 S.W.2d 163 (Mo. App. 1993). State laws vary on check-off bargaining. A majority of courts upheld limiting check-off privileges to the certified bargaining agent. San Lorenzo Educ. Assn. v. Wilson, 32 Cal. 3d 841 (1983); Memphis A.F.T. v. Board of Educ., 534 F.2d 699 (6th Cir. 1976); Conn. State Fed'n of Teachers v. Board of Educ. Members, 538 F.2d 471 (2d Cir. 1976). *But see contra:* Board of School Directors v. Wis. Employment Relations Comm'n, 168 N.W.2d 92 (Wis. 1969).

97. Chicago Teachers Union v. Hudson, 475 U.S. 292 (1986); Abood v. Detroit Board of Educ., 431 U.S. 209 (1977). To like effect, *see* Crommley v. Mich. Educ. Assn., 843 F. Supp. 1147 (Mich. 1994); Grunwald v. San Bernardino City Unified School Dist., 994 F.2d 1370 (9th Cir. 1993); New Jersey Ed. Assn. v. New Jersey Public Empt. Relations Comm., 628 A.2d 789 (N.J. Super. 1993). Where the state legislation is silent on union security bargaining, the decision rests with the courts. *See, e.g.,* School Board of Escombia County v. PERB, 350 So. 2d 819 (Fla. 1978) (check-off, a mandatory subject of bargaining); Kentucky Educ. Public Affairs Council v. Ky. Registry of Finance, 667 F.2d 1125 (6th Cir. 1982) (check-off without employee consent—prohibited).

98. *See also* Weissenstein v. Burlington School Comm'rs, 543 A.2d 691 (Vt. 1988).

99. Perry Educ. Assn. V. Perry Local Educ. Assn., 460 U.S. 37 (1983). *Accord:* Davidson v. Community Cons. School Dist., 130 F.3d 265 (7th Cir. 1997).Uncertified minority unions may be excluded from collective negotiation sessions, but not from public board meetings. City of Madison Joint School Dist. No. 8 v. Wis. Employment Relations Comm'n, 429 U.S. 167 (1976).

100. *E.g.,* Board of Educ. v. Chicago Teachers Union, 412 N.E.2d 587 (Ill. 1980). A third form, "final offer" arbitration, is not covered in this text.

101. School Comm. of Springfield v. Springfield Admrs. Assn., 628 N.E.2d 33 (Mass. App. 1994) (appointment of teachers); North Star School Dist. v. North Star Educ. Assn., 625 A.2d 159 (Pa. Cmwlth. 1993) (teacher suspension proceedings); Sup. School Comm. v. Portland Teachers Assn., 338 A.2d 155 (Me. 1975) (work-day issue—restricted to meet-and-discuss consultation).

102. *Position elimination:* School Comm. of Hanover v. Curry, 325 N.E.2d 282 (Mass. 1975). *Teacher files:* Board of Educ. v. Areman, 363 N.Y.S.2d 437 (1975). *Teacher evaluation:* Proviso Council of W. Suburban Teachers Union v. Board of Educ., 513 N.E.2d 996 (Ill. 1987). *Leaves of absence:* Tucson Unified School Dist. No. 1 v. Tucson Educ. Assn., 747 P.2d 602 (Ariz. App. 1987). *Teacher nonrenewal:* Newman v. Board of Educ., 325 A.2d 387 (Del. 1975). *Discharge for cause:* Local 8599 United Steelworkers v. Board

of Educ., 209 Cal. Rptr. 16 (1984). *See also* Port Huron Area School Dist., 393 N.W.2d 811 (Mich. 1986); Annot., *Statutory Arbitration for Public Employees,* 68 A.L.R. 3d 885 (1976) and pkt. part.

103. *Supervisory disputes: Compare* School Comm. of W. Springfield v. Korbut, 358 N.E.2d 831 (Mass. 1976) (denying arbitrability), *with* Scranton School Board v. Scranton Fed'n of Teachers, 365 A.2d 1339 (Pa. 1976) (enforcing arbitration). New Jersey courts upheld arbitration on teacher duty changes, but voided arbitration on class schedule changes. Red Bank Board of Educ. v. Warrington 351 A.2d 778 (N.J. 1976); Ridgefield Park Educ. Assn. v. Ridgefield Board of Educ., 393 A.2d 278 (N.J. 1978).

Union agreements on class size and seniority credits were held enforceable in arbitration. Board of Educ. v. Greenburgh Teachers Fed'n, 381 N.Y.S.2d 517 (1976).

Some courts held that boards may agree to arbitrate teacher evaluations. Central Pt. School Dist. v. Emp. Relations Board, 555 P.2d 1269 (Or. 1976); Board of Educ. v. Harrison Assn. of Teachers, 360 N.Y.S.2d 49 (1974); Milberry v. Board of Educ., 345 A.2d 559 (Pa. 1976).

Teacher termination was subject to grievance arbitration in several states where the bargained agreement limited termination to "just cause." Board of Directors v. Merrymeeting Educ. Assn., 354 A.2d 169 (Me. 1976); Board of Educ. v. Niagara Wheatfield Teachers, 388 N.Y.S.2d 459 (1976); Board of Educ. v. Philadelphia Fed'n of Teachers, 346 A.2d 35 (Pa. 1975); Danville Board of School Directors v. Fifield, 315 A.2d 473 (Vt. 1975); Kaleva-Norman Dickson School Dist. No. 6 v. Kaleva-Norman-Dickson School Teachers Assn., 227 S.W.2d 500 (Mich. 1975).

Agreements to arbitrate board promotion decisions, and to arbitrate sabbatical salaries other than those specified in education statutes were held unenforceable. Board of Educ. v. N. Bergen Educ. Assn., 357 A.2d 302 (N.J. 1976); Cumberland Valley Educ. Assn., v. Cumberland Valley School Dist., 354 A.2d 265 (Pa. 1976).

104. Kentwood Public Schools v. Kent County Educ. Assn., 520 N.W.2d 682 (Mich. App.

1994); Matter of Clarkstown Cent. School Dist., 558 N.Y.S.2d 704 (1990) (presumption of intent to arbitrate). *Re* the essence test, *see* Mahoning County Board v. Mahoning County TMR Educ. Assn., 500 N.E.2d 872 (Ohio 1986). The question of whether a particular proceeding is arbitrable may itself be subject to arbitration. Piercy v. School Board of Washington County, 576 So. 2d 806 (D. Fla. 1991).

105. Sup. School Comm. v. Portland Teachers Assn., 338 A.2d 155 (Me. 1975); Rylke v. Portage Area School Dist., 341 A.2d 233 (Pa. 1975).

106. Canon School Dist. v. W.E.S. Constn. Co., Inc., 868 P.2d 1014 (Ariz. App. 1993).

107. Board of Educ. of Rockford School Dist. v. Illinois Educ. Labor Relations Board, 629 N.E.2d 797 (Ill. App. 1994); Midland Borough School Dist. v. Midland Educ. Assn., 616 A.2d 633 (Pa. 1992).

108. Board of Educ. v. Bellemore-Merrick Soc. Teachers, 347 N.E.2d 603 (N.Y. 1976); School Comm. of Danvers v. Tyman, 360 N.E.2d 877 (Mass. 1977).

109. Piquard v. Board of Educ., 610 N.E.2d 757 (Ill. App. 1993); Board of Trustees v. Cook County College Teachers Union, 318 N.E.2d 202 (Ill. 1974).

110. Board of Directors of Starmont Comm. School Dist. v. Banks, 498 N.W.2d 697 (Iowa 1993) (automatic stay); Chester Upland Educ. Assn. v. Pa. Labor Relations Board, 631 A.2d 723 (Pa. Cmwlth. 1993) (court review of stay order).

111. Martin v. Montezuma-Cortez School Dist., 809 P.2d 1010 (Colo. App. 1990); Jefferson County Board of Educ. v. Jefferson County Educ. Assn., 393 S.E.2d 653 (W. Va. 1990).

112. *See* Annot., *Right of Public Employees to Engage in Work Stoppage,* 37 A.L.R. 3d 1147, Section 12 (1971; Supp. 1988).

113. *Compare, e.g.,* Rapid City Educ. Assn. v. Rapid City School Dist., 442 N.W.2d 926 (S.D. 1989), *with* N.E.A.-Goodland v. Board of Educ., 775 P.2d 675 (Kan. App. 1989).

114. City of Rockford v. Local 113, 240 N.E.2d 705 (1968) (speech); Board of Educ. v. Ohio Educ. Assn., 235 N.E.2d 538 (Ohio 1967); Board of Educ. v. Kankakee Fed'n of Teachers, 264 N.E.2d 18 (Ill. 1970) (conduct).

115. Reichley by Wall v. North Penn School Dist., 626 A.2d 123 (Pa. 1993); Joint School Dist. No. 1 v. Wis. Rapids Educ. Assn., 234 N.W.2d 289 (Wis. 1975); Rockwell v. Board of Educ., 226 N.W.2d 596 (Mich. 1976).

116. State v. Del. Educ. Assn., 326 A.2d 868 (Del. 1974).

117. Timberlane Regional School Dist. v. Timberlane Regional Educ. Assn., 317 A.2d 555 (N.H. 1974).

118. *See* Annot., *Damage Liability of Public Employee Union or Union Officials for Unlawful Work Stoppage*, 84 A.L.R. 3d 336 (1978) and pkt. part. Courts use fines and injunctions sanctions sparingly, lest severe penalties harden labor conflict.

119. Hortonville Joint School Dist. No. 1 v. Hortonville Educ. Assn., 426 U.S. 481 (1976).

120. The courts of California, Florida, Idaho, Indiana, Kentucky, Louisiana, Nevada, New Jersey, Ohio, and Pennsylvania uphold the majority view terminating tenure by resignation, notwithstanding later reemployment by the district. *See* Annot., *Termination of Teacher Tenure—Resignation*, 9 A.L.R. 4th 729 (1981) and pocket part.

121. Petrella v. Siegel, 537 N.Y.S.2d 124 (1988) (statute requirement that resignation be in writing).

122. Mullen v. Fayetteville-Perry L. School Dist., 557 N.E.2d 1235 (Ohio App. 1988).

123. Schwartz v. Board of Educ., 358 N.Y.S.2d 49 (1974); Cords v. Window Rock School Dist., No. 8, 526 P.2d 757 (Ariz. 1974) (failure to perform sabbatical leave agreement—held a resignation). *Implied resignation:* Miller v. Noe, 432 S.W.2d 818 (Ky. 1968) (taking unauthorized leave).

    Re formal resignation, *see* Trumansburg Cent. School Dist. v. Chalone, 499 N.Y.S.2d 92 (1982).

124. *E.g.*, Rockwell, *supra* note 115; Shiffen v. Board of Educ., 206 N.W.2d 250 (Mich. 1973).

125. Babitzke v. Silverton Union High School, 695 P.2d 93 (Or. App. 1985). *But see* Kearns v. Lower Merion School Dist., 346 A.2d 875 (Pa. 1975) (failure to report for work).

126. Wiljama v. Board of Educ., 213 N.W.2d 830 (Mich. 1975).

127. Gould v. Board of Educ., 616 N.E.2d 142 (N.Y. 1993) (mistaken belief on resignor's tenure rights); Boulder Valley School Dist. v. Price, 805 P.2d 1085 (Colo. 1991) (resignation by teacher in weakened mental condition).

128. Booth v. Argenbright, 731 P.2d 1318 (Mont. 1987); Knee v. School Dist., 676 P.2d 727 (Idaho 1984).

129. Leithliter v. Board of Trustees, 91 Cal. Rptr. 215 (1971).

130. Mohn v. Indep. School Dist., 471 N.W.2d 723 (Minn. App. 1991) (resignation as teacher did not surrender status as principal).

131. *Board acceptance required:* Braught v. Board of Educ., 483 N.E.2d 623 (Ill. 1985) (acceptance indicated by replacement of resigning teacher); Sherman v. Board of Educ., 389 N.Y.S.2d 515 (1976); Hart v. School Board of Wakalla County, 340 So. 2d 121 (Fla. 1976).

    Board acceptance not required: Teague v. Walnut Ridge Schools, 868 S.W.2d 56 (Ark. 1993); Mitchell v. Jackson County Board of Educ., 582 So. 2d 1128 (Ala. 1991); Sinkevich v. School Committee of Raynham, 530 N.E.2d 173 (Mass. 1988); Booth v. Argenbright, 731 P.2d 1318 (Mont. 1987); Warren v. Buncome City Board of Educ. 343 S.E.2d 225 (N.C. 1986).

132. Palone v. Jefferson Parish School Board, 297 So. 2d 208 (La. 1974). Martin v. School Committee of Natick, 480 N.E.2d 625 (Mass. 1985) (hearing not required for RIF dismissal); Dailey v. Board of Educ., 327 N.W.2d 321 (Mich. 1982) (nonrenewal not applicable to RIF); Minn. Assn. Public Schools v. Hanson, 178 N.W.2d 846 (Minn. 1970) (tenure cannot freeze RIF reorganization).

133. *See* Hartmeister and Russo, *Taxing the System When Selecting Teachers for Reduction-In-Force*, 130 Ed. Law Rep. (No. 3) 989 (1999).

134. E. York School Dist. v. Long, 430 A.2d 267 (Pa. 1981).

135. Unlike many states, RIFs are not authorized for budgetary shortfalls in Pennsylvania. E. York School Dist. v. Long, 430 A.2d 267 (Pa. 1981).

136. Palone v. Jefferson Parish School Board, 297 So. 2d 208 (La. 1974); Karbach v. Board of Educ., 114 Cal. Rptr. 84 (1974); Geduldig v. Board of Educ., 351 N.Y.S.2d 167 (1974).

137. Palos Verses Faculty Assn. v. Governing Board, 183 Cal. Rptr. 196 (1982); Dykeman v. Board of Educ., 316 N.W.2d 69 (Neb. 1982); E. Detroit Fed'n of Teachers v. Board of Educ., 223 N.W.2d 9 (Mich. 1974).

For application of overlapping statutes, *see* Works v. Abrahamson Union High School Dist. Board of Directors, 483 A.2d 258 (Vt. 1984); Gassman v. Governing Board of Rincon Valley School Dist., 128 Cal. Rptr. 273 (1976).

138. *See* authorities discussed in Sullivan v. Teague Superintendent of Educ., 424 So. 2d 574 (Ala. 1982). DeSimone v. Board of Educ., 612 F. Supp. 1568 (E.D. N.Y. 1985).

139. Young v. Board of Educ., 315 N.E.2d 768 (N.Y. 1974); Jordahl v. Ind. School Dist. No. 129, 225 N.W.2d 224 (Minn. 1974).

140. Holmes v. Board of Trustees, 792 P.2d 10 (Mont. 1990); Strand v. Spec. School Dist., 361 N.W.2d 369 (Minn. App. 1984); Coates v. Board of Educ., 662 P.2d 1279 (Kan. 1983). For an exceptional view in declining enrollments, *see* Underwood v. Henry County School Board, 427 S.E.2d 330 (Va. 1993)

141. Walkowski v. Duquesne City School Dist., 644 A.2d 1277 (Pa. Cmwlth. 1994); Jenson v. Jt. Ind. School Dist., 408 N.W.2d 203 (Minn. App. 1987) (seniority under collective bargaining agreement).

142. McManus v. Indep. School Dist., 321 N.W.2d 891 (Minn. 1982).

143. *Re* military leave, *see* Rochester Area School Board v. Duncan, 528 A.2d 48 (Pa. 1987); *Re* maternity leave, *see* Somon v. School Committee of Boston, 478 N.E.2d 137 (1985); *Re* approved leave, *see* Andresky v. W. Allegheny School Dist., 437 A.2d 1075 (Pa. Cmwlth. 1981).

144. Dreyfuss v. Board of Educ., 339 N.Y.S.2d 547 (1972).

145. Triggs v. Berkeley County Board of Educ., 425 S.E.2d 111 (W. Va. 1992).

146. Dilley v. Slippery Rock Area School Dist., 625 A.2d 153 (Pa. Cmwlth. 1993).

147. Gill v. Duchess County Board of Coop. Educ. Services, 472 N.Y.S.2d 435 (1984).

148. Beckett v. Roderick, 251 A.2d 427 (Me. 1969).

149. Klein v. Board of Educ., 497 N.W.2d 620 (Minn. App. 1993). *Compare, e.g.,* Rappold v. Board of Educ., 464 N.Y.S.2d 240 (1983), *with* Dykeman v. Board of Educ., 316 N.W.2d 69 (Neb. 1982). Butler v. Board of Educ., 769 P.2d 651 (Kan. 1989), held that a board need not rearrange class schedules to create enough part-time positions in order to retain tenured teacher. The case law also varies as to whether the board or the complaining teacher has the burden of proving that a particular realignment was reasonable or unreasonable. Musorofiti v. Board of Educ., 482 N.E.2d 1226 (N.Y. 1985); Hayes v. Board of Educ., 431 N.E.2d 690 (Ill. 1982).

150. *Exclusive statutory grounds:* W. Va. Dept. of Human Services v. Boley, 358 S.E.2d 438 (W. Va. 1987) (child abuse statute, not ground for teacher discharge); Schultz v. Board of Educ., 315 N.W.2d 633, 635 (Neb. 1982).

Hearing requirements: see McMillrn v. U.S.D. Preate, 855 P.2d 896 (Kan. 1993); Janke v. Community School Board, 587 N.Y.S. 2d (N.Y. 1992).

151. See cases authorities collected in *Annots., Modern Status of Rule That Employer May Discharge At-Will Employee,* 12 A.L.R. 4th 544 (1982) and pkt. part; *Damages—Teacher's Wrongful Discharge,* 22 A.L.R. 3d 1047 (1968) and pkt. part.

152. Chicago Board of Educ. v. Payne, 430 N.E.2d 310 (Ill. 1981); Wishart v. McDonald, 500 F.2d 1110 (1st Cir. 1974); Denton v. S. Kitsap School Dist., 516 P.2d 1080 (Wash. 1973).

Other grounds for discharge in some states include disloyalty, intemperance, cruelty, willful misconduct, good and sufficient cause, evident unfitness, and neglect of duty. Roberts v. Rapides Par. School Board, 617 So. 2d 187 (La. App. 1993) (neglect of duty); Stansberry v. Argensbright, 738 P.2d 478 (Mont. 1987); Blaine v. Moffat County School Dist., 709 P.2d 96 (Colo. App. 1985) (drinking with students); Board of School Directors, 353 A.2d 898 (Pa. 1976) (cruelty).

153. Nat'l Gay Task Force v. Board of Educ., 729 F.2d 1270 (10th Cir. 1984). *See generally* Delon and VanZandt, *Statutory Grounds for Dismissal Survive Vagueness Challenges,* 17 West Ed. Rep. 313 (1984).

154. *Compare, e.g.,* Goldin v. Board of Central School Dist. No. 1, 359 N.Y.S.2d 384 (1973) (consensual sexual activity bewteen teacher and former student—held insufficient for discharge), with Sullivan v. Meade County Indep. School Dist. No. 101, 387 F. Supp. 1237 (D.S.D. 1975), *aff'd,* 530 F.2d 799 (8th Cir. 1976) (teacher discharged for cohabitation with married man). *But see* Board of Educ. v. Jennings, 651 P.2d 1037 (N.M. 1982) (reinstatement of principal discharged for adulterous affair with school secretary).

155. Schulz v. Board of Educ., 315 N.W.2d 633, 637 (Neb. 1983); Board of Educ. of Baltimore County, 507 A.2d 192 (Md. 1986).

156. West v. Tangipahoa Par. School Board, 615 So. 2d 979 (La. App. 1993) (failure to screen offensive movies for class viewing, held not ground for dismissal in light of teacher's past record).

157. *Re* warning letter procedure, *see* Shepard v. South Harrison R-II School Dist., 718 S.W.2d 195 (Mo. App. 1986). *Re* remediation, *see* Mott v. Endicotta School Dist. No. 308, 713 P.2d 98 (Wash. 1986); Hanlon v. Board of Educ., 695 S.W.2d 930 (Mo. App. 1985).

    Compare Board of Educ. v. State Board of Educ., 577 N.E.2d 575 (Ill. App. 1991) (sexual letters to students—held irremediable); McCullough v. Ill. State Board of Educ., 562 N.E.2d 430 (Ill. App. 1990) (criminal tax conviction—held irremediable), *with* Board of Educ. of Chicago v. Johnson, 570 N.E.2d 869 (Ill. App. 1991) (violation of board rule—held remediable).

158. *See* Annot., *Teachers' Incompetency, Inefficiency,* 4 A.L.R. 3d 1090 (1965) and pkt. part.

159. (1) Singleton v. Iberville Parish School Board, 136 So. 2d 809 (La. 1961); (2) Rainwater v. Board of Educ., 645 S.W.2d 172 (Mo. App. 1983); (3) Jones v. Jefferson Parish School Board, 688 F.2d 837 (5th Cir. 1982); (4) Fender v. School Dist. No. 25, 347 N.E.2d 270 (Ill. 1976); (5) Sutherby v. Gobels Board of Educ., 348 N.W.2d 277 (Mich. App. 1984); (6) Spano v. School Dist. of Brentwood, 316 A.2d 162 (Pa. 1974) (refusal to consult superiors on curriculum); (7) Pratt v. Ala. State Tenure Comm'n, 394 So. 2d 18 (Ala. 1980); (8) Mortweet v. Ethan Board of Educ., 241 N.W.2d 580 (S.D. 1976) (insensitivity to student needs; reluctance to try new teaching methods); Di Leo v. Greenfield, 541 F.2d 949 (2d Cir. 1976) (neglect of professional duties); (9) Phillips v. Board of Educ., 330 A.2d 151 (Del. 1975); (10) Katz v. Ambach, 472 N.Y.S.2d 492 (1984).

160. Dusanek v. Hannon, 677 F.2d 538 (7th Cir. 1982); Fitzpatrick School Administrative Dist., 465 N.Y.S.2d 240 (1983).

161. *See* Annot., *What Constitutes Insubordination,* 78 A.L.R. 3d 83 (1977) and pkt. part. *Defiance of direct orders:* Alinovi v. Worcester School Committee, 777 F.2d 776 (1st Cir. 1985); Weaver v. Board of Educ., 514 N.Y.S.2d 473 (1987). *Violation of school rules:* Simmons v. Vancouver School Dist., 704 P.2d 648 (Wash. 1985); Thompson v. Board of Educ., 688 P.2d 954 (Colo. App. 1983).

162. *Unauthorized absence:* Christopherson v. Spring Valley Elem. School Dist., 413 N.E.2d 199 (Ill. 1980); Anderson v. Indep. School Dist., 292 N.W.2d 562 (Minn. 1980); Willis v. School Dist., 606 S.W.2d 189 (Mo. 1980). *Encouraging disrespect:* Jacker v. School Board, 426 So. 2d 1149 (Fla. App. 1983); Birdwell v. Hazelwood School Dist., 491 F.2d 490 (8th Cir. 1973) (inciting students to "get the R.O.T.C. off campus"). *Disregard of corporal punishment policy:* Burton v. Kirby, 775 S.W.2d 834 (Tex. 1989).

163. Calvin v. Rupp, 334 F. Supp. 358 (N.D. Mo. 1971).

164. Rumora v. Board of Educ., 335 N.E.2d 378 (Ohio 1973).

165. Beverlin v. Board of Educ., 216 S.E.2d 544 (W. Va. 1975); Howell v. Winn Parish School Board, 321 So. 2d 420 (La. 1975).

166. Elvin v. City of Waterville, 573 A.2d 381 (Me. 1990); Roberts v. Santa Cruz Unified School Dist., 778 P.2d 1294 (Ariz. 1989); Myers v. Orleans Parish School Board, 423 So. 2d 1030 (La. 1983); Kurlander v. School Comm., 451 N.E.2d 138 (Mass. 1983).

167. Scott County School Dist. v. Dietrich, 499 N.E.2d 1170 (Ind. App. 1986); Brubaker v. Board of Educ., 502 F.2d 973 (7th Cir. 1974); Carrao v. Board of Educ., 360 N.E.2d 536 (Ill. 1977).

168. Clayton v. Board of Educ., 375 N.Y.S.2d 169 (1975).

169. Wishart v. McDonald, 500 F.2d 110 (1st Cir. 1974).

170. Stansberry v. Argensbright, 738 P.2d 478 (Mont. 1987); Rogliano v. Fayette City Board of Educ., 347 S.E.2d 220 (W. Va. 1986). *Compare* Jefferson County School Dist. v. Fair Dismissal Appeals Board, 812 P.2d 1384 (Or. 1991); School Dist. of Philadelphia v. Puljer, 500 A.2d 905 (Pa. Cmwlth. 1985); Schmidt v. Board of Educ., 712 S.E.2d 45, 48 (Mo. App. 1986).

171. *E.g.,* Woo v. Putnam County Board of Educ., 504 S.E.2d 644 (W. Va. 1998) (notorious publicity and public uproar on teacher use of marijuana). *See generally* C. Hooker, *Terminating Teachers for Conduct Beyond the Schoolhouse Gate,* 96 Ed. Law Rep. 1 (1995).

172. Westley v. Terrebone Parish School Board, 665 F. Supp. 499 (E.D. La. 1987) (outside theft); McBroom v. Board of Educ., 494 N.E.2d 1191 (Ill. 1986) (locker theft); Bolentine v. Ark. State Board of Educ., 684 S.W.2d 246 (Ark. 1985) (school record falsification).

173. Appeal of Flannery, 178 A.2d 751 (Pa. 1963); Beterson v. Stewart, 140 S.E.2d 482 (S.C. 1965).

174. Rado v. Board of Educ., 583 A.2d 102 (Conn. 1990) (phone tampering and eavesdropping).

175. *Compare, e.g.,* Adams v. State Professional Practices Council, 406 So. 2d 1170 (Fla. 1980); Chicago Board of Educ. v. Payne, 430 N.E.2d 310 (Ill. 1981); *with* Rogliano v. Fayette City Board of Educ., 347 S.E.2d 220 (W. Va. 1986); Comings v. State Board of Educ., 100 Cal. Rptr. 73 (1972).

176. DeMichele v. Greenburch Centennial School Dist., 167 F.3d 784 (2d Cir. 1999); Parker v. Byron Center Board of Educ., 582 N.W.2d 859 (Mich. 1998) (sexual relations with fifth grader). *See also* Fisher v. Ind. School Dist. No. 622, 357 N.W.2d 152 (Minn. 1984)

177. *See* cases collected in Annots., *Dismissal of Teachers—Sexual Conduct,* 78 A.L.R. 3d 19 (1977) and pkt. part; and *Dismissal of Teachers—Illegal Drugs,* 47 A.L.R. 3d 754 (1973) and pkt. part; Stredonsky v. Sobol, 572 N.Y.S.2d 445 (1991); Ulrich v. State, 555 N.E.2d 172 (Ind. 1990); Sauter v. Mt. Vernon School Dist., 791 P.2d 549 (Wash. 1990).

178. Hamm v. Poplar Bluff R-1 School Dist., 955 S.W.2d 27 (Mo. 1997).

179. Ponton v. Newport News School Board, 632 F. Supp. 1056 (E.D. Va. 1986); Avery v. Homewood City Board of Educ., 674 F.2d 337 (5th Cir. 1982) (unwed pregnancy, not a per se "cause" for discharge).

180. Erb v. Iowa State Board of Pub. Instruction, 216 N.W.2d 339 (Iowa 1974).

181. Bowers v. Hardwick, 478 U.S. 186 (1986).

182. Board of Educ. v. Nat'l Gay Task Force, 729 F.2d 1270 (10th Cir. 1984), *aff'd,* 105 S. Ct. 1858 (1985); Rowland v. Mad River School Dist., 730 F.2d 444 (6th Cir. 1984) (self-proclaimed lesbian love affair).

183. Pettit v. State Board of Educ., 513 P.2d 889 (Cal. 1973) (public discussion of "swinger" conduct); McConnell v. Anderson, 451 F.2d 193 (8th Cir. 1971) (publicized request for homosexual marriage license); *in re* Grossman, 316 A.2d 39 (N.J. 1974) (publicized sex change surgery); Weissbaum v. Hannon, 439 F. Supp. 873 (N.D. Ill. 1977) (posing nude for a magazine); Wishart v. McDonald, 500 F.2d 1110 (1st Cir. 1974) (lewd gestures with mannequin in public view).

184. *Cf.* Board of Educ. v. State Board of Educ., 577 N.E.2d 575 (Ill. App. 1991) (sexual letters to students).

185. Jarvella v. Willoughby-Eastlake City School Dist. Board of Educ., 233 N.E.2d 143 (Ohio 1967).

186. de Groat v. Newark Unified School Dist., 133 Cal. Rptr. 225 (1976).

187. Gross v. Board of Educ., 571 N.Y.S.2d 200 (1991); Greater Clark County School Corp. v. Myers, 493 N.E.2d 1267 (Ind. App. 1986); Annot., *Damages—Teacher's Wrongful Discharge,* 22 A.L.R. 3d 1047 (1968) and pkt. part.

188. Annotation, *supra* note 187 at p. 1051.

189. Annotation, *supra* note 187 at p. 1052.

190. *Re* supervisors, *see* Williams v. Banning, 72 F.3d 552 (7th Cir. 1995) (supervisor not liable); Grant v. Lone Star Co., 21 F.3d 649 (5th Cir. 1995). *Re* union liability, *see* Greene v. Pomona Unified School Dist., 38 Cal. Rptr. 2d 770 (1995).

191. For a review of the authorities on shifting burdens of proof, *see* St. Mary's Honor Center

v. Hicks, 113 S. Ct. 2742 (1992); Jones v. School Dist. of Phila.,—F.3d—(3d Cir. 2000) (Title VII), *accord:* Crim v. Board of Educ., 147 F.3d 535, 557–8 (7th Cir. 1998); *semble:* Green v. School Board of Hillborough County, 25 F.3d 974 (11th Cir. 1994); Fairbairn v. Board of Educ., 876 F. Supp. 432 (E.D. N.Y. 1995) (Title IX and 42 U.S.C. § 1981); Thomas v. Contoocook Valley School Dist., 150 F.3d 31 (1st Cir. 1990) (ADA); Geary v. Visitation of Blessed Virgin Mary Parish School, 7 F.3d 324 (3d Cir. 1993) (age discrimination); Cliff v. Board of School Commissioners, 42 F.3d 403 (7th Cir. 1994) (age discrimination).

192. Turic v. Holland Hospitality Inc., 85 F.3d 1211, at p. 1213 (6th Cir. 1996).

193. Schurr v. Resorts International Hotel Inc., 196 F.3d 486 (3d Cir. 1999).

194. Mendoza v. Borden Inc., 195 F.3d 1238 (11th Cir. 1999).

195. Farber v. Massillon Board of Educ., 908 F.2d 65 (6th Cir. 1990); Burns v. Gadsden State Comm. College, 908 F.2d 1512 (11th Cir. 1990).

196. Farber v. Massillon Board of Educ., 908 F.2d 65 (6th Cir. 1990); McCullar v. Ill. Human Rights Comm'n, 511 N.E.2d 1375 (Ill. 1987) (pay differential for boys' basketball coach and girls' volleyball coach—upheld).

197. Kindred v. Northome/Ind. School Dist., 983 F. Supp. 835 (D. Minn. 1997).

198. Los Angeles v. Manhart, 435 U.S. 702 (1978); Norris v. Arizona Governing Comm., 463 U.S. 1073 (1983); Spirit v. TIAA-CREF, 735 F.2d 23 (2d Cir. 1984).

199. Board of Regents, Univ. of Nebraska v. Dawes, 522 F.2d 380 (8th Cir. 1975).

200. Berry v. Board of Supervisors, 715 F.2d 971 (5th Cir. 1983).

201. Sutton v. United Air Lines Inc., 119 S. Ct. 2139 (1999); Murphy v. United Parcel Service, 119 S. Ct. 2133 (1999).

This text does not cover the special questions on drug addicts and alcoholics, and their possible rehabilitation—questions on which the federal courts are currently divided. *See, e.g.,* Zenor v. El Paso Healthcare System, 176 F.3d 847 (5th Cir. 1999)

202. Doe v. Dekalb County School Dist., 145 F.3d 1441 (11th Cir. 1998) (teacher with HIV infection), citing School Board of Nassau County v. Arline, 480 U.S. 273 (1987) (teacher with tuberculosis, in remission, decided prior to ADA under Rehabilitation Act).

203. Sullivan v. River Valley School Dist., 197 F.3d 804 (6th Cir. 1999).

204. See Comment, R.D. Wenkart, *Public Employment, Reasonable Accommodation and the ADA,* 133 Ed. Law Rep. 647 (1999).

205. *Change of work schedule:* Jacobsen v. Tillman, 17 F. Supp. 2d 1018 (1998) (change that would not defeat job utility—held reasonable). *But see* the *Salmon* case at the end of this chapter for instances where a change of hours would defeat job purpose and therefore is not a "reasonable accommodation."

Leave of absence: Cehrs v. Northeast Ohio Alzheimer's Res. Center, 155 F.3d 775 (6th Cir. 1998).

Transfer to open position: Jackson v. N.Y. State Division of Labor, 205 F.3d 562 (2d Cir. 2000).

206. *See* Smith v. Midland Brake Inc., 158 F.3d 1060 (10th Cir. 1999) and authorities cited in McMackins v. Elk Grove, 21 F. Supp. 2d 1202 (E.D. Cal. 1998); Gaul v. Lucent Technology, 134 F.3d 596 (3d Cir. 1998).

207. Alsbrook v. City of Maumelle, 184 F.3d 999 (8th Cir. 1999), *cert. granted sub nom,* Ashbrook v. Arkansas,120 S. Ct. 1003 (2000); Kimel v. Fla. Board of Regents, 139 F.3d 1427 (11th Cir. 1998), *cert. granted sub nom,* Fla. Dept. of Corrections v. Dickson, 120 S. Ct. 976 (2000).

208. Reeves v. Sanderson, 127 S. Ct. 2097 (2000); Sanchez v. Denver Public Schools, 164 F.3d 527, 531 (10th Cir. 1998); Widoe v. District No. 111 Otoe County School, 147 F.3d 726 (8th Cir. 1998).

209. Reeves, *supra* note 208.

210. Wooden v. Board of Educ., 931 F.2d 376 (6th Cir. 1919) (hiring younger more qualified person); Spring v. Sheboygan Area School Dist., 865 F.2d 883 (7th Cir. 1989) (change of school assignment); Phair v. Montgomery County Public Schools, 3 F. Supp. 2d 644 (D. Md. 1997) (unfavorable rating).

211. Hodgson v. First Federal Savings & Loan Assn., 455 F.2d 818 (5th Cir. 1972)

(disapproving refusal to hire 47-year-old woman as bank teller).

212. E.E.O.C. v. School Board of Pinellas County, 742 F. Supp. 622 (M.D. Fla. 1990); Geller v. Markham, 635 F.2d 1027 (2d Cir. 1980).

213. E.E.O.C. v. Comm. Unit School Dist., 642 F. Supp. 902 (S.D. Ill. 1986) (reclassification of putative retirees—held discrimination); Trans World Airlines v. Thurston, 105 S. Ct. 613, 621 (1985).

214. E.E.O.C. v. State of Ill., 69 F.3d 167 (7th Cir. 1995) (ban on mandatory age retirement);

E.E.O.C. v. Newport Mesa Unified School Dist., 893 F. Supp. 927 (C.D. Cal. 1995) (age-based salary differentials violate ADEA).

215. Pub. L. 101-521 (1990) [overruling the effect of Pub. Employees Ret. System v. Betts, 492 U.S. 158 (1989)].

216. *Cf.* Oubre v. Entergy Operations Inc., 522 U.S. 422 (1998). *See also* 68 U.S.L.W. 2243 (11-2-99).

217. Kimel v Fla. Board of Regents, 120 S. Ct. 631 (2000). *See, e.g.,* Duke v. Grady Mun. Schools, 127 F.3d 972 (10th Cir. 1997); Doe,—U.S.—, 117 S. Ct. 900–4 (1997).

CHAPTER 6

Personal Civil Rights—Teachers

❖ **CHAPTER DISCUSSION QUESTIONS**

❖ **CASES**

❖ **ENDNOTES**

[†]Indicates case with review questions.

BACKGROUND NOTE

The preceding chapter dealt largely with the laws governing employment rights and duties. This chapter deals with broader personal rights of teachers and school employees. Constitutional rights differ in nature and scope from rights created by federal or state statutes. Constitutions are concerned only with protecting individuals against infringements by governments and government actors, as in state-operated public schools, but statutes may create rights and remedies not created by the Constitution. Further, state laws often create civil rights beyond those guaranteed by federal law. State-to-state variations on state-created rights are too great to permit adequate summarization in this text, but the following discussion will mention some examples of significant state law supplements to federal civil rights.

The law regarding civil rights developed piecemeal, over time, in response to historical experience. It does not form a unified or coordinated code. The following sections treat each branch of relevant law separately though many suits arising from a common set of events allege multiple, concurrent civil rights violations under different statutes and different constitutional provisions. The *Lacks* and *Curtis* cases at the end of this chapter exemplify the confluence of constitutional and statutory claims.

The Fourteenth Amendment is the principal source of constitutional rights for public school teachers. It reads:

> *No State* shall make or enforce any law which shall abridge the privileges or immunities of citizens . . .; nor shall any *state* deprive any *person* of life, *liberty* or property without *due process* of law; nor deny to any person . . . the *equal protection of the laws.* (Emphasis added.)

As interpreted by the Supreme Court, the Fourteenth Amendment covers two kinds of rights—*unwritten* fundamental rights that are rooted in historical notions of liberty (such as parental, familial, and privacy rights) and rights derived from the language of the Fourteenth Amendment and of those parts of the original Bill of Rights, particularly the First and Fourth Amendments, which the Supreme Court held to be encompassed by the Fourteenth Amendment Due Process and Equal Protection Clauses. These rights are both procedural and substantive, and court doctrines determine their scope and operation in the school setting.

CONSTITUTIONAL PROCEDURAL RIGHTS

Due Process under Federal Law

A Supreme Court Justice once observed that "[T]he history of liberty has largely been the history of observance of procedural safeguards." *McNabb v. U.S.*, 318 U.S. 332, 347 (1943). School decisions that deny *procedural* due process are invalid and will be overturned, even though they would have been lawful had due process been afforded. This consequence leads to the questions whether, in a given case, a teacher is entitled to constitutional (as distinguished from statutory or regulatory) procedures and, if so, what procedures are constitutionally due? An individual must, of course, request due process procedures or risk waiving them. A due process claim may also be denied where the teacher failed to seek an available hearing under union grievance procedures.[1]

Cases Entitled to Due Process

Constitutional procedures are due only where the affected party has a constitutionally recognized *liberty* or *property* interest in the proceedings. The existence of such a protected interest is often an issue.

Liberty Interests. The obvious example of a liberty interest is seen when school authorities move to punish a teacher for exercising freedom of speech. A less obvious instance is seen when school actions injure the teacher's professional reputation or opportunity to pursue his or her occupation. To command due process, school actions must not only affect a constitutional liberty, but must *sufficiently* affect them. Not all uncomplimentary reports sufficiently affect reputation to support a liberty interest claim. Thus, courts have not found any injury to a liberty interest from statements regarding (a) poor work habits; (b) noncooperation; (c) tardiness, absence, and failure to maintain discipline; (d) unsatisfactory work performance; and (e) aggressive behavior.[2] Derogatory comments or findings against a teacher were held not sufficiently stigmatizing as to require due process hearings where (a) the charges were undisclosed to the public, or (b) were undisputed or admitted by the teacher, or (c) asserted a personal opinion but not an official fact, for instance, where a board member opined to a nonofficial that "We need to get rid of that SOB."[3] That statement may show personal bias, but not official stigma injury to a liberty interest. A district's failure to provide a public explanation for suspending and not renewing a teacher was found not to rise to the level of stigmatizing a teacher's reputation where the district did not publicize its actions or its reasons for those actions.[4]

On the other hand, contested charges of dishonesty, emotional instability, and insubordination sufficiently affect an interest in professional reputation to require due process hearings.[5] In sum, the right to due process will depend on the impact of specific circumstances, including the nature, disclosure, and denial or admission of particular conduct.

Property Interests. Unlike liberty interests, which are grounded in the Constitution itself, "property interests" must be founded in state law.

> Property interests . . . are not created by the Constitution. Rather they are created and their dimensions are defined by existing rules and understandings that stem

> from an independent source such as state law–rules or regulations. . . . [*Board of Regents v. Roth,* 408 U.S. 564, 577 (1972)]

As noted elsewhere, teacher tenure and certification are classic species of property interest that cannot be withdrawn without due process.[6] An administrator whose position was not protected under state law could not assert a constitutional property interest in continuation of employment.[7] As seen in the nonrenewal cases in Chapter 5 and in the *Curtis* case at the end of this chapter, many employment positions do not encompass a property interest. Tenure and certification statutes usually vest rights that courts recognize as a species of property interest.[8] In exceptional circumstances, a court may find a property interest that is not expressly conferred by state law, but derived from state official custom, but most courts have refused to do so.[9]

Due Process Procedures

"Once due process is required, the question remains—what process is due?"[10] There is no uniform answer; only a formula.

> The very nature of due process negates any concept of inflexible procedures universally applicable to every imaginable situation. [*Goss v. Lopez,* 419 U.S., at 578 (1975)]

> Due process . . . is not a technical conception with a fixed content unrelated to time, place and circumstances. . . . [*Ingraham v. Wright,* 430 U.S. 651, 675 (1977)]

As explained by the Supreme Court in the above *Goss* case, due process does not require school authorities to employ the same procedures in every case or adopt the same procedures used by courts.

The core requirement of constitutional due process is *fair treatment,* and "some kind of hearing" to afford a teacher an opportunity to respond to adverse proposals or charges. But the quantum and formality of procedures needed for a fair hearing will vary with the nature of each case. In exigent cases, due process may be satisfied even without a prior hearing where prehearing suspensions and removal of a teacher are made on credible allegations of serious misconduct that could threaten school stability or safety, as long as a fair hearing on those allegations is offered the teacher with reasonable promptness following his or her removal.[11]

Unless waived by the affected party, due process requires at a minimum the first three of the following elements:

1. Reasonable *notice* of the charges or subject of the hearing, which allows a fair *opportunity to prepare* for the hearing,
2. A *reasonably prompt hearing,*
3. An *impartial tribunal* to hear and decide the charges,
4. The right to present *evidence* and to *confront* adverse witnesses and evidence,

5. The right to be represented by legal *counsel,*
6. The right to an *official record* of the proceeding, and
7. The right to *appeal* the hearing decisions to higher authority.

As to the need for additional procedures beyond notice, a hearing, and an impartial tribunal, the Supreme Court prescribed the following test, which balances the need for progressively greater formalities to protect the individual's interest against the administrative fiscal and operational burdens that additional procedures would entail:

> First, the private interest that will be affected . . .; second, the risk of erroneous deprivation of such interest . . . and the probable value, if any, of additional or substitute procedural safeguards; and, finally, the [public] interests, including the functions involved and the fiscal or administrative burdens that the additional or substitute procedural requirements would entail. [*Mathews v. Eldridge,* 424 U.S. 319, 335 (1976)]

Concrete guidance on applying this formula to various case circumstances can only be gathered from court decisions.[12]

Notice and Hearing. A hearing must be provided unless it is waived or would be pointless, i.e., where the pertinent facts are undisputed and the school board has no discretion but to take legally prescribed action on those facts.[13] If the timing and location of hearings are unfairly set, such as within 24 hours or with only several hours notice, the hearing and resulting teacher discharge are legally void and subject to reversal.[14]

A hearing notice must contain sufficient information to enable the addressee reasonable opportunity to ascertain and respond to the charges. While school authorities need not provide teachers with minute specification of all evidence, unreasonably vague notices or denial of teacher access to essential evidence will nullify the proceedings and any action based on them.[15] Adding new charges that potentially support additional penalties that were not mentioned in a prior notice may in fairness require new notices on those charges, even though they are based on the same conduct covered by the prior notice.[16]

The fair notice principle also underlies the void for vagueness doctrine, which invalidates statutes and regulations that do not contain sufficient notice and information to enable persons of ordinary intelligence to ascertain that the sanctioned conduct was prohibited and punishable.[17] Courts are particularly apt to void unclear laws or regulations that could chill freedom of speech.

Prehearing Terminations and Suspensions. Notice and hearing must normally be afforded *before* adverse action is taken against a teacher, but as noted above, that right may be postponed and subordinated to overriding needs of school safety and security that require immediate action, provided a hearing is set as promptly as practical thereafter.[18] The question whether alleged threats to school interests are sufficiently grave or imminent to forego a prior hearing is a matter for court determination.[19] Courts have nullified prehearing actions that, if later disclosed, would irreparably damage an employee's reputation and future employment prospects.[20]

Impartial Tribunal.   Hearings by biased officials or tribunals are by definition unfair, but the constitutional standard of an impartial tribunal is much looser for school decisions than for court decisions. School boards and their members are presumed to be impartial, and the burden of rebutting that presumption lies with the party challenging their impartiality. The Supreme Court thus ruled that a teacher who was discharged by a school board for participating in an illegal strike did not establish board bias by showing that the board was involved in heated labor negotiations that led to the strike. Because the interest of board members in the labor negotiations did not involve their personal or financial interests, the Court held that their presumed impartiality was not disproven.[21] In like vein, prehearing board investigations or public statements regarding a teacher's personal conduct or performance did not alone void later board hearings, absent proofs that board members' opinions were not open to reconsideration on the basis of evidence presented at a later hearing.[22] However, if a teacher satisfies a court that a board member or hearing officer irrevocably prejudged a case, the holding of a later hearing will not restore impartiality or validate the board's decision.[23]

The presumption of impartiality may be rebutted by evidence of malice, fixed prejudgment, or conflict of interest on the part of a hearing officer or board members, for instance, where a board member involved in a fight with a teacher participated in a later hearing involving that teacher.[24] In stark circumstances, a court may conclude that even the appearance of personal bias denied due process and nullified a board decision, for instance, where a board member's wife testified against a school principal in a demotion hearing and was present during board deliberations and vote on the principal's demotion.[25] Other common grounds for destroying impartiality include hearings where the same person acted as both judge and witness against the teacher, or as both hearing prosecutor and legal counsel to the deciding tribunal.[26] However, the participation of school solicitors as prosecutors in school board hearings does not automatically destroy the board's impartiality if the solicitor does not counsel the board in its deliberations.[27]

Right to Present and Confront Evidence.   The right to cross-examine adverse witnesses, a fixture in formal court hearings, does not extend to all school hearings. In the *Goss* case, which is discussed in Chapter 7, cross-examination was not required for summary hearings on minor infractions that involve minor penalties. Many hearing issues and affected interests are not so weighty as to require cross-examination, but the cases reveal no pattern of opinion as to which circumstances or teacher interests are sufficiently weighty to require cross-examination or prohibit the use of hearsay evidence (statements of absent third parties who cannot be cross-examined).[28] Examples of situations where due process requires confrontation of adverse evidence include board failure to disclose information essential to a defense, or exclusion of a party from a hearing where evidence adverse to that party is presented, or board refusal to produce a requested material witness (examining doctor).[29]

Right to Counsel.   The right to have legal counsel present and participate in a hearing, like the right of cross-examination, will depend on whether such assistance is fairly needed.

> The requirement of counsel as an ingredient of fairness is a function of all of the other aspects of the hearing. Where the proceeding is non-criminal in nature, where the hearing is investigative and not adversarial and the government does not proceed through counsel, where the individual concerned is mature and educated, where his knowledge of the events . . . should enable him to develop the facts adequately through available sources, and where the other aspects of the hearing taken as a whole are fair, due process does not require representation by counsel. [*Wasson v. Trowbridge*, 383 F.2d 807 (2d Cir. 1967)]

As this statement indicates, the participation or absence of school district counsel at a hearing may influence court decision on this question.

Hearing Record and Appeal.   The right to a written or electronic record of a particular proceeding is strongest where the teacher interests are substantial and where the teacher has a right to appeal the hearing decision to a higher tribunal.[30] In such cases, courts may require that an adequate hearing record be prepared and available to ensure a fair and informed review of the case by the appellate tribunal.[31]

School authorities may cure due process omissions by timely substitute procedures, provided such substituted procedures do not unfairly burden the affected parties or prejudice their ability to be heard as effectively as they could have done originally.[32] A party may waive all or part of procedural due process elements, and any such waiver would foreclose the right to later complain of those omissions.[33]

Due Process under State Law

State laws provide significant procedural protections over and above those required for constitutional due process. They may also specify remedies, such as automatic reinstatement, money damages, or rehearings for denial of state-legislated due process. State requirements vary with the subject of school decisions, e.g., those pertaining to teacher certification, ratings, nonrenewal, demotion, and tenure. For example, the laws of some states bar local school boards, no matter how impartial, from conducting teacher discharge hearings; expressly grant rights to a hearing record; and subject local board procedures to regulations by central state agencies.[34] State laws may also deny, grant, or limit a right of appeal for particular school decisions.[35] As with federal due process, a party may waive or relinquish state law due process rights, provided the waiver is made freely, without coercions, and with full knowlege of the waiver circumstances.[36]

CONSTITUTIONAL SUBSTANTIVE RIGHTS

There are two general categories of substantive rights. The first involves the general right to be free from official restraints or punishments that do not rationally serve a valid school *purpose,* or whose *means* do not rationally achieve justified school purposes. Because public school actions are presumptively rational, a party alleging violation of this right has the burden of proving that such actions lack the required rational connection to school purposes.[37]

The second category involves particularized rights, such as freedom of speech and association, freedom from unreasonable search and seizure, freedom of religion, rights to bodily security, and autonomy in making certain personal decisions regarding familial relations and reproduction. For these rights, courts require stricter justifications than mere rationality. The *Lacks* and *Curtis* opinions at the end of this chapter raised and explained the foregoing classes of substantive rights.

Freedom of Expression

The scope of speech rights and protections depends on the content, manner, and context of its utterance. Attempts to control expression take two forms, namely, *prior restraints,* which prohibit particular speech, and retaliatory punishment of completed speech. Free speech rights protect public school teachers from retaliation by school supervisors against protected speech.

Prior restraints are particularly disfavored and usually require clear proof of overriding school interests to justify them.[38] Courts have overturned school policies that (a) prohibited teacher criticism of coworkers, even though such criticism if improperly made might be ground for school punishment, and (b) forbade a teacher's right to acknowledge her (lesbian) sexual orientation outside the classroom.[39] On the school's "don't ask, don't tell" policy for homosexuals, the court further held that the refusal to renew her appointment as a volleyball coach was an unconstitutional retaliation against her freedom of speech. Similarly, a school's blanket prior restraint against teacher comment or press statements was voided and held not justified by the desire to avoid partisan tensions or to maintain confidentiality of school desegregation plans.[40]

Coercion as well as prohibition of expression violates freedom of speech: "[T]he right to remain silent . . . is as much a part of First Amendment protections as the right to speak out in the face of an illegitimate demand for silence." *Russo v. Central School Dist. No. 1,* 469 F.2d 623, 634 (2d Cir. 1972). The court there upheld a teacher right to decline to salute the flag in school exercises. However, where a teacher refuses not only to salute the flag, but also to conduct required pledge of allegiance exercises, the courts must decide whether her right of expression or her classroom duty should prevail in the balance. Some courts solved that problem by allowing teachers to have a student or other person conduct the exercise while respectfully standing aside, on the reasoning that the teacher's expressive silence did not disrupt or undermine the school's program.[41]

In claiming that school authorities violated one's constitutional right by taking retaliatory action, a teacher must prevail on two issues. First, the teacher must provide proof that the adverse school decision arose from an unconstitutional motive to retaliate. Thus, a court dismissed the claim of a teacher that her work was outsourced and her position eliminated in retaliation for her exposure several years earlier of wrongdoing in her department. She did not produce sufficient evidence that her reports of wrongdoings were a substantial or motivating factor behind the challenged school decision.[42] Second, if the employee carries the burden of demonstrating unconstitutional motive, the school authorities may still defeat the claim by proof that they would have reached the same decision, even in the absence of the disapproved speech.[43]

Scope of Constitutional Protection

Time, Place, and Manner of Speech Regulation.   First Amendment restrictions do not apply to nondiscriminatory, reasonable regulations that are adopted to ensure orderly scheduling, use, and management of school facilities, though they incidentally limit speech opportunities. Where use restrictions control the time, place, and manner of individual expression, without targeting particular speakers, speech content, or viewpoints, they need only be reasonable in light of their housekeeping purposes to be constitutionally valid. Thus, while school authorities may not declare school premises off limits for all teacher personal speech, they may reserve certain times and places exclusively for the conduct of school programs or for school-related programs. Teachers may clearly be prohibited from, and punished for, using the class sessions for personal expression unrelated to class duties.[44]

Classes of Protected Speech.   As a general proposition, individual speech is protected against retaliation unless school needs to control it outweigh the individual's free speech interest. Under the lead Supreme Court decisions discussed below, the balance between teacher freedom of speech and school interests depends on the speech classification as involving *matters of public concern* or *matters of personal concern.* For speech on public concerns, teachers may not be penalized unless that speech materially *disrupts* or *interferes* with school operations. For speech on personal concerns, teachers may be punished if school authorities reasonably believe that the speech would undermine the efficient operation of the school, whether or not the speech is disruptive. Proving that speech threatens actual or imminent disruption of school functions is significantly more difficult than proving reasonable grounds to believe that speech will reduce the efficiency of school operations.

In *Pickering v. Board of Educ.,* 391 U.S. 563, 568 (1968), the Supreme Court held that a teacher could not be dismissed for writing a letter to a newspaper during a school election campaign which criticized the school board's management of school revenues and its allocation of school resources. The court set the constitutional standard as follows:

> [T]he State has interests as an employer in regulating the speech of its employees that differ significantly from those it possesses in connection with regulation of speech of the citizenry in general. The problem in any case is to arrive at a balance between the interests of the teacher, as a citizen, in commenting upon matters of public concern and the interest of the State, as an employer, in promoting the efficiency of the public services it performs through its employees.

In *Connick v. Myers,* 461 U.S. 138 (1983), the Court upheld dismissal of an assistant district attorney for circulating criticisms of the operation of the district attorney's office, on finding that her speech involved a matter of a personal employment grievance, notwithstanding her claim that she was speaking on a matter of public concern.

> We hold only that when a public employee speaks not as a citizen upon matters of public concern, but instead as an employee upon matters only of personal interest, absent the most unusual circumstances, a federal court is not the appropriate forum in which to review the wisdom of a personnel decision. . . .

Thus, a teacher's right as a citizen to communicate his or her views to the public on a matter of *public concern* is outweighed by school interests only if the speech is shown to "materially and substantially interfere with the requirements of appropriate discipline in the operation of the school."[45] But as held in *Connick* and later cases, the *Pickering* disruption standard does not apply to personal concern speech. A school supervisor who *reasonably believed* that a given speech undermined the efficiency of school operations could discipline a teacher, even if the supervisor's belief later proved to have been mistaken.[46]

The protection of public concern speech was extended by the Supreme Court to oral, face-to-face teacher criticisms to her principal of the school's racial policies. That subject involved a matter of public concern and her encounters with her principal were private and not disruptive of school work.[47]

Educators and courts thus face two critical issues: Does the disapproved expression involve a matter of public or personal concern; and under the applicable test for each class of speech, does the penalized speech *sufficiently* threaten or undermine school functions to justify its punishment? These fact-bound questions are difficult to resolve.

> Whether an employee's speech addresses a matter of public concern must be determined by the content, form, and context of a given statement, as revealed by the whole record. . . . Because of the enormous variety of fact situations in which critical statements . . . may be thought . . . to furnish grounds for dismissal, we do not deem it either appropriate or feasible to lay down a general standard against which all such statements may be judged. . . . . . . Although such particularized

balancing is difficult, the courts must reach the most appropriate possible balance of the competing interests. . . . (*Connick v. Myers, supra*)

As illustrated by the following sampling and by the authorities in the endnote, the cases have been very mixed on the classification of employee speech. Even the Supreme Court Justices disagreed 5–4 in a startling decision that a police clerk's statement that she wished an attempt to assassinate President Reagan would succeed was protected speech of public concern.[48] Teachers and supervisors should, therefore, err on the side of caution when judging whether particular statements are of personal or public concern.

A teacher who questioned the accuracy of school attendance records was held to speak on a matter of public concern, but was nevertheless subject to school punishment because the statements (which proved to be inaccurate) were found to be disruptive of school working relationships. Another court held that a teacher charge that school authorities misrepresented student scores on standardized achievement tests was not disruptive and therefore protected from school discipline.[49] Teacher criticism of superiors on matters found to involve personal concerns may be grounds for discharge,[50] but a teacher's remark at a union meeting that the board was attempting to buy off teachers with small concessions was held not constitutionally punishable.[51]

The manner and context of criticisms are important factors. Orderly criticisms of school policies at a school-sponsored public forum and in scholarly journals were protected expression, but a teacher could not claim protection for abusive remarks impugning his superintendent as a liar at a public school board meeting.[52] Similarly, a teacher who helped distribute a pamphlet containing false accusations against a school principal was punishable though she did not author the pamphlet, while a teacher who encouraged students to print an underground newspaper, without instigating its particular content, was not found to be disruptive.[53] Easier examples of disruptive speech are found in activities that threaten personal safety and security at school.[54]

Political Speech. Teacher wearing of an armband to school, as a passive antiwar expression, was found nondisruptive protected speech, but a teacher who left the school in order to join an antiwar rally lacked constitutional protection.[55] A teacher request for permission to sponsor a political symposium was not so threatening to justify a school penalty, but the use of class time to promote union activity or to organize civil rights groups did not qualify as protected expression.[56] A teacher discharged for falsely denying he made certain statements cannot thereafter avoid dismissal on a claim that the statements if not denied were protected.[57]

The line between protected political speech and unprotected partisan political activity was recently illustrated in a case where a school district prohibited teachers from wearing, during instructional time, political buttons to campaign against a California initiative to adopt a voucher system of financing elementary and secondary education. The district cited a state law that prohibited public school districts from sponsoring or subsidizing the distribution of partisan campaign materials. The court upheld the ban insofar as it applied to employees while engaged in curricular activities, but held that it could not be constitutionally applied to noninstructional settings.[58]

Curriculum-Related Speech.   School sanctions for teacher use of disapproved class materials or exercises commonly test the limits of freedom of speech. Teacher initiative to organize pedagogical materials and instructional methods, however desirable, should not be mistaken for a constitutional right. Most cases have upheld punishment of teachers for curricular practices that violated school directives,[59] and most cases that reversed such punishments rested on grounds other than a free speech right, such as unfairness or arbitrariness of the imposed punishments.[60] The Supreme Court *Pico* opinion reported in Chapter 2 and its following statement in a college labor case undercut arguments for a *constitutional right* of academic freedom that would limit school authority to dictate curricular expression.

> Appellees [teachers] have no constitutional right to force the government to listen to their views. . . . The academic setting . . . does not alter this conclusion. To be sure there is a strong . . . tradition of faculty participation in school governance. . . . *But this Court has never recognized a constitutional right of faculty to participate in policymaking in academic institutions.* [*Minn. State Bd. of Comm'y Colleges v. Knight*, 485 U.S. 271, 283, 287 (1985)] (Emphasis added)

The *Lacks* case, which appears at the end of this chapter, also rejected the implicit teacher claim of academic leeway, if not right, to conduct disapproved classroom assignments. Courts have denied constitutional shelter to extemporaneous classroom discussions of sex topics, and even to a teacher's decision to discipline an 11-year-old girl for using a vulgar word during school recess, by having her write the vulgar word 1,000 times.[61]

The difficulty of importing into public schools the higher education model of academic freedom that developed in private European universities by and for communities of adult scholars is manifest in three decisions of the First Circuit Court of Appeals.[62] In groping for a constitutional foothold for public school teacher academic freedom, the court began by preliminarily enjoining discharge of a high school English teacher for refusing to obey a school order that he discontinue classroom discussion of an offensive epithet following his assignment of a class reading that explored its uses. One year later the same court refused to enjoin a university from closing down a campus art exhibit by one of its professors though the university previously authorized the exhibit. The university concluded that the vulgar captions of the art would be exposed to women and children passing through the campus.[63] Still later, the same court skirted the constitutional question while reversing a teacher discharge for making a transitory reference to a vulgar word (for sexual intercourse) during a class discussion of taboo words, but only because the school regulation against the practice was unconstitutionally vague. It insisted that it "in no way" regretted its prior decisions, but signaled a retreat by stating: "We confess that we are not of one mind as to whether the plaintiff's conduct fell within the protection of the First Amendment."[64] To which spin, the neighboring Second Circuit Court of Appeals commented: "While the First Circuit has indicated that it does not 'regret' its decision in *Keefe v. Geanakos, supra,* its enthusiasm for intrusion into academic issues seems to be lessening."[65] Perhaps the trend against a theory of free-standing constitutional academic freedom[66] reflects a general shift in sentiment, away from expanded liberties toward greater official control of school activities.

While the above discussion does not cover the full range of potential issues on teacher classroom autonomy, it cautions against loose reliance on extralegal arguments about academic freedom.

Associational Freedom. The First Amendment protects the right to associate and to express oneself through associations, be they political, labor related, familial, or social. School employment decisions that favor or disfavor individuals solely because of their affiliation with a particular political party are classic examples of unconstitutional abridgements.[67] As with personal speech, associational expression may be limited by overriding school interests. Group expression that diverts a teacher from assigned teaching duties[68] or incites disharmony and disruption of school working relationships is not constitutionally protected.[69]

The constitutional rights of personal association include rights to belong to a religious order, marry a civil rights activist, and elect to send a child to a private, rather than to a public, school. School board denial of employment opportunities or benefits to teachers for electing such associations were overturned as unconstitutional infringements.[70] A board's refusal to renew a teacher's contract because she was living with a person she intended to marry was held to violate her constitutional right of intimate association.[71]

Symbolic Expression. As noted above, nonverbal acts (e.g., armbands, political buttons, picketing, flag burning) may be used to express ideas. However, courts do not give even weight to all types of symbolic expression. They give greater weight to political symbolic expression than to personal symbolic expression by choice of appearance and dress.

The case law on the right to determine one's appearance is limited and varies by region. More recent cases tend to follow the guideline adopted by the Supreme Court for male hair regulation for police employees, notwithstanding the material differences between police and teacher work.[72] That decision treated choice of hair style as a generalized substantive liberty that is subject to reasonable regulation, rather than an elemental First Amendment freedom of expression. The Supreme Court there stated: "Thus the question is not . . . whether the State can establish a genuine public need for the specific regulation. . . . The constitutional issue . . . is whether the petitioner's [employer's] determination . . . is so irrational that it may be branded 'arbitrary,' and therefore a deprivation of respondent's 'liberty' interest in freedom to choose his own hair style."[73] Under this approach, appearance regulations are prima facie valid with the burden on challengers to show that they lack a rational basis.

Appearance regulation penalties have been overturned on due process grounds where they did not afford teachers fair notice or warning that certain attire or grooming was prohibited and subject to disciplinary penalty.[74]

Liberty interests in choice of dress have also been subordinated to educational interests.[75] Courts upheld nonrenewal of a teacher who refused to lengthen her miniskirt, and sustained male dress code requirements of jackets and ties.[76] Prohibitions of religious garb or symbols while at school have not been extensively tested, but the Supreme Court dismissed an appeal seeking to overturn an Oregon statute that prohibited religious garb in public schools. While not a formal ruling, that action suggests that a legislature may constitutionally ban or limit teacher religious garb in public schools, assuming the details of the ban are not unreasonable or unduly vague.[77] A federal court later upheld a similar Pennsylvania law as not violating the antidiscrimination provisions of Title VII or its requirement of "reasonable" religious accommodation of employees.[78] In balancing the individual's interest in choice of dress with school interest in avoiding sectarian influence in public schools, courts may yet clarify whether some clothing accessories or jewelry are not sufficiently obtrusive to render their ban unreasonable.[79] The wearing of small pins, bracelets, or insignia has not stimulated school bans or test litigation. On balance, they may command greater protection than overtly religious habits or prominent sectarian symbols.[80]

Rights of Privacy

The law on privacy rights in schools is also undergoing significant shifts as school authorities intensify efforts to monitor and control school violence. Because much of that experience is attributed to weapons, drugs, and other contraband, school authorities have adopted sweeping search policies not featured in older case law. The following discussion reflects ongoing developments of the law on teacher searches, but not the more highly specialized law on "seizure" of property that is disclosed by a search.

The Constitution protects three distinct kinds of privacy, namely:

Spatial privacy, such as protection from unreasonable government search of persons and places;

Informational privacy, such as protection from compelled disclosure of certain types of personal information; and

Decisional privacy, such as protection from government interference with certain personal decisions.

Each of these has a separate history and doctrinal foundation. Spatial privacy is governed by the express language of the Fourth Amendment and is far more developed than the newer law on decisional and informational privacy.

Spatial Privacy

The Fourth Amendment guarantees persons "the right . . . to be secure in their persons, houses, papers and effects against *unreasonable* searches and seizures." (Emphasis added) However, the Fourth Amendment only applies to parties who have a reasonable expectation of privacy in the subject of the search. Only then must the search be "reasonable" to be constitutional. Searches undertaken in accordance with a court order or "warrant" automatically satisfy the Fourth Amendment, but most school searches are undertaken without a court warrant.

The courts have recognized several situations that constitutionally justify warrantless searches, namely searches that are made with the consent of the affected party[81]; searches made upon observation of contraband material that was left "in plain view" by the owner; searches made in emergencies to avoid a serious threat of harm; searches made to identify, inventory, or preserve property that comes into government custody following the owner's official confinement (jailed) or disability (accident victim); and searches that are part of routine government inspection and maintenance of public property.

A party who consents to a search or leaves material exposed to "plain view" of passersby cannot be said to have a reasonable expectation of privacy, any more than a party who knows or should know that school authorities reserve the right to make reasonable, routine inspections of government-owned enclosures. Courts have also found that teachers have no reasonable expectation of privacy in areas of a school that are subject to normal supervisory monitoring. School videotaping of a teacher's classroom has been found to not violate anyone's Fourth Amendment rights.[82]

The use of evidence produced by unconstitutional school searches, though barred in criminal proceedings, is allowed by some courts in school disciplinary proceedings.[83] Nevertheless, the potential personal monetary liability for violations of an individual's right to be free from unconstitutional searches is a powerful reason to avoid unlawful searches.

Property Searches.   The Supreme Court first considered search rights of educational employees in *O'Connor v. Ortega,* which appears at the end of this chapter. That opinion should be read for its own authority, because it supersedes the older scant law on teacher desk searches. *O'Connor* upheld a warrantless search by state hospital administrators of a physician's workplace office, desk, and files even though the affected employee had some expectation of privacy in these enclosures. The Court noted that the occupant's expectation was reduced by the nature of his hospital work and workplace. It opted for a soft rule of reason rather than a fixed rule:

> We hold, therefore, that public employer intrusions on the constitutionally protected privacy interests of government employees for noninvestigatory, work-related purposes, as well as for investigations of work-related misconduct, should be judged by the standard of reasonableness under all the circumstances.

The *O'Connor* case fixed two important points that undercut prior law. First, it applied the same test of a reasonable search to both *investigatory* and *noninvestigatory* searches. Second, it held that searches of government-owned enclosures could be made upon a reasonable, individualized suspicion of a violation of law *or of employer regulations,* without a showing of probable cause of illegal action.

Personal Searches.   Routine, nonintrusive medical examinations do not involve a constitutional expectation of privacy and are not subject to Fourth Amendment restrictions. However, unusual intrusive medical examinations or tests that are not understood to be part of routine medical checkups do implicate privacy expectations, as would a search for materials hidden in or on a person's body, clothing, or personal effects. The bounds of protected privacy expectations are being narrowed in many cases, as concerns over school violence, drugs, and sexual abuse increase the pressure to expand the zone of constitutional searches. Several recent cases mark this trend. The *Aubrey* opinion, which appears at the end of this chapter, upheld suspicionless drug testing of a school custodian, while another circuit court[84] upheld suspicionless drug testing (by urinalysis) of applicants for teaching positions and of employed teachers and principals who applied for a transfer or promotion. Both cases adopted the position that the employees occupied "safety sensitive" positions for which suspicionless drug testing by urinalysis was a "reasonable" search under the Fourth Amendment. These cases extended to teachers the safety sensitive rationale that the Supreme Court previously applied to uphold suspicionless drug testing of high school student athletes in a peculiarly drug-ridden school (*Vernonia* case, presented at the end of Chapter 7), and of trainmen and federal customs agents.

The safety sensitive rationale has uncharted potential to undercut prior case law, which condemned mandatory urinalysis and blood testing unless such were required by state law, or unless school authorities could show (1) an individualized "reasonable" suspicion that the condition of the tested individual threatened work performance or the well-being of others, or threatened a specific school need that outweighed the teacher's privacy interest[85]; and further (2) that such need could not be met by less intrusive means than the drug test.[86] The difference between the latter fact-bound justifications[87] and the recent classification of particular school positions as being "safety sensitive" is qualitative, and it remains to be seen whether or to what extent the new approach will take hold in other courts.

Increased concern over teacher drug use has led to stricter school surveillance. The Eleventh Circuit Court of Appeals recently upheld discharge of a teacher for refusing to take a drug test after marijuana was found in her car during a police drug sweep.[88] The court found that the school policy of mandatory testing within two hours of the incident was valid in that the police discovery of marijuana itself created a reasonable suspicion that the teacher violated the school's drug and alcohol policy.

An equally important requisite for a valid search is that it be reasonable in scope as well as in purpose. The lead student search case *(New Jersey v. T.L.O.),* which is discussed in the next chapter, established this principle.

Search challenges often raise separate due process objections that the selected examination and testing procedures are unreliable or inaccurate either in the manner of gathering, preserving, or transmission of specimens to be tested or in the methods of testing and evaluating such specimens. If such defects are shown, they alone will invalidate any action based on the search.

Informational Privacy

The constitutional law on informational privacy is relatively new and incomplete, both with respect to the types of information that qualify for privacy protections and the types of public needs for its disclosure that would outweigh and subordinate the individual's privacy claim (e.g., to ensure employee fitness or safety).[89] Courts have not pushed for a broad doctrine in this area:

> Virtually every governmental action interferes with personal privacy to some degree. . . . Inferring very broad "constitutional" rights where the Constitution itself does not express them is an activity not appropriate to the judiciary. . . . . . . [We] conclude that the Constitution does not encompass a general right to nondisclosure of private information. . . .
>
> . . .
>
> Our opinion does not mean that we attach little significance to the right of privacy, or that there is no constitutional right to nondisclosure of private information. . . . Our opinion simply holds that not all rights of privacy or interests in nondisclosure of private information are of constitutional dimension. . . . [*J.P. v. DeSanti*, 653 F.2d 1080, 1090–1091 (6th Cir. 1981)]

Under statutes that open school records to public inspection, courts are likely to reject claims of informational privacy in school personnel files.[90] Conversely, they are likely to enforce statutes that shield items of personal information from public disclosure. In many instances, state laws entrust to courts and administrators the task of judging whether a teacher's privacy interest in personal information should outweigh or be subordinated to public needs for its disclosure.[91] The law in each state must be consulted on these points.[92]

Decisional Privacy

The full range of personal decisions that might qualify for constitutional protection has also not been fully canvassed by the courts. The Supreme Court recognized that certain decisions are a part of fundamental constitutional "liberty" that is protected against official interference, namely, the right to make decisions regarding marriage, reproduction, and traditional family relationships.[93] Various statutes provide supplemental protections, but their selective coverage of different subjects of personal decision do not project a general pattern of protected decisional privacy.[94]

Substantive Rights under State Law

As noted in the above discussions, state statutes are sources of rights that are not guaranteed by the federal Constitution,[95] and they must accordingly be considered.

Chapter 6 Discussion Questions

Where the answer to a question may be qualified by special circumstances, explain the potential qualification.

1. What are the limits of teacher due process rights under the following?
    a.   The Constitution
    b.   State education statutes
    c.   Union agreements
    Explain your answer for each part.

2. Do all teachers have identical due process rights under the Constitution? Explain.

3. When, if ever, may a teacher be suspended without a prior hearing? Explain.

4. When, if ever, may school authorities lawfully search a teacher's desk without the teacher's consent where there is no reasonable basis to suspect that the searched desk contains evidence of the teacher's violation of law or of employment rules? Explain.

5. When, in your opinion, may school authorities lawfully require teachers to submit to random collection and analysis of their urine specimens?

6. What is the difference between constitutional protection afforded teachers against school penalties for uttering
    a.   Speech of "personal" concern.
    b.   Speech of "public" concern.

7. How have courts generally treated teacher claims of "academic freedom" as a shield against school control of classroom speech?

8. May school authorities constitutionally dictate teacher class assignments? Explain.

9. When, if ever, may a teacher invoke constitutional protection against school penalty for refusing to conduct a prescribed class flag salute and pledge of allegiance?

10. Does a teacher have a constitutional right to the following?
    a.   To join a union
    b.   To join the communist party
    c.   To participate in partisan school board election campaigns

❖ CASES

Case 6.1

LACKS v. FERGUSON REORGANIZED SCHOOL DISTRICT R-2
147 F.3d 718 (8th Cir. 1998)

[**Focus Note**. *The limits of teacher academic freedom. Lacks sued to overturn her termination on a charge of violating school board policy against allowing student use of profanity at school. She claimed that the termination violated her constitutional rights to due process and freedom of speech, and subjected her to racial discrimination in violation of Title VII of the civil rights act. The trial court ordered Lacks's reinstatement with back pay, attorneys' fees, and costs, and in addition, the jury returned a verdict in her favor for $500,000 on her constitutional claims and $250,000 on her race discrimination claim. The Court of Appeals reversed the trial court judgment and the jury verdicts on all counts.*]

RICHARD S. ARNOLD, CHIEF JUDGE.

✧ ✧ ✧

. . . Lacks taught English and journalism classes, and she sponsored the school newspaper. In October 1994, Lacks divided her junior English class into small groups and directed them to write short plays, which were to be performed for the other students in the class and videotaped. The plays written by the students contained profanity, including the repeated uses of the words "fuck," "shit," "ass," "bitch," and "nigger." When the plays were videotaped, these words were used more than 150 times in approximately forty minutes. . . . Lacks later admitted that the plays contained an unusual amount of profanity. . . . . . . Lacks was aware of the content of the plays . . . because she had previously reviewed at least one of the scripts and had attended rehearsals of the plays the day before. . . . On October 10, the students performed their plays and were videotaped at the direction of Lacks. . . .

The following January, as a result of complaints . . . the existence of the videotapes came to the attention of Vernon Mitchell, the principal. . . . Mitchell initiated an inquiry. . . . During the investigation, the administrators learned that . . . Lacks had permitted a student to read aloud in a classroom two of his poems which contained profanity and graphic descriptions of oral sex. . . .

Following the investigation, Dr. Robert Fritz, the district superintendent, formally charged Lacks with "willful or persistent violation of and failure to obey [the school district's] policies" . . . . Fritz . . . recommended her termination. . . . Lacks requested a hearing, and the school board heard testimony from Lacks and fifteen other witnesses over five evenings. . . . . . . On March 23, the board issued a decision which found that Lacks was aware of the school board's policy . . . that she could have chosen teaching methods which prohibited profanity, and that her failure to do so constituted a "willful and persistent practice violative of Board policy. . . ." . . . [T]he school board terminated Lacks's teaching contract.

. . . [T]he District Court held that Lacks did not willfully violate board policy 3043, because she believed that profanity was permitted in the context of creative expression in the classroom. . . .

✧ ✧ ✧

. . . After a careful review of the evidence, we hold that the record contains sufficient evidence for the school board to have concluded that Lacks willfully violated board policy.

Lacks admitted that she allowed students to use profanity in the classroom in the context of performing the plays . . . and reading aloud the poems they had composed. . . . Lacks defended this practice by arguing that she thought that the board's policy . . . applied only to "student behavior" and not to students' creative assignments. She also argued that her teaching method . . . required her to allow her students creative freedom, which included the use of profanity. . . . Lacks could not say with certainty that she would be able to teach at Berkeley High School if her students were not given the freedom to use profanity in their creative activities. . . .

✧ ✧ ✧

The school board also heard testimony from Lacks's principal, Vernon Mitchell, that he told Lacks that profanity was not permitted in the school newspaper. . . . Mitchell testified that he discussed the use of profanity in the newspaper with Lacks "[t]wo or three times." . . . Mitchell also noted that signs posted in Lacks's classroom read "No Profanity." . . .

Lacks claimed that Mitchell never warned her. . . . However . . . assessing the credibility of witnesses is the function of the school board, not the reviewing court. . . . The policy prohibiting profanity was explicit and contained no exceptions. . . . We think it was not unreasonable for the board to treat student writing for the newspaper and student writing for the class as alike. . . . We hold that the board's decision was reasonable and supported by substantial evidence on the record as a whole. The judgment in the plaintiff's favor on this claim must be reversed.

When the jury returned a verdict in favor of Lacks on her First Amendment claim, it provided answers to two interrogatories posed by the District Court's instructions. . . . With respect to the first interrogatory—"Did [Lacks] have reasonable notice that allowing students to use profanity in their creative writing was prohibited?"—the jury answered "no." With respect to the second interrogatory—"Did defendant school district have a legitimate academic interest in prohibiting profanity by students in their creative writing, regardless of any other competing interests?"—the jury also answered "no." . . . We reverse and hold, as a matter of law, that the answer to both of those questions was "yes."

❖ ❖ ❖

. . . In *Bethel School District No. 403 v. Fraser*, 478 U.S. 675 . . . (1986), a student was disciplined for using sexually suggestive language in a speech before a high school assembly. Before the student gave the speech, he told some of his teachers what he was going to say, and he was told that the speech was "inappropriate and that he probably should not deliver it" and that giving the speech could have "severe consequences." . . . The Court rejected the student's argument that his due process rights had been violated because he had not received sufficient notice. . . . In the present case, not only did Lacks admit that she was familiar with the school district's disciplinary rules . . . her principal also testified that he told her that the rules applied to one form of student creative activity. Therefore, as a matter of law, Lacks had sufficient notice. . . .

We also hold, as a matter of law, that the school board had a legitimate academic interest in prohibiting profanity by students in their creative writing. . . .

A flat prohibition on profanity in the classroom is reasonably related to the legitimate pedagogical concern of promoting generally acceptable social standards. . . . Allowing one student to call another a "fucking bitch" and a "whore" in front of the rest of the class, and allowing a student to read aloud a poem that describes sexual encounters in the most graphic detail . . . hardly promotes these shared social standards. We consider the matter too plain for argument.

. . . Therefore, the judgment in the plaintiff's favor on her First Amendment claim is reversed.

. . . The jury found that Lacks had proved . . . that race was a motivating factor in the school board's decision to terminate her. . . . We reverse, and hold as a matter of law that race was not a motivating factor in the school board's decision to terminate Lacks. . . .

. . . Mitchell admitted that when he saw the videotape with the students performing their plays, his reaction was that it was "black students acting a fool and white folks videotaping it." . . . Lacks also elicited testimony from another teacher . . . that in the past Mitchell had displayed signs of hostility toward white teachers . . . because Mitchell believed that some white teachers did not care about the students. . . . And Lacks produced some evidence which arguably showed that Dr. John Wright, an assistant superintendent for personnel, viewed the videotaping incident in racial terms. Lacks is white; Mitchell, Wright, and the students are black.

However, Mitchell and Wright did not make the decision to terminate Lacks; that decision was made by the school board. Lacks responds . . . by arguing that the school board was influenced by the bias of the administrators, and that the board consequently served as the conduit, or "cat's paw," of the racial animus of the school administration. . . . But Lacks produced no evidence that the school board deferred to the opinion or judgment of Mitchell or Wright. . . . . . .

. . . The evidence . . . unequivocally shows that the board made an independent determination. . . . Lacks's "cat's paw" theory must therefore fail.

Lacks offers one piece of evidence which allegedly shows direct racial bias . . . a four-page press release issued by the board after it terminated Lacks's teaching contract. The press release reads in part:

> . . . The video produced in Ms. Lacks' class demonstrates a serious and extreme lack of direction from the teacher. Teachers do not have the right to abdicate their responsibility to set standards under the guise of creativity. The content of the video is a violation of our black community; it is a violation of our white community; it is a violation of the values within our community and it is a violation of the ethical teaching standards. . . .

Lacks argues that the references to "white community" and "black community" provide direct evidence that the board "had race on its mind" when it fired Lacks. . . . That proposition is questionable. . . . Moreover, having race on one's mind is not the same thing as acting because of race. At any rate, the single reference in the school board's press release is not sufficient to sustain the jury verdict on the race discrimination claims. . . .

The judgment of the District Court is reversed, and the cause remanded with directions to dismiss the complaint with prejudice.

Review Question 6.1

1. What does the above opinion reveal on the power of courts regarding the following?
   a. Overruling jury fact findings
   b. Judicial review of sufficiency of evidence
   c. The sufficiency of notice to satisfy due process
   d. The scope of "academic freedom"

   _____

Case 6.2

CURTIS v. OKLAHOMA CITY PUBLIC SCHOOLS BOARD OF EDUCATION
147 F.3d 1200 (10th Cir. 1998)

> [*Focus Note*. *This case illustrates the confluence of constitutional and statutory claims based on alleged discrimination. Following his termination by the district for willful neglect of duty and incompetence, and the superintendent's charge that he*

misdirected a district advisory committee in the aftermath of court-ordered school desegregation, Curtis sued the Oklahoma City Public Schools alleging that his termination (1) denied him procedural due process, (2) violated his substantive constitutional right to be free of arbitrary government action, (3) retaliated against him for his constitutionally protected speech, and (4) amounted to employment discrimination in violation of Title VII of the Civil Rights Act.]

OPINION BY MURPHY, CIRCUIT JUDGE.

✧ ✧ ✧

The Board continued to operate its schools in substantial conformity with the 1972 court-ordered desegregation plan until 1985, when the Board adopted the Student Reassignment Plan ("SRP"). . . .

Under the SRP, a number of previously desegregated schools were returned to primarily one-race status for the asserted purposes of increasing parental involvement and alleviating greater busing burdens on young black children. . . . . . .

✧ ✧ ✧

. . . [T]he plaintiffs in the original Dowell [desegregation] litigation challenged the SRP . . . seeking to . . . enjoin the Board from implementing the SRP. . . . This . . . litigation continued through 1993, when . . . this court affirmed the district court's 1991 ruling dismissing the case. . . .

✧ ✧ ✧

. . . In 1987, Plaintiff was employed as the Equity/Affirmative Action Officer. . . . Plaintiff's "job goals" included assisting the School District in achieving equity under the SRP. . . . Plaintiff was to achieve these goals in part by . . . serving as a "communication link" between the Committee, Board, and the Superintendent of the School District. . . .

In early 1989, Sylvia Little became Plaintiff's immediate supervisor. Plaintiff experienced a number of conflicts with Little and began to receive written reprimands and other criticisms . . . from Little. Plaintiff contends the disciplinary actions were retaliatory. . . .

On September 25, 1989, Plaintiff testified at a hearing . . . on behalf of a colleague, Belinda Biscoe, who alleged she had been subjected to harassment and salary discrimination by [Superintendent] Steller. . . .

On November 14, 1989, Plaintiff was placed on a Plan for Improvement ("PFI"), a vehicle to correct his alleged performance deficiencies. Plaintiff asserts this was in retaliation for his testimony at the Biscoe hearing. In January 1990, Plaintiff . . . gave testimony to a grand jury investigating the School District. In March 1990, Plaintiff filed a racial discrimination and harassment charge with the EEOC. . . .

✧ ✧ ✧

On December 4, 1989, the Board officially adopted a new charge ("1989 charge"). The . . . 1989 charge stated that the Equity Officer and Committee were "appoint[ed] and charge[d] . . . with ensuring that black [students] and students of other racial groups are not adversely affected as a result of the Board's 1985 adoption of a Student Reassignment Plan." . . .

❖ ❖ ❖

In September 1990, the Committee issued its report on equity. . . . . . . The report concluded the Dowell schools were generally "worse than" the group of comparison schools. . . .

In a memorandum to the Board . . . Superintendent Steller criticized the report as inconsistent with the Board's 1989 charge. Under the 1989 charge, the Committee was to monitor all sub-districts to determine if students of all racial and ethnic backgrounds were receiving equity. . . . The report also examined a number of different factors than those set out in the 1989 charge. . . . Steller expressly rejected the Committee's conclusion that the Dowell schools were deficient. . . . Steller further suggested the Committee was biased and stated that "[t]he timing of this report [was] . . . suspiciously close to the date when the oral arguments [were] to be heard [in the Dowell litigation] by the U.S. Supreme Court [in October 1990]."

❖ ❖ ❖

. . . On November 6, Steller notified Plaintiff in writing that he was recommending . . . that Plaintiff be discharged for "willful neglect of duty and incompetence." The reasons cited for the discharge recommendation included Plaintiff's alleged failure to guide the Equity Committee . . . consistent with the Board's 1989 charge. . . . Steller subsequently sent a letter to the Board containing his recommendation and an outline of the reasons and supporting evidence.

A pretermination hearing . . . was scheduled for January 19, 1991. Plaintiff informed the Board that he would not attend the scheduled hearing. At the scheduled hearing, the Board voted to deny Plaintiff's prior request for a continuance until the EEOC acted and then voted . . . to terminate Plaintiff's employment with the School District.

In July 1992, the EEOC dismissed Plaintiff's discrimination complaint. . . . . . .

❖ ❖ ❖

1. Protected Speech Under the First Amendment

❖ ❖ ❖

. . . [T]he threshold question is whether the speech may be "fairly characterized as constituting speech on a matter of public concern" as opposed to speech upon matters of only personal interest. . . .

❖ ❖ ❖

2. Public Concern

. . . In determining whether the speech in question addressed a matter of public concern, we consider the "content, form, and context of [the] . . . statement[s], as revealed by the whole record." . . .

"In deciding how to classify particular speech, courts focus on the motive of the speaker and attempt to determine whether the speech was calculated to redress personal grievances or whether it had a broader public purpose." . . .

❖ ❖ ❖

This court agrees that Plaintiff's speech, both his pre-charge advocacy and his post-charge guidance, involved a matter of public concern. . . .

3. Pickering Balancing

Having concluded Plaintiff's speech involved a matter of public concern, this court next applies the *Pickering* balancing test to determine whether Plaintiff's interest in commenting on such matters was outweighed by his government employer's interest in restricting the speech. . . .

❖ ❖ ❖

After reviewing the record and balancing the interests of Plaintiff and Defendants, this court concludes Plaintiff's pre-charge advocacy was protected. . . .

In addition, Defendants have not identified any actual disruption attributable to Plaintiff's pre-charge advocacy. . . .

We reach a different conclusion, however, with respect to Plaintiff's post-charge guidance. Given the inconsistencies between the Board-approved charge and the Committee's Blueprint . . . Defendants were entitled to consider Plaintiff's post-charge guidance . . . as reflecting negatively upon Plaintiff's competence and willingness to perform his job responsibilities. . . . Further, there is evidence that Plaintiff's post-charge guidance had a detrimental impact on the working relationship between the Board, Plaintiff's Supervisors, and the Equity Committee. . . . Additionally, Plaintiff's failure to guide the Committee consistent with the charge disrupted the Board's effective and efficient functioning. . . . . . . Based on the above factors, this court concludes Defendants' interests outweigh Plaintiff's interests with respect to Plaintiff's post-charge guidance and this speech is therefore not constitutionally protected. . . .

B. Due Process Claims

❖ ❖ ❖

Plaintiff asserts the Board's decision to terminate his employment violated substantive due process. "In order to present a claim of denial of 'substantive' due process . . . a liberty or property interest must be present to which the protection of due process can attach." . . . Plaintiff asserts he had a property interest in continued employment. . . . Assuming a protected property interest, " '[s]ubstantive' due process requires only that termination of that interest not be arbitrary, capricious, or without a rational basis." . . . "The Due Process Clause of the Fourteenth Amendment is not a guarantee against incorrect or ill-advised personnel decisions." *Bishop v. Wood,* 426 U.S. 341, 350 . . . (1976).

❖ ❖ ❖

Plaintiff has not established a genuine issue of material fact underlying his substantive due process claim. . . .
. . . The fact that the Board members relied on Steller's evaluation and referenced supporting evidence . . . does not render the Board's decision arbitrary or capricious.
. . . The district court therefore properly granted summary judgment to Defendants on Plaintiff's due process claims.

❖ ❖ ❖

. . . In his Title VII claim, Plaintiff asserted Defendants terminated him in retaliation for filing a discrimination complaint with the EEOC. The ultimate question to be decided . . . in a Title VII case is " 'which party's explanation of the employer's motivation it believes.' " . . . [quoting *United States Postal Serv. Bd. of Governors v. Aikens,* 460 U.S. 711, 716 . . . (1983)]. The plaintiff always has the burden of persuading the trier of fact that the defendant intentionally discriminated against the plaintiff. . . .
Our review of the record establishes there was evidence supporting the court's determination of no retaliation. . . . [W]e affirm the district court's ruling on Plaintiff's Title VII claim. . . .

III. Conclusion

The district court did not err in granting Defendants' motions for summary judgment on Plaintiff's due process claims, § 1983 claim, and Title VII claim. . . . The district court did, however, improperly conclude that Plaintiff's pre-charge advocacy . . . concerning the need to focus on the Dowell schools . . . was not protected by the First Amendment. The matter is therefore remanded to the district court for further proceedings consistent with this opinion.

Case 6.3

O'CONNOR v. ORTEGA
480 U.S. 709 (1987)

[***Focus Note***. *Search of employee's state-supplied office. Magno Ortega, Chief of Professional Education at a state hospital, brought suit following his dismissal for im-*

proprieties, alleging that the dismissal resulted from an unconstitutional search of his office, desk, and files.]

JUSTICE O'CONNOR . . . *delivered an opinion in which* THE CHIEF JUSTICE, JUSTICE WHITE, *and* JUSTICE POWELL *join.*

This suit . . . presents two issues concerning the Fourth Amendment rights of public employees. First . . . whether the respondent . . . had a reasonable expectation of privacy in his office, desk, and file cabinets at his place of work. Second, we must address the appropriate Fourth Amendment standard for a search conducted by a public employer in areas in which a public employee is found to have a reasonable expectation of privacy.

✧ ✧ ✧

. . . [W]e have held in the past that the Fourth Amendment governs the conduct of school officials. . . . Searches and seizures by government employers or supervisors of the private property of their employees, therefore, are subject to the restraints of the Fourth Amendment.

. . . Our cases establish that Dr. Ortega's Fourth Amendment rights are implicated only if the conduct of the Hospital officials . . . infringed "an expectation of privacy that society is prepared to consider reasonable." . . .

✧ ✧ ✧

Because the reasonableness of an expectation of privacy, . . . is understood to differ according to context, it is essential first to delineate the boundaries of the workplace context. The workplace includes those areas and items that are related to work and are generally within the employer's control. . . . These areas remain part of the workplace context even if the employee has placed personal items in them. . . .

✧ ✧ ✧

Public employees' expectations of privacy in their offices, desks, and file cabinets, like similar expectations of employees in the private sector, may be reduced by virtue of actual office practices and procedures, or by legitimate regulation. . . .

Given the great variety of work environments . . . the question of whether an employee has a reasonable expectation of privacy must be addressed on a case-by-case basis.

✧ ✧ ✧

. . . In the case of searches conducted by a public employer, we must balance the invasion of the employee's legitimate expectations of privacy against the government's need for supervision, control, and the efficient operation of the workplace.

✧ ✧ ✧

There is surprisingly little case law on the appropriate Fourth Amendment standard of reasonableness for a public employer's work-related search of its employee's offices, desks, or file cabinets. . . .

❖ ❖ ❖

The legitimate privacy interests of public employees in the private objects they bring to the workplace may be substantial. Against these privacy interests, however, must be balanced the realities of the workplace, which strongly suggest that a warrant requirement would be unworkable. . . . [E]mployers most frequently need to enter the offices and desks of their employees for legitimate work-related reasons wholly unrelated to illegal conduct. . . . An employer may have need for correspondence, or a file or report available . . . while the employee is away from the office. Or . . . employers may need to safeguard or identify state property or records . . . in connection with a pending investigation into suspected employee misfeasance.

In our view, requiring an employer to obtain a warrant whenever the employer wished to enter an employee's office, desk, or file cabinets for a work-related purpose would seriously disrupt the routine conduct of business and would be unduly burdensome. . . .

❖ ❖ ❖

. . . Because the parties in this case have alleged that the search was either a noninvestigatory work-related intrusion or an investigatory search for evidence of suspected work-related employee misfeasance, we undertake to determine the appropriate Fourth Amendment standard of reasonableness *only* for these two types of employer intrusions. . . .

❖ ❖ ❖

To ensure the efficient and proper operation of the agency, therefore, public employers must be given wide latitude to enter employee offices for work-related, noninvestigatory reasons. We come to a similar conclusion for searches conducted pursuant to an investigation of work-related employee misconduct. . . .

In our view, therefore, a probable cause requirement for searches of the type at issue here would impose intolerable burdens on public employers. . . .

❖ ❖ ❖

. . . We hold, therefore, that public employer intrusions on the constitutionally protected privacy interests of government employees for noninvestigatory, work-related purposes, as well as for investigations of work-related misconduct, should be judged by the standard of reasonableness under all the circumstances. Under this reasonableness standard, both the inception and the scope of the intrusion must be reasonable. . . .

❖ ❖ ❖

In the procedural posture of this case, we do not attempt to determine whether the search of Dr. Ortega's office and the seizure of his personal belongings satisfy the standard of reasonableness. . . . No evidentiary hearing was held in this case. . . .

❖ ❖ ❖

On remand, therefore, the District Court must determine the justification for the search and seizure, and evaluate the reasonableness of both the inception of the search and its scope.

❖ ❖ ❖

Case 6.4

AUBREY v. SCHOOL BOARD OF LAFAYETTE PARISH
148 F.3d 559 (5th Cir. 1998)

> [*Focus Note*. *Mandatory random employee urinalysis. Aubrey, an elementary school custodian, brought suit alleging that he was subjected to a random, urinalysis drug test in violation of his Fourth Amendment rights. The trial court dismissed the case and the Court of Appeals affirmed the dismissal, holding that the school board's need to conduct suspicionless searches of persons in safety sensitive positions outweighed the privacy interests of Aubrey and other safety sensitive employees.]*

POLITZ, CHIEF JUDGE.

❖ ❖ ❖

As a custodian at the Prairie Elementary School, Aubrey's duties included cleaning . . . bathrooms each day, using various chemicals. He . . . was responsible for securing the premises . . . making minor repairs to buildings, furniture and equipment. . . . He constantly was in the presence of the young students.

In December 1992, the Board adopted an Employee Drug Testing Policy. In August 1993, Aubrey attended an in-service training . . . in which the drug testing policy was distributed and reviewed.

Each year the Board submitted a list of "safety sensitive" employees to Security Concepts International, Inc. for random selection and drug testing. On September 28, 1994, the Board requested that Aubrey and fourteen other employees submit to a urinalysis screening. Aubrey's test indicated the presence of tetrahydrocannabinol, the active chemical in marijuana. As an alternative to termination, the Board required that Aubrey attend a substance abuse program. . . .

Denying that he had used marijuana, Aubrey sought an injunction barring the Board from firing him, or requiring that he continue to attend the substance abuse program. ....

❖ ❖ ❖

. . . Further, the fourth amendment . . . extends to all government searches. . . . This restraint . . . generally bars officials from undertaking a search or seizure absent individualized suspicion. Searches conducted without grounds for suspicion of particular individuals have been upheld, however, in certain limited circumstances. See *National Treasury Employees v. Von Raab,* 489 U.S. 656 . . . (1989); *Skinner v. Railway Labor Executives Assn.,* 489 U.S. 602 . . . (1989); *Vernonia School District 47J v. Acton,* 515 U.S. 646 . . . (1995); *Chandler v. Miller,* 520 U.S. 305 (1997).

A program which compels government employees to submit to urinalysis is a search. . . . Such a drug test therefore must meet the reasonableness requirement. ....

The Supreme Court has found that special needs may outweigh the privacy interests of individuals. In *Skinner v. Railway Labor Executives' Association,* the Court stated:

The Government's interest in regulating the conduct of railroad employees to ensure safety, like its supervision of probationers . . . or its operation of a government office, school, or prison, "likewise presents 'special needs' beyond normal law enforcement that may justify the departures from the usual warrant and probable-cause requirements." [fn. 19. *Skinner,* 489 U.S. at 620. . . .]

Similarly in *National Treasury Employees v. Von Raab,* the Court found permissible the U.S. Customs Service's drug testing program analyzing urine specimens of employees applying for promotions to positions involving interdiction of illegal drugs and requiring the carrying of firearms.

In *Vernonia School District 47J v. Acton,* a policy adopted by a school district to test student athletes was held non-violative of fourth amendment protections. The Court stated that "[d]eterring drug use by our Nation's schoolchildren is at least as important as enhancing efficient enforcement of the Nation's laws against the importation of drugs, which was the governmental concern in *Von Raab* or deterring drug use in engineers and trainmen, which was the governmental concern in *Skinner.*"

❖ ❖ ❖

. . . The Board contends that the urinalysis was obtained to maintain the safe and efficient operation of its schools . . . and decrease the potential spread of drug use among its students. . . . The Board also asserts that it "has a compelling interest and commitment to eliminate illegal and unauthorized drug use . . . drug users, drug activities, and drug effects from all of its workplaces." The Board has not produced any summary judgment evidence to demonstrate a problem of drug abuse or use in its schools, and although such a showing would be of persuasive value, it is not mandatory. . . . . We find the Board's interests to be substantial indeed.

The Board's valid and compelling public interests must be weighed against the intrusion and interference with individual liberty. . . .

First, Aubrey had notice that his position . . . was specifically designated as safety sensitive. . . . The custodial position was considered safety sensitive because of the handling of potentially dangerous machinery and hazardous substances in an environment including a large number of children ranging in age from three to eleven. . . .

Second, the intrusiveness of the search was minimal. . . . Aubrey produced the sample in privacy. . . . [H]e was not required to disclose any personal medical information, nor was the urinalysis used to determine the presence of anything other than the presence or absence of drugs. . . .

It is clear that . . . the special need in this case is substantially more than symbolic. . . . . . . In Orleans Parish School Board, we held that the School Boards' policies, requiring all employees to submit to a drug abuse and alcohol screening panel following an accident during the course and scope of their employment, were violative of the fourth amendment. The Boards [in New Orleans] failed to articulate a special need for the testing. . . . The Lafayette Parish School Board has demonstrated that it is motivated by the special incentive to protect our most important resource—children. Although the facts in this case differ from Acton [Vernonia] in that the [Vernonia] school was testing student athletes as opposed to employees, the most significant element in both this case and Acton is that "the Policy was undertaken in furtherance of the government's responsibilities, under a public school system, as guardian and tutor of children entrusted to its care." . . .

We therefore conclude and hold that the Board's need to conduct the suspicionless searches pursuant to the drug testing policy outweighs the privacy interests of the employees in an elementary school who interact regularly with students, use hazardous substances, operate potentially dangerous equipment, or otherwise pose any threat or danger to the students.

❖ ENDNOTES

1. Alba v. Ansonia Board of Educ., 999 F. Supp. 687 (D. Conn. 1998).

2. Dudley v. Augusta School Dept., 23 F. Supp. 2d 85 (D. Me. 1998) (demotion as possible stigmatization of teacher); Alba, *supra* note 1 (nonrenewal decision did not stigmatize teacher).
   (a) Bristol Va. School Bd. v. Quarles, 366 S.E.2d 82 (Va. 1988); Cogdill v. Comal Indep. School Dist., 630 F. Supp. 47 (W.D. Tex. 1985). "... [T]he competence of teachers, and the standards of its measurement are not, without more, matters of constitutional dimensions." *See* Scheelhaase v. Woodbury Central Comm. School Dist., 488 F.2d 237, 244 (8th Cir. 1973).
   (b) Irby v. McGowan, 380 F. Supp. 1024 (S.D. Ala. 1974) (teacher allowed to resign with removal of dismissal charges from her record).
   (c) Cooper v. Curry, 399 F. Supp. 372 (S.D. Miss. 1975).
   (d) Coen v. Boulder Valley School Dist., 402 F. Supp. 1335 (D. Colo. 1975).
   (e) Gray v. Union County Int. Educ. Dist., 520 F.2d 803 (9th Cir. 1975).

3. (a) *Undisclosed charges:* Brandt v. Bd. of Coop. Educ. Services, 845 F.2d 416 (2d Cir. 1988); Buhr v. Buffalo Public School Dist. No. 38, 509 F.2d 1196 (8th Cir. 1974).
   (b) *Undisputed charges:* Codd v. Velger, 429 U.S. 624 (1977); Carpenter v. City of Greenfield School Dist., 358 F. Supp. 220 (E.D. Wis. 1973).
   (c) *Expression of opinion:* Strasburger v. Board of Educ., 143 F.3d 351 (7th Cir. 1998).

4. Lancaster v. Ind. School Dist., 149 F.3d 1228 (10th Cir. 1998).

5. Supan v. Michelsfeld, 468 N.Y.S.2d 384 (1983) (dishonesty); Bomhoff v. White, 526 F. Supp. 488 (D. Ariz. 1981) (instability); Morris v. Board of Educ., 401 F. Supp. 188 (D. Del. 1975) (insubordination); Lombard v. Board of Educ., 502 F.2d 631 (2d Cir. 1974) (emotional instability).

6. Petron v. Dept. of Educ., 726 A.2d 1091 (Pa. 1999) (suspension of certification required a due process hearing).

7. Crim v. Board of Educ., 147 F.3d 535 (7th Cir. 1998) (superintendent); Bailey v. Floyd County Board of Educ., 106 F.3d 135 (6th Cir. 1997) (Head Start administrator); Board of Educ. v. Harrell, 882 P.2d 511 (N.M. 1994).

8. Mazurek v. Wolcott Board of Educ., 815 F. Supp. 71 (D. Conn. 1993); McCreery v. Babylon Unified Free School Dist., 827 F. Supp. 136 (E.D. N.Y. 1993); Cotnoir v. U. of Maine System, 35 F.3d 6 (1st Cir. 1994).

9. *Finding of promise of tenure from school customs and practices:* Perry v. Sindermann, 408 U.S. 593 (1972). *Semble:* Soni v. Board of Trustees, 376 F. Supp. 289 (E.D. Tenn. 1974) (implied "entitlement"). *Refusal to find unexpressed property right:* Gregory v. Hunt, 24 F.3d 781 (6th Cir. 1994).

10. Goss v. Lopez, 419 U.S., at 577 (1975).

11. Mustafa v. Clark County School Dist., 157 F.3d 1169 (9th Cir. 1998).

12. Bostean Los Angeles Unified School Dist., 73 Cal. Rptr. 2d 253 (Cal. 1998).

13. Coleman v. Reed, 147 F.3d 751 (8th Cir. 1998).

14. Cleveland Board of Educ. v. Loudermill, 470 U.S. 532 (1985); Bates v. Hinds, 334 F. Supp. 528 (N.D. Tex. 1971).

15. Cleveland Board of Educ., *supra* note 14; Okeson v. Tolley School Dist. No. 25, 766 F.2d 378 (8th Cir. 1985); Brown v. State Board of Educ., 391 So. 2d 866 (S.C. 1990).

16. *Cf.* Montoya v. Sanger Unified School Dist., 502 F. Supp 209 (E.D. Cal. 1980).

17. Board of Trustees v. Landry, 638 N.E.2d 1261 (Ind. App. 1994).

18. Dixon v. Love, 431 U.S. 105 (1977); Janke v. Comm. School Board, 587 N.Y.S.2d 733 (1992).

19. Gilbert v. Homar, 117 S. Ct. 1807 (1997) (prehearing suspension without pay—held consistent with due process); Andresky v. W. Allegheny School Dist., 437 A.2d 1074 (Pa. Cmwlth. 1981).

20. Kirschling v. Lake Forest School Dist., 687 F. Supp. 927 (D. Del. 1988); Huntley v. Comm. School Board of Brooklyn, 543 F.2d 979 (2d Cir. 1976).

21. Hortonville Dist. v. Hortonville Educ. Assn., 426 U.S. 483 (1976). To like effect, *see* Byrd v. Greene County School Dist., 633 So. 2d 1018 (Miss. 1994).

22. Larsen v. Oakland Community School Dist., 416 N.W.2d 89 (Iowa 1987). The law is reviewed in Withrow v. Larkin, 421 U.S. 35 (1975). Penn-Delco School Dist. v. Urso, 382 A.2d 162 (Pa. 1978); Weissman v. Board of Educ., 547 P.2d 1267 (Colo. 1976).

23. *Ex Parte* Concuh County Board of Educ., 495 So. 2d 1108 (Ala. 1986); Staton v. Mayes, 552 F.2d 908 (10th Cir. 1977).

24. Kamjathy v. Board of Educ., 348 N.Y.S.2d 28 (1973).

25. Katruska v. Dept. of Educ., 727 A.2d 612 (Pa. 1999).

26. Keith v. Comm. School Dist., 262 N.W.2d 249 (Iowa 1978); English v. Northeast Board of Educ., 348 A.2d 494 (Pa. 1975) (solicitor as hearing officer); Miller v. Board of Educ., 200 N.E.2d 838 (Ill. 1964) (solicitor as prosecutor and counsel to board on admissibility of evidence).

27. Harmon v. Mifflin County School Dist., 651 A.2d 681 (Pa. 1994).

28. On the varied treatment of hearsay evidence, *see* Kinkle v. Garrett-Keyser-Butler School Dist., 5667 N.E.2d 1171 (Ind. App. 1991); Casada v. Booneville School Dist. No. 65, 686 F. Supp. 730 (W.D. Ark. 1988).

29. Brown v. South Carolina Board of Educ., 391 So. 2d 866 (S.C. 1990); Springfield School Dist. v. Shellem, 328 A.2d 535 (Pa. 1974).

30. *See, e.g.,* Tucker v. Board of Educ., 492 A.2d 839 (Conn. 1985) (no universal constitutional right of appeal); Mason v. Thetford School Board, 457 A.2d 647 (Vt. 1982) (no right of appeal). For cases where right of appeal allowed, *see* Racine Unified School Dist. v. Thompson, 321 N.W.2d 334 (Wis. 1982).

31. Smith v. Board of Educ., 484 N.Y.S.2d 602 (1985).

32. Board of Educ. of Charles County v. Crawford, 395 A.2d 835 (Md. 1979); Alexander v. School Dist. No. 17, 248 N.W.2d 335 (Neb. 1976).

33. *See, generally,* Westley v. Terrebone Parish School Board, 656 F. Supp. 499 (E.D. La. 1987). *General waiver of hearing:* Ferguson v. Board of Trustees, 564 P.2d 971 (Idaho 1977) (intentionally leaving hearing); Cords v. Window Rock School Dist., 526 P.2d 757 (Ariz. 1974) (waiver by abandonment).

   Waiver of specific aspect of hearing: McDonough v. Kelly, 329 F. Supp. 144 (D. N.H. 1971) (right to counsel); Hickey v. Board of School Directors, 328 A.2d 529 (Pa. 1974) (right to have witness testify); Pyle v. Wash. County School Board, 238 So. 2d 121 (Fla. 1970) (of a hearing record); Mullally v. Board of Educ., 164 N.W.2d 742 (Mich. 1968) (of prior notice); Williams v. Cody, 545 P.2d 905 (Or. 1976) (of appeal).

34. Schmidt v. Indep. School Dist. No. 1, 349 N.W.2d 563 (Minn. App. 1984); Holland v. Board of Educ., 327 S.E.2d 155 (W. Va. 1985).

35. Turner v. Board of Trustees, 121 Cal. Rptr. 715 (1975).

36. Thombleson v. Board of School Trustees, 492 N.E.2d 327 (Ind. App. 1986); Scotchlas v. Board of School Directors, 496 A.2d 916 (Pa. Cmwlth. 1985).

37. Strasburger v. Board of Educ., 143 F.3d 351 (7th Cir. 1998).

38. *Unconstitutional rule against teacher communications with school board members:* Knapp v. Whitaker, 757 F.2d 827 (7th Cir. 1985); Anderson v. Central Point School Dist., 746 F.2d 505 (9th Cir. 1984). *Unconstitutional prohibitions against school-site distribution of literature:* Hall v. Board of School Comm'rs., 681 F.2d 965 (5th Cir. 1983).

39. (a) Westbrook v. Teton County School Dist., 918 F. Supp. 1475 (D. Wyo. 1996).
    (b) Weaver v. Nebo School Dist., 29 F. Supp. 2d 1279 (S.D. N.Y. 1998).

40. Hall, *supra* note 38; Davis v. E. Baton Rouge Par. School Board, 78 F.3d 920 (5th Cir. 1996) (order barring news media disclosure of labor strategy meetings—overturned).

41. Russo v. Central School Dist., 469 F.2d 623 (2d Cir. 1972).

42. Brady v. Houston Independent School Dist., 113 F.3d 1419 (5th Cir. 1997). *See also* Bailey v. Floyd County Board of Educ., 106 F.3d 135 (6th Cir.

1997) (failure to prove termination decision was based on employee's speech).

43. Dudley v. Augusta School Dept., 23 F. Supp. 2d 85 (Me. 1998); Harris v. Shelby County Board of Educ., 99 F.3d 1078 (11th Cir. 1996).

44. Ward v. Hickey, 996 F.2d 448 (1st Cir. 1993); Miles v. Denver Public Schools, 944 F.2d 773 (10th Cir. 1991) (sanctions for classroom comments on rumors of sexual misconduct); Pelozo v. Capistrano Unified School Dist., 37 F.3d 517 (9th Cir. 1994) (restriction on teacher discussions of religion during school day).

45. Tinker v. Des Moines Ind. School Dist., 393 U.W. 503, 506–9 (1969). *See also* Piver v. Pender County Board of Educ., 835 F.2d 1076 (4th Cir. 1987).

46. Connick v. Myers, 461 U.S. 138 (1983); Waters v. Churchill, 62 U.S.L.W. 4397 (1994).

47. Givhan v. Western Line Cons. School Dist., 439 U.S. 410 (1979).

48. The Supreme Court justices divided 5–4 in holding that a low-level employee of a police department spoke on a matter of public, not private concern, in expressing her disappointment that the attempted assassination of President Reagan failed. Rankin v. McPherson, 483 U.S. 378 (1987).

    For skillful manipulation of public–personal balancing factors, *see* Piver *supra* note 45 (teacher advocacy of tenure for fellow teacher and encouraging students to circulate petitions in support of tenure candidate—held justified as training in civic action).

    Speech ruled of public concern: Mazurek v. Wolcott Board of Educ., 815 F. Supp. 71 (D. Conn. 1993) (comments on teacher quality); Ratliff v. Wellington Exempted Village Schools Board of Educ., 820 F.2d 792 (6th Cir. 1987) (principal's report to school board on poor school conditions and atmosphere of mistrust); Cox v. Dardanelle Public School Dist., 790 F.2d 668 (8th Cir. 1986) (teacher grievances against principal).

    Speech held to be of personal and not public concern: Callaway v. Hafeman, 832 F.2d 414 (7th Cir. 1987) (sexual harassment complaint—held motivated by personal concern); Day v. S. Park Indep. School Dist., 768 F.2d 696 (5th Cir. 1985) (complaint of principal's evaluation); Roberts v. Van Buren Pub. Schools, 773 F.2d 949 (8th Cir.

1985) (complaints on management of field trips); Saye v. St. Vrain Valley School Dist., 785 F.2d 862 (10th Cir. 1986) (teacher complaints to parents on "aide time").

49. *Compare* Brewster v. Board of Educ., 149 F.3d 971 (9th Cir. 1998), *with* Bernheim v. Litt, 79 F.3d 318 (2d Cir. 1996).

50. *Unprotected criticism of superiors:* Khuans v. School Dist., 123 F.3d 1010 (7th Cir. 1997) (psychologist's statements to school superiors critical of psychologist's supervisor—held not to involve matter of public concern); Stevenson v. Lower Marion County School Dist., 327 S.E.2d 656 (S.C. 1985) (incitement against school superior).

51. Roberts v. Lake Central School Dist., 317 F. Supp. 63 (N.D. Ind. 1970); Gieringer v. Central School Dist., 477 F.2d 1164 (8th Cir. 1973).

52. *Compare* Copp v. Unified School Dist., 882 F.2d 1547 (10th Cir. 1989); Seemuller v. Fairfax County School Board, 878 F.2d 1578 (4th Cir. 1989); Thompson v. Board of Educ. City of Chicago, 711 F. Supp. 394 (N.D. Ill. 1989); Adcock v. Board of Educ., 513 P.2d 900 (Cal. 1973); *with* Jones v. Battles, 315 F. Supp. 601 (D. Conn. 1970).

53. *Compare* Gilbertson v. McAlister, 403 F. Supp. 1 (D. Conn. 1975), *with* Bertot v. School Dist., 522 F.2d 1171 (10th Cir. 1975).

54. Solmitz v. Maine School Admin. Dist. No. 59, 495 A.2d 812 (Me. 1985).

55. *Passive armband:* James v. Board of Educ., 461 F.2d 566 (2nd Cir. 1972). *Leaving school:* Petition of Davenport, 283 A.2d 452 (Vt. 1971).

56. *Protected expression:* Petition of Davenport, *supra* note 55. *Unprotected conduct:* Knarr v. Board of School Trustees, 317 F. Supp. 832 (N.D. Ind. 1970). *Cf.* Cooley v. Board of Educ., 327 F. Supp. 454 (E.D. Ark. 1971) (civil rights rally). Johnson v. Branch, 364 F.2d 177 (4th Cir. 1966).

57. Fogarty v. Boles, 121 F.3d 886 (3d Cir. 1997); Jones v. Collins, 132 F.3d 1048 (5th Cir. 1998).

58. California Teachers Assn. v. Governing Board of San Diego Unified School Dist., 53 Cal. Rptr. 2d 474 (1996).

59. Boring v. The Buncombe County Board of Educ., 136 F.3d 364 (4th Cir. 1998) (drama teacher play selection); Board of Educ. of

Jefferson County School Dist. R-1 v. Wilder, 960 P.2d 695 (Colo. 1998) (showing controversial film without required school approval); Bradley v. Pittsburgh Board of Educ., 910 F.2d 1171 (3d Cir. 1990) (choice of class management techniques); Kirkland v. Northside Indep. School Dist., 890 F.2d 794 (5th Cir. 1989) (selection of class materials); Milliken v. Board of Directors, 611 P.2d 414 (Wash. 1980) (disapproved teaching method).

See M. Yudof, *The Three Faces of Academic Freedom,* 32 Loyola L. Rev. 831 (1987); E. Bjorklun, *Regulating the Use of Theatrical Movies in the Classroom: Academic Freedom Issues,* 100 Edlaw Rep. 1 (1995); *Symposium on Academic Freedom,* 66 Tex. L. Rev. 1274 (1988); J. Tuner-Egner, *Teacher's Discretion in Selecting Instructional Materials and Methods,* 53 Educ. L. Rep. 365 (1989).

60. Bradley v. Pittsburgh Board of Educ., 910 F.2d 1172 (3d Cir. 1990) (unfair notice to teacher); Proposed Termination of James Johnson's Teaching Contract, 451 N.W.2d 343 (Minn. App. 1990) (arbitrary directive).

61. Celestine v. Lafayette Parish School Board, 284 So. 2d 650 (La. 1973). *See also* Moore v. School Board of Gulf County, 364 F. Supp. 355 (N.D. Fla. 1973) (teacher's reference to personal sexual attitudes and to student sexual development); State v. Board of Directors, 111 N.W.2d 198 (Wis. 1961) (teacher discussion of sex in class). *Cf.* Simon v. Jefferson Davis Par. School Board, 289 So. 2d 511 (La. 1974). *Compare* Palo Verde Unified School Dist. v. Hensey, 9 Cal. App. 2d 967 (1970), *with* Lindros v. Governing Board of Torrance Unified School Dist., 9 Cal. 3d 524 (1973).

62. Keefe v. Geanakos, 418 F.2d 359 (1st Cir. 1969); Close v. Lederle, 424 F.2d 988 (1st Cir. 1970); Mailloux v. Kiley, 436 F.2d 565 (1st Cir. 1970).

63. Close, *supra* note 62.

64. Mailloux, *supra* note 62.

65. From footnote 7 of the opinion in President's Council v. Comm. School Board, 457 F.2d 289 (2d Cir. 1972).

66. *See* survey of cases in Cary v. Board of Educ., 598 F.2d 535 (10th Cir. 1979).

Later cases denying academic freedom claim: Fisher v. Fairbanks N. Star Borough School Dist., 704 P.2d 213 (Ala. 1985) (use of supplemental materials); Meckley v. Kanawha County Board of Educ., 383 S.E.2d 839 (W. Va. 1989) (order directing teacher to reevaluate student grade did not violate academic freedom); Milliken v. Board of Directors of Everett, 611 P.2d 414 (Wash. 1980) (board authority to prescribe teaching method as well as content—upheld); Parker v. Board of Educ., 237 F. Supp. 222 (D. Md.), *aff'd,* 348 F.2d 464 (4th Cir. 1966) (teacher dismissed for insubordination for insistent class assignment of *Brave New World*); *accord:* Harris v. Mechanicsville Cent. School Dist., 380 N.E.2d 313 (N.Y. 1978); Adams v. Campbell County School Dist., 511 F.2d 1242 (10th Cir. 1975); Hetrick v. Martin, 480 F.2d 705 (6th Cir. 1973) (teacher not protected from nonrenewal based on teaching methods and philosophy); Alinovi v. Worcester School Comm., 777 F.2d 776 (1st Cir. 1985) (dismissal for refusal to allow principal to read teacher's paper about students).

Cases recognizing academic freedom claims: Kingsville Indep. School Dist. v. Cooper, 611 F.2d 1109 (5th Cir. 1980); Lindros v. Governing Board, 510 P.2d 361 (Cal. 1973); Parducci v. Rutland, 316 F. Supp. 352 (N.D. Ala. 1970) (teacher reinstated).

"The cases which held for the teachers and placed emphasis upon the teachers' rights to exercise discretion in the classroom, seemed to be situations where school authorities acted in the absence of a general policy . . . and [where they] had little to charge against the teacher other than the assignment with which they were unhappy. [citations] . . . *See* Cary v. Board of Educ., 598 F.2d 535, 541–2 (10th Cir. 1979).

67. Rutan v. Republican Party of Ill., 110 S. Ct. 2729 (1990); Branti v. Finkel, 445 U.S. 507 (1980). For the school context, *see, e.g.,* Wichert v. Walter, 606 F. Supp. 1516 (D. N.J. 1985); Piazza v. Aponte Roque, 909 F.2d 35 (1st Cir. 1990) (nonrenewal based on party affiliation).

68. Opdahl v. Zeeland Pub. School Dist., 512 N.W.2d 444 (N.D. 1994) (associational activities during teacher work time).

69. Raposa v. Meade School Dist., 790 F.2d 1349 (8th Cir. 1986) (teacher transfer for speech that created disharmony in small community).

70. Buford v. Southeast Dubois County School Corp., 472 F.2d 890 (7th Cir. 1972); Rawlings v.

Butler, 290 S.W.2d 801 (Ky. 1956); Hysong v. School Dist., 30 A.2d 482 (Pa. 1894). *Cf.* McDaniel v. Patty, 435 U.S. 618 (1978); Randle v. Indianola Sep. School Dist., 373 F. Supp. 766 (N.D. Miss. 1974); Fyfe v. Curlee, 902 F.2d 401 (5th Cir. 1990); Brantley v. Surles, 765 F.2d 478 (5th Cir. 1985); Stough v. Crenshaw County Board of Educ., 744 F.2d 1479 (11th Cir. 1984).

71. Lasota v. Town of Topsfield, 979 F. Supp. 45 (D. Mass. 1997).

72. *Later cases:* Domico v. Rapides Par. School Board, 675 F.2d 100 (5th Cir. 1982); Morrison v. Hamilton County Board of Educ., 494 S.W.2d 770 (Tenn. 1973); Miller v. School Dist. No. 167, 495 F.2d 658 (7th Cir. 1974).

    Earlier cases: see Conard v. Goolsby, 350 F. Supp. 713 (N.D. Miss. 1972); Ball v. Kerriville Indep. School Dist., 529 S.W.2d 792 (Tex. 1975) (refusal to shave beard—held not to be grounds for dismissal).

73. *See* Kelley v. Johnson, 425 U.S. 238, 247–8 (1976).

74. Ramsey v. Hopkins, 320 F. Supp. 477, remanded on other grounds, 447 F.2d 128 (5th Cir. 1970); Lucia v. Duggan, 303 F. Supp. 112 (D.C. Mass. 1969).

75. Ball v. Board of Trustees, 584 F.2d 684 (5th Cir. 1978); Miller v. School Dist. No. 167, 495 F.2d 658 (7th Cir. 1974). *See* cases collected in Annot., *Teacher Dress,* 58 A.L.R. 3d 1227 (1974).

76. Tardif v. Quinn, 545 F.2d 761 (1st Cir. 1976). *Cf.* E. Hartford Educ. Assn. v. Board of Educ., 405 F. Supp. 94 (D. Conn. 1975) (upholding teacher dress code); E. Hartford Educ. Assn. v. Board of Educ., 562 F.2d 838 (1st Cir. 1977) (dismissal for refusing to wear necktie).

77. Cooper v. Eugene School Dist. No. 4J, 723 P.2d 298 (Or. 1986), *appeal dismissed* 480 U.S. 942 (1987).

78. United States v. Board of Educ., School Dist. of Philadelphia, 911 F.2d 882 (3d Cir. 1990) (Pa. religious garb statute—upheld).

79. Moore v. Board of Educ., 212 N.E.2d 833 (Ohio 1965); O'Connor v. Hendrich, 77 N.E. 612 (N.Y. 1906).

80. *Ibid. See* early cases in Annot., *Wearing of Religious Garb by Public School Teachers,* 60 A.L.R. 2d 300 (1958).

81. *Teacher union representatives may not consent to a search of a represented teacher:* McDonnell v. Hunter, 809 F.2d 1302, 1310 (8th Cir. 1987) (purported consent in union bargained contract).

82. MR by RR v. Lincolnwood Board of Educ., 843 F. Supp. 1236 (N.D. Ill. 1994) (videotape of public area); Roberts v. Houston Indep. School Dist., 788 S.W.2d 107 (Tex. 1990) (videotape of classroom).

83. Gordon J. v. Santa Ana Unified School Dist., 208 Cal. Rptr. 657 (Cal. App. 1984); Ross v. Springfield School Dist., 641 P.2d 600, 610 (Or. 1981).

84. Knox County Educ. Assn. v. Knox County Board of Educ., 158 F.3d 361 (6th Cir. 1998); Aubrey v. School Board of Lafayette Parish, 148 F.3d 559 (5th Cir. 1998); Contra Loder v. Glendale, 28 Cal. App. 4th 796 (1997) (overturned *suspicionless* mandatory urinalysis for employees seeking promotions).

85. *Cf.* Vernonia School Dist. v. Acton, 515 U.S. 646 (1995).

86. *E.g.,* Patchogue-Medford Cong. of Teachers v. Board of Educ., 510 N.E.2d 325 (N.Y. 1987); Schaill by Kross v. Tippecanoe County School Corp., 864 F.2d 1309 (7th Cir. 1988); *Dragnet Drug Testing in Public Schools,* 86 Col. L. Rev. 852 (1986).

87. Jones v. McKenzie, 833 F.2d 335 (D.C. Cir. 1987) (testing of school bus aides upheld against a background of widespread drug abuse).

88. Hearn v. Board of Public Educ., 191 F.3d 1329 (11th Cir. 1999).

89. Child Protection Group v. Cline, 350 S.E.2d 541 (W. Va. 1986) (parents granted access to medical records of school bus driver whose actions raised questions of student safety); *cf.* Strong v. Board of Educ. of Uniondale Unified Free School Dist., 902 F.2d 208 (2d Cir. 1990); Daury v. Smith, 842 F.2d 9 (1st Cir. 1988) (teacher refusal to undergo reasonable request for psychiatric examination—not protected as constitutional privacy). *See, generally,* Turkington, *The Emerging Unencumbered Constitutional Right to Informational Privacy,* 10 N. Ill. U. L. Rev. 479 (1990); Note, *The Constitutional Right of Informational Privacy,* 14 Fordham Urban L. Rev. 927 (1986).

90. Teachers Local 59 v. Special School Dist., 512 N.W.2d 107 (Minn. App. 1994); Klein Ind. School Dist. v. Mattox, 830 F.2d 576 (5th Cir. 1987); Brouillet v. Cowles Publishing Co., 791 P.2d 526 (Wash. 1990); Hovet v. Hebron Public School Dist., 419 N.W.2d 189 (N.D. 1988).

91. *Cf.* Whalan v. Roe, 429 U.S. 589 (1977).

92. See the state authorities in Robinson v. Merritt, 375 S.W.2d 204 (W. Va. 1988); Annot., *What Constitutes Personal Matters Exempt from Disclosure . . . under State Freedom of Information Act*, 26 A.L.R. 4th 666 (1983).

93. Bowers v. Hardwick, 478 U.S. 186 (1986) (rejecting privacy claim for consensual, adult homosexual relations); *accord:* Ross v. Springfield School Dist., 657 P.2d 188 (Or. 1982).

94. The amorphous state law on decisional privacy is not surveyed here.

95. *See* authorities reviewed in W.D. Valente, *Education Law—Public and Private,* Vol. I, § 13.11 (1985 and Pkt. Pt. 1989) and in Johnson v. San Jacinto Jr. College, 498 F. Supp. 555 (S.D. Tex. 1980) (denying privacy immunity to adulterous relationship between registrar and teacher). Littlejohn v. Rose, 768 F.2d 765 (6th Cir. 1985) (nonrenewal for divorce action infringed right of privacy). *Compare also* Ponton v. Newport News School Board, 632 F. Supp. 1056 (E.D. Va. 1986) (right of privacy regarding out-of-wedlock birth), *with* Chambers v. Omaha Girls Club, 834 F.2d 697 (8th Cir. 1987) (discharge of pregnant unmarried employee—upheld); Hollenbaugh v. Carnegie Free Library, 578 F2d. 1374 (3d Cir. 1979) (public extramarital cohabitation not protected as privacy right).

CHAPTER 7

Student Rights and Discipline

❖ **CHAPTER DISCUSSION QUESTIONS**

❖ **CASES**
7.1 Gonzales v. McEuen, 435 F. Supp. 460 (1977)[†]
7.2 Bethel School District No. 403 v. Fraser, 478 U.S. 675 (1986)
7.3 Hazelwood School District v. Kuhlmeier, 484 U.S. 260 (1988)[†]
7.4 Vernonia School District v. Acton, 515 U.S. 646 (1995)[†]
7.5 Miller v. Wilkes, 172 F.3d 574 (8th Cir. 1999)
7.6 ABC School v. Mr. and Mrs. M., 1997 Mass. Super. Lexis 43
7.7 Hendrick Hudson Dist. Board of Educ. v. Rowley, 458 U.S. 176 (1982)

❖ **ENDNOTES**

[†] Denotes cases with review questions.

BACKGROUND NOTE

Chapters 1 to 3 considered student rights under state education laws. This chapter deals with student civil rights, primarily under the federal Constitution and federal education subsidy statutes. The following discussion does not canvass the many variations of state laws on civil rights, but will refer briefly to some examples of state law rights that are not guaranteed by federal law. The next chapter will deal with the interplay between laws governing substantive civil rights and laws providing remedies for the violation of these rights.

PROCEDURAL RIGHTS OF DUE PROCESS

Federal Law

The same two-part inquiry discussed in Chapter 6 for teacher constitutional due process claims governs student claims; i.e., does the student have a constitutionally recognized *liberty or property interest* that entitles the student to constitutional due process? If so, what process is due the student in particular case circumstances?

Interests That Qualify for Due Process

Not all school benefits and restrictions implicate a liberty or property interest. It is now settled that a student's entitlement under state law to a public education or to state-mandated educational benefits is a property interest that entitles students who face educational penalties to due process. But state laws that leave educational decisions, such as admission or grade promotion, to school board discretion do not create a right or entitlement as to require due process hearings on those decisions.[1] Student access to an honor society, student office, or to participation in graduation ceremonies, as distinguished from the right to receive a diploma, have, with rare exception, been held not a constitutional interest.[2] Most cases find that student interest in participation in extracurricular activities, or school athletics does not qualify for constitutional due process, but a court may in exceptional circumstances require it, e.g., for a uniquely talented athlete whose exclusion from varsity sports would potentially jeopardize his opportunity to pursue a life career in professional sports.[3]

Elements of Due Process

The quantum of procedures required for due process will vary with the nature of each proceeding.[4]

Notice and Hearing.   In *Goss v. Lopez*, 419 U.S. 565 (1975), the Supreme Court invalidated a 10-day suspension for lack of a due process hearing because the student's property interest in receiving public education and liberty interest in avoiding loss of reputation through suspension entitled him to "some kind of hearing." The Court stressed that only minimal due process is required for minor disciplinary cases, and stated that an immediate conference between the student and school principal or other superior, with oral advice of the disciplinary charge and an opportunity for the student to respond to the charge, would suffice for short suspensions. A student who declined an oral request to give his version of a reported marijuana use incident may not thereafter complain when the school principal, upon further investigation, suspended him on that charge.[5]

For cases of severe charges or penalties, due process would require correspondingly greater procedures, such as written notice of charges, right to legal counsel, and right to cross-examine adverse witnesses. Such procedures may be required where a short suspension is a prelude to expulsion for the same conduct.[6] Transfers between schools of comparable quality were recently treated as having the same effect as a short-term suspension and thus subject to some informal process, while transfers to less desirable schools or classes involved stronger student educational interests, hence requiring a more formal hearing.[7] *Goss* and later cases noted several other examples of disciplines that are too minimal to implicate a need for any due process hearings:

> Certainly . . . measures such as after-school detention, restriction to classroom during free periods, reprimand or admonition do not per se involve matters rising to the dignity of constitutional magnitude.[8]

Emergency exclusions of a student from school without a prior hearing, in order to ensure school safety or stable school operations, do not violate due process as long as a postexclusion hearing is provided as soon as practicable.[9]

Two years after deciding *Goss*, the Supreme Court held that corporal punishment may be administered without a due process hearing. It held that the punishment would not seriously interrupt or affect the student's right to public education, or materially abridge a "liberty" interest in avoiding a beating.[10] The Court concluded that any benefit of a prior hearing in such cases is outweighed by the state's interest in prompt, effective discipline, and noted that state tort law provided an adequate remedy for any unlawful use of force. The Court further held that corporal punishment is not "cruel and unusual punishment," which is prohibited by the Eighth Amendment to the Constitution.

It appears that no prior hearing is required for academic decisions[11] unless penalties for academic failure are so severe as to implicate a student's property or liberty interest. The case variations manifest the reluctance of courts to interfere with educational decisions.

Where due process requires advance written notice, the notice must be given in a timely manner and must provide sufficient information to afford the student a fair opportunity to prepare a defense, but the amount and detail of notice required to meet the fairness test can only be determined by the nature and complexity of the disciplinary charge.[12] Whether due process includes a right to demand an open or a closed hearing also depends on the demands of fairness to all affected parties unless that right is conferred by a state statute. Absent controlling legislation, fairness may require a closed hearing to protect a person's reputation from unproven charges, but in other circumstances, fairness to the parties may require that the hearing be open to the public.[13]

As noted in Chapter 6, the fair notice principle finds expression in "void for vagueness" doctrine, which nullifies statutes and regulations that do not provide sufficient information to inform persons of ordinary intelligence as to what conduct is prohibited and what penalties such conduct will incur. Under the *Hazelwood* and *Bethel* cases, which appear at the end of this chapter, students cannot complain of lack of notice regarding conduct that is obviously wrongful.

The fair notice element of due process does not require schools to publish advance, narrowly drawn written regulations for every conceivable restriction on student conduct or expression. Courts may disagree on the fairness of notice in varied school environments. The word "misconduct" was held unconstitutionally vague for student discipline in some cases, but not in others. The prohibition against "behavior . . . inimical to the welfare, safety, or morals of other pupils" was held not unduly vague in Colorado, while the failure to specify criteria of "substantial disruption" was deemed fatal in Puerto Rico.[14] Courts are inclined to uphold terms that are customarily understood, such as willful disobedience, intentional disruption, student walkouts, boycotts, incorrigible behavior, profanity, excessive absenteeism, and vulgarity.[15] Though weakened by later case trends, some strict decisions caution against casual reliance on arguably vague regulations.[16]

Impartial Tribunal.   As reported in Chapter 6, school boards are presumed to be impartial tribunals so that a party alleging board bias has the burden of proving that charge.[17] A party may not attempt to provoke tribunal bias, e.g., by calling board members "fascist pigs" in order to disqualify the tribunal as biased by the party's insults.[18]

Impartiality was clearly destroyed, however, where a prosecution witness also served as a member of the judging panel.[19] There is some case division on the extent to which school board counsel can lawfully participate in school board hearings and deliberations.[20] The *Gonzales* decision, which appears at the end of this chapter, cautions against administrative staff performing potentially inconsistent roles in school board hearings and deliberations. This problem is avoided where state law or board regulations require that disciplinary hearings be conducted by persons other than school board members, and which permit the participation of school attorneys as prosecutor or counsel to the board, but not both.

Right to Present and Confront Evidence.   The right to present evidence is universal, but the right to be notified of adverse evidence and to cross-examine witnesses is not. In *Goss*, noted above, the Supreme Court rejected the suggestions that students have a right of cross-examination or to legal counsel in all student disciplinary hearings. Courts do not require these elements for minor infractions or punishments, but have held them essential in cases that involve potential serious penalties, especially where the hearing outcome would turn on the credibility of conflicting witnesses.[21] In such cases courts held that the board had to disclose and to produce adverse witnesses for cross-examination, though a court could excuse such failure as harmless error if the testimony of the absent witness could not have affected the hearing outcome.[22]

Decisions on the use or exclusion of hearsay evidence also vary with case circumstances.[23]

> Other federal courts are divided on the issue of confrontation and cross-examination. Some have held that a hearing incorporating that safeguard must be afforded in school expulsion proceedings. . . . Others have declined to accord that right. . . . In *Dillon v. Pulaski City Special Sch. Dist.* (E.D. Ark.) 468 F. Supp. 54, 58, the court held that a student not permitted to confront and cross-examine teachers or administrators who accused him of wrongdoing was denied due process, but stated in dicta that confrontation and cross-examination of student accusers might be disallowed consistent with due process if reprisals were likely. [*Aguirre v. San Bernadino City Unified School,* 170 Cal. Rptr. 206, 215 (1981)]

Right to Counsel.   Like cross-examination, the right to have an attorney present and participate in hearings depends on the nature of each hearing.

> Where the proceeding is non-criminal in nature, where the hearing is investigative and not adversarial and the government does not proceed through counsel, where the individual concerned is mature and educated, where his knowledge of the events . . . should enable him to develop the facts adequately through available sources, and where the other aspects of the hearing taken as a whole are fair, due process does not require representation by counsel. . . . See *Wasson v. Trowbridge,* 382 F.2d 807, 812 (2d Cir. 1967).

In line with the foregoing approach, no right to counsel was found where the school attorney was not present or where the hearing was considered advisory and not adversary.[24] But exclusion of a student's attorney from a hearing on charges of academic cheating that if proven would disqualify the student from taking a scholarship examination was held to deny due process.[25]

Hearing Record and Appeal.   Constitutional due process does not include a universal right of appeal from an administrative hearing, and a state legislature may grant or deny it.[26] Where a right of appeal is conferred by law, some kind of hearing record (stenographic or electronic) is required in order to provide the appellate tribunal a sufficient record for a fair review.[27] Where such a right is not so conferred, courts must decide whether a record is needed for fair consideration of the case.[28]

Waiver and Cure of Procedural Defects.   Students may waive due process rights expressly or by conduct, such as failure to pursue available procedures. Because waiver requires an *intentional* relinquishment or abandonment of a *known* right or privilege, school authorities should document, where possible, such waivers as having been freely and intelligently made. Procedural deficiencies can also be cured by substitute, corrective procedures. Finally, errors that are not waived or corrected but that do not materially affect the fairness or outcome of the case may still be excused as "harmless" errors.[29]

Statutory Procedures

In addition to constitutional due process, Congress may, as a condition of federal grants of aid, require school districts to adopt special procedures on matters affecting federally aided programs. For example, the Individuals with Disabilities Education Act discussed below prescribed special procedures that school administrators must follow for students with disabilities.

State Law

State laws often mandate procedures for specified school board actions that are not required by the federal Constitution, e.g., those dealing with student placement and assignment, or student access to extracurricular programs, student offices, or student organizations. Failure to observe state-mandated procedures is also grounds to overturn school decisions.

SUBSTANTIVE CONSTITUTIONAL RIGHTS

The National Constitution

The constitutional protections reviewed in Chapter 6 apply to students; however, student rights are not coextensive with those of teachers.

> In *New Jersey v. T.L.O.*, 469 U.S. 325, 340–342, . . . we reaffirmed that the constitutional rights of students in public school are not automatically coextensive with the rights of adults in other settings. . . . *See Bethel School District No. 403 v. Fraser*, 478 U.S. 675 at p. 682 (1986).

General Right to Rational Treatment

Constitutional liberty includes a general right to be free from government restraints or punishments that do not rationally serve a valid school *purpose*, or that employ *means* that do not rationally achieve a proper purpose. That right outlaws school restraints that are irrational in either purpose or in the means to achieve a rational purpose. With limited exceptions school actions are presumptively rational, so that a challenging party has the burden of establishing that the school's action lacked rational foundations. The determination whether an action is or is not "reasonable" calls for judgments on specific case facts. Courts may differ in their assessment whether case circumstances render particular student disciplines rational or irrational. A threatening outburst by a student occasioned by school bureaucratic shuffles was not deemed so serious as to justify her suspension when she promptly apologized for it, whereas in other circumstances, expulsion of a student who was deemed to pose danger to other students or teachers was held reasonable.[30]

Out-of-school misconduct that threatens student welfare, such as sale or use of drugs or alcohol or assaults on other students, is punishable as rationally connected to school missions.[31] On the other hand, other courts overturned, as irrational, punishment for being arrested away from school on a charge of drug possession absent proof of the student's guilt, and for being a passenger in a car that contained alcoholic beverages.[32] A manifest violation of the rational nexus test occurred where the school board expelled a student because his parent assaulted a board member.[33]

The cases on the rationality of academic penalties are mixed. A few courts sustained forfeiture of credits or privileges for serious student misconduct,[34] while academic penalties were overturned on nonconstitutional grounds, i.e., for abuse of discretion or for lack of authority (ultra vires).[35] Where automatic penalties are set by statute, courts tend to find them reasonable, even though the statute makes no allowance for mitigating circumstances.[36]

Right to Bodily Security

Fourteenth Amendment "liberty" encompasses the fundamental right to be secure in one's person and body. That right covers a broad range of unprivileged conduct—from uninvited, unwelcome nonsexual physical contact to sexual abuse and assault.

Corporal Punishments and Restraints. While a number of states have laws that prohibit or limit the use of corporal punishment,[37] the Supreme Court rejected the argument that normal discipline of corporal punishment infringed the right to bodily security.[38] However, the Court there did not reach the narrow question whether corporal punishment may be so severe and shocking as to violate a substantive constitutional right to bodily security. The circuit courts have recognized such a right against shockingly severe or brutal physical punishments, though their assessment whether particular punishments are sufficiently shocking to trigger constitutional protection may differ. Those authorities are listed in the endnote.[39] The Supreme Court recognition of a right to bodily security under federal laws in cases of teacher sexual abuse of students may well forecast its acceptance of a like constitutional right in cases of shocking corporal punishments.

Sexual Abuse and Molestation. The right to be free from sexual molestation is recognized in state tort law, under federal civil rights statutes which are reviewed in Chapter 8, and as a matter of constitutional right in cases of shocking sexual abuse.[40]

Freedom of Expression

Time, Place, and Manner Restrictions.   As explained in Chapter 6, the strongest school justification for restricting free speech is the need to maintain orderly scheduling and use of school facilities. "Time, place, and manner" regulations need only be reasonable in purpose and scope to be constitutional.[41] School authorities may confine student rallies to reasonably prescribed times and places, and may punish student protesters for occupying or obstructing facilities that are reserved for other school uses.

Scope of Constitutional Protection.   Both the First Amendment and the Equal Protection Clause of the Fourteenth Amendment forbid school authorities to suppress expression solely on the basis of its content or viewpoint. As with religious speech (considered in Chapter 3), school authorities may not deny school resources or the use of school facilities to disfavored student expression while granting such benefits to favored student communications, unless they can show an overriding school need that justifies the different treatment.

Freedom of speech and of the press apply on school premises, but the protection of student speech depends on its legal classification as *personal speech* that is *not of pedagogical concern,* or as *school-sponsored speech* that is *of pedagogical concern.* The Constitution affords greater protection to purely personal student speech than to speech that is either school sponsored or of pedagogical concern. The Supreme Court's explanation of the difference is presented in the *Bethel* opinion, which appears at the end of this chapter.

In *Tinker v. Des Moines Ind. Community School Dist.,*[42] the Supreme Court established a disruption test for limiting purely personal student expression. In this case the court found for a student First Amendment right to wear a war protest armband to school, because the school board did not demonstrate that the symbolic armband expression materially interfered with the work of the school. But, as noted there and in other cases,[43] even passive symbols can in some contexts threaten to disrupt school functions so as to justify their prohibition. Wearing confederate flag clothing patches or symbols in racially tense schools is one example.[44] The disruption issue presents kindred problems to those noted for teachers in Chapter 6, namely, what kinds and degrees of physical or psychological interference or distraction make expression "disruptive"?

In *Bethel,* the Supreme Court held that the *Tinker* disruption test does not govern student speech that is school related or of school pedagogical concern, and that school authorities could constitutionally suspend a student for delivering a lewd nominating speech to a school-sponsored assembly which the authorities reasonably considered to be "inappropriate." In later extending the *Bethel* rationale to school censorship of a school-sponsored student newspaper, the Supreme Court restated its personal/pedagogical speech dichotomy:

[T]he question that we addressed in *Tinker*—is different from the question whether the First Amendment requires a school. . . to promote particular student speech. The former question addresses educators' ability to silence a student's personal expression. . . . The latter question concerns educators' authority over school-sponsored publications, theatrical productions, and other expressive activities that students . . . and members of the public might reasonably perceive to bear the imprimatur of the school. These activities may fairly be characterized as part of the school curriculum, whether or not they occur in a traditional classroom setting. . . . See *Hazelwood School Dist. v. Kuhlmeier,* 484 U.S. 260, 271 (1988).

Lower courts have accordingly upheld school suppression of student plays and supplemental class readings whose content they deemed educationally inappropriate.[45] The standards set by *Tinker* and by *Bethel* and *Hazelwood* remain contentious. Some commentators argue that *Bethel* applies only to "school-sponsored" speech, and not to all speech "of pedagogical concern," but several courts have read *Bethel* more broadly to uphold school bans of vulgar, lewd and offensive student expression, whether or not it is school sponsored.[46]

In deciding whether a given speech and its circumstances render the speech constitutionally subject to the stricter *Tinker* test or to the deferential *Bethel* test, school authorities are best guided by decisions whose facts most closely proximate the case in question. Under either test, the balance between student and school interest is based on the specific mode and context of expression. For example, courts tend to give stricter constitutional protection to political communication than to student choice of personal appearance as a mode of expression. The following case samplings illustrate these contextual variables.

Critical Speech. Orderly student criticisms of school policies or practices qualify as protected speech, but disruptive messages that incite insubordination or disorder, such as abusive speech to school superiors or speech calling for a student strike or takeover of school buildings, are constitutionally punishable.[47]

Student Press, Plays, and Literature. School authorities may control the time, place, and manner of school-site distribution of student literature, by reasonable, nondiscriminatory regulations.[48] They may constitutionally ban obscene or libelous publications that lack First Amendment protections and may also suppress them as pedagogically inappropriate.[49]

The authority of court decisions from the roaring 1970s,[50] has been undercut by the Supreme Court decisions in *Bethel* and *Hazelwood. Hazelwood* subjected student yearbooks to greater school content control[51] and mooted the authority of an earlier college student press case that had been much invoked to advocate broad press freedoms for high school students.[52] It further undercut prior cases that required prior written school regulations to specify what expression was forbidden.

We reject respondent's suggestion that school officials be permitted to exercise prepublication control over school-sponsored publications only pursuant to specific written regulations. . . .[53]

The authority of prior cases on the question whether written regulations are required for non-sponsored student publications is further clouded by the Court's refusal in the *Bethel* case to require prior *written* regulations to punish lewd oral student speech.

The *Hazelwood* opinion expressly equated school control over school-sponsored plays with school control over school newspapers, and confirmed lower court decisions that squarely upheld school suppression of student plays that were deemed educationally inappropriate.[54]

Political and commercial advertisements: School prohibitions of politically partisan or socially controversial ads in student newspapers also generate case conflicts,[55] but once a public school student newspaper accepts outside advertisements it may not refuse other advertisements solely on the disapproval of the ad's message unless that message defeats school needs or purposes.[56] The cases are mixed on the question whether and under what test school authorities may regulate school site *distribution* of independently produced newspapers.[57]

As illustrated by the *Dawson* case at the end of Chapter 1, control over student distribution of commercial literature is to be differentiated from school use of educational material that happens to have a commercial component.

Anonymous student publications: Freedom of the press generally includes a right of anonymous publication, but school superiors may demand disclosure of the authors of communications distributed on school grounds.[58]

Appearance and Dress. Symbolic constitutional expression may be made by a passive display of symbols (as in the *Tinker* armband case) or by use of symbols bracketed with active conduct (such as flag burning[59] or draft-card burning). However,

> [W]hen speech and non-speech elements are combined in the same course of conduct, a sufficiently important governmental interest in regulating the non-speech element can justify incidental limitation of First Amendment freedoms. [*United States v. O'Brien*, 391 U.S. 367, 376 (1968)]

Students may express ideas by refusing to act, e.g., declining to participate in a flag salute, and courts have overturned laws and regulations that require students to stand or leave the room during flag salute ceremonies.[60] The expressive right to "opt out" of school requirements does not extend to the point of interfering with school functions. Student boycotts, walkouts, and sit-ins at sites designated for other school uses are not constitutionally protected.[61]

Student choice of personal appearance, grooming, and dress implicates a general liberty interest, but it is not as weighty as that of verbal expression.[62] Following the Supreme Court ruling that shifted the constitutional balance in the direction of upholding school regulation of student verbal expression, courts may afford similar leeway in school regulation of student dress. Nevertheless, appearance and dress regulations must still be sufficiently clear and be reasonably connected to proper school purposes.[63]

Grooming cases have centered largely on male hair length restrictions, and the federal circuits remain divided on their constitutionality.[64] The Supreme Court has declined to review or resolve that conflict, hence school authorities must observe the prevailing constitutional law in their particular circuit. Hair style restrictions in extracurricular activities (e.g., for athletes during the playing season) are more readily upheld as serving school interests in the health, safety, and effective performance of student participants.[65]

The factors that may determine the validity of a school dress code were illustrated by a recent case which upheld a ban against attire that featured certain colleges or sports teams at one high school, because the banned attire was found to be emblematic of school gangs that intimidated other students, but overturned the imposition of a like ban at other schools where that attire was not shown to be a source of trouble.[66] Another court upheld a dress code provision barring T-shirts that contained sexually vulgar, though not disruptive, messages, while voiding a different provision of the same dress code that barred garb that contained allegedly harassing messages.[67]

Where school districts adopt uniform dress requirements, courts will have to decide whether they rationally serve school educational and disciplinary interests in different grade levels of elementary and secondary schools.

Different hair and dress restrictions for male and female students have generally withstood sex discrimination challenges but courts in Alaska, Ohio, and Oregon held them void under their state law.[68]

Dress regulations designed to protect student health and safety are valid, but courts may differ in their assessment whether these justifications exist in fact. Bans against jeans for female students were upheld in Kentucky but overturned in Idaho and New Hampshire, while tight skirts, pants, or mini-skirts were found to be sufficiently immodest to justify school bans in Arkansas.[69]

Case variations on transsexual and gender identity issues also reflect the varied attitudes of courts in different states and regions with regard to sex-related issues. One court upheld a school decision to bar a male student from attending a prom dressed in girls' clothing, while another court upheld a male student's right to bring a male date to the school prom.[70]

Freedom of Association—Student Organizations. The First Amendment right to form and join organizations[71] may be subordinated to overriding school interests. To foster tolerance and democratic values, school authorities may prohibit secret or separatist fraternities, sororities, or clubs.[72] To prevent student injury, they may prohibit hazardous hazing rites.[73] To maintain proper oversight of student clubs, they may demand that student organizations disclose and file with school superiors the organization's bylaws and officers.[74]

Rights of Privacy

School Searches. The influx of drugs, weapons, and other contraband into schools and the concurrent escalation of school violence has triggered zero-tolerance policies and has intensified school searches. Some recent cases allowed school searches that were previously disapproved. The Chapter 6 overview of the constitutional principles on school search authority will not be repeated here, save to note their peculiar applications to students.[75] Searches allegedly undertaken with a student's consent are more likely to raise fact issues as to whether the student gave that consent freely and knowingly, or whether the consent was obtained by subtle intimidation, or in student ignorance of the possible consequences of the search.[76] Student expectations of privacy and freedom from search may be further narrowed by school rules. For example, a student may not claim a protected privacy interest where the school announced that school chaperones would conduct random searches of their hotel rooms on a school-sponsored field trip.[77]

The Supreme Court set different bounds for student searches in two separate decisions dealing with distinct circumstances. In the first case, *New Jersey v. T.L.O.*, 469 U.S. 325 (1985), it affirmed that students have some expectation of privacy at school that is protected by the Fourth Amendment, and it adopted the following requirements for a "reasonable" constitutional search:

- school authorities must have a reasonable individualized suspicion that the searched student violated a law or school rule;
- The scope and extent of the search must be limited to what is reasonable to serve the search purpose of preventing a suspected infraction of law or school rules; and
- The search must not be excessively intrusive in light of the student's age and sex and of the gravity of the suspected infraction.

The *T.L.O.* ruling expanded previously uncertain limits of a valid search to include searches for violations of school rules that do not involve crimininal acts. *T.L.O.* further made clear that the gravity of a suspected infraction, while a factor in limiting the scope or *intrusiveness* of a search, is not relevant to the question whether grounds exist to undertake a search.

> . . . [A] highly intrusive [e.g. strip] search in response to a minor infraction would similarly not comport with the sliding scale [of reasonableness] advocated by the Supreme Court in T.L.O. See *Cornfield v. School District No. 230*, 991 F.2d 1316 (7th Cir. 1993).

T.L.O. further clarified prior law in holding that a search justifying reasonable suspicion could be based on many sources, e.g., observation or information supplied by faculty, students, police officers, or anonymous informers, and suspect student conduct such as furtive movements, presence at suspicious locations, or flight when approached by school superiors.[78]

The Court in *T.L.O.* declined to address several questions on which lower courts disagreed; namely, whether students have a constitutional expectation of privacy in school desks, lockers, or other enclosures supplied for their convenience; whether searches undertaken jointly with police officers are governed by stricter constitutional standards,[79] and whether evidence uncovered in an unlawful police search by non-school officials could be used in school disciplinary proceedings, though that evidence would be inadmissible in a court of law.[80]

With regard to school enclosures, the Supreme Court's decision in the *O'Connor* case (Case 6.3) which upheld hospital search of an employee's desk, together with its relaxed standards for a student personal search suggests that students have even less expectation of privacy than teachers in school-supplied lockers and desks, and that schools could constitutionally search student desks and lockers even without reasonable suspicion if the purpose is to ensure proper use and maintenance of school property, especially if such searches are undertaken under an announced policy that periodic inspections will be made of school desks and lockers.

In the second search case, decided 10 years after *T.L.O.*, the Supreme Court adopted a second test for a constitutional search. In upholding mandatory, random, suspicionless urinalysis drug testing (admittedly a search) of student athletes in a drug-troubled school, the *Vernonia* case, which appears at the end of this chapter, held that the *T.L.O.* individualized suspicion standard is not the sole test for a "reasonable" search. *Vernonia* held that the school's strong interest in curtailing drug use outweighed the students' privacy interest, but it added a significant warning: "We caution against the assumption that suspicionless drug testing will readily pass constitutional muster in other contexts." That warning appears to rule out dragnet mandatory drug testing of entire school populations, but it provides no concrete guidance on the crucial question: In what circumstances will *T.L.O.* govern and in what circumstances will *Vernonia* govern? In confronting that question, lower courts have arrived at conflicting conclusions. The *Miller* opinion, which also appears at the end of this chapter, read *Vernonia* expansively to validate mandatory, suspicionless, random drug searches for students who wished to participate in *any* extracurricular activity, not just athletics in untroubled as well as troubled schools. On the other hand, other courts found that *T.L.O.* rather than *Vernonia* governed cases involving suspicionless drug testing absent exigent danger.[81] One case overturned search of band members whom the court found to have a higher expectation of privacy than athletes. Another overturned mandatory testing of students suspended for fighting, absent grounds to suspect that the suspended students used illegal substances. A third case voided a school search of a tardy student's pockets as lacking any reasonable basis to suspect that the student's lateness stemmed from an infraction of law or school rules. However, where a student arrived with dilated pupils and acted unruly, the court considered those circumstances sufficient for individualized suspicion to justify subjecting the student to a medical assessment and to removal of his shirt to search for drugs.[82]

Body Searches. The strong privacy interest in one's person requires weighty justification for intruding upon it, whether by patting down, removal of clothing, or canine sniffing. The legislatures in a number of states have absolutely prohibited strip searches of students.[83] Where not so prohibited, courts agree that strip searches might be reasonable in circumstances of suspected grave misconduct or threat; that body searches must be conducted by an authorized person of the same sex as the searched student; and that the intrusion on the student's person be no greater than is reasonably required to achieve the specific search purpose. Beyond agreeing on those factors, the courts are not agreed on the degree of danger and evidence required to satisfy those tests.[84]

Exploratory canine sniffing of closed containers (lockers and cars) is viewed differently than canine sniffing of a student's body. A canine sniff of a student's body was held to be a search by the Fifth, Ninth, and Tenth Circuit Courts of Appeal, but not by the Seventh Circuit, whose view may represent a waning minority.[85] Notwithstanding the few recent cases that upheld random drug searches in troubled schools, canine sniffing of students continues to be held unreasonable and invalid in the absence of a school-site drug problem or of "individualized suspicion" of serious misconduct.[86]

Informational Privacy—Student Records and Reports.   A free-standing right to privacy regarding sensitive personal information exists as a substantive constitutional liberty, independently of Fourth Amendment limitations on government searches. It is also created by certain statutes, such as the student records statutes that are discussed below. A majority of federal courts have recognized a federal constitutional right to informational privacy for intensely personal information, and a number of state courts found such a right under their state constitutions and laws.[87]

Recognized rights of informational privacy can be protected against school encroachment by court injunctions.[88] Such rights, however, are not absolute, either under constitutional or statutory law. Courts must elaborate the *nature* and *limits* of informational privacy—limits which may differ with regard to attempts to *acquire* or gain access to information that is deemed useful or necessary to school functions, and with regard to official authority to *disclose* such information once obtained. In setting the bounds of informational privacy, courts must determine whether school needs for particular information outweighs the student or family interests in keeping it private. The judicial balance of public need for personal information versus privacy protection of that information will generally depend on the factual particulars in each case, i.e., the type and detail of sought information, its relative importance to achieving significant school goals, and the countervailing personal interests in preserving its privacy.

Detailed school surveys undertaken to ascertain student attitudes and conduct, and to assess the impact of school programs are flashpoints of parental opposition and litigation. A recent case in point involved a school classroom questionnaire for all 1,200 high school students and all 800 sixth and eighth graders of the school district. The questionnaire consisted of 90 detailed questions that, among other things, inquired whether the student respondent was gay or bisexual; had engaged in oral or group sex (using and explicitly defining the terms "fellatio" and "cunnilingus"); had AIDs; or had used co-caine or any of a long list of drugs presented by the questionnaire.[89] Following vociferous parental complaints that the survey intruded into family matters and that it provided an almanac for bad behavior and planted seeds for youth misconduct, the school authorities issued an apology, softened by the custom-ary explanation that the questionnaire was relevant to student mental health, was voluntary and anonymous, and that the parents were given or should have received, advance notice of the survey with a right to withhold their chil-dren from participation in it.

Leaving aside the inevitable mishaps and defaults of meaningful parental notice, and the fact that even proper notice may not suffice in all circumstances to avoid liability for infringement of informational privacy, school administra-tors could entertain safer legal procedures beyond pro-forma notice to parents. For example, in *federally funded* school surveys federal law requires that no stu-dent be subjected to a questionnaire that relates to sexual conduct, family rela-tionships, or illegal activities, unless that student's parent gives advance written consent to the child's participation—a requirement that is enforced by the U.S. Department of Education.[90] For school surveys that are not federally funded, school authorities may find it prudent to adopt the federal requirement as a fur-ther safeguard against liability for violations of privacy rights.

State statutes on informational privacy also require judicial interpreta-tion, especially with relation to other statutes that mandate public access to some school records. See, for example, the discussion of "sunshine" laws, which are noted in Chapter 1 under Local School Boards. In the absence of clear legislative direction, courts must decide how state privacy and student records statutes interact and set the balance between allowing or forbidding public ac-cess to particular student information.[91]

The federal Family Educational Rights and Privacy Act of 1974 (FERPA) which applies to all schools receiving federal aid, partially nationalized the law on student records. It does not prevent states from regulating school records in a manner that is consistent with FERPA. FERPA governs only "educational records" of students who have been admitted to a school. It ensures students and their guardians control over "personally identifying" student information by barring third-party access to, and school disclosure of, student records that con-tain such information without the written consent of affected students or their guardians. Specified exceptions of privileged access and uses of student records are made for persons with recognized interests in student records, such as school board members, teachers, and medical and law enforcement professionals.[92]

The law entitles parents and students over 18 years of age to inspect, re-produce, and challenge the accuracy of educational records, and to control the release of personally identifiable information by forbidding its release without their written authorizations for each release. Authorizations for release and waiver of rights must be specific as to content, recipient, and purposes of use, and schools may not demand waivers. Parental waivers may be revoked by a student upon attaining 18 years of age. The law permits release of test data and other "directory information" in a form that precludes student identification if the release of such information is authorized by state law.

FERPA authorizes school authorities to presume that a natural parent is entitled to record access unless they receive evidence that state law, court order, or other legally binding instrument negates that presumption.[93] A parent is, therefore, presumptively entitled under FERPA to obtain the forwarding address of his child from school records. The governing state law on rights of separated parents is discussed in the final section of this chapter. In any event, school districts should require official documentation of loss of a parent's rights where one parent or guardian requests a school to deny record access to the other parent or guardian, if only to avoid liability for denying a right of access under FERPA.[94]

FERPA leaves general record administration to the states, including their preservation or destruction, with the important restriction that student records may not be altered or destroyed while a valid request for their inspection or release is outstanding.

Disclosure of confidential information that has not been entered in student records is not covered by FERPA and presents broader issues of informational privacy. Whether "confidential" information may be lawfully withheld and not reported to school authorities or in school records presents a double-edged problem. Should damaging confidential information be wrongfully placed in a student's record, its author and possibly the school district would be exposed to possible liability for defamation or for breach of confidentiality. Conversely, should that information be wrongfully *withheld,* however innocently, the withholding party could be subject to legal penalties for failure to report it, especially under statutes that mandate reporting of information regardless of its source.[95] The foregoing dilemma is not adequately resolved by the older law on privileges of confidentiality, which applied only to ministers, doctors, and lawyers, or by laws on "testimonial privileges," which govern only rights to withhold information in court proceedings.[96] A professional confidante of students must initially decide what communicated information qualifies as "confidential" in a legal sense, regardless of its classification as confidential under professional ethics standards. He or she must then ascertain if state law extends a privilege of confidentiality. For example, nontherapeutic counseling does not generally create a privileged confidence, and information on infectious social diseases may be subject to reporting obligations by health professionals in particular states. Some states exonerate doctors and treating agencies that provide specified medical services to minors (e.g., pregnancy, venereal disease, and drug-related illnesses) from the normal obligation to notify parents or obtain their consent to disclosure. In the absence of such specific statutory coverage, school employees—especially in allied health professions—may encounter a gap between their legal and ethical obligations. In light of the possible variations of law in each state, school professionals may want to seek legal counsel in serious cases.

The risks of failing to report information increase when that information relates to child abuse, suicide, or threats of injuries to third parties (targets of pathological fear or hatred). Three decisions illustrate the risk of liability for failure to give protective warnings, notwithstanding traditional patient–doctor confidentiality. Psychotherapists were held legally obligated to take some steps to protect persons threatened by their patients.[97] In sum, a grave emergency can suspend even classical privileges of confidentiality. A further exception to rights of confidentiality or informational privacy is indicated by the emerging law on special school duties to protect vulnerable students, such as suicidal students, by alerting appropriate parties of the danger or by adopting school preventive programs, whether or not the danger was discovered from private or confidential sources. See for example, the suicide cases discussed in Chapter 8.

Decisional Privacy (Autonomy).   Decisional privacy rights, including the right to marry and to beget children, have been extended to students and their parents.[98] These developments narrow school authority to exclude pregnant or married students from normal school benefits, unless they can demonstrate that such exclusion is justified by overriding school interests.[99] Such a justification was found where a student athlete was disciplined and disqualified from school-sponsored athletics for engaging in sexual conduct with another student while on a school trip.[100] Sex discrimination statutes, as discussed in Chapter 8, raise additional barriers to school constraints on pregnant students, but they do not forbid measures to protect a pregnant student's health or safety.

As noted in Chapters 1 through 3, parental rights must be balanced against the school interests. Recent cases illustrate how courts must strike that balance, especially in situations where a student requires medical care. The *ABC* case, which appears at the end of this chapter, presented, for the first time, the question whether a school could refuse the parents' demand that the school refrain from attempting to resuscitate their four-year-old disabled child if the child went into cardiac arrest while at school. In that case, the court recognized the constitutional right of parents to refuse medical treatment for a child and to demand that the school take no "active measures" to treat the child's heart failure. The court distinguished its prior rulings that a parent does not have a right to compel *affirmative* medical measures that are contrary to the school's view of its ethical duty to the student. The distinction between demand for inaction and demand for action was apparent in another federal circuit which upheld the school's right to refuse parents' demands that a school nurse administer medication to their child in amounts that exceeded the recommended daily dosage listed in the Physician's Desk Reference, even though the child's physician prescribed that dosage.[101]

Where separated parents cannot agree on a specific decision, a majority of state jurisdictions vest the decision with the custodial parent.[102] In questionable cases school authorities should seek legal counsel and perhaps request that the parents submit their dispute to an appropriate court.

CHILDREN WITH DISABILITIES—IDEA AND § 504

The Americans with Disabilities Act of 1990 (ADA), the Rehabilitation Act of 1973 (known as § 504), and the Individuals with Disabilities Education Act of 1990 (IDEA) are the major federal statutes regarding persons with disabilities. The ADA and § 504 are essentially negative prohibitions against disability-based discrimination. The IDEA alone is an affirmative rights-conferring statute that applies to the education of children with disabilities between the ages of 3 and 21.[103] Despite some clarifying amendments in 1997, the IDEA's long, complex, and technical provisions breed many interpretive issues and disputes. The numerous refinements of this law cannot be adequately distilled here, and fuller treatment must be sought in specialized texts on the IDEA.[104] The following general overview indicates the more common problems that arise in the routine administration of IDEA.

Under IDEA states must provide children who have disabilities with a "free appropriate public education" (hereafter FAPE), with emphasis on special education and on educationally related services that are needed to enable them to benefit from a FAPE.[105] The law defines "children with disabilities" broadly to include children with physical, mental, and health impairments, serious emotional disturbance, specific learning disabilities, and for children aged 3 to 9, certain kinds of developmental limitations.[106] AIDS conditions are covered,[107] but the point at which an AIDS condition becomes sufficiently disabling to qualify for IDEA benefits is a matter for case determination.

The Supreme Court identified IDEA obligations in the *Rowley* case, which appears at the end of this chapter. These obligations include the duty to:

- Identify children with educational handicaps;
- Evaluate their educational needs;
- Prepare and provide them with an "individualized educational program" (IEP) that is tailored to their particular disability needs;
- Provide them with "education-related services";
- Provide parents and children specified due process procedures in disputes with their servicing school district.

The required IEPs must be developed jointly by the local educational agency (generally the school district), the child's teacher, and the child's parents or guardian. The IEP must be reviewed at least annually and be revised if necessary to maintain the essentials of a FAPE.

FAPE Requirements

The adequacy of a disputed FAPE is left ultimately to the courts, but a FAPE does not require school districts either to achieve fixed levels of achievement or to "maximize the potential of each child," or even to provide optimal education for each child. Rather, as *Rowley* held, it requires "meaningful" access to an education that confers "some educational benefit" consistent with the particular child's abilities and potential. *Rowley* thus rejected a fixed FAPE standard since what is "appropriate" for one child with a disability is not "appropriate" for another.[108] The district must, however, preserve FAPE benefits by such measures as are needed to prevent educational regression and backsliding, such as special or extended classes beyond the normal school year, week, or day.[109] An extracurricular IEP component may also be required if the child with a disability can benefit educationally from it.[110]

IDEA does not exempt students with disabilities from general test requirements for a regular high school diploma. Nor are such tests deemed discriminatory under the Rehailitation Act (§ 504) or the Americans with Disabilities Act (ADA) unless the student can show that he or she was in fact "otherwise qualified" to pass the test but prevented from doing so by some discriminatory element in the test makeup or administration.[111]

The need for educationally "related services" to enable a child to receive FAPE benefits remains a chronic point of dispute. Such services may include transportation, developmental, corrective and other supportive services, health-related, psychological and counseling services, physical and occupational therapy, recreational programs, or other forms of accommodations.[112]

Specific child need determines what related services are required. Thus, the Supreme Court held in *Rowley* that the bright Amy Rowley did not need a sign language interpreter to benefit from her FAPE, but it later implicitly ruled that a deaf student who required a classroom sign language interpreter to benefit from a FAPE could be entitled to one as an education-related service.[113]

The issue whether health-related care is a required "related service" or in "medical service" that is not required by IDEA, was resolved in *Cedar Rapids Community School Dist. v. Garrett*, 119 S. Ct. 992 (1999), where the Supreme Court held that the school district must provide one-on-one assistance throughout the school day to a ventilator-dependent student who required continuous monitoring and treatment, including urinary catheterization, suctioning of the student's tracheotomy, lowering and lifting the student every hour to and from a reclining and upright position, and monitoring the student's ventilator for possible malfunction. The Court ruled that those services were education related because they were essential to enable the student to receive educational benefits of a FAPE and because the services could be provided by a competently trained person other than a physician. *Cedar Rapids* thus established that IDEA-related services include all health-related services that are essential for a child's FAPE, no matter how continuous or costly they may be, as long as they could be competently performed by someone other than a licensed physician. The case considerably extended the Court's prior decision in *Irving Ind. School Dist. v. Tatro*, 468 U.S. 883 (1984) that required school-site intermittent catheterization (CIC) of a student with a disability.

Placement Rules

IDEA requires appropriate educational placement of a child with a disability at public expense, including placement at a "private" facility when an appropriate public facility is not available.[114] A facility need not be the preferred, superior, or best available facility to be appropriate, and a parent cannot demand an alternative placement if an appropriate one is offered by the school district. Where school authorities fail to place a child in an appropriate facility, parents who directly arrange an appropriate placement may recover reimbursement of that expense and other equitable relief as long as the placement is reasonable, even if the placement school or facility is not on the state's approved list.[115] Conversely, if the court finds that a parent made an inappropriate placement, the parent cannot claim reimbursement or other IDEA relief.

> Courts fashioning discretionary equitable relief under IDEA must consider all relevant factors, including the appropriate and reasonable level of reimbursement that should be required. Total reimbursement will not be appropriate if the court determines that the private placement was unreasonable. [*Florence County School Dist. v. Carter,* 114 S. Ct. 361, 366 (1993)]

Private school student entitlements to IDEA benefits are discussed below.

IDEA "stay put" provisions generally prohibit a change from a challenged placement until IDEA administrative procedures are exhausted. Unexcused failure to pursue those procedures is grounds to defeat claims that a party might otherwise have. Courts have, however, allowed exceptions to the "stay put" mandate where resort to further administrative procedures would seriously delay and jeopardize the rights and education of the affected child.[116]

IDEA further requires that a FAPE be provided in "the least restrictive" educational environment "to the maximum appropriate extent." The 1997 IDEA amendments elevated this mainstreaming "preference" to a "presumption" that such placement should be made. Those Amendments did not clarify or change prior law that mainstreaming be limited to what is "appropriate" for the child's condition and to what is "reasonable" in light of the cost of regular classroom placement. Mainstreaming is not required for a child whose conditions prevent the child from benefiting from regular classroom placement or whose condition renders the child disruptive to a regular classroom.[117]

> For [some] children, mainstreaming does not provide an education designed to meet their unique needs. . . .
>
> . . . The Act does not, however, provide any substantive standards for striking the proper balance between its requirement for mainstreaming and its mandate for a free appropriate public education. . . .
>
> . . . we decline to adopt the approach that other circuits have taken. . . .
>
> . . . [W]e discern a two part test for determining compliance with the mainstreaming requirement. First, we ask whether education in the regular classroom . . . can be achieved satisfactorily. . . . If it cannot . . . we ask, second, whether the school has mainstreamed the child to the maximum extent appropriate. *See Daniel R.R. v. State Board of Educ.,* 874 F.2d 1036, 1044–5, 1048 (5th Cir. 1989).

In the absence of further clarification, the determination of the appropriateness of complete or partial mainstreaming for each child must be guided by current government regulations and the case law in each federal circuit. While the courts have not agreed on a formula to assess the cost limits of mainstreaming, they have rejected the view that mainstream placements must be made "at all cost."[118]

Equitable Participation in IDEA Benefits by Private School Students

As noted above, courts may enforce the FAPE requirement against a school district that cannot or refuses to provide a required FAPE, by authorizing an appropriate placement at a private school. However, where parents elect to enroll a child in a private school for reasons other than a school district failure to provide a FAPE, the question whether the school districts must provide other special services or benefits at the private school has not been finally settled. The 1997 IDEA Amendments state that such services "may" (rather than "must") be provided to students at private school sites, and that amounts spent for such services equal "a proportionate amount of federal funds made available for such services." The cases suggest different readings of the amendments. Most courts held that the amendments give school districts discretion to decide whether or not to provide special services to children with disabilities at private school sites when the particular service is made available at a public school site, and further that states are required to provide such children only those services that can be purchased with their proportionate amount of the federal funds received by the state for such services.[119] Under that reading, a district need not pay the full costs of off-site services if it exceeds the average cost of like services for all children with disabilities in the state.

Discipline of Children with Disabilities

Prior to the 1997 amendments, the permissible school punishments for misbehaving students with disabilities were left largely to court determination. The 1997 IDEA amendments addressed that issue. Briefly stated, the amendments confirmed case holdings that children with disabilities could be subjected to discipline only for conduct that was within their reasonable control and that was not a manifestation of their disability, so long as the selected form of discipline did not defeat the FAPE purposes of IDEA.[120] The 1997 amendments also removed some procedural obstacles that the Supreme Court had previously found to exist[121] by providing administrative mechanisms to facilitate removal of students with disabilities to interim alternative settings for up to 45 days for weapons or drug infractions, or upon a showing of likely injury by a child with a disability, whether or not the child's behavior was a manifestation of the child's handicap. The 1997 amendments also settled court conflicts by requiring FAPE services for all children with disabilities including those lawfully suspended or expelled from school.[122]

Procedural Requirements

To ensure parents the right to challenge administrative decisions relating to their child, IDEA prescribed due process procedures of notice, hearing, and appeal. *Unexcused* failure to follow IDEA administrative procedures will normally foreclose a party from further relief or appeals to higher tribunals.[123] However, failure to exhaust those procedures may be excused if their use would defeat the Act's purposes, e.g., where one party thwarted administrative appeals or where school safety required prompt removal of a child with a disability.[124] Many states provide special education benefits that are not afforded by federal law.[125] States often grant different benefits for different categories of disability.

SUBSTANTIVE RIGHTS UNDER STATE LAW

State laws provide independent sources of student rights. Student suspensions may be overturned for violating state procedural requirements, though those procedures are not required for federal due process. School searches that pass federal constitutional muster may still be void under stricter state law requirements, such as those which prohibit strip searches or corporal punishment. School administrators must therefore observe the peculiarities of their state laws on student rights.

Rights of Separated Parents

State law generally governs the rights of separated and divorced parents relative to the education of their children. The federal FERPA law on student records is not intended to displace state law.[126] This would seem especially true of child custody and visitation rights (including protective orders that bar a delinquent or abusive parent from contact with a child) presumably to serve the "best interest" of the child. Child custody rights, whether full, temporary, shared, or nonexistent, thus remain an important, though not exclusive, factor in determining a parent's right to be involved in educational decisions.[127] Where separated parents cannot agree on a specific educational question, a majority of state courts hold that the decision of the custodial parent will prevail.[128] In cases of shared or split custody or in doubtful cases, the respective authority of each parent must be resolved by the state tribunal entrusted with custody disputes. In doubtful cases school authorities should seek counsel on the respective rights of disputing parents.

Chapter Discussion Questions

Where the answer to a question may be qualified by special circumstances, explain the potential qualification.

1. On what basis may school authorities or teachers lawfully confiscate weapons taken to school by a student without violating the student's property rights?

2. When, if ever, must a student be excused from school-prescribed courses or activities on the student's plea of religious objection? Explain.

3. On what grounds may school districts lawfully interfere with or penalize the following?
   a. Student speech
   b. Student dress
   c. Student hair style
   d. Student makeup or jewelry

4. How, in your opinion, should school authorities strike a constitutional balance between student liberty and school interests in requiring students to wear school-approved uniforms?

5. What limits does federal law place on public access to and disclosure of student records?

6. What guarantees do state laws provide for public access to school records?

7. When federal and state laws on student records come into conflict, which law governs? Why?

8. Does a school district demand that a student perform community service to graduate from high school infringe upon student liberty? See Chapter 2, page 36.

9. Why are student rights not coextensive with those of teachers with respect to the following?
   a. Freedom of expression
   b. Freedom from unreasonable searches

10. What factors do courts consider in deciding whether to uphold the following?
    a.   A student claim of reasonable expectation of privacy
    b.   A school claim of a reasonable suspicion to justify a student search

11. Is canine sniffing for drugs considered a "search" when directed against school lockers? When directed against a student's person? Explain.

12. Under current case law, what factors do courts consider in determining whether school policies of random, suspicionless, urinalysis of students are reasonable and constitutional?

13. With regard to the federal statute for the education of children with disabilities, when, if ever, may public school authorities refuse to:
    a.   Mainstream a handicapped child?
    b.   Decline to provide a "related service"?
    c.   Reimburse a parent for placement of a child with a disability in a private school or facility?
    d.   Provide a due process hearing on parent objections to the child's educational program?

❖ C A S E S

Case 7.1

GONZALES v. McEUEN
435 F. Supp. 460 (1977)

*[**Focus Note.** Due process in student disciplinary hearings. This opinion addresses questions whether school boards and administrators who are directly concerned with establishing school discipline can act as impartial tribunals in hearings on student misconduct. The high school students facing suspension and expulsion did not think so.]*

Takasugi, District Judge

❖ ❖ ❖

Impartiality of the Board

Plaintiffs' strongest and most serious challenge is to the impartiality of the Board. They contend that they were denied their right to an impartial hearing. . . . The basis for this claim is, first, overfamiliarity of the Board with the case; second, the multiple role played by defendants' counsel; and, third, the involvement of the Superintendent of the District, Mr. McEuen, with the Board of Trustees during the hearings.

No one doubts that a student charged with misconduct has a right to an impartial tribunal. . . . There is doubt, however, as to what this means. . . . Bias is presumed to exist, for example, in cases in which the adjudicator has a pecuniary interest in the outcome . . . or in which he has been the target of personal attack or criticism from the person before him. . . . The decision maker may also have such prior involvement with the case so as to acquire a disqualifying bias. . . . The question before the Court is not whether the Board was actually biased, but whether, under the circumstances, there existed probability that the decision maker would be tempted to decide the issues with partiality. . . .

Overfamiliarity

. . . Depositions . . . show that the members of the Board met with school officials prior to the hearings. Plaintiffs contend that this prior involvement . . . deprived plaintiffs of the opportunity for a fair hearing. The court rejects this contention. Exposure to evidence presented in a nonadversary investigative procedure is insufficient in itself to impugn the fairness of the Board members. . . . Nor is a limited combination of investigatory and adjudicatory functions in an administrative body necessarily unfair, absent a showing of other circumstances such as malice or personal interest in the outcome. . . . . . . Some familiarity with the facts . . . does not disqualify a decision maker. *Hortonville Dist. v. Hortonville Ed. Assoc.,* 426 U.S. 482, 491 . . . (1976).

Multiple Roles of Counsel

. . . It is undisputed that attorneys . . . who prosecuted the charges . . . in the expulsion proceedings, also represent the Board members in this action. . . . Counsel for defendants admit that they advised the Board . . . with respect to its obligations regarding these expulsions, but they deny that they advised the Board during the proceedings themselves.

A reading of the transcripts reveals how difficult it was to separate the two roles. . . .

It is the opinion of this court that the confidential relationship between the attorneys for the District and the members of the Board, reinforced by the advisory role played by the attorneys for the Board, created an unacceptable risk of bias. . . .

Involvement of Superintendent McEuen

. . . Superintendent McEuen was present with the Board for approximately forty-five minutes during its deliberations on the issue of expelling these plaintiffs. The plaintiffs contend that their due process rights were violated by this involvement of Mr. McEuen with the Board. This court agrees.

✧ ✧ ✧

The court concludes that the process utilized by the Board was fundamentally unfair. . . .

Discussion of Individual Students

. . . Plaintiffs Barrington and Munden were expelled . . . on November 10, 1976. Neither Barrington nor Munden was present; neither was represented by either parent or counsel.

On October 29, 1976, letters had been sent to the parents advising them that the principal was recommending expulsion of the students. . . . The letters contained no notice . . . of the student's right to be present at the hearing, to be represented by counsel, and to present evidence. This was a clear violation of . . . the California Education Code. . . .

. . . The defendants maintain that the notices . . . complied, at least, with *federal* due process. . . . They contend that since a hearing was held and there was notice to the parents of the charges against the students, the requisites of procedural due process were satisfied. The court disagrees. . . .

Goss clearly anticipates that where the student is faced with the severe penalty of expulsion he shall have the right to be represented by and through counsel, to present evidence on his own behalf, and to confront and cross-examine adverse witnesses.

Other courts have held that a hearing incorporating these safeguards must be held before or shortly after a child is suspended for a prolonged or indefinite period. *Black Coalition v. Portland School District No. 1,* 484 F.2d 1040, 1045 (9th Cir. 1973); *Esteban v. Central Missouri State College,* 277 F. Supp. 649 (W.D. Mo. 1967). This court agrees.

. . . Defendants next argue that even if the notice was defective, the court must still determine whether the plaintiffs were given a fair and impartial hearing. Defendants misapprehend the meaning of notice. It is not "fair" if the student does not know, and is not told, that he has certain rights which he may exercise at the hearing.

❖ ❖ ❖

It follows that their expulsions were improper.

❖ ❖ ❖

Review Question 7.1

1. How does the foregoing decision differ from the Supreme Court *Hortonville* case, which the above opinion cited and which held that school boards are presumed to be impartial?

Case 7.2

BETHEL SCHOOL DISTRICT NO. 403 v. FRASER
478 U.S. 675 (1986)

[**Focus Note.** *The limits of student freedom of speech at school were tested by Fraser, a high school student who relied on the expansive language of the landmark armband (Tinker) case. His nominating speech for student elective office at a school-organized assembly of some 600 adolescent students was laced with elaborate, graphic, and explicit sexual innuendos, notwithstanding prior advice of two teachers that the speech was inappropriate and should not be given. The assistant principal later notified Fraser orally that his speech was considered a violation of the school rule against disruptive, obscene, and vulgar conduct, and that he would be* *suspended for two days and disqualified as a candidate for commencement speaker. Fraser and his father appealed to the courts for injunctive relief and monetary damages claiming violation of his free speech and due process rights. Identify the various reasons which the Supreme Court advanced to reject those challenges.]*

CHIEF JUSTICE BURGER *delivered the opinion of the Court.*

. . . [A] school counselor observed the reaction of students to the speech. Some students hooted and yelled; some by gestures graphically simulated the sexual activities pointedly alluded to in respondent's speech. Other students appeared to be bewildered and embarrassed. . . . A Bethel High School disciplinary rule prohibiting the use of obscene language in the school provides:

> Conduct which materially and substantially interferes with the educational process is prohibited, including the use of obscene, profane language or gestures.

This Court acknowledged in *Tinker v. Des Moines Independent Community School Dist., supra,* that students do not "shed their constitutional rights to freedom of speech or expression at the schoolhouse gate."

❖ ❖ ❖

The marked distinction between the political "message" . . . in *Tinker* and the sexual content of respondent's speech in this case seems to have been given little weight by the Court of Appeals. . . .

It is against this background that we turn to consider the level of First Amendment protection accorded to Fraser's utterances and actions. . . .

The role and purpose of the American public school system were well described by two historians, who state: "[P]ublic education must prepare pupils for citizenship in the Republic . . . It must inculcate the habits and manners of civility as values in themselves conducive to happiness and as indispensable to the practice of self-government in the community and the nation." . . .

❖ ❖ ❖

. . . It does not follow, however, that simply because the use of an offensive form of expression may not be prohibited to adults . . . the same latitude must be permitted to children in a public school. In *New Jersey v. T.L.O.,* 469 U.S. 325, 340–342 . . . we reaffirmed that the constitutional rights of students in public school are not automatically coextensive with the rights of adults in other settings. . . .

Surely it is a highly appropriate function of public school education to prohibit the use of vulgar and offensive terms in public discourse. . . .

The determination of what manner of speech in the classroom or in school assembly is inappropriate properly rests with the school board.

. . . The schools . . . may determine that the essential lessons of civil, mature conduct cannot be conveyed in a school that tolerates lewd, indecent, or offensive speech and conduct such as that indulged in by this confused boy.

The pervasive sexual innuendo in Fraser's speech was plainly offensive to both teachers and students—indeed to any mature person. By glorifying male sexuality, and in its verbal content, the speech was acutely insulting to teenage girl students.

. . . The speech could well be seriously damaging to its less mature audience, many of whom were only 14 years old and on the threshold of awareness of human sexuality. . . .

❖ ❖ ❖

. . . Unlike the sanctions imposed . . . in *Tinker,* the penalties imposed . . . were unrelated to any political viewpoint. The First Amendment does not prevent the school officials from determining that to permit a vulgar and lewd speech . . . would undermine the school's basic educational mission. . . . . . .

Respondent contends that his suspension violated due process because he had no way of knowing that the delivery of the speech in question would subject him to disciplinary sanctions. This argument is wholly without merit. . . . Given the school's need to be able to impose disciplinary sanctions for a wide range of unanticipated conduct disruptive of the educational process, the school disciplinary rules need not be as detailed as a criminal code which imposes criminal sanctions. . . .

Two days' suspension from school does not rise to the level of a penal sanction calling for the full panoply of procedural due process protections. . . . The school disciplinary rule proscribing "obscene" language and the pre-speech admonitions of teachers gave adequate warning to Fraser that his lewd speech could subject him to sanctions.

Case 7.3

HAZELWOOD SCHOOL DISTRICT v. KUHLMEIER
484 U.S. 260 (1988)

[*Focus Note. This case represented the first Supreme Court decision on students' rights of freedom of the press in student publications. The unusual case circumstances, namely, deletion of two pages of a high school newspaper by school administrators without consulting the student editors, on a plea of time constraints to have the paper published before end of school term, may limit the decision's impact.*]

Justice White delivered the opinion of the Court.

This case concerns the extent to which educators may exercise editorial control over the contents of a high school newspaper produced as part of the school's journalism curriculum.

I

Petitioners are the Hazelwood School District. . . . ; various school officials; Robert Eugene Reynolds, the principal of Hazelwood East High School; and Howard Emerson, a teacher in the school district. Respondents are three former Hazelwood East students who were staff members of Spectrum, the school newspaper. . . .

Spectrum was written and edited by the Journalism II class at Hazelwood East. . . .

❖ ❖ ❖

The Journalism II course was taught by Robert Stergos . . . . Stergos left Hazelwood East on April 29, 1983, when the May 13 edition of Spectrum was nearing completion, and petitioner Emerson took his place as newspaper adviser. . . .

The practice at Hazelwood East . . . was for the journalism teacher to submit page proofs of each Spectrum issue to Principal Reynolds for his review prior to publication. On May 10, Emerson delivered the proofs of the May 13 edition to Reynolds, who objected to two of the articles. . . . One of the stories described three Hazelwood East students' experiences with pregnancy; the other discussed the impact of divorce on students at the school.

Reynolds was concerned that, although the pregnancy story used false names . . . the pregnant students still might be identifiable from the text. He also believed that the article's references to sexual activity and birth control were inappropriate for some of the younger students at the school. In addition, Reynolds was concerned that a student identified by name in the divorce story had complained that her father "wasn't spending enough time with my mom, my sister and I" prior to the divorce, "was always out of town on business or out late playing cards with the guys," and "always argued about everything" with her mother. . . .

Reynolds believed that the student's parents should have been given an opportunity to respond to these remarks. . . . He was unaware that Emerson had deleted the student's name from the final version of the article.

Reynolds believed that there was no time to make the necessary changes . . . before the scheduled press run and that the newspaper would not appear before the end of the school year if printing were delayed. . . . He concluded that his only options . . . were to publish a four-page newspaper . . . eliminating the two pages on which the offending stories appeared, or to publish no newspaper at all. Accordingly, he directed Emerson to withhold from publication the two pages containing the stories on pregnancy and divorce. He informed his superiors of the decision, and they concurred.

❖ ❖ ❖

Students . . . do not "shed their constitutional rights to freedom of speech or expression at the schoolhouse gate." *Tinker.* . . .

We have nonetheless recognized that the First Amendment rights of students . . . "are not automatically coextensive with the rights of adults in other settings" . . . A school need not tolerate student speech that is inconsistent with its "basic educational mission," . . . even though the government could not censor similar speech outside the school. . . .

A

We deal first with the question whether Spectrum may appropriately be characterized as a forum for public expression. . . .

. . . [S]chool facilities may be deemed to be public forums only if school authorities have "by policy or by practice" opened those facilities "for indiscriminate use by the general public," or by some segment of the public, such as student organizations. . . . If the facilities have instead been reserved for other intended purposes, then no public forum has been created, and school officials may impose reasonable restrictions on the speech of students, teachers, and other members of the school community. . . . . . .

❖ ❖ ❖

School officials did not deviate in practice from their policy that production of Spectrum was to be part of the educational curriculum and a "regular classroom activit[y]." The District Court found that Robert Stergos, the journalism teacher. . ."... in fact exercised a great deal of control over Spectrum." . . . For example, Stergos selected the editors . . . scheduled publication dates, decided the number of pages for each issue, assigned story ideas . . . advised students on the development of their stories, reviewed the use of quotations, edited stories, selected and edited the letters to the editor, and dealt with the printing company. Many of these decisions were made without consultation with the Journalism II students.

❖ ❖ ❖

The evidence relied upon by the Court of Appeals in finding Spectrum to be a public forum . . . is equivocal at best. . . . In sum, the evidence . . . fails to demonstrate the "clear intent to create a public forum". . . .

. . . Instead, they "reserve[d] the forum for its intended purpos[e]," . . . as a supervised learning experience. . . . Accordingly, school officials were entitled to regulate the contents of Spectrum in any reasonable manner. . . . It is this standard, rather than our decision in Tinker, that governs this case.

The question whether the First Amendment requires a school to tolerate particular student speech . . . is different from the question whether the First Amendment requires a school to affirmatively promote particular student speech. . . . The latter question concerns educators' authority over school-sponsored publications, theatrical productions, and other expressive activities that students, parents, and members of the public might reasonably perceive to bear the imprimatur of the school. These activities may fairly be characterized as part of the school curriculum, whether or not they occur in a traditional classroom setting. . . .

Educators are entitled to exercise greater control over this second form of student expression. . . . Hence, a school may in its capacity as publisher of a school newspaper or producer of a school play "disassociate itself," . . . not only from speech that would "substantially interfere with [its] work . . . or impinge upon the rights of other students," . . . but also from speech that is, for example, ungrammatical, poorly written, inadequately researched, biased or prejudiced, vulgar or profane, or unsuitable for immature audiences. A school . . . may refuse to disseminate student speech that does not meet those standards. In addition, a school must be able to take into account the emotional maturity of the intended audience in determining whether to disseminate student speech on potentially sensitive topics. . . .

❖ ❖ ❖

. . . [W]e hold that educators do not offend the First Amendment by exercising editorial control over the style and content of student speech in school-sponsored expressive activities so long as their actions are reasonably related to legitimate pedagogical concerns.

. . . It is only when the decision to censor . . . has no valid educational purpose that the First Amendment is so "directly and sharply implicate[d]," as to require judicial intervention to protect students' constitutional rights.

❖ ❖ ❖

The judgment of the Court of Appeals for the Eighth Circuit is therefore Reversed.

Review Question 7.3

1. What general guidelines does the above opinion offer for school control of student publications?

Case 7.4

VERNONIA SCHOOL DISTRICT v. ACTON
515 U.S. 646 (1995)

> [*Focus Note. Suspicionless student searches. In the following opinion, the Supreme Court upheld a school requirement that in order to participate in school interscholastic athletic programs students must submit to random, suspicionless urinaly-*

*sis testing for amphetamines, cocaine, and marijuana, or be excluded from partici-
pation in those activities. Note the detailed safeguard procedures that the school district adopted in order to avoid constitutional objections that the gathering, processing, and testing of urine specimens were overly intrusive, unfair, or unreliable.]*

JUSTICE SCALIA *delivered the opinion of the Court.*

. . . In the mid-to-late 1980s, however, teachers and administrators observed a
sharp increase in drug use. Students began to speak out about their attraction
to the drug culture, and to boast that there was nothing the school could do
about it. . . . Between 1988 and 1989 the number of disciplinary referrals in Vernonia schools rose to more than twice the number reported in the early
1980s. . . . . . .

. . . [A]s the District Court found, athletes were the leaders of the drug culture. . . . Expert testimony . . . confirmed the deleterious effects of drugs on motivation, memory, judgment, reaction, coordination, and performance. . . .

Initially, the District responded . . . by offering special classes, speakers,
and presentations designed to deter drug use. It even brought in a specially
trained dog to detect drugs, but the drug problem persisted. . . .

. . . District officials began considering a drug-testing program. . . . The
school board approved the Policy. . . .

. . . Students wishing to play sports must sign a form consenting to the
testing and must obtain the written consent of their parents. Athletes are tested
at the beginning of the season for their sport. In addition, once each week of the
season the names of the athletes are placed in a "pool" from which a student
. . . blindly draws the names of ten percent of the athletes for random testing. . . .

The student to be tested completes a specimen control form which bears
an assigned number. Prescription medications that the student is taking must
be identified. . . . The student then enters an empty locker room accompanied
by an adult monitor of the same sex. Each boy selected produces a sample at a
urinal, remaining fully clothed with his back to the monitor. . . . . . . Girls produce samples in an enclosed bathroom stall, so that they can be heard but not
observed. After the sample is produced, it is given to the monitor, who checks
it for temperature and tampering. . . .

The samples are sent to an independent laboratory, which routinely
tests them. . . . The laboratory's procedures are 99.94% accurate. The District
follows strict procedures regarding the chain of custody and access to test results. The laboratory does not know the identity of the students whose samples it tests. . . . Only the superintendent, principals, vice-principals, and athletic directors have access to test results, and the results are not kept for more
than one year.

If a sample tests positive, a second test is administered as soon as possible to confirm the result. If the second test is negative, no further action is
taken. If the second test is positive, the athlete's parents are notified, and the

school principal convenes a meeting with the student and his parents, at which the student is given the option of (1) participating . . . in an assistance program that includes weekly urinalysis, or (2) suffering suspension from athletics. . . . The student is then retested prior to the start of the next athletic season. . . . . . . a second offense results in automatic imposition of option (2); a third offense in suspension for the remainder of the current season and the next two athletic seasons.

. . . James Acton signed up to play football. . . . He was denied participation, however, because he and his parents refused to sign the testing consent forms.

. . . In *Skinner v. Railway Labor Executives' Assn.*, 489 U.S. 602, 617, . . . we held that state-compelled collection and testing of urine . . . constitutes a "search" subject to the demands of the Fourth Amendment. . . .

. . . [T]he ultimate measure of the constitutionality of a governmental search is "reasonableness." . . . [W]hether a particular search meets the reasonableness standard "is judged by balancing its intrusion on the individual's Fourth Amendment interests against its promotion of legitimate governmental interests." *Skinner*, supra, at 619. . . .

❖ ❖ ❖

. . . The school search we approved in *T.L.O.* . . . was based on individualized suspicion of wrongdoing. . . . We have upheld suspicionless searches and seizures to conduct drug testing of railroad personnel involved in train accidents . . .; to conduct random drug testing of federal customs officers who carry arms or are involved in drug interdiction . . . ; and to maintain automobile checkpoints looking for illegal immigrants and contraband . . . and drunk drivers, *Michigan Dept. of State Police v. Sitz*, 496 U.S. 444, 110 S.Ct. 2481, 110 L.Ed.2d 412 (1990).

. . . The Fourth Amendment does not protect all subjective expectations of privacy, but only those that society recognizes as "legitimate." *T.L.O.*, 469 U.S., at 338. . . . What expectations are legitimate varies, of course, with context, id., at 337. . . . In addition, the legitimacy of certain privacy expectations vis-a-vis the State may depend upon the individual's legal relationship with the State. . . . Central . . . to the present case is the fact that the subjects of the Policy are (1) children, who (2) have been committed to the temporary custody of the State as schoolmaster.

. . . Fourth Amendment rights, no less than First and Fourteenth Amendment rights, are different in public schools than elsewhere; the "reasonableness" inquiry cannot disregard the schools' custodial and tutelary responsibility for children. For their own good and that of their classmates, public school children are routinely required to submit to various physical examinations, and to be vaccinated against various diseases. . . .

Legitimate privacy expectations are even less with regard to student athletes. School sports are not for the bashful. . . . Public school locker rooms . . . are not notable for the privacy they afford. . . .

There is an additional respect in which school athletes have a reduced expectation of privacy. By choosing to "go out for the team," they voluntarily subject themselves to a degree of regulation. . . . In Vernonia's public schools, they must submit to a preseason physical exam . . . they must . . . comply with any "rules of conduct, dress, training hours and related matters as may be established . . . by the head coach and athletic director. . . .

❖ ❖ ❖

Having considered the scope of the legitimate expectation of privacy. . ., we turn next to the character of the intrusion. . . . Under the District's Policy, male students produce samples at a urinal along a wall. They remain fully clothed and are only observed from behind, if at all. Female students produce samples in an enclosed stall, with a female monitor standing outside listening only for sounds of tampering. These conditions are nearly identical to those typically encountered in public restrooms. . . . Under such conditions, the privacy interests . . . are in our view negligible.

The other privacy-invasive aspect of urinalysis is . . . the information it discloses concerning the state of the subject's body, and the materials he has ingested. . . . it is significant that the tests . . . here look only for drugs, and not for whether the student is, for example, epileptic, pregnant, or diabetic. . . . Moreover, the drugs . . . screened are standard, and do not vary according to the identity of the student. And finally, the results of the tests are disclosed only to a limited class of school personnel who have a need to know; and they are not turned over to law enforcement authorities or used for any internal disciplinary function. . . .

Respondents argue, however, that the District's Policy is in fact more intrusive . . . because it requires the students, to identify in advance prescription medications they are taking. . . . [W]e have never indicated that requiring advance disclosure of medications is per se unreasonable. . . .

❖ ❖ ❖

Finally, we turn to consider the nature . . . of the governmental concern . . . and the efficacy of this means for meeting it. . . . . . . [T]he District Court held that because the District's program also called for drug testing in the absence of individualized suspicion, the District "must demonstrate a 'compelling need' for the program.". . . It is a mistake, however, to think that the phrase "compelling state interest," . . . describes a fixed, minimum quantum of governmental concern. . . . Rather, the phrase describes an interest which appears important enough to justify the particular search at hand. . . . Whether that relatively high degree of government concern is necessary . . . or not, we think it is met.

That the nature of the concern is important—indeed, perhaps compelling—can hardly be doubted. . . . And of course the effects of a drug-infested school are visited not just upon the users, but upon the entire student body and faculty. . . .
. . . [T]he necessity for the State to act is magnified by the fact that this evil is

being visited . . . upon children for whom it has undertaken a special responsibility. . . . Finally . . . this program is directed more narrowly to drug use by school athletes, where the risk of immediate physical harm to the drug user or those with whom he is playing his sport is particularly high. . . .

✧ ✧ ✧

. . . Respondents argue that a "less intrusive means end" was available, namely, "drug testing on suspicion of drug use." . . . We have repeatedly refused to declare that only the "least intrusive" search practicable can be reasonable under the Fourth Amendment.

Taking into account all the factors we have considered above . . . we conclude Vernonia's Policy is reasonable and hence constitutional.

We caution against the assumption that suspicionless drug testing will readily pass constitutional muster in other contexts. . . .

Review Question 7.4

1. How broad an exception did *Vernonia* carve from the Court's prior requirement of individualized suspicion for a valid student search? The *Miller* case which follows represents one extreme of the range of possible readings of *Vernonia*.

Case 7.5

MILLER v. WILKES
172 F.3d 574 (8th Cir. 1999)

[*Focus Note. This decision extended the Vernonia rationale to uphold a school district requirement that, notwithstanding the absence of any drug problem in the district, students wishing to participate in any school extracurricular programs must undergo random, suspicionless drug testing, including the student's participation in the Radio Club, prom committees, the quiz bowl, and school dances.*]

BOWMAN, CHIEF JUDGE.

✧ ✧ ✧

. . . [T]he search at issue . . . is not supported by a warrant, probable cause, or individualized suspicion. . . . The Supreme Court has held that the public school environment provides the requisite "special needs" so that a school district may dispense with those Fourth Amendment protections. *Vernonia*, 515 U.S. at 653. . . .

❖ ❖ ❖

Pathe argues that the fact that the policy in Vernonia applied only to student athletes was more significant . . . than was the fact that the policy applied to students who were attending public school. We read the case differently. . . .

❖ ❖ ❖

We must acknowledge, however, that there is not the same "immediacy" here as there was in Vernonia. . . . There is no "immediate crisis" in Cave City public schools. . . . . . .

. . . We see no reason that a school district should be compelled to wait until there is a demonstrable problem . . . before the district is constitutionally permitted to take measures that will help protect its schools against the sort of "rebellion" proven in Vernonia. . . .

❖ ❖ ❖

. . . [W]e come now to the final step in our analysis: the balancing. Weighing the minimal intrusion on the lowered expectation of privacy against the district's concern and the essentially unchallenged efficacy of its policy, we conclude that the School District's interest is "important enough to justify the particular search at hand." . . .

We hold that the challenged portion of the Chemical Screen Test Policy for Cave City Schools . . . is constitutional. . . .

❖ ❖ ❖

Case 7.6

ABC SCHOOL v. MR. & MRS. M.
1997 Mass. Super., Lexis 43

> [*Focus Note.* Parent/school conflict on control of student medical treatment. Parents delivered to school authorities a "Do Not Resuscitate" Order ("DNR Order") on behalf of their child, Minor M, who has severe disabilities. The school brought suit requesting a court order allowing it to refuse to honor the order, and the parents requested a court ruling and order that school refusal to honor the DNR Order would violate a constitutional right to refuse medical treatment.]

> Opinion by: RICHARD F. CONNON.

❖ ❖ ❖

Background

ABC School educates disabled children between the ages of 3 and 22 who reside in member towns and whose educational needs exceed the capabilities of their own public school.

. . . Minor M is a four-year-old girl who is severely disabled both mentally and physically. At present, Minor M weighs only twenty pounds. . . . . . . While at ABC School, Minor M receives physical, occupational and speech therapies and vision stimulation activities. She is transported to and from school . . . provided by DEF Schools.

During the past year, Minor M's medical condition deteriorated significantly. In March of 1997, Minor M had an apneic spell, meaning her breathing ceased. The school nurse administered care to Minor M until she was transported to the local hospital via ambulance. Following this incident, Minor M was evaluated by her private physician, Dr. Nedda Hobbs, M.D., in Boston. On April 10, 1997, after consultation with Mr. and Mrs. M, Dr. Hobbs issued a DNR Order which states in relevant part:

> Should Minor M have a cardiorespiratory arrest, she may receive oxygen, suction and stimulation. She should receive rectal valium if she appears to be having a prolonged seizure. Minor M should not receive cardiopulmonary resuscitation, intubation, defibrillation, or cardiac medications. Invasive procedures such as arterial or venous puncture should only be done after approval of her parents. Should Minor M have an apneic spell at school, she should receive oxygen, suction and stimulation. If she responds to this, her parents should be contacted and she can be transported home. If she does not respond, she should be transported by ambulance to the local hospital.

The DNR Order was submitted to ABC School and Mr. and Mrs. M were informed that ABC School would not honor it. . . .

❖ ❖ ❖

Prior to Minor M's enrollment at ABC School, Mr. and Mrs. M were notified of the institution's preservation of life policy and Mrs. M stated that no DNR Order was in effect. . . .

Discussion

This case presents an issue of first impression in Massachusetts. Most of the case law concerning DNR Orders are in the context of health care facilities and not educational institutions. Plaintiffs argue that their ethical and professional obligations both as an internal matter and as a matter of statutory duty prohibit them from honoring the DNR Order for Minor M. Minor M's parents argue that the DNR Order was obtained for the benefit of their daughter and that their right to refuse medical treatment on behalf of Minor M is constitutionally protected and must be honored by ABC School. For the following reasons, this court finds that Mr. and Mrs. M have the right to refuse medical treatment on behalf of their daughter and that, based on an assessment of the likelihood of success on the merits, the plaintiffs' [School's] request for declaratory and injunctive relief is denied. Defendants' [Parents'] request for declaratory relief is allowed.

Plaintiffs argue that case law in Massachusetts establishes that a treating facility cannot be forced to honor a DNR Order if transfer to another facility which would honor that order is available. See *Brophy v. New England Sinai Hospital*, 398 Mass. 417, 497 N.E.2d 626 (1986). The string of cases relied upon by the plaintiffs are distinguishable on a critical point. The cases cited by plaintiffs hold that individual medical personnel and medical institutions cannot be compelled "to take active measures which are contrary to their view of their ethical duty toward their patient." *Brophy*, 398 Mass. at 441.

Unlike those cases which involved medical personnel taking active measures to potentially hasten death, ABC School and its staff are being asked to refrain from giving unwanted and potentially harmful medical treatment to Minor M. The DNR Order does not prohibit all life-saving measures, but rather prohibits the use of cardiopulmonary resuscitation, intubation, defibrillation, and other invasive procedures in the event that Minor M suffers cardiac arrest. Moreover, as the guardians of their minor child, Mr. and Mrs. M have the right to refuse unwanted medical treatment on her behalf. See *Superintendent of Belchertown v. Joseph Saikewicz*, 373 Mass. 728, 370 N.E.2d 417 (1977) (right to refuse medical treatment stems from constitutional right to privacy) . . . This court is not in a position to find that such a refusal is not in the best interests of Minor M . . .

ABC School argues that Mr. and Mrs. M were notified of the preservation of life policy prior to Minor M's enrollment, Mrs. M specifically stated that no DNR Order was in effect before Minor M began attending the program and therefore no argument of detrimental reliance can be made by Mr. and Mrs. M. In light of Minor M's physical condition, however, the possibility that a change in circumstance could give rise to DNR Order was not so remote that ABC School was not apprised of the possibility.

ABC School argues that equitable considerations weigh in ABC School's favor because of the undue burden that would be placed on the R.N. in charge of the program who does not have the ability to confer with other medical personnel concerning Minor M. However, the DNR Order at issue is very specific in what is prohibited: cardiopulmonary resuscitation, intubation, defibrillation, and cardiac medication. Based on plaintiffs' argument, it appears that the R.N. at ABC School does not have the capability to conduct intubation or defibrillation and, therefore the only concern is the prohibition of CPR and medication. An order prohibiting CPR and medication does not require consultation with other medical personnel.

Finally, ABC School argues that even if this court refuses to grant the requested injunctive relief, this court should issue a declaratory judgment shielding ABC School personnel from liability in the event that they violate the DNR Order and administer aid pursuant to G.L.C. 71, 55A. Section 55A reads in relevant part:

No collaborative school teacher . . . or other . . . collaborative employee who, in good faith, renders emergency first aid or transportation to a student who has become injured or incapacitated . . . shall be liable in a suit for damages as a result of his acts or omissions either for such first aid or as a result of providing such emergency transportation to a place of safety. . . .

. . . [T]his court will not issue a declaratory judgment that any action taken in violation of the DNR Order would be "in good faith." To do so would vitiate the DNR Order and essentially constitute an end-run around this court's denial of the request for injunctive relief.

✧ ✧ ✧

Order

. . . The plaintiffs are hereby ORDERED to honor the terms of the Do Not Resuscitate Order for the care and treatment of Minor M pending adjudication of this case on its merits.

Case 7.7

HENDRICK HUDSON DIST. BOARD OF EDUC. v. ROWLEY
458 U.S. 176 (1982)

[***Focus Note.*** *Special educational services that must be provided to satisfy the basic FAPE mandate of the IDEA. What guidelines can you derive from the opinion?*]

JUSTICE REHNQUIST delivered the opinion of the Court.

This case arose in connection with the education of Amy Rowley, a deaf student. . . . Amy has minimal residual hearing and is an excellent lipreader. . . .

As required by the Act, an IEP was prepared for Amy. . . . The Rowleys agreed with parts of the IEP but insisted that Amy also be provided a qualified sign-language interpreter in all her academic classes. . . . Such an interpreter had been placed in Amy's kindergarten class for a 2-week experimental period, but the interpreter had reported that Amy did not need his services at that time. The school administrators likewise concluded that Amy did not need such an interpreter in her first-grade classroom. . . .

. . . Pursuant to the Act's provision for judicial review, the Rowleys then brought an action . . . claiming that the administrators' denial of the sign-language interpreter constituted a denial of the "free appropriate public education" guaranteed by the Act.

The District Court found that Amy "is a remarkably well adjusted child" who interacts and communicates well with her classmates and has "developed an extraordinary rapport" with her teacher. . . . It also found that "she performs better than the average child in her class and is advancing easily from grade to grade," . . . but "that she understands considerably less of what goes on in class than she could if she were not deaf" and thus "is not learning as much, or performing as well academically, as she would without her handicap,". . . . This disparity between Amy's achievement and her potential led the court to decide that she was not receiving a "free appropriate public education.". . .

✧ ✧ ✧

. . . It is beyond dispute that . . . the Act does expressly define "free appropriate public education":

> The term "free appropriate public education" means *special education* and *related services* which (A) have been provided at public expense, under public supervision and direction, and without charge, (B) meet the standards of the State educational agency, (C) include an appropriate preschool, elementary, or secondary school education in the State involved, and (D) are provided in conformity with the individualized education program required under section 1414(a)(5) of this title. § 1401(18) (Emphasis added).

"Special education," as referred to in this definition, means "specially designed instruction, at no cost to parents or guardians, to meet the unique needs of a handicapped child, including classroom instruction, . . . home instruction, and instruction in hospitals and institutions." § 1401(16). "Related services" are defined as "transportation, and such developmental, corrective, and other supportive services . . . as may be required to assist a handicapped child to benefit from special education." § 1401(17).

. . . Thus, if personalized instruction is being provided with sufficient services to permit the child to benefit from the instruction, and the other items on the definitional checklist are satisfied, the child is receiving a "free appropriate education" as defined by the Act.

Noticeably absent from the language of the statute is any substantive standard prescribing the level of education to be accorded handicapped children. Certainly the language of the statute contains no requirement . . . that States maximize the potential of handicapped children "commensurate with the opportunity provided to other children." . . .

. . . Respondents contend that "the goal of the Act is to provide each handicapped child with an equal educational opportunity." . . . We think, however, that the requirement that a State provide specialized educational services . . . generates no additional requirement that the services so provided be sufficient to maximize each child's potential "commensurate with the opportunity provided other children.". . .

. . . The theme of the Act is "free appropriate public education," a phrase which is too complex to be captured by the word "equal" whether one is speaking of opportunities or services.

The District Court and the Court of Appeals thus erred when they held that the Act requires New York to maximize the potential of each handicapped child commensurate with the opportunity provided nonhandicapped children. Desirable though that goal might be, it is not the standard that Congress imposed upon States which receive funding under the Act. . . .

Implicit in the congressional purpose . . . is the requirement that the education . . . be sufficient to confer some educational benefit upon the handicapped child. . . . The statutory definition of "free appropriate public education," . . . expressly requires the provision of "such . . . supportive services . . . as may be required to assist a handicapped child to *benefit* from special education." § 1401(17). We therefore conclude that the "basic floor of opportunity" provided by the Act consists of access to specialized instruction and related services which are individually designed to provide educational benefit to the handicapped child.

The determination of when handicapped children are receiving sufficient educational benefits to satisfy the requirements of the Act presents a more difficult problem. . . . We do not attempt today to establish any one test for determining the adequacy of educational benefits conferred upon all children covered by the Act. . . .

. . . Insofar as a State is required to provide . . . a "free appropriate public education," we hold that it satisfies this requirement by providing personalized instruction with sufficient support services to permit the child to benefit educationally from that instruction. Such instruction and services must be provided at public expense, must meet the State's educational standards, must approximate the grade levels used in the State's regular education, and must comport with the child's IEP. . . . In addition the IEP . . . should be reasonably calculated to enable the child to achieve passing marks and advance from grade to grade.

❖ ❖ ❖

The parties disagree sharply over [other] provisions, petitioners contending that courts are given only limited authority to review for state compliance . . . and no power to review the substance of the state program, and respondents contending that the Act requires courts to exercise de novo review over state educational decisions and policies. . . .

❖ ❖ ❖

. . . [A] court's inquiry is twofold. First, has the State complied with the procedures set forth in the Act? And second, is the individualized educational program . . . reasonably calculated to enable the child to receive educational benefits? If these requirements are met, the State has complied with the obligations . . . and the courts can require no more.

In assuring that the requirements of the Act have been met, courts must be careful to avoid imposing their view of preferable educational methods upon the States. . . .

Entrusting a child's education to state and local agencies does not leave the child without protection. . . . As this very case demonstrates, parents and guardians will not lack ardor in seeking to ensure that handicapped children receive all of the benefits to which they are entitled by the Act.

❖ ENDNOTES

1. Erik v. Causby, 977 F. Supp. 384 (E.D.N.C. 1997) (no right to grade promotion).

2. *Re honor societies:* Dangler v. Yorktown Cent. Schools, 771 F. Supp. 625 (S.D.N.Y. 1991); 777 F. Supp. 1177 (S.D.N.Y. 1991); *accord:* Price v. Young, 580 F. Supp. 1 (E.D.Ark. 1983); Karnstein v. Pewaukee School Board, 557 F. Supp. 565 (E.D.Wis. 1983). For a rare instance where a court found a "liberty" interest in honorary society membership, *see* Warren v. National Assn. of Sec. School Principals, 375 F. Supp. 1043 (N.D.Tex. 1974). *Cf.* Ector County Ind. School Dist. v. Hopkins, 518 S.W.2d 576 (Tex. 1975).

   Re student office: Bull v. Dardanelle Pub. School Dist., 745 F. Supp. 1455 (E.D. Ark. 1990) (no right to run for student council). *See also* Moore v. Hyche, 761 F. Supp. 112 (N.D. Ala. 1991).

3. *Hearing not required:* Farver v. Board of Educ., 40 F. Supp. 2d 323 (D. Md. 1999) (extracurricular activities); Spring Branch I.S.D. v. Stamos, 695 S.W.2d 556 (Tex. 1985) (exclusion for grade deficiency); Palmer v. Merluzzi, 689 F. Supp. 400 (D. N.J. 1988).

   Hearing required: Duffley v. N.H. Interscholastic Athletic Assn., 446 A.2d 462 (N.H. 1982).

4. Goss v. Lopez, 419 U.S. 565 (1975); *accord:* Baxter v. Round Lake Area Schools, 856 F. Supp. 438 (N.D. Ill. 1994).

5. Atcitty v. San Juan County School Dist., 967 P.2d 1261 (Utah 1998).

6. Baxter, *supra* note 4.

7. *Transfers to comparable schools:* Everett v. Marcase, 426 F. Supp. 397 (E.D. Pa. 1977); *but see* Madera v. Board of Educ., 386 F.2d 778 (2d Cir. 1967).
   Transfers to less desirable schools: Mills v. Board of Educ., 348 F. Supp. 866 (D.D. Colo. 1972); Pa. Assn. for Retarded Children v. Cmwlth., 343 F. Supp. 279 (E.D. Pa. 1972).

8. Linwood v. Board of Educ., 462 F.2d, at 770 (7th Cir. 1972).

9. Hill v. Rankin County Mississippi Sch. Dist., 843 F. Supp. 1112 (S.D. Miss. 1993); McClain v. Lafayette Cty. Board of Educ., 673 F.2d 106 (5th

Cir. 1982) (carrying weapon); Gardenshire v. Chalmers, 326 F. Supp. 1200 (D. Ky. 1971) (carrying firearms).

10. Ingraham v. Wright, 430 U.S. 651 (1997).

11. *cf.* Board of Curators v. Horowitz, 435 U.S. 78 (1978) (medical school student).

12. LaBrosse v. St. Bernard Parish School Board, 483 So.2d 1253 (La. App. 1986). *Compare,* Rucker v. Colonial School Dist., 517 A.2d 703 (Del. Super. 1976) (4 days' notice of expulsion hearing—held adequate), *with* Vought v. Van Buren Pub. Schools, 306 F. Supp. 1388 (E.D. Mich. 1969) (5 days' notice required).

13. *Closed hearing upheld:* Racine Unified School Dist. v. Thomas, 321 N.W.2d 334, 338 (Wis. 1982) (statutory right); Pierce v. School Comm. of New Bedford, 322 F. Supp. 957 (D. Mass. 1971).
    Closed hearing disapproved: DeJesus v. Penberthey, 334 F. Supp. 70–77 (D. Conn. 1972).

14. People in the interest of K.P., 514 P.2d 1131 (Colo. 1973); Intron v. State Board of Educ., 384 F. Supp. 674 (D. Puerto Rico 1974).

15. Williams v. Board of Educ., 626 S.W.2d 361 (Ark. 1982). *See also* Murray v. W. Baton Rouge School Board, 472 F.2d 438 (5th Cir. 1973); Alex v. Allen, 409 F. Supp. 379 (W.D. Pa. 1976); Fielder v. Board of Educ., 346 F. Supp. at 730 (D. Neb. 1972).

16. *See also* Clairborne v. Beebe School Dist., 687 F. Supp. 1358 (E.D. Ark. 1988) (phrase "prior to"—held vague); Leibner v. Sharbaugh, 429 F. Supp. 744 (D. Va. 1977).

17. *See, e.g.,* Newsome v. Batavia Local School Dist., 842 F.2d 920 (6th Cir. 1988); Murray v. W. Baton Rouge School Board., 472 F.2d 438 (5th Cir. 1973).

18. *See* Pierce v. School Comm. of New Bedford, 322 F. Supp. 957, at 962 (D. Mass. 1971).

19. Warren v. Nat'l Assn. of Secondary School Principals, 375 F. Supp. 43 (N.D. Tex. 1974).

20. Harrall v. Wilson County Schools, 293 S.E.2d 687 (N.C. 1932); *contra:* Alex v. Allen, 409 F. Supp. 379 (W.D. Pa. 1976).

21. *Cross examination denied:* Jones v. Board of Trustees, 524 So.2d 968 (Miss. 1988)

(suspension); Texarkana Indep. School Dist. v. Lewis, 470 S.W.2d at 736 (Tex. Civ. App. 1971) (expulsion), and cases there cited.

Cross-examination and counsel allowed: Stone v. Prosser Cons. School Dist., 971 P.2d 125 (Wash. App. 1999) (expulsion); Newsome v. Batavia Local School Dist., 842 F.2d 920 (6th Cir. 1988); Casada v. Booneville School Dist. No. 65, 686 F. Supp. 730 (W.D. Ark. 1988).

22. Fielder v. Board of Educ., 346 F. Supp. 722 (D. Neb. 1972). *But see contra:* Jones, *supra* note 21; Greene v. Moore, 373 F. Supp. 1194 (N.D. Tex. 1974). *Re harmless denial of confrontation:* Paredes by Koppenhoefer v. Curtis, 864 F.2d 426 (6th Cir. 1988).

23. *Hearsay testimony allowed:* Tasby v. Estes, 643 F.2d 1103 (5th Cir. 1981); Boykins v. Fairfield Board of Educ., 492 F.2d 697 (5th Cir. 1974). *Hearsay testimony not allowed:* Fielder v. Board of Educ., 346 F. Supp. 722 (D. Neb. 1972); DeJesus v. Penberthey, 344 F. Supp. 70 (D. Conn. 1972).

24. *School counsel not present:* Texarkana, *supra* note 21. *Advisory hearing:* Madera v. Board of Educ., 380 F.2d 778 (2nd Cir. 1967).

25. *Re* Goldwyn, 281 N.Y.S.2d 199 (1967). *Cf.* Givens v. Poe, 346 F. Supp. 202 (W.D.N.C. 1972).

26. *Compare* Mason v. Thetford School Board, 457 A.2d 647, 649 (Vt. 1982) (denying right of appeal), *with cases finding statutory right of appeal:* Ross v. Disare, 500 F. Supp. 928, at p. 931 (S.D.N.Y. 1977).

27. Racine Unified, *supra* note 13 (board minutes as record of hearing); Ross, *supra* note 26.

28. *Compare* Mills v. Board of Educ. 348 F. Supp. 866 (D.D.C. 1972) (record required), *with* S. v. Board of Educ., 97 Cal. Rptr. 422 (1971).

29. Pace v. Dryden Cent. School Dist., 574 N.Y.S.2d 142 (1991).

30. Lovell v. Poway Unified School Dist., 847 F. Supp. 780 (S.D. Cal. 1994); Hill v. Rankin County Mississippi School Dist., 843 F. Supp. 1112 (S.D. Miss. 1993).

31. *See Annot., Discipline of Pupil for Non-School Conduct,* 53 A.L.R. 3d 1124 (1973). *Re* drugs and assaults, *see* Rucker v. Colonial School Dist., 517 A.2d 703 (Del. Super. 1976); Fisher v. Burkburnett Indep. School Dist., 419 F. Supp. 1200 (N.D. Tex. 1976).

Re vandalism, see Clinton Mun. Sep. School Dist. v. Byrd, 477 So.2d 237 (Miss. 1985).

32. Howard v. Clark, 299 N.Y.S.2d 65 (1969); Bunger v. Iowa H.S. Athletic Assn., 197 N.W.2d 555 (Iowa 1972).

33. St. Ann v. Palisi, 495 F.2d 423 (5th Cir. 1974).

34. Slocum v. Holton Board of Educ., 429 N.W. 2d 607 (Mich. App. 1988) (grade reduction); Jacobs v. School Board of Lee County, 519 So.2d 1002 (Fla. App. 1987) (expulsion from honor society); *Compare* Board of Educ. v. Ambach, 465 N.Y.S.2d 77 (1983) (overturning expulsion for summertime crime).

35. *Abuse of discretion:* Katzman v. Cumberland Valley School Dist., 479 A.2d 671 (Pa. Cmwlth. 1984).

Ultra vires: Hamer v. Board of Educ., 383 N.E.2d 231 (Ill. 1978); Guitirrez v. School Dist. R-1, 585 P.2d 935 (Colo. 1978).

36. Fisher, *supra* note 31; Dunn v. Tyler Indep. School Dist., 460 F.2d 137 (5th Cir. 1972).

37. Recent studies report that 25 states enacted laws to prohibit corporal punishment. *See* J. Dayton, *Corporal Punishment in the Public Schools,* 89 Ed.Law Rep. 729 (1994) at p. 730, n.7.

38. Ingraham v. Wright, 430 U.S. 651 (1977) at n. 47. *For recent developments, see* Jefferson v. Ysleta Indep. School Dist., 817 F.2d 303 (5th Cir. 1987); I. M. Rosenberg, *A Study in Irrationality, Refusal to Grant Substantive Due Process Protection Against Excessive Corporal Punishment in the Public Schools,* 27 Hous. L. Rev. 399 (1990).

39. *Cases finding a substantive due process right against shocking corporal punishment:* Metzger v. Osbeck, 841 F.2d 518 (3d Cir. 1988); Garcia v. Miera, 817 F.2d 650 (10th Cir. 1987); Webb v. McCullough, 828 F.2d 1151 (6th Cir. 1987); Hall v. Tawney, 621 F.2d 607, 610 (4th Cir. 1980). *Cases finding punishment not sufficiently shocking:* Brown by Brown v. Johnson, 710 F. Supp. 183 (E.D. Ky. 1989); Wise v. Pea Ridge School Dist., 855 F.2d 560 (8th Cir. 1988) (paddlings that caused severe bruises).

Cases rejecting substantive due process claim against corporal punishment: See Fee v. Herndon, 900 F.2d 804 (5th Cir. 1990).

40. Stoneking v. Bradford Area School Dist., 882 F.2d 720 (3rd Cir. 1989); Thelma D. by Delores A. v. Board of Educ., 934 F.2d 929 (8th Cir. 1991); J.O. v. Alton Comm. Unit School Dist., 909 F.2d

267 (7th Cir. 1990); D.T. v. Indep. School Dist. No. 16 of Pawnee County, 894 F.2d 1176 (10th Cir. 1990). *See* Sorenson, *Sexual Abuse in Schools,* 27 Educ. Ad. Q., 460 (1991); Valente, *School District and Official Liability for Teacher Sexual Abuse of Students,* 57 Educ. L. Rep. 645 (1990).

41. *See* Grayned v. City of Rockford, 408 U.S. 104 (1972).

42. 393 U.S. 503 (1969).

43. West v. Derby Unified School Dist., 23 F. Supp. 2d 1223 (D. Kan. 1998) (school ban on possession of confederate flag symbols at racially tense school—upheld); *accord:* Crosby v. Holsinger, 852 F.2d 801 (4th Cir. 1988) (ban on "Johnny Reb" symbol).

44. Idem.

45. Vigil v. School Board, 862 F.2d 1517 (11th Cir. 1989) (board disapproval of text containing passages deemed inappropriately vulgar, from Chaucer's "A Miller's Tale" and Aristophanes' "Lysistrata"); Bystrom v. Fridley H.S. Indep. School Dist., 822 F.2d 747 (8th Cir. 1987) (upholding school-site ban on vulgar speech and school preclearance of off-campus publications); Seyfried v. Walton, 668 F.2d 214 (3d Cir. 1981) (upholding ban on school production of play, *Pippin*). *Contra:* Burch v. Barker, 861 F.2d 1149 (9th Cir. 1988).

46. *Ibid.* Pyle v. So. Hadley School Dist., 861 F. Supp. 157 (D. Mass. 1994), *citing* Chandler v. McMinnville School Dist., 978 F.2d 524 (9th Cir. 1992).

47. *Disruptive incitement:* Gano v. School Dist. 411, 674 F. Supp. 796 (D. Idaho 1987) (portraying school superiors as drunkards); Scoville v. Board of Educ., 425 F.2d 10 (7th Cir. 1970) (criticism of school policies). *Compare* Hatter v. L.A. City H.S. Dist., 452 F.2d 673 (9th Cir. 1971) (peaceful protest against school dress code).

Call for a strike and takeover: Williams v. Spencer, 622 F.2d 1206 (4th Cir. 1980); Lake Park Educ. Assn. v. Lake Park H.S. Dist., 526 F. Supp. 719 (N.D. Ill 1981); Ring v. Reorganized School Dist., 609 S.W.2d 241 (Mo. 1980).

48. Nelson v. Moline School Dist., 725 F. Supp. 965 (C.D. Ill. 1989).

49. *Obscenity is not protected expression under the First Amendment.* Miller v. Cal., 413 U.S. 15 (1973).

Libelous (defamatory) expression is not protected speech: Special defenses of public news media to libel claims are not relevant to school-related publications.

50. Nitzberg v. Park, 525 F.2d 378 (4th Cir. 1975); Jacobs v. Board of School Comm'rs, 490 F.2d 601 (7th Cir. 1973), vacated as moot following plaintiff graduations, 420 U.S. 128 (1975); Shanley v. Northeast Indep. School Dist., 462 F.2d 960 (5th Cir. 1972); Eisner v. Stamford Board of Educ., 440 F.2d 803 (2d Cir. 1971); Riseman v. School Comm. of Quincy, 439 F.2d 148 (1st Cir. 1971).

Pre-*Hazelwood* cases that disapproved school suppression of sex-related student articles are weakened by *Hazelwood.*

51. Perumal v. Saddleback Valley Unified School Dist., 243 Cal. Rptr. 545 (1988).

52. The college press cases [*e.g.,* Papish v. Board of Curators, Univ. of Mo., 410 U.S. 667 (1973)] are clearly inapposite for public schools and were barely noted in *Hazelwood.*

53. 484 U.S. 260, 272.

54. *See, e.g.,* Seyfried v. Walton, 668 F.2d 214 (3d Cir. 1981) (ban on play, *Pippin*) and cases at note 45, supra.

55. *Exclusion of ads—held constitutional:* Planned Parenthood of Southern Nevada v. Clark County School Dist., 941 F.2d 817 (9th Cir. 1991) (family planning); Zucker v. Panitz, 299 F. Supp. 102 (E.D.N.Y. 1969) (partisan political ads).

Exclusion held unconstitutional: San Diego Comm. v. Governing Board, 790 F.2d 1471 (9th Cir. 1986) (antidraft ad); Searcey v. Crim, 642 F. Supp. 313 (N.D. Ga. 1986), *modified on appeal,* Searcey v. Crim, 815 F.2d 1398 (11th Cir. 1987).

56. *Upholding ban:* Katz v. McAulay, 438 F.2d 1058 (2d Cir. 1970); Hernandez v. Hanson, 430 F. Supp. 1154 (D. Neb. 1977). *Overturning ban:* Cintron v. State Board of Educ., 384 F. Supp. 674 (D. Puerto Rico 1974).

57. *Compare* Peterson v. Board of Educ., 370 F. Supp. 1208 (D. Neb. 1973) *with* Jacobs, *supra* note 50; the Bystrom and Burch cases, *supra* note 45.

58. Talley v. Cal., 362 U.S. 60 (1960); Healy v. James, 408 U.S. 169 (1972).

59. Texas v. Johnson, 491 U.S. 397 (1989).

60. Sheldon v. Fannin, 221 F. Supp. 766 (Ariz. 1963). *Compare* Caldwell v. Craighead, 432 F.2d 213 (6th Cir. 1970), *with* Frain v. Barron, 307 F. Supp. 27 (E.D.N.Y. 1969).

61. *Unprotected class boycotts and walkouts:* Sapp v. Renpoe, 511 F.2d 172 (5th Cir. 1975); Rhyne v. Childs, 359 F. Supp. 1085 (N.D. Fla. 1973); Tate v. Board of Educ., 453 F.2d 975 (8th Cir. 1972).

62. Hatch v. Goerke, 502 F.2d 1189 (10th Cir. 1974); Richards v. Thursten, 424 F.2d 128 (1st Cir. 1970).

63. Crossen v. Fatsi, 309 F. Supp. 114 (D. Conn. 1970); Bannister v. Paradis, 316 F. Supp. 185 (D.N.H. 1970).

64. *The Third, Fifth, Sixth, Ninth and Tenth circuits upheld school male hair length restrictions:* Zeller v. Donagel School Dist. Board of Educ., 517 F.2d 600 (3d Cir. 1975); Murray v. W. Baton Rouge Parish School Board., 472 F.2d 438 (5th Cir. 1973); Ferrel v. Dallas Indep. School Dist., 392 F.2d 697 (6th Cir. 1968); Gfell v. Rickelman, 441 F.2d 444y (6th Cir. 1971); Olff v. E. Side H.S. Dist., 445 F.2d 932 (9th Cir. 1971); Hatch v. Goerke, note 62; Freeman v. Flake, 448 F.2d 258 (10th Cir. 1971).

    The First, Fourth, Seventh and Eighth circuits nullified them as unconstitutional. Richards, *supra* note 62; Long v. Zopp, 476 F.2d 180 (4th Cir. 1973); Holsapple v. Woods, 500 F.2d 49 (7th Cir. 1974); Torvik v. Deborah Comm. Schools, 453 F.2d 779 (8th Cir. 1972).

65. Humphries v. Lincoln Parish School Board, 467 So.2d 870 (La. App. 1985); Long v. Zopp, *supra* note 64.

66. Jeglin v. San Jacinto Unified School Dist., 827 F. Supp. 1459 (Cal. 1993).

67. Pyle v. So. Hadley School Com., 861 F. Supp. 157 (D. Mass. 1994).

68. **Upheld:** Board of Trustees of Bastrop Independent School Dist. v. Toungate, 958 S.W.2d 365 (Tex. 1997) (male pony-tail ban) and cases there cited; Jones v. W.T. Henning, 721 So.2d 530 (La. App. 1998) (male earring ban) and cases there cited; Barber v. Colo. Ind. School Dist., 901 S.W.2d 447 (Tex. App. 1995).

    But see Breese v. Smith, 502 P.2d 159 (Alaska 1972) (state constitutional violation); Jacobs v. Benedict, 316 N.E.2d 898 (Ohio 1974); Neuhaus v. Federico, 505 P.2d 939 (Or. 1972) (as unauthorized by school statutes).

69. Dunkerson v. Russell, 502 S.W.2d 64 (Ky. 1973); Murphy v. Pocatello School Dist., 480 P.2d 878 (Idaho 1971); Bannister v. Paradis, 316 F. Supp. 185 (D.N.H. 1970); Wallace v. Ford, 346 F. Supp. 156 (E.D. Ark. 1972). *See also* Graber v. Kniola, 216 N.W.2d 925 (Mich. 1974) (*re* bikinis); Fowler v. Williams, 251 S.E.2d 889 (N.C. 1979) (graduation dress requirement—upheld).

70. Harper v. Edgewood Board of Educ., 655 F. Supp. 1353 (S.D. Ohio 1987) (male student wishing to dress as female); Fricke v. Lynch, 491 F. Supp. 381 (D.R.I. 1980) (same sex date to school prom).

71. Wilson v. Abilene Indep. School Dist., 190 S.W.2d 406 (Tex. 1945); Burkitt v. School Dist. No. 1, 246 P.2d 566, 578 (Or. 1952).

72. Passel v. Ft. Worth Indep. School Dist., 453 S.W.2d 888 (Tex. 1970). For statute and case authorities in more than 25 states, *see* Robinson v. Sacramento Unified School Dist., 53 Cal. Rptr. 781, 788–9 (1966).

73. McNaughton v. Circleville Board of Educ., 345 N.E.2d 649 (C.D. Ohio 1974) (belt beatings and rubbing of hot pepper into their faces).

74. Healy v. James, 408 U.S. 169 (1972); *cf.* Eisen v. Regents, Univ. of Cal., 75 Cal. Rptr. 45 (1969).

75. *General exception to search limitations: Consent to search,* Carter v. Raybuck, 742 F.2d 977 (6th Cir. 1984); Jones v. Latexo Indep. School Dist., 449 F. Supp. 223, 236–7 (E.D. Tex. 1980).

    Plain view exception: State v. D.T.W., 425 So.2d 1383 (Fla. 1983).

    Police search incident to arrest: State v. Kimball, 503 P.2d 176 (Hawaii 1972) (student loitering on school grounds).

    Identification or preservation of lost property: Illinois v. Lafayette, 462 U.S. 640 (1983) (warrantless inventory search by police).

76. *In* Interest of Feazell, 360 So.2d 907 (La. App. 1978) (upheld consent following school threat to call police); *In re* Scott K, 595 P.2d 105 (Cal. 1979) (voiding police search on parent consent, but

against consent of minor owner). *See also* Tartar v. Raybuck, 742 F.2d 977 (6th Cir. 1984).

77. Rhodes v. Guarricino, 54 F. Supp. 2d 186 (S.D.N.Y. 1999).

78. State v. Whorley, 720 So.2d 282 (Fla. App. 1998) (student tip); Coronado v. State, 806 S.W.2d 302 (Tex. 1991); Comm. v. Carey, 554 N.E.2d 1199 (Mass. 1990); Appeal in Pima County Juvenile Action, 733 P.2d 316 (Ariz. App. 1987); State v. Joseph T., 886 S.E.2d 728 (W. Va. 1985); Martens v. Dist. No. 220, 620 F. Supp. 29 (N.D. Ill. 1985); *In re* State in Interest of G.C., 296 A.2d 102 (N.J. 1972). *But see* Waters v. U.S., 311 A.2d 835 (D.C. Cir. 1973).

The personal history of the searched student bears upon the sufficiency of furtive action to support a search. *Compare, e.g., In re* Bobby B., 218 Cal. Rptr. 253 (1985) (presence in lavatory during class hour—held sufficient) *with In re* William G, 709 P.2d 1287 (Cal. 1985) (furtive gestures—held insufficient basis for suspicion).

79. T.L.O., 469 U.S. 337, 341. *Cases that held that school searches on police request did not require probable cause:* Illinois v. Dilworth, 661 N.E.2d 310 (Ill. 1996); Cason v. Cook, 810 F.2d 188 (8th Cir. 1987); Martens v. Dist. No. 220, 620 F. Supp. 29 (N.D. Ill. 1985). *Cases that required showing of probable cause:* Picha v. Wilgos, 410 F. Supp. 1214, 1219–21 (N.D. Ill. 1976); People v. Bowers, 356 N.Y.S.2d 432 (1974) (school security officer).

80. T.L.O., 409 U.S., at p. 333. *Several courts allowed schools to act on such evidence.* Gordon J. v. Santa Ana Unified School Dist., 208 Cal. Rptr. 657 (1984); Bellnier v. Lund, 438 F. Supp. 437 (N.D.N.Y. 1977); Morale v. Grigel, 422 F. Supp. 988 (D.N.H. 1976).

81. *Cases upholding random, suspicionless drug testing for extracurricular participants:* Miller v. Wilkes, 172 F.3d 574 (8th Cir. 1999); Todd v. Rush County Schools, 133 F.3d 984 (7th Cir. 1998). *Cases overturning suspicionless student searches:* Trinidad School Dist. No. 1 v. Lopez, 963 P.2d 1095 (Colo. 1998) (band members); Willis by Willis v. Anderson Comm. School Corp., 158 F.3d 415 (7th Cir. 1998) (mandatory search rule for students suspended for fighting); D.I.R. v. State of Indiana, 683 N.E.2d 251 (Ind. 1997) (search of tardy student's pockets).

82. Bridgman v. New Trier H.S. Dist., 128 F.3d 146 (7th Cir. 1997).

83. California, Iowa, Washington, and Wisconsin enacted statutes that bar or restrict strip searches, and similar legislation is pending in other states. J. Stefkovich, *Strip Searching after Williams: Reactions to the Concern for School Safety,* 93 Ed.Law Rep. 1107 (1994).

84. *Ibid. Cases upholding such searches:* Cornfield v. School District No. 230, 991 F.2d 1316, 1321 (7th Cir. 1993);Widener v. Frye, 809 F. Supp. 35 (S.D. Oh. 1992); Williams by Williams v. Ellington, 936 F.2d 881 (6th Cir. 1991).

Cases disapproving such searches: State ex rel Galford v. Mark Anthony B., 433 S.E.2d 41 (W.Va. 1993); M.M. v. Anker, 607 F.2d 588 (2d Cir. 1979).

85. B.C. v. Plumas Unified School Dist., 192 F.3d 1260 (9th Cir. 1999); Horton v. Goose Creek Indep. School Dist., 690 F.2d 470 (5th Cir. 1982); Burnham v. West, 681 F. Supp. 1160 (E.D. Va. 1987); Zamora v. Pomeroy, 639 F.2d 662 (10th Cir. 1981). *Contra:* Doe v. Renfrow, 631 F.2d 91 (7th Cir. 1980) (nude search).

86. B.C. v. Plumas, *supra* note 85.

87. *Re the federal constitution, see, e.g.,* Flanagan v. Munger, 890 F.2d 1557 (2d Cir. 1989) (discussion of constitutional right of privacy). *But see contra:* A.M. Fed of Govt. Employees v. Dept. of Housing, 118 F.3d 786, 791 (D.C.Cir. 1997) *and* J.P. v. DeSanti, 653 F.2d 1080, 1090–1 (6th Cir. 1981) where the court declared: "Our opinion does not mean . . . that there is no constitutional right to nondisclosure of private information. . . . Our opinion simply holds that not all rights of privacy or interests in nondisclosure of private information are of constitutional dimension."

Re potential state constitutional grounds, see, e.g., Falcon v. Alaska Pub. Offices Comm'n, 570 P.2d 469 (Alaska 1977); People v. Stritzinger, 668 P.2d 738 (Cal. 1983).

The cases on informational privacy are collected in R. Turkington, *Legacy of the Warren and Brandeis Article: The Emerging Unencumbered Constitutional Right to Informational Privacy,* 10 N.Ill.U.L.Rev. 479, 493–510 (1990); Note, *The Constitutional Protection of Informational Privacy,* 71 B.U.L.Rev. 133, 145–50 (1991).

88. *E.g.,* Merriken v. Cressman, 364 F. Supp. 913, 916 (E.D. Pa. 1973) (intensely personal questionnaire about student family—enjoined as invasion of privacy).

89. *See* Report, *School Sex and Drug Survey Angers 6th Graders' Parents,* New York Times, B-6 (May 26, 2000).

90. Pupil Protection Rights Amendment, General Education Provisions Act, Sec. 439, 20 U.S.C.A. Sex. 1232(h); 34 Code of Federal Regulations, Part 98, Sections 98.1–98.5 (7-1-99). A district that conducted a similar, but federally funded, questionnaire was the target of a federal complaint and investigation under the foregoing law and regulation. *See* Report, *Supra* note 89. On the inapplicability of the federal law to surveys that are not federally funded, *see* Altman v. Bedford Cent. School Dist., 45 F. Supp. 2d 368, 391 (S.D.N.Y. 1999).

91. State law variations are noted in Sargent School Dist. No. RE 33J v. Western Services Inc., 751 P.2d 56 (Colo. 1988). Webster Groves School Dist. v. Pulitzer Pub. Co., 898 F.2d 1371 (8th Cir. 1990) (barring disclosure of information hurtful to child with disability); Young v. Armstrong School Dist., 344 A.2d 738 (Pa. 1975) (citizen entitled to copy names and addresses of school parents to prepare a petition on school proposals); Hendricks v. Board of Trustees, 525 S.W.2d 930 (Tex. 1975) (taxpayer right to copy school district financial records).

92. 20 U.S.C. § 1232(g). *See Annot: Validity, Construction and Application of Family Educational Rights and Privacy Act,* 112 A.L.R. Fed 1 (1993).

    The FERPA definition of educational records excludes the following: records of applicants who are not admitted to the school; personal notes of teachers that are not discussed with others; and records of treating physicians and certain law enforcement agencies.

    "Personally identifiable educational records" are those that "would make the reader . . . reasonably certain of the identity of the student." 45 C.F.R. Pt. 99 (1976). But contests can arise as to what is nonpersonal data. Sargent School Dist. No. RE 33J v. Western Services Inc., 751 P.2d 56 (Colo. 1988). Many states have similar laws. *See, e.g.,* Bowie v. Evanston Comm. Cons. School Dist., 522 N.E.2d 669 (Ill. 1988).

    Examples of FERPA exemptions: Release of records under court order; to protect public safety; to a parent of dependent student; certain government officials, and teachers and principals for their work with the student.

    Excepted from student access: financial records or data of parents, doctor's records, and

information on which they validly waived a right of access.

93. FERPA regulations (34 C.F.R., part 99); Page v. Rotterdam-Mohonasen Central School Dist., 441 N.Y.S.2d 323 (1981).

94. Dachs v. Board of Educ., 277 N.Y.S.2d 449 (1967); Fay v. South Colonie Cent. School Dist., 802 F.2d 21 (2d Cir. 1986).

95. Pesce v. J. Sterling Morton H.S. Dist. 201, 830 F.2d 789 (7th Cir. 1987).

96. The Supreme Court recently extended testimonial privilege to communications between patients and licensed psychotherapists. Jaffee v. Redmond, 116 S. Ct. 1923 (1996).

97. Hedlund v. Superior Ct., 34 Cal. 3d 695 (1982); McIntosh v. Milano, 403 A.2d 500 (N.J. 1979); Tarasoff v. Regents of the Univ. of Cal., 551 P.2d 334 (Cal. 1976).

98. *See* Indiana H.S. Athletic Assn. v. Raike, 329 N.E.2d 66 (Ind. 1975) for a survey of the cases.

99. *Exclusions disapproved:* Shull v. Columbus Mun. Separate School Dist., 338 F. Supp. 1376 (N.D. Miss. 1972); Ordway v. Hargraves, 323 F. Supp. 1155 (D. Mass. 1971).

    Extracurricular activities exclusions: Beeson v. Kiowa City School Dist., 567 P.2d 801 (Colo. 1977); Bell v. Lone Oak Indep. School Dist., 507 S.W.2d 636 (Tex. 1974); Holt v. Shelton, 341 F. Supp. 821 (M.D. Tenn. 1972).

100. Brands v. Shelton Comm. School, 671 F. Supp. 627 (N.D. Iowa 1987).

101. DeBord v. Board of Educ., 126 F.3d 1102 (8th Cir. 1997).

102. Leahy v. Leahy, 858 S.W.2d 221 (Mo. 1993); Von Tersch v. Von Tersch, 455 N.W.2d 130 (Neb. 1990); Connelly v. Connelly, 409 So.2d 175 (Fl. App. 1982).

103. 20 U.S.C.A. § 1400.

104. *Students with Disabilities and Special Education,* (Oakston Pub. Co. 16th ed. 1999); J. Mead, *Expressions of Congressional Intent: Examining the 1997 Amendments to the IDEA,* 127 Ed. Law Rep. 511 (1998).

105. Smith v. Robinson, 468 U.S. 992, 1019–20 (1984); Morton Comm. Unit School Dist., 152 F.3d 583 (7th Cir. 1998); 20 U.S.C. § 1400 *et seq.*

106. (3) Child with a disability—
    (A) In general—The term "child with a disability" means a child—
    (i) with mental retardation, hearing impairments (including deafness), speech or language impairments, visual impairments (including blindness), serious emotional disturbance (hereinafter referred to as "emotional disturbance"), orthopedic impairments, autism, traumatic brain injury, other health impairments, or specific learning disabilities; and (ii) who, by reason thereof, needs special education and related services.
    (B) Child aged 3 through 9
    The term "child with a disability" for a child aged 3 through 9 may, at the discretion of the State and the local educational agency, include a child—
    (i) experiencing developmental delays, as defined by the State and as measured by appropriate diagnostic instruments and procedures, in one or more of the following areas: physical development, cognitive development, communication development, social or emotional development, or adaptive development; and (ii) who, by reason thereof, needs special education and related services. (Sec. 101 of 1977 Amendments). 20 U.S.C.A. § 1401 et se.

107. Martinez v. School Board of Hillsborough County, 711 F. Supp. 1066 (M.D. Fla. 1989). Such children are also protected against discrimination by § 504. See Chapter 8 discussion of § 504.

108. See Ridgewood Board of Educ. V. N.E. for M.E., 172 F.3d 238, 247 (3d Cir. 1999) and authorities there cited.

109. Williams v. Gering Pub. Schools, 463 N.W.2d 799 (Neb. 1990) (year-round program— required); Yaris v. Special School Dist., 728 F.2d 1005 (8th Cir. 1984); Crawford v. Pittman, 708 F.2d 1028 (5th Cir. 1983); Georgia Assn. of Retarded Citizens v. McDaniel, 511 F. Supp. 1263 (N.D. Ga. 1981); (requiring extended school year). See also Abrahamson v. Hershman, 701 F.2d 233 (1st Cir. 1983) (round-the-clock training for child with severe retardation).

110. Rettig v. Kansas City School Dist., 720 F.2d at pp. 466–7.

111. *Re IDEA:* Brookhart v. Ill. State Board of Educ., 697 F.2d 179, 1983 (7th Cir. 1983); Board of Educ. v. Ambach, 458 N.Y.S.2d 680, 684–5 (1982).

    Re Section 504: Southeastern Comm. College v. Davis, 442 U.S. 397, 411–2 (1979).

112. Ojai Unified School Dist. v. Jackson, 4 F.3d 1467 (9th Cir. 1994) (blind student housing 80 miles from parents' residence, held a reimburseable related-service expense).

    Facilities modification for transportation: Dubois v. Connecticut State Board of Educ., 727 F.2d 44 (2nd Cir. 1984); Hurry v. Jones, 734 F.2d 829 (1st Cir. 1984); Hawaii Dept. of Educ. v. Kathryn D., 727 F.2d 809 (9th Cir. 1983).

113. Zobrest v. Catalina Foothills School Dist., 509 U.S. 1 (1993). See also Woolcott v. State Board of Educ., 351 N.W.2d 601 (Mich. 1984).

114. Florence County School Dist. v. Carter, 114 S. Ct. 361 (1993); Tice v. Botetourt County School Board, 908 F.2d 1200 (4th Cir. 1990). *Within the district:* Barnett v. Fairfax County School Board, 927 F.2d 146 (4th Cir. 1991).

    Outside the district: Union School Dist. v. Smith, 15 F.3d 1519 (9th Cir. 1994) (placement at private counseling clinic—upheld); Jackson, *supra* note 112.

115. School Committee, Twn. of Burlington v. Dept. of Educ., 4671 U.S. 359 (1985); Florence County School Dist. v. Carter, 114 S. Ct. 361 (1993); Muller v. Comm'ee on Special Educ., 145 F.3d 95 (2d Cir. 1998); Matthew J. v. Massachusetts Dept. of Educ., 989 F. Supp. 380 (D. Ma. 1998).

116. Burlington, *supra* note 115; Anderson v. Thompson, 658 F.2d at pp. 1213–4 (emergency change of placement); Christopher N. v. McDaniel, 569 F. Supp., at p. 294. *Compare:* Marvin H. v. Austin Indep. School Dist., 714 F.2d 1348, 1356 (5th Cir. 1983) and authorities cited there; William S. v. Gill, 572 F. Supp. 509, 516 (N.D. Ill. 1983); Doe v. Anrig, 728 F.2d 30 (1st Cir. 1984).

117. Hartmann v. Loudoun County Board of Educ., 118 F.3d 996 (4th Cir. 1997).

118. The different tests adopted by the Third, Fifth and Eleventh Circuits on one hand, and the Fourth, Sixth, and Eighth Circuits on the other, are explained in Sacramento City Unified

School Dist. v. Rachel H., 14 F.3d 1398, 1403–4 (9th Cir. 1994). Where appropriate, a court may require only part-time mainstreaming to meet particular child's needs. Springdale School Dist. v. Grace, 693 F.2d 41, 43 (8th Cir. 1982).

Compare, e.g., Pinkerton v. Moye, 509 F. Supp. 107, 112–4 (W.D. Pa. 1981), *with* Espino v. Besteiro, 520 F. Supp. 905 (S.D. Tex. 1981) [*rev'd* on unrelated grounds, 708 F.2d 1002 (5th Cir. 1983)], where the court required classroom placement, even though it would require air conditioning the entire classroom.

119. The Second, Fifth, Seventh, Eighth, and Ninth Circuit Courts of Appeal held that special education services are not required at private school sites if they are made available elsewhere. KDM v. Reedsport School Dist., 196 F.3d 1046 (9th Cir. 1999); K.R. by M.R. v. Anderson Community School Corp., 125 F.3d 1017 (7th Cir. 1997); Russman v. City of Watervliet, 150 F.3d 219 (2d Cir. 1998); Cefalu v. E. Baton Rouge Parish School Board, 117 F.3d 231 (5th Cir. 1997). The Eighth Circuit held that the 1977 amendments gave no individual right to related services at a private site, but only proportional funding for the same class of students. The Tenth Circuit held that such services are required, but that the district need only pay the average cost of such service in a public school setting. Fowler v. Unified School Dist., 128 F.3d 1431 (10th Cir. 1997); Peter v. Wedl, 155 F.3d 992 (8th Cir. 1998). The Sixth Circuit upheld provision of special services to a child with a disability at a private school. Peck v. Lansing School Dist., 148 F.3d 619 (6th Cir. 1998). *See also* Morton Comm. Unit School Dist., 152 F.3d 583 (7th Cir. 1998).

120. S-1 v. Turlington, 635 F.2d 342, 347 (5th Cir. 1981); Thomas v. Davison Academy, 846

F. Supp. 611 (M.D. Tenn. 1994) (reversing expulsion for conduct attributable to handicap); Kaelin v. Grubbs, 682 F.2d 595 (6th Cir. 1982), and cases cited there.

121. 20 U.S.C. § 1415(k). Under the prior law, the Supreme Court held that a suspension of more than 10 days constituted a change in placement subject to "stay put," and other statutory due process procedures. Honig v. Doe, 484 U.S. 305 (1988).

122. 20 U.S.C. § 1412(a).

123. Charlie F. v. Board of Educ. of Skokie School Dist. 68, 98 F.3d 989 (7th Cir. 1996); Garro v. State of Conn., 23 F.3d 734, 737 (2d Cir. 1994).

124. Meehan v. Pachogue-Medford School, 25 F. Supp. 2d 129 (E.D.N.Y. 1998) (thwarting delays); Gadsden City Board of Educ. v. B.P., 3 F. Supp. 2d 1299 (N.D. Ala. 1998) (school safety); Weil v. Board of Elementary & Secondary Educ., 931 F.2d 1069 (5th Cir. 1991) (statutory procedures tolled as futile where district lacked necessary placement facility).

125. *See, e.g.,* Fowler v. Unified School Dist., 128 F.3d 1431 (10th Cir. 1997).

126. Fay v. S. Colonie Cent. School Dist., 802 F.2d 21 (2d Cir. 1986), ruled that federal courts deciding FERPA issues should follow state court decisions under state law. *Accord:* P. Edward A. v. Williams, 696 F. Supp. 1432 (C.D. Utah 1988).

127. Strosnider v. Strosnider, 686 P.2d 981 (Ariz. 1984). *See generally* Annot., *Non-custodial Parent Rights re Education of Child,* 36 A.L.R. 3d 1093 (1971) and latest pkt.

128. Leahy v. Leahy, 858 S.W.2d 221, 226 (Mo. 1993); Von Tersch v. Von Tersch, 455 N.W.2d 130 (Neb. 1990); Connelly v. Connelly, 409 So.2d 175 (Fl. App. 1982).

The Pyramid of Discrimination Remedies

B. Specific Statute Remedies
    1. Title VII Remedies
    2. ADA and Rehabilitation Act Remedies
    3. Age Discrimination Remedies
    4. Titles VI and IX Remedies
    5. IDEA Remedies
    6. Attorneys Fees Awards
C. State Statutes

❖ CHAPTER DISCUSSION QUESTIONS

❖ CASES

8.1 Missouri v. Jenkins, 515 U.S. 70 (1995)
8.2 Davis v. Monroe County Board of Education, 119 S. Ct. 1661 (1999)[†]
8.3 Debra P. by Irene P. v. Turlington, 730 F.2d 1405 (11th Cir. 1984)
8.4 Doe v. Board of Educ. of Cons. School Dist. 230, 18 F. Supp. 2d 954 (N.D. Ill. 1998)
8.5 Hasenfus v. LaJeunesse, 175 F.3d 68 (1st Cir. 1999)[†]
8.6 Walker v. District of Columbia, 969 F. Supp. 794 (D. D.C. 1997)

❖ APPENDIX

Federal Antidiscrimination Statutes

❖ ENDNOTES

[†]Indicates cases with review questions.

BACKGROUND NOTE

This chapter deals principally with major federal laws that cover various fronts of discrimination, unlike the discussion in Chapters 5 and 6, which deal with discrimination against employees only. Many of the laws reviewed here created a new species of federal liability: Their elements of liability differ markedly from the traditional state tort laws reviewed in Chapter 4.

The array of discrimination laws grew incrementally in response to isolated political movements and experience. That fact explains why each law created different grounds of liability and different remedies, and why each law requires separate study. Congress has not enacted legislation to harmonize the interaction of these laws with the result that one set of events often gives rise to alternative or multiple claims under different statutes and under the Constitution.

The chapter also discusses the operation of these laws with respect to specific subjects of discrimination. The last part discusses the allowed remedies when more than one law covers the same conduct, that is, whether recovery is allowed under only one statute, or whether alternative or cumulative recoveries may be allowed for separate claims under overlapping statutes.[1]

SUBJECTS OF SPECIAL REMEDIES

Racial and Ethnic Discrimination

Constitutional Protections

The Equal Protection Clause of the Fourteenth Amendment prohibits the states and their agencies, including school districts, from denying the equal protection of the law to any person. The Fourteenth Amendment applies only to government (called *de jure)* discrimination, whether by enactment of discriminatory laws or by official conduct. The Fourteenth Amendment does *not* apply to private (*de facto*) discrimination. As seen later, this *de jure–de facto* distinction defines constitutionally remediable racial segregation on one hand, and constitutionally nonremediable societally caused segregation on the other. The distinction also sets limits on permissible affirmative action programs.

De jure discrimination arises in two ways, by *legal classifications* and by *discriminatory treatment.* Laws, regulations, or official directives that classify rights and obligations according to racial or ethnic traits are presumptively unconstitutional and void. The government authority must establish that a suspect trait classification is necessary to meet a *compelling state interest* to overcome that presumption—a burden that is almost impossible to meet. *Intentional* discriminatory treatment is equally unconstitutional even where the laws themselves are racially neutral.

The Supreme Court observed that all laws classify and, to that extent, differentiate (sic discriminate) the rights and obligations of different societal groups:

> The . . . promise that no person shall be denied the equal protection of the laws must coexist with the practical necessity that most legislation classifies . . . with resulting disadvantages to various groups of persons. . . . We have attempted to reconcile the principle with the reality by stating that, if a law neither burdens a fundamental right nor targets a *suspect* class, we will uphold the legislative classification so long as it bears a rational relation to some legitimate end. [*Romer v. Evans*, 116 S. Ct. 1620 (1996)] (Emphasis added)

The Court's distinction between *suspect* and *nonsuspect* classification thus becomes critical because *suspect* classifications are presumptively unconstitutional while nonsuspect classifications are presumptively constitutional, with the burden of proof on the challenger to show that a *nonsuspect* classification has no rational basis.

In outlawing official racial segregation of public schools, *Brown v. Board of Education*[2] established that race is a suspect classification. Racial segregation of students and staff within particular schools is also unconstitutional.[3] The participation of government officials, as administrators of a private trust that contains racially restrictive provisions, is also unconstitutional and unenforceable.[4] The constitutional ban against racial classifications and racially discriminatory treatment applies to all races so that Caucasians may obtain court relief against race-based laws or conduct that disfavor them,[5] such as the displacement of white employees to make way for new or less senior minority race employees.[6]

Interdistrict Segregation.   Severe disparities between the racial makeup of students in adjoining urban and suburban school districts do not, alone, prove government intent to segregate those schools. Parties seeking to void interdistrict racial imbalances on constitutional grounds must prove that the interdistrict racial difference was caused by official action rather than by *de facto* population shifts.

> . . . Before the boundaries of separate . . . school districts may be set aside . . . for remedial purposes . . . it must first be shown that there has been a constitutional violation within one district that produces a significant segregative effect in another district. Specifically it must be shown that racially discriminatory acts of the state or local school districts, or of a single school district have been a substantial cause of inter-district segregation. [*Milliken v. Bradley*, 418 U.S. 717 (1974)]

When a court found official causation of interdistrict segregation and ordered cross-boundary desegregation, the Supreme Court let the decision stand by declining to take it or appeal.[7]

Discrimination by Conduct. Discriminatory *treatment* that is motivated by racial hostility or segregative intent is unconstitutional. Administrative selection of school sites, attendance zones, or school transfer plans that are intended to foster racial separation are therefore unconstitutional.[8] But unlike the case of disfavoring *laws*, the alleged victim of discriminatory conduct must prove that the discriminatory treatment was *intentional*.[9] Discriminatory purpose may be inferred from the totality of the relevant facts, but the courts have not agreed on how unusual or severe disproportionate racial treatment must be to support an inference of discriminatory intent. This is particularly true with reference to statistical evidence.[10]

> Our cases have not embraced the proposition that a law or other official act . . . is unconstitutional *solely* because it has racially disproportionate impact. [*School Dist. of Omaha v. United States*, 433 U.S. 667, at p. 668 (1977)]

Affirmative Action Remedies.   Courts use their equity powers to compel affirmative action to redress unconstitutional racial discrimination because the legal remedy of monetary compensation is inadequate to terminate or undo the injurious effects of *de jure* segregation.[11] Courts may thus employ, as a remedial tool, special race-based treatment for members of the injured racial group, including reassignment to nonsegregated schools, busing to non-neighborhood schools, compensatory education, and provision of educational resources or facilities that are needed to undo the adverse effects of past segregation.

> Just as the race of students and teachers must be considered in determining whether a constitutional violation has occurred, so also must race be considered in formulating a remedy. [*N.C. State Board of Educ. v. Swann*, 402 U.S. 43 (1971)]

Courts may revise or suspend their affirmative action orders to meet changing circumstances, and to prevent or permit school closures that affect desegregation efforts.[12] The *Jenkins* opinion at the end of this chapter illustrates the broad sweep of court equitable powers, and also their limits. The Supreme Court indicated three major limitations:

1. As in the above discussed interdistrict segregation cases, a court may not order remedies that go beyond the scope or bounds of a constitutional violation.
2. Courts must exercise their powers of discretion reasonably in fashioning desegregation remedies, and higher courts will reverse desegregation orders that are found to be arbitrary.
3. Court desegregation jurisdiction terminates when desegregation is achieved to the fullest practical extent.[13]

The Supreme Court further ruled that courts may terminate their oversight jurisdiction *in stages* though "unitary status" in all facets of school operations is not fully achieved.[14] Some courts have ceded back to school districts control over some school functions while retaining jurisdiction over other school functions.

Once desegregation jurisdiction terminates, it cannot be reasserted unless a new case establishes a new *de jure* violation.[15] A court may not order a previously desegregated school district to undo racial imbalances caused by subsequent *de facto* population shifts.[16]

Affirmative Action Issues.   Compensatory education programs that are not racially exclusive or preferential are constitutional though they incidentally benefit more children of a particular race.[17] Difficulties arise where affirmative action programs intended to redress *de facto* racial disadvantages employ fixed race-based set-asides or quotas. The Supreme Court has invalidated such programs as unconstitutional classifications in cases that involved medical school admission preferences, layoff preferences, and preferential access to municipal contracts.[18] In those cases, the Court rejected the claim that the programs served a "compelling state interest" that would justify those programs constitutionally.

In the public school setting, however, the "compelling state interest" argument continues to be pressed in the lower courts on the more specialized argument that the state's interest in achieving effective education by ensuring a racially diverse student body and teaching staff in public schools is a constitutional "compelling" interest. A number of lower courts rejected that argument in striking down public school policies of minority racial preference in admitting students to select elementary and high schools and in the allowance of student transfers from urban to suburban schools.[19] However, because the Supreme Court has not squarely considered whether the educational value of racial diversity in public school classes is sufficiently compelling to justify a racial classification, the federal courts remain divided on the constitutionality of such affirmative action programs:

> Relying largely on the Fifth Circuit Courts decision in *Hopwood v. Texas*, 78 F.3d 932 (5th Cir.) . . . the District Court concluded that remedying past wrongs by the governmental entity is the only compelling state interest to justify racial classifications. . . .

> However, notwithstanding the Fifth Circuit's holding . . . there is much disagreement among the circuit courts as to whether this is, in fact, the state of the law. . . . As the First Circuit has recently acknowledged, "[t]he question of precisely what interests government may legitimately invoke to justify race-based classifications is largely unsettled." *Wessman v. Gittens*, 160 F.3d 790, 795 (1st Cir. 1998). . . . The confusion stems from the absence of a clear majority of the Supreme Court on this issue. [*Brewer v. West Irondequoit Cent. School Dist.*, 212 F.3d 738, at p. 747 (2d Cir. 2000)]

Proponents of affirmative action continue to fashion new programs to test affirmative action limits under both the federal and state constitutions. For example, the use of racial criteria for admission to an experimental public school that was operated by a university as a research laboratory to improve urban education was recently upheld under the federal Constitution. The court found that the admission criteria were necessary to produce a proper laboratory environment for useful research, which served a valid state interest to improve education in urban schools.[20] The Supreme Court of Connecticut recently found that the racial and economic isolation of black students in Hartford public schools in relation to white students in adjoining suburbs deprived the urban students of a substantially equal educational opportunity in violation of the *state* constitution.[21]

Statutory Protections

The antidiscrimination statutes hereafter discussed are listed and described in the Appendix to this chapter for convenient reference. These laws fall into two historical groups, namely, the reconstruction statutes of the Civil War era (42 U.S.C. §§ 1981–1988) and the civil rights statutes of the modern era. Their coverage, remedies, procedures, and proof requirements differ from those derived from the Constitution.

The principal reconstruction era statute on race is known as *42 U.S.C. § 1981* and that of the modern era is known as *Title VI*. Section 1981 prohibits *purposeful* discrimination on account of race, whereas Title VI prohibits discrimination on account of race, color, or national origin, but only in federally aided programs. Title VI suit for alleged racial discrimination could not be brought against a city and city planning board whose activities were not a "program or activity" receiving federal funds.[22]

Like Title VII, which was reviewed in Chapter 5, Title VI permits an inference of discrimination from disproportionate racial disadvantages without proof of actual racial animus, which inference a defendant can rebut by showing a nondiscriminatory reason for its action.[23] Claims of discriminatory treatment in public schools often turn on particular case facts.[24] A school board's bypassing a white teacher candidate to appoint a black candidate was held not to be animated by bias because the appointee's racial identification with a predominantly black student body was deemed a legitimate consideration for the employment decision.[25] But other cases hold that the reassignment of white and Latino coaches to make way for a black candidate to coach a predominantly black team, and the appointment of a white teacher over a black candidate purportedly because the white teacher could better identify with a predominantly white student body were discriminatory in the circumstances of those cases.[26] Racial minority complaints objecting to school curriculum as discriminatory could be brought on constitutional grounds, but not under Title VI if the challenged programs were not federally aided.[27] Failure of school authorities to stop known ongoing racial ridicule, slurs, and epithets by many school students against African-Americans was held to be actionable discrimination under Title VI.[28]

Racial Disparities in Testing and Placement. Test requirements for school or course placements that result in greatly disparate failure or lower grades of identified racial or ethnic minorities, with consequent placement in racially dominant classes or in inferior educational programs, have been challenged on various grounds, namely, that the group disparate results evidence discriminatory treatment, that the tests are unfair because students were not provided adequate instruction and preparation to pass them, that the test content was culturally biased, or that the test indicators to measure student learning capacity are unsound. The *Debra P.* opinion at the end of this chapter illustrates the convergence of these issues in the context of competency tests for the award of a diploma. As that case illustrates, racially disparate results alone may not suffice to prove a constitutional or a statutory violation, and test validation or fairness can only be assessed in terms of specific test purposes, content, and background circumstances. There can be no single validating standard for tests that measure aptitude, educability, ability grouping, remedial deficiencies, and achievement for graduation. Indeed, as *Debra P.* held, a challenged test may be valid for some purposes and invalid for others.

The mixed decisions on ability grouping tests that result in racially disparate grading and placement[29] further confirm the importance of test purposes and circumstances to determine whether a challenged test denies equal protection, or due process, or amounts to discrimination under Title VI.

Similar issues underlie challenges to teacher testing and promotion, whether under Title VII (as reviewed in Chapter 5), or under Title VI or § 1981. In challenges to the California Basic Educational Skills Test (CBEST) for teacher certification, which produced racially disparate results, the court held that the disparate impact claim could be raised under Title VI as well as under Title VII.[30]

The remedies of Title VI and § 1981 are narrower than that of Title VII. Section 1981 remedies only *purposeful* racial discrimination, for instance, where a teacher is denied promotion because of her race or forced to relinquish her job by racially hostile treatment.[31]

Linguistically Disadvantaged Minorities. The use of standard English for school instruction or testing has not been disapproved as unconstitutional *solely* because of disparate impacts on students who lack good command of English, unless such adverse results are attributable to past unconstitutional discrimination.[32] More hopeful avenues for the linguistically disadvantaged are provided by federal and state statutes.[33] The Bilingual Education Act, the Equal Education Opportunities Act (EEOA), and Title VI provide federal fiscal incentives for affirmative programs to assist students who lack adequate language skills, regardless of their racial identity.[34] Under these statutes, claimants must establish that school authorities failed to take statutorily required action to overcome language learning barriers.[35] The federal laws allow states to determine what is "appropriate action" to remedy language barriers, but state standards may themselves be subject to challenge. In the only test case to reach the Supreme Court in this area, it held that denial of affirmative special English instruction to a large community of acutely disadvantaged Chinese-American students would violate Title VI as well as the law of California.

> . . . the [school] district must take affirmative steps to rectify the language defi-ciency in order to open its instructional program to these students. . . . Any abil-ity grouping or tracking system employed . . . to deal with the special language skill needs of . . . children must be designed to meet such language skill needs . . . and must not operate as an educational deadend or permanent track. [*Lau v. Nichols*, 414 U.S. 563, 568 (1974)]

The *Lau* opinion did not answer the critical question: How large must the num-ber of disadvantaged students be, or how severe must the linguistic deficiency be, to trigger a need for group affirmative action, as against the remedy of in-dividualized special language instruction for students with identified linguis-tic problems? Lower courts later indicated that the need for affirmative action will depend on several factors, such as the size of the needful student group, the degree of their linguistic handicaps, the utility of bilingual communication, and the availability of instructors with required language skills. Where the number of needful children was small, and the school district addressed their problems individually, some courts declined to order affirmative action pro-grams.[36] More recently, however, a Circuit Court construed *Lau* more broadly to indicate that Title VI bars English language policies that caused a disparate adverse impact on non-English speakers, in that case, adult applicants for a state driver's license.[37] The sparsity of cases on language remedies in the school context probably reflects the fact that schools continue to develop pro-grams to improve student facility in the English language, on their own initia-tive especially in districts with large numbers of students whose primary lan-guage is other than English.

Gender Discrimination

Constitutional Protections

Gender classifications are "quasi-suspect" and subject to heightened scru-tiny under the Equal Protection Clause.[38] The constitutional shadings between "strict" scrutiny for racial classification and "intermediate" heightened scrutiny for gender classifications are not significant for school administration purposes. School officials still have the burden of justifying a gender-based classification. The constitutional and statutory prohibitions against gender dis-crimination apply to either sex.[39]

The Supreme Court had not as of the end of its year 2000 session ruled di-rectly on the proper level of constitutional scrutiny for homosexual orientation. It did overturn a state initiative that prohibited a state and its subdivisions from treating homosexual orientation as a protected civil right, finding that the voided law failed the broader constitutional test in that the law did not ration-ally serve a legitimate government purpose.[40]

Statutory Protections

As discussed in Chapter 5, Title VII bars gender-based employment discrimination. Title IX of the Education Amendments of 1972 prohibits gender discrimination by school district recipients of federal aid against any beneficiary of the federally aided program. Like its Title VI twin on race, it does not subject *individuals* to liability for sexual discrimination.[41] Title IX discrimination may be shown by disparate gender impacts, subject to rebuttal proof of valid reasons for the challenged action. In the *Davis* case, to be discussed shortly, the Supreme Court held that Title IX gender discrimination includes sexual abuse and harassment committed by a member of the opposite or the same sex as the victim; by a supervisor; or by a peer (whether teacher on teacher or student on student); or against a homosexual (gay or lesbian) person.[42] As the Court there ruled, Title IX (and implicitly its Title VI twin on race) authorized an implied private right of action for discrimination victims to recover monetary damages beyond employment or educational injuries against an offending school district, a remedy not *directly* authorized by Title VII. On the other hand, the *Davis* decision adopted stricter liability standards for Title IX (and implicitly for Title VI) than those governing claims under other statutes, such as § 1983, which is reviewed later in this chapter.

Gender-Segregated Schools.   Official segregation by gender violates both the Constitution and Title IX,[43] but the cases left open the possibility that single-gender schools might be found constitutionally justified to achieve a compelling state purpose and to be nondiscriminatory in purpose or effect in special circumstances. As advocates of single-gender education continue to press for their use, especially in troubled coed urban schools, courts may yet develop exceptions to the general ban against single-gender public schools.

Disparate Gender Treatment.   Discrimination has been found where school programs, especially for sports, do not provide reasonably comparable programs, resources, or services for girls as for boys, or where schools fail reasonably to accommodate kindred interests and abilities of each gender group.[44] The perennial issue in such cases is whether dissimilar arrangements for each sex are reasonable or reasonably comparable rather than discriminatory.[45] Single-gender teams in contact sports are deemed lawful under Title IX regulations and under one line of cases, as a reasonable accommodation of physical and psychological differences between the sexes, and of different skills of each gender.[46] Some courts, however, have insisted that individual student capability should determine access to any school activity, regardless of the applicant's sex.[47] Title IX's implementing regulations also leave room for argument as to which school sports fit the category of contact sports.[48] A recent case held that a university that opted to allow a member of the opposite sex to try out for a single-gender team in a contact sport cannot under Title IX thereafter discriminate against the admitted tryout candidate.[49] Whether that view would extend to primary or secondary schools may be doubted.

In the uncertain borders of gender law, school authorities face a Catch-22 situation. If they create single-gender teams, someone may view that as a Title IX violation, but if they permit mixed male/female teams or competition, they run a risk that an injured student will sue under state tort law for negligent mismatching of student competitors. In jurisdictions whose courts require that "competent" girls (of sufficient strength and dexterity) be allowed to try out with boys for a contact sport team (football),[50] school authorities must trust to the good judgment of coaches plus a dash of good fortune.

Sexually disproportionate exclusion or failure of tested students in state scholarship examinations has been overturned under Title IX,[51] as has exclusion from school programs on the basis of pregnancy-related restrictions where those restrictions are not shown to be a reasonable means of protecting student health or safety.

More difficult gender discrimination issues are posed in cases where a pregnant student expelled from or denied admission to a national honor society claims a violation of her rights under Title IX, the federal constitutional or state constitutions and laws. In view of the high value placed on honor society membership as an aid to admittance to more prestigious colleges for which the competition is intense, these cases present lively, controversial issues.

Under Title IX, a threshold question is whether nomination to or membership in a national honor society, under rules set by that national organization but which are administered by the local high school, constitutes a program or educational benefit within the meaning and protection of Title IX. If not, Title IX does not apply. On the one hand, since the National Honor Society by its constitution and rules sets the prerequisites for admission, including a finding of good character and leadership qualities, student membership is arguably an extramural, rather than a school, award. On the other hand, the school's administration and authority to grant or withhold membership under national society rules may well be viewed as a school "program" covered by Title IX, even if the award itself is found not to be a school educational "benefit." The few cases in this area assume, without extensive discussion, that honor society claims are covered by Title IX.[52]

Where Title IX is considered to apply, courts must decide whether disqualification of an unmarried pregnant student for honor society membership constitutes gender discrimination under a theory of disparate impact or treatment of females since only they can become pregnant, or whether their disqualification is gender neutral because it is based, not on pregnancy, but on premarital sexual activity which led to the pregnancy, an activity that may defeat the requirement of good student character and leadership qualities. These claims thus turn essentially on questions of evidence and of *fact*, namely, whether the school authorities were motivated solely to address disqualifying sexual activity or to penalize the resulting pregnancy. For disparate treatment claims, as noted in previous discussions, the complaining student has the difficult burden of proving that the school authorities acted improperly either to penalize the pregnancy, or to disqualify females but not unmarried male candidates who were known by the selection committee to have engaged in pre-marital sex, and thus be similarly situated with pregnant students. The courts have divided in their assessment of the evidence presented by complainants and school defendants on these factual issues.[53]

Constitutional claims typically accompany Title IX claims in the honor society cases. A clear violation of equal protection rights occurs where school selection committees admit male students known to have engaged in premarital sex while excluding pregnant female students for premarital sexual conduct. But the claim that school authorities violate equal protection rights by failing to inquire into male premarital sexual conduct absent some indication or notice of such conduct is more questionable, notwithstanding the fact that pregnant students cannot escape notice of their sexual activity. Constitutional claims other than equal protection, i.e., of a right to reproductive autonomy or privacy and association have been notably unsuccessful, if only because student desire for national honor society membership does not itself implicate a fundamental constitutional right.

There always remains the possibility that state courts may find broader grounds for relief against exclusion of pregnant students from national honor societies under their state constitutions and gender discrimination laws.

Sexual Abuse and Harassment.   For the sake of brevity, the phrase "sexual abuse" is used here to include both physical abuse and nonphysical harassment. The major body of Title IX cases involves sexual abuse, mostly of female students. Student and teacher victims have sought concurrent relief under Title IX, under the Constitution (right to bodily security), and under state tort law, with teachers having possible recourse to Title VII where the abuse involved their employment.[54] The Supreme Court decision in the *Davis* case (Case 8.2 at the end of this chapter) reviews sex abuse cases and merits direct reading as part of this discussion. The elements of Title IX liability there promulgated may be summarized as follows:

1. Title IX only governs recipients of federal aid for gender discrimination in the federally aided program. For this reason, school districts, but not individual wrongdoers, are liable for Title IX violations.
2. Under Title IX, school districts are not subject to vicarious liability for the personal misconduct or negligent supervision of their employees, but only for injuries caused by the district's own official policies or customs.
3. School district policies or customs may be established inferentially by the district's *deliberate indifference to known acts* of sexual abuse *by someone whom the district has legal authority to control.* However, a supervisor's knowledge of sexual abuse can be treated as knowledge by the district for purposes of establishing a school policy based on "deliberate indifference" to known violations of federal rights, but supervisor negligence in hiring a sexual harasser has been held not to establish a "policy" for § 1983 purposes.[55]

4. To be liable under Title IX, the district's policy or custom must be found to *cause*, albeit indirectly, the victim to suffer the sexual abuse, and the sexual abuse must be sufficiently *severe, pervasive,* and *objectively offensive* to *bar the victim's access to an educational opportunity or benefit.*

Gender-related oppressive teasing or ridicule by employees that is not so severe as to result in a deprivation of educational opportunity or benefit is not a Title IX violation.[56] The *Davis* decision left several unanswered questions, which are noted in the review questions following that opinion. For example, would calling a student a prostitute in class, over a period of several weeks, be sufficiently severe and shocking to violate Title IX? One court thought not.[57]

Disability Discrimination

Despite a few unappealed trial court decisions, a trait of disability has not commanded heightened constitutional protection.[58] The special protections given to school employees with disabilities against employment discrimination are covered in Chapter 5. The special educational protections given to children with handicaps are discussed in Chapter 7. In addition to those specialized laws, other statutes provide broader protections to individuals with disabilities. Under these statutes, "disability" is more broadly defined to include any impairment that "substantially limits" a major life activity.

Title II of the Americans with Disabilities Act provides that an individual with a covered disability cannot be excluded from or denied the benefits of public services, programs, or activities by a public entity because of his or her disability. Similarly, the Rehabilitation Act of 1973 (§ 504) provides that an individual with a covered disability cannot be denied access to or the benefits of any federally assisted programs or facilities because of such disability. These laws remedy discrimination by public entities, including school districts, but do not reach or sanction individual actors, such as school teachers.[59] School decisions that deny benefits to a person with a disability for reasons other than their disability are not considered discriminatory under these laws.[60]

Title II and Section 504 authorize recovery of money compensatory damages for intentional discrimination.[61] Examples of disability discrimination include exclusion from school of an HIV-infected student (under § 504) where the student's condition did not pose a material threat to others,[62] and exclusion of a student from participation in a school choir or school play because of her severe depression (under Title II of the ADA).[63]

Alien Discrimination

Aliens are not a protected class under major antidiscrimination statutes, but alien status is a subject of some constitutional protection against discrimination. The degree of that protection depends on several factors, such as the age, immigration status (temporary, permanent, or illegal entrant), and nature of the denied benefit or opportunity that is alleged to be discriminatory.

Alien Children

Alien children who lawfully reside within a school district have a constitutional right to receive public education on equal terms with citizen students, even when they were illegally brought to the United States by their parents. In *Plyler v. Doe*,[64] the Supreme Court ruled that a school district could not constitutionally exclude alien children from public schools because of the parents' illegal entry, even though the parents could be denied government benefits. The narrow scope of that decision became clear when the Supreme Court later held that a school district could exclude an alien child who was sent by his Mexican parents to reside with a relative in the United States for the purpose of securing a free public education. The court explained that the school district did not discriminate in denying admission because it excluded any child who was not a bona fide resident of the district.[65]

Alien Teachers and Employees

The Supreme Court took a different stance on adults. For aliens *lawfully admitted* to the United States, noncitizenship, like race and gender, was held to be a suspect trait entitled to strict scrutiny against state discrimination in the provision of public benefits and employment, with one notable exception. For *public function* activities from, could constitutionally exclude noncitizens. The Court defined a "public function" as one that requires *citizen* participation and control in order to maintain democratic government, and held that public school teaching encompassed a "public function." It therefore concluded that states could constitutionally exclude aliens from employment as public school teachers.[66] Courts now have to decide which nonteaching school positions fall within or outside the public function exception in order to determine whether aliens may be constitutionally denied consideration for those positions. Such decisions are not readily predictable. The wide and varied spectrum of possible duties of ancillary school positions, such as teacher aides, librarians, school psychologists, counselors, nurses, therapists, or even truant officers, which will require case by case analysis.

Other Traits

Age

Age, like disability, is not a suspect trait entitled to heightened constitutional protection. Any rationally age-based school policy or decision would be constitutional.[67] The Age Discrimination in Employment Act (ADEA), which was discussed in Chapter 5, remains the principal statutory protection against age discrimination. Although the Eleventh Amendment renders states immune from suit under the ADEA,[68] that immunity, as explained in Chapter 5, does not cover school districts in the majority of states whose laws do not consider school districts to be covered by state sovereign immunity. As further noted in

Chapter 5 and in the following discussion of other federal civil rights statutes, the broader law of immunity under different federal statutes is too checkered and complex to ensure school district reliance on federal claims of immunity even in the small minority of states that do clothe their school districts with sovereign immunity.

Religion

The major *constitutional* protections for and against religious discrimination in public schools are covered in Chapters 3, 6, and 7. The major *statutory* protections against related religious discrimination are provided by Title VII, which is reviewed in Chapter 5.

Poverty

Like age and disability, poverty is not a constitutionally suspect trait, so that constitutional protection for poverty classes is limited to acts of *irrational* or *intentional* government discrimination.[69] The federal antidiscrimination laws do not target economic need conditions for special protections. More promising relief is afforded in those states whose constitutions are interpreted by their courts to require affirmative state actions to overcome educational barriers in poor school districts, but not in states whose courts refused to construe their state constitutions more liberally than the national Constitution. State-to-state variations and legislative developments in this important field of school finance are noted in the endnote.[70]

OVERLAPPING STATUTORY REMEDIES

Where discrimination statutes overlap to cover the same case, courts must decide which of the statutory remedies is to be allowed.

> We begin with the Supreme Court's recent reminder that we should not confuse the availability of a private right of action with the availability of various remedies. [*See W.B. v. Matula,* 67 F.3d 484, 494 (3d Cir. 1995)]

Equitable (sic injunctive) relief poses no problem, since courts may always grant such relief. However, as to availability of *legal* relief for monetary compensation under different statutes that prescribe different liability standards and measures of recovery, courts must determine how those statutes were intended to interact. Of course, courts will not allow double recovery for the same injury,[71] but they must first decide tricky questions that various Congresses did not trouble to anticipate or answer, namely, does the same conduct cause the same or separate, different injuries under different statutes; if different theoretical injuries arise under different statutes, is any part of the monetary remedy allowed under one statute subsumed by the allowance of similar monetary remedy under another statute[72]; and ultimately, did Congress intend a particular statute to govern particular grievances to the exclusion of all other statutes, i.e., to *preclude* application of other statutes? These are questions for legal experts, but awareness of them may help school administrators to recognize the need for expert counsel in multiple claim cases.

The following sections consider the problems of exclusive or alternative remedies. The first section describes the operation of the umbrella remedial statute known as § 1983, which redresses deprivation of *any* federal right under *any* federal law. The ensuing section considers whether or how relief under § 1983 enhances or is limited by the more specialized remedies of other statutes.

General § 1983 Remedies for Deprivation of Federal Rights

> Section 1983 . . . *does not create substantive rights.* . . . *It provides a remedy for the violation of rights created elsewhere.* . . . § 1983 *provides a remedy for actions* . . . *whether those rights derive from the Constitution or from a federal statute.* [*Day v. Wayne County Board of Auditors*, 749 F.2d 1199, 1202 (6th Cir. 1984)] (Emphasis added)

As seen in the cases reported at the end of this and other chapters, § 1983 is a favored source of civil rights litigation. But even this action may be precluded if Congress intended another substantive statute to provide the sole remedy for the same right violation.[73]

By its terms, § 1983 covers only deprivations caused by "state action," i.e., an act of the state or its subdivisions such as a school district. The following points stress the "limited action" of § 1983.

- Neither negligence nor vicarious liability amounts to a "deprivation" of federal rights. School districts can only be liable for deprivations *caused by* their own *policies* or *customs,* and not for the wrongs of their individual employees.[74]
- There is no *universal* federal right to school district protection against injury in all circumstances, however foreseeable that injury might have been.
- For an individual to be personally liable under § 1983 his or her actions must have been taken "under color of law." As hereafter explained, many wrongful acts of school employees are not clothed with "color of law."

School District Liability and Defenses

Although the states themselves have been held immune from liability under § 1983, state subdivisions such as school districts are not so immune and have been held liable for § 1983 violations.[75]

District liability and defenses under § 1983 are distinct from the personal liability and defenses of their supervisors and staff. Suits against board members in their capacity as board members are treated as suits against the school district "entity" and not against them personally.[76]

Official Policy or Custom Requirements.   A school district could only be liable for actions attributable to it by way of its own policy or custom, and only when such policy or custom provides a causative "affirmative link" to the right deprivation.[77] Official policy is readily found in school board resolutions, written regulations, and officially authorized decisions either by the school board or by someone who is legally empowered to make a *final* decision on behalf of the district.[78] School superiors may thus create an official policy for the district, but that authority does not attach automatically to all supervisors. To be a policymaker with reference to a specific decision, the actor must have been authorized to make that decision as a final decision for the school district.[79] An *unwritten* official policy may also be inferred from school practices that are so "well settled as to constitute a 'custom or usage' with the force of law."[80] The existence of an alleged policy or custom attributable to the district can only be decided on the basis of the facts of each case. These points are illustrated in the *Doe* case, which appears at the end of this chapter.

Under the foregoing limitations, a district cannot be held liable for a bus driver's assault of student passengers because the assault was not taken pursuant to an official policy or custom, and supervisor carelessness will not render a district liable.[81] Even where a supervisor negligently failed to carry out the district's security policy of screening school entrants for weapons, the use of that weapon was held not to be caused by the district policy, but by the negligence of those who failed to carry it out.[82]

Right to Protection Claims.   With the escalation of violence, sexual abuse, and student suicides in the schools, victims and their parents have pressed on the courts two new theories of a federal right to school protection. One is based on an alleged school special relationship to its students; the other is based on the contention that deliberate supervisor indifference to known dangers amounts to an official policy that causes federal rights deprivations. The first theory has been less productive than the second.

Special Relationship Duties.   The thesis that a special duty to protect their students creates a corresponding federal right to that protection originated in cases involving government confined prisoners and mental hospital inmates.[83] As of 2000, most courts had refused to extend those cases to public school children, including those who were sexually assaulted by their teachers and others.[84]

The *Hasenfus* case at the end of this chapter contains a thoughtful review of the special protection thesis in the context of a school's failure to protect a suicidal child. Although the court there declined to find a duty to protect in that case, it left open the possibility that a special relationship duty-to-protect might be found in special circumstances.[85] The weakness of the special relationship thesis was highlighted by another suicide decision that found no school district duty to protect a special education student who committed suicide at home after being suspended and driven home without parental notification.[86] The court did allow the parents to attempt to hold the school principal and counselor personally liable under § 1983 on a theory that their actions actively created the suicide danger. The student suicide cases under state tort law have no bearing on a deprivation of federal right claim under § 1983.

Deliberate Indifference Claims. Section 1983 claimants have had better success with the theory of deliberate indifference. The Supreme Court explained and approved that theory in the *Davis* case, which appears at the end of this chapter. Briefly stated, *deliberate* indifference by a government entity to *known* or reasonably discoverable threats of assaults at school or school-sponsored functions may support an inference of an official policy or custom that is a *causative* element of consequent assaults.[87] On the essential requirement of knowledge of the threat or pattern of abuse,[88] the question in many cases is whether official inaction constituted deliberate indifference or only negligence. As the court noted in another case alleging failure to screen out or properly train assaultive employees, negligence alone does not amount to deliberate indifference:

> Only where a municipality's failure to train its employees in a relevant respect evidences a "deliberate indifference" to [individual rights] can such a shortcoming be properly thought of as a city "policy or custom" that is actionable under § 1983. [*See City of Canton v. Harris,* 489 U.S. 378 (1989)]

The Eleventh Circuit held that the mother of a student who committed suicide at home after twice attempting to do so at school had a § 1983 cause of action for school deliberate indifference if she could prove that the district failed to address known suicidal dangers at its school, that it failed to train school personnel in suicide intervention/prevention, and that it failed to warn parents of known student suicide attempts.[89]

In sexual assault cases, recovery against a school district will require proof that school supervisors knew of sexual harassment and assault, and with deliberate indifference failed to protect the student victim.[90] In cases alleging deprivation of due process rights, a school district may escape § 1983 liability even for an admitted denial of due process if its omission was rendered harmless by equivalent substitute due process under state law.[91]

School District Immunity School districts are not accorded any form of governmental immunity from § 1983. Their immunity under state tort law cannot defeat the federal law claim.[92]

Individual Liability and Defenses

Unlike the policy or custom basis for school district liability, personal liability of school superiors, teachers, and other employees under § 1983 can only arise where they acted under "color of law," that is, where their actions were taken under authority conferred on them by state law through their school district.

Thus a bus driver would be personally liable under § 1983 for physical or sexual abuse of students during a school term,[93] but a teacher would not be liable under § 1983 for sexually molesting a student during summer recess.[94] Similarly, a teacher who failed to report child abuse by a teacher at another school lacked the "color of law" connection to activity at the other school.[95] These distinctions make it clear that § 1983 is not a full substitute for tort recovery under state tort law.

Individual Immunity   School superiors and employees are accorded a qualified immunity from § 1983 liability where they have no reason to know that their conduct interferes with a federal right, such as where the law establishing that right was not settled at the time of the alleged deprivation.[96]

> We therefore hold that government officials performing discretionary functions generally are shielded from liability for civil damages insofar as their conduct does not violate clearly established statutory or constitutional rights of which a reasonable person would have known. . . . Reliance on the objective reasonableness of an official's conduct, as measured by reference to clearly established law, should avoid excessive disruption of government. [*Harlow v. Fitzgerald*, 457 U.S. 800, 817–9 (1982)]

Under this objective standard, a person's subjective ignorance and innocent mistake are not grounds for qualified personal immunity. Only if the law establishing the asserted right was not clearly settled would qualified immunity be allowed.

Specific Statute Remedies

The still developing law on the interaction of federal remedial statutes leaves many still unanswered questions. The following notes sketch the current case trends.

Title VII Remedies

Where conduct concurrently violates Title VII rights and a *constitutional* right, Title VII does not preclude suit or recovery under § 1983 for deprivation of the constitutional right.[97] However, as to other claims for employment discrimination, a majority of federal circuits appear to agree that the Title VII remedies are exclusive and preclude alternative remedies for *employment injuries* under § 1983, or under Titles VI and IX.[98] In 1991 Congress expanded Title VII remedies to include monetary damages for *intentional* discrimination,[99] thereby narrowing its differences with § 1983 recovery.

While Title VII might affect the application of employee suits under Title VI or IX, it has no bearing on suits by students who are not employed by the district.

ADA and Rehabilitation Act Remedies

The Civil Rights Act of 1991 amended the Americans with Disabilities Act (ADA) and the Rehabilitation Act to authorize the same monetary remedies as are provided for Title VII violations. The same limitations above noted for Title VII were held to apply to ADA suits. One federal circuit also held that compensatory damages are not available under Title II of ADA and the Rehabilitation Act absent showing of discriminatory intent.[100]

Age Discrimination Remedies

The Age Discrimination in Employment Act (ADEA) tracks Title VII standards, so that the Title VII remedies limitations may also be adopted under this law to preclude alternative suits or recoveries under § 1983. A majority of the federal circuit courts that addressed this issue have held that the ADEA provides the exclusive remedy for age discrimination, but there is some conflict in a minority of other circuits.[101]

Titles VI and IX Remedies

Under the *Davis* case (presented at the end of this chapter), monetary damages may be recovered under Title IX for gender discrimination, such as student sexual abuse by a teacher. In so ruling the Supreme Court commented that a like private right of action would exist under Title VI for racial discrimination.[102] The Supreme Court did not there consider whether a right to sue under Title IX or Title VI would preclude suit under § 1983 for a deprivation of the constitutional right to bodily security. The lower courts are divided on this question.[103]

With reference to teacher claims under these titles, the preclusive effect of Title VII, which was noted in the prior section on Title VII, might apply as well to Titles VI or IX where the discrimination is employment related.

IDEA Remedies

As reported in the *Walker* case at the end of this chapter, the Handicapped Children's Protective Act of 1986 amended IDEA to provide that IDEA equitable remedies do *not* preclude private damage actions for IDEA violations. While some disagreements persist among the federal circuits, the position taken by the *Walker* court, that such damages may be sought under § 1983, reflects the position of a majority of federal circuits.[104]

Attorneys Fees Awards

Congress has by various laws authorized courts to award attorneys fees to prevailing parties in actions to vindicate federal rights, and to deny fee requests that they consider unjust.[105] The Supreme Court construed the major fee shifting statute as favoring the award of fees to a prevailing plaintiff, but not to prevailing defendants unless the plaintiff's suit were found to be "frivolous, unreasonable, and without foundation."[106] The distinction was made on its view that the purpose of fee shifting was to encourage victims to seek court redress, and not to deter *bona fide* claimants from bringing suit out of fear that they be liable for defendant's attorney fees if they failed.

State Statutes

State civil rights laws do not reflect any general pattern of coverage for different types of discrimination, or of remedies for state law violations.[107] The laws of each state must accordingly be consulted.

Chapter 8 Discussion Questions

Where the answer to a question may be qualified by special circumstances, explain the potential qualification.

1. Which of the following areas of discrimination receive heightened constitutional scrutiny: race, gender, disability, age, alien status?

2. What is the constitutional basis and limit of court powers to order schools to adopt "affirmative action" programs?

3. When may schools voluntarily adopt "affirmative action" racial or gender preferences for teacher appointments or student assignments under the Constitution? Under discrimination statutes?

4. When must a court surrender and terminate its jurisdiction over school desegregation? Explain.

5. In what circumstances will physical sexual abuse by a teacher of a student amount to a violation of the following?
   a. A constitutional right of bodily security
   b. A statutory right under Title IX

6. What laws allow a student victim of unconstitutional discrimination or unconstitutional invasion of bodily security to recover monetary damages against the following?
   a. The person who committed that wrong
   b. The school district of student attendance
   Explain.

7. Do students have any constitutional or statutory rights to be protected from their own suicidal tendencies? Explain.

8. How do the following laws differentiate between the liability of individuals and of school districts for discrimination violations?
   a. Title VII
   b. Titles VI and IX
   c. The Americans with Disabilities Act
   d. The Age Discrimination in Employment Act
   e. The Individuals with Disabilities Education Act

9. Is allowance of attorneys fees for a civil rights violation a matter of constitutional right? Statutory right? Discretion of the court? Explain.

10. How does "deliberate indifference" differ from negligence in civil rights law?

11. What is the meaning of "public function" positions in public school employment and how does that meaning affect the constitutional protection of noncitizen school employees?

12. Why do courts allow recovery of punitive damages under Section 1983 against individual defendants, but not against school district defendants?

❖ CASES

Case 8.1

MISSOURI v. JENKINS
515 U.S. 70 (1995)

> [**Focus Note.** *The limits of court authority to control desegregation and to order affirmative action remedies. The following opinion covers one of the longest, most intensive exercises of court segregation supervision of local and state school officials. The 5–4 division among the justices forecasts continuing controversy over the limits of court desegregation jurisdiction.]*

CHIEF JUSTICE REHNQUIST *delivered the opinion of the Court.*

. . . This case has been before the same United States District Judge since 1977. . . .

After a trial that lasted 7 1/2 months, the District Court determined that the State and the KCMSD [Kansas City, Missouri School District] . . . operated a segregated school system within the KCMSD. . . .

In June 1985, the District Court issued its first remedial order. . . . . . .

. . . First, the District Court ordered that the KCMSD be restored to an AAA classification. . . . . . . Second, it ordered that the number of students per class be reduced so that the student-to-teacher ratio was below the level required for AAA standing. . . . The District Court also ordered programs to expand educational opportunities for all KCMSD students: full-day kindergarten; expanded summer school; before- and after-school tutoring; and an early childhood development program. . . . Finally, the District Court implemented a state-funded "effective schools" program . . . .

. . . The total cost for these . . . programs has exceeded $220 million. . . .

❖ ❖ ❖

. . . In November 1986, the District Court approved a comprehensive magnet school and capital improvements plan. . . . . . . Under the . . . plan, every senior high school, every middle school, and one-half of the elementary schools were converted into magnet schools. . . .

In June 1985, the District Court ordered substantial capital improvements. . . . . . . In November 1986, the District Court approved further capital improvements . . . "to . . . attract non-minority students back to the KCMSD." . . .

In September 1987, the District Court adopted . . . KCMSD's long-range capital improvements plan. . . . . . . The plan called for the renovation of approximately 55 schools, the closure of 18 facilities, and the construction of 17 new schools. . . . The District Court rejected what it referred to as the "patch and repair" approach . . . because it "would not achieve suburban comparability. . . ." . . . As of 1990, the District Court had ordered $260 million in capital improvements. . . . Since then, the total cost of capital improvements ordered has soared to over $540 million.

. . . Since that time, however, the District Court has ordered salary assistance to all but three of the approximately 5,000 KCMSD employees. The total cost of this component . . . is over $200 million.

The District Court's desegregation plan has been described as the most ambitious and expensive remedial program in the history of school desegregation. . . . The annual cost per pupil . . . far exceeds that of . . . any school district in Missouri. Nevertheless, the KCMSD, which has pursued a "friendly adversary" relationship with the plaintiffs has continued to propose ever more expensive programs. . . . Not surprisingly, the cost . . . has "far exceeded KCMSD's budget, or its authority to tax." . . . The State . . . has borne the brunt of these costs. The District Court candidly has acknowledged that it has "allowed the District planners to dream" . . . .

❖ ❖ ❖

. . . [W]e granted certiorari to consider the following: (1) whether the District Court exceeded its constitutional authority when it granted salary increases to virtually all instructional and noninstructional employees of the KCMSD, and (2) whether the District Court properly relied upon the fact that student achievement test scores had failed to rise to some unspecified level when it declined to find that the State had achieved partial unitary status as to the quality education programs.

❖ ❖ ❖

. . . The ultimate inquiry is " 'whether the [constitutional violator] ha[s] complied in good faith with the desegregation decree since it was entered, and whether the vestiges of past discrimination ha[ve] been eliminated to the extent practicable.' " . . . (quoting *Dowell*, supra, 498 U.S., at 249–250. . . .)

❖ ❖ ❖

The State argues that the order approving salary increases . . . was crafted to serve an "interdistrict goal" . . . .

Here, the District Court has found . . . that this case involved no interdistrict constitutional violation that would support interdistrict relief. . . .

❖ ❖ ❖

The District Court's remedial plan . . . is not designed solely to redistribute the students within the KCMSD in order to eliminate racially identifiable schools. . . . Instead, its purpose is to attract nonminority students from outside the KCMSD schools. But this interdistrict goal is beyond the scope of the intradistrict violation. . . .

❖ ❖ ❖

. . . A district court seeking to remedy an intradistrict violation that has not "directly caused" significant interdistrict effects . . . exceeds its remedial authority if it orders a remedy with an interdistrict purpose. This conclusion follows directly from Milliken II. . . .

❖ ❖ ❖

. . . In this posture, we conclude that the District Court's order of salary increases . . . is simply too far removed from an acceptable implementation of a permissible means to remedy previous legally mandated segregation. . . .

Similar considerations lead us to conclude that the District Court's order requiring the State to continue to fund the quality education programs because student achievement levels were still "at or below national norms at many grade levels" cannot be sustained. . . .

❖ ❖ ❖

[JUSTICES STEVENS, SOUTER, GINSBURG, and BREYER dissented.]

Case 8.2

DAVIS v. MONROE COUNTY BOARD OF EDUCATION
119 S. Ct. 1661 (1999)

[***Focus Note.*** *Title IX remedies. Action by LaShonda, a fifth-grade student and her parent (Davis) against the county school board (Board) and school officials individually to recover monetary damages under Title IX for failing properly to protect her from sexual harassment by her classmate, G.F., over a period of five months. The lower courts held that Title IX did not provide a private cause of action for student-on-student sexual harassment. The Supreme Court reversed, and resolved several Title IX questions on which the lower courts were in disagreement.]*

JUSTICE O'CONNOR *delivered the opinion of the Court.*

. . . We consider here whether a private damage action may lie against the school board in cases of student-on-student harassment. We conclude that it may, but only where the funding recipient acts with deliberate indifference to known acts of harassment in its programs or activities. Moreover, we conclude that such an action will lie only for harassment that is so severe, pervasive, and objectively offensive that it effectively bars the victim's access to an educational opportunity or benefit.

❖ ❖ ❖

Petitioner's minor daughter, LaShonda, was allegedly the victim of a prolonged pattern of sexual harassment by one of her fifth-grade classmates at Hubbard Elementary School. . . . According to petitioner's complaint, the harassment began in December 1992, when the classmate, G.F., attempted to touch LaShonda's breasts and genital area and made vulgar statements. . . . . . . Similar conduct allegedly occurred on or about January 4 and January 20, 1993. . . . LaShonda reported each of these incidents to her mother and to her classroom teacher, Diane Fort. . . . Petitioner [parent], in turn, also contacted Fort, who allegedly assured petitioner that the school principal, Bill Querry, had been informed. . . . Petitioner contends that, notwithstanding these reports, no disciplinary action was taken against G.F. . . .

G.F.'s conduct allegedly continued for many months. . . .

❖ ❖ ❖

The string of incidents finally ended in mid-May, when G.F. was charged with, and pleaded guilty to, sexual battery for his misconduct. . . . The complaint alleges that LaShonda had suffered during the months of harassment . . . specifically, her previously high grades allegedly dropped . . . and, in April 1993, her father discovered that she had written a suicide note. . . . . . .

❖ ❖ ❖

There is no dispute here that the Board is a recipient of federal education funding for Title IX purposes. . . .

❖ ❖ ❖

. . . We must determine whether a district's failure to respond to student-on-student harassment in its schools can support a private suit for money damages. See *Gebser v. Lago Vista Independent School Dist.*, 524 U.S. 274, 283 . . . (1998). . . . This Court has indeed recognized an implied private right of action under Title IX . . . and we have held that money damages are available in such suits, *Franklin v. Gwinnett County Public Schools*, 503 U.S. 60 . . . (1992). . . .

. . . Respondents contend, specifically, that the statute only proscribes misconduct by grant recipients, not third parties. . . .

We agree . . . that a recipient of federal funds may be liable in damages under Title IX only for its own misconduct. . . .

We disagree . . . however, that petitioner seeks to hold the Board liable for G.F.'s actions instead of its own. . . . In *Gebser,* we concluded that a recipient of federal education funds may be liable in damages under Title IX where it is deliberately indifferent to known acts of sexual harassment by a teacher. . . .

Accordingly, we rejected the use of agency principles to impute liability to the district for the misconduct of its teachers. . . . Liability arose, rather, from "an official decision by the recipient not to remedy the violation." *Gebser v. Lago Vista Independent School Dist.*, supra, at 290. By employing the "deliberate indifference" theory . . . we concluded in *Gebser* that recipients could be liable in damages only where their own deliberate indifference effectively "cause[d]" the discrimination, 524 U.S., at 291. . . . . . .

❖ ❖ ❖

. . . Deliberate indifference makes sense as a theory of direct liability . . . only where the funding recipient has some control over the alleged harassment. . . .

. . . If a funding recipient does not engage in harassment directly, it may not be liable for damages unless its deliberate indifference "subject[s]" its students to harassment. That is, the deliberate indifference must, at a minimum, "cause [students] to undergo" harassment or "make them liable or vulnerable" to it. . . . Moreover, because the harassment must occur "under" "the operations of" a funding recipient . . . the harassment must take place in a context subject to the school district's control . . . .

. . . The dissent consistently mischaracterizes this standard to require funding recipients to "remedy" peer harassment . . . and to "ensur[e] that . . . students conform their conduct to" certain rules . . . Title IX imposes no such requirements. . . . [T]he recipient must merely respond to known peer harassment in a manner that is not clearly unreasonable. This is not a mere "reasonableness" standard, as the dissent assumes. . . . . . .

❖ ❖ ❖

. . . Courts, moreover, must bear in mind that schools are unlike the adult workplace and that children may regularly interact in a manner that would be unacceptable among adults. . . . Indeed, at least early on, students are still learning how to interact appropriately with their peers. It is thus understandable that . . . students often engage in insults, banter, teasing, shoving, pushing, and gender-specific conduct that is upsetting to the students subjected to it. Damages are not available for simple acts of teasing and name-calling among school children, however, even where these comments target differences in gender. Rather . . . damages are available only where the behavior is so severe, pervasive, and objectively offensive that it denies its victims the equal access to education that Title IX is designed to protect.

. . . [The dissent's] Comparisons to an "overweight child who skips gym class because the other children tease her about her size," the student "who refuses to wear glasses to avoid the taunts of 'four-eyes,' " and "the child who refuses to go to school because the school bully calls him a 'scaredy-cat' at recess," . . . are inapposite and misleading. Nor do we contemplate, much less hold, that a mere "decline in grades is enough to survive" a motion to dismiss. . . . The drop-off in LaShonda's grades provides necessary evidence of a potential link . . . but petitioner's ability to state a cognizable claim here depends equally on the alleged persistence and severity of G.F.'s actions. . . . We trust that the dissent's characterization of our opinion will not mislead courts to impose more sweeping liability than we read Title IX to require.

   . . . Although, in theory, a single instance of sufficiently severe one-on-one peer harassment could be said to have such an effect, we think it unlikely that Congress would have thought such behavior sufficient to rise to this level. . . .

❖ ❖ ❖

On this complaint, we cannot say "beyond doubt that [petitioner] can prove no set of facts in support of [her] claim which would entitle [her] to relief." . . . Accordingly, the judgment of the United States Court of Appeals for the Eleventh Circuit is reversed, and the case is remanded for further proceedings consistent with this opinion. . . .

Review Questions 8.2

1. Why were the involved teachers and supervisors not subject to liability under Title IX? Could they be liable under the § 1983 statute discussed later in the chapter?

2. How can a school board protect itself against false oral claims that it was notified or had knowledge of alleged sexual harassment? Would an official announcement of a policy requiring the filing of written harassment complaints with school personnel and a prompt official investigation of such complaints be useful? See the Title VII cases at the end of Chapter 5.

3. The Supreme Court limited Title IX liability "only for harassment that is so severe, pervasive, and objectively offensive that it effectively bars the victim's access to an educational opportunity or benefit." Can lower courts disagree in what kinds of student heckling is nonactionable banter rather than "severe," "objectively offensive" conduct that "effectively bars" access to educational opportunity? Can courts buck that question to a jury?

4. How would knowledge or ignorance of a victim's fragile condition affect the prior question?

Case 8.3

DEBRA P. BY IRENE P. v. TURLINGTON
730 F.2d 1405 (11th Cir. 1984)

> [**Focus Note.** High school graduation competency tests. Suit challenging Florida's Educational Accountability Act which required students to pass a competency test in order to receive the state high school diploma. The Eleventh Circuit Court of Appeals held that under conditions prevailing in 1984, the racially disproportionate impact of the competency test did not make it discriminatory and unlawful.]

R. LANIER ANDERSON III, CIRCUIT JUDGE.

❖ ❖ ❖

The district court held that use of the SSAT-II for diploma denials violated the due process and equal protection clauses, Title VI, and the EEOA. . . .

The court enjoined the test's use as a diploma sanction until the 1982–83 school year. . . . . . . The district court found that the SSAT-II's content was valid, which would allow the state to use it as a diploma sanction after 1982. The district court issued the four-year injunction for two reasons. First, the court found that the examination violated the equal protection clause, Title VI, and the EEOA by perpetuating past discrimination against black students who had attended segregated schools for the first four years of their education. . . . Second, the court held that the test's implementation schedule provided insufficient notice, in violation of the due process clause. . . . The court determined that . . . four to six years should intervene between announcement of the test and implementation of the diploma sanction. . . .

On appeal, the former Fifth Circuit Court of Appeals upheld the district court's injunction, but remanded for further findings on two issues. . . .

❖ ❖ ❖

On remand, the district court tried the two issues separately. . . . [O]n the first issue, the district court concluded that the state had met its burden of proving . . . that the competency examination is "instructionally valid," *i.e.*, a fair test of that which is taught in Florida's schools. . . .

. . . [O]n the second issue, the court found that although vestiges of past segregation still exist to some extent, and although the test still has a racially discriminatory impact, there is no causal link between the disproportionate failure rate of black students and those present effects of past segregation. . . . The court found, moreover, that even if there were a causal connection, the defendants had carried their burden of showing that the diploma sanction would remedy those effects. . . . The propriety of these findings forms the basis for this appeal. . . .

I. Instructional Validity

❖ ❖ ❖

B. Factual Findings

Appellants challenge on several grounds the district court's factual finding that students are afforded an adequate opportunity to learn the SSAT-II skills. . . .

1. The Focus on the 1981–82 School Year
The appellants object that the IOX study . . . is invalid because it evaluated only the 1981–82 school year. . . .

❖ ❖ ❖

To the extent that the IOX study relies on an inference that what was taught in 1981–82 was taught as far back as 1971, we acknowledge some concern . . . .

❖ ❖ ❖

On the other hand, there was a clearly reasonable inference that the instruction revealed in the 1981–82 survey was substantially the same as the post-Act instruction, *i.e.,* beginning in 1977. . . . There was evidence that "the bulk of the [SSAT-II] instruction occurs in the latter years" of a child's educational career, which in this case would be the years since 1977. . . .

❖ ❖ ❖

Florida's remedial efforts are extensive. . . . Students have five chances to pass the SSAT-II between 10th and 12th grades, and if they fail, they are offered remedial help. Students may also elect to remain in school for an additional year on a fulltime or parttime basis to receive, at the state's expense, "special instruction designed to remedy [their] identified deficiencies." . . . If they then pass the SSAT-II, they are awarded their diplomas. . . .

❖ ❖ ❖

The results of the student survey are also impressive. Ninety to ninety-nine percent of the students surveyed statewide said they had been taught the test skills. . . . Dr. Popham found this "very powerful evidence" of instructional validity. . . .

The remedial efforts and the student survey . . . persuade us that there was adequate evidence to support the district court's finding of instructional validity, notwithstanding our reservations . . . concerning the pre-1977 instruction. We are also persuaded . . . by the SSAT-II pass rate in the Class of 1983. After four of five test administrations, 99.84 percent of the class had passed the communications portion of the test and 97.23 percent had passed the math portion. . . .

❖ ❖ ❖

II. "Vestiges" of Past Discrimination

. . . Use of the test as a diploma sanction would be permissible only if the state satisfied the test set forth in *McNeal v. Tate County School District* . . . by demonstrating either (1) that the disproportionate failure of blacks was not caused by the present effects of past intentional segregation, or (2) that the use of the test as a diploma sanction would remedy those effects. . . .

. . . [T]he district court concluded that vestiges of past purposeful segregation still exist to some extent in Florida schools. . . . The court also noted the plaintiffs' evidence "that black students are still being suspended more often than white students . . . . that racial stereotypes still persist, and that blacks are being assigned to EMR [educable mentally retarded] classes more readily than whites." . . .

The court also noted the undisputed fact that the SSAT-II failure rate among black students is still disproportionately high. . . . However, the court found . . . that there is no causal link between the present effects of past school segregation and the disproportionate failure rate. . . . The district court found, moreover, that even if there were a causal connection, the state had proven that the test will help remedy those effects. . . .

A. The Finding of No Causal Link

The district court based its finding . . . partly on the testimony of Dr. Barbara Lerner, an expert witness for the state. . . .

❖ ❖ ❖

We think that this was sufficient evidence upon which to base a finding that whatever vestiges of discrimination remain do not cause the disproportionate failure rate among black students. . . .

. . . The fact that ninety-one to ninety-nine percent of the black students nonetheless pass the SSAT-II is strong evidence that the vestiges do not cause blacks to fail the test.

❖ ❖ ❖

B. The Finding That the Diploma Sanction Remedies Vestiges

The district court also found that, even assuming there was a causal link between vestiges and disparate impact, the state had satisfied the second prong of the *McNeal* test by demonstrating that use of the SSAT-II as a diploma sanction would remedy the vestiges of past intentional segregation. . . .

❖ ❖ ❖

The remarkable improvement in the SSAT-II pass rate among black students over the last six years demonstrates that use of the SSAT-II as a diploma sanction will be effective in overcoming the effects of past segregation. Appellants argue that the improvement has nothing to do with diploma sanctions. . . . However, we think it likely that the threat of diploma sanction . . . contributed to the improved pass rate, and that actual use of the test . . . will be equally, if not more, effective in helping black students overcome discriminatory vestiges. . . .

✧ ✧ ✧

Conclusion

We affirm the district court's findings (1) that students were actually taught test skills, (2) that vestiges of past intentional segregation do not cause the SSAT-II's disproportionate impact on blacks, and (3) that use of the SSAT-II as a diploma sanction will help remedy the vestiges of past segregation. Therefore, the State of Florida may deny diplomas to students (beginning with the Class of 1983) who have not yet passed the SSAT-II.

Affirmed.

Case 8.4

DOE v. BOARD OF EDUC. OF CONS. SCHOOL DIST. 230
18 F. Supp. 2d 954 (N.D. Ill. 1998)

[**Focus Note.** *High school students sued school district and district administrators and teachers, alleging numerous violations of constitutional, statutory, and common law rights arising from teacher's sexual activity with them. The following opinion illustrates why so many such cases require a trial to determine whose version of teacher–student relationships is true.*]

Memorandum Opinion and Order

GETTLEMAN, DISTRICT JUDGE.

✧ ✧ ✧

Plaintiffs . . . have brought a six count . . . complaint against defendants Board of Education of Consolidated School District 230 ("District") and Arlene See, Daniel Romano, Patrick Vasquez, Charles Cummings, Lisa Otto, Cyndie Skroch and Dr. Timothy Brown. . . . The suit alleges that "while acting as [their] instructor, Vasquez engaged in sexual relations with plaintiffs who were minor students." . . .

✧ ✧ ✧

Facts

. . . [A]ll of the parties . . . agree that Vasquez, who was an Instructor for the Andrew High School Winter Guard and Marching Band ("Winter Guard"), had a sexual relationship with two of his students. . . . The first student, identified as Jane Doe I, was 16 in late April 1994 when the relationship began. That relationship ended June 3, 1995. Jane Doe I was a member of the Winter Guard throughout that time period. Jane Doe II was 15 in late October 1994 when her relationship with Vasquez began. That relationship ended in February 1996. Jane Doe II was also a member of the Winter Guard throughout that period. . . .

Vasquez was originally hired . . . in 1985. He was approximately 20 years old at that time. He continued in that position until 1990. He took the 1990 season off. . . . He was rehired in Fall 1991, apparently on defendant Romano's [Band Director] recommendation, and remained an instructor until February 14, 1996, when he was arrested as a result of his relationships with [plaintiffs] Jane Doe I and Jane Doe II.

It is also uncontested that plaintiffs, as well as Vasquez, worked hard at keeping the relationships secret. Indeed, neither plaintiff knew of the other's involvement with Vasquez. Nor, apparently, were they aware that between April 1993 through August 1994 Vasquez had a sexual relationship with Skroch, a teacher-supervisor of the Winter Guard. There is also nothing in the record to demonstrate that any of the individual board members had actual knowledge of the situation.

Discussion

Federal Claims

Count I

In Count I, brought pursuant to 42 U.S.C. § 1983, plaintiffs charge the individual defendants with having "promulgated and maintained policies which fostered sexual abuse of minor female high school students at Andrew High School by Vasquez. . . ." The doctrine of respondeat superior cannot be used to impose § 1983 liability on a supervisor for the conduct of a subordinate violating a plaintiff's constitutional rights. . . . "Personal involvement is a prerequisite for individual liability in a § 1983 action. Supervisors who are simply negligent in failing to detect and prevent subordinate misconduct are not personally involved. Rather, supervisors must know about the conduct and facilitate it . . . condone it, or turn a blind eye for fear of what they might see. They must in other words act either knowingly or with deliberate, reckless indifference." . . .

In the instant case, there is no evidence clearly demonstrating that any of the individual defendants had actual knowledge of the sexual relationships between plaintiffs and Vasquez. . . . Therefore, they can be liable only if there are facts to support an inference that they acted with deliberate, reckless indifference, i.e., that they turned a blind eye to the evidence before them.

The facts regarding what each of the individual defendants knew are hotly contested. . . . At most, the record reveals that: (1) the individual defendants were aware of rumors about Vasquez and plaintiffs . . . (2) defendants knew that plaintiffs were helping Vasquez chart Winter Guard programs at his house after school hours; (3) Skroch and Otto discussed their own personal, sexual and marital lives with Winter Guard members; and (4) Skroch was having sexual relations with Vasquez. There is also testimony from one plaintiff that Skroch was aware of the situation between Vasquez and plaintiffs. This testimony was denied by Skroch. In addition, all of the individual defendants knew that Vasquez had married a former student shortly after her graduation.

Although there is no direct evidence establishing that any of the individual defendants had actual knowledge of Vasquez's relationships with plaintiffs, the evidence set forth above, if true, could lead a reasonable jury to conclude that some or all of the individual defendants had enough knowledge to suspect some improper activity and did nothing about it. Because the extent of that knowledge is in dispute and material to any claim that "they turned a blind eye" to Vasquez's abuse of plaintiffs, summary judgment for either party on Count I is inappropriate and denied.

The individual defendants also argue that they are entitled to the defense of qualified immunity. Under this defense, "government officials performing discretionary functions are shielded from liability for civil damages in so far as their conduct does not violate clearly established statutory or constitutional rights of which a reasonable person would have known." *Harlow v. Fitzgerald*, 457 U.S. 800, 818 . . . (1982). . . .

There is no dispute that plaintiffs had a clearly established constitutional right to be free from Vasquez's sexual abuse. Defendants argue, however, that under existing case law . . . they can be liable . . . only if they had actual notice of Vasquez's unconstitutional acts and then demonstrated deliberate indifference to those acts. . . . At that time, several courts had held that an official's failure to act upon rumors does not constitute deliberate indifference. . . . Other courts had held that an official's failure to act, by itself, does not show condonation, encouragement, approval, or authorization of a subordinate's conduct. . . . Therefore, defendants argue that . . . no reasonable school official in their positions would have understood that he or she would be violating plaintiff's constitutional rights. . . .

As noted above, however, the record regarding what each individual defendant knew about plaintiffs' relationships with Vasquez, and when he/she knew it, is replete with disputed facts. . . . [T]he court is persuaded that there is enough evidence in the record for a reasonable jury to decide that some or all of the individual defendants were aware of or "turned a blind eye" to Vasquez's unconstitutional conduct. . . . Because a material question of fact remains in dispute, defendants are not entitled to summary judgment . . . based on the defense of qualified immunity.

Count II

In Count II, plaintiffs allege that the District violated § 1983 by acquiescing and/or ratifying the actions or inactions of the individual defendants, resulting in policies, customs and/or practices that facilitated Vasquez's abuse of plaintiffs. . . .

In their memorandum, plaintiffs identify two specific policies of the District. . . . Those "policies" asserted by plaintiffs are the District's decisions to: (1) rehire and retain Vasquez after he married Amy, his former student; and (2) designate Otto and Skroch as Vasquez's supervisors.

❖ ❖ ❖

In the instant case, plaintiffs' claim against the District is based predominately on the District's decision to rehire Vasquez knowing that he had recently divorced his first wife and married Amy, a former Winter Guard member and recent graduate with whom he may have had physical contact while she was a student. Plaintiffs . . . argue that this single decision by the District constitutes a policy. . . .

Recently, in *Board of County Commissioners of Bryan County, Okl. v. Brown*, 520 U.S. 397 . . . (1997), the Supreme Court examined the issue of whether a municipality can be liable under § 1983 for a single hiring decision. In *Brown*, an arrestee brought a § 1983 action against the county, the county sheriff, and a reserve deputy seeking to recover for injuries sustained while being forcibly removed from an automobile after it was stopped. . . . The deputy, who was the son of the sheriff's nephew, had a record of driving infractions and had pleaded guilty to various driving-related and other misdemeanors including assault and battery, resisting arrest, and public drunkenness. The jury found in favor of the plaintiff, and the appellate court affirmed, based on the sheriff's decision to hire the deputy. The Supreme Court reversed, holding that the county was not liable for the sheriff's isolated decision to hire the deputy without adequate screening because the plaintiff had not demonstrated that the sheriff's decision reflected a "conscious disregard for a high risk that [the deputy] would use excessive force in violation of [the plaintiff's] federally protected right." 117 S. Ct. at 1394.

❖ ❖ ❖

. . . [T]he Court stated that although inadequate screening of an applicant's record may reflect indifference to an applicant's background, that is not the indifference relevant for purposes of a legal inquiry into municipal liability under § 1983. . . . The Court emphasized, id. at 1392 (emphasis added):

> A finding of culpability simply can not depend on the mere probability that any officer inadequately screened will inflict any constitutional injury. Rather it must depend on the finding that *this officer* was highly likely to inflict the *particular injury* suffered by the plaintiff. The connection between the background of the particular applicant and the specific constitutional violation alleged must be strong.

... [T]here is evidence in the record to suggest that the District decided to rehire Vasquez with some knowledge that he may have engaged in an extra-marital sexual relationship with a student (Amy). If plaintiffs can prove that to be true, Vasquez would have been violating Amy's constitutional rights. From that, a jury could conclude that a decision to ignore Vasquez's relationship with Amy would reflect more than just an indifference to Vasquez's record, but a deliberate indifference to plaintiffs constitutional rights, and that it was highly likely that Vasquez would do the same thing with other students that he had done with Amy. ... Accordingly, the District's motion for summary judgment on Count II is denied.

State Claims

In Counts III and IV, plaintiffs allege that *the District* willfully and wantonly hired and retained Vasquez in violation of Illinois common law and the Illinois School Code.... In Count VI, plaintiffs allege that the *individual defendants* willfully and wantonly failed to supervise Vasquez, and failed to report Vasquez's conduct in violation of the School Code and the Abused and Neglected Child Reporting Act.... Defendants have moved for summary judgment ... arguing that they are immune from liability under the Local Governmental Employees Tort Immunity Act....

Section 3-108(a) of the Tort Immunity Act provides:

> Except as otherwise provided by this Act ... neither a local public entity nor a public employee is liable for an injury caused by a failure to supervise an activity on or the use of any public property.

The section unambiguously grants immunity from liability that would otherwise arise from both negligent and willful and wanton conduct. ...

Plaintiffs argue that § 3-108 applies only to physical injuries occurring in the use of public property ... Plaintiffs are wrong. ... Accordingly, the court concludes that the section applies to plaintiffs' claims.

Section 2-201 of the Tort Immunity Act provides:

> ... [A] public employee serving in a position involving the determination of a policy or the exercise of discretion is not liable for an injury resulting from his act or omission in determining policy when acting in the exercise of such discretion even though abused.

Plaintiffs do not argue that the District's decision to hire Vasquez is not an exercise of discretion covered by the section. Instead, they argue that § 2-201 (and § 3-108) do not apply to allegations of willful and wanton conduct....

This argument was recently rejected by the Illinois Appellate Court in *Henrich v. Libertyville High School*, 289 Ill.App.3d 809 ... 683 N.E.2d 135 (2d Dist. 1997). ... Because the legislature did not express any exceptions to the immunity provided by § 3-108(a), the court refused to read one in. ...

Finally, plaintiffs argue that defendants' duty to report sexual abuse is a ministerial act, not a discretionary act covered by § 2-201. . . . It is undisputed that defendants are mandated by state law to report suspected sexual abuse. However, the reporter must first determine what constitutes "suspect sexual abuse" within the meaning of the reporting act, and whether such abuse likely occurred. Reaching such a conclusion clearly entails the exercise of a degree of judgment and discretion. Accordingly, the court concludes that § 2-201 applies to plaintiffs' claims based on failure to report under the Reporting Act.

Conclusion

For the reasons set forth above, plaintiffs' motion for partial summary judgment is denied. Defendants' motion for summary judgment is denied as to Counts I and II and granted as to Counts III, IV and VI.

Case 8.5

HASENFUS v. LAJEUNESSE
175 F.3d 68 (1st Cir. 1999)

*[**Focus Note.** Student suicide—right to protection. The parents of Jamie, a 14-year-old student, sued the town, the board of education, the district superintendent, the school principal, and her gym teacher, Carlo Kempton, following Jamie's attempted suicide, while alone in an unsupervised locker room to which she had been sent by Kempton, her gym teacher, following his reprimanding her for misconduct during a class on the school athletic field. She survived but suffered permanent physical impairments. The complaint alleged several state law tort claims, and federal law civil rights claims. The court dismissed the state tort claims under an order that permitted her to pursue them in state court. The following opinion on the federal law claim elaborates on several § 1983 requisites. Key phrases are shown here in italics.]*

BOUDIN, CIRCUIT JUDGE.

❖ ❖ ❖

The complaint describes two other incidents as background to the attempted suicide. One was that Jamie had been raped when she was 13 and later underwent the further trauma of testifying against the rapist. School officials were aware of the rape. Jamie had reported it to the school nurse, Jackie Kempton (wife of the gym teacher, Carlo Kempton), and was later counseled by the school nurse and school guidance counselor. According to the complaint, Carlo Kempton knew or should have known of the rape and should not have sent Jamie "alone and unsupervised away from the area he was monitoring when he knew or should reasonably have known that she was despondent or distressed."

The other background event was that seven other students in the Winthrop Middle School had also attempted suicide in the three months prior to May 1996. Several of those attempts had occurred at school or school events, and Jamie apparently knew or was associated with at least two of those students. . . .

. . . The counts with which we are centrally concerned were based upon section 1983; they charged that specific acts and omissions by defendants acting *under color of state law* deprived Jamie of her Fourteenth Amendment rights, including, inter alia, rights to life and physical safety. . . .

The gist of the wrongful acts . . . were the failure to take a range of preventive actions . . . to cope with the suicide epidemic and, specifically as to Jamie, three narrower failures or mistakes discussed at the end of this opinion. Carlo Kempton's alleged wrongful acts were reprimanding Jamie in front of her classmates and sending her alone to the locker room. . . .

. . . On review, we take the factual allegations of the complaint as true. . . .

The central question for us . . . is whether the conduct attributed to the defendants violates the federal Constitution so far as it protects against state action depriving one of life or liberty without "due process of law." . . .

❖ ❖ ❖

In the complaint, the principal conduct charged against the defendants—apart from Kempton—was their failure to take measures to cope with the rash of attempted suicides at the school. Under common law, inaction rarely gives rise to liability unless some special duty of care exists. . . . In *DeShaney v. Winnebago County*, 489 U.S. 189, 109 S. Ct. 998, 103 L.Ed.2d 249 (1989), the Supreme Court took the same view of substantive due process obligations, holding that *ordinarily a state's failure to intervene to prevent harm to an individual by a private actor is not a constitutional violation.*

The main exceptions to this proposition are incarcerated prisoners or involuntarily committed mental patients. . . . In such cases, failures to act . . . may comprise a due process or other constitutional violation because the state-imposed circumstance of confinement prevents such individuals from helping themselves. Liability then arises under section 1983 if the plaintiff shows that the inaction was malicious or reflected the official's "deliberate indifference" to the welfare of the prisoner or inmate. . . .

The plaintiffs urge that Jamie is similar to the prisoners and patients because school attendance is compulsory and because in some measure the school authorities act in loco parentis. The circuits that have confronted this issue have uniformly rejected this argument. . . . The Hasenfuses' position is especially difficult to accept outright since the Supreme Court has come pretty close to rejecting it in a recent dictum . . . :

[W]e do not, of course, suggest that public schools as a general matter have such a degree of control over children as to give rise to a constitutional "duty to protect." Vernonia Sch. Dist. v. Acton, 515 U.S. 646, 655 . . . (1995). See also Wyke, 129 F.3d at 569.

Nevertheless, we are loath to conclude . . . that inaction by a school toward a pupil could *never* give rise to a due process violation. From a common-sense vantage, *Jamie is not just like a prisoner in custody. . . . But neither is she just like the young child in DeShaney who was at home in his father's custody. . . .* For limited purposes and for a portion of the day, students are entrusted by their parents to control and supervision of teachers in situations where—at least as to very young children—they are manifestly unable to look after themselves.

Thus, *when Vernonia says that the schools do not "as a general matter" have a constitutional "duty to protect," perhaps in narrow circumstances there might be a "specific" duty.* If Jamie had suffered a heart attack in the classroom, and the teacher knew of her peril, could the teacher merely leave her there to die without summoning help? . . .

Yet *even if* we assume arguendo that in narrow circumstances *the Supreme Court might find a due process obligation of the school or school employees to render aid to a student in peril—*and Vernonia invites some caution—*it would require pungent facts. The basic due process constraint . . . where substance . . . is involved, is against behavior so extreme as to "shock the conscience." County of Sacramento v. Lewis,* 523 U.S. 833 . . . (1998). . . . . . . [T]his means conduct that is truly outrageous, uncivilized, and intolerable. *Lewis,* 118 S. Ct. at 1717.

. . . *The few circuit cases* that have found or posited possible liability under a shock-the-conscience rubric . . . have usually *involved egregious facts.* . . . The omissions charged against the school authorities here are not even close to violating this outrageousness standard.

❖ ❖ ❖

Attempted suicide by school-age children is no slight matter; but it has no single cause and no infallible solution. See Governor's Task Force on Adolescent Suicide & Self-Destructive Behaviors, Adolescent Suicide 42–61 (1996). . . . Possibly there was school negligence here . . . *but negligence is not a due process violation. Daniels v. Williams,* 474 U.S. 327, 332–33 (1986).

We turn now from the charge of inaction . . . to the claims against Carlo Kempton that do charge him with affirmative acts, specifically, the public reprimand of Jamie and her banishment to the unsupervised locker room. . . . Where a state official acts so as to create or even markedly increase a risk, due process constraints may exist. . . . But once again, the behavior must be conscience-shocking or outrageous. See *Lewis,* 118 S. Ct. at 1717–19.

❖ ❖ ❖

. . . [I]t is not alleged that Jamie threatened to kill herself then or at any other time known to Kempton. . . . . . . To say that Kempton acted maliciously to cause harm to Jamie, or otherwise acted in a way that should shock the conscience, is not a remotely plausible interpretation of the facts alleged. . . .

Only one circuit case cited to us has found a triable issue on anything remotely like these facts and its own facts were more aggravated. In *Armijo*, 159 F.3d 1253, school officials sent home a 16-year-old special education student for violent behavior at school. The student had earlier threatened to kill himself and, contrary to school policy, the officials did not notify his parents that he had been sent home, where the student had access to firearms—a fact school officials were alleged to have known. Alone at home, the student shot himself. His parents then sued, alleging inter alia a substantive due process claim, and the case went to the Tenth Circuit. . . .

The Tenth Circuit held that *DeShaney* barred any affirmative duty to protect based on a "custodial relationship" between student and school. *Armijo*, 159 F.3d at 1261–62. But the court also said liability might be based on the school's affirmative act—sending the student home alone—if it increased the danger to the child and also met the "shocks-the-conscience" test. . . . The court said that the latter test might be met if at trial the school officials were also shown to have known that the child in question had previously threatened suicide, was now distraught, was a special education pupil not fully able to care for himself, and had access at home to firearms. . . .

Whether or not one agrees with the Tenth Circuit that such behavior would be conscience-shocking . . . the assumed facts are at least very troubling . . . . If sound, the Tenth Circuit decision is at the outer limit, and does not come close to embracing Kempton's actions.

✧ ✧ ✧

In closing, we emphasize again that the due process clause is not a surrogate for local tort law or state statutory and administrative remedies. . . .

Review Questions 8.5

1. The hindsight determination of what is conscience-shocking conduct rests with judges and not juries. Could courts disagree in their hindsight review?

2. Had Jamie been sent to a lab or shop that contained dangerous material or equipment would that conduct be conscience shocking?

3. On the state tort claim that was referred to the state court, would the defendants face higher risks of an adverse negligence verdict?

Case 8.6

WALKER v. DISTRICT OF COLUMBIA
969 F. Supp. 794 (D. D.C. 1997)

[**Focus Note.** *IDEA and § 1983 remedies. Student and his guardian sued the District of Columbia and the superintendent of schools under the Individuals with Disabilities Education Act (IDEA), the Rehabilitation Act, and § 1983, alleging failure to provide special education. The court decided the following questions: (1) whether the IDEA authorizes recovery of damages beyond reimbursement for special education expenses; (2) whether § 1983 authorizes recovery of monetary damages for deprivation of IDEA rights; (3) whether the burden was on plaintiffs to establish that the school district had a custom or practice that was the moving force behind the alleged IDEA violations; (4) whether damages would be available under the Rehabilitation Act; and (5) whether in any allowance of damages, punitive damages were allowable against a school district.]*

PAUL L. FRIEDMAN, DISTRICT JUDGE.

Phillip Walker is a sixteen year-old student . . . who has been diagnosed as mildly mentally retarded. He complains that for many years he was not given the special education to which he was entitled under the Individuals with Disabilities Education Act ("IDEA"). . . . Specifically, he claims that he was misdiagnosed, that the statutorily-required due process hearings . . . were not held in a timely manner, that his educational evaluations were conducted improperly, and that he was deprived of services related to his special educational needs. On March 26, 1996, a Hearing Officer awarded Phillip a private placement at the Kennedy School and two years of compensatory education and ordered an occupational therapy evaluation and a neurological screening. Plaintiffs sought damages but the Hearing Officer concluded that he lacked authority to award them.

I. Background

❖ ❖ ❖

Defendants maintain (1) that damages are not available for violations of the IDEA; (2) that plaintiffs cannot bring a Section 1983 action based on IDEA violations; (3) that even if plaintiffs could bring a Section 1983 action, they have failed to state a claim because they have not alleged a custom or practice of IDEA violations; and (4) that plaintiffs have failed to state a claim under the Rehabilitation Act.

The Court concludes that damages are not available under the IDEA itself but that plaintiffs can bring a Section 1983 claim for damages to vindicate their rights under the IDEA. The Court further finds that plaintiffs have raised an allegation of a custom or practice of IDEA violations on the part of the District sufficient to survive defendants' motion to dismiss on that basis. Plaintiffs have also alleged a valid Rehabilitation Act claim. Whether the District of Columbia in fact has a custom or practice of failing to enforce the IDEA or whether the Rehabilitation Act was actually violated in this case are questions of fact not susceptible to summary judgment on this record. This case therefore shall be set for trial.

II. Discussion

A. The IDEA and Section 1983

❖ ❖ ❖

Where a school system fails to provide special education or related services, a student is entitled to compensatory education. See *Hall v. Knott County Board of Education,* 941 F.2d 402, 407 (6th Cir. 1991). . . . If a parent pays for educational placements or related services to which a child is later found to be entitled, the school system must reimburse the parent. *Town of Burlington School Committee v. Department of Education,* 471 U.S. 359, 369 (1985). Reimbursement is considered an equitable remedy, and compensatory damages beyond reimbursement are not provided for by the IDEA. . . . In sum, while Phillip can and has been awarded compensatory education, he cannot obtain money damages under the IDEA for the education that the District allegedly failed to provide.

Plaintiffs maintain, however, that they can obtain compensatory damages under 42 U.S.C. § 1983, as could any civil rights plaintiff. Defendants respond that a Section 1983 cause of action is unavailable because the IDEA establishes a comprehensive remedial scheme that precludes such an action. Defendants' argument, however, ignores the 1986 amendments to the IDEA . . . and the legislative history accompanying those amendments. See The Handicapped Children's Protection Act of 1986, . . . Section 1415(f) of the IDEA provides:

> Nothing in this chapter shall be construed to restrict or limit the rights, procedures, and remedies available under the Constitution, title V of the Rehabilitation Act of 1973, or other Federal statutes protecting the rights of children and youth with disabilities. . . . 20 U.S.C. § 1415(f).

Congress added this section to the IDEA in order to overturn the Supreme Court's decision in *Smith v. Robinson,* 468 U.S. 992 . . . (1984), in which the Court held that the IDEA precluded claims under the Rehabilitation Act and the Equal Protection Clause. . . . The Third Circuit has held that with Section 1415(f), Congress intended to permit Section 1983 actions to vindicate rights under the IDEA and that money damages may be awarded under Section 1983 for an IDEA violation. See *W.B. v. Matula,* 67 F.3d at 494–95. The Seventh Circuit also appears to assume . . . that damages are available in Section 1983 actions for IDEA violations. See *Charlie F. v. Bd. of Education of Skokie School District 68,* 98 F.3d 989, 991–93 (7th Cir. 1996). . . . See also *Doe v. Alfred,* 906 F. Supp. 1092, 1098–1100 (S.D. W.Va. 1995) (discussing the circuits' split over whether plaintiffs must exhaust their IDEA administrative remedies when filing a Section 1983 claim for damages). By contrast, the Sixth Circuit has held that damages are not available under Section 1983 because the IDEA does not provide for them directly, see *Crocker v. Tennessee Secondary Sch. Athletic Assoc.*, 980 F.2d 382, 386–87 (6th Cir. 1992), but the Sixth Circuit in Crocker did not address the legislative history of Section 1415(f). The D.C. Circuit has not addressed the issue of damages in a Section 1983 action brought for alleged violations of the IDEA. The Court is persuaded by the reasoning of the Third Circuit. The plain language of Section 1415(f) indicates that Congress intended to preserve all alternative civil rights remedies, including those available under Section 1983, to vindicate the rights created by the IDEA. . . . Accordingly, plaintiffs may maintain a Section 1983 action here.

As in any Section 1983 action . . . the burden is on the plaintiffs in this case to establish that the District of Columbia has a custom or practice that is the moving force behind the alleged IDEA violations. . . . . . . [P]laintiffs' submissions do not establish that the District of Columbia has or had such a custom or practice. Accordingly, plaintiffs' motion for partial summary judgment must be denied.

B. The Rehabilitation Act

Plaintiffs also allege a violation of Section 504 of the Rehabilitation Act. . . . In the context of children who receive benefits pursuant to the IDEA, the D.C. Circuit has noted that " 'in order to show a violation of the Rehabilitation Act, something more than a mere failure to provide the "free and appropriate education" required by the [IDEA] must be shown.' " . . . "[E]ither bad faith or gross misjudgment must be shown before a Section 504 violation can be made out. . . ." . . . Plaintiffs have alleged sufficient facts to raise a genuine dispute over whether District officials exercised gross misjudgment in Phillip's case, a dispute that can only be resolved at trial. . . .

✧ ✧ ✧

C. Punitive Damages

Plaintiffs also seek punitive damages but such damages are not available against the District as a matter of law. See *City of Newport v. Fact Concerts*, 453 U.S. 247 . . . (1981). . . . The claim for punitive damages therefore will be dismissed.

III. Conclusion

The Court concludes that if plaintiffs prove their case at trial compensatory damages are available under Section 1983 for violations of the IDEA. Damages are also available under Section 504 of the Rehabilitation Act if plaintiffs prove at trial that the District of Columbia demonstrated bad faith or gross misjudgment in exercising its responsibilities under the IDEA. Punitive damages are not available.

✧ ✧ ✧

APPENDIX
Federal Antidiscrimination Statutes

Part I—Summary List

Post–Civil War Statutes

Civil Rights Acts of 1866, 1870, 1871

Modern Era Statutes

Civil Rights Act of 1964
Education Amendments of 1972
Equal Pay Act of 1964
Age Discrimination in Employment Act
Equal Educational Opportunities Act
Rehabilitation Act of 1973
Individuals with Disabilities Education Act
Americans with Disabilities Act. (42 U.S.C. § 12143)
Civil Rights Restoration Act of 1991

Part II—Core Provisions

Reconstruction Era Statutes (42 U.S.C. §§ 1981–1988)

42 U.S.C. § 1981 *All persons* . . . shall have the same right . . . to the full and equal benefit of all laws and proceedings for the security of persons and property as is enjoyed by white citizens. . . .

42 U.S.C. § 1983 Every person who, under color of any [state law, regulation, custom or usage] . . . subjects . . . any . . . person . . . to the *deprivation of any rights* . . . *secured by the Constitution and laws,* shall be liable to the party injured. . . .

42 U.S.C. §§ 1985 and 1986 [provides in part that any persons conspiring to deprive "any person or class of persons of the *equal protection of the laws,* shall be liable to the party so injured. . . ."]

42 U.S.C. § 1988 authorizes recovery of attorney fees by a prevailing party in the following suits:

. . . In any . . . proceeding to enforce a provision of sections 1981, 1982, 1983, 1985, and 1986 of this title, title IX of Public Law 92-318, or Title VI of the Civil Rights Act of 1964, the court . . . may allow the prevailing party . . . *a reasonable attorney's fee as part of the costs.*

Modern Era Statutes

Equal Educational Opportunities Act (EEOA) (20 U.S.C. § 1703) prohibits denial of equal *educational opportunity* on account of *race, color, sex, or national origin.*

Title VI [Civil Rights Act of 1964; 42 U.S.C. § 2000(d)] prohibits discrimination on account of race, color, or national origin.

Title IX (Education Amendments of 1972, 42 U.S.C. § 1681) prohibits *sexual* discrimination.

Rehabilitation Act (Section 504) (29 U.S.C. § 794) prohibits discrimination solely by reason of handicap.

Individuals with Disabilities Education Act (IDEA) (20 U.S.C. § 1401) requires states to provide free appropriate public education to children with handicaps.

Title VII (42 U.S.C. § 2000(e) prohibits employment discrimination on account of *race, color, religion, sex, or national origin.*

Equal Pay Act (29 U.S.C. § 206(d)) prohibits wage discrimination on account of *sex.*

Americans with Disabilities Act (ADA) (42 U.S.C. § 12101) prohibits employment discrimination because of *disability.*

Age Discrimination in Employment Act (ADEA) (29 U.S.C. § 621) prohibits employment discrimination because of an individual's *age.*

ENDNOTES

1. *See, e.g.,* the reproduced opinions at the end of this chapter and Ridgewood Board of Educ. v. N.E. ex. El. M.E., 172 F.3d 238 (3rd Cir. 1999) wherein the courts had to adjudicate numberous separate claims under overlapping federal statutes.

2. Brown v. Board of Educ. I, 347 U.S. 483 (1954); Brown v. Board of Educ. II, 349 U.S. 294 (1955).

3. *Segregated teacher and staff assignments:* Bradley v. School Board, 382 U.S. 103 (1965); Rogers v. Paul, 382 U.S. 198 (1965).

4. Pennsylvania v. Board of Trusts, 353 U.S. 230 (1957).

5. Fairbairn v. Board of Educ., 876 F. Supp. 432 (E.D. N.Y. 1995).

6. Covington v. Beaumont School Dist., 714 F. Supp. 1402 (E.D. Tex. 1989) (displacement of white coaches to employ black coaches—held unconstitutional); Cunico v. Pueblo Pub. School Dist., 693 F. Supp. 954 (D. Colo. 1988) (retention of black administrator over senior white administrator—held unconstitutional). Seniority adjustments that do not cause loss of employment are not here covered. *See* Int'l. Brotherhood of Teamsters v. United States, 431 U.S. 324 (1977).

7. Evans v. Buchanan, 555 F.2d 373 (3d Cir. 1977), which the Supreme Court declined to review. Delaware State Board of Educ. v. Evans, 434 U.S. 880, 994 (1977).

8. *Discriminatory treatment:* Lee v. Washington County Board of Educ., 682 F.2d 894, 895 (11th Cir. 1982). *Segregative site selections:* Lee v. Autanga County Board of Educ., 514 F.2d 646 (5th Cir. 1975). *Segregated attendance zones:* Keyes v. School Dist. No. 1, Denver, 413 U.S. 189 (1973). *Segregative school choice plans:* Green v. County School Board, 391 U.S. 430 (1968).

9. Washington v. Davis, 426 U.S. 229 (1976); *cf.* Villanueva v. Carere, 85 F.3d 481 (10th Cir. 1996); Austin Indep. School Dist. v. United States, 429 U.S. 990 (1977).

10. *Cases accepting statistical evidence:* Johnson v. Transportation Agency, 480 U.S. 616 (1987) (Title VII claim); United States v. Midland Indep. School Dist., 519 F.2d 60 (5th Cir. 1975). *Cases*

finding statistics of disparate impact insufficient: Washington v. Davis, 426 U.S. 229 (1976) (constitutional claim).

11. "In fashioning . . . the decrees, the courts will be guided by equitable principles. Traditionally equity has been guided by a practical flexibility in shaping its remedies and by a facility for adjusting and reconciling public and private needs." Brown v. Board of Educ. (Brown II), 349 U.S. 294 (1955). *See also* Swan v. Charlotte-Mecklenberg Board of Educ., 402 U.S. 1 (1971).

12. *School closures enjoined:* Fisher v. Lohr, 821 F. Supp. 1342 (D. Ariz. 1993). *School closure permitted as assisting desegregation:* Higgins v. Grand Rapids Board of Educ., 508 F.2d 779, 793–5 (6th Cir. 1974).

13. Pasadena City Board of Educ. v. Spangler, 427 U.S. 424 (1976). "The District Court should address itself to whether the board had complied *in good faith* with the desegregation decree . . . and whether the vestiges of past discrimination had been eliminated *to the extent practicable. . . .* The . . . court should *look . . . to every facet of school operations—faculty,* staff, transportation, extracurricular activities and facilities. Board of Educ. of Okla. Pub. Schools v. Dowell, 498 S. Ct. 237, 249, 250 (1991) (Emphasis added)

14. Freeman v. Pitts, 112 S. Ct. 1430 (1992).

15. Board of Educ. of Okla. Pub. Schools v. Dowell, 111 S. Ct. 630 (1991).

16. Pasadena City Board of Educ. v. Spangler, 427 U.S. 424 (1976).

17. Anderson v. San Francisco Unified School Dist., 357 F. Supp. 248 (N.D. Cal. 1972); *cf.* Villanueva v. Carere, 85 F.3d 481 (10th Cir. 1996) (charter school for "at risk" students did not violate equal protection).

18. Regents, Univ. of California v. Bakke, 438 U.S. 912 (1978) (voiding fixed racial quota for medical school admissions); Wygant v. Jackson Board of Educ., 467 U.S. 267 (1986) (voiding minority retention preference in layoffs); Adarand Constructors, Inc. v. Pena, 115 S. Ct. 2097 (1995) (voiding fixed percentage quota of public contracts for African-American businesses).

19. Hopwood v. State of Texas, 78 F.3d 932 (5th Cir.), *cert denied,* 518 U.S. 1033 (1996); [Brewer v. W. Irondequoit Cent. School Dist., 32 F. Supp. 2d 619 (W.D. N.Y. 1999) (interdistrict transfers)]; *semble:* Equal Enrollment Assn. v. Board of Educ., 937 F. Supp. 700 (N.D. Ohio 1996); Tuttle v. Arlington County School Board, 189 F.3d 431 (4th Cir. 1999) (special admissions).

20. Hunter v. Regents of the Univ. of Calif., 190 F.3d 1061 (9th Cir. 1999).

21. Sheff v. O'Neill, 678 A.2d 1267 (Conn. 1996).

22. Hodges v. Public Bldg. Com'n of Chicago, 873 F. Supp. 128 (N.D. Ill. 1995).

23. Sandoval v. Hagan, 197 F.3d 484 (11th Cir. 1999).

24. *See also* Smith v. Board of Educ., 365 F.2d 770 (8th Cir. 1966) (compensatory action).

25. Council of Supervisory Assns. v. Board of Educ., 245 N.E.2d 204 (N.Y. 1969); Porcelli v. Titus, 431 F.2d 1254 (3d Cir. 1970). *Cf.* Morton v. Mancari, 417 U.S. 535 (1974) (employment preference of Native Americans in U.S. Bureau of Indian Affairs—held constitutional). *But see* Auerbach v. African-American Teachers Assn., 356 F. Supp. 1046 (E.D. N.Y. 1973).

26. Covington v. Beaumont School Dist., 714 F. Supp. 1402 (E.D. Tex. 1989) (black displacement of white and Latino coaches); NAACP v. Allen, 493 F.2d 614 (5th Cir. 1974) (white displacement of black teacher).

27. Grimes by and through Grimes v. Sobol, 832 F. Supp. 704 (S.D. N.Y. 1993).

28. Monteiro v. Tempe Union High School District, 158 F.3d 1022 (9th Cir. 1998).

29. *Tests upheld notwithstanding racially disproportionate results:* Quarles v. Oxford Mun. Separate School Dist., 868 F.2d 750 (5th Cir. 1989); Castaneda by Castaneda v. Pickard, 781 F.2d 456 (5th Cir. 1986); Morales v. Shannon, 516 F.2d 411 (5th Cir. 1975); Parents in Action in Special Educ. v. Hannon, 506 F. Supp. 831 (N.D. Ill. 1980).

  Tests voided as producing racially disproportionate results: Larry P. Riles, 793 F.2d 969 (9th Cir. 1984) (under Title VI and Rehabilitation Act).

  The required severity of adverse racial impact remains unresolved. *See* Morales v. Shannon, *supra* this note (statistical results held not sufficiently unusual to require court interference).

30. Association of Mexican-American Educators ("AMAE") v. State of Cal., 836 F. Supp. 1534 (N.D. Cal. 1993).

31. Fairbairn v. Board of Educ., 876 F. Supp. 432 (E.D. N.Y. 1995) (Title VII tests for employment discrimination apply under § 1981, Title IX, and the Disabilities Act); *cf.* Reynolds v. School Dist., 69 F.3d 1523 (10th Cir. 1995) (§ 1981 claim for racial discrimination in promotion, failed for lack of proof of intent to discriminate).

32. United States v. Texas, 466 F.2d. 519 (5th Cir. 1976).

33. Bilingual education laws were enacted in Alaska, Massachusetts, Michigan, Arizona, Arkansas, California, Colorado, Illinois, Iowa, Maine, New Mexico, New York, Oregon, Pennsylvania, Rhode Island, and Texas, among others.

34. Castaneda by Castaneda v. Pickard, 648 F.2d 989 (5th Cir. 1981); Aspira v. Board of Educ., 394 F. Supp. 1161 (S.D. N.Y. 1975) (consent decree); Serna v. Portales Mun. Schools, 499 F.2d 1147 (10th Cir. 1975) (under Title VI). Bilingual Educ. Act, as amended. 20 U.S.C. § 880(b).

35. Teresa P. v. Berkeley Unified School Dist., 724 F. Supp. 698 (N.D. Cal. 1989)

36. Otero v. Mesa County Valley School Dist., 408 F. Supp. 162 (D. Colo. 1975); Morales, *supra* note 29. Note, *Bilingual Education Problems—A Problem of Substantial Numbers,* 77 U. Fordham L. Rev. 561 (1977).

37. Sandoval v. Hagan, 197 F.3d 484 (11th Cir. 1999).

38. "The State must show 'at least that the [challenged] classification served 'important governmental objectives and that the discriminatory means employed' are 'substantially related to the achievement of those objectives.' . . . And it must not rely on overbroad generalizations about the different talents, capacities or preferences of males and females. . . . " *United States v. Virginia et al.,* 116 S. Ct. 2264, at p. 2275 (1996).

39. Grant v. Bullock County Board of Educ., 895 F. Supp. 1506 (M.D. Ala. 1995); Meritor Sav. Bank v. Vinson, 477 U.S. 57 (1986); United Teachers v. Board of Educ., 712 F.2d 1349 (9th Cir. 1983).

40. Romer v. Evans, 116 S. Ct. 1620 (1996).

41. Doe v. Beaumont I.S.D., 8 F. Supp. 2d 596 (E.D. Tex. 1998).

42. *See also* Kinman v. Omaha Public School Dist., 171 F.3d 607 (8th Cir. 1999); Murrell v. School Dist. No. 1, 186 F.3d 1238 (10th Cir. 1999); Haines v. Metropolitan Gov't of Davidson County, 32 F. Supp. 2d 991 (M.D. Tenn. 1998); H.M. v. Jefferson County Board of Educ., 719 So. 2d 793 (Ala. 1998).

43. United States v. Virginia, 116 S. Ct. 2264 (1996); Mississippi Univ. for Women v. Hogan, 458 U.S. 718 (1982); Garrett v. Board of Educ., 775 F. Supp. 1004 (E.D. Mich. 1991) (boys-only high school enjoined under Title IX).

44. Alston v. Va. High School League, 176 F.R.D. 220 (W.D. Va. 1997); Roberts v. Colo. State Board of Agric., 998 F.2d 824 (10th Cir. 1993); Hoover v. Meiklejohn, 430 F. Supp. 164 (Colo. 1977) (Soccer). Annot., *Application of State Law to Sex Discrimination in Sports*, 66 A.L.R. 3d 1262 (1975) and pkt part.

45. *Upheld:* Barnett v. Texas Wrestling Assn., 16 F. Supp. 2d 690 (N.S. Tex. 1998); Clark v. Ariz. Interscholastic Assn., 695 F.2d 1126 (9th Cir. 1989); Jones v. Okla. Secondary School Activities Assn., 424 F. Supp. 732 (D. Tenn. 1976).
    Disapproved: Noncomparable softball programs for girls and boys. Israel v. W. Va. Secondary Schools Activities Comm'n, 388 S.E.2d 480 (W. Va. 1989).

46. Kleczek v. Rhode Island Int. League, 768 F. Supp. 951 (D. R.I. 1991) (exclusion of male student from girls' field hockey team); Clark, *supra* note 45; Ruman v. Eskew, 343 N.E.2d 806 (Ind. 1976) (tennis); Bucha v. Ill. High School Assn., 351 F. Supp. 69 (N.D. Ill. 1972) (swimming).

47. Force v. Pierce City R-VI School Dist., 570 F. Supp. 1020 (W.D. Mo. 1983); Morris v. Michigan State Board of Educ., 472 F.2d 1207 (6th Cir. 1973) (tennis); Bednar v. Neb. School Activities Assn., 531 F.2d 922 (8th Cir. 1976); Gilpin v. Kansas State High School Activities Assn., 377 F. Supp. 1233 (D. Kan. 1973) (cross-country).

48. Petrie v. Ill. High School Assn., 394 N.E.2d 855 (Ill. 1985) (exclusion of boys from girls' volleyball team). *But see* Williams v. School Dist. of Bethlehem, 998 F.2d 168 (3d Cir. 1993) (remand for determination whether field hockey is a contact sport); Saint v. Neb. School Activities Assn., 684 F. Supp. 626 (D. Neb. 1988) (requiring girl tryout for boys' high school wrestling team). Note, *The Application of Title IX to School Athletic Programs*, 68 Cornell L. Rev. 222 (1983).
    One year after ruling that a high school must permit a girl to try out for the varsity football team, the New Jersey State Commissioner of Education ruled that a high school need not permit a boy to play on the girls' field hockey team. New York Times, May 22, 1986, at B7.

49. Mercer v. Duke Univ., 190 F.3d 643 (4th Cir. 1999).

50. Force v. Pierce City, *supra* note 47; Darrin v. Gould, 540 P.2d 882 (Wash. 1975) (state ERA ruling); Opinion of the Justices, 371 N.E.2d 426 (Mass. 1977) (state ERA ruling).

51. Sharif v. New York State Educ. Dept., 709 F. Supp. 345 (S.D. N.Y. 1989).

52. *See, e.g.*, Pfeiffer v. School Board for Marion Center Area, 917 F.3d 779, 783 (3d Cir. 1990). The pertinent cases and issues are reviewed in T. A. Schweitzer, *"A" Students Go to Court: Is Membership in the National Honor Society a Cognizable Legal Right?*, 50 Syracuse L. Rev. 63 (2000).

53. Compare, *e.g.*, Pfeiffer, *supra* note 52, at 784 (upholding disqualification) *with* cases reversing student disqualification: Wort v. Vierling, No. 82-3169, slip op. (C.D. Ill. Sept. 14, 1984), *aff'd* on other grounds, 778 F.2d 1233 (7th Cir. 1985); Chipman v. Grant County School Dist., 30 F. Supp. 2d 975 (E.D. Ky. 1998); Cazares v. Barber, Case No. CIV-90-0128-TUC-ACM, slip op. (D. Ariz. May 31, 1990).

54. Davis v. Monroe County Board of Educ., 119 S. Ct. 1661 (1999); Rosa H. v. San Elizario Ind. School Dist., 106 F.3d 648 (5th Cir. 1997); S.B.L. v. Evans, 80 F.3d 307 (8th Cir. 1996); Doe v. Petaluma City School Dist., 830 F. Supp. 1560 (N.D. Cal. 1993); Patricia H. v. Berkeley Unified School Dist., 830 F. Supp. 1288 (N.D. Cal. 1993). *See* G. Sorenson, *Peer Sexual Harassment: Remedies and Guidelines under Federal Law*, 92 E. Law Rep. 1 (1994).

55. Doe v. Beaumont I.S.D., 8 F. Supp. 2d 596 (E.D. Tex. 1998).

56. The Davis rulings were anticipated by some federal circuits. Murrell v. School Dist. No. 1, 186 F.3d 1239 (10th Cir. 1999); Smith v. Metropolitan School District Perry Township, 128 F.3d 1014 (7th Cir. 1997).

57. Abeyta v. Chama Ind. School Dist., 77 F.3d 1253 (10th Cir. 1996).

58. Pa. Assn. for Retarded Children v. Commonwealth, 343 F. Supp. 279 (E.D. Pa. 1972) (consent decree); Mills v. Board of Educ., 348 F. Supp. 866 (D. D.C. 1972).

59. Baird v. Rose, 192 F.3d 462 (4th Cir. 1999).

60. Sandison v. Mich. High School Athletic Assn., 64 F.3d 1026 (6th Cir. 1995) (exclusion based on age rule did not violate ADA); Urban v. Jefferson County School Dist., 870 F. Supp. 1558 (D. Colo. 1994) (denial of desired placement did not violate Rehabilitation Act).

61. Ferguson v. City of Phoenix, 157 F.3d 668 (9th Cir. 1998).

62. Ray v. School Dist. of DeSoto County, 666 F. Supp. 1524 (N.D. Fla. 1987).

63. Baird v. Rose, 192 F.3d 462 (4th Cir. 1999).

64. 457 U.S. 202, 210 (1982).

65. Martinez v. Bynum, 461 U.S. 321 (1983).

66. Ambach v. Norwick, 441 U.S. 68 (1979).

67. Mass. Board of Retirement v. Murgia, 427 U.S. 307 (1976); Weisbrod v. Lynn, 383 F. Supp. 933 (D. D.C. 1974), aff'd, 420 U.S. 940 (1975).

68. Kimel v. Florida Board of Regents, 120 S. Ct. 63 (2000). Owen v. City of Independence, 445 U.S. 622 (1980).

69. San Antonio Ind. School Dist. v. Rodriguez, 411 U.S. 1 (1973).

70. Abbott v. Burke, 710 A.2d 450 (N.J. 1998); Claremont School District v. Governor, 138 N.H. 183, 635 A.2d 1375 (1993); McDuffy v. Secretary of the Executive Office of Education, 415 Mass. 545, 615 N.E.2d 516 (1993); New Haven v. State Board of Educ., 228 Conn. 699, 638 A.2d 589 (1994). For a general review of individual states, see ACIR, Symposium on the Property Tax, 19 Intergovernmental Perspective 10 (1993); Underwood and Sparkman, *School Finance Litigation: A New Wave of Reform,* 14 Harv. J.L. & Pub. Policy, 517 (1991).

71. Guerra v. Manchester Terminal Corp., 498 F.2d 641 (5th Cir. 1974).

72. *See, e.g.,* Johnson v. Railway Express Agency, 421 U.S. 454, 460 (1975).

73. Middlesex County Sewerage Authority v. National Sea Clammers Assn., 453 U.S. 13 (1981); Maine v. Thibotout, 448 U.S. 1 (1980).

74. Smith v. Metropolitan School Dist., 128 F.3d 1014 (7th Cir. 1997); Doe v. Claiborne County, 103 F.3d 495 (6th Cir. 1996).

75. Owen v. City of Independence, 445 U.S. 622 (1980); X. v. Fremont County School Dist., 162 F.3d 1175 (10th Cir. 1998).

76. Busek v. State, 785 P.2d 855 (Wyo. 1990); Clay v. Conlee, 815 F.2d 1164, 1170 (8th Cir. 1987).

77. Doe v. Beaumont I.S.D., 8 F. Supp. 2d 596 (E.D. Tex. 1998); Doe v. Board of Educ., 18 F. Supp. 2d 954 (N.D. Ill. 1998); Ware v. Unified School Dist., 902 F.2d 815, 819 (10th Cir. 1990).

78. St. Louis v. Praprotnik, 485 U.S. 112 (1988); Hall v. Marion School Dist. No. 2, 31 F.3d 183 (4th Cir. 1994).

79. *See e.g.,* Doe, *supra* note 77 (teacher sexual abuser held not a policymaker); Dallas Ind. School Dist., 153 F.3d 212 (5th Cir. 1998) (principal not a policymaker in the presented circumstances).

80. *See* Monell v. Dept. of Social Services, 436 U.S. 658 (1978). Williams v. Ellington, 936 F.2d 881 (6th Cir. 1991) (school principal order for an unconstitutional student search was not sufficient to prove a school policy to authorize that search).

81. R.L.R. v. Prague Pub. School Dist., 838 F. Supp. 1526 (W.D. Okla. 1993); Jones v. Board of Educ., 854 P.2d 1386 (Colo. App. 1993); Daniels v. Williams, 474 U.S. 327 (1986); Davidson v. Cannon, 474 U.S. 344 (1986); Enright v. Board of School Directors, 346 N.W.2d 771 (Wis. 1984).

82. Johnson v. Dallas Ind. School Dist., 38 F.3d 198 (5th Cir. 1994).

83. The confinement cases are reviewed in Deshaney v. Winnebago Co. Dept. of Social Services, 489 U.S. 189 (1989). *See also* Wood v. Ostrander, 851 F.2d 1212 (9th Cir. 1988).

84. Doe v. Claiborne County, 103 F.3d 495 (6th Cir. 1996); D.R. v. Middle Bucks Area Vo-Tech.

School, 972 F.2d. 1364 (3d Cir. 1991) (no constitutional duty to prevent sexual harassment by a student); *accord:* J.O. v. Alton Comm. Unit School Dist., 909 F.2d 267 (7th Cir. 1990). The contrary Fifth Circuit view that the school had a special relationship and constitutional duty to protect 14-year-old student against teacher sexual assault is a distinct minority. Doe v. Taylor Ind. School Dist., 15 F.3d 443 (5th Cir. 1994).

85. "Rather the existence of a legal right of control is the linchpin in all cases in which we have found Section 1983 liability based on breach of duty to act, even where private actors committed the injurious harm." *See* Doe v. Rains County Ind. School Dist., 66 F.3d 1402, 1414 (5th Cir. 1995). The same court found no special relationship duty to protect a sexually assaulted deaf student who *voluntarily* resided at a state school for the deaf. Walton v. Alexander, 44 F.3d 1297 (5th Cir. 1995).

86. Armijo by and through Chavez v. Wagon Mound Public Schools, 159 F.3d 1253 (10th Cir. 1998).

87. City of Canton v. Harris, 489 U.S. 378 (1989) (recognized that deliberate indifference might be found in some circumstances from a failure to train an employee). Ware, *supra* note 77.

88. Johnson v. Dallas Ind. School Dist., 38 F.3d 198 (5th Cir. 1994) (alleged failure to prevent shooting of student); Leffall v. Dallas Ind. School Dist., 28 F.3d 521 (5th Cir. 1994) (deliberate indifference not shown by failure to protect student from a shooting following a school dance); Rosa H. v. San Elizario Ind. School Dist., 887 F. Supp.149 (W.D. Tex. 1995) (negligent placement of abusive student who injured other students). *See also* Gonsalez v. Ysleta Ind. School Dist., 996 F.2d 745 (5th Cir. 1993) (transfer but not removal of teacher accused of sexual assault—held not to constitute deliberate indifference).

89. Wyke v. Polk County School Board, 129 F.3d 560 (11th Cir. 1997).

90. *Compare* Doe v. Claiborne County, 103 F.3d 495 (6th Cir. 1996) (insufficient allegations), *with* Murrell v. School Dist. 1, Denver, Colorado, 186 F.3d 1238 (10th Cir. 1999) (sufficient allegations). Doe v. Board of Educ., 18 F. Supp. 2d 954 (N.D. Ill. 1998).

91. Parrat v. Taylor, 451 U.S. 527 (1981); Coriz v. Martinez, 915 F.2d 1469 (10th Cir. 1990) (meaningful state remedy for excessive punishment satisfies claim of constitutional injury).

92. Owen v. City of Independence, 445 U.S. 622 (1980); Stoddard v. School Dist., 590 F.2d 829 (10th Cir. 1979); Craig v. Columbus City Schools, 760 F. Supp. 128 (S.D. Ohio 1991).

93. Jane Doe v. Special School Dist., 682 F. Supp. 451 (E.D. Mo. 1988).

94. D.T. v. Ind. School Dist., 894 F.2d 1176 (10th Cir. 1990).

95. Doe v. Raines County Ind. School Dist., 66 F.3d 1402 (5th Cir. 1995).

96. W.B. v. Matula, 67 F.3d 484, 499 (3d Cir. 1995) [quoting Harlow v. Fitzgerald, 457 U.S. 800 (1982)]; Doe v. Taylor Ind. School Dist., 15 F.3d 433 (5th Cir. 1994).

97. The Second, Third, Fourth, Fifth, Sixth, Seventh and Tenth Circuits directly or by dicta found no preemption by Title VII of § 1983 suits for claims of constitutional rights deprivations. *See* W.B. v. Matula, *supra* note 96, and similar rulings there cited from other federal circuits. Lakoski v. James, 66 F.3d 751 (5th Cir. 1995); Beardsley v. Webb, 30 F.3d 524 (4th Cir. 1994); Keller v. Prince Georges County Dept. of Social Services, 827 F.2d 952 (4th Cir. 1987); Trigg v. Ft. Wayne Comm. Schools, 766 F.2d 299 (7th Cir. 1985); Day v. Wayne County Board of Auditors, 749 F.2d 1199, 1204 (6th Cir. 1984); Vulcan Society v. Civil Service Commission, 490 F.2d 387, 390 (2d Cir. 1973); Poulson v. Davis, 895 F.2d 705 (10th Cir. 1990).

98. *Ibid;* Gibson v. Kickman, 2 F. Supp. 2d 1481 (M.D. Ga. 1998); Duello v. Board of Regents, 487 N.W.2d 56 (Wis. 1998).
    Re preclusion of § 1983 relief for a pure Title VII statutory claim: *e.g.,* Poulson, *supra* note 97, at p. 710; Day, *supra* note 97, at p. 1204; Lakoski, *supra* note 97, at p. 755 (citing Irby v. Sullivan, 737 F.2d 1418; 1428 (5th Cir. 1984); Keller, *supra* note 97, at p. 956 (dicta reference to Supreme Court statements that Title VII precludes alternate remedies under other civil war reconstruction statutes [42 USC §§ 1981, 1985(3)]; Walker v. City of Little Rock, 787 F.2d 1223 (8th Cir. 1986).

99. The Civil Rights Act of 1991, 42 U.S.C. § 2000e, 105 Stat. 1071 (see Appendix to this chapter).

    Not covered in this text are the following issues: Liability of nonemployer individuals under § 1981 or § 1983 for employment related discrimination. *See, e.g.,* Johnson v. Railway Express Agency, 421 U.S. 454, 460 (1975); Lee v. Washington County Board of Educ., 625 F.2d 1235 (5th Cir. 1980); Runyan v. McCrary, 427 U.S. 160 (1976).

    The statutes codified as 42 U.S.C. §§ 1982 and 1985 have rare operation in public schools.

    Preclusion of § 1981 suits where § 1983 suit is available. *See* Jett v. Dallas Ind. School Dist., 109 S. Ct. 2702 (1989).

    On the question whether the Civil Rights Act of 1991 permits direct § 1981 damage suits, *see* Federation of American Contractors v. Oakland, 96 F.3d 1204 (9th Cir. 1996).

100. Ferguson v. City of Phoenix, 157 F.3d 668 (9th Cir. 1998).

101. The case law is summarized in Bond v. Board of Educ. of the City of New York, 1999 WL 151702 (E.D. N.Y. 1999). *See also* Zombro v. Baltimore City Police Dept., 868 F.2d 1364, 1369 (4th Cir.), *cert. denied,* 493 U.S. 850 (1989); Prieto v. Rosa, 894 F.2d 467, 470 (1st Cir. 1990). The Second Circuit has not addressed the preclusion issue, and its district courts are split. *Compare* Reed v. Town of Branford, 949 F. Supp. 87, 90 (D. Conn. 1996) (no ADEA preclusion of § 1983 claim), *with* Gregor v. Dewinski, 911 F. Supp. 643, 651 (W.D. N.Y. 1996) (ADEA provides the exclusive remedy for age discrimination).

102. In Franklin v. Gwinnett County Public Schools, 112 S. Ct. 1028, 1035 (1992), the Court offered the view that like damage remedies would also be available for intentional violations of Title VI.

103. *Cases holding § 1983 actions are not precluded by Title IX remedies:* Oona R-S by Kate S. v. Santa Rosa City Schools, 890 F. Supp. 1452 (N.D. Cal. 1995); Seamons v. Snow, 84 F.3d 1126,1233 (10th Cir. 1996); Lillard v. Shelby County Board of Educ., 76 F.3d 716, 722–4 (6th Cir. 1996); Mann. v. Univ. of Cincinnati, 864 F. Supp. 44 (S.D. Ohio 1994).

    Cases holding that § 1983 claims are subsumed and precluded by Title IX remedies: Boulahanis v. Board of Regents, 198 F.3d 33 (7th Cir. 1999); Ridgewood Board of Educ. v. N.E., 172 F.3d 238 (3rd Cir. 1999); Mennone v. Gordon, 889 F. Supp.

53 (D. Conn. 1995); Mabry v. State Board of Comm. Colleges, 597 F. Supp. 1235, 1239 (D. Colo. 1984).

104. "Initially we note that the Court of Appeals for the Fourth Circuit recently held that a plaintiff may not sue under 42 U.S.C. § 1983 for IDEA violations because IDEA provides a comprehensive remedial scheme for violations of its own requirements. Sellers v. School Board, 141 F.3d 524, 529 (4th Cir. 1998). But we must follow our decision in W.B. v. Matula, 67 F.3d 484 (3d Cir. 1995), which held that IDEA claims may be actionable under § 1983" *See* Ridgewood, *supra* note 103, at p. 252.

105. The Civil Rights Attorneys Fees Award Statute codified at 42 U.S.C. § 1988 authorizes fee recovery in actions brought under §§ 1981, 1983, Titles VI, VII, and IX.

    Re IDEA, *see* The Handicapped Children's Protective Act of 1986, 20 U.S.C. § 1415.

    Re § 504 and ADA, see The Civil Rights Act of 1991; New York City Fire Dept. v. Civil Service Commission, 490 F.2d 387, 390 (2d Cir. 1973); Poulson v. Davis, 895 F.2d 705 (10th Cir. 1990). These and other authorities are reviewed in detail in the Keller case, *supra* note 97; Annot., *Civil Rights Act—Attorneys Fees,* 16 A.L.R. Fed 621 (1973) and pkt. part.

    "A party 'prevails' . . . if his or her lawsuit is a substantial factor or significant catalyst in achieving the primary relief sought." Robinson v. Kimbrough, 652 F.2d 458, 465 (5th Cir. 1981).

    The fact that a party prevails through settlement rather than through trial does not prevent the awarding of fees. Maher v. Gagne, 448 U.S. 122, 129 (1980). *See* Barlow-Gresham Unified High School Dist. v. Mitchell, 940 F.2d 1280 (9th Cir. 1991) (prelitigation settlement); McSomebodies v. San Mateo City School Dist., 897 F.2d 975 (9th Cir. 1989) (successful administrative hearings).

106. Christiansburg Garment Co. v. EEOC, 434 U.S. 412 (1978); Oldring v. School Board of DuVal County, 567 So. 2d 519 (Fla. 1990) (denying fees to defending board); Dahlem v. Board of Educ., 901 F.2d 1508 (10th Cir. 1990) (court discretion to deny fees).

107. Brennan, *State Constitutions and the Protection of Individual Rights,* 90 Harv. L. Rev. 489 (1977); Annot., *Recovery of Damages as Remedy for Wrongful Discrimination under State or Local Civil Rights Provisions,* 85 A.L.R. 3d 351 (1978).

❖ CHAPTER 9

Private Education: Alternatives to Public Schools

❖ **CHAPTER OUTLINE**
I. Background Note
    A. State Regulation of Private Education
        1. Constitutional Constraints on State Regulation
        2. State Approval Requirements
            a. Home Schooling
        3. School Location and Construction Requirements
II. Tort Liability
    A. Immunity Defenses and Dollar Recovery Caps
    B. Topical Tort Situations
        1. Premises Liability
        2. Duties of Supervision
        3. Affirmative Defenses
        4. First Aid
        5. Defamation Liability
        6. Educational Malpractice
III. Rights of Teachers and Students
    A. Teacher Rights and Duties
        1. Contract Rights
        2. Statutory Rights
    B. Student Rights and Duties
        1. Contract Rights
        2. Student Discipline
        3. Statutory Rights
    C. Rights under Antidiscrimination Laws
        1. Background Note
        2. Subjects of Discrimination
            a. Race and Ethnicity
            b. Gender
            c. Disability
            d. Age
            e. Religion
        3. State Antidiscrimination Laws
IV. Government Aids to Private Education
    A. Background Note

B. Forms of Government Aid
  1. Aid Directed to Church Institutions
  2. Aid Directed to Students and Parents
    a. School Transportation
    b. Instructional Materials and Equipment
    c. Remedial Services
    d. Tuition, Vouchers, and Tax Relief
V. Charter Schools
  A. Legal Status of Charter Schools
  B. Charter Grants, Renewal, and Revocation
    1. Eligible Parties
    2. Application and Approval Procedures
    3. Charter Renewal and Revocation
  C. Charter School Funding
  D. Statutory Control Issues
    1. Admissions Criteria
      a. Open vs. Selective Admissions
      b. Gender-Based Selection
      c. School Service Area
    2. Curriculum and Teacher Qualifications
    3. Transportation

❖ **CHAPTER DISCUSSION QUESTIONS**

❖ **CASES**
9.1 Geraci v. St. Xavier High School, 3 Ohio Op. 3d 146 (1978)
9.2 Catholic High School Assn. of Archdiocese of New York v. Culvert, 753 F.2d 1161 (2nd Cir. 1985)[†]
9.3 Agostini v. Felton, 521 U.S. 203 (1997)
9.4 Mitchell v. Helms,—U.S.—(2000)[†]

❖ **APPENDIX**
State Charter Statutes

❖ **ENDNOTES**

———
[†]Indicates cases with review questions.

BACKGROUND NOTE

This chapter discusses the law on alternative forms of private education: non-public schools, home education, and charter schools, which combine some features of public and private schools. Many state and federal laws affecting these sources were unknown before 1950, and many of their operations require collaboration with public school authorities, an effort that often occasions misunderstandings regarding the differences between the rights and obligations of public and nonpublic schools.

The general makeup of private schools and other alternative education programs varies from state to state, as the number of and enrollments in non-public schools, home education programs, and charter schools continue to change. Dual enrollment or share-time classes with public schools were discussed in Chapter 3 and will not be repeated here.

Private schools, the dominant alternative to public education, may for present purposes be defined as follows:

> A school which is controlled by an individual or by an agency other than a State, subdivision of a State, or the federal government, usually which is supported primarily by other than public funds, and the operation of whose programs rests with other than publicly elected or appointed officials. [*The Condition of Education* 248 (1982 ed.), National Center for Education, U.S. Dept. of Education]

State Regulation of Private Education

Private schools predated the creation of public school systems in the early nineteenth century, and states did not attempt substantial direct regulation of nonpublic education until the twentieth century. That regulation continues to evolve with statutory changes and changes in constitutional law.

Constitutional Constraints on State Regulation

As explained in past chapters, the First and Fourteenth Amendments apply to *state action,* but not to private action. Therefore, the constitutional constraints that govern actions of state governments and public schools do not govern private educational activities. For this reason, the *constitutional* rights of teachers and students in public schools, such as due process, equal protection of the laws, freedom of speech, association, and religion, and freedom from unreasonable search do not attach to teachers, employees, and students in private schools for lack of the "state action" prerequisite. Only in rare instances are private school actions sufficiently bracketed with government action to be treated as state action. General state regulation and contracts with private schools and most forms of state aid to those schools have been held insufficient to create a state action foundation for the assertion of constitutional rights against them.[1] The failure to note this stark contrast of constitutional obligations between public and nonpublic education leads to unnecessary frictions and disagreements between persons who serve or are served by private schools. On the other hand, individuals affiliated with private schools retain their constitutional rights as citizens against government education-related laws or regulations that infringe those rights. Thus, state attempts to require all parents to send their children to public schools and federal laws prohibiting the use of foreign languages in private schools were struck down as infringing fundamental constitutional liberties of parents.[2] Contrary to popular impression, those landmark rulings involved nonsectarian as well as church-related schools and were founded on unenumerated fundamental liberties, rather than freedom of religion.

Nevertheless, the Supreme Court made clear that states may constitutionally regulate private schools to ensure adequate citizen education as long as their regulations are reasonable and do not impinge on protected civil rights.[3]

The general principles regarding the religion (Establishment and Free Exercise) clauses of the First Amendment were discussed in past chapters and will not be repeated here, except with reference to their unique applications to religiously affiliated schools and school groups. For example, the Establishment Clause remains a principal focus of continuing challenges to federal and state financial aid to religious schools, whereas the Free Exercise Clause remains the focus of recurring challenges to state refusal to grant such aid. The Free Exercise limit on state compulsory education that surfaced in the Amish children case, *Wisconsin v. Yoder,* as discussed in Chapter 2, has been invoked by other private educators, but courts have refused to broaden the Amish exemption to cover parties whose religious objections are not sufficiently substantial to outweigh the state's strong interest in assuring minimal child education.[4] A state may not only insist that private schools meet reasonable state requirements, but may also enforce such requirements by ordering unapproved schools to report on and identify the children in attendance at such schools.[5]

State prosecutions of parents who violate compulsory education laws raise ancillary but important evidentiary questions. In criminal enforcement proceedings, the presumption of innocence casts on the state the burden of proving parental intent to violate the law beyond a reasonable doubt,[6] but in civil enforcement proceedings, the courts in a number of states held that parents of children not in a qualified school are *prima facie* guilty unless they prove that they are entitled to an exemption from the law, or that the child was being educated in a state-qualified school or program.[7] Parental failure to seek state approval or exemption will, however, support prosecution.[8] Where public authorities seek the ultimate sanction of terminating parental custodial rights to their children, courts may require the state to prove their unfitness by "clear and convincing" evidence and that the drastic remedy serves the child's best interests.[9]

Constitutional differences aside, statutory regulation of private schools is often less restrictive and detailed than the laws governing public schools, though, as noted later, some civil rights and antidiscrimination statutes apply as well to private schools.

State Approval Requirements

State approval or licensure requirements vary considerably from state to state with regard to different classes of nonpublic schools, e.g., nondenominational and church-related schools, schools for exceptional children, residential schools, and home education.[10] The report of the Education Commission of the States[11] and reports on charter schools illustrate the diversity of regulated education systems. Where an attendance law refers only to a "school," courts have to decide whether nontraditional programs such as home instruction can be considered "schools."[12] In most cases, however, specialized statutes cover such questions.

In cases that challenge state requirements for approval and certification of nonpublic schools or home education programs, the courts have taken two antithetical approaches, namely, whether the state is limited constitutionally to setting only minimal "output" standards that ensure adequate educational achievement, or whether the state may set higher "input" standards of educational resources and effort that are "equivalent" or "comparable" to those required of public schools. A majority of state courts have upheld state laws that specify approval standards for nonpublic schools, including requirements that private school instructors be state approved or certified and that such schools or home education programs meet state prescribed curriculum requirements.[13] Parties may seek exemption from particular parts of state requirements if those requirements coerce religious conscience and if the state does not have an overriding "compelling" interest to insist on that requirement.[14] Courts have generally rejected contentions that state approval regulations are discriminatory or interfere with private rights of contract, association, and privacy as unsubstantiated by the evidence.[15]

Several state courts struck down, as unreasonable or unconstitutional, requirements that private schools provide equivalent or substantially comparable resources, programs, and goals as provided by public schools.[16] An Ohio court reversed convictions of parents affiliated with a Christian Bible school for defying regulations that required the school to have teacher certification, instructional time allocation, educational philosophy, and community involvement requisites comparable to those of public schools on the grounds that those "input" requirements were not necessary to achieve necessary educational goals and therefore infringed religious freedom under the federal and state constitutions.[17]

The broader objection that approval standards are too vague to provide fair notice and due process met with mixed responses and ultimately depends on the specific language of the challenged law.[18] The cases are also mixed on the kindred objection that approval statutes unconstitutionally delegate legislative power to administrators because they lack adequate legislative guidelines to control administrative discretion. See discussion of the delegation doctrines in Chapter 1.

Where state standards satisfy the foregoing objections, a court may still overturn an official approval decision on administrative law grounds, i.e., that the decision is *ultra vires,* erroneously applies the law, or is an arbitrary abuse of discretion. Thus a state board's attempt to supervise private schools where the statute only authorized it to approve the school's instructional program, was overturned as *ultra vires.*[19]

Home Schooling.   With regard to home schooling, all states and the District of Columbia now allow it in some form, but their regulatory schemes vary. Recent studies indicate that 30 states have statutes or regulations dealing explicitly with home education; that 13 states allow home schooling without imposing specific approval requirements; and that 8 states regulate home schooling much as they do private schools.[20] State approval standards also vary, with 26 states employing "output" achievement standards and standardized tests to evaluate pupil progress, and the remainder favoring "input" standards of teacher competency or certification, curriculum, and instructional time controls to approach equivalence or comparability to public school instruction.

A West Virginia statute that made children ineligible for further home schooling if their standardized test scores fall below the 40th percentile and they do not improve after remedial home schooling was upheld against the constitutional challenge that it infringed parental rights and denied parents equal protection.[21] Studies of state home schooling regulations are listed in the endnote.[22]

Objections to home education standards, such as the mandate for "equivalent" education, were sustained in six states, five of which thereafter enacted new laws on home schooling.[23] Challenges based *solely* on asserted parental interests failed almost universally in light of the state's acknowledged interest in assuring adequate home education. Many cases have sustained state requirements that home school teachers meet state degree standards, and that home schooled children pass standardized tests or reenter public schools.[24] Where, however, the challengers claimed a right to religious exemption under the Free Exercise Clause, the courts have divided in the balancing of state and religious interests. Two recent cases illustrate that division. In Michigan, the court held that an otherwise valid requirement of state certification of home education teachers could not be constitutionally applied to parents whose religious convictions prohibited the use of certified teachers. It concluded that the state's demand of a teaching certificate was not so essential to its educational purpose as to justify the restraint on religious conscience, while a court in Iowa rejected that reasoning and found that the state's interest in mandating certified teachers was sufficient to outweigh the religious objections.[25]

The authority of public school boards to allow home-schooled students to participate in public school extracurricular activities raises an interesting but unsettled question for school districts that consider an open door policy to allow such access.[26]

Private schools are generally allowed to set their own admission standards and to prefer, sic discriminate, students of a particular religion, gender, or social class, except in the limited situations, to be discussed later, where antidiscrimination laws bar such preferences.

School Location and Construction Requirements

Private schools are subject to state and local land use and building regulations,[27] as long as those regulations reasonably relate to public health, safety, or welfare and are nondiscriminatory.[28] Zoning exclusions of private schools from the entire municipality have been voided as unreasonable, as has the imposition of oppressive use conditions, such as the requirement that a private school be located on at least 50 acres of land.[29] The cases are split on the question whether zoning restrictions for different kinds of schools (i.e., nursery and elementary schools, profit and nonprofit schools) are discriminatory or reasonable.[30]

Schools may be lawfully excluded from selected residential areas,[31] but where private but not public schools were so excluded, a majority of cases voided the differential treatment, while some courts upheld them on the ground that public schools are exempt from municipal regulation, or that municipal burdens created by public schools in residential areas are different from those created by private schools.[32] A few states and localities enacted laws and ordinances that expressly prohibit different zoning treatment of public and nonpublic schools.[33] As with all administrative decisions, zoning decisions may be challenged as *ultra vires* or for abuse of discretion.[34]

Reasonable building construction and use conditions also govern school buildings,[35] but arbitrary conditions may be overturned for abuse of discretion such as forbidding school use of on-site water, or raising official objections after issuance of official approvals and a certificate of occupancy.[36] School use denials may also be overturned where the official stated reasons for denial of school uses are not supported by substantial evidence.

Zoning disputes often turn on the contested meaning of key terms in the law, requiring courts to decide whose interpretation is correct.

> . . . the zoning ordinance issue in this case reduces to whether Washington Christian Academy is "church" use . . . sufficient to bring it within the excepted prior use. The church maintains that since the school is an integral and inseparable part of their religious faith, the use for church and school are one and the same. The City views the uses as separable. [*City of Sumner v. First Baptist Church*, 639 P.2d 1358, 1365 (Wash. 1982)]

The zoning classification of institutions that provide mixed school and related functions, e.g., education services with temporary housing or treatment, varies with use standards of individual laws. Mixed-purpose institutions were excluded from school zones in New York, as being more in the nature of treatment centers than private schools, while courts in Massachusetts and New Jersey ruled that a rehabilitative and educational center retained its status as a school for zoning purposes.[37]

The eminent domain power of governments to take private property for public uses extends to private school properties, but in such cases, the government must pay the school owner just compensation for the taken property.[38]

TORT LIABILITY

Except as modified by statute, the general tort principles reviewed in Chapter 4 also apply to private schools. Those principles, though not repeated here, form the basis of the following discussion.

Immunity Defenses and Dollar Recovery Caps

The *entity* immunity of private schools differs from the *personal* immunity of their staff. Personal tort immunity did not exist at common law, but has been created by legislation in a growing number of states.

At common law, private schools operated not for profit were treated as charitable organizations and were held immune from tort liability. A growing number of states have, by court decision or legislation, abrogated or delimited charitable tort immunity. Those limitations vary with the law of each state.[39] For example, Illinois law immunizes public and private schools and their teachers from liability for negligence, but not for willful, reckless, or wanton misconduct.[40] Many states deny immunity for injuries caused by nuisances or defective conditions of school property.[41] In some states the law grants tort immunity for conduct in the performance of educational functions but not for conduct arising out of activities that are deemed "proprietary" or commercial in nature.

Aside from immunity, state legislatures may, as indicated in Chapter 4, limit liability by fixing the amount of monetary damages that may be recovered from private schools for particular torts, by setting a maximum dollar ceiling or cap of allowed recovery, or by limiting any greater recovery to the amount of liability insurance covering the defendant.[42] These recovery caps have been largely sustained against constitutional attack. Even so, the best shield against tort losses is prevention and minimization of tort hazards in school operations.

Topical Tort Situations

Premises Liability

As noted in Chapter 4, schools are liable to invitees (students, staff, and visitors on school business) for injuries caused by hazardous conditions of buildings, equipment, and grounds if those conditions could have been prevented by reasonable care in their inspection and maintenance. That duty of care extends only to the physical areas to which students or other persons are invited.

The duty of care with respect to noninvitees, such as *licensees* who enter the premises lawfully but without invitation, or *trespassers,* who enter the premises unlawfully, differs from the duty to invitees. As to licensees the only school duty is to refrain from intentionally harming them and to warn them of known latent dangers. As to trespassers, a school generally owes no duty of care or prior warning, except where their exposure to particular harm becomes known to school authorities. A special rule applies to child licensees or trespassers in states that adopt the doctrine of *attractive nuisance,* which makes schools liable for injuries arising from dangerous property conditions that are reasonably known to attract unwitting children into hazardous entry.[43] The determination whether a condition of school property constitutes an attractive nuisance is a pivotal issue in such cases.

Liability for negligence or lack of due care is ascertained by the foreseeability of a risk of harm from particular conduct or conditions and the existence or nonexistence of a reasonable opportunity to ascertain and prevent that harm.[44] The lack-of-notice defense does not apply, however, where the school affirmatively created the dangerous condition (e.g., by using glass panels rather than thick plate glass in a school door).[45] Issues of foreseeability and timely notice of danger are often left to jury determination. Examples of conditions for which private schools may be held liable in negligence include slippery floors, unstable equipment or furnishings, defective elevators, inadequate lighting in walkways and parking lots, and unsafe machinery, ramps, and fire extinguishers.[46]

The known increase of school-site assaults creates the duty to minimize such conduct by reasonable security and protection measures, and failure to take them has rendered schools liable for injuries suffered from such assaults.[47]

Duties of Supervision

Under the doctrine of *respondeat superior,* the school is liable for the negligence or tortious misconduct of its agents and employees when acting within the scope of their employment or authority. Vicarious liability may extend to conduct of unpaid aides who work under the direction of school staff.[48] A school would, therefore, be liable for negligent bus operation along the driver's assigned route, but was not liable for negligence of its bus driver after he left his assigned route for his own purposes. "Scope of employment" issues are not always so clear. Where a school medical doctor caused injury in the negligent exercise of his medical judgment, a court held that the school was not liable since it had no control over that judgment.[49]

The school duty to provide reasonable supervision includes a duty of prudent care in selecting individuals who are entrusted with supervisory authority. Schools are liable for negligent hiring of incompetent persons who cause injuries,[50] but they are not ensurers of continuing competence of all employees, e.g., where future lapses of previously competent employees are not reasonably foreseeable.

The duty of supervision was well stated in the following case that involved a second grader whose holiday costume was ignited by a nearby candle:

> Negligent supervision . . . involves a breach of a duty defendant owes plaintiff which causes plaintiff to suffer damages. . . . To recover, plaintiff need not show that the very injury resulting from defendant's negligence was foreseeable, but merely that a reasonable person could have foreseen that injuries of the type suffered would be likely to occur under the circumstances. . . . . . . The defendant is not an insurer of plaintiff's safety . . . nor is defendant required to maintain a constant vigil over each member of the class by keeping every student within eyesight. . . . The duty of defendant . . . was merely to exercise reasonable or ordinary care in the supervision of plaintiff. . . . The exercise of ordinary care where children are involved, however, requires more vigilance and caution than might the exercise of ordinary care where adults are concerned. . . . This is particularly true when a potentially dangerous condition exists and the supervisor is or should be aware of it. [*Smith v. Archbishop of St. Louis,* 632 S.W.2d 516, 521, 522 (Mo. 1982)]

Courts and juries must consider all relevant circumstances in determining issues of negligence and proximate cause, including such factors as (1) the nature of the activity, (2) the age and past conduct history of the students, and (3) the practicability and probable effect of general or special supervision. A jury could readily find negligence for lack of supervision where a young child fell from a schoolyard merry-go-round,[51] but another court dismissed a tort suit for an unsupervised child who fell from monkey bars in the schoolyard. Still another court refused to dismiss suit for a child's fall from a four-foot railing in the schoolyard.[52] Courts often leave these and other fact-bound questions to jury determination, and they seldom overrule jury findings since so much depends on the assessment of specific circumstances.

Tort claimants have the burden of proving negligence and proximate cause, i.e., that a supervisor should have foreseen the risk of harm, and the lack of supervision caused the harm. This burden is difficult in unexplained accidents, such as where a young retarded student was drowned in a pond on a 50-acre rural campus. The court held that because the child had been at the school for some weeks and had often walked near the pond, there was no indication of any risk and consequent need to provide more direct supervision against the child falling or jumping into the pond.[53]

Discharge of a firearm by a student in the presence of a supervising teacher was ground for finding negligent supervision.[54] Circumstantial evidence of negligent supervision may support tort recovery. Where a private nursery school student was found by her mother at the end of the school day to have suffered a brain concussion and the school failed to explain what had occurred,[55] the court applied the doctrine of *res ipsa loquitur,* meaning "the thing speaks for itself," to uphold tort liability.

Because school personnel cannot observe every movement of every child at all times, reasonable general supervision rather than special, direct supervision of students is all that is required in most cases. Knowledge of special danger, however, triggers more stringent duties of special supervision.

General supervision is required in situations where students are engaged in many activities which are not usually dangerous. Specific supervision is required when activities are unusually dangerous or the supervisor is instructing an activity with which students are not familiar. (See Note, *School Liability for Athletic Injuries*, 21 Washburn L.J. 315, 321, n. 52.)

Reasonable general supervision is sufficient in most cases. Schools are not liable for unforeseeable student violations of school rules, for instance, where students cycled across school grounds in violation of regularly enforced school rules.[56] Similarly, a student who returned to school before he was directed to do so could not recover for injuries sustained while playing on a snow-covered bush.[57] Recovery was also denied students placed on disciplinary assignment (to pull weeds) who decided to play football and were thereby injured.[58] However, a school may be held liable for schoolyard injuries where school superiors had notice of, but made no effort to prevent, injurious student activities (students throwing pebbles at each other).[59]

Courts repeatedly stress that schools are not liable for unavoidable accidents. A child spectator at a school baseball game who was struck by a bat that slipped from the batter's hands had no claim in tort.[60] While courts recognize a supervisory duty of coaches to provide safe athletic equipment, the cases on the extent of care in inspecting and fitting such equipment are not consistent.[61]

The Chapter 4 discussion of student injuries during a teacher's temporary absence from class is equally pertinent here. Such cases present two issues: whether the supervisor's absence was itself reasonable or negligent; and if negligent, whether that absence was a proximate cause of the student injury, i.e., whether the supervisor's presence could have prevented the injury. A teacher's 25-minute absence from class rendered the school liable for a classroom assault,[62] but in other cases, the absence of a teacher or supervisor did not render the school liable.[63]

Negligence from lack of supervision is more readily found where students are permitted to engage in risky activities with other students. A jury could find actionable negligence for injury from a hurled discus during schoolyard discus-throwing practice.[64] But with respect to nonhazardous after-school activities, a private high school was held to have no duty of supervision.[65]

The duty of special (direct) supervision clearly attaches where a student is affirmatively directed by a school superior to perform a potentially dangerous task. But where the need for such supervision is unclear, courts may leave the question to the jury.

Private schools are duty bound to supervise school-sponsored activities. Where a school superior authorized an off-duty employee to transport a student to a field trip, the school was held liable for the driver's negligence.[66]

Affirmative Defenses

As explained in Chapter 4, an injured party may be totally or partially barred from recovering for another's tort under the doctrines of contributory negligence or assumption of risk. The burden of proving these defenses lies with the defending school or teacher. Findings of contributory negligence and assumption of risk depend on inferences to be drawn from widely varying circumstances. A high school freshman who was permitted to work in a chemistry lab without supervision could not recover for injuries arising from his unauthorized attempt to concoct gunpowder.[67] Juries were also permitted to find student contributory negligence where the student attempted to board a school vehicle by stepping on the side wheel before it started up,[68] and where an adolescent student climbed a tree to gather pecans on instructor's order, but negligently put his weight on a shaky branch.[69]

In a majority of states, the legislatures and courts have modified the defenses of contributory negligence and assumption of risk to permit partial recovery based on the degree of the victim's contributory or comparative negligence. A private school may thus be liable for injuries in the proportion that *its* negligence contributed to the injury.[70]

First Aid

A duty to render reasonable first aid to students arises only when the need is apparent, but that duty is limited and does not require an individual to venture a diagnosis, treatment, or procedure that requires special training not received by that individual.[71] However, when teachers volunteer medical assistance to students, they will be held liable for injuries caused by their well-intentioned but negligent actions.[72]

Defamation Liability

The Chapter 4 discussion of liability for defamation pertains equally to private schools and their employees.

Educational Malpractice

For the reasons explained in Chapter 4, courts have refused to recognize a general tort duty that schools ensure adequate educational achievement, or to interpret private school enrollment contracts as creating a special duty to ensure adequate educational achievement.[73] In the absence of a clear and specific undertaking to different effect, courts only require schools to make reasonable, good-faith instructional efforts.[74]

RIGHTS OF TEACHERS AND STUDENTS

The law of contracts is the dominant source of individual rights of teachers, students, and parents in their dealings with private schools. A contract is a legally enforceable agreement, but not all agreements are valid and enforceable as contracts. The major disputes between private schools and their teachers or students revolve around the interpretation of employment or admissions contracts. The usual question is which party breached the contract? Less prominent, but substantial statutory rights, particularly under antidiscrimination statutes, must also be considered.

Teacher Rights and Duties

Contract Rights

Unexcused termination of employment by a school before the expiration of the contract period would be a contract breach for which the terminated teacher employee could recover lost contract salary.[75] Conversely, *material* defaults by a teacher on his or her employment terms would be a contract breach that would release the school from its contract obligations and thus justify termination of the teacher without further pay.[76] Contracts may create procedural rights that are not created by statutes.[77]

Courts play a crucial role in deciding what rights and duties are created by employment contracts and which party breached its respective obligations thereunder.[78] In determining the fair contract expectations of the parties, courts consider all circumstances surrounding the making of the contract, including the parties' past course of dealings and the nature of the school and of the job duties of the position in question. They may imply terms and obligations, though not expressly specified in the written contract, as being within the fair contemplation of the contract. Courts will not, however, imply an obligation that contradicts express contract terms.[79] To avoid uncertainty, private school contracts increasingly refer to and incorporate obligations specified in other school documents, such as school handbooks and regulations that specify teacher obligations more fully.

An individual or union agreement with a church-sponsored high school may contain a stipulation that teachers are subject to discharge for publicly contradicting, by word or action, the moral teachings of the sponsoring church. Where no such duty is stipulated, different case histories produce different results. One case overturned the discharge of a Catholic school teacher for marrying a Catholic priest contrary to church law because the school failed to specify that observance of church law was a condition of continued employment,[80] whereas other cases upheld nonrenewal or dismissal of Catholic teachers who remarried contrary to precepts of the church school sponsor,[81] or who intentionally concealed material facts regarding their marriage situation which contravened the moral teaching of the sponsoring church.[82] The implication of a contract duty not to undermine a school's value goals may also be made in contracts of nonreligious private schools.[83] Courts will not question the accuracy or validity of asserted religious precepts since such investigation would entangle the government with religion in violation of the First Amendment.

Private schools may voluntarily negotiate collective contracts with teacher associations where such bargaining by them is not mandated by a labor statute, as in Pennsylvania.[84] Where private school teachers and employees assert bargaining rights, the first question that must be answered is whether the state or the national labor relations law governs them. The courts have answered that question differently for religious and nonreligious schools, with the Supreme Court holding that the National Labor Relations Act (NLRA) does not apply to religious private schools because Congress did not intend to cover them, while the First Circuit Court of Appeals held that the NLRA does apply to nonreligious private schools.[85]

Religiously affiliated schools in some states opposed state regulation of their employment relations on the further ground that state labor laws could not constitutionally apply to them, because state regulation would interfere with their religious liberty under the First Amendment. That question has not reached the Supreme Court and the federal circuit courts are divided on that issue. The *Culvert* case, which appears at the end of this chapter, notes the split between the First and Seventh Circuits. *Culvert* held that religious schools were constitutionally subject to the New York labor law, with the proviso that the state's control over their bargaining could not extend to issues that involved religious belief or motivation. The Seventh Circuit arrived at a contrary conclusion and found that state bargaining oversight would create an unconstitutional entanglement of government and religion. Until the Supreme Court resolves the conflict on the constitutional issue, it remains open to decision in other circuits. The constitutional issue has been rendered largely academic in states where church schools are either exempt from state labor oversight or have elected to accede to state labor jurisdiction.

The courts of New York and New Jersey have also found no federal law barrier, either by preemption of the NLRA or by constitutional principles, to state mandated bargaining by church schools.[86] However, as the *Culvert* opinion declared, courts still have to decide on a case-by-case basis whether a disputed official labor decision intrudes unconstitutionally into a religious question or function of the affected school.

Statutory Rights

The prime statutory rights of teachers in private schools are provided by the laws against employment discrimination, which are discussed later in this chapter.

Student Rights and Duties

Contract Rights

The rights of private school students and their parents are defined by the express and implied terms of the admission contract. Student enrollment generally connotes agreement to abide by the documents of admission and by incorporated or implied terms of the school's catalogs, regulations, handbooks, and generally understood customs of the school.

The importance of such terms is evident in parent–school disagreements over tuition owed, tuition refunds, school release of academic grades and records, and the legality of school disciplinary sanctions. The *Geraci* case at the end of this chapter illustrates these points. Courts enforce payment of contract tuition provisions unless they are found to be unconscionable or against public policy,[87] including agreements that call for full tuition payment without refund, notwithstanding a later parent decision not to have a child attend the school, or student failure or inability to complete a covered semester.[88] Nor can parents claim tuition refund where the student was dismissed for violating school rules, or was withdrawn on school request pursuant to the school's reserved contract right to request withdrawal for stated reasons.[89] A parent's failure to pay agreed charges in breach of a contract relieves the school of any further obligations, including any duty to prepare or release the student's academic records.[90] A court may reach a contrary result if it finds an implied school promise that the school would release grade records on courses that were satisfactorily completed.[91] Where a school breached an implied contract duty, that breach precluded recovery of unpaid tuition, for instance, where a vocational school failed to maintain educational records required for student licensure to practice the skills there taught.[92] Courts will not generally second-guess school academic decisions, but if they find that a school acted in bad faith, they can treat its action as a contract breach.[93]

Student Discipline

Contract limitations on student discipline and punishment are often unclear. Sanctions, including expulsion, for conduct that is "immoral" or "detrimental" to the school or its interests have been upheld as within the fair understanding of the parties, even though such terms might be considered unconstitutionally vague in a public school.[94] Although courts are not inclined to question school conduct standards or to overturn student punishments,[95] they are likely to question and overturn disciplinary procedures or severe punishments that are patently unfair, as beyond the fair contemplation of the school's contract.[96] The limitations placed on discipline of students with handicaps by the IDEA and Rehabilitation Act, as discussed in Chapter 7, apply as well to children with handicaps who are attending private schools.

Statutory Rights

Private schools that admit students with disabilities must comply with the IDEA, including disciplinary limitations that interfere with students' access to the education and other rights conferred by that law. See the Chapter 7 review of the IDEA. They must also observe the obligations imposed by other antidiscrimination laws discussed later in this chapter.

A school's duty to maintain confidentiality of student information, beyond that required by the Family Education Rights and Privacy Act of 1974 (FERPA), will depend on the nature of the information and any governing statutes. See the discussion of confidentiality issues in Chapter 7. The possibility that a court might imply a contract obligation of confidentiality should incline administrators to keep student information confidential wherever practicable.

Most private schools must comply with FERPA regulations, which are discussed in Chapter 7, because that law governs any school that receives *any* assistance from the federal Commissioner of Education. In addition, all schools must generally comply with state laws on maintaining and filing required records with state education agencies, such as those dealing with student health, attendance, testing, and graduation.

Rights under Antidiscrimination Laws

Background Note

The excerpts and text discussion on antidiscrimination statutes in Chapters 5 and 8 provide the basic coverage information for discussing their application to private schools. Those sources should be referenced in reading the following discussion.

One major statute that has practically no application to private schools is the umbrella remedial statute known as § 1983, which, as explained in Chapter 8, does not operate against private individuals or private schools.[97] It only covers deprivation of federal rights by state agents or actions taken "under color of law." The instances where private school activity qualifies as "state action" or action "under color of law" are relatively rare.

Subjects of Discrimination

Race and Ethnicity.   Federal *constitutional* protections against racial or ethnic segregation and discrimination do not apply to private actions except where they are so closely bracketed with government action as to color the school action as "state action." The classic illustration of this exception arose in the case of Girard College, a private primary and secondary school created by and administered under a will that limited admissions to Girard College to "white male orphans." Because that will involved extensive state and city contributions to the construction and the operation of the school (by a city board of trustees) over many decades, the courts enjoined the school's exclusion of African-American students as unconstitutional state action.[98]

Statutory protections against discrimination have broader reach into private schools. Under the Act of 1866 (§ 1981), which prohibits racial discrimination in the making of contracts, the Supreme Court enjoined a private school from refusing admission to African-American applicants after the school had publicly advertised for public patronage.[99] That case did not raise or decide the broader question whether private schools are bound to contract with persons who are not publicly invited to do business with them. The constitutional bar against government interference with free exercise of religion may prevent the application of § 1981, such as where the school expelled students for violating its religiously dictated rule against interracial dating.[100] That limitation, however, does not prevent the government from denying affirmative government benefits to segregated religious schools, such as the denial of tax exemptions to the private institution that barred interracial dating. The Supreme Court in upholding that denial noted the important distinction between affirmative government interference with religion, on one hand, and government denial of public benefits to a school whose practices violate legislative policy.[101]

Title VII.   This law applies to private schools, subject to the exceptions noted in Chapters 5 and 8 for religiously based employment decisions. The Supreme Court upheld the constitutionality of those exemptions against the challenge that they aided religion in violation of the Establishment Clause.[102] However, as there noted, the bare fact of church affiliation is not automatic grounds for Title VII exemption. To qualify for the religious exemption, a private school employer must establish two basic facts, namely, that the school has the required religious character, and that the challenged employment decision involved a bona fide employment qualification to preserve the school's religious purposes. As to the requisite religious character issue, courts have held that the school must be supported or controlled in substantial part by a religious association (not necessarily a church or religious order) and must pursue the claimed religious goals.[103] A qualified school could, therefore, adopt hiring preferences that are essential to the school mission even though that preference excludes an otherwise protected class, such as race or gender, and it may discharge a teacher for conduct contrary to the school's religious tenets.[104]

Title VI.   Unlike Title VII, this law only covers conduct that involves federally aided programs. To the extent that Title VI does apply, however, the Chapter 8 discussion of its coverage and remedies is equally pertinent to all nonpublic schools.

Gender.   With regard to employment discrimination claims under Title VII, the above comments on Title VII coverage regarding racial discrimination apply as well to gender discrimination. With regard to the Equal Pay Act, the courts are divided on the question whether that law, as discussed in Chapter 5, applies to private schools.[105] With regard to Title IX coverage of gender discrimination, it, like Title VI, is confined to federally aided activities, be they public or private. The review of Title IX in Chapter 8 is, therefore, equally pertinent here, with the added limitation of constitutional exemption for religiously dictated gender preferences.

Disability.   A private school that accepts government funds under any program for students with disabilities must comply with the funding conditions and requirements. Hence a private school that has state-funded teachers must comply with the salary ceilings set by state law,[106] and must adopt expense reimbursement limits and conditions that are set by the grantor government.[107] Though private schools are not required by law to admit and serve students with disabilities, those that do so become subject to the same obligations under the Individuals with Disabilities Education Act and the Rehabilitation Act, which are discussed in Chapter 7. But a school that accepts a child with a disability without prior official reference under the IDEA assumes the risk that payment of its charges will be made by the parent.[108]

The Americans with Disabilities Act (ADA) and Rehabilitation Act oblige private schools not to discriminate against their employees with disabilities and to provide them with *reasonable* accommodation of their disabilities. However, as explained in Chapters 5 and 8, the ADA does not require employers to retain employees whose disabilities render them incapable of performing the "essential functions" of their job, where no reasonable accommodation would enable them to do so.[109]

Age.   The federal statute (ADEA) barring age discrimination in employment applies to government-subsidized schools,[110] but the federal courts are not agreed on the question whether it could be constitutionally applied to church-related schools. The Second and Third Circuits found no constitutional barrier, but courts from some other circuits held that the religious schools could not be governed by the act under the religion clauses of the Constitution.[111] Where a church-sponsored school defended its dismissal of teachers (who claimed they were fired because of their age) on the grounds that the teachers breached their employment contract not to violate church law, the court ruled that it could try the age discrimination claim on the narrow issue of the school's motivation in firing them, without inquiring into the validity of church doctrine.[112] The religious exemption claim can thus be defeated if an employee proves that the school's claim of religious exemption is a pretext for age discrimination.[113] Subject to these qualifications, the discussion of age discrimination in Chapters 5 and 8 pertains to private schools.

Religion.   The *constitutional* prohibitions against religious discrimination by public schools, as reviewed in Chapter 3, do not apply to private schools (religious or not) for lack of the requisite "state action." As previously noted, Title VII provides a kindred exemption for religiously based employment decisions. Under that exemption, the Supreme Court held that a religiously affiliated school may lawfully limit its hiring to persons who are affiliated with the sponsoring church.[114] State attempts to impose an *absolute* duty on religious institutions to provide religious accommodation for all its employees were nullified as unconstitutional by the Supreme Court.[115]

The Chapter 8 discussion on allowable remedies under the foregoing statutes is equally pertinent to nonpublic schools whose activities are embraced by any of those laws.

State Antidiscrimination Laws

State antidiscrimination laws often parallel federal laws,[116] and many prohibit forms of private discrimination that are not prohibited or remedied by the federal laws. State-to-state variations in this area[117] prevent generalization, hence the law of the resident state must be consulted for its specific coverage and remedies.

GOVERNMENT AIDS TO PRIVATE EDUCATION

Background Note

Nonpublic education is predominantly financed by student tuition and fees and by private contributions. Private schools are free to adopt their own fiscal policies as to those private source funds. They must comply with general tax and welfare laws, such as employer contributions for social security, unemployment compensation, workers' compensation, minimum wages, and administration of employee pension plans.[118]

Government financial assistance to religiously affiliated schools and government oversight of the uses of such assistance raise perennial challenges that they violate the federal or state constitutional prohibitions against government aid to religion or against the use of public funds for private purposes.

Challenges under state constitutions have drawn conflicting responses reflecting different court interpretations of each state's constitution. Some forms of state aid that survive federal constitutional challenge may still be overturned under a state constitution. The following discussion deals primarily with the national Constitution, which applies uniformly to all states.

Court rulings on aid to private schools under the Establishment and Free Exercise Clauses have taken different turns and twists over time. The Chapter 3 discussion of those developments with reference to public schools has kindred relevance for religiously affiliated private schools. What kinds of government assistance unconstitutionally aid religion or impermissibly involve the government with religion? On that question, the courts draw a sharp distinction between aid to higher education and aid to primary and secondary education. Direct government grants and loans to church-related colleges and their students have been uniformly upheld, whereas similar grants and subsidies to parochial schools, their students, and student parents have received mixed treatment, with some forms of aid upheld and others struck down.[119]

The shifting constitutional guidelines espoused in sharply divided Supreme Court opinions were reexamined by the Supreme Court in the *Agostini* case, which appears at the end of this chapter. The oft criticized and equally oft ignored three-part "Lemon" test, that an aid law must serve a secular legislative purpose, have a "primary effect" that neither advances nor inhibits religion, and pose no "excessive" government–religion entanglements,[120] has never been flatly repudiated but its wavering applications continue to be debated within the Court. A secular legislative purpose is readily found in the goal of improving education, while the elusive and argumentative third element of avoiding *excessive* government–religion entanglements has waned more than waxed in recent cases. The "primary effect" element remains a dominant point of contention.

> It is well to emphasize, however, that the tests must not be viewed as setting the precise limits to the necessary constitutional inquiry, but serve only as guidelines with which to identify instances in which the objectives of the Establishment Clause have been impaired. . . . Primary among the evils against which the Establishment Clause protects "have been sponsorship, financial support, and active involvement of the sovereign in religious activity." . . . But it is clear that not all legislative programs that provide indirect or incidental benefit to a religious institution are prohibited by the Constitution. [*Meek v. Pittinger*, 421 U.S., at 358–59 (1975)]

> We have consistently held that government programs that neutrally provide benefits to a broad class of citizens defined without reference to religion are not readily subject to an Establishment Clause challenge just because sectarian institutions may also receive an attenuated financial benefit. [*Zobrest v. Catalina Foothills School Dist.*, 113 S. Ct., at p. 2466 (1993)]

Because a majority of Supreme Court Justices have not agreed on a universal test for all forms of government aid, the safest course is to consider the current Supreme Court view on each class of aid in light of decisions that deal most closely with each form of aid.

Forms of Government Aid

Aid Directed to Church Institutions

Direct government grants to church-related private schools for building maintenance in poverty areas and for instructional expenses in secular courses have been overturned as unconstitutional.[121] No constitutional challenge has been pressed to the Supreme Court to invalidate comparable direct government subsidies to church-related orphanages or protectories, and the lower courts have generally held such assistance to be constitutional.[122] With regard to grants of federal *surplus* property, the Supreme Court held that disposition of surplus property does not involve government spending and therefore is not subject to challenge by a taxpayer for lack of taxpayer "standing" to question that disposition.[123]

State reimbursement of church school expenses to conduct and report results of state-mandated student achievement tests, though initially voided were later upheld when the tests were prepared and scored by state agencies. Finally such reimbursement was ruled constitutional even though parochial school teachers scored, as well as conducted, the tests.[124]

Indirect government benefits, such as property tax exemptions on houses of worship, have been held constitutional.[125] That ruling *permits* but does not *require* states to grant such tax exemptions to church schools. Most taxes challenges by private schools rest on the statutory grounds that the tax law was not intended to apply to the school's property or income.[126]

Aid Directed to Students and Parents

Some government benefits for students or parents that are provided through school channels (such as student lunch programs, special educational services, course texts and library books, job training, and transportation), or directly to students or parents through grants, tax benefits, or publicly provided educational services have been upheld. However, as noted later, the limits of such aid remain sorely debated within the Supreme Court.

School Transportation.   In *Everson v. Board of Education*,[127] the Supreme Court upheld public subsidies for student transportation to church-related schools as a child-benefit welfare measure. It later overturned state-funded field trip transportation for such students because the presence of religious school teachers on such trips was thought to risk support of the school's religious teaching.[128] That reasoning was undercut by the later Supreme Court decision (*Zobrest*) which held that the Establishment Clause did not prohibit state provision of a sign language interpreter for a child with a hearing impairment in a parochial school classroom under the children with handicaps statute (IDEA). That law is reviewed in Chapter 7. The *Zobrest* decision was cited prominently in the *Mitchell* case that appears at the end of this chapter.

Though the *federal* Constitution *permits* state provision of school transportation to church schools, it does not *require* states to do so. Individual states have adopted different limits on the routes, distances, and allowed public expenditures for private school transportation. Parents may not demand transportation services beyond that required by the transportation statute.[129] Courts have also rejected the argument that denial of school transportation to nonpublic school children would violate their rights to equal protection or penalize their free exercise of religion in attending church schools.[130]

In a majority of states, courts have held nonpublic school transportation to be valid under their state constitutions, but a significant minority of state courts found such transportation impermissible under their state constitution.[131] Where state legislatures authorize interdistrict transportation to both public and nonpublic school students, the law was sustained even though nonpublic school students made much greater use of the interdistrict transportation.[132] Where the law permits interdistrict transportation only for nonpublic school students, the state courts have divided on the validity of that arrangement, with Iowa and Rhode Island invalidating it and Pennsylvania permitting it.[133]

Discriminatory application of a valid law, e.g., by denying transportation services based on the enrollment in public or private schools, may be enjoined.[134] Nor can school administrators ignore specific statutory restrictions, such as where a statute limited the authority to provide parochial school transportation to "the nearest available public school."[135] Where a statute expressly mandates (rather than merely permits) private school transportation, state administrators have no discretion to deny it.[136]

Where the agency charged with providing nonpublic school transportation elects, in lieu thereof, to pay parents funds to obtain substitute transportation, some courts allowed the practice as authorized by busing statutes, as long as the fare payment is reasonable and less than the district's cost of providing busing service.[137]

Administrative decisions on transportation arrangements may always be challenged for abuse of discretion,[138] but parents must make timely application for school transportation or be foreclosed from complaining.[139]

Instructional Materials and Equipment.   State loans of secular textbooks to nonpublic school children have been upheld under the federal Constitution,[140] under the state constitutions of New York, Ohio, and Pennsylvania, but such loans were held unconstitutional under the state constitutions of Massachusetts, Kentucky, California, Michigan, Missouri, Nebraska, Oregon, and South Dakota.[141]

The Supreme Court initially distinguished government loans of books, which it upheld, from loans of other instructional materials and equipment, which it found unconstitutional. That distinction was later rejected by the Supreme Court in the *Mitchell* case, which is reported at the end of this chapter. The Court there held that state loan of instructional materials and computers for use by students in religiously affiliated schools is constitutional although the materials and computers were placed in the custody of those schools.[142] *Mitchell* removed a major barrier to government efforts to wire all primary and secondary schools for computer education in the Internet age.

Remedial Services.   The *Mitchell* decision also changed prior law on government provision of "auxiliary services" to students of church-related schools. After previously invalidating the use of federal funds for remedial services to disadvantaged children at church-related schools,[143] the Court later split three ways on the constitutionality of providing counseling, diagnostic, therapeutic, and remedial services to needful students at church schools; one bloc of Justices viewed such services as valid in all circumstances, another bloc viewed them as invalid in all circumstances, and the third swing bloc concluded that *some* diagnostic and health services could be validly provided but not on church-school premises.[144] A few years later, one coalition of majority Justices held that state provision of *diagnostic services* (speech, hearing, and psychological testing) inside parochial schools by publicly employed professionals was constitutional, while another coalition of majority Justices held that such on-site *therapeutic services*, often provided by the same public school professionals, was unconstitutional.[145] In 1985 the Court, by 5–4 vote, nullified laws that provided for *remedial instruction* by public school teachers *inside* parochial schools,[146] but the Court thereafter upheld public provision of on-site education-related services (sign-language interpreter) inside a parochial school classroom under the IDEA. That case, *Zobrest*, figured prominently in later Supreme Court decisions that upheld government aid for students at religiously affiliated schools. In *Agostini*, the Supreme Court ruled that the provision of *remedial instruction* to disadvantaged children inside parochial schools by publicly employed professionals under Title I of the federal education aid statute was constitutional. The Court then followed up in the above-noted *Mitchell* case by holding that the loan of computers and instructional materials for student use inside religious school classrooms was constitutional. Both *Agostini* and *Mitchell* mark a shift away from the school site test of constitutionality. They expressly overruled and confined earlier contrary Supreme Court decisions. As the latest word on these issues, the *Agostini* and *Mitchell* opinions, which appear at the end of this chapter, merit close reading. These decisions do not discuss or involve government tuition voucher grants, which are discussed below.

For states whose constitutions prohibit state delivery of valid federal aid programs, Congress has enacted "bypass" legislation that authorizes federal officials to deliver such aid through sources other than state or local government agencies.[147]

Tuition, Vouchers, and Tax Relief.   In 1973, the Supreme Court held that state reimbursement to parents of part of their tuition costs at church-related schools was an unconstitutional aid to the religious mission of those schools.[148] Several states thereafter enacted broader educational subsidies that extend to all parents, on the theory that a program of general assistance available to all parents could pass constitutional muster regardless of their choice of schools. A Wisconsin law that provided tuition grants to students of low-income families for use in public or nonsectarian private schools was upheld under the federal and Wisconsin constitutions, but a federal court in Ohio later overturned an Ohio law that granted school tuition vouchers to low-income parents for use in parochial as well as nonsectarian schools.[149] A similar tuition voucher law was struck down by a Florida state court on state constitutional grounds.[150] Both the Ohio and Florida decisions have been appealed and at this writing are pending further court decision. The Supreme Court has to date declined petitions for it to review the constitutionality of tuition vouchers that could be used for education expenses at religiously affiliated schools.

The *Agostini* and *Mitchell* decisions did not consider or discuss the constitutionality of tuition relief programs for parents of students attending religiously affiliated schools, their potential relevance to the constitutionality of tuition relief programs continues to be debated by parties who support and oppose such programs.

A variant on the tuition grant issue appeared in Maine and Vermont laws that granted tuition and tax relief benefits to parents in districts that lacked public schools for use in nonsectarian private schools, but denied those benefits for parents of children in parochial schools. In cases that did not reach the Supreme Court, those laws were upheld against the challenge that they were discriminatory and violated Fourteenth Amendment equal protection and First Amendment free exercise of religion.[151]

In 1973, the Supreme Court voided a New York tax relief provision as an indirect form of subsidy for church school tuition,[152] but it later sustained a Minnesota law that allowed all parents a state income tax deduction for educational expenses, though church school parents gained the most benefit from the deduction.[153] The Court concluded that because the tax scheme was a law of general application, its prior precedents did not control:

> . . . this case is vitally different from the scheme struck down in *Nyquist*. There, public assistance amounting to tuition grants, was provided only to parents of children in *nonpublic* schools. [Moreover] we intimated that "public assistance (e.g., scholarships) made available generally without regard to the sectarian-nonsectarian or public-nonpublic nature of the institution benefitted," might not offend the Establishment Clause. We think the tax deduction adopted by Minnesota is more similar to this latter type of program than it is to the arrangement struck down in *Nyquist*. [*Mueller v. Allen*, 463 U.S. 388, 397, 398 (1983)]

More recently the Arizona Supreme Court upheld that state's law which provided tax credit up to $500 for taxpayer contributions to organizations that provide tuition support to private schools, including church-related schools.[154] The thesis that governments could constitutionally employ tax policy to lessen parental financial burdens of educating children in sectarian as well as other schools continues to be debated and litigated.

The Supreme Court has been asked on several recent occasions to review the above voucher cases, but it has declined to do so.[155]

Tax relief laws that satisfy the federal Constitution must still satisfy state constitutions, but the effect of state constitutions on tax relief laws remains largely untested in most states.

CHARTER SCHOOLS

Legal Status of Charter Schools

The state statutes and regulations on charter schools are too fresh, evolving, and varied to indicate any single pattern of legal treatment. The structure, powers, and operational requirements of charter schools and their elemental characteristics thus vary with the peculiarities of law in each state. Some charter schools may be described as new school districts,[156] or as public schools operating within an existing district,[157] or as private, nonprofit corporations.[158] Their goals, funding mechanisms, and degree of official oversight vary widely. Some are highly specialized and dedicated to improving the education of a narrow class of students, such as "at-risk" or "special needs" children who are not successful in a normal public school environment.[159] Some charter schools mimic special-purpose academies in the way they tailor their organization, curriculum, and teaching methods to particular goals.

As shown in Figure 9.1, 37 states have enacted laws for the grant of a state charter to eligible schools or associated individuals since 1991, when charter schools were first authorized.

The web site source of the study by the Center for Education Reform also notes that as of the 1999–2000 school year the charter schools in 31 states and the District of Columbia served about 400,000 students. The total number of 1,689 charter schools for the 1999–2000 school year, an increase from a total of 1,129 previously reported by the Center for the 1998–1999 school year (at the same web site), is a further indication of the rapid growth of charter schools.

One common purpose or policy of such laws is to allow charter schools greater legal autonomy than is accorded to traditional public schools with the hope of encouraging them to develop innovative educational programs and practices, and through the force of competition, to improve the quality of public education by stimulating like or new educational reforms in public schools. However, the laws in many states have reserved such a high degree of state and local school district oversight and control of charter schools as to raise the criticism that such laws defeat the purpose by encouraging local initiative by granting authority on one hand and taking it back with the other. Researchers have noted that "weak" charter laws reflect a political compromise to accommodate opponents of the charter school movement.[160]

State	Number	State	Number
Alaska	17	Michigan	173
Arizona	352	Minnesota	59
California	239	Mississippi	1
Colorado	65	Nevada	5
Connecticut	16	New Jersey	48
Delaware	5	New Mexico	3
District of Columbia	31	New York	5
Florida	111	North Carolina	75
Georgia	32	Ohio	48
Hawaii	2	Pennsylvania	47
Idaho	8	Rhode Island	2
Illinois	19	South Carolina	8
Kansas	15	Texas	167
Louisiana	17	Wisconsin	55
Massachusetts	39	Total	1,689

FIGURE 9.1   Charter Schools in Operation, by State, 1999–2000 School Year
Source: Center for Education Reform, "Charter School Highlights and Statistics," published on the center's web site: http://edreform.com.

> For charter schools to have a positive impact on public education as a whole, policymakers will need to go back to the drawing boards of charter school legislation. . . . And regulators will need to retool systems of oversight to ensure accountability while minimizing the administrative burdens. . . . They [charter schools] have surprised many by surviving . . . despite philosophical opposition. . . . . . . Perhaps despite the host of political and operational challenges they face, charter schools will surprise skeptics yet again. [B.C. Hassel, *The Charter School Challenge*, 162, 163 (Brookings Institution Press, Washington, D.C. 1999)]

In view of the substantial differences in state charter laws, the following overview can only indicate the general range of their terms. It does not represent either the precise content or direction of legal developments and administrative practice. Readers who desire specific information regarding the charter school operations in a particular state may refer to the Appendix to this chapter, which lists the statutory source for each state.

The grant and receipt of a charter may be likened to a contract between the state and the chartered school whereby the charter terms define the school's purposes, educational methods, organization, management, students to be educated, and standards for measuring achievement of the school's purposes. Charter obligations incorporate criteria on admissions, testing, teacher qualifications, and student transportation. Those criteria differ in many significant respects from the criteria that govern public schools.

In some states a charter school may operate independently of local school board control, but in most states, charter schools remain subject to ongoing oversight by state or local school boards. Thus, although they offer an alternative to public schooling, charter schools remain one form of state-sponsored school.

Experimental innovations in public school, such as "schools within schools" or school district "academies" mimic some charter schools. In one school district,[161] 95 such intramural units were instituted in 22 public schools to spur new approaches to meet special student problems or interests. Such subdivided groups may even involve participation and funding support by private organizations. The National Education Association has supported the development of these intramural academies to "restructur[e] the governance, instruction, parent involvement, and assessment practices" of public schools. One purpose of charter schools is to stimulate improvements in the quality of public education by creating competition with them.[162] Many statutes expressly require active participation by teachers, staff, parents, and/or local community groups in the creation and administration of charter schools.

Charter Grants, Renewal, and Revocation

Eligible Parties

Charter laws prescribe eligibility standards for parties that desire to obtain a charter. Some states allow an existing public school, nonprofit organization, group of teachers, or parents[163] to apply for a charter.[164] Other states limit applications to existing public schools and to new nonsectarian schools.[165] A few permit an existing private school to convert to a charter school, provided that the charter school is nonsectarian and nondenominational.[166] A hybrid approach has been to require the local school district to receive the charter and to then contract with other parties to operate the chartered school within the district.[167]

Application and Approval Procedures

Procedures for applying for a charter are usually specified by charter statutes. Some states authorize state officials to establish application procedures[168] and, less commonly, local school boards.[169] Similar state variations appear for charter approvals, with some laws vesting that authority in state officials, and others vesting it in local school boards, or in state officials on the recommendation of the local school board.[170] In some states, charter approval may be made by any one of several entities, including a community college or state university.[171] Where an existing school seeks to convert to a charter school, the law may require that its application be approved by a specified percentage of the teachers, employees, parents, or members of the local community who participate in the meetings to discuss the proposed conversion.[172]

Public hearings are required in some instances, as part of the application and grant process.[173] The right to seek court review of administrative denials of charters or charter renewals is granted in some states, but denied in others.[174]

Charter Renewal and Revocation

The law in most states sets the term or length of a charter grant, commonly three to five years,[175] with an opportunity for successive charter renewals. Some statutes also specify other circumstances in which charters will be revoked or not be renewed. Statutory grounds to revoke or deny renewal of a school charter include failure to meet its own or state-imposed achievement standards;[176] violation of applicable laws or charter provisions;[177] or the school's teachers, parents, or the local community vote to revoke or block renewal of a charter.[178]

Charter School Funding

Funding methods may be set by the charter terms[179] or may require approval of the agency empowered to approve school charters.[180] In addition to their tuition charges, charter schools frequently receive public assistance through a combination of state, federal, and local monies, usually determined on a per-student formula, and state funding was held not to violate the state constitution of California.[181] Depending on state law, charter tuition may be paid by the state or by the local district.[182] In Connecticut, charter schools may charge local districts up to the amount they spend per student. Public funding adjustments are often required for special education students, particularly those with handicaps.[183] Charter school may also seek and receive grants from private sources.[184]

Statutory Control Issues

Admissions Criteria

Charter school admissions criteria involve several basic issues that vary with the type of charter school and with the admissions standards of governing state law.

Open vs. Selective Admissions.   A state charter may require charter schools to admit all students, subject only to restrictions based on the grade levels, curriculum offering, or residence of the student,[185] or it may require charter schools to have a student racial and ethnic makeup reflective of the general population of its served area, or it may authorize such schools expressly to serve an identified minority student body.[186] The allowance of competitive admissions may be part of the charter itself,[187] but a few states permit significant leeway for competitive admissions practices.[188]

Some of the states allow a charter school to serve specific *special education* or *"at-risk" students*,[189] give preference to applications for schools dedicated to helping at-risk students,[190] or require that a specified percentage of chartered schools must be devoted to at-risk students.[191] Some also require that every charter proposal indicate how the school will address special educational needs of at-risk students.[192] Louisiana went further to require that the percentage of charter school "at-risk" students equal or exceed the percentage of such students in the local district.

Gender-Based Selection.   Although public schools may not adopt gender-based admissions, it remains unclear and unsettled whether states may constitutionally permit the establishment of single-sex charter schools. As noted in Chapter 8, some educators advocate single-sex education in the belief that it would benefit at-risk students, particularly in urban areas with distressed schools.

School Service Area.   State laws also vary on the question whether a charter school may serve only students residing within the bounds of its overlying school district, and the extent to which schools that serve target disadvantaged students must give admission preference to students living in the "home" district.[193]

Curriculum and Teacher Qualifications

Charter laws may authorize specialized elective curricula alongside traditional curricula, e.g., in performing arts or computer science.[194] Some states have also exempted charter schools from state or local regulation of textbook and curriculum requirements.[195] Most states require that charter school teachers be certified by state educational authorities, but a few allow some teachers not to be so certified.[196]

Transportation

School transportation service is critical to economically disadvantaged students who seek admission to charter schools. Some states require charter schools[197] or local districts[198] to provide such transportation. Where a student resides outside of the charter school's "home" district, a state may provide or pay for such transportation.[199]

Chapter 9 Discussion Questions

Where the answer to a question may be qualified by special circumstances, explain the potential qualification.

1. What is the principal difference between the constitutional rights and obligations of public schools, their teachers, and students and those of private schools, their teachers, and students?

2. What is the principal difference between state regulation of public schools, their teachers, and students and that of private schools, their teachers, and students?

3. What is the principal difference between the law of public school relations with their teachers and students and that of private school relations with their teachers and students?

4. Is receipt by private schools and their students of publicly paid school transportation and health services a constitutional right? Determined by legislation? Explain.

5. In what circumstances may a parent satisfy compulsory education laws by educating a child at home? Explain.

6. May nonpublic school pupils be admitted part time to a public school class? To a public school extracurricular activity? Explain.

7. Does the general law of tort duties and liabilities that apply to public schools also apply to private schools? Explain.

8. Are the tort immunity doctrines that apply to public schools the same for private schools? Explain.

9. List the forms of government aid to church-related education which under the latest Supreme Court decisions are:
   a. Prohibited by the national Constitution.
   b. Allowed by the national Constitution.
   c. Whose validity under the national Constitution remains unsettled.

10. How do charter schools differ from public schools?

11. How do charter schools differ from private schools?

12. Are the charter school laws and regulations uniform among the states? Explain.

13. In your opinion, will charter schools withstand challenge as impermissible uses of public funds under the national Constitution? Under state constitutions? Explain.

❖ C A S E S

Case 9.1

GERACI v. ST. XAVIER HIGH SCHOOL
3 Ohio Op. 3d 146 (1978)

> [**Focus Note**. *Competing claims of contract breach. Suit by expelled parochial school student seeking reinstatement.*]

BETTMAN, J.

. . . This appeal raises basically two issues. First, whether appellants' constitutional right to due process has application to the conduct of disciplinary proceedings by a private school. Secondly, whether appellees' handling of Mark's expulsion was arbitrary and unreasonable and therefore a breach of appellants' contract of enrollment.

❖ ❖ ❖

The due process requirements of the Fourteenth Amendment are only applicable to situations involving "state action." . . .

Where . . . the enterprise in question is regulated by the state, state action will be found if there is "a sufficiently close nexus between the State and the challenged action of the regulated entity so that the action of the latter may be fairly treated as that of the State itself." . . . This mode of analysis would here focus on the specific action of expulsion from St. Xavier. The state regulation of St. Xavier is relatively minimal. Our attention has been directed to nothing indicating state involvement in St. Xavier's disciplinary process. . . .

Even without state involvement in the disciplinary proceedings, state action may still be found if the state is so entwined with the administration and operation of the school that a "symbiotic relationship" has developed. . . .

St. Xavier is approved by the state as a high school. It files annual reports with the state dealing with its curriculum, class loads, number of teachers, etc. The teachers at St. Xavier all have state certificates of qualification. The state provides, on loan, certain standard textbooks and furnishes transportation to students. The school is exempted from state taxation. However, other than ascertaining that the school meets minimum state standards for a high school, the state exercises no control over the school whatsoever. This is certainly not the sort of pervasive state involvement required for a finding of a symbiotic state action. . . .

Our conclusion that there is no state action in the disciplinary proceedings of a private high school such as St. Xavier is supported by *Wisch v. Sanford School, Inc.,* 420 F. Supp. 1310 (D.C. Del. 1976); *Bright v. Isenbarger,* 314 F. Supp. 1382 (N.D. Ind. 1970); and a long line of federal cases involving private universities. The assignment is, accordingly, overruled.

Appellants' assignments of error . . . maintain that the trial court erred in finding that the contract between the parties was breached by Mark's conduct and not by the procedures used by appellees in determining to expel him.

Mr. Geraci had paid Mark's tuition for his junior year and made the required deposit toward the senior year tuition. The parties are in agreement that this gave rise to a contract that St. Xavier would continue to provide education to Mark so long as he met its academic and disciplinary standards. They are further in agreement that the catalogue, describing St. Xavier High School's academic program and its standards and requirements constituted a part of the terms and conditions of such contract. The catalogue . . . provides in pertinent parts:

> By the act of registering at St. Xavier High School, a student and his parents (or guardians) understand and agree to pursue the educational objectives and practices as stated in this catalogue and to observe the disciplinary code of the school. . . .

> Disciplinary Norms

> The St. Xavier norms of conduct are predicated on two premises: first, that every student has the right to certain situations (such as the protection of his personal property, the physical integrity of the facilities, an atmosphere conducive to personal growth and development) and, second, that every student has the duty to preserve these rights for others. . . . Since no list of norms can cover every situation, the administration presumes that common sense, mature judgment, and Christian charity are the guides by which every St. Xavier student should measure his actions.

> The assistant principal is in charge of all matters of discipline. . . .

> Expulsion

> The following offenses are grounds for expulsion:

> 1. conduct detrimental to the reputation of the school. . . .
> 8. immorality in talk or action.

Appellants understood that Xavier maintained high standards of deportment. The evidence before the trial court was as follows. On the final day of the school year Tom McKenna, a student at Moeller High School, entered St. Xavier

High School, went to the classroom where Mark Geraci and his classmates were taking a final test and threw a meringue pie in the face of Mr. Downie, the teacher. Pandemonium ensued. . . . By Mark's own testimony, several weeks before he and some fellow students had decided it would be a "funny prank" to get McKenna to "pie" Mr. Downie. . . . The original plan was that Mark would collect $50.00 from the group to pay McKenna. He did not, however, collect any money. Nevertheless, the evening preceding the last day of school . . . McKenna asked "whatever happened about the pie throwing." Geraci told him he had not collected any money and McKenna said "he might come over and do it anyway." Mark made no response to this statement. On McKenna's inquiry Geraci told him the room number of the class where Mr. Downie would be teaching and, on further inquiry, which door of the building to enter. At McKenna's request, Geraci called another Moeller student to arrange for transportation for McKenna.

The very recital of the above facts makes abundantly clear that Geraci aided and abetted McKenna's throwing of the pie in the face of his teacher, Mr. Downie, an act patently "immoral," "detrimental to the reputation of the school" and violative of Geraci's acknowledged duty to exercise "common sense, mature judgment, and Christian charity." The trial court's finding that Geraci's acts constituted a breach of the contract with St. Xavier is, therefore, fully supported by the evidence.

Although . . . a private school's disciplinary proceedings are not controlled by the due process clause, and accordingly such schools have broad discretion in making rules and setting up procedures for their enforcement, nevertheless, under its broad equitable powers a court will intervene where such discretion is abused or the proceedings do not comport with fundamental fairness. . . .

The record shows that Mr. Meyer, the Assistant Principal of Xavier . . . called Mark to his office several hours after the event. At that time Mark, though protesting that he did not really expect McKenna to go through with it, admitted substantially all the elements of his involvement. . . . Meyer forthwith advised him that he was expelled. The transcript further shows that before this decision was finalized Mr. Meyer, Mr. Trainor, the Principal, and Father Borgmann, President of St. Xavier, all discussed and considered the matter; that Meyer discussed it with Mr. Geraci; that Trainor discussed it with Mr. Geraci and that Father Borgmann discussed it with both father and son. The testimony as to these discussions shows an appreciation and consideration by appellees of Mark's previously unblemished disciplinary record and his academic excellence. . . . On the basis of the record we cannot say that appellees abused their discretion nor that the procedures were unfair.

The trial court did not err in holding that Mark's expulsion was just, proper, and in accordance with the contract between the parties and did not constitute an abuse of discretion. . . .

The judgment of the trial court must accordingly be affirmed.

Case 9.2

CATHOLIC HIGH SCHOOL ASSN. OF ARCHDIOCESE OF NEW YORK v. CULVERT
753 F.2d 1161 (2nd Cir. 1985)

[**Focus Note**. *Limits of state control over religious school labor relations. After Catholic schools teachers' union filed unfair labor charges against the association managing those schools, the association brought suit seeking declaratory judgment that state labor relations law and state jurisdiction were preempted by the National Labor Relations Act (NLRA) and alternatively that the state's asserted jurisdiction violated the religion clauses of the First Amendment. The following opinion notes and discusses the split of opinion between it and the 7th Circuit Court of Appeals on the constitutional question.*]

CARDAMONE, CIRCUIT JUDGE.

This appeal presents delicate issues involving the relationship between church and state. . . . The issue in this case is whether the Religion Clauses of the First Amendment made applicable to the states by the Fourteenth Amendment prohibit the New York State Labor Relations Board from exercising jurisdiction over the labor relations between parochial schools and their lay teachers. This "difficult and sensitive" question, expressly left open by the Supreme Court in *NLRB v. Catholic Bishop*, 440 U.S. 490 . . . is one of first impression in this Circuit. . . .

The New York State Labor Relations Board (State Board or Board) administers the New York State Labor Relations Act (SLRA or Act). As originally enacted in 1937 the Act's provisions did not apply to employees of charitable, educational or religious associations and corporations. In 1968 the Act was amended to bring these employees within its scope. . . .

The parties agree that the schools are "church-operated". . . . The faculty of the Association is composed of both lay and religious teachers, all of whom are directly involved in the transmission of religious values to the students. . . . The by-laws of the Union specifically exclude religious faculty, and each of the agreements was expressly limited to nonreligious issues. . . .

In 1980 . . . the Union filed unfair labor practice charges against the Association for the first time. . . . None of these charges raised a religious issue. . . .

. . . As a result of its investigation the Board issued a formal complaint. The Association immediately brought an action seeking a declaratory judgment and injunctive relief against the State Board. It challenged the State Board's assertion of jurisdiction, alleging that it violates the Religion Clauses of the First Amendment and that jurisdiction by the Board over lay teachers in church-operated schools is preempted by the National Labor Relations Act. . . . The Union and the Board opposed the Association's motion for summary judgment. . . . The Association's motion was granted by United States District Judge Morris E. Lasker upon his conclusion that the State Board's assertion of jurisdiction violated the Establishment Clause. . . .

The virtually identical issue was presented but left unresolved in *Catholic Bishop.* There a closely-divided Supreme Court held that the National Labor Relations Board (NLRB) lacked jurisdiction over lay teachers because Congress had not affirmatively indicated that it intended them to be covered by the National Labor Relations Act (NLRA).

. . . Judge Lasker then reached the First Amendment issues and held that application of the Act to lay teachers violated the Establishment Clause because it "threatens to produce excessive entanglement between church and state." . . . He specifically limited his holding to lay teachers, as opposed to other church employees . . . and found it unnecessary to rule on the Association's free exercise claim. . . .

The district court also held that limitations in the collective bargaining agreement would not cure the conflict with the Establishment Clause. . . . Finally, Judge Lasker held that the NLRA does not preempt the State Board from asserting jurisdiction over parochial schools. . . .

◇ ◇ ◇

We turn first to the Association's argument that the State's assertion of jurisdiction violates the Establishment Clause. The Supreme Court has made it clear . . . that "total separation is not possible in an absolute sense, [for s]ome relationship between government and religious organizations is inevitable." *Lemon v. Kurtzman,* 403 U.S. 602, 614 . . . (1971). It explained that "the line of separation, far from being a 'wall,' is a blurred, indistinct, and variable barrier depending upon all the circumstances of a particular relationship." . . . The Court has often found it useful to use the familiar three-pronged test in determining whether there has been a violation of the Establishment Clause.

◇ ◇ ◇

. . . The parties do not dispute that the Act has a secular purpose and that its primary effect is not to advance or inhibit religion. Nonetheless, the district court found that assertion of jurisdiction under the Act violates the Establishment Clause because it threatens to produce an excessive administrative entanglement of government with religion.

. . . First, it found that there was an "imminent possibility" that the Association would be required to bargain with lay teachers on religious subjects. Second, it found that . . . the State Board might have to determine whether an asserted religious reason was a valid part of church doctrine. . . .

. . . The State Board's relationship with the religious schools . . . does not involve the degree of "surveillance" necessary to find excessive administrative entanglement. In the three key Supreme Court cases addressing excessive administrative entanglement . . . states attempted to provide aid to support certain secular aspects of classroom instruction in parochial schools. In these three cases the Supreme Court held that the aid resulted in excessive administrative entanglement, finding that the restrictions imposed would inevitably require "comprehensive, discriminating, and continuing state surveillance." . . . This is quite unlike the situation here where the State Board's supervision over the collective bargaining process is neither comprehensive nor continuing.

. . . A "church-operated" school believing itself aggrieved by such an [Labor Board] order may refuse to comply and raise a First Amendment defense when and if the Board seeks judicial enforcement of its order.

The Association relies, as did the Seventh Circuit in *Catholic Bishop,* on a passage from an article on collective bargaining in colleges and universities:

❖ ❖ ❖

We decline to follow the Seventh Circuit down this slippery slope. . . . In effect the Association contends that the state would be compelling it to do something that it must choose to do voluntarily or not at all. But as the Fifth Circuit stated in *EEOC v. Mississippi:* "That faculty members are expected to serve as exemplars of practicing Christians does not serve to make the terms and conditions of their employment matters of church administration and thus purely of ecclesiastical concern." 626 F.2d at 485. Thus, the duty to bargain does not involve excessive administrative entanglement between church and state.

The second ground for the district court's finding of excessive administrative entanglement was that the State Board's jurisdiction would require it to determine the validity of asserted religious motives as part of church doctrine. . . .

In the present case it is not the inquiry into whether a belief is sincerely held by an individual that is at issue. Rather, it is the possibility of recurrent questioning of whether a particular church actually holds a particular belief. . . . One of the primary purposes of the Establishment Clause was to avoid just this result. Thus, the First Amendment prohibits the State Board from inquiring into an asserted religious motive to determine whether it is pretextual.

The question remains whether this limitation of the State Board's powers should preclude it from asserting jurisdiction. We think not. . . . It is still free to determine, using a dual motive analysis, whether the religious motive was in fact the cause of the discharge. . . . Other circuits have made a similar accommodation by permitting the EEOC to assert jurisdiction but precluding it from determining whether an asserted reason is pretextual. See, e.g., *EEOC v. Mississippi College,* 626 F.2d at 485.

. . . We agree with the Seventh Circuit that in cases involving lay faculty the Board should not be allowed to find a violation simply because anti-union animus motivated a discharge "in part." Nonetheless, we adopt the accommodation that the Seventh Circuit rejected. . . . Were the Board allowed to apply an "in part" test in addressing an asserted religious motive, an order based on such a finding would violate the First Amendment. . . . To avoid this unconstitutional result, the Board therefore may order reinstatement of a lay teacher at a parochial school only if he or she would not have been fired otherwise for asserted religious reasons.

Where a principled basis exists . . . to limit state aid to or regulation of parochial schools, an attempt should be made to accommodate the interests of church and state under the Establishment Clause. . . .

For basically the same reasons, we reach the same result with respect to the Association's Free Exercise claim. The Association, quoting the Seventh Circuit . . . first argues that "the very threshold act of certification of the union necessarily alters and impinges upon the religious character of all parochial schools." . . . Support for such an absolute view is found neither in case law nor the history of the First Amendment. . . .

A determination of whether state regulation of the way the Association acts in its relations with its lay teachers violates free exercise requires a balancing test. The burden the state imposes on the Association's exercise of its religious beliefs must be weighed against the State's interests in enforcing the Act. We must consider whether: . . . (2) the State action burdened the religious exercise; and (3) the State interest was sufficiently compelling to override the constitutional right of free exercise of religion. See *Wisconsin v. Yoder*, 406 U.S. 205. . . .

We first turn to whether the claims presented here are religious and not secular. . . . Many matters that pertain to private schools are already subject to governmental regulation. The Association must meet state requirements for fire inspections, building and zoning regulations and compulsory school attendance laws, all of which regulate the conduct of the Association's schools. . . .

❖ ❖ ❖

The Association does not contend that collective bargaining is contrary to the beliefs of the Catholic Church. . . .

. . . To find that an enactment violates the right to free exercise of religious beliefs, "it is necessary . . . for one to show the coercive effect of the enactment as it operates against him in the practice of his religion." *School District v. Schempp*, 374 U.S. 203, 223 . . . . The injury must be "a demonstrable reality," not merely a speculative possibility . . . and compliance with the regulation must be directly contrary to claimant's religious beliefs. . . . For the reasons discussed [above] . . . and because of the restrictions we have placed on the Board's power, these claims do not burden freedom of religious exercise.

But a lingering question remains as to whether State Board jurisdiction may impermissibly chill free exercise rights; whether ". . . [t]o minimize friction . . . prudence will ultimately dictate that the bishop tailor his conduct and decisions to 'steer far wider of the unlawful zone' of impermissible conduct." 559 F.2d at 1124. . . .

It is necessary, then, to decide whether this indirect and incidental burden on religion is justified by a compelling state interest. . . . Here a compelling state interest exists. State labor laws are essential to the preservation of industrial peace and a sound economic order. . . . . . . Thus, even if the exercise of Board jurisdiction has an indirect and incidental effect on employment decisions in parochial schools involving religious issues, this minimal intrusion is justified by the State's compelling interest in collective bargaining.

The judgment appealed from insofar as it held there was no preemption by the National Labor Relations Act is affirmed. . . . Insofar as the judgment granted summary judgment . . . in favor of the plaintiff Association upon a finding of a First Amendment violation, it is reversed. . . .

GEORGE C. PRATT, CIRCUIT JUDGE, dissenting.

Although I agree with the majority opinion on the preemption issue, I dissent on the constitutional issue for the reasons set forth in Judge Lasker's opinion below . . . and in the seventh circuit's opinion in *Catholic Bishop v. NLRB*, 559 F.2d 1112 (7th Cir. 1977). . . .

Review Questions 9.2

1. Consider the First and Seventh Circuit court positions. Which approach do you think will be more persuasive in other federal circuits?

2. Under the above opinion, what limits does the Constitution place on state labor board decisions affecting religious schools?

3. As the above opinion notes, the New York labor statute initially excluded religious school employees from its coverage, but was amended to cover them. Does this suggest that state legislatures have a constitutional choice, as a matter of policy, either to include them, as in New York, or exclude them as in Pennsylvania?

4. On the preemption issue, the above opinion contained the following important footnote: "2. If *Catholic Bishop* had held that teachers are within the jurisdiction granted by the NLRA but are not "employees" within the meaning of that Act, the State Board would be plainly preempted from exercising jurisdiction. . . . In this case, the State Board has validly asserted jurisdiction because Congress did not indicate that the NLRB had jurisdiction." Does this mean Congress can still preempt the state laws by enacting a law that clearly confers jurisdiction on the NLRB?

Case 9.3

AGOSTINI v. FELTON
521 U.S. 203 (1997)

> *[**Focus Note**. Constitutional criteria on government aid to church-related education. Twelve years after deciding that the New York City Board of Education could not constitutionally send public school teachers into parochial schools to provide remedial education to disadvantaged children under a federally funded program, the Supreme Court overruled that decision in the following opinion and took occasion to review in some detail its changing approach to measuring the constitutional limits on government aids to church-related education.]*

JUSTICE O'CONNOR *delivered the opinion of the Court.*

In *Aguilar v. Felton*, 473 U.S. 402 . . . (1985), this Court held that the Establishment Clause of the First Amendment barred the city of New York from sending public school teachers into parochial schools to provide remedial education to disadvantaged children. . . . . . . Petitioners maintain that *Aguilar* cannot be squared with our intervening Establishment Clause jurisprudence. . . . We agree with petitioners that *Aguilar* is not consistent with our subsequent Establishment Clause decisions and further conclude that, on the facts presented here, petitioners are entitled . . . to relief [lifting of the injunction against allowing public school teachers from providing remedial services inside a parochial school]. . . .

In 1965, Congress enacted Title I of the Elementary and Secondary Education Act of 1965 . . . to "provid[e] full educational opportunity to every child regardless of economic background." . . . Toward that end, Title I channels federal funds, through the States, to "local educational agencies" (LEA's). . . . Title I funds must be made available to all eligible children, regardless of whether they attend public schools . . . and the services provided to children attending private schools must be "equitable in comparison to services and other benefits for public school children." . . .

. . . The Title I services themselves must be "secular, neutral, and nonideological," § 6321(a)(2), and must "supplement, and in no case supplant, the level of services" already provided by the private school. . . .

Petitioner Board of Education of the City of New York (Board), an LEA . . . has grappled ever since with how to provide Title I services. . . . . . . Recognizing that more than 90% of the private schools within the Board's jurisdiction are sectarian . . . the Board initially arranged to transport children to public schools for after-school Title I instruction. But this enterprise was largely unsuccessful. Attendance was poor, teachers and children were tired, and parents were concerned for the safety of their children. . . . The Board then moved the after-school instruction onto private school campuses, as Congress had contemplated when it enacted Title I. . . .

After this program also yielded mixed results, the Board implemented the plan we evaluated in *Aguilar v. Felton*. . . . . . . Assignments to private schools were made on a voluntary basis and without regard to the religious affiliation of the employee or the wishes of the private school. . . . . . . Before any public employee could provide Title I instruction at a private school, she would be given a detailed set of written and oral instructions. . . . Specifically, employees would be told that (i) they were employees of the Board and accountable only to their public school supervisors; (ii) they had exclusive responsibility for selecting students for the Title I program and could teach only those children who met the eligibility criteria for Title I; (iii) their materials and equipment would be used only in the Title I program; (iv) they could not engage in team-teaching or other cooperative instructional activities with private school teachers; and (v) they could not introduce any religious matter into their teaching or become involved in any way with the religious activities of the private schools. . . . All religious symbols were to be removed from classrooms used for Title I services. . . . The rules acknowledged that it might be necessary for Title I teachers to consult with a student's regular classroom teacher to assess the student's particular needs and progress, but admonished instructors to limit those consultations to mutual professional concerns regarding the student's education. . . . To ensure compliance . . . a publicly employed field supervisor was to attempt to make at least one unannounced visit to each teacher's classroom every month. . . . In 1978 . . . taxpayers—respondents here—sued the Board claiming that the Board's Title I program violated the Establishment Clause. . . . . . . The District Court granted summary judgment for the Board, but the Court of Appeals for the Second Circuit reversed. While noting that the Board's Title I program had "done so much good and little, if any, detectable harm," . . . the Court of Appeals nevertheless held that *Meek v. Pittenger*, 421 U.S. 349 . . . (1975), and *Wolman v. Walter*, 433 U.S. 229 . . . (1977), compelled it to declare the program unconstitutional. In a 5–4 decision, this Court affirmed on the ground that the Board's Title I program necessitated an "excessive entanglement of church and state in the administration of [Title I] benefits." 473 U.S., at 414. . . . . . . On remand, the District Court permanently enjoined the Board "from using public funds for any plan or program under [Title I] to the extent that it . . . permits public school teachers and guidance counselors to provide teaching and counseling services on the premises of sectarian schools. . . .

❖ ❖ ❖

In order to evaluate whether *Aguilar* has been eroded by our subsequent Establishment Clause cases, it is necessary to understand the rationale upon which *Aguilar*, as well as its companion case, *School Dist. of Grand Rapids v. Ball*, 473 U.S. 373 . . . (1985), rested.

In Ball, the Court evaluated two programs. . . . The district's Shared Time program . . . provided remedial and "enrichment" classes, at public expense, to students attending nonpublic schools. The classes were taught during regular school hours by publicly employed teachers, using materials purchased with public funds, on the premises of nonpublic schools. The Shared Time courses were in subjects designed to supplement the "core curriculum" of the nonpublic schools. . . .

. . . The Court acknowledged that the Shared Time program served a purely secular purpose. . . . . . . Nevertheless, it ultimately concluded that the program had the impermissible effect of advancing religion. . . .

✧ ✧ ✧

Distilled to essentials, the Court's conclusion that the Shared Time program in *Ball* had the impermissible effect of advancing religion rested on three assumptions: (i) any public employee who works on the premises of a religious school is presumed to inculcate religion in her work; (ii) the presence of public employees on private school premises creates a symbolic union between church and state; and (iii) any and all public aid that directly aids the educational function of religious schools impermissibly finances religious indoctrination, even if the aid reaches such schools as a consequence of private decisionmaking. Additionally, in *Aguilar* there was a fourth assumption: that New York City's Title I program necessitated an excessive government entanglement with religion because public employees who teach on the premises of religious schools must be closely monitored to ensure that they do not inculcate religion.

Our more recent cases have undermined the assumptions upon which *Ball* and *Aguilar* relied. To be sure, the general principles we use . . . have not changed. . . . For example, we continue to ask whether the government acted with the purpose of advancing or inhibiting religion. . . . . . . Likewise, we continue to explore whether the aid has the "effect" of advancing or inhibiting religion. What has changed since we decided *Ball* and *Aguilar* is our understanding of the criteria used to assess whether aid to religion has an impermissible effect.

. . . First, we have abandoned the presumption erected in *Meek* and *Ball* that the placement of public employees on parochial school grounds inevitably results in the impermissible effect of state-sponsored indoctrination or constitutes a symbolic union between government and religion. In *Zobrest v. Catalina Foothills School Dist.*, 509 U.S. 1 (1993), we examined whether the IDEA . . . was constitutional as applied to a deaf student who sought to bring his state-employed sign-language interpreter with him to his Roman Catholic high school. We held that this was permissible, expressly disavowing the notion that "the Establishment Clause [laid] down [an] absolute bar to the placing of a public employee in a sectarian school." . . . We refused to presume that a publicly employed interpreter would be pressured by the pervasively sectarian surroundings to inculcate religion. . . . In the absence of evidence to the contrary, we assumed instead that the interpreter would dutifully discharge her responsibilities as a full-time public employee. . . . . . . *Zobrest* also implicitly repudiated another assumption on which *Ball* and *Aguilar* turned: that the presence of a public employee on private school property creates an impermissible "symbolic link" between government and religion. . . .

Second, we have departed from the rule relied on in *Ball* that all government aid that directly aids the educational function of religious schools is invalid. In *Witters v. Washington Dept. of Servs. for Blind*, 474 U.S. 481 . . . (1986), we held that the Establishment Clause did not bar a State from issuing a vocational tuition grant to a blind person who wished to use the grant to attend a Christian college and become a pastor, missionary, or youth director. . . . The grants were disbursed directly to students, who then used the money to pay for tuition at the educational institution of their choice. . . . The same logic applied in *Zobrest* . . . because the IDEA's neutral eligibility criteria ensured that the interpreter's presence in a sectarian school was a "result of the private decision of individual parents" and " [could] not be attributed to state decision-making." 509 U.S., at 10. . . . . . . *Zobrest* and *Witters* make clear that, under current law, the Shared Time program in *Ball* and New York City's Title I program in *Aguilar* will not, as a matter of law, be deemed to have the effect of advancing religion through indoctrination. . . . Certainly, no evidence has ever shown that any New York City Title I instructor teaching on parochial school premises attempted to inculcate religion in students. . . .

. . . We do not see any perceptible (let alone dispositive) difference in the degree of symbolic union between a student receiving remedial instruction in a classroom on his sectarian school's campus and one receiving instruction in a van parked just at the school's curbside. To draw this line based solely on the location of the public employee is neither "sensible" nor "sound," and the Court in *Zobrest* rejected it. . . . In all relevant respects, the provision of instructional services under Title I is indistinguishable from the provision of sign-language interpreters under the IDEA. . . .

✧ ✧ ✧

. . . A number of our Establishment Clause cases have found that the criteria used for identifying beneficiaries are relevant in a second respect. . . . Specifically, the criteria might themselves have the effect of advancing religion by creating a financial incentive to undertake religious indoctrination. . . . This incentive is not present, however, where the aid is allocated on the basis of neutral, secular criteria that neither favor nor disfavor religion, and is made available to both religious and secular beneficiaries on a nondiscriminatory basis. . . .

. . . [W]e have sustained programs that provided aid to all eligible children regardless of where they attended school. See, e.g., *Everson v. Board of Ed. of Ewing*, 330 U.S. 1 . . . (1947) (sustaining local ordinance authorizing all parents to deduct from their state tax returns the costs of transporting their children to school on public buses); *Board of Ed. of Central School Dist. No. 1 v. Allen*, 392 U.S. 236 . . . (1968) (sustaining New York law loaning secular textbooks to all children); *Mueller v. Allen*, 463 U.S. 388 . . . (1983) (sustaining Minnesota statute allowing all parents to deduct actual costs of tuition, textbooks, and transportation from state tax returns); *Witters*, 474 U.S., at 487–488 . . . (sustaining Washington law granting all eligible blind persons vocational assistance); *Zobrest,* 509 U.S., at 10 (sustaining section of IDEA providing all "disabled" children with necessary aid).

❖ ❖ ❖

We now turn to *Aguilar*'s conclusion that New York City's Title I program resulted in an excessive entanglement between church and state. ...

Not all entanglements, of course, have the effect of advancing or inhibiting religion. Interaction between church and state is inevitable ... and we have always tolerated some level of involvement between the two. Entanglement must be "excessive" before it runs afoul of the Establishment Clause. ... As discussed previously, the Court's finding of "excessive" entanglement in *Aguilar* rested on three grounds: (i) the program would require "pervasive monitoring by public authorities" to ensure that Title I employees did not inculcate religion; (ii) the program required "administrative cooperation" between the Board and parochial schools; and (iii) the program might increase the dangers of "political divisiveness." 473 U.S., at 413–414. ... Under our current understanding of the Establishment Clause, the last two considerations are insufficient by themselves to create an "excessive" entanglement. ... Since we have abandoned the assumption that properly instructed public employees will fail to discharge their duties faithfully, we must also discard the assumption that pervasive monitoring of Title I teachers is required. ... Moreover, we have not found excessive entanglement in cases in which States imposed far more onerous burdens on religious institutions than the monitoring system at issue here. ...

❖ ❖ ❖

To summarize, New York City's Title I program does not run afoul of any of three primary criteria we currently use to evaluate whether government aid has the effect of advancing religion: it does not result in governmental indoctrination; define its recipients by reference to religion; or create an excessive entanglement. We therefore hold that a federally funded program providing supplemental, remedial instruction to disadvantaged children on a neutral basis is not invalid under the Establishment Clause when such instruction is given on the premises of sectarian schools by government employees pursuant to a program containing safeguards such as those present here. The same considerations ... require us to conclude that this carefully constrained program also cannot reasonably be viewed as an endorsement of religion. ... Accordingly, we must acknowledge that *Aguilar,* as well as the portion of *Ball* addressing Grand Rapids' Shared Time program, are no longer good law.

❖ ❖ ❖

For these reasons, we reverse the judgment of the Court of Appeals and remand to the District Court with instructions to vacate its September 26, 1985 order.

Case 9.4

MITCHELL v. HELMS
—U.S.—(2000)

> [**Focus Note**. *State aid to religious schools and their students. After 15 years of litigation in lower courts on the constitutionality of a Louisiana law that authorized state loans of instructional materials and computer equipment for student use in religious schools, the Supreme Court Justices split three ways on the proper meaning and application of the Establishment Clause. The following opinion, rather than decisively settling the aid issues, invites further debate within and outside the Court.]*

Justice Thomas announced the judgment of the Court and delivered an opinion, in which THE CHIEF JUSTICE, JUSTICE SCALIA, *and* JUSTICE KENNEDY *join.*

As part of a longstanding school aid program known as Chapter 2, the Federal Government distributes funds to state and local governmental agencies, which in turn lend educational materials and equipment to public and private schools, with the enrollment of each participating school determining the amount of aid that it receives. The question is whether Chapter 2, as applied in Jefferson Parish, Louisiana, is a law respecting an establishment of religion, because many of the private schools receiving Chapter 2 aid in that parish are religiously affiliated. We hold that Chapter 2 is not such a law.

I

A

Chapter 2 of the Education Consolidation and Improvement Act of 1981 . . . has its origins in the Elementary and Secondary Education Act of 1965 (ESEA) . . . and is a close cousin of the provision of the ESEA that we recently considered in *Agostini v. Felton,* 521 U.S. 203 . . . (1997). Like the provision at issue in *Agostini,* Chapter 2 channels federal funds to local educational agencies (LEA's), which are usually public school districts, via state educational agencies (SEA's), to implement programs to assist children in elementary and secondary schools. Among other things, Chapter 2 provides aid

> "for the acquisition and use of instructional and educational materials, including library services and materials (including media materials), assessments, reference materials, computer software and hardware for instructional use, and other curricular materials." 20 U.S.C. § 7351(b)(2).

LEA's and SEA's must offer assistance to both public and private schools (although any private school must be nonprofit). . . . Participating private schools receive Chapter 2 aid . . . and allocations of Chapter 2 funds for those schools must generally be "equal (consistent with the number of children to be served) to expenditures for programs . . . for children enrolled in the public schools. . . ." Further, Chapter 2 funds may only "supplement and, to the extent practical, increase the level of funds that would . . . be made available from non-Federal sources." § 7371(b). LEA's and SEA's may not operate their programs "so as to supplant funds from non-Federal sources." . . .

Several restrictions apply to aid to private schools. Most significantly, the "services, materials, and equipment" provided to private schools must be "secular, neutral, and nonideological." . . . In addition, private schools may not acquire control of Chapter 2 funds or title to Chapter 2 materials, equipment, or property. . . . A private school receives the materials and equipment . . . by submitting to the LEA an application detailing which items the school seeks and how it will use them; the LEA, if it approves the application, purchases those items from the school's allocation of funds, and then lends them to that school.

. . . [P]rivate schools have primarily used their allocations for nonrecurring expenses, usually materials and equipment. In the 1986–1987 fiscal year, for example, 44% of the money budgeted for private schools in Jefferson Parish was spent by LEA's for acquiring library and media materials, and 48% for instructional equipment. Among the materials and equipment provided have been library books, computers, and computer software, and also slide and movie projectors, overhead projectors, television sets, tape recorders, VCR's, projection screens, laboratory equipment, maps, globes, filmstrips, slides, and cassette recordings.

It appears that, in an average year, about 30% of Chapter 2 funds spent in Jefferson Parish are allocated for private schools. For the 1985–1986 fiscal year, 41 private schools participated in Chapter 2. For the following year, 46 participated, and the participation level has remained relatively constant since then. . . . Of these 46, 34 were Roman Catholic; 7 were otherwise religiously affiliated; and 5 were not religiously affiliated.

B

Respondents filed suit in December 1985, alleging, among other things, that Chapter 2, as applied in Jefferson Parish, violated the Establishment Clause of the First Amendment of the Federal Constitution. The case's tortuous history over the next 15 years indicates well the degree to which our Establishment Clause jurisprudence has shifted in recent times, while nevertheless retaining anomalies with which the lower courts have had to struggle.

In 1990 . . . Chief Judge Heebe of the District Court . . . granted summary judgment in favor of respondents. . . . He held that Chapter 2 violated the Establishment Clause because . . . the program had the primary effect of advancing religion. . . .

Two years later, Chief Judge Heebe having retired, Judge Livaudais received the case. Ruling . . . on postjudgment motions, he reversed the decision of former Chief Judge Heebe and upheld Chapter 2, pointing to several significant changes in the legal landscape over the previous seven years. . . .

Judge Livaudais also relied heavily on a 1995 decision of the Court of Appeals for the Ninth Circuit, *Walker v. San Francisco Unified School Dist.*, 46 F.3d 1449, upholding Chapter 2. . . . The Ninth Circuit acknowledged in *Walker* . . . that *Meek* and *Wolman* appeared to erect a constitutional distinction between providing textbooks (permissible) and providing any other in-kind aid (impermissible). 46 F.3d, at 1464–1465; . . . The Court of Appeals viewed this distinction, however, as "thin" and . . . more importantly, as "rendered untenable" by subsequent cases. . . .

Finally, in addition to relying on our decision in *Zobrest* and the Ninth Circuit's decision in *Walker*, Judge Livaudais invoked *Rosenberger v. Rector and Visitors of Univ. of Va.*, 515 U.S. 819 . . . (1995), in which, a few months after *Walker*, we held that the Establishment Clause does not require a public university to exclude a student-run religious publication from assistance available to numerous other student-run publications.

✧ ✧ ✧

The Fifth Circuit [in this case] thus faced a dilemma between . . . the Ninth Circuit's holding and analysis in *Walker* and our subsequent decisions in *Rosenberger* and *Agostini*, and, on the other hand, our holdings in *Meek* and *Wolman*. . . . The Fifth Circuit acknowledged that *Agostini* . . . had rejected a premise of *Meek*, but that court nevertheless concluded that *Agostini* had neither directly overruled *Meek* and *Wolman* nor rejected their distinction between textbooks and other in-kind aid. The Fifth Circuit therefore concluded that *Meek* and *Wolman* controlled, and thus it held Chapter 2 unconstitutional. . . .

II

The Establishment Clause of the First Amendment dictates that "Congress shall make no law respecting an establishment of religion." In the over 50 years since *Everson*, we have consistently struggled to apply these simple words in the context of governmental aid to religious schools. . . .

In *Agostini*, however, we brought some clarity to our case law, by overruling two anomalous precedents . . . and by consolidating some of our previously disparate considerations under a revised test. Whereas in *Lemon* we had considered whether a statute (1) has a secular purpose, (2) has a primary effect of advancing or inhibiting religion, or (3) creates an excessive entanglement between government and religion . . . in *Agostini* we modified *Lemon* for purposes of evaluating aid to schools and examined only the first and second factors, see 521 U.S., at 222–223. . . . We acknowledged that our cases discussing excessive entanglement had applied many of the same considerations as had our cases discussing primary effect, and we therefore recast *Lemon*'s entanglement inquiry as simply one criterion relevant to determining a statute's effect. *Agostini, supra*, at 232–233. . . . We also acknowledged that our cases had pared somewhat the factors that could justify a finding of excessive entanglement. 521 U.S., at 233–234. . . . We then set out revised criteria for determining the effect of a statute: . . .

In this case, our inquiry under *Agostini*'s purpose and effect test is a narrow one. Because respondents do not challenge the District Court's holding that Chapter 2 has a secular purpose, and because the Fifth Circuit also did not question that holding . . . we will consider only Chapter 2's effect. Further, in determining that effect, we will consider only the first two *Agostini* criteria, since neither respondents nor the Fifth Circuit has questioned the District Court's holding . . . that Chapter 2 does not create an excessive entanglement. Considering Chapter 2 . . . we conclude that it neither results in religious indoctrination by the government nor defines its recipients by reference to religion. We therefore hold that Chapter 2 is not a "law respecting an establishment of religion." In so holding, we acknowledge what both the Ninth and Fifth Circuits saw was inescapable—*Meek* and *Wolman* are anomalies in our case law. We therefore conclude that they are no longer good law.

A

As we indicated in *Agostini* . . . the question whether governmental aid to religious schools results in governmental indoctrination is ultimately a question whether any religious indoctrination that occurs in those schools could reasonably be attributed to governmental action. . . . We have also indicated that the answer to the question of indoctrination will resolve the question whether a program of educational aid "subsidizes" religion, as our religion cases use that term. See *Agostini,* 521 U.S., at 230–231. . . .

In distinguishing between indoctrination that is attributable to the State and indoctrination that is not, we have consistently turned to the principle of neutrality, upholding aid that is offered to a broad range of groups or persons without regard to their religion. If the religious, irreligious, and areligious are all alike eligible for governmental aid, no one would conclude that any indoctrination that any particular recipient conducts has been done at the behest of the government. . . . If the government is offering assistance to recipients who provide, so to speak, a broad range of indoctrination, the government itself is not thought responsible for any particular indoctrination. To put the point differently, if the government, seeking to further some legitimate secular purpose, offers aid on the same terms, without regard to religion, to all who adequately further that purpose, see *Allen*, 392 U.S., at 245–247 . . . then it is fair to say that any aid going to a religious recipient only has the effect of furthering that secular purpose. The government, in crafting such an aid program, has had to conclude that a given level of aid is necessary to further that purpose among secular recipients and has provided no more than that same level to religious recipients.

As a way of assuring neutrality, we have repeatedly considered whether any governmental aid that goes to a religious institution does so "only as a result of the genuinely independent and private choices of individuals." *Agostini, supra,* at 226. . . . . . . For if numerous private choices, rather than the single choice of a government, determine the distribution of aid pursuant to neutral eligibility criteria, then a government cannot, or at least cannot easily, grant special favors that might lead to a religious establishment. . . .

The principles of neutrality and private choice, and their relationship to each other, were prominent not only in *Agostini* . . . but also in *Zobrest, Witters,* and *Mueller.* The heart of our reasoning in *Zobrest,* upholding governmental provision of a sign-language interpreter to a deaf student at his Catholic high school, was as follows:

> "The service at issue in this case is part of a general government program that distributes benefits neutrally to any child qualifying as 'disabled' under the [statute], without regard to the 'sectarian-nonsectarian, or public-nonpublic nature' of the school the child attends. By according parents freedom to select a school of their choice, the statute ensures that a government-paid interpreter will be present in a sectarian school only as a result of the private decision of individual parents. In other words, because the [statute] creates no financial incentive for parents to choose a sectarian school, an interpreter's presence there cannot be attributed to state decisionmaking." 509 U.S., at 10, 113 S.Ct. 2462.

. . . *Witters* and *Mueller* employed similar reasoning. In *Witters,* we held that the Establishment Clause did not bar a State from including within a neutral program providing tuition payments for vocational rehabilitation a blind person studying at a Christian college to become a pastor, missionary, or youth director. . . .

❖ ❖ ❖

The tax deduction for educational expenses that we upheld in *Mueller* was, in these respects, the same as the tuition grant in *Witters.* We upheld it chiefly because it "neutrally provides state assistance to a broad spectrum of citizens," 463 U.S., at 398–399 . . . and because "numerous, private choices of individual parents of school-age children," id., at 399 . . . determined which schools would benefit from the deductions. . . .

Agostini's second primary criterion for determining the effect of governmental aid is closely related to the first. The second criterion requires a court to consider whether an aid program "define[s] its recipients by reference to religion." 521 U.S., at 234. . . . In *Agostini* we set out the following rule for answering this question:

> "This incentive is not present, however, where the aid is allocated on the basis of neutral, secular criteria that neither favor nor disfavor religion, and is made available to both religious and secular beneficiaries on a nondiscriminatory basis. Under such circumstances, the aid is less likely to have the effect of advancing religion." Ibid.

❖ ❖ ❖

We hasten to add, what should be obvious from the rule itself, that simply because an aid program offers private schools, and thus religious schools, a benefit that they did not previously receive does not mean that the program, by reducing the cost of securing a religious education, creates, under *Agostini*'s second criterion, an "incentive" for parents to choose such an education for their children. For any aid will have some such effect. . . .

B

Respondents inexplicably make no effort to address Chapter 2 under the *Agostini* test. Instead, dismissing *Agostini* as factually distinguishable, they offer two rules that they contend should govern our determination. . . . They argue first, and chiefly, that "direct, nonincidental" aid to the primary educational mission of religious schools is always impermissible. Second, they argue that provision to religious schools of aid that is divertible to religious use is similarly impermissible. Respondents' arguments are inconsistent with our more recent case law, in particular *Agostini* and *Zobrest*, and we therefore reject them.

Although some of our earlier cases, particularly *Ball*, 473 U.S., at 393–394 . . . did emphasize the distinction between direct and indirect aid, the purpose of this distinction was merely to prevent "subsidization" of religion. . . . As even the dissent all but admits . . . (opinion of SOUTER, J.), our more recent cases address this purpose not through the direct/indirect distinction but rather through the principle of private choice. . . . . . .

Indeed, *Agostini* expressly rejected the absolute line that respondents would have us draw. We there explained that "we have departed from the rule relied on in *Ball* that all government aid that directly assists the educational function of religious schools is invalid." 521 U.S., at 225. . . . *Agostini* relied primarily on *Witters*. . . . It was undeniable in *Witters* that the aid (tuition) would ultimately go to the Inland Empire School of the Bible and would support religious education. We viewed this arrangement, however, as no different from a government issuing a paycheck to one of its employees knowing that the employee would direct the funds to a religious institution. Both arrangements would be valid, for the same reason: "[A]ny money that ultimately went to religious institutions did so 'only as a result of the genuinely independent and private choices of individuals." *Agostini, supra,* at 226 . . . (quoting *Witters,* 474 U.S., at 487. . .). . . .

As *Agostini* explained, the same reasoning was at work in *Zobrest*, where we allowed the government-funded interpreter to provide assistance at a Catholic school, "even though she would be a mouthpiece for religious instruction," because the interpreter was provided according to neutral eligibility criteria and private choice. . . .

✧ ✧ ✧

Further, respondents' formalistic line breaks down in the application to real-world programs. In Allen, for example, although we did recognize that students themselves received and owned the textbooks, we also noted that the books provided were those that the private schools required for courses, that the schools could collect students' requests for books and submit them to the board of education, that the schools could store the textbooks, and that the textbooks were essential to the schools' teaching of secular subjects. See 392 U.S., at 243–245. . . . Whether one chooses to label this program "direct" or "indirect" is a rather arbitrary choice, one that does not further the constitutional analysis.

Of course, we have seen "special Establishment Clause dangers," . . . when money is given to religious schools or entities directly rather than . . . indirectly. . . . But direct payments of money are not at issue in this case, and we refuse to allow a "special" case to create a rule for all cases.

2

Respondents also contend that the Establishment Clause requires that aid to religious schools not be impermissibly religious in nature or be divertible to religious use. We agree with the first part of this argument but not the second. Respondents' "no divertibility" rule is inconsistent with our more recent case law and is unworkable. . . .

Our recent precedents, particularly *Zobrest*, require us to reject respondents' argument. For *Zobrest* gave no consideration to divertibility or even to actual diversion. Had such things mattered . . . we would have found the case to be quite easy—for striking down rather than, as we did, upholding the program. . . . . . . Quite clearly, then, we did not, as respondents do, think that the use of governmental aid to further religious indoctrination was synonymous with religious indoctrination by the government or that such use of aid created any improper incentives.

Similarly, had we, in *Witters*, been concerned with divertibility or diversion, we would have unhesitatingly, perhaps summarily, struck down the tuition-reimbursement program, because it was certain that *Witters* sought to participate in it to acquire an education in a religious career from a sectarian institution. . . .

Justice O'CONNOR acknowledges that the Court in *Zobrest* and *Witters* approved programs that involved actual diversion. . . . The dissent likewise does not deny that *Witters* involved actual diversion. . . . The dissent does claim that the aid in *Zobrest* "was not considered divertible," . . . but the dissent in *Zobrest*, which the author of today's dissent joined, understood the case otherwise. . . .

❖ ❖ ❖

In *Agostini* itself, we approved the provision of public employees to teach secular remedial classes in private schools partly because we concluded that there was no reason to suspect that indoctrinating content would be part of such governmental aid. . . . Relying on *Zobrest*, we refused to presume that the public teachers would " 'inject religious content' " into their classes . . . especially given certain safeguards that existed; we also saw no evidence that they had done so. . . .

In *Allen* we similarly focused on content, emphasizing that the textbooks were preapproved by public school authorities and were not "unsuitable for use in the public schools because of religious content." . . . Although it might appear that a book, because it has a pre-existing content, is not divertible . . . it is hard to imagine any book that could not, in even moderately skilled hands, serve to illustrate a religious message. . . . A teacher could, for example, easily use Shakespeare's King Lear, even though set in pagan times, to illustrate the Fourth Commandment. See Exodus 20:12 ("Honor your father and your mother"). Thus, it is a non-sequitur for the dissent to contend that the textbooks in *Allen* were "not readily divertible to religious teaching purposes". . . .

A concern for divertibility, as opposed to improper content, is misplaced not only because it fails to explain why the sort of aid that we have allowed is permissible, but also because it is boundless—enveloping all aid, no matter how trivial—and thus has only the most attenuated (if any) link to any realistic concern for preventing an "establishment of religion." Presumably, for example, government-provided lecterns, chalk, crayons, pens, paper, and paintbrushes would have to be excluded from religious schools under respondents' proposed rule. But we fail to see how indoctrination by means of (i.e., diversion of) such aid could be attributed to the government. . . .

It is perhaps conceivable that courts could take upon themselves the task of distinguishing among the myriad kinds of possible aid based on the ease of diverting each kind. But it escapes us how a court might coherently draw any such line. It not only is far more workable, but also is actually related to real concerns about preventing advancement of religion by government, simply to require, as did *Zobrest, Agostini,* and *Allen,* that a program of aid to schools not provide improper content and that it determine eligibility and allocate the aid on a permissible basis.

C

The dissent serves up a smorgasbord of 11 factors that, depending on the facts of each case "in all its particularity" . . . could be relevant to the constitutionality of a school-aid program. And those 11 are a bare minimum. We are reassured that there are likely more. . . . The dissent resurrects the concern for political divisiveness that once occupied the Court but that post-*Aguilar* cases have rightly disregarded. . . . As Justice O'CONNOR explained in dissent in *Aguilar:* "It is curious indeed to base our interpretation of the Constitution on speculation as to the likelihood of a phenomenon which the parties may create merely by prosecuting a lawsuit." 473 U.S., at 429. . . .

One of the dissent's factors deserves special mention: whether a school that receives aid (or whose students receive aid) is pervasively sectarian. The dissent is correct that there was a period when this factor mattered, particularly if the pervasively sectarian school was a primary or secondary school. . . . But that period is one that the Court should regret, and it is thankfully long past.

There are numerous reasons to formally dispense with this factor. First, its relevance in our precedents is in sharp decline. Although our case law has consistently mentioned it even in recent years, we have not struck down an aid program in reliance on this factor since 1985, in *Aguilar* and *Ball. Agostini* of course overruled *Aguilar* in full and *Ball* in part, and today Justice O'CONNOR distances herself from the part of *Ball* with which she previously agreed, by rejecting the distinction between public and private employees that was so prominent in *Agostini.* . . . In *Witters*, a year after *Aguilar* and *Ball*, we did not ask whether the Inland Empire School of the Bible was pervasively sectarian. In *Bowen*, a 1988 decision, we refused to find facially invalid an aid program (although one not involving schools) whose recipients had . . . included pervasively sectarian institutions. . . . Then, in *Zobrest* and *Agostini*, we upheld aid programs to children who attended schools that were not only pervasively sectarian but also were primary and secondary. . . . In disregarding the nature of the school, *Zobrest* and *Agostini* were merely returning to the approach of *Everson* and *Allen*, in which the Court upheld aid programs to students at pervasively sectarian schools. . . .

Second, the religious nature of a recipient should not matter to the constitutional analysis, so long as the recipient adequately furthers the government's secular purpose. . . . If a program offers permissible aid to the religious (including the pervasively sectarian), the areligious, and the irreligious, it is a mystery which view of religion the government has established, and thus a mystery what the constitutional violation would be. The pervasively sectarian recipient has not received any special favor, and it is most bizarre that the Court would, as the dissent seemingly does, reserve special hostility for those who take their religion seriously, who think that their religion should affect the whole of their lives, or who make the mistake of being effective in transmitting their views to children.

Third, the inquiry into the recipient's religious views required by a focus on whether a school is pervasively sectarian is not only unnecessary but also offensive. It is well established, in numerous other contexts, that courts should refrain from trolling through a person's or institution's religious beliefs. See *Employment Div., Dept. of Human Resources of Ore. v. Smith*, 494 U.S. 872, 887 . . . (collecting cases). Yet that is just what this factor requires. . . . Although the dissent welcomes such probing . . . we find it profoundly troubling. In addition . . . the application of the "pervasively sectarian" factor collides with our decisions that have prohibited governments from discriminating in the distribution of public benefits based upon religious status or sincerity. See *Rosenberger v. Rector and Visitors of Univ. of Va.*, 515 U.S. 819 . . . ; *Lamb's Chapel v. Center Moriches Union Free School Dist.*, 508 U.S. 384 . . . ; *Widmar v. Vincent*, 454 U.S. 263. . . .

Finally, hostility to aid to pervasively sectarian schools has a shameful pedigree that we do not hesitate to disavow. . . . Although the dissent professes concern for "the implied exclusion of the less favored" . . . the exclusion of pervasively sectarian schools from government-aid programs is just that, particularly given the history of such exclusion. Opposition to aid to "sectarian" schools acquired prominence in the 1870s with Congress's consideration (and near passage) of the Blaine Amendment, which would have amended the Constitution to bar any aid to sectarian institutions. Consideration of the amendment arose at a time of pervasive hostility to the Catholic Church and to Catholics in general, and it was an open secret that "sectarian" was code for "Catholic." See generally Green, *The Blaine Amendment Reconsidered*, 36 Am. J. Legal Hist. 38 (1992). Notwithstanding its history, of course, "sectarian" could, on its face, describe the school of any religious sect, but the Court eliminated this possibility of confusion when, in *Hunt v. McNair*, 413 U.S., at 743, 93 S.Ct. 2868, it coined the term "pervasively sectarian"—a term which, at that time, could be applied almost exclusively to Catholic parochial schools and which even today's dissent exemplifies chiefly by reference to such schools. . . .

In short, nothing in the Establishment Clause requires the exclusion of pervasively sectarian schools from otherwise permissible aid programs, and other doctrines of this Court bar it. This doctrine, born of bigotry, should be buried now.

III

Applying the two relevant *Agostini* criteria, we see no basis for concluding that Jefferson Parish's Chapter 2 program "has the effect of advancing religion." . . . Chapter 2 does not result in governmental indoctrination, because it determines eligibility for aid neutrally, allocates that aid based on the private choices of the parents of schoolchildren, and does not provide aid that has an impermissible content. Nor does Chapter 2 define its recipients by reference to religion.

Taking the second criterion first, it is clear that Chapter 2 aid "is allocated on the basis of neutral, secular criteria that neither favor nor disfavor religion, and is made available to both religious and secular beneficiaries on a nondiscriminatory basis." . . . Aid is allocated based on enrollment: . . . and allocations to private schools must "be equal (consistent with the number of children to be served) to expenditures for programs under this subchapter for children enrolled in the public schools of the [LEA]," 20 U.S.C. § 7372(b). . . . The allocation criteria therefore create no improper incentive. Chapter 2 does, by statute, deviate from a pure per capita basis for allocating aid to LEA's, increasing the per-pupil allocation based on the number of children within an LEA who are from poor families, reside in poor areas, or reside in rural areas. §§ 7312(a)-(b). But respondents have not contended, nor do we have any reason to think, that this deviation . . . leads to deviation in the allocation among schools within each LEA . . . and, even if it did, we would not presume that such a deviation created any incentive one way or the other with regard to religion.

. . . The program makes a broad array of schools eligible for aid without regard to their religious affiliations or lack thereof. . . . We therefore have no difficulty concluding that Chapter 2 is neutral with regard to religion. . . . Chapter 2 aid also, like the aid in *Agostini, Zobrest,* and *Witters*, reaches participating schools only "as a consequence of private decisionmaking." . . . Private decisionmaking controls because of the per capita allocation scheme. . . . It is the students and their parents—not the government—who, through their choice of school, determine who receives Chapter 2 funds. The aid follows the child.

Because Chapter 2 aid is provided pursuant to private choices, it is not problematic that one could fairly describe Chapter 2 as providing "direct" aid. . . . Nor, for reasons we have already explained, is it of constitutional significance that the schools themselves, rather than the students, are the bailees of the Chapter 2 aid. The ultimate beneficiaries of Chapter 2 aid are the students who attend the schools that receive that aid, and this is so regardless of whether individual students lug computers to school each day or, as Jefferson Parish has more sensibly provided, the schools receive the computers. Like the Ninth Circuit, and unlike the dissent . . . we "see little difference in loaning science kits to students who then bring the kits to school as opposed to loaning science kits to the school directly." *Walker, supra,* at 1468, n. 16. . . .

Finally, Chapter 2 satisfies the first *Agostini* criterion because it does not provide to religious schools aid that has an impermissible content. The statute explicitly bars anything of the sort, providing that all Chapter 2 aid for the benefit of children in private schools shall be "secular, neutral, and nonideological" . . . and the record indicates that the Louisiana SEA and the Jefferson Parish LEA have faithfully enforced this requirement insofar as relevant to this case. The chief aid at issue is computers, computer software, and library books. The computers presumably have no pre-existing content, or at least none that would be impermissible for use in public schools. Respondents do not contend otherwise. Respondents also offer no evidence that religious schools have received software from the government that has an impermissible content.

There is evidence that equipment has been, or at least easily could be, diverted for use in religious classes. . . . In any event, for reasons we discussed . . . *supra,* the evidence of actual diversion and the weakness of the safeguards against actual diversion are not relevant to the constitutional inquiry, whatever relevance they may have under the statute and regulations.

Respondents do, however, point to some religious books that the LEA improperly allowed to be loaned to several religious schools, and they contend that the monitoring programs of the SEA and the Jefferson Parish LEA are insufficient to prevent such errors. The evidence, however, establishes just the opposite, for the improper lending of library books occurred—and was discovered and remedied—before this litigation began almost 15 years ago. . . .

The District Court found that prescreening by the LEA coordinator of requested library books was sufficient to prevent statutory violations . . . and the Fifth Circuit did not disagree. Further, as noted, the monitoring system appears adequate to catch those errors that do occur. We are unwilling to elevate scattered de minimis statutory violations, discovered and remedied by the relevant authorities themselves prior to any litigation, to such a level as to convert an otherwise unobjectionable parishwide program into a law that has the effect of advancing religion.

IV

In short, Chapter 2 satisfies both the first and second primary criteria of *Agostini.* It therefore does not have the effect of advancing religion. For the same reason, Chapter 2 also "cannot reasonably be viewed as an endorsement of religion," . . . Accordingly, we hold that Chapter 2 is not a law respecting an establishment of religion. Jefferson Parish need not exclude religious schools from its Chapter 2 program. To the extent that *Meek* and *Wolman* conflict with this holding, we overrule them.

Our conclusion regarding *Meek* and *Wolman* should come as no surprise. The Court as early as *Wolman* itself left no doubt that *Meek* and *Allen* were irreconcilable. . . . Today we simply acknowledge what has long been evident and was evident to the Ninth and Fifth Circuits and to the District Court.

The judgment of the Fifth Circuit is reversed.

It is so ordered.

Concurring Opinion

JUSTICE O'CONNOR, with whom JUSTICE BREYER joins, concurring in the judgment.

. . . Since 1965, Congress has reauthorized the Title I and Title II programs several times. Three terms ago, we held in *Agostini v. Felton,* 521 U.S. 203 . . . that Title I . . . did not violate the Establishment Clause. I believe that *Agostini* likewise controls the constitutional inquiry respecting Title II presented here, and requires the reversal of the Court of Appeals' judgment that the program is unconstitutional as applied in Jefferson Parish, Louisiana. To the extent our decisions in *Meek v. Pittenger* . . . and *Wolman v. Walter* . . . are inconsistent with the Court's judgment today, I agree that those decisions should be overruled. I therefore concur in the judgment.

I

I write separately because, in my view, the plurality announces a rule of unprecedented breadth for the evaluation of Establishment Clause challenges to government school-aid programs. Reduced to its essentials, the plurality's rule states that government aid to religious schools does not have the effect of advancing religion so long as the aid is offered on a neutral basis and the aid is secular in content. The plurality also rejects the distinction between direct and indirect aid, and holds that the actual diversion of secular aid by a religious school to the advancement of its religious mission is permissible. Although the expansive scope of the plurality's rule is troubling, two specific aspects of the opinion compel me to write separately. First, the plurality's treatment of neutrality comes close to assigning that factor singular importance in the future adjudication of Establishment Clause challenges to government school-aid programs. Second, the plurality's approval of actual diversion of government aid to religious indoctrination is in tension with our precedents and, in any event, unnecessary to decide the instant case.

✧ ✧ ✧

I agree with Justice SOUTER that the plurality, by taking such a stance, "appears to take evenhandedness neutrality and in practical terms promote it to a single and sufficient test for the establishment constitutionality of school aid." . . .

I do not quarrel with the plurality's recognition that neutrality is an important reason for upholding government-aid programs against Establishment Clause challenges. . . . Nevertheless, we have never held that a government-aid program passes constitutional muster solely because of the neutral criteria it employs as a basis for distributing aid. . . .

. . . Even if we at one time used the term "neutrality" in a descriptive sense to refer to those aid programs characterized by the requisite equipoise between support of religion and antagonism to religion, Justice SOUTER's discussion convincingly demonstrates that the evolution in the meaning of the term in our jurisprudence is cause to hesitate before equating the neutrality of recent decisions with the neutrality of old. As I have previously explained, neutrality is important, but it is by no means the only "axiom in the history and precedent of the Establishment Clause." *Rosenberger v. Rector and Visitors of Univ. of Va.,* 515 U.S. 819, 846 . . . (concurring opinion). Thus, I agree with Justice SOUTER's conclusion that our "most recent use of 'neutrality' to refer to generality or evenhandedness of distribution . . . is relevant in judging whether a benefit scheme so characterized should be seen as aiding a sectarian school's religious mission, but this neutrality is not alone sufficient to qualify the aid as constitutional." . . .

I also disagree with the plurality's conclusion that actual diversion of government aid to religious indoctrination is consistent with the Establishment Clause. . . . Although "[o]ur cases have permitted some government funding of secular functions performed by sectarian organizations," our decisions "provide no precedent for the use of public funds to finance religious activities." *Rosenberger, supra,* at 847 . . . (O'CONNOR, J., concurring). At least two of the decisions at the heart of today's case demonstrate that we have long been concerned that secular government aid not be diverted to the advancement of religion. . . .

The plurality bases its holding that actual diversion is permissible on *Witters* and *Zobrest.* . . . Those decisions, however, rested on a significant factual premise missing from this case, as well as from the majority of cases thus far considered by the Court involving Establishment Clause challenges to school-aid programs. Specifically, we decided *Witters* and *Zobrest* on the understanding that the aid was provided directly to the individual student who, in turn, made the choice of where to put that aid to use. . . . Accordingly, our approval of the aid in both cases relied to a significant extent on the fact that "[a]ny aid . . . that ultimately flows to religious institutions does so only as a result of the genuinely independent and private choices of aid recipients." *Witters, supra,* at 487 . . . ; see *Zobrest, supra,* at 10 . . . ("[A] government-paid interpreter will be present in a sectarian school only as a result of the private decision of individual parents"). This characteristic of both programs made them less like a direct subsidy, which would be impermissible under the Establishment Clause, and more akin to the government issuing a paycheck to an employee who, in turn, donates a portion of that check to a religious institution. . . .

Recognizing this distinction, the plurality nevertheless finds *Witters* and *Zobrest*—to the extent those decisions might permit the use of government aid for religious purposes—relevant in any case involving a neutral, per-capita-aid program. . . . Like Justice SOUTER, I do not believe that we should treat a per-capita-aid program the same as the true private-choice programs considered in *Witters* and *Zobrest*. . . . First, when the government provides aid directly to the student beneficiary, that student can attend a religious school and yet retain control over whether the secular government aid will be applied toward the religious education. The fact that aid flows to the religious school and is used for the advancement of religion is therefore wholly dependent on the student's private decision. . . .

Second, I believe the distinction between a per-capita school-aid program and a true private-choice program is significant for purposes of endorsement. . . . In terms of public perception, a government program of direct aid to religious schools based on the number of students attending each school differs meaningfully from the government distributing aid directly to individual students who, in turn, decide to use the aid at the same religious schools. In the former example, if the religious school uses the aid to inculcate religion in its students, it is reasonable to say that the government has communicated a message of endorsement. Because the religious indoctrination is supported by government assistance, the reasonable observer would naturally perceive the aid program as government support for the advancement of religion. That the amount of aid received by the school is based on the school's enrollment does not separate the government from the endorsement of the religious message. . . . Rather, endorsement of the religious message is reasonably attributed to the individuals who select the path of the aid.

Finally, the distinction between a per-capita-aid program and a true private-choice program is important when considering aid that consists of direct monetary subsidies. . . . If, as the plurality contends, a per-capita-aid program is identical in relevant constitutional respects to a true private-choice program, then there is no reason that, under the plurality's reasoning, the government should be precluded from providing direct money payments to religious organizations (including churches) based on the number of persons belonging to each organization. And, because actual diversion is permissible under the plurality's holding, the participating religious organizations (including churches) could use that aid to support religious indoctrination. To be sure, the plurality does not actually hold that its theory extends to direct money payments. . . . That omission, however, is of little comfort. In its logic—as well as its specific advisory language . . .—the plurality opinion foreshadows the approval of direct monetary subsidies to religious organizations, even when they use the money to advance their religious objectives.

Our school-aid cases often pose difficult questions at the intersection of the neutrality and no-aid principles and therefore defy simple categorization under either rule. As I explained in *Rosenberger*, "[r]esolution instead depends on the hard task of judging—sifting through the details and determining whether the challenged program offends the Establishment Clause. Such judgment requires courts to draw lines, sometimes quite fine, based on the particular facts of each case." 515 U.S., at 847, 115 S.Ct. 2510 (concurring opinion). *Agostini* represents our most recent attempt to devise a general framework for approaching questions concerning neutral school-aid programs. *Agostini* also concerned an Establishment Clause challenge to a school-aid program closely related to the one at issue here. For these reasons, as well as my disagreement with the plurality's approach, I would decide today's case by applying the criteria set forth in *Agostini*.

II

. . . Looking to our recently decided cases, we articulated three primary criteria to guide the determination whether a government-aid program impermissibly advances religion: (1) whether the aid results in governmental indoctrination, (2) whether the aid program defines its recipients by reference to religion, and (3) whether the aid creates an excessive entanglement between government and religion. Id., at 234. . . . Finally, we noted that the same criteria could be reviewed to determine whether a government-aid program constitutes an endorsement of religion. Id., at 235. . . .

Respondents neither question the secular purpose of the Chapter 2 (Title II) program nor contend that it creates an excessive entanglement. . . . [W]e need ask only whether the program results in governmental indoctrination or defines its recipients by reference to religion.

Taking the second inquiry first, it is clear that Chapter 2 does not define aid recipients by reference to religion. . . .

Agostini next requires us to ask whether Chapter 2 "result[s] in governmental indoctrination." . . .

. . . First, we explained that the Court had since abandoned "the presumption erected in *Meek* and *Ball* that the placement of public employees on parochial school grounds inevitably results in the impermissible effect of state-sponsored indoctrination or constitutes a symbolic union between government and religion." . . . Rather, relying on *Zobrest,* we explained that in the absence of evidence showing that teachers were actually using the Title I aid to inculcate religion, we would presume that the instructors would comply with the program's secular restrictions. See *Agostini,* 521 U.S., at 223–224, 226–227. . . .

Second, we noted that the Court had "departed from the rule relied on in *Ball* that all government aid that directly assists the educational function of religious schools is invalid." . . .

❖ ❖ ❖

. . . Although respondents claim that Chapter 2 aid has been diverted to religious instruction, that evidence is de minimis, as I explain at greater length below. . . .

III

Respondents contend that *Agostini* is distinguishable. . . . Here, in contrast, federal funds pay for instructional materials and equipment that LEA's lend to religious schools for use by those schools' own teachers in their classes. Because we held similar programs unconstitutional in *Meek* and *Wolman*, respondents contend that those decisions, and not *Agostini*, are controlling. . . . . . . Like respondents, Justice SOUTER also relies on *Meek* and *Wolman* in finding the character of the Chapter 2 aid constitutionally problematic. . . .

At the time they were decided, *Meek* and *Wolman* created an inexplicable rift within our Establishment Clause jurisprudence concerning government aid to schools. . . .

In *Meek* and *Wolman*, we adhered to *Allen*, holding that the textbook lending programs at issue in each case did not violate the Establishment Clause. See *Meek*, 421 U.S., at 359–362, (plurality opinion); *Wolman*, 433 U.S., at 236–238 . . . (plurality opinion). . . .

✧ ✧ ✧

The inconsistency between the two strands of the Court's jurisprudence did not go unnoticed. . . . . . .

Indeed, technology's advance since the *Allen, Meek,* and *Wolman* decisions has only made the distinction between textbooks and instructional materials and equipment more suspect. . . . Because computers constitute instructional equipment, adherence to *Meek* and *Wolman* would require the exclusion of computers from any government school aid program that includes religious schools. Yet, computers are now as necessary as were schoolbooks 30 years ago, and they play a somewhat similar role in the educational process. . . .

Respondents insist that there is a reasoned basis . . . for the distinction between textbooks and instructional materials and equipment. They claim that the presumption that religious schools will use instructional materials and equipment to inculcate religion is sound because such materials and equipment, unlike textbooks, are reasonably divertible to religious uses. . . .

I would reject respondents' proposed divertibility rule. First, respondents cite no precedent of this Court that would require it. The only possible direct precedential support for such a rule is a single sentence contained in a footnote from our *Wolman* decision. . . . Indeed, if anything, the *Wolman* footnote confirms the irrationality of the distinction between textbooks and instructional materials and equipment. . . . [T]he [*Wolman*] Court explained the continuing validity of *Allen* solely on the basis of stare decisis: . . . Thus, the *Wolman* Court never justified the inconsistent treatment it accorded the lending of textbooks and the lending of instructional materials and equipment based on the items' reasonable divertibility.

Justice SOUTER's attempt to defend the divertibility rationale . . . fares no better. . . .

In any event, even if *Meek* and *Wolman* had articulated the divertibility rationale urged by respondents and Justice SOUTER, I would still reject it for a more fundamental reason. Stated simply, the theory does not provide a logical distinction between the lending of textbooks and the lending of instructional materials and equipment. An educator can use virtually any instructional tool, whether it has ascertainable content or not, to teach a religious message. In this respect, I agree with the plurality that "it is hard to imagine any book that could not, in even moderately skilled hands, serve to illustrate a religious message." . . . In today's case, for example, we are asked to draw a constitutional distinction between lending a textbook and lending a library book. Justice SOUTER's try at justifying that distinction only demonstrates the absurdity on which such a difference must rest. . . . Moreover, if the mere ability of a teacher to devise a religious lesson involving the secular aid in question suffices to hold the provision of that aid unconstitutional, it is difficult to discern any limiting principle to the divertibility rule. For example, even a publicly financed lunch would apparently be unconstitutional under a divertibility rationale because religious-school officials conceivably could use the lunch to lead the students in a blessing over the bread. . . .

To the extent Justice SOUTER believes several related Establishment Clause decisions require application of a divertibility rule in the context of this case, I respectfully disagree. Justice SOUTER is correct to note our continued recognition of the special dangers associated with direct money grants to religious institutions. . . . It does not follow, however, that we should treat as constitutionally suspect any form of secular aid that might conceivably be diverted to a religious use. . . .

Justice SOUTER also relies on our decisions in *Wolman* . . . *Levitt v. Committee for Public Ed. & Religious Liberty* . . . *Tilton v. Richardson* . . . and *Bowen.* None requires application of a divertibility rule in the context of this case. . . . Finally, our decision in *Bowen* proves only that actual diversion, as opposed to mere divertibility, is constitutionally impermissible. . . .

IV

. . . I would adhere to the rule that we have applied in the context of textbook lending programs: To establish a First Amendment violation, plaintiffs must prove that the aid in question actually is, or has been, used for religious purposes. . . .

. . . Relying on both the majority opinion and my separate opinion in *Ball,* respondents therefore contend that we must presume that religious-school teachers will inculcate religion in their students. If that is so, they argue, we must also presume that religious-school teachers will be unable to follow secular restrictions on the use of instructional materials and equipment lent to their schools by the government. . . .

I disagree, however, that the latter proposition follows from the former. First . . . the Court's willingness to assume that religious-school instructors will inculcate religion has not caused us to presume also that such instructors will be unable to follow secular restrictions on the use of textbooks. I would similarly reject any such presumption regarding the use of instructional materials and equipment. When a religious school receives textbooks or instructional materials and equipment lent with secular restrictions, the school's teachers need not refrain from teaching religion altogether. Rather, the instructors need only ensure that any such religious teaching is done without the instructional aids provided by the government. . . .

❖ ❖ ❖

V

Respondents do not rest, however, on their divertibility argument alone. . . . First, respondents claim that the program's safeguards are insufficient to uncover instances of actual diversion. . . . Second, they contend that the record shows that some religious schools in Jefferson Parish may have used their Chapter 2 aid to support religious education (i.e., that they diverted the aid). . . . Third, respondents highlight violations of Chapter 2's secular content restrictions. . . . And, finally, they note isolated examples of potential violations of Chapter 2's supplantation restriction. . . . [T]he plurality appears to contend that the Chapter 2 program can be upheld only if actual diversion of government aid . . . is permissible under the Establishment Clause. . . . Justice SOUTER concludes that the Chapter 2 program, as applied in Jefferson Parish, violated the Establishment Clause. I disagree with both the plurality and Justice SOUTER. The limited evidence amassed by respondents during 4 years of discovery (which began approximately 15 years ago) is at best de minimis and therefore insufficient to affect the constitutional inquiry.

. . . [T]he plurality, and Justice SOUTER all appear to proceed from the premise that, so long as actual diversion presents a constitutional problem, the government must have a failsafe mechanism capable of detecting any instance of diversion. We rejected that very assumption, however, in *Agostini*. . . . I see no constitutional need for pervasive monitoring under the Chapter 2 program.

The safeguards employed by the program are constitutionally sufficient. . . .

❖ ❖ ❖

Justice SOUTER contends that any evidence of actual diversion requires the Court to declare the Chapter 2 program unconstitutional as applied in Jefferson Parish. . . . I know of no case in which we have declared an entire aid program unconstitutional on Establishment Clause grounds solely because of violations on the miniscule scale of those at issue here. . . . While extensive violations might require a remedy along the lines asked for by respondents, no such evidence has been presented here. To the contrary, the presence of so few examples over a period of at least 4 years (15 years ago) tends to show not that the "no-diversion" rules have failed, but that they have worked. Accordingly, I see no reason to affirm the judgment below and thereby declare a properly functioning aid program unconstitutional.

❖ ❖ ❖

. . . As in *Agostini,* the Chapter 2 aid is allocated on the basis of neutral, secular criteria; the aid must be supplementary and cannot supplant non-Federal funds; no Chapter 2 funds ever reach the coffers of religious schools; the aid must be secular; any evidence of actual diversion is de minimis; and the program includes adequate safeguards. Regardless of whether these factors are constitutional requirements, they are surely sufficient to find that the program at issue here does not have the impermissible effect of advancing religion. For the same reasons, "this carefully constrained program also cannot reasonably be viewed as an endorsement of religion." Accordingly, I concur in the judgment.

JUSTICE SOUTER, with whom JUSTICE STEVENS and JUSTICE GINSBURG join, dissenting.

❖ ❖ ❖

So far as the line drawn has addressed government aid to education, a few fundamental generalizations are nonetheless possible. There may be no aid supporting a sectarian school's religious exercise or the discharge of its religious mission, while aid of a secular character with no discernible benefit to such a sectarian objective is allowable. Because the religious and secular spheres largely overlap in the life of many such schools, the Court has tried to identify some facts likely to reveal the relative religious or secular intent or effect of the government benefits in particular circumstances. We have asked whether the government is acting neutrally in distributing its money, and about the form of the aid itself, its path from government to religious institution, its divertibility to religious nurture, its potential for reducing traditional expenditures of religious institutions, and its relative importance to the recipient, among other things.

In all the years of its effort, the Court has isolated no single test of constitutional sufficiency, and the question in every case addresses the substantive principle of no aid: what reasons are there to characterize this benefit as aid to the sectarian school in discharging its religious mission? Particular factual circumstances control, and the answer is a matter of judgment.

❖ ❖ ❖

Today, the substantive principle of no aid to religious mission remains the governing understanding of the Establishment Clause as applied to public benefits inuring to religious schools. The governing opinions on the subject in the 35 years since *Allen* have never challenged this principle. The cases have, however, recognized that in actual . . . litigation over school aid legislation, there is no pure aid to religion and no purely secular welfare benefit; the effects of the laws fall somewhere in between, with the judicial task being to make a realistic allocation between the two possibilities. . . .

❖ ❖ ❖

II

A

The most deceptively familiar of those considerations is "neutrality," the presence or absence of which, in some sense, we have addressed from the moment of *Everson* itself. I say "some sense," for we have used the term in at least three ways in our cases, and an understanding of the term's evolution will help to explain the concept as it is understood today, as well as the limits of its significance in Establishment Clause analysis. "Neutrality" has been employed as a term to describe the requisite state of government equipoise between the forbidden encouragement and discouragement of religion; to characterize a benefit or aid as secular; and to indicate evenhandedness in distributing it.

❖ ❖ ❖

The shift from equipoise to secular was not, however, our last redefinition, for the Court again transformed the sense of "neutrality" in the 1980s. Reexamining and reinterpreting *Everson* and *Allen,* we began to use the word "neutral" to mean "evenhanded," in the sense of allocating aid on some common basis to religious and secular recipients. . . .

❖ ❖ ❖

In sum, "neutrality" originally entered this field of jurisprudence as a conclusory term, a label for the required relationship between the government and religion as a state of equipoise between government as ally and government as adversary. Reexamining *Everson*'s paradigm cases to derive a prescriptive guideline, we first determined that "neutral" aid was secular, non-ideological, or unrelated to religious education. Our subsequent reexamination of *Everson* and *Allen,* beginning in *Nyquist* and culminating in *Mueller* and most recently in *Agostini,* recast neutrality as a concept of "evenhandedness."

❖ ❖ ❖

In the days when "neutral" was used in *Everson*'s sense of equipoise, neutrality was tantamount to constitutionality. . . . This is not so at all, however, under the most recent use of "neutrality" to refer to generality or evenhandedness of distribution. This kind of neutrality is relevant in judging whether a benefit scheme so characterized should be seen as aiding a sectarian school's religious mission, but this neutrality is not alone sufficient to qualify the aid as constitutional. It is to be considered only along with other characteristics of aid, its administration, its recipients, or its potential that have been emphasized over the years as indicators of just how religious the intent and effect of a given aid scheme really is. . . . Thus, the basic principle of establishment scrutiny of aid remains the principle as stated in *Everson,* that there may be no public aid to religion or support for the religious mission of any institution.

B

The insufficiency of evenhandedness neutrality as a stand-alone criterion of constitutional intent or effect has been clear from the beginning of our interpretative efforts, for an obvious reason. Evenhandedness in distributing a benefit approaches the equivalence of constitutionality in this area only when the term refers to such universality of distribution that it makes no sense to think of the benefit as going to any discrete group. Conversely, when evenhandedness refers to distribution to limited groups within society, like groups of schools or schoolchildren, it does make sense to regard the benefit as aid to the recipients. . . .

Hence, if we looked no further than evenhandedness, and failed to ask what activities the aid might support, or in fact did support, religious schools could be blessed with government funding as massive as expenditures made for the benefit of their public school counterparts, and religious missions would thrive on public money. This is why the consideration of less than universal neutrality has never been recognized as dispositive. . . .

At least three main lines of enquiry addressed particularly to school aid have emerged to complement evenhandedness neutrality. First, we have noted that two types of aid recipients heighten Establishment Clause concern: pervasively religious schools and primary and secondary religious schools. Second, we have identified two important characteristics of the method of distributing aid: directness or indirectness of distribution and distribution by genuinely independent choice. Third, we have found relevance in at least five characteristics of the aid itself: its religious content; its cash form; its divertibility or actual diversion to religious support; its supplantation of traditional items of religious school expense; and its substantiality.

❖ ❖ ❖

C

This stretch of doctrinal history leaves one point clear beyond peradventure: together with James Madison we have consistently understood the Establishment Clause to impose a substantive prohibition against public aid to religion and, hence, to the religious mission of sectarian schools. Evenhandedness neutrality is one, nondispositive pointer toward an intent and (to a lesser degree) probable effect on the permissible side of the line between forbidden aid and general public welfare benefit. Other pointers are facts about the religious mission and education level of benefited schools and their pupils, the pathway by which a benefit travels from public treasury to educational effect, the form and content of the aid, its adaptability to religious ends, and its effects on school budgets. The object of all enquiries into such matters is the same whatever the particular circumstances: is the benefit intended to aid in providing the religious element of the education and is it likely to do so?

The substance of the law has thus not changed since *Everson*. Emphasis on one sort of fact or another has varied depending on the perceived utility of the enquiry, but all that has been added is repeated explanation of relevant considerations, confirming that our predecessors were right in their prophecies that no simple test would emerge to allow easy application of the establishment principle.

The plurality, however, would reject that lesson. The majority misapplies it.

❖ ❖ ❖

IV

The plurality would break with the law. The majority misapplies it. That misapplication is, however, the only consolation in the case, which reaches an erroneous result but does not stage a doctrinal coup. But there is no mistaking the abandonment of doctrine that would occur if the plurality were to become a majority. It is beyond question that the plurality's notion of evenhandedness neutrality as a practical guarantee of the validity of aid to sectarian schools would be the end of the principle of no aid to the schools' religious mission. And if that were not so obvious it would become so after reflecting on the plurality's thoughts about diversion and about giving attention to the pervasiveness of a school's sectarian teaching.

The plurality is candid in pointing out the extent of actual diversion of Chapter 2 aid to religious use in the case before us . . . and equally candid in saying it does not matter. . . . To the plurality there is nothing wrong with aiding a school's religious mission; the only question is whether religious teaching obtains its tax support under a formally evenhanded criterion of distribution. The principle of no aid to religious teaching has no independent significance.

And if this were not enough to prove that no aid in religious school aid is dead under the plurality's First Amendment, the point is nailed down in the plurality's attack on the legitimacy of considering a school's pervasively sectarian character when judging whether aid to the school is likely to aid its religious mission. . . . The plurality nonetheless condemns any enquiry into the pervasiveness of doctrinal content as a remnant of anti-Catholic bigotry (as if evangelical Protestant schools and Orthodox Jewish yeshivas were never pervasively sectarian), and it equates a refusal to aid religious schools with hostility to religion (as if aid to religious teaching were not opposed in this very case by at least one religious respondent and numerous religious amici curiae in a tradition claiming descent from Roger Williams). My concern with these arguments goes not so much to their details as it does to the fact that the plurality's choice to employ imputations of bigotry and irreligion as terms in the Court's debate makes one point clear: that in rejecting the principle of no aid to a school's religious mission the plurality is attacking the most fundamental assumption underlying the Establishment Clause, that government can in fact operate with neutrality in its relation to religion. I believe that it can, and so respectfully dissent.

Review Questions 9.4

1. Why did the concurring and dissenting Justices reject the view of the Court opinion that government "neutrality" in dispensing educational aid is all that the Establishment Clause requires?

2. What would the concurring and dissenting Justices require beyond the neutrality standard of the plurality opinion?

3. What is the difference between the constitutional test espoused by the concurring Justices and that espoused by the dissenting Justices?

4. Was the *Lemon* test of purpose and effect very helpful in the *Mitchell* case?

❖ APPENDIX

State Charter School Laws

The following list of state charter laws requires further updating, as state legislatures continue to enact new charter school laws or amend existing laws.

Alaska—Alaska Statutes 14.03.250 to 290

Arizona—Arizona Revised Statutes 15-181 to 189

Arkansas—Arkansas Statutes Annotated 6-10-116

California—California Educational Code 47600 to 47625

Colorado—Colorado Revised Statutes 22-30.5-101 to 114

Connecticut—1996 Connecticut Senate Bill 59 (effective 7/1/96)

Delaware—Delaware Code 501 to 516

Florida—1996 Florida House Bill 403 (effective 7/1/96)

Georgia—Official Code of Georgia Annotated 20-2-255

Hawaii—Hawaii Revised Statutes 296-101 to 102

Illinois—105 ILCS 5/27A-1 to 13

Kansas—Kansas Statutes Annotated 72-1901 to 1910

Louisiana—Louisiana Revised Statutes 17:3971 to 3982

Massachusetts—Massachusetts Annotated Laws ch. 71 sec. 89

Michigan—Michigan Statutes Annotated 15.4501 to 4515

Minnesota—Minnesota Statutes 120.06400

New Hampshire—Revised Statutes Annotated 194-B:1 to B:22

New Jersey—1996 N.J. Advance Legislative Service 426 (Jan. 10)

New Mexico—New Mexico Statutes Annotated 22-28A-1 to 7

Rhode Island—Rhode Island General Laws 16-77-4 to 6, 8, 11

Texas—Texas Educational Code 12.101 to 12.118

Wisconsin—Wisconsin Statutes 118.40

Wyoming—Wyoming Statutes 21-3-201 to 207

Sources: Sara Godshall and Jennifer Hill, seamonkey@ed.asu.edu; Stuart Biegel, *School Choice Policy and Title VI*; Thomas Maughs-Pugh, *Charter Schools 1995: A Survey and Analysis* (Dartmouth); J. A Peyser, *School Choice: When, Not If*, B.C Law Review (1994).

❖ ENDNOTES

1. Rendell-Baker v. Kohn, 457 U.S. 830 (1982); Huff v. Notre Dame High School, 456 F. Supp. 1145 (D. Conn. 1978).

2. Pierce v. Society of Sisters; Pierce v. Hill Military Academy, both reported at 268 U.S. 510 (1925); Meyer v. Nebraska, 262 U.S. 390 (1923); Farrington v. Tokushige, 273 U.S. 284 (1927).

3. State v. Vietto, 247 S.E.2d 298 (N.C. 1978); Scoma v. Chicago Board of Educ., 391 F. Supp. 452 (N.D. Ill. 1974).

4. Scoma, *supra* note 3; State v. Kasuboski, 275 N.W.2d 101 (Wis. 1978).

5. Atty. Gen. v. Bailey, 436 N.E.2d 139 (Mass. 1982).

6. State v. Massa, 231 A.2d 252 (N.J. 1967); *In re* Monnig, 638 S.W.2d 782 (Mo. 1982); *cf.* In interest of Sawyer, 672 P.2d 1093 (Ky. 1983) (need "clear and convincing" evidence); *in re* Contempt of Liles, 349 N.W.2d 377 (Neb. 1984).

7. *Re challenge to law:* State v. Shaver, 294 N.W.2d 883 (N.D. 1980); Scoma, *supra* note 3; State v. Lowry, 383 P.2d 962 (Kan. 1963).
   Re compliance by alternative education: In re H., 357 N.Y.S.2d 384 (1974).

8. Cmwlth. v. Renfrow, 126 N.E.2d 109 (Mass. 1955); State ex rel. Shoreline School Dist. v. Superior Ct., 346 P.2d 999 (Wash. 1959).

9. Santosky v. Kremer, 450 U.S. 993 (1982).

10. Grigg v. Comm., 297 S.E.2d 799 (Va. 1982) and cases there cited; Glenmore Academy v. State Board of Private Academic Schools, 385 A.2d 1049 (Pa. 1978) (separate licensure of private academies); DelConte v. State, 308 S.E.2d 898, 901–2 (N.C. 1983) (legislative differentiation between church-related and nonsectarian private schools). Annot., *Attendance at Private or Parochial Schools,* 65 A.L.R. 3d 1222 (1975).

11. *State Regulation of Private Religious Schools,* 25 Ariz. L. Rev. 123 (1983); Comment, *The State and Sectarian Education: Regulation to Deregulation,* Duke L.J. 801 (1980); Annot., *Validity of State Regulation of Curriculum and Instruction in Private and Parochial Schools,* 18 A.L.R. 4th 649 (1982).

"Acceptable ways of meeting the schooling requirement vary widely among states. Some states require certification of teachers and schools, some only approval and some only minimal evidence that schooling takes place. . . . Some states, such as Alaska, Arizona, Georgia and Ohio give state and local school officials wide discretionary authority to excuse a child from the compulsory attendance requirement. . . . Some states have consciously deregulated their private schools. . . ." P. Lines, *Private Education Alternatives and State Regulation,* pp. 3–4 (Education Commission of the States, March 1982).

12. The meanings given to "school" under state statutes are discussed in DelConte, *supra* note 10, and Grigg, *supra* note 10; Lines & Bray, *What Is a School?* 16 West Ed. L. Rep. 371 (1984).

13. *Re certification for schools:* People v. DeJonge, 470 N.W.2d 433 (Mich. 1991); Fellowship Baptist Church v. Benton, 815 F.2d 485 (8th Cir. 1987).

    Re certification for home education: State v. Moorehead, 308 N.W.2d 60 (Iowa 1981); State v. Riddle, 285 S.E.2d 359 (W. Va. 1981).

    Re curriculum requirements: Shaver, *supra* note 7.

    These cases rested decision on their state constitutions, and thus avoided deciding any federal question that could lead to federal court review.

14. Fellowship Baptist Church, *supra* note 13; State v. Calvary Academy, 348 N.W.2d 898 (Neb. 1984); State v. Andrews, 651 P.2d 473 (Hawaii 1982); Jernigan v. State, 412 So. 2d 1242, 1246 (Ala. 1982); Brown v. Dade Christian Schools Inc., 556 F.2d 310 (5th Cir. 1977).

15. *Re rights of contract, association and privacy, see* Tollefson v. Roman Catholic Bishop, 268 Cal. Rptr. 550 (1990); Bailey, *supra* note 5; State v. McDonough, 448 A.2d 977, 979 (Me. 1983).

    Re discrimination claim, see Bailey, *supra* note 5; State v. Edgington, 663 P.2d 74 (N.M. 1983); State v. Bowman, 653 P.2d 254 (Or. 1982).

16. State of Ohio v. Whisner, 351 N.E.2d 750 (Ohio 1976); Kentucky State Board of Elementary & Secondary Educ. v. Rudasill, 589 S.W.2d 877 (Ky. 1979); State of North Carolina v. Columbus Christian Academy, Sup. Ct., Div. No.78 CUS

1678 (N.C. 1978). The Kentucky court echoed the Whisner output theme:

Expert testimony . . . established that there is not the slightest connection between teacher certification and enhanced educational quality. . . . . . . [P]laintiffs . . . have shown that . . . their educational product is at least equal to if not somewhat better than that of the public schools. . . .

17. Whisner, *supra* note 16.

18. *Cases sustaining vagueness objections:* State v. Popanz, 332 N.W.2d 750 (Wis. 1983) ("private school"—held impermissibly vague); Roemhild v. State, 308 S.E.2d 154 (Ga. 1983).

    Cases rejecting vagueness challenges: Bangor Baptist Church v. State, 549 F. Supp. 1208 (D. Me. 1982) ("equivalent" education—held not vague); Moorehead, *supra* note 13; ("equivalent instruction" and "certified teacher"—held not vague).

19. Santa Fe Comm. School v. New Mexico State Board of Educ., 581 P.2d 272 (N.M. 1977).

20. C. J. Klicka, *The Right to Home School* 161 (1995); Gordon, William MacGuire, *The Law of Home Schooling* (1994); Neal Devins, *Fundamentalist Christian Educators v. State: An Inevitable Compromise,* 60 Geo. Wash. L. Rev. 818 (1992).

    States exempting home education include: Connecticut, Maine, Massachusetts, and New York. *States treating home education same as private schools:* Alabama, Kansas, Michigan, and Nebraska.

21. Null v. Board of Educ., 815 F. Supp. 937 (S.D. W.Va. 1993).

22. C. J. Klicka, *Home Schooling in the United States: A Statutory Analysis,* pp. i, ii (1989). *States referring to "equivalent" time of instruction:* Connecticut, Indiana, New Jersey, and Nevada. *States requiring "regular and thorough" instruction:* Maryland, Delaware, and Rhode Island. *States referring to instruction "comparable" to public schools:* Idaho and Michigan.

23. Roemhild, *supra* note 18; State v. Popanz, *supra* note 18; State v. Newstrom, 371 N.W.2d 525 (Minn. 1985); Ellis v. O'Hara, 612 F. Supp. 379 (E.D. Mo. 1985); Iowa; Benton, *supra* note 13; Jeffery v. O'Donnell, 702 F. Supp. 516 (M.D. Pa. 1988).

24. *Certification requirements—upheld:* People v. Bennett, 501 N.W.2d 106 (Mich. 1993); Crites v. Smith, 826 S.W.2d 459 (Tenn. App. 1991).

    Competency achievement—upheld: Null v. Board of Educ. of the County of Jackson, 815 F. Supp. 937 (S.D. W. Va. 1993).

25. People v. DeJonge, 501 N.W.2d 127 (Mich. 1993) (upholding religious objection); State v. Riviera, 497 N.W.2d 878 (Iowa 1993) (rejecting religious objection defense).

26. *See* article, *Students Schooled at Home Welcome,* The Philadelphia Inquirer (Maine Line Ed., 10-19-99), p. RE-6.

27. Seward Chapel, Inc. v. City of Seward, 655 P.2d 1293, 1297–8 (Alaska 1982); Johnson & Wales College v. DiPrete, 448 A.2d 1271, 1279 (R.I. 1982). *See* Annot., *Zoning Regulations—Private Schools,* 74 A.L.R. 3d 14 (1976).

28. Lakewood, Ohio Congregation of Jehovah's Witnesses Inc. v. City of Lakewood, 699 F.2d 303, 305 (6th Cir. 1983).

29. *Total exclusion from the municipality:* Brookville v. Paulgene Realty Corp., 180 N.E.2d 905 (N.Y. 1960); Roman Catholic Welfare Corp. v. Piedmont, 289 P.2d 438 (Cal. 1955).

    Oppressive requirements: Westbury Hebrew Congregation Inc. v. Downer, 302 N.Y.S.2d 923 (1969).

30. *Compare* Three L. Corp. v. Board of Adjustment, 288 A.2d 312 (N.J. 1972) (held valid), *with* Chicago v. Sachs, 115 N.E.2d 762 (Ill. 1953).

31. Roman Catholic Diocese v. Ho-Ho-Kus, 220 A.2d 97 (N.J. 1966).

32. Annot., *Zoning Regulations—Private Schools,* 74 A.L.R. 3d 14 (1976). *Zoning exclusion voided:* Diocese of Rochester v. Planning Board, 136 N.E.2d 827 (N.Y. 1956); Phillips v. Homewood, 50 So. 2d 267 (Ala. 1951).

    Exclusion sustained: Tustin Heights Assn. v. Board of Supervisors, 339 P.2d 914 (Cal. 1954); State v. Sinar, 65 N.W.2d 43 (Wis. 1954).

33. St. Cassian's Catholic Church v. Allen, 190 A.2d 667 (N.J. 1963); City of Concord v. New Testament Baptist Church, 382 A.2d 377 (N.H. 1978).

34. Johnson & Wales College v. DiPrete, 448 A.2d 1271, 1280–2 (R.I. 1982); Saddle River Country

Day School v. Saddle River, 144 A.2d 425, *aff'd per curiam,* 150 A.2d 34 (N.J. 1959).

35. First Assembly of God v. City of Alexandria, 739 F.2d 942 (4th Cir. 1984); St. Cassian's Catholic Church, *supra* note 33.

36. *After-the-fact school "noise" objection—overturned:* Alpine Christian Fellowship v. County Commissioners, 870 F. Supp. 991 (D. Colo. 1994). *On-site water requirement—overturned:* W. Goshen Twp. v. Bible Baptist Church, 313 A.2d 177 (Pa. 1973).

37. *Compare* Brandt v. Zoning Board of Appeals of New Castle, 393 N.Y.S.2d 264 (1977), *with* Harbor Schools v. Board of Appeals of Haverhill, 366 N.E.2d 764, 767–9 (Mass. 1977); Areba School Corp. v. Mayor and Council of Twp. of Randolph, 376 A.2d 1273 (N.J. 1977).

38. *See* Annot., *Eminent Domain: Right to Condemn Property Owned or Used by Private Educational, Charitable or Religious Organization,* 80 A.L.R. 3d 833 (1977).

39. For varied treatment of private school charitable immunity, *see* Annots., *Tort Immunity—Nongovernmental Charities,* 25 A.L.R. 4th 517 (1983); *Tort Immunity—Private Schools,* 38 A.L.R. 3d 480 (1971).

States that abrogated private school tort immunity, in whole or in part, include Arizona, California, District of Columbia, Idaho, Illinois, Indiana, Iowa, Kansas, Kentucky, Louisiana, Massachusetts, Minnesota, Missouri, New Jersey, New York, Ohio, Oklahoma, Pennsylvania, Rhode Island, South Carolina, Texas, Utah, Vermont, Washington, and Wisconsin. Some states substituted limited or partial immunity, including Arkansas, Connecticut, Colorado, Maryland, Nebraska, Nevada, Tennessee, and Virginia.

40. Bernesak v. Catholic Bishop, 409 N.E.2d 287 (Ill. 1980); Merrill v. Catholic Bishop of Chicago, 290 N.E.2d 259 (Ill. 1972).

41. Love v. Nashville A. and Normal Inst., 243 S.W.304 (Tenn. 1922). *See also* discussion of nuisances in Chapter 4.

42. On statutory waiver of immunity to amount of liability insurance, *see, e.g.,* Maine Rev. Stat. Ann. title. 14, § 158 (1980); Kobylanski v. Chicago Board of Educ., 347 N.E.2d 705, 709 (Ill. 1976).

43. Yeske v. Aron Old Farm Schools, 470 A.2d 705 (Conn. 1984) (child trespasser injured by a cable); Saul v. Roman Catholic Church, 402 P.2d 48 (N.M. 1965) (child fall into school site excavation). *But see contra,* Siver v. Atlantic Union College, 154 N.E.2d 360 (Mass. 1958).

44. Velez v. Our Lady of Victory Church, 486 N.Y.S.2d 302 (1985).

45. Wilkinson v. Hartford Acc. & Ind. Co., 411 So. 2d 22 (La. 1982).

46. Garofoli v. Salesianum School, Inc., 208 A.2d 308 (De. 1965), and case authorities in 68 Am. Jur. 2d § 324.

47. Kim v. State, 616 P.2d 1376 (Hawaii 1980) (duty to prevent criminal assault by students); James v. Charlotte-Mecklenburg Board of Educ., 300 S.E.2d 21, 24 (N.C. 1983).

48. *See* Annot., *Liability of Charitable Organization for Tort of Unpaid Volunteer,* 82 A.L.R. 3d 1213 (1978).

49. Cramer v. Hoffman, 390 F.2d 19 (2d Cir. 1968).

50. For a discussion of administrative negligence in hiring school personnel, *see* J. v. Victory Tabernacle Baptist Church, 372 S.E.2d 391 (Va. 1988).

51. Roman Catholic Church v. Keenan, 243 P.2d 455 (Ariz. 1952).

52. Hillman v. Greater Miami Hebrew Academy, 72 So. 2d 668 (Fla. 1954) (case dismissed); Mlynarski v. St. Rita's Congregation, 142 N.W.2d 207 (1966) (trial granted).

53. Hunter v. Evergreen Presbyterian Vocational School, 338 So. 2d 164 (La. 1976).

54. Noland v. Colorado School of Trades, Inc., 386 P.2d 358 (Colo. 1963).

55. Fowler v. Seaton, 394 P.2d 697 (Cal. 1964).

56. Selleck v. Insurance Co. of North America, 182 So. 2d 547 (La. 1966).

57. Shanahan v. St. James' Roman Catholic Church, 223 N.Y.S.2d 519 (1960).

58. Martin v. Roman Catholic Archbishop, 322 P.2d 31 (Cal. 1958).

59. Bernesak, *supra* note 40 (permitting children to play "crack the whip" during class recess);

Sheehan v. St. Peter's Catholic School, 188 N.W.2d 868 (Minn. 1971) (students throwing pebbles at each other); Titus v. Lindberg, 288 A.2d 65 (N.J. 1967).

60. Benedetto v. Travelers Insurance Co., 172 So. 2d 354 (La. 1965).

61. *Compare* Everett v. School Dist., 380 N.E.2d 653 (Mass. 1978) (liability for use of defective hockey helmets), *with* Brackman v. Adrian, 472 S.W.2d 735 (Tenn. 1971) (no liability for coach's failure to require catcher's mask in softball game).

62. Christofides v. Hellenic Eastern Orthodox Christian Church, 227 N.Y.S.2d 946 (1962). *But see* Kim *supra* note 47 (female teacher not negligent in leaving class to seek help to stop a fight).

63. Townsend by Benavente, 339 F.2d 421 (9th Cir. 1964) (student struck by nut thrown by another student during noon recess); Kos v. Catholic Bishop, 45 N.E.2d 1006 (Ill. 1942).

64. Marques v. Riverside Military Academy, 73 S.E.2d 574 (Ga. 1952).

65. *See* Martin v. Roman Catholic Archbishop, 322 P.2d 31 (Cal. 1958).

66. Sharpe v. Quality Educ. Inc., 296 S.E.2d 661 (N.C. 1982); Brokaw v. Black-Foxe Military Inst., 231 P.2d 816 (Cal. 1951).

67. Moore v. Order Minor Conventuals, 267 F.2d 296 (4th Cir. 1959).

68. Beardsell v. Tilton School, 200 A. 783 (N.H. 1938).

69. Bryant v. Thunderbird Academy, 439 P.2d 818 (Ariz. 1968).

70. Faber v. Roelofs, 212 N.W.2d 856 (Minn. 1973).

71. Applebaum v. Nemon, 678 S.W.2d 533 (Tex. 1984) (no duty to provide CPR). *See* Stineman v. Fontbonne College, 664 F.2d 1082 (8th Cir. 1981), and the authorities there cited from other states.

72. O'Brien v. Twp. High School Dist., 392 N.E.2d 615 (Ill. 1980); Guerrieri v. Tyson, 24 A.2d 468 (Pa. 1942).

73. Helm v. Professional Children's School, 431 N.Y.S.2d 246 (1980).

74. Pietro v. St. Joseph's School, N.Y. Sup. Ct., Suffolk County (1979), reported at 48 U.S. Law Week 2229.

75. Dunn v. Bessie F. Heirn School, Inc., 209 So. 2d 538 (La. 1968).

76. Story v. San Rafaele Military Academy, 3 Cal. Rptr. 847 (1960).

77. Reardon v. Lemoyne, 454 A.2d 428 (N.H. 1982); *cf.* Toussaint v. Blue Cross, 292 N.W.2d 880 (Mich. 1980).

78. Odem v. Pace Academy, 510 S.E.2d 326 (Ga. App. 1998). *See* Chapter 5 discussion of implied duties of teachers.

79. Mullan v. Bishop of the Diocese, 540 So. 2d 174 (Fla. App. 1989) (termination without hearing—reversed); Tollefson v. Roman Catholic Bishop, 268 Cal. Rptr. 550 (Cal. App. 1990) (contract provision precluded finding of contrary implied duty).

80. Wiethoff v. St. Veronica's School, 210 N.W.2d 108 (Mich. 1973).

81. Little v. Wuerl, 929 F.2d 944 (3d Cir. 1991); Little v. St. Mary Magdalen Parish, 739 F. Supp. 1003 (W.D. Pa. 1990); Bishop Carrol High School v. Unemployment Compensation Board of Review, 557 A.2d 1141 (Pa. Cmwlth. 1989). *But see* St. Pius X Parish v. Murray, 557 A.2d 1214 (R.I. 1989).

82. Bischoff v. Brothers of Sacred Heart, 416 So. 2d 348 (La. 1982) (intentional concealment of remarriage contrary to teaching of sponsoring church); Ostrolenk v. Louise S. McGhee School, 402 So. 2d 237 (La. 1981) (failure to disclose discharge by another private school).

83. Martin v. Coral Gables Academy, 369 So. 2d 255 (La. 1979) (discharge for opposing school's disciplinary policy).

84. Assn. of Catholic Teachers v. Pennsylvania Labor Relations Board, 692 A.2d 1039 (Pa. 1997); *cf.* Central Catholic Educ. Assn. v. Archdiocese of Portland, 891 P.2d 1318 (Or. App. 1995) (state statutory exemption premised on existence of federal NLRA jurisdiction).

85. NLRB v. Catholic Bishop, 440 U.S. 490 (1979); Edward Street Daycare Center, Inc. v. NLRB, 189 F.3d 40 (1st Cir. 1999).

86. New York State Emp. Relations Board v. Christ the King Regional High School, 90 N.Y.2d 244 (1997); So. Jersey Catholic School Teachers Assn. v. St. Teresa of the Infant Jesus Church Elementary School, 675 A.2d 1155 (N.J. Super. 1996). The New Jersey court relied on the state constitution as creating a compelling state interest in compulsory bargaining as the ground to subordinate the church school's federal constitutional claim to a religious exemption. For special applications of the NLRA in special situations, *see* Universidad Central de Bayamon v. Natl. Labor Relations Board, 793 F.2d 383 (1st Cir. 1986) (church-related university); Natl. Labor Relations Board v. Hanna Boys Center, 940 F.2d 1295 (9th Cir. 1991) (nonteaching employees at residential school).

87. King v. Dramatic Arts, 102 Misc. 2d 1111 (N.Y. 1980) (contract permitting student dismissal without justification while retaining tuition— voided as unconscionable). *See also* Annot., *School Tuition or Board,* 20 A.L.R. 4th 303 (1983).

88. *Change of mind:* Moyse v. Runnels School, Inc., 457 So. 2d 767 (La. App. 1984). *Failure to complete:* St. Margaret's-McTernan v. Thompson, 617 A.2d 449 (Conn. App. 1993); Lake Ridge Academy v. Carney, 613 N.E.2d 183 (Ohio 1993); Princeton Montessori Society, Inc. v. Leff, 591 A.2d 685 (N.J. Super. 1991); Leo Found'n., Inc. v. Kiernan, 240 A.2d 218 (Conn. 1967).

89. Thomas Jefferson School Inc. v. Kapros, 728 S.W.2d 315 (Mo. App. 1987) (discharge for misconduct); Wentworth Military Academy v. Marshall, 283 S.W.2d 868 (Ark. 1955) (withdrawal on school request).

90. Girardier v. Webster College, 563 F.2d 1267 (8th Cir. 1977).

91. McKee v. Southfield School, 613 So. 2d 659 (La. App. 1993).

92. Sciortino v. Leech, 242 So. 2d 269 (La. 1971).

93. Village Comm. School v. Adler, 478 N.Y.S.2d 546 (1984) (suit to recover tuition met by counterclaim that school misrepresented and breached its contract); Paladino v. Adelphia Univ., 454 N.Y.S.2d 246 (1980) (contract breach claim based on failure to provide a quality education—rejected).

94. Blaine v. Savannah Country Day School, 491 S.E.2d 446 (Ga. App. 1997) (upheld expulsion of high school senior prior to graduation for violation of academic honor code).

95. *Expulsion upheld:* Hutcheson v. Grace Lutheran School, 517 N.Y.S.2d 760 (1987); Bloch v. Hillel Torah N. Sub. Day School, 426 N.E.2d 976 (Ill. 1981). *Compare* Aronson v. N. Park College, 418 N.E.2d 776 (Ill. 1981) (damages recovered for wrongful expulsion).

96. Fiedler v. Marumsco Christian School, 631 F.2d 1144 (4th Cir. 1980) (reinstatement of student expelled for interracial dating).

97. Powe v. Miles, 407 F.2d 73 (2d Cir. 1968).

98. Pa. v. Brown, 270 F. Supp. 782 (E.D. Pa. 1967), *aff'd* 392 F.2d 120 (3rd Cir. 1968).

99. Runyon v. McCrary, 427 U.S. 160 (1976).

100. Fielder, *supra* note 96; Bob Jones Univ. v. United States, 468 F. Supp. 890 (D.S.C. 1978), *rev'd,* 461 U.S. 574 (1983).

101. Bob Jones University v. United States, 461 U.S. 574 (1983).

102. Corp. of Presiding Bishop v. Amos, 483 U.S. 327 (1987).

103. EEOC v. Kamehameha Schools/Bishop Estate, 990 F.2d 458 (9th Cir. 1993) (exemption denied). *See also,* Dolter v. Ahlert High School, 483 F. Supp. 266 (N.D. Iowa 1980); Pime v. Loyola Univ. of Chicago, 585 F. Supp. 435 (N.D. Ill. 1984).

104. Little v. Wuerl, 929 F.2d 944 (3d Cir. 1991); Little v. St. Mary Magdalen Parish, 739 F. Supp. 1003 (W.D. Pa. 1990).

105. EEOC v. Tree of Life Christian Schools, 751 F. Supp. 700 (S.D. Ohio 1990); Horner v. Mary Inst., 613 F.2d 706, 713 (8th Cir. 1980). On case divisions regarding application of the Equal Pay Act, *compare* Russell v. Belmont College, 554 F. Supp. 667 (M.D. Tenn. 1982), *with* Ritter v. Mt. St. Mary's College, 495 F. Supp. 724 (D. Md. 1980).

106. Org. to Assure Services v. Ambach, 434 N.E.2d 1329 (N.Y. 1982).

107. Idem. *See, e.g.,* N.J. Stat. Ann. title. 18A, §§ 46-19.1 *et seq.*

108. Newport-Mesa Unified School Dist. v. Hubert, 183 Cal. Rptr. 334 (1982).

109. McMackins v. Elk Grove Unified School Dist., 21 F. Supp. 2d 1201 (E.D. Cal. 1998).

110. Sacred Heart School Board v. Labor & Industry Review Comm'n, 460 N.W.2d (Wis. 1990).

111. *Held not exempt:* DeMarco v. Holy Cross High School, 4 F.3d 166 (2d Cir. 1993); *cf.* Geary v. Visitation of the Blessed Virgin Mary Parish School, 7 F.3d 324 (3d Cir. 1993).

    Held exempt: Powell v. Stafford, 859 F. Supp. 1343 (D. Colo. 1994); Cochran v. St. Louis Prep. Seminary, 717 F. Supp. 1413 (E.D. Mo. 1989).

112. Basinger v. Pilarczyk, 707 N.E.2d 1149 (Ohio Ct. App. 1997).

113. Sacred Heart School Board v. L.I.R.C., 460 N.W.2d 430 (Wis. App. 1990).

114. Amos, *supra* note 102.

115. Estate of Thornton v. Caldor, 472 U.S. 703 (1985).

116. VanScoyk v. St. Mary's Assumption Parochial School, 580 P.2d 1315 (Kans. 1978) (state antidiscrimination exemption for religious preferences).

117. *Compare* Marchioro v. Chaney, 582 P.2d 487 (Wash. 1978) (expansive scope of Washington State equal rights amendment, distinguished from Pennsylvania and Massachusetts laws). *Cf.* Lowell v. Kowalski, 405 N.E.2d 135 (Mass. 1980); Henderson v. Henderson, 327 A.2d 60 (Pa. 1974).

118. *Minimum wage coverage:* Donovan v. Shenandoah Baptist Church, 573 F. Supp. 320 (W.D. Va. 1983); *cf.* Tony and Susan Alamo Found. v. Secretary of Labor, 105 S. Ct. 1953 (1985). *Workers' compensation coverage:* Victory Baptist Temple v. Industrial Comm'n, 442 N.E.2d 819 (Ohio 1982). Larson, *Workmen's Compensation Law,* V, 1C, §§ 50.40–.44(a) (1983), reported that six states (Alaska, Arkansas, Georgia, Idaho, Mississippi, and North Dakota) exempted to some extent charitable and religious employers from workers' compensation obligations. *Social security coverage:* United States v. Lee, 455 U.S. 252 (1982). *Unemployment compensation coverage and exemptions for private schools: see, e.g.,* St. Martin's Evangelical Lutheran Church and

Northwestern Lutheran Academy v. South Dakota, 451 U.S. 772 (1981); California v. Grace Brethren Church, 457 U.S. 393, 403 (1982).

119. *Upheld:* Roemer v. Md. Pub. Works Board, 426 U.S. 734 (1976). *Struck down:* Comm. for Public Educ. and Religious Liberty v. Nyquist, 413 U.S. 756 (1973).

    Higher education grants and loans, held constitutional: Tilton v. Richardson, 403 U.S. 672 (1971); Hunt v. McNair, 413 U.S. 736 (1973); Americans United for Separation of Church and State v. Blanton, 434 U.S. 803 (1977).

    Elementary and secondary school expense reimbursement, held unconstitutional: Lemon v. Kurtzman, 403 U.S. 602 (1971); Sloan v. Lemon, 413 U.S. 825 (1973); Nyquist, this note.

120. *See* Lemon, *supra* note 119.

121. Nyquist, *supra* note 119 (facilities maintenance expenses); Lemon, *supra* note 119 (instructional expense reimbursement).

122. *Compare* Opinion of Justices, 258 N.E.2d 779 (Mass. 1970) (voiding state purchases of educational services), *with* Cmwlth. v. School Comm. of Springfield, 417 N.E.2d 408 (Mass. 1981) (upholding state purchase of special educational services).

123. Valley Forge Christian College v. Americans United for Separation of Church and State, 454 U.S. 464 (1982).

124. Levitt v. Comm. for Public Educ., 413 U.S. 472, 480 (1973); Wolman v. Walter, 433 U.S. 229 (1977); Comm. for Public Educ. v. Regan, 444 U.S. 646 (1980).

125. *See* Walz v. Tax Comm'n, 397 U.S. 664, 674 (1970).

126. Board of Appraisal Review v. Protestant Episcopal Church Council, 676 S.W.2d 616 (Tex. 1984), finding that 185 acres of 392-acre tract was "reasonably necessary" to operate a school for purposes of the tax statute. Summit United Methodist Church v. Kinney, 7 Ohio St. 3d 13 (1983) (church educational unit not entitled to property tax exemption when part of same building was rented for use as a child care center).

127. 330 U.S. 1 (1947).

128. Wolman, *supra* note 124.

129. *See, e.g.,* Reed v. Atty. Gen., 478 A.2d 788 (N.J. 1984); Atty. Gen. v. School Comm. of Essex, 439 N.E.2d 770 (Mass. 1982); Cook v. Griffin, 364 N.Y.S.2d 632 (1975); Dickinson P.S. Dist. No. 1 v. Scott 252 N.W. 2d 216 (N.D. 1977); Rickmyer v. Gates-Chili Central School Dist., 368 N.Y.S.2d 636 (1975).

130. Luetkemeyer v. Kaufmann, 364 F. Supp. 376 (W.D. Mo.); *aff'd* 419 U.S. 888 (1974).

131. *See* Annot., *Private Schools—Public Aid—Bus Service,* 41 A.L.R. 3d 344 (1972) and latest pkt part. For variations in state law arrangements, *see* Janasiewicz v. Board of Educ., 299 S.E.2d 34, 37, 38 (W. Va. 1982).

   States which upheld parochial school busing: Bowker v. Baker, 167 P.2d 256 (Cal. 1946); Snyder v. Town of Newtown, 161 A.2d 770 (Conn. 1960); Board of Educ. v. Bakalis, 299 N.E.2d 737 (Ill. 1973); Neal v. Fiscal Court, 986 S.W.2d 907 (Ky. 1999); Board of Educ. of Baltimore County v. Wheat, 199 A. 628 (Md. 1938); Bloom v. School Comm., 379 N.E.2d 578 (Mass. 1978); Alexander v. Bartlett, 165 N.W.2d 445 (Mich. 1968); Americans United, Inc., as Protestants v. Indep. School Dist., No. 622, 179 N.W.2d 146 (Minn. 1970); W. Morris Regional Board of Educ. v. Sills, 279A.2d 609 (N.J. 1971); Board of Educ. of Central School Dist. No. 1 v. Allen, 228 N.E.2d 791 (N.Y. 1967); Honohan v. Holt, 244 N.E.2d 537 (Ohio 1968); Springfield School Dist. v. Dept. of Educ., 397 A.2d 1154 (Pa. 1979); Members of Jamestown School Comm. v. Schmidt, 405 A.2d 16 (R.I. 1979); Janasiewicz v. Board of Educ., 299 S.E.2d 34 (W. Va. 1982); O'Connell v. Kniskern, 484 F. Supp. 896, 899 (E.D. Wis. 1980).

   States which invalidated parochial school busing: Matthews v. Quinton, 362 P.2d 932 (Alaska 1961); Opinion of the Justices, 216 A.2d 668 (Del. 1966); Spears v. Honda, 449 P.2d 130 (Hawaii 1968); Epeldi v. Engelking, 488 P.2d 860 (Idaho 1971); Mallory v. Barrera, 544 S.W.2d 556 (Mo. 1976); Board of Educ. v. Antone, 384 P.2d 911 (Okla. 1963); Visser v. Nooksack Valley School Dist., No. 506, 207 P.2d 198 (Wash. 1949).

132. Members of the Jamestown School Comm. v. Schmidt, 669 F.2d 1 (1st Cir. 1983); Springfield School Dist. v. Pennsylvania Dept. of Educ., 397 A.2d 1154, *appeal dismissed sub nom.,* School Dist. of Pittsburgh v. Pennsylvania Dept. of Educ., 443 U.S. 901 (1979).

133. Idem; Americans United for Separation of Church and State v. Benton, 413 F. Supp. 955 (S.D. Iowa 1975).

134. *See* Young v. Board of Educ., 246 N.W.2d 230 (Wis. 1976).

135. Rickmyer, *supra* note 129.

136. O'Connell v. Kniskern, 484 F. Supp. 896 (E.D. Wis. 1980); Cook, *supra* note 129.

137. St. John Vianney School v. Board of Educ., 336 N.W.2d 387 (Wis. 1983) (school board could use mass transit); Janasiewicz, *supra* note 131 (monetary stipends in lieu of school transportation—upheld).

138. Refusal to transport child to private school that lay 400 feet beyond the district boundary— held arbitrary and overturned. Deutsch v. Teel, 400 F. Supp. 598, 600 (E.D. Wis. 1975).

139. Board of Educ., Hauppauge Union Free School Dist. v. Ambach, 462 N.Y.S.2d 294 (1983).

140. Board of Educ. v. Allen, 392 U.S. 236 (1968).

141. California Teachers Assn. v. Riles, 172 Cal. Rptr. 300 (1981); Fannin v. Williams, 655 S.W.2d 480 (Ky. 1983); Bloom v. School Comm., 379 N.E.2d 578 (Mass. 1978); McDonald v. School Board of Yankton, 246 N.W.2d 93 (S.D. 1976); Paste v. Tussey, 512 S.W.2d 97 (Mo. 1974); Gaffney v. St. Dept. of Educ., 220 N.W.2d 550 (Neb. 1974); *In re* Advisory Opinion, 228 N.W.2d 772 (Mich. 1975); Dickman v. School Dist. No. 62C, 366 P.2d 533 (Or. 1961).

142. Mitchell v. Helms,—U.S.—(2000).

143. Meek v. Pittinger, 421 U.S. 349 (1985).

144. Woman, *supra* note 124.

145. *Id.*

146. Aguilar v. Felton, 473 U.S. 402 (1985); Ball, *supra* note 143.

147. School Dist. of the City of Grand Rapids v. Ball, 473 U.S. 373 (1985). Wheeler v. Barrera, 417 U.S., at 402 (1974).

148. Sloan v. Lemon, 413 U.S. 825 (1973) (voiding state tuition subsidies for children in church-related primary and secondary schools). *Compare* Americans United for the Separation of Church and State v. Blanton, 434 U.S. 803 (1977), *aff'd* 433 F. Supp. 97 (M.D. Tenn. 1977)

(upholding state scholarship subsidies to students in higher education, including church-related colleges).

149. *Compare* Jackson v. Benson, 578 N.W.2d 602 (Wis. 1998), *cert. denied,* 119 S. Ct. 466 (1998) (upholding the law), *with* Simmons-Harris v. Zelman, 72 F. Supp. 2d 834 (N.D. Ohio 1999) (holding voucher law unconstitutional).

150. Holmes v. Bush, 2d Judicial Circuit, Leon County, Florida, CV 99-3370 (March 14, 2000).

151. Strout v. Albanese, 178 F.3d 57 (1st Cir. 1999), *cert. denied,* 120 S. Ct. 329 (1999); Bagley v. Raymond School Dept., 728 A.2d 127 (Me. 1999), *cert denied,* 120 S. Ct. 364 (1999); Chittenden Town School Dist. v. Dept. of Educ., 738 A.2d 539 (Vt. 1999), *cert. denied, sub nom.* Andrews v. Vermont Dept. of Educ., 120 S. Ct. 626 (1999).

152. Comm. for Public Educ. and Religious Liberty v. Nyquist, 413 U.S. 756 (1973).

153. Mueller v. Allen, 463 U.S. 388 (1983).

154. Kotterman v. Killian, 972 P.2d 606 (Ariz. 1999), *cert. denied,* 120 S. Ct. 283 (1999).

155. Kotterman, *supra* note 154; Strout, *supra* note 151;Bagley, *supra* note 151; Jackson, *supra* note 149.

156. The source of all state references in this and following endnotes is NEA: *Charter Schools* (update of May 1996), and B. C. Hassel, *The Charter School Challenge* (Brookings Institution Press, Washington, D.C. 1999).

157. New Hampshire.

158. Louisiana, Massachusetts, Michigan, New Hampshire.

159. California, Michigan, Minnesota, Colorado, and Massachusetts.

160. Hassel, *supra* note 156.

161. Philadelphia, Pennsylvania.

162. Kansas statute. Philadelphia Inquirer, Oct 10, 1996, p. b1 (South Jersey edition).

163. Louisiana requires that a group seeking a charter have at least three individuals holding valid Louisiana teaching certificates. In Minnesota, only one organizer must be a certified teacher.

164. Arizona, New Hampshire.

165. Arkansas, New Jersey, Georgia, Illinois, Wyoming.

166. Florida.

167. Wisconsin.

168. Arkansas.

169. In Alaska, local school districts are to proscribe application procedures.

170. *Approval by state officials:* Massachusetts, Hawaii, Connecticut, Texas. *Approval by local officials:* Wyoming, Kansas, Colorado. *Approval by state officials on recommendation of local boards:* Illinois, Georgia, New Jersey, New Mexico, Florida, Arkansas.

171. *Alternative approval authority:* Delaware, Arizona. *Approval by a college or university:* Michigan.

172. New Hampshire, Wisconsin, New Jersey, Hawaii, Georgia, Florida, California, Arkansas. Minnesota requires that 90% of the faculty at a school sign a petition in order for conversion to charter school status to occur.

173. Delaware.

174. Right of appeal allowed in Florida, but denied in Illinois and Delaware.

175. Arizona, California, Colorado (five years); Connecticut (maximum of five years); Delaware (initially granted for three years, renewable every five years after that).

176. California, Florida (charter proposal should contain termination clause allowing for revocation if appropriate progress is not being made and not likely to be made in the near future).

177. Delaware.

178. Arkansas (revocation for failure to fulfill charter's terms or if two-thirds of employees ask for revocation); Georgia (revocation on vote of majority of faculty and parents present at meeting to discuss charter or when state law violated; renewal requires majority support of parents and faculty).

179. Illinois (with condition that funding allow rough equivalence between the charter school's per-pupil expenditures and that of the local school district).

180. Arizona.

181. Hawaii; Florida; Delaware; Texas; Rhode Island (in addition, school receives any federal and state aid as if it were a local district); New Jersey (local district pays amount roughly equal to what it spends per student in public schools); Minnesota (charter school paid per pupil as if it were a school district).

182. *By the state:* Massachusetts. *By the local district:* Louisiana.

183. Hawaii, Delaware, Illinois.

184. Illinois, Connecticut.

185. New Jersey, Arizona, Connecticut.

186. California, Florida.

187. Alaska.

188. New Hampshire is an exception.

189. Florida.

190. Colorado, Wisconsin.

191. Rhode Island.

192. Delaware.

193. Delaware, Illinois, New Hampshire, New Jersey, Florida, Colorado.

194. Kansas. This type of curriculum specialization is permitted in Pennsylvania, which does not strictly speaking have "charter schools" but uses the "academies" or "schools within schools" model.

195. Alaska; California (exemptions from state and local policies, if approved as part of proposed charter, are valid).

196. For instance, in Louisiana, only 75% of teachers at a school need be certified; in New Hampshire, 50% must be certified or have three years' experience.

197. Texas, New Hampshire, and Florida impose the burden of transportation on the school itself. California requires that the charter proposal indicate how transportation issues, particularly for low-income students, are to be addressed.

198. Rhode Island, New Jersey, Massachusetts, Kansas (required for economically disadvantaged students only; optional for others); Delaware (local district must provide in-district transport; charter school must assist students residing outside district); Connecticut (only to students residing within the "home" district).

199. New Jersey, Minnesota (provide transportation aid if student resides outside of "home" district).

❖ SELECTED PROVISIONS—CONSTITUTION OF THE UNITED STATES

We the people of the United States, in Order to form a more perfect Union, establish Justice, insure domestic Tranquility, provide for the common defence, promote the general Welfare, and secure the Blessings of Liberty to ourselves and our Posterity, do ordain and establish this Constitution for the United States of America.

Article I

❖ ❖ ❖

Section 8. [1] The Congress shall have Power to lay and collect Taxes, Duties, Imposts and Excises, to pay the Debts and provide for the common Defence and general Welfare of the United States; . . .

[3] To Regulate Commerce with foreign Nations, and among the several States, and within the Indian Tribes; . . .

[18] To make all Laws which shall be necessary and proper for carrying into Execution the foregoing Powers, and all other Powers vested by this Constitution in the Government of the United States, or in any Department or Officer thereof. . . .

Section 10. [1] No State shall . . . pass any . . . Law impairing the Obligation of Contracts. . . .

Article III

Section 1. The judicial Power of the United States, shall be vested in one supreme Court, and in such inferior Courts as the Congress may from time to time ordain and establish. The Judges, both of the supreme and inferior Courts, shall hold their Offices during good Behaviour, and shall, at stated Times, receive for their Services a Compensation, which shall not be diminished during their Continuance in Office. . . .

Section 2. [1] The judicial Power shall extend to all Cases, in Law and Equity, arising under this Constitution, the Laws of the United States and Treaties made, or which shall be made, under their Authority; . . . to Controversies to which the United States shall be a party; — to Controversies between two or more States; — between a State and Citizens of another State;—between Citizens of different States; — between Citizens of the same State claiming Lands under the Grants of different States, and between a State, or the Citizens thereof, and foreign States, Citizens or Subjects. . . .

Article VI

❖ ❖ ❖

[2] This Constitution, and the Laws of the United States which shall be made in Pursuance thereof; and all Treaties made, or which shall be made, under the Authority of the United States, shall be the supreme Law of the Land; and the judges in every State shall be bound thereby, any Thing in the Constitution or Laws of any State to the Contrary notwithstanding.

❖ ❖ ❖

Amendment I [1791]

Congress shall make no law respecting an establishment of religion, or prohibiting the free exercise thereof; or abridging the freedom of speech, or of the press; or the right of the people peaceably to assemble, and to petition the Government for a redress of grievances.

❖ ❖ ❖

Amendment IV [1791]

The right of the people to be secure in their persons, houses, papers, and effects, against unreasonable searches and seizures, shall not be violated, and no Warrants shall issue, but upon probable cause, supported by Oath or affirmation, and particularly describing the place to be searched, and the persons or things to be seized.

Amendment V [1791]

No person shall be . . . compelled in any criminal case to be a witness against himself, nor be deprived of life, liberty, or property, without due process of law; nor shall private property be taken for public use, without just compensation.

❖ ❖ ❖

Amendment VIII [1865]

Excessive bail shall not be required, . . . nor cruel and unusual punishments inflicted.

Amendment IX [1791]

The enumeration in the Constitution, of certain rights, shall not be construed to deny or disparage others retained by the people.

Amendment X [1791]

The powers not delegated to the United States by the Constitution, nor prohibited by it to the States, are reserved to the States respectively, or to the people.

❖ ❖ ❖

Amendment XIII [1865]

Section 1. Neither slavery nor involuntary servitude, except as a punishment for crime whereof the party shall have been duly convicted, shall exist within the United States, or any place subject to their jurisdiction.

Section 2. Congress shall have power to enforce this article by appropriate legislation.

Amendment XIV [1868]

Section 1. All persons born or naturalized in the United States, and subject to the jurisdiction thereof, are citizens of the United States and of the State wherein they reside. No State shall make or enforce any law which shall abridge the privileges or immunities of citizens of the United States; nor shall any State deprive any person of life, liberty, or property, without due process of law; nor deny to any person within its jurisdiction the equal protection of the laws.

❖ ❖ ❖

❖ GLOSSARY

This glossary briefly explains selected legal terms that are commonly used as shorthand descriptions of particular legal principles and proceedings. The first part of the glossary lists phrases that have endured in law since their original coinage from Latin, Old French, and Early English. The second part lists English words and phrases that have peculiar meaning and usage in the law. This glossary covers only terms encountered in this book. Fuller coverage would require a lengthy text such as that of legal dictionaries.

Legal Phrases Drawn from Latin and French

Ab initio. From the very beginning.

Ad valorem. To the value. The phrase is used to describe property taxes based on the property's assessed value.

Amicus curiae. Friend of the court. Refers to one, who though not a party to a court case, submits a legal brief and arguments requesting the court to take a particular position in the matter.

Arguendo. For the sake of argument, stating and analyzing a point without admitting its validity.

Assumpsit. Form of lawsuit alleging a contract.

Bona fide. In good faith. Refers to action taken innocently and without notice of legal error or of affected third-party rights.

Caveat. A warning to take care or guard against some contingency or risk.

Certiorari. A form of petition to have a case reviewed by a higher court.

De facto. A situation arising from situational facts, not created by law. Used in contrast to *de jure*.

De jure. Derived from law; founded in written laws or in official action.

De minimis. A matter of minimal importance; insufficient to command judicial attention or relief.

De novo. Proceeding anew, independent of prior legal findings or proceedings.

Dicta. Remarks in court opinions not essential to the decision and therefore not legally authoritative as a precedent. Synonym of *obiter*.

Ejusdem generis. Of the same class. A rule of statutory construction, where general words following a list of specific items are construed to refer only to matters of the same nature as the specified items.

En banc. By the full bench; a hearing by all of the judges of a particular court rather than an individual or panel of judges who belong to that court.

Et alii (et al.). And others.

Et sequentes (et seq.). And the following. Usually refers to pages following a referenced page.

Ex officio. By reason of holding a public office.

Ex parte. From one party only. Refers to proceeding brought without notice to or participation by an adverse party.

Ex rel. Out of relation. Refers to proceeding instigated by an individual that is brought in the name of the state.

Ibidem (ibid.). In the same place.

Idem (id.). The very same. Refers to a prior citation, to avoid repetition.

In loco parentis. In the place of the parent.

In pari materia. On like subject matter.

In re. In the matter of; regarding.

Inclusio unius est exclusio alterius. A rule of construction where coverage or authorization of one matter is deemed to exclude other matters.

Infra. Below, usually referring to later text or citation.

Inter alia. Among other things.

Ipsi dixit. The thing (or person) speaks for itself.

Ipso facto. By reason of the stated fact.

Mandamus. Action to compel an official to perform a ministerial duty imposed by law.

Modus operandi. The mode or method of operation.

Non obstante verdicto (N.O.V.). Notwithstanding the verdict. A judgment N.O.V. reverses the jury verdict as unsupported by fact or law.

Non sequitur (non seq.). It does not follow. A fallacy in logic.

Nunc pro tunc. Now for then. A retroactive ruling.

Per curiam. By the court; usually signifying an unsigned judicial opinion.

Per se. By or of itself; not requiring further support.

Prima facie. At first impression. A sufficient case subject to defense or disproof by rebuttal evidence or argument.

Quantum meruit. The merited value of a claim for goods or services received; recovery of reasonable value in equity to avoid unjust enrichment by one with an otherwise sound legal defense.

Quasi. Nearly but not legally the same.

Quo warranto. By what authority. Name of an action to test another's title to a public office.

Ratio decidendi. The rationale or reason for a judicial decision.

Res ipsa loquitur. The thing speaks for itself. A rule of proof based on circumstantial evidence.

Res judicata. Adjudicated matter that binds the parties to the suit and bars their further suit on the same subject.

Respondeat superior. Let the master answer [for the acts of his servant]. The basis for tort liability of a master or principal for the acts of his or her servant or agent.

Scienter. Knowledge (of operative facts).

Sine die. Without a fixed day. An adjournment without appointing a future time for reconvening.

Stare decisis. To stand by the decision. The basis of deciding cases on the basis of prior decisions (precedents).

Sua sponte. Of its own volition; on its own motion.

Subpoena. Court order to appear at a designated time and place, under penalty for refusal to do so.

Supra. Above, referring to preceding text or cases.

Ultra vires. Beyond (in excess of) official authority.

Vel non. Or not.

Volenti non fit injuria. A volunteer may not incur or claim injury from his or her volunteered conduct.

English Terminology Having Special Meaning in the Law

Abandonment. Knowing relinquishment of one's legal right to property or position.

Abatement. Reduction, suspension, or termination of a legal obligation or proceeding.

Abridge. To shorten; in constitutional law, to interfere with.

Abuse of discretion. Capricious exercise of administrative judgment or authority, and the basis for reversal by a court.

Action (at law). A lawsuit.

Affidavit. A written declaration under oath.

Affirmative action. Intentional preference, usually of a disadvantaged person or minority group.

Agency shop. Employment situations in which employees are by law required to pay service fees to the union representative, even though they elect not to join and become members of the union.

Appearance. Entry of a party to a legal proceeding.

Appellant. A party who appeals a decision to a higher court.

Appellee. A party against whom an appeal is taken.

Arbitrator. A person chosen to resolve a dispute.

Assault. An offer or threat to inflict physical harm.

Assignment. A transfer.

Battery. Unlawful contact with the person of another.

Bond. A written promise containing guarantees or security to perform a contract or debt obligation.

Brief. Written argument presented by lawyers to a court.

Cause of action. A legal ground to institute a lawsuit and to obtain a legal remedy.

Class action. A suit brought on behalf of a large class of individuals by one or more representative members of that class.

Cohabitation. A state of living together, often referring to extramarital relations.

Color of law. Under the appearance or aegis of legal authority.

Common law. Law developed by courts through case decisions, independently of written laws.

Complainant. See *plaintiff.*

Complaint. The written pleading of the party plaintiff stating the grounds for seeking relief by a court.

Consideration. In contract law, the bargained-for value given in exchange for another's promise.

Contempt of court. Conduct that interferes with or disobeys a court order or proceedings.

Contract. A legally enforceable promise or set of promises.

Corporation. A fictional legal entity that is created by law.

Counterclaim. A demand by a sued party (defendant) against the original suing party (plaintiff).

Covenant. An agreement or promise.

Damages. Monetary compensation to redress a legal injury.

Defendant. The party against whom a legal proceeding is brought.

Delegation. The transfer of authority.

Demurrer. Objection to a pleading as legally insufficient.

Deposition. Record of written testimony under oath, not taken at trial.

Directory. A legal instruction that is not "mandatory."

Discretion. An exercise of judgment and choice.

Duress. Unlawful coercion.

Emancipation. Legal release from another's control, such as of a married child from parents.

Eminent domain. The sovereign power of government to take private property for public use.

Enjoin. To order forbearance or action.

Estoppel. Equitable doctrine to preclude assertion or denial of a fact or promise.

Excise. A tax on a privilege or on a transaction.

Executory. An incomplete transaction or interest.

Expunge. Delete completely, as from a court record.

Felony. A class of serious crimes, as distinguished from lesser offenses called *misdemeanors.*

Fornication. Sexual intercourse between unmarried persons.

Forum. The court or place where disputes are heard.

Grievance. A claim of injury. In collective bargaining a procedure to resolve disputes.

Holding. A court's decision on specific facts.

Hung jury. A jury whose members cannot agree on a verdict.

Immunity. Exemption from legal obligations or liability, based on legal status.

Implied. Not expressed, but inferred.

Infancy. The age below that of legal majority.

Invitee. A visitor by invitation, as distinguished from a trespasser.

Judgment. The final finding in a legal proceeding.

Jurisdiction. The lawful authority to manage or decide particular activities or disputes.

Latent defect. A defect not reasonably ascertainable by normal observation.

Libel. An unprivileged defamatory publication.

Licensee. In tort law, a party permitted to enter property for his or her own purposes, not an invitee.

Mandate. A legal command.

Ministerial. A directed act that does not involve discretionary decision.

Minority. Not of legal age.

Misdemeanor. See *felony.*

Mitigation of damages. Duty of injured person to minimize losses caused by another's breach of obligation.

Motion. A request for a court ruling.

Opinion. A court's case report, explaining its decision.

Petitioner. Party asking for relief by a trial or appeals court.

Plagiarism. Use of another's composition as one's own product.

Plaintiff. The party who brings a lawsuit.

Police power. The inherent power of government to promote public welfare.

Privilege. An advantage accorded by law to a particular class of persons.

Probative. Having evidentiary value.

Quorum. The number of members required for lawful action by an official assembly.

Remand. A return of a case, for further proceedings, to the tribunal from which it was appealed.

Respondent. The party answering a complaint or petition.

Restitution. The restoration of value received, in kind or money, to make good another's loss.

Review. Judicial consideration of a decision by an administrative agency or a lower court.

Slander. Defamation by oral communication, as distinguished from *libel.*

Syllabus. An abridged statement of a court's decision that precedes the full court opinion.

Tender. An offer to perform a particular act.

Trespass. An unlawful interference with another's person or property; in pleading, a form of action to recover damages for such interference.

Unilateral. Action taken by one party only.

Venue. A place selected for trial.

Verdict. The finding of a jury.

Vested. Complete and fixed; not contingent.

Vicarious. A party's right or obligation imputed from the actions of another. See, e.g., *respondeat superior.*

Void. Without any legal force.

Voidable. Capable of being voided under certain circumstances.

Waiver. A voluntary and knowing surrender of particular rights or immunities.

Writ. Official order of a court or tribunal commanding a response or action.

Zoning. Legislative restrictions on locality, uses, and construction of particular classes of real property.

❖ SELECT TABLE OF CASES

The following Table lists the Cases that are reproduced at the end of each chapter and selected cases of special import. The principal Cases are referenced by chapter and page number. All other cases are referenced by the chapter and endnote number in which they appear. The principal and select cases, and all cases from the United States Supreme Court, are listed in bold type.

❖ INDEX

ISBN 0-13-030546-4

9 780130 305466

90000>